This book focuses on the "after-life" of historical texts in the period between the arrival of printing in England and the early eighteenth century.

Whereas previous studies of historical writing during this period have focused on their authors and on their style or methodology, this work examines the history book from a number of other perspectives. The intention is to situate the study of history books within the current literature on the history of the book and the history of print culture.

After discussing the process whereby the inheritance of the medieval chronicle was broken down into a variety of different historical genres during the sixteenth century, the author turns to the questions of how and why history books were read, who owned them, the borrowing and lending of them, their production and printing, and methods for marketing and distributing them.

D. R. WOOLF is Professor of History and Dean of Humanities, McMaster University, Ontario. He is the author of *The Idea of History in Early Stuart England* (1990), and coeditor of two volumes, *Public Duty and Private Conscience in Seventeenth-Century England* (1993) and *Rhetorics of Life-Writing in Early Modern Europe* (1995).

Cambridge Studies in Early Modern British History

Series editors

ANTHONY FLETCHER
Professor of History, University of Essex

JOHN GUY
Professor of Modern History, University of St. Andrews

and JOHN MORRILL
*Professor of British and Irish History, University of Cambridge,
and Vice-Master of Selwyn College*

This is a series of monographs and studies covering many aspects of the history of the British Isles between the late fifteenth century and the early eighteenth century. It includes the work of established scholars and pioneering work by a new generation of scholars. It includes both reviews and revisions of major topics and books, which open up new historical terrain or which reveal startling new perspectives on familiar subjects. All the volumes set detailed research into our broader perspectives and the books are intended for the use of students as well as of their teachers.

For a list of titles in the series, see end of book.

READING HISTORY IN EARLY MODERN ENGLAND

D. R. WOOLF

CAMBRIDGE
UNIVERSITY PRESS

PUBLISHED BY THE PRESS SYNDICATE OF THE UNIVERSITY OF CAMBRIDGE
The Pitt Building, Trumpington Street, Cambridge, United Kingdom

CAMBRIDGE UNIVERSITY PRESS
The Edinburgh Building, Cambridge CB2 2RU, UK   www.cup.cam.ac.uk
40 West 20th Street, New York, NY 10011–4211, USA   www.cup.org
10 Stamford Road, Oakleigh, Melbourne 3166, Australia
Ruiz de Alarcón 13, 28014 Madrid, Spain

© Cambridge University Press 2000

First published 2000

Printed in the United Kingdom at the University Press, Cambridge

Typeset in Sabon 10/12pt [VN]

A catalogue record for this book is available from the British Library

Library of Congress Cataloguing in Publication data
Woolf, D. R. (Daniel R.)
Reading History in early modern England / by D. R. Woolf.
p.   cm. (Cambridge studies in early modern British history)
ISBN 0 521 78046 2 (hardback)
1. Great Britain – Historiography.   2. Great Britain – History – Tudors, 1485–1603
– Historiography.   3. Great Britain – History – Stuarts, 1603–1714 – Historiography.
4. Historiography – Great Britain – History – 16th century.   5. Historiography – Great
Britain – History – 17th century.   6. Books and reading – England – History – 16th
century.   7. Books and reading – England – History – 17th century.   8. History publishing –
Great Britain – History.   I. Title.   II. Series.

DA1.W665 2000   941'.007'2 – dc21   00-023593

ISBN 0 521 78046 2 hardback

CONTENTS

ILLUSTRATIONS

Maps

Plates

PREFACE

One of the central themes of this study is that historians do not create books on their own but within a social context. In the case of the present book, that social context includes a great number of friends and colleagues who have generously volunteered their thoughts and their time, reading draft chapters, offering references, or providing suggestions. I cannot possibly acknowledge every such debt here, but must mention, among early modern historians and literary scholars in North America and in Great Britain, Robert Tittler, Fritz Levy, David Dean, Sara Mendelson, John Craig, Paul Christianson, Ian Dyck, W. J. Sheils, Zachary Schiffman, Penny Gouk, Melinda Zook, Sears McGee, Gerald Aylmer, Vivienne Larminie, Tom Mayer, Annabel Patterson, Brian Levack, Fiona Black, Lois G. Schwoerer, Ian Maxted, Derek Hirst, Kevin Sharpe (whose own recent book, *Reading Revolutions*, regrettably appeared while this work was at the page proof stage), Gordon Schochet, David Harris Sacks, and John Salmon. Among scholars of the history of the book, some working in libraries or in literature departments, Elisabeth Leedham-Green was generous with her time during a visit to Cambridge in 1992, and R. J. Fehrenbach kindly answered my queries concerning the Private Libraries in Renaissance England project, providing diskettes of information that only space constraints have prevented me from having exploited more fully.

Although I have recently moved to McMaster University (the institution of the late R. M. Wiles, whose study of serialization features prominently in chapter 6), nearly all of the book was researched and written during a dozen years at Dalhousie University in Halifax, Nova Scotia. I would like to thank my former Dalhousie colleagues in history and other departments, in particular Jack Crowley, Cynthia Neville, Norman Pereira, Jane Parpart, Bertrum MacDonald, Trevor Ross, and Christina Luckyj for their many suggestions and for the opportunity to present some of the materials herein in a variety of forms. I thank also Tina Jones and Mary Wyman-Leblanc for many years of superb secretarial support in History, and Dean Peter Ricketts and his staff in the Faculty of Graduate Studies, where I passed my last two years at Dalhousie most congenially.

xi

Chapters 1 and 2 were aired, in earlier forms, at the Sixteenth-Century Studies conference in 1986 and the North American Conference of British Studies in 1993. Portions of chapters 5 and 6 were presented as a lecture at the Harry Ransom Humanities Research Center at the University of Texas at Austin in 1994. Material particularly pertaining to the reading habits of women was presented at the 1995 meeting of the Society for the History of Authorship, Reading and Publishing. I am grateful to the audiences and commentators at these events for their insights.

Another theme of the book is the economic constraints on the production of historical knowledge. While I have had no patron like the late Elizabethan historians, nor the gentry income and leisure to study and compose without employment, neither have I been compelled to issue this work serially, or by subscription, in contrast to many of the authors mentioned herein. In a work such as this, that involves travel to a good many archives and libraries, travel support is essential, and it is a pleasure to acknowledge several successive small grants from Dalhousie's Faculty of Graduate Studies Research Development Fund, and two larger research grants from the Social Sciences and Humanities Research Council (1990–93 and 1993–96), which considerably defrayed the cost of travel to and within Britain and the United States; the first of these SSHRCC grants also included a coveted research time stipend that enabled me to spend the two winter terms of 1991 and 1992 free of undergraduate teaching duties; the second included a substantial budget for research assistance that made possible the work represented in appendix B. Short-term fellowships from the Folger Shakespeare Library and the Harry Ransom Center (the latter sojourn sponsored by the American Society for Eighteenth-Century Studies) enabled me to spend several weeks at each of those libraries, and I thank the staffs of both for their assistance. The Board of Governors of Dalhousie University approved a sabbatical leave in 1993–94 enabling me to take up the Folger and Ransom fellowships and make two further trips to England, during which I several times enjoyed the hospitality of Zena Oster and the late Victor Oster. The Institute for Advanced Study in Princeton provided me with a membership in its School of Historical Studies in 1996–97, and it is a pleasure to acknowledge the assistance of its faculty (in particular Peter Paret and Irving Lavin) and staff (especially Marian Zelazny, Linda Stewart, Elliot Shore and Marsha Tucker) in making that such a wonderful experience, during which the book achieved close to its final form. My colleagues at the Institute that year provided many more good ideas than I have been able to pursue, in particular Donald R. Kelley, Tom Gieryn, Diane Vaughan, Martina Kessel, Harry Liebersohn, Richard Sharpe, Fernando Cervantes, and Deborah Klimburg-Salter.

In the making of a book that in large measure concerns libraries of the past, those of the present have played a significant role. The staffs of the several libraries and record offices whose holdings form the bedrock of this study assisted in a variety of ways, both in answering queries promptly, and in assisting me while I was finding my way around their resources. I wish to acknowledge the kind permission of His Grace the Duke of Beaufort to quote from the Berkeley papers in his possession, and similarly the permission of the Society of Antiquaries of Newcastle-upon-Tyne to quote a number of their manuscripts on deposit at the Northumberland Record Office. Above all in this category, I pay tribute to the staff of the Killam Memorial Library at Dalhousie (in particular Karen Smith, Oriel MacLennan, Gwyn Pace, Phyllis Ross and Holly Melanson) whose labours on behalf of scholarship and teaching, in the face of interminable cutbacks, have been herculean. Carl Spadoni and the staff of the Mills Memorial Library at McMaster have been equally generous to a newcomer, not least in assisting me with the reproduction of illustrations at short notice.

Although the last two chapters are replete with war stories of authors' conflicts and negotiations with their publishers, my experience with Cambridge University Press has been a very happy one. I thank the series editors, John Morrill, Anthony Fletcher and John Guy, for their careful reading of the manuscript and their suggestions, and William Davies, Hilary Hammond, and Michelle Williams for shepherding the work through the press. Much of chapter 1 appeared, in an earlier version, as "Genre into Artifact: the Decline of the English Chronicle in the Sixteenth Century," *Sixteenth Century Journal*, 19 (1988), 321–54, and the opening section of chapter 2 contains matter that appeared in "Speech, Text, and Time: The Sense of Hearing and the Sense of the Past in Renaissance England," *Albion*, 18 (1986), 159–93. I am grateful to the editors of both journals for permission to reprint this material in revised form.

I had the pleasure at Dalhousie of a great number of extremely perceptive students. In particular I would like to acknowledge my former undergraduate student David Adams, and past and present graduate students Aki Beam, Lorraine Gallant, Ruth McClelland-Nugent, Krista Kesselring (who assisted in the subscription list analysis in chapter 6), Greg Bak (who graciously assisted me in the identification of many of the works listed in appendix B) and Kathryn Brammall. Several of these students participated in my 1994 graduate seminar on print culture in England, during which many of my own ideas were put to the test. My debt to Susan Hunter and Paula MacKinnon, the two graduate library science students who were full collaborators in the study summarized in appendix B, is more fully acknowledged there.

During the long period of research and writing, I should also like to thank my parents for their continued interest in matters historiographical, and for their many years of personal support. The book is dedicated to my three children, Sarah, Sam and David, none of whom was born when I began the project, but all of whom are now quite happily reading books of their own.

ABBREVIATIONS AND NOTE ON THE TEXT

Alum. Cant.	*Alumni Cantabrigienses: a biographical list of all known students, graduates and holders of office at the University of Cambridge, from the earliest times to 1900*, compiled by John Venn and J. A. Venn, 2 parts in 10 vols. (Cambridge, 1922–54)
Borth.	Borthwick Institute, York
BL	British Library
Bodl.	Bodleian Library, Oxford
Camden Soc.	Camden Society
CKS	Centre for Kentish Studies
CUL	Cambridge University Library
CWE	*Collected Works of Erasmus*
DNB	*Dictionary of National Biography*
EHR	*English Historical Review*
EETS	Early English Text Society
ESTC	*Eighteenth-Century Short-Title Catalogue*
Folger	Folger Shakespeare Library, Washington, DC
Hist. MSS Comm.	Historical Manuscripts Commission
HRC	Harry Ransom Humanities Research Centre, Austin, Texas
MLGB	N. R. Ker, *Medieval Libraries of Great Britain: a list of surviving books*, 2nd edn (1964)
MMBL	N. R. Ker and A. J. Piper, *Medieval Manuscripts in British Libraries*, 4 vols. (Oxford, 1969–92)
NUC	*National Union Catalogue, Pre-1956 Imprints*
Pepys, *Diary*	*The Diary of Samuel Pepys*, ed. R. Latham and W. Matthews, 11 vols. (Berkeley and Los Angeles, 1970–82)
Plomer, i	R. B. McKerrow, H. R. Plomer *et al.*, *A Dictionary of the Printers and Booksellers who were at Work in England Scotland and Ireland from 1475–1640*

Plomer, ii	H. R. Plomer *et al.*, *A Dictionary of the Printers and Booksellers who were at Work in England Scotland and Ireland from 1641–1667*
Plomer, iii	H. R. Plomer *et al.*, *A Dictionary of the Printers and Booksellers who were at Work in England Scotland and Ireland from 1668–1725*
Plomer, iv	H. R. Plomer *et al.*, *A Dictionary of the Printers and Booksellers who were at Work in England Scotland and Ireland from 1726–1775*
PRO	Public Record Office
RO	Record Office
SAL	Society of Antiquaries, London
STC	*A Short-Title Catalogue of Books Printed in England, Scotland, and Ireland and of English Books Printed Abroad, 1475–1640*, compiled by A. W. Pollard and G. R. Redgrave (2nd edn revised and enlarged, begun by W. A. Jackson and F. S. Ferguson and completed by Katharine F. Pantzer, London: Bibliographical Society, 1976–91)
Surtees Soc.	Surtees Society
TC	*The Term Catalogues*, ed. Edward Arber, 3 vols. (1905)
TRHS	*Transactions of the Royal Historical Society*
Wing	Donald Wing, *Short-Title Catalogue . . . 1641–1700*

Contractions from manuscript sources have been modernized unless the precise text is needed (for instance to notebook annotations). Spelling is otherwise as in original. Dates are Old Style, but the year is calculated from 1 January. On occasion, where clarity requires it, dates are written 1687/88. Place of publication in bibliographical footnote references is London unless otherwise stated.

Introduction

This is a history book about the history of history books, and about the experiences of some of their readers in the two and a half centuries following the arrival of printing in England. As readers, we now take it for granted that history is to be found principally in books. Yet that is a matter of practice, and has not always been the case.[1] There is, in fact, no law, natural or otherwise, that necessitates the placing of historical discourse into a hard or paperbound codex. Nor does it take place there exclusively, for all our stress on the book. Historical knowledge can be acquired in other forms also, ranging from the academic or popular journal (closest cousin of the book), to television, film, Internet discussion groups, and military board games. Other academic disciplines, especially in the natural and social sciences, have already deprived the book of its status as the dominant vessel for the communication of knowledge. Humanists, and especially professional historians and literary scholars, are especially wedded to its preservation. In large part this is because the cultural and economic structures of honour and reward (promotion, prizes and fellowships, merit increases) that we have erected within our academic micro-society still privilege the book above all other forms of presentation – most notoriously in the now commonplace requirement of a monograph, published with a reputable press, in order to secure tenure in most North American departments of history. While rumors of the "death of the book" appear to have been greatly exaggerated, there is no question that the turn of the millennium and the advent of the Information Age have rendered the status of books in general, and expensive academic books in particular, uncertain at best.

It is somewhat surprising, therefore, that there is very little available in print about the history of the history book *as* book. This is all the stranger if one considers that there are two well-developed, if entirely unconvergent,

---

[1] For the significance of the transition from roll to codex in the history of access to information, see Michael Hobart and Zachary Schiffman, *Information Ages* (Baltimore, 1998); Roger Chartier, *Forms and Meanings: Texts, Performances, and Audiences from Codex to Computer* (Philadelphia, 1995).

1

grand streams of modern humanist scholarship that deal with areas related to each of the terms in the phrase "history book." The more recent is the history of the book in general, and its related subfields, the history of reading and the history of libraries. The first has been pioneered in American and especially French scholarship, in particular the work of certain *Annales*-influenced historians, beginning with Lucien Febvre and Henri-Jean Martin's famous *The Coming of the Book*.[2] The second has a more complicated parentage, deriving not just from intellectual history, but also from continental (especially German) and American literary theory (reader-response theory in particular), cognitive psychology, philosophy and hermeneutics.[3] The third, library history, has a slightly older history and has now wedded an older, Anglo-American textual tradition and physical bibliography (focused mainly on issues of provenance, ownership, watermarks, bindings, and so on) with a social history approach that pays attention to the owners as well as their collections. With articles on book history appearing daily, and the advent of journals such as *Libraries and Culture, Book History*, and *Publishing His-*

[2] The literature on all these topics is enormous, and growing by the day, and I shall not attempt a complete bibliography here. The modern history of the book may be said to have begun with Lucien Febvre and Henri-Jean Martin, *L'Apparition du Livre* (Paris, 1958), trans. D. Gerard and ed. D. Nowell-Smith and D. Wootton as *The Coming of the Book* (1984). Since Febvre and Martin, the historiography of the book has taken off, especially in the past twenty years. Martin himself has been among the leaders of the *histoire du livre* in France: see, for instance, his *Le livre français sous l'Ancien Régime* (Paris, 1987) and *Print, Power, and People in Seventeenth-Century France*, trans. David Gerard (Metuchen, NJ, 1993). The most wide-ranging recent studies, and most influential because of their frequent translation into English are those of Roger Chartier, including *The Cultural Uses of Print in Early Modern France*, trans. Lydia G. Cochrane (Princeton, 1987) and his briefer study of libraries and their users, *The Order of Books: Readers, Authors and Libraries in Europe Between the Fourteenth and Eighteenth Centuries*, trans. Lydia G. Cochrane (Oxford, 1994). A similarly important study of a particular type of cheap-print book is Robert Mandrou's still untranslated *De la culture populaire aux XVIIe et XVIIe siècles: La Bibliothèque Bleue de Troyes*. Chartier's approach, unlike Martin's and others, emphasizes the cultural uses of books (and print in general) rather than relying on quantification of such issues as book ownership and production rates. In North America, Robert Darnton has adopted both approaches in a series of important studies, beginning with *The Business of Enlightenment: a Publishing History of the Encyclopédie, 1775–1800* (Cambridge, MA, 1979); his subsequent studies include essays collected in *The Kiss of Lamourette: Reflections in Cultural History* (New York and London, 1990) and *The Forbidden Best-Sellers of Pre-Revolutionary France* (New York, 1995). While she has not published a monograph on the subject, the essays of Natalie Zemon Davis have also been profoundly influential beyond French borders, in particular *Society and Culture in Early Modern France* (Stanford, 1975). Although much criticized and controverted, Elizabeth Eisenstein's enormous *The Printing Press as an Agent of Change* (Cambridge, 1979) is an important and seminal work from or against which much of the scholarship of the 1980s and 1990s has emerged.

[3] See, e.g., Wolfgang Iser, *The Act of Reading: a Theory of Aesthetic Response* (Baltimore, 1978); Philip Davis, *The Experience of Reading* (London and New York, 1992); Hans Robert Jauss, *Toward an Aesthetic of Reception,* trans. Timothy Bahti (Minneapolis, 1982). The high tide of reader response in the United States came in the 1980s in the wake of such works as Stanley Fish, *Is There a Text in This Class? The Authority of Interpretive Communities* (Cambridge, MA, 1980) and Susan Suleiman and Inge Crosman (eds.), *The Reader in the Text: Essays on Audience and Interpretation* (Princeton, 1980).

tory, not to mention collaborative projects such as the British Reading Experience Database (RED), the history of what has collectively, if uneasily, been called "print culture" is clearly booming. It has also been given considerable attention by scholars of early modern England, both historical and literary, the fruits of whose efforts are obvious in important studies by Margaret Spufford and Tessa Watt.[4]

The other grand stream is the history of history, a major part of the overall activity that is usually called "historiography." Historians are proud of their discipline and its achievements. As a resolutely backward-looking lot we have never been shy about examining the origins of our discipline, though we have generally done so in a highly whiggish way that celebrates the pioneers of modern critical methods and historicist appreciation of change and individuality. These are assumed, rather than demonstrated, to have been the illuminated chamber of truth toward which our more courageous and visionary predecessors were feeling their way, stumbling grittily through a maze of half-lit passages blocked by myth, error, anachronism, and partisan or religious bigotry. We have evaluated past historians and historical scholars (including some, such as antiquaries, philologists, and epigraphers, who are not always deemed historians-proper) almost entirely according to the standards practiced by our discipline in its post-Rankean, modern shape. In Anglo-American historiography, this tendency has been especially noticeable, from early twentieth-century surveys by the likes of James T. Shotwell, James Westfall Thompson, and Harry Elmer Barnes, up to the more recent textbook by Ernst Breisach, which is at least more guarded in picking winners and losers among the historians of past eras.[5]

---

[4] Margaret Spufford, *Small Books and Pleasant Histories: Popular Fiction and its Readership in Seventeenth-Century England* (1981); Tessa Watt, *Cheap Print and Popular Piety, 1550–1640* (Cambridge, 1991); for an influential study of the press and German popular literature, see Robert Scribner, *For the Sake of Simple Folk: Popular Propaganda for the German Reformation* (Cambridge, 1981). An early and still valuable study is H. S. Bennett, *English Books and Readers*, 3 vols. (Cambridge, 1952–70). Most recently the entire subject of what precisely is meant by "print culture" has been unpacked by Adrian Johns in his *The Nature of the Book* (Chicago, 1998).

[5] James T. Shotwell, *The History of History* (New York, 1939); James Westfall Thompson, *A History of Historical Writing*, 2 vols. (New York, 1942); Harry Elmer Barnes, *A History of Historical Writing* (Norman, OK, 1937); Ernst Breisach, *Historiography: ancient, medieval, and modern*, 2nd edn (Chicago, 1993). A briefer, English account exhibiting many of the same whiggish features can be found in a book by Herbert Butterfield (the very author who coined the phrase "Whig interpretation of history"), *Man on His Past: the Study of the History of Historical Scholarship* (Cambridge, 1955). Most recently, a focus on not simply method but on the even narrower question of the creation of a modern "profession" can be found in John Kenyon's *The History Men: the historical profession in England Since the Renaissance* (1983). For alternative approaches, highlighting the social context of history-writing in the nineteenth and twentieth centuries, and especially the hitherto neglected issue of gender, see Maxine Berg, *A Woman in History: Eileen Power, 1889–1940* (Cambridge, 1996) and Bonnie G. Smith, *The Gender of History* (Cambridge, MA, 1998). Cf. Billie Melman's essay, "Gender, History and Memory: The Invention of a Women's Past in the Nineteenth and Early Twentieth Centuries," *History and Memory*, 5 (1993), 5–41.

Within the narrower compass of histories of early modern English history-writing, one sees laid out the steps in this passage to modern scholarship from the end of the Middle Ages to the early Hanoverian period (the unit of time taken by the present book). From David Douglas' *English Scholars, 1660–1730*, first published just before World War II, through F. Smith Fussner's *The Historical Revolution* (1962) and F. J. Levy's *Tudor Historical Thought* (1967), right up to recent works by scholars such as Joseph M. Levine, Michael Hunter, and Arthur Ferguson, scholars of early modern English historiography have, to varying degrees, bought into a progressive account of the development of English history writing, antiquarian research, and archaeological methods, and by extension, of the main currents in the history of what we now call the "discipline" in other countries.[6] Most of these works also deal with briefer spans of time. The year 1640, which marks the end of Pollard and Redgrave's *Short-Title Catalogue* and the beginning of the Long Parliament, has often provided the dividing line between the Tudor and early Stuart period of Renaissance historiography (Levy, Fussner, Ferguson), and its Restoration and Augustan successor (Douglas, Levine). Levine's *Humanism and History* covers the whole period, but its essays are discrete snapshots rather than a continuous account, and the greater weight of its material is drawn from the later, Augustan age.[7]

Works concerned with the development of ancillary studies have also concentrated on advances in the development of historical conceptualization or historical method, though not in quite the same way. J. G. A. Pocock's classic *The Ancient Constitution and the Feudal Law*,[8] an incisive study of the formation of the modern notion of feudalism within the context of seventeenth-century political debates and arguments about the development of law, has the virtue of placing the texts it dissects within a richly defined contemporary context. Pocock's work covers the legal side of antiquarianism, and though its analysis of this is both incisive and balanced, it is still

---

[6] David C. Douglas, *English Scholars 1660–1730* (revised edn, 1951); T. D. Kendrick, *British Antiquity* (1950); F. J. Levy, *Tudor Historical Thought* (San Marino, CA, 1967); Arthur B. Ferguson, *Clio Unbound: Perception of the Social and Cultural Past in Renaissance England*, (Durham, NC, 1979); Joseph M. Levine, *Humanism and History: Origins of Modern English Historiography* (Ithaca, NY, 1987) and *The Battle of the Books: History and Literature in the Augustan Age* (Ithaca, NY, 1991); D. R. Woolf, *The Idea of History in Early Stuart England* (Toronto, 1990); J. A. I. Champion, *The Pillars of Priestcraft Shaken: the Church of England and its Enemies, 1660–1730* (Cambridge, 1992), pp. 25–98.

[7] The period between 1640 and 1660 has been rather less well-served, but see Royce MacGillivray, *Restoration Historians and the English Civil War* (The Hague, 1974); R. C. Richardson, *The Debate on the English Revolution*, 3rd edn. (Manchester, 1998); and Nicholas von Maltzahn, *Milton's History of Britain: Republican Historiography in the English Revolution* (Oxford, 1991). A detailed study of the historical writing of the civil war and interregnum is badly needed.

[8] J. G. A. Pocock, *The Ancient Constitution and the Feudal Law: a Study of English Historical Thought in the Seventeenth Century. A Reissue with a Retrospect* (Cambridge, 1987).

framed in terms of identifying how the "correct" interpretation of English feudalism and of the origins of the common law emerged from political and legal debates of the seventeenth century.[9] Michael Hunter's exemplary works on the connections between archaeology, history, and natural history avoid judging contemporaries by modern standards, but remain focused on issues of methodology, albeit well situated within their social context.[10]

There can be little doubt that there were, in fact, important methodological and conceptual developments during the Tudor and Stuart centuries. These are rather more obvious on the antiquarian and philological side than in mainstream narrative historiography, where the degree of change has been considerably overstated, as classical and Renaissance models of history writing and ideas about the proper functions of a good history remained influential. Recent studies of late seventeenth-century histories by Martine Watson Brownley and Philip Hicks have quite properly emphasized the rhetorical and stylistic boundaries of historical form during this period, and have thereby dropped some much-needed, sobering rain on the celebratory parade leading from the early Tudor chroniclers to Enlightenment masters such as Edward Gibbon.[11]

There is little need to revisit most of these topics here. The present work is less concerned with the sense of the past than with "history proper," but *not* with historical texts as such: my goal, quite simply, is to combine historiography with the history of books, readers, and libraries. The focus is on early modern England, though the same approach could just as easily be applied, *mutatis mutandis*, to eighteenth-century France, nineteenth-century Germany, or twentieth-century Japan and the United States.[12] This is not, in

---

[9] The archaeological side, focusing on the study of old objects (coins, fossils, and great monuments like Stonehenge) has been dealt with in a parallel literature by Levine (in *Humanism and History*) and by authors such as Stuart Piggott (a practicing archaeologist with a highly positivist view of the development of his discipline), Graham Parry (a literary scholar), and Michael Hunter, a historian of knowledge and latterly science who offers a somewhat cooler evaluation of early modern archaeology, especially in the published and unpublished writings of John Aubrey. These works do not suffer from the same fixation on the text of the authors they study, but nor do they address questions of readership, ownership and contemporary reception of such works. See in particular Stuart Piggott, *Ruins in a Landscape: Essays in Antiquarianism* (Edinburgh, 1976) and *Ancient Britons and the Antiquarian Imagination: Ideas from the Renaissance to the Regency* (London, 1989); Graham Parry, *The Trophies of Time: English antiquarians of the seventeenth century* (Oxford and New York, 1995); Stan A. E. Mendyk, *"Speculum Britanniae": Regional Study, Antiquarianism and Science in Britain to 1700* (Toronto, 1989); Michael Hunter, in particular in his *John Aubrey and the Realm of Learning* (1975).

[10] Hunter, *John Aubrey* and *Science and the Shape of Orthodoxy: Intellectual Change in Late Seventeenth-Century Britain* (1995).

[11] Martine W. Brownley, *Clarendon and the Rhetoric of Historical Form* (Philadelphia, 1985); Philip Hicks, *Neoclassical History and English Culture: from Clarendon to Hume* (New York, 1996).

[12] An enormously important, but underused, work of this sort is Bernard Guenée's *Histoire et culture historique dans l'Occident médiéval* (Paris, 1980).

other words, a book about historians. Although the familiar names of early modern historiography from Polydore Vergil through Raphael Holinshed, from William Camden to William Stukeley, feature prominently herein, I am not in the least concerned with their interpretations of the past, their methods, their literary style, or even the social environment within which they wrote their texts. Nor, unlike Pocock, Quentin Skinner, John Dunn and the "Cambridge School" of political thought am I much interested (here) in the linguistic context of those texts. Rather, the present work is devoted to the after-life of historical texts, as words written on paper or parchment made their way from author through printer and publisher and into book form; how those books then were distributed and marketed; who was collecting them and for what reasons; where and how they were stored, retrieved and shared; and how readers made sense of them.

Those questions are, for reasons made clear in chapter 2, answered in reverse order, beginning with readers, after an opening study of the emergence of various historical genres from the medieval and Tudor chronicle. My reason for doing this is to avoid falling into another trap, that of regarding the transmission of historical knowledge as a vector in one direction, from author to reader, with every step along the way being simply that of a retransmitter. On the contrary, readers very clearly used what they read, revised it in various ways, lent their books to others, and ultimately shaped the commercial boundaries of what could be published. Readers represent not the end of a line, but a component in an on-going system of knowledge production that Robert Darnton once called a communications circuit, but which is far more dynamic and complex than even that useful metaphor suggests. This is not to say that the historians themselves will pass unmentioned, but where they and their antiquarian and biographical colleagues figure in this account (other than simply being identified as the authors of a particular book owned, read, annotated, printed, or sold) it is as then-living humans, actively engaged themselves in reading other works, and interacting with their booksellers, printers, and colleagues.

In his magisterial recent study *The Nature of the Book*, the emphasis of which is on scientific books (and, to a lesser extent, on early histories of printing), Adrian Johns has argued forcefully that the text conceived of and written by authors, even very famous and influential authors, is not necessarily identical to the text that is finally presented in book form. Moreover, Johns contends, authors and readers alike were aware of this and thus deeply skeptical of what they read in print, tending to place greater trust, as the seventeenth-century wore on, in works attributed to authors of high social standing or at least of unimpeachable moral character.[13] All manner of

---

[13] In this argument, Johns has been influenced by recent studies of the social construction of early modern science, especially Steven Shapin's *A Social History of Truth: Civility and Science in Seventeenth-Century England* (Chicago, 1994).

influences could intrude to shape, revise, and alter an author's words. These could be relatively minor, as in the revisions enforced by copyeditors and proofreaders, or much more serious, as in cases of outright piracy, where a book was printed allegedly without its author's permission, or with the wrong author's name attached. Johns' account of the mechanics of book production and dissemination apply largely to the history of science, but it is not at all difficult to extend them to another major branch of *scientia*, broadly defined, namely history, which by the eighteenth century had become for most lay readers the single most important branch of literature other than fiction or religion. By the time of Addison and Defoe, and *a fortiori* a few decades later at the time of Hume and Robertson, historical knowledge had become an essential mark of respectability, ease in its discussion an essential part of the training of young men and, for slightly different reasons, young ladies.[14]

How it got that way has, of course, a great deal to do with the work of the chroniclers, historians, biographers, and antiquaries who wrote the texts that became books, but they were certainly not the only authors of this development. F. Smith Fussner was probably right to suggest in 1962 that there was a "historical revolution" in England. Unfortunately, he identified the wrong things as revolutionary (history-writing) and he located his revolution in far too brief, and early, a span of time between 1580 and 1640. The true historical revolution in England was not the late Elizabethan and early Stuart working-out of proper historical method, or, as Arthur Ferguson would have it, that era's discovery of the idea of long-term social change. Rather, the revolution, which was a slow one, lay in the much longer-lasting change in sensibility, taste, and manners that turned history first from the minor pastime of a small number of monastic chroniclers and civic officials into a major area of study and leisurely pursuit of university students, lawyers, aspiring courtiers, and ordinary readers, and thence into a much more broadly appealing genre that straddled the worlds of scholarship and literary culture. One has simply to compare the smallish number of historical texts listed in Pollard and Redgrave's *Short-Title Catalogue* up to 1640 with the immense growth in historical titles registered by Donald Wing's successor catalogue, and the explosion of titles in the *Eighteenth-Century Short-Title Catalogue*. Alternatively, one can compare the limited, classically and biblically focused historical discussions of a very small segment of highly educated people, mainly men, in the sixteenth century with the almost daily conversations, familial readings, public performances, and correspondence discussions of historical issues in the eighteenth century, among both men and women, involving nearly everything about the past, British, European, and Asian, as well as the older classical and biblical material.

[14] D. R. Woolf, "A Feminine Past? Gender, Genre, and Historical Knowledge in England, 1500–1800," *American Historical Review*, 102.3 (June 1997), 645–79.

The chronological boundaries of the present book are, with occasional glances earlier and later, from the beginnings of printing in England in 1475 to the year 1730, the latter a somewhat arbitrary date but one, as it turns out, that fits well with some of the materials used, for example the bookseller's stockbook analyzed in appendix A. The story told within those dates, which is really several interlocking stories, begins with the Indian summer of the earliest form of history book in England, the chronicle. The definitive and indeed virtually only form of history book available to most history readers throughout the Middle Ages, the chronicle at first appeared to have adapted itself quite happily to the age of print. A significant number of new chronicles were produced for the press in the first three-quarters of the sixteenth century, and the chroniclers at first had little competition other than a handful of ancient historians. Unlike the case in Europe, where classically inspired humanist historiography was already half a century old at the advent of print (especially in Italy and to a lesser extent in France and Germany), there was at first no rival to the English chroniclers. Humanist history did not take hold, the work of early Tudor Italian emigrés such as Polydore Vergil notwithstanding, until the very end of the sixteenth century, and the chronicle thus seemed to have the field to itself. Yet by the 1570s the chronicle had begun a final and precipitate fall from grace. It virtually vanished as a printed genre (editions of older medieval chronicles excepted) in the seventeenth century, even while its annalistic format remained popular as a means for private readers to organize what they had themselves read elsewhere. Yet one must be very cautious in assigning too clear a link between the demise of the chronicle and the influence of humanism. The chronicle's eclipse owed a good deal to its humanist competition, to be sure, but also to a much-changed marketplace for history, and to the fact that many of the functions it had previously served could now be better served by other historical genres whose authors freely borrowed the contents of the chroniclers while eschewing their literary form. My account pays due attention to the conventional humanist critiques of the faults of chroniclers, but attempts to set these against broader social and economic trends that made the chronicle not simply a literary and methodological but also a commercial dinosaur. To put it another way, humanist historiography was indeed the mortal enemy of the chronicle, but not in the rather simplistic way that this has usually been understood.[15]

From the carcass of the chronicle there emerged many other, complementary forms of historical work: poems, plays, antiquarian tracts, humanist "politic histories," and, via a slightly different route connected more directly with religious concerns, biographies of humbler sorts of folk. Chapter 2

---

[15] For an attempt to redress this balance, from a different perspective than that offered here, see Annabel Patterson, *Reading Holinshed's Chronicles* (Chicago, 1994).

looks at the sorts of books that readers were reading and, in particular, at *how* they read them, paying close attention to note-keeping techniques, and linkages made between the reader's own knowledge of other work and the words he or she was reading. A recent and influential school of thought, associated primarily with Anthony Grafton, Lisa Jardine, and William H. Sherman, has stressed the careful, deliberate and focused reading, rereading and rereading performed by certain classically trained scholars such as Gabriel Harvey and John Dee, who made of the texts in front of them not what the author said, but what they required the author to have said at that particular moment.[16] Individual sentences or paragraphs would be glossed and reglossed, contextualized within several different webs of meaning generated by other texts. I believe this to be a correct interpretation of the methods and motives of a good many well-documented late Renaissance readers, and offer one or two similar seventeenth-century examples. But it was not the only style of reading at play in England during this period, and it diminished in relative importance as the Renaissance petered out. Accordingly, I argue here for a rather more pluralistic model of history-reading in early modern England, a model which allows for Grafton, Jardine, and Sherman's version of what is sometimes called (though not by them) "intensive" reading, but also for a much more leisurely form of "extensive" reading that follows little pattern beyond the individual reader's tastes, personal concerns, and daily whims.[17] I suggest that by the end of the period covered here, in the early eighteenth century, the more informal style of history-reading was considerably more widely practiced than the "humanist" style so much in evidence a century before, though one could still find both practiced at different times by the same reader.

With chapter 3 the present study begins to become more quantitative, examining the issue of history-book ownership: how many people possessed what sort of books. The sources for this include published and unpublished wills and inventories, and private library lists. The methods used are extended in chapter 4, which deals with the related topic of the place of history

---

[16] Anthony Grafton and Lisa Jardine, "'Studied for Action': How Gabriel Harvey Read his Livy," *Past and Present*, 129 (1990), 30–78; Anthony Grafton, *Commerce with the Classics: Ancient Books and Renaissance Readers* (Ann Arbor, MI, 1997); William H. Sherman, *John Dee: the Politics of Reading and Writing in the English Renaissance* (Amherst, MA, 1995).

[17] The idea of a shift from intensive to extensive reading is not a new one and is in some danger of being oversimplified. Taken up by Darnton and by Chartier, it originates in the idea of a "reading revolution" promulgated by the German scholar Rolf Engelsing in his *Der Bürger als Leser: Lesergeschichte in Deutschland, 1500–1800* (Stuttgart, 1971). The two modes are not, of course, incompatible since the same reader might well study one work repeatedly while perusing many others in less detail. For an eighteenth-century illustration, see John Brewer, "Reconstructing the Reader: prescriptions, texts, and strategies in Anna Larpent's reading," in James Raven, Helen Small, and Naomi Tadmor (eds.), *The Practice and Representation of Reading in England* (Cambridge, 1996), pp. 226–45.

books in libraries, but with the focus now less on individual than on institutional owners, and on the challenges, physical and intellectual, of storing, retrieving, and accessing a swelling stream of historical works during the two centuries between the dissolution of the monastic libraries and the advent of the Hanoverian circulating libraries. In neither of these chapters is the goal to discover exactly what copy of which edition of what author belonged to a particular reader, and where it came from. Exhaustive reconstruction of the libraries of major bibliophiles from John Dee to Jonathan Swift and his lesser-known contemporary, Thomas Baker, has been the valuable work of a number of skilled bibliographers. Rather than reinvent these wheels, I have chosen instead to draw upon modern critical editions of library catalogs and, in one important case, a major edited collection of book-owners' probate inventories, supplementing these with analysis of other library catalogs, inventories, account books, and related documents that have come to light in central and local archives.[18] Rather than continuously interrupt the text with details of every history book contained in such lists, I have generally confined such listing activities to footnotes and, on occasion, to a number of tables and appendices.

In chapter 5 I move further along in the process that separates reader from author, to the production and economics of history-book production, revisiting at length a theme first raised in the chapter on chronicles. In this chapter I illustrate the prices at which different histories are known to have been bought and sold, arguing that publishers increasingly catered to social and economic inequalities by producing books that could sell, or that could be watered down into cheaper formats such as epitomes and abstracts. Chapter 6 continues in this vein, exploring the means by which history books, once written, were drawn to the attention of prospective readers (sometimes, as in the case of subscription, before publication), and how, in the physical sense, they were distributed from the center to the periphery. Here again, my task has been considerably eased by the work of previous scholars who have studied such features of the book trade as auctions, subscription, and serialization.

The marketing techniques just mentioned were very much the creatures of a highly literate, book-oriented age in which historians had to compete with each other commercially as well as intellectually, and in which history itself was under threat by other types of writing, especially the novel. In order to understand how the historiographical marketplace of the eighteenth century came about, we must look first to an earlier time, at the dawn of the age of printing in England, when readers' choices were considerably more limited. We begin, therefore, with the rather tangled story of the decline and fall of the English chronicle.

[18] Elisabeth Leedham-Green, *Books in Cambridge Inventories: Book-lists from Vice-Chancellor's Court Probate Inventories in the Tudor and Stuart Periods* (2 vols., Cambridge, 1986).

The death of the chronicle

I ha' beene here ever since seven a clock i' the morning to get matter for one page, and I thinke I have it compleate; for I have both noted the number and the capacity of the degrees here; and told twice over how many candles there are i' th' roome lighted, which I will set you downe to a snuffe precisely, because I love to give light to posteritie in the truth of things.

> Ben Jonson, *News from the New World Discovered in the Moon*[1]

Jonson's caricature of a chronicler desperate to find news with which to stuff his tome, having promised his stationer to use at least three reams of paper, may well have amused his audience, but it would scarcely have surprised them. The chronicler had provided easy prey for wits for at least three decades by the time Jonson wrote. A tongue even sharper than his own, that of Thomas Nashe, had lashed out against the hapless recorder of events as early as 1592. Characteristically, Nashe managed to present his victim in the worst possible light, warning his gentle readers against "lay chronigraphers, that write of nothing but of mayors and sheriefs, and the dere yere, and the great frost."[2] Digression, irrelevance, and triviality seemed to many seventeenth-century historians and their readers to be the essence of chronicles. Most modern scholars have agreed with the thrust of Nashe's and Jonson's statements, even while making the more subtle distinctions among different chroniclers that the perspective of four centuries provides.

While there is considerable agreement on the fact of the chronicle's decline, there is little in the way of an explanation for that decline; nor (ironically, given the subject) is its chronology very clear. The standard works on Renaissance historiography round up the usual suspects, among which "humanism" is by far the leading contender. The chronicle lost status

---

[1] Jonson, *News from the New World Discovered in the Moon*, in *Ben Jonson*, ed. C. H. Herford, P. Simpson and E. Simpson (11 vols., Oxford, 1925–52), VII, 514. Herford (X, 596) redates this from 6 January 1621 to the same date in 1620. This chapter was previously published, in a different form, as "Genre into Artifact: the Decline of the English Chronicle in the Sixteenth Century," *Sixteenth Century Journal*, 19 (1988), 321–54. It has been considerably revised since then, in particular by the addition of archival material not then known to me.   [2] *The Works of Thomas Nashe* ed. R. B. McKerrow (Oxford, 1904–10), I, 194.

in the sixteenth century, we are told, because historians were no longer satisfied with its rigid, annalistic structure, or because they found its style barbaric, or because its providential mode of explanation had ceased to provide a satisfactory interpretation of the unfolding of events now perceived as having immediate, contingent causes, human or natural. Historians evolved other forms such as the "politic" history (itself a return to a Latin, particularly Tacitean style of historiography), which transcended the confines of the annal and which sought the causes of the events it depicted in human nature rather than providence, fate, or fortune; or the antiquarian treatise in which remnants of the past were organized topographically or topically rather than chronologically.[3]

Such generalizations contain an element of truth, but they leave much unnoticed. A number of other factors must be taken into any account of the decay of the chronicle from its former stature as a living, growing genre into a remnant of the past useful mainly as evidence for the modern historian.[4] I suggest that the social, cultural, and technological changes that affected other forms of studying or representing the past also lie behind the transformation of the chronicle, and that the advent of humanist historical writing in the later sixteenth century is not so much a cause of the chronicle's demise as one among several consequences of the broader developments that occasioned this.[5] The present chapter accordingly opens our inquiry into the early modern history book with an exploration of how it emerged from, and eclipsed, its medieval predecessor.

---

[3] On antiquities and history in ancient and Renaissance times, see Arnaldo Momigliano, "Ancient History and the Antiquarian," *Studies in Historiography* (1966).

[4] A terminological note: in the present work I have taken history, in all its many, and increasing, types, as a "subject" (a "discipline" being grossly anachronistic at this juncture). Where I use the term "genre" it is nearly always in reference to *types* of historical writing: chronicles, politic histories, antiquarian works, biographies, and so on, with occasional finer distinctions of subgenre having to be made, in particular where quantitative analysis has been employed (for instance in appendix B, below). "Format" (or sometimes, more colloquially, "size") reflects the bibliographical and printing distinction among works published as folio, quarto, octavo, and so on.

[5] Annabel Patterson's *Reading Holinshed's Chronicles* (Chicago, 1994) is the first serious attempt to deal with the question of what Holinshed and his collaborators were trying to do, and to what audience they were appealing, without looking at that book either as the fount of Shakespeariana or as a sign of the decadence of a medieval genre. I have found Patterson's discussion stimulating, in particular her emphasis on the polyvocality inherent in so many-authored a work. I agree with much of it, not least her justified criticism of earlier books on Tudor and Stuart historiography (including one by the present author) for not taking the chronicles on their own merits. On the other hand, I find less convincing her reading of the *Chronicles* as a manifesto of early modern liberalism, and would want to argue that whatever the intrinsic merits of the *Chronicles* and its clear appeal to contemporaries (Shakespeare among them), it was nevertheless part of a genre that was already on its last legs; where my own differs from older accounts is in the reasons for that decline, which is really a sign of transmutation into something else, the modern genres of history, fiction, and news.

INTO THE AGE OF PRINT: HIGDEN'S "POLYCHRONICON"
AND ITS IMITATORS

There is no space in the current book for a lengthy review of the origins and history of the chronicle in its various medieval forms. The progress over nearly two centuries of the best-known late medieval chronicle, Ranulf Higden's *Polychronicon*, however, offers an excellent example of the changing social role of the chronicle in the later Middle Ages. There is no reason to suppose that Higden (d. 1364), a Benedictine monk of Chester, wrote his universal chronicle for any other than the Latinate monastic orders for which such chronicles were usually written, or at most for the benefit of a highly select audience around the king, yet the *Polychronicon* proved to be the medieval equivalent of a best-seller.[6] Many chronicles began with the Creation or with Brutus the Trojan, but Higden's was the first truly "universal" history written in England. Divided into seven books (for the seven ages of man) which dealt with a wide variety of topics including social customs, religion, geography, natural history, and numerology, it was a true encyclopedia in the earlier medieval tradition of Isidore of Seville and Vincent of Beauvais. Higden was influenced by the homiletic impulses of his day,[7] but he could not resist telling entertaining stories, often without an obvious moral, and all these features combined to make the *Polychronicon* so popular that, in the words of a recent scholar, it "killed the demand for the older histories."[8] Later chroniclers often found it easier to write their own works as continuations of Higden's. Others imitated its form, though they failed to achieve its popularity. So well known was Higden's work that by 1387 it had been translated by John de Trevisa, a secular clerk, for the benefit of the fourth Baron Berkeley; another translation was made in the fifteenth century.[9] In Trevisa's version, the *Polychronicon* became one of the most familiar accounts of both universal and English history, rivaling the popularity of Geoffrey of Monmouth and the *Brut* family of chronicles.

Trevisa's translation became even better known when Caxton chose it as one of the first historical works to emerge from his press, publishing part of it in 1480 and the whole work in 1482, with a continuation covering the period from 1377 to 1461. Caxton's successor, Wynkyn de Worde, published another edition in 1495 and Peter Treveris a third in 1527, the latter

---

[6] Higden, who was probably his abbey's librarian, was summoned in 1352 to appear at Westminster "with all his chronicles" to advise the council: J. G. Edwards, "Ranulph, Monk of Chester," *English Historical Review*, 47 (1932), 94; John Taylor, *The Universal Chronicle of Ranulf Higden* (Oxford, 1966), p. 1.

[7] Margaret Jennings, "Monks and the *Artes Praedicandi* in the Time of Ranulf Higden," *Revue Bénédictine*, 86 (1976), 119–28.   [8] Taylor, *Universal Chronicle of Ranulph Higden*, p. 16.

[9] Antonia Gransden, *Historical Writing in England* (2 vols., Ithaca, N.Y., 1974–82), II, 220; D. C. Fowler, "New Light on John Trevisa," *Traditio*, 18 (1962), 289–317.

sponsored jointly by the bookseller and a London mercer named Roger Thomye.[10] The survival of a trial title page for that edition, and its revision, with the title itself considerably enlarged, demonstrates that the *Polychronicon* had already achieved a kind of "brand-name" recognition which the publisher was keen to accentuate.[11] Printed versions of Higden's book retained a certain marketability even in the late seventeenth century, while manuscripts of it – rather more commonplace than for most medieval historical texts – changed hands throughout the period. The manuscript now in the Somerset Record Office, for instance, began the sixteenth century in the Augustinian abbey of Keynsham before being acquired after the dissolution by Richard Godwyn; later in the century, one Robert Rosewell would pay 7s 6d for it, and a new owner purchased it in the seventeenth century.[12]

Throughout the Middle Ages the limitations on reproduction imposed by a chirographic technology had restricted the medieval chronicle, monastic, secular or lay, chivalric or urban, to a comparatively small audience of readers (or listeners) in the present and future. The developing appetite for history among a lay audience slowly drew the records of the past out of the *scriptoria* and abbey libraries, into scriveners' shops and noble and gentry collections – a process which the dissolution of the monasteries in the 1530s completed rather than began. But such expansion was severely limited by the cost and slowness of reproducing and distributing manuscripts.[13] A 1333 version of the *Brut*, now in the Inner Temple Library, cost a total of 6s 9d for its nineteen quires, including the parchment and the scribe's fee, a sum certainly beyond the range of most buyers below the aristocracy.[14]

The coming to England of movable type in the last quarter of the fifteenth century did not initiate the dissemination of historical books like the *Polychronicon*, but it amplified it enormously. Tudor printers found a market for the mass reproduction of historical texts, some, like Bede (trans. 1565), written centuries earlier, others, like Fabyan's chronicle (1516), written very recently. One must be careful neither to minimize nor to overstate the impact of print, which in this case was longer-term rather than immediate. Up to the

---

[10] James Kelsey McConica, *English Humanists and Reformation Politics Under Henry VIII and Edward VI* (Oxford, 1965), p. 63.

[11] Percy Simpson, *Proof-Reading in the Sixteenth, Seventeenth, and Eighteenth Centuries* (1935, reprinted 1970), p. 65 and plates III and IV.

[12] *MMBL*, IV, 488, referring to Somerset RO (Taunton), DD/SAS C/1193/66. Another manuscript was being used by a Bath provisioner to wrap butter, cheese, and other foods as late as the 1860s: *MMBL*, II, 223.

[13] For the distribution of literature to provincial households in the later Middle Ages, see A. I. Doyle in *English Court Culture in the Later Middle Ages*, ed. V. J. Scattergood and J. W. Sherborne (New York, 1983), pp. 163–81; for historical interests among the aristocracy, see R. F. Green, *Poets and Princepleasers: Literature and the English Court in the Late Middle Ages* (Toronto, 1980), pp. 135–42.

[14] *MMBL*, I, 88, referring to Inner Temple Lib., MS 511.19.

1550s, historical works as a whole constituted only a tiny fraction of the output of printers, even of those specifically interested in history, like Caxton; and among the many different types of work claiming to be "historical," allegorical, didactic works like the ancient *Gesta Romanorum* or *The Seven Wise Masters of Rome*, and vernacular romances such as Guy of Warwick and Bevis of Southampton clearly surpassed the chronicles in popularity. Nevertheless, under the stimulus of a revival of chivalric values under Edward IV and Henry VIII, a steady trickle appeared of editions of medieval chronicles hitherto available only in manuscript, accompanied by translations such as Lord Berners' of Froissart (1523–25) and an English life of Henry V (1513) by an anonymous author claiming to "translate" Titus Livius Frulovisi's fifteenth-century *Vita Henrici Quinti*.[15] The *Brut* was published in 1480 and again in 1482, with four more editions before 1500 and seven others over ensuing decades, and manuscripts of this, like the *Polychronicon*, circulated throughout the sixteenth and seventeenth centuries.[16] Caxton himself commented on the increasing availability of chronicles as early as 1480, noting that "in many and diverse places the comyn cronicles of englond ben had and also now late enprinted at Westmynstre."[17] The next step was the production of chronicles specifically for the press, initially in the form of updating existing ones. Although Caxton contributed little of his own material to the *Brut*, it soon became known as "Caxton's Chronicle."[18] He added an eighth book to the *Polychronicon* in 1482, "to thentente that such thynges as have ben don syth the deth or ende of the sayd boke of polycronicon shold be had in remembraunce and not putte in oblyvyon ne forgetynge." Successive printers of Fabyan's chronicle similarly brought that work forward in time at every edition until early in Elizabeth's reign.[19]

A further by-product of the printing of chronicles was the creation, really for the first time in England, of a public identity for the chronicler. This is

---

[15] A second edition of Berners' translation appeared in 1545, and an epitome of it in 1608; *The First English Life of King Henry the Fifth*, ed. C. L. Kingsford (Oxford, 1911). A new Latin life was written in the 1570s by Robert Redmayne: *Memorials of Henry the Fifth*, ed. C. A. Cole, Rolls Series (1858), pp. 3–59; R. R. Reid, "The Date and Authorship of Redmayne's Life of Henry V," *English Historical Review*, 30 (1915), 691–98.

[16] Syon College acquired a fifteenth-century English version in the mid-seventeenth century: *MMBL*, I, 289–90.

[17] Caxton, *The Chronicles of England* (1480 et seq.). E. Gordon Duff, *Fifteenth-Century English Books* (Bibliographical Society, Oxford, 1917), nos. 97–102. Other editions were published by Caxton's apprentice, Wynkyn de Worde, and by alien rivals in London and St. Albans, such as the Frenchman Julian Notary and the Fleming William de Machinlia: E. J. Worman, *Alien Members of the Book Trade* (1906); E. Gordon Duff, *Wynkyn de Worde and his Contemporaries* (1925).

[18] Stow pointed out in the 1590s that "Caxton's Chronicle" had in fact acquired that name only because Caxton had printed it: Kingsford, *English Historical Literature* (Oxford, 1913), p. 137.

[19] Higden, *Polycronicon*, ed. Caxton (1482), fo. 449r. The several continuations of Fabyan in 1516, 1533, 1542, and 1559 are reproduced in Ellis' edition of 1811.

signified in the practice, standard from this time, of identifying individual chronicles as the work of an author: "Caxton's Chronicle" and "Fabyan's Chronicle," then "Hall's Chronicle," "Holinshed's Chronicle[s]," and finally, in the seventeenth century, "Baker's Chronicle" join European favorites like "Carion's Chronicle" as standard citations in marginal glosses and references to history reading. As polemic and argumentation increased with the confessional and dynastic quarrels of the day, so the shoulder of an author's printed name in the margins was increasingly put to the wheel of argument.[20] The identity of many medieval chroniclers had of course been known for some time (even if attributions were wrong), but the authors remained shadowy figures compared with knowledge of ancient historians, who had generally been more notable figures. The publication of chronicles in general would serve to promote the identification of particular chronicles with their authors, whether or not they were in print. An early anticipation of the engraved or woodcut authorial portraits in histories of the late sixteenth and seventeenth centuries can be found in the peculiar decision of one sixteenth-century reader, in possession of a late fifteenth-century manuscript of Hardyng's chronicle, to supply an author's portrait for his book (pl. 1.1). Since no likeness of Hardyng himself was at hand, the owner pasted in a woodcut by Lucas Cranach the younger of a German prince, decoratively colored for the purpose and with invented coats of arms superimposed, together with the legend "The portrature of John Harding: maker of these chronicles."[21]

ADAPTING TO CHANGE: THE TUDOR CHRONICLE

At this stage in its relations with print, the chronicle was still a thriving genre whose individual examples were subject to editorial modification by author/ printers attempting to keep them current. About 1530 the lawyer and

---

[20] For the early development of reference to authority in early modern historical texts, see Anthony Grafton, *The Footnote: a Curious History* (Cambridge, MA, 1997), especially ch. 6.

[21] Bodl. MS Ashm. 34 (Hardyng's chronicle), facing fo. 1r. The MS was purchased for twenty shillings in 1604, probably with the portrait already in it, by Peter Fanwood (see note at fo. 177v). For description of the Hardying MS and identification of the portrait, see the handwritten annotations to W. H. Black, *A Descriptive, Analytical and Critical Catalogue of the Manuscripts bequeathed to the University of Oxford by Elias Ashmole* (Oxford, 1845) in Duke Humfrey's library, Bodleian Library, Oxford.

Plate 1.1 (*opposite*)   An early example of an authorial image, in this case contrived: "The portrature of John Harding: maker of these chronicles." The illustration in fact is a colored woodcut by Lucas Cranach the younger portraying George the Pious, prince of Anhalt, from the latter's *Conciones et scripta* (Wittenberg, 1520).

printer, John Rastell, compiled and printed a completely new chronicle, *The pastyme of people*.[22] Robert Wyer probably compiled the short chronicle, distilled from *Brut* and Lydgate, which he printed some time before 1535.[23] Short chronicles such as these enjoyed some popularity until the mid-sixteenth century,[24] but the production of larger works for the press would peak under Elizabeth in the activities of the prodigious printer and chronicler Richard Grafton and in the even better-known works of John Stow. The consequence of all these developments was to make the chronicle more widely accessible than it had ever been or would be again. Paradoxically, this very accessibility may also have contributed to its demise.

The structure of the chronicle had proved remarkably resistant to change over the centuries. Typography replaced the illumination with the woodcut, the roll with the folio or quarto page, but little else changed in the form in which chronicles were written, at least until the mid-Tudor period. Typical entries almost always record a miscellany of events under a given year. Some merely list these events; others offer some elaboration, perhaps even occasional references backwards or forwards to other events. Charles Wriothesley appended his own chronicle for Henry VIII's reign to a paraphrase of that of Richard Arnold for the reign of Henry VII, published in 1502 and 1521 and often known as *The Customes of London*. Arnold in turn had taken the early portions of his account from a manuscript chronicle that survives in the British Library.[25] A few entries give some idea of the flavor of Wriothesley's work and of such annals in general:

Henrici VII. Anno 5.
   This yeare Creplegate was new made, and E. Francke and other put to death.
Henrici VII. Anno 6.
This yeare, in June, Kinge Henrie the Eight was borne at Greenewich, which was second sonne to King Henry the VIIth, named Duke of Yorke. Sir Robert Chamberlayne beheaded. A conduict begun at Christ Churche.[26]

---

22 John Rastell, *The pastyme of people. The cronycles of dyvers realmes and most specyally of Englond compyled & emprynted* (ca. 1530).

23 [Robert Wyer], *The Cronycle begynnynge at the vii ages of the worlde with the comynge of Brute & the reygne of all the kynges* (n.d., but pre-1535): see STC 9984; F. J. Levy, *Tudor Historical Thought* (San Marino, CA, 1967), p. 25.

24 See, for example: J. Byddell (printer), *A short cronycle, wherein is mencioned all names of all the kings* (1539); J. Judson (printer), *A cronicle of years, wherein ye shall find the names of all the kings* (ca. 1552), a work which ends with a list of the principal roads of England; and an anonymous broadsheet, *The cronycle of all the kynges, syth Wyllyam Conqueroure* (ca. 1590).   25 BL MS Cott. Jul. B I.

26 *Wriothesley's Chronicle*, ed. W. D. Hamilton Camden Soc., n.s. XI, XX (2 vols., 1875–77), I, 2. Compare these entries with Arnold, *The Customs of London, otherwise called Arnold's Chronicle*, ed. F. Douce (1811), p. xxxviii. The section of Arnold that is specifically historical runs only from p. xix to p. liii, with the annals increasing substantially in length from 1499. The remaining nine-tenths of the volume contains charters, customs, and various documents concerning the city, with incidental reference to national politics and ecclesiastical matters.

In each annal, events of national importance are accorded no more significance than those of purely local interest. In the entry for 1491–92, Wriothesley is able to describe the birth of a royal child who by his own time had indeed become king; he thus exploits hindsight to see in the event more than it could have signified at the time that Henry, a second son, had been born, and thereby adds a detail absent in Arnold's annal for the same year.[27] But there is no attempt to relate any of these events one to another, no evidence that either Wriothesley or Arnold perceived these events as anything other than interesting, discrete occurrences related solely by chronology. To read either work, the only event of any importance to occur in 1498 was the repairing of the weathercock, cross, and bowl of St. Paul's in December and their solemn hallowing and reattachment six months later.[28] Only when these writers came to compose their own annals for the very recent past do their entries begin to fill out and gain value as independent sources.

Entries in the latest surviving monastic chronicles, those of Thornton Abbey (1139–1526) and Butley Priory (1509–35), are a little fuller.[29] One of the last monastic chronicles to be written in England, that of the Grey Friars of Newgate, began in the late fifteenth century and survived the dissolution of the house in 1538 only to expire in 1556. Commencing in 1189, it is virtually indistinguishable from a London chronicle, and scarcely less parochial:

xxii Ao. This yere was chosyn [sheriff] by the citte one Jonson a goldesmythe, and he made hys fest; but within iiii dayes he was dyschargyd at the commandment of the kynge, and William Fitzwilliam chosyn, and so kepte alle the hole yere, and the other toke soche a thowthe [*sic*] that he dyde. Item the bakeres howse in Warwyke lane burnyd. And twelve herynges a jd. And a gally burnyd at Hamton.[30]

The same chronicle's entry for 1536 reports on the rebellions in Lincolnshire and Yorkshire; that for the following year, however, is concerned with the murder of a mercer in Cheapside and the mayoral proclamation promising a reward for the capture of the killer. The executions of Thomas More

---

[27] *Arnold's Chronicle*, p. xxxviii. The bringing of such hindsight to annal entries is not uncommon and provides a reminder that the date of entry generally lagged behind the date of the event, often by several years. A similar example can be found in the chronicle of Lynn where again the chronicler records "And in this yere Kyng henrye the VIIIth was borne": Flenley, *Six Town Chronicles* (Oxford, 1911), p. 187, from Bodl. MS Top. Norfolk c.2.

[28] *Wriothesley's Chronicle*, I, 3; *Arnold's Chronicle*, p. xxxix.

[29] *Historia abbatiae sive monasterii de Thornton super Humbriam in comitatu Lincoln*, Bodl. MS Tanner 166, fos. 4r–20r; this was used by Wharton in the late seventeenth century as the text for his collection *Anglia Sacra*, as was the mid-sixteenth century chronicle of Lichfield, *Chronicon Lichefeldensis Ecclesiae*, in BL MS Cott. Vesp. E.xvi, art 2, fos. 26–37, annotated in the late sixteenth century by John Stow (fo. 29v) and Thomas Talbot (fos. 46–7).

[30] *Chronicle of the Grey Friars of London* ed. J. G. Nichols, Camden Soc. original series 53 (1852), p. 29.

and Anne Boleyn, in 1535 and 1536, are mentioned in passing without elaboration.[31]

Like Wriothesley's lay chronicle, the Grey Friars' annals were not written for publication, so it is not surprising that they are somewhat more simple than some published chronicles of about the same date. The surprising thing is that many of those that *were* written expressly for the press are hardly more polished or sophisticated, while their form of presentation is little different; the authors of the newer chronicles, like most printers and readers, did not at first grasp that print was more than simply a fast method of replicating manuscripts. When Thomas Lanquet died in 1545 at the age of twenty-four, he left his *Epitome of Cronicles* completed only to the birth of Christ. It remained for Thomas Cooper (d. 1594), later the bishop of Winchester, to complete the work and publish it. The preface makes it clear that Cooper was not simply engaged in an amusing pastime. He intended this book, complete with an index and a healthy dose of protestant polemic, for the public. So did Robert Crowley, who published a pirated version and forced Cooper into producing a second edition of his own. Even with a wider audience, Cooper remained true to the rudimentary annals of Lanquet's book:

[AD 1399] 5360/5339
A great noumbre of people in Fraunce, were vexed and dyed of the plague Ipedimie.
A blasing sterre was sene at the same tyme wyth beames of most fervent fire.
Henrye the .iiii was ordeyned kynge of Englande more by force, as it appeared, than by lawful succession or election, which thing turned him to muche unquietnesse, & caused often rebellion in this realme[.] of courage he was noble and valiant, and after the civil warres was appeased, shewed him selfe very gentil and lovinge to his subjectes. Henrie his sonne was made prince of Wales.[32]

Richard Grafton, who had experienced success with his editions of Hall (1548, 1550, 1552) and the metrical chronicle by John Hardyng (1543), which he continued to the year 1509, published his own *Chronicle at Large* in 1569, in order to correct what he believed to be gross errors in Cooper's work. Only one edition of this exists, and it was alone among Grafton's works in failing to be reprinted. Grafton may have found that this relatively large volume could not compete in popularity with the various abridgments of the chronicles that he published between 1562 and 1576, works of the same shape and size as Cooper's *Epitome*.

For most readers, at least until the latter part of Elizabeth I's reign, accounts such as Cooper's proved adequate. In the citizen's perception of the unfolding of events, each occurrence held some significance, and each was

---

[31] This is sometimes considered the last monastic chronicle written in England but later chronicles by Catholic authors and members of religious orders on mission in England, occur, often in Latin, well into the seventeenth and even eighteenth centuries.

[32] Thomas Lanquet (ed. Cooper), *Epitome of cronicles* (1549; 2nd edn, 1559), fo. 250v.

equally comprehensible in terms of the will of God. Indeed, this last point was so obvious to contemporaries that it needed little in the way of a formal statement; few chroniclers bothered to make explicit the providential aspect of all but the most wonderful or strange events. Nowadays we pay attention each day to national events, local occurrences, and to matters that involve our immediate circle of friends and relatives. The difference is that these are not usually recorded together: even the daily newspaper is divided into world, national, and local sections, thereby dissecting and prearranging our perception of experience by reducing it into discrete categories of varying significance.[33] The town chronicler of the fifteenth or sixteenth centuries shaped his reader's perception in a different way: he wrote a kind of civic commonplace book in which the entire spectrum of urban experience was represented as a whole, precisely as the monastic chronicler of early centuries had done. Robert Fabyan (d. 1513) divided his *New Chronicles*, the primary vehicle through which Hall and Holinshed received the London chronicles, into seven books, not to represent a variety of topics in a logical arrangement, but to symbolize the Seven Joys of the Virgin Mary, whose cult was particularly important in pre-reformation London. Earlier chroniclers had, of course, often adopted this seven-book arrangement to reflect the Seven Ages of Man or the Seven Days of Creation; such strategies for the periodization of history endured well into the sixteenth century. Fabyan's chronicle, unlike the *Great Chronicle of London*, which may also be by him,[34] was not specifically written about the city, though Fabyan, a prominent citizen who had been sheriff in 1493, could not resist according London pride of place in his accounts of events.

THE TUDOR CHRONICLE: FRIENDS AND FOES

As a vendible genre, designed for public consumption rather than for institutional or corporate record-keeping, the Tudor chronicle was at the whim of a market that was to prove both soft and short-lived. Peaking at mid-century, the market had largely been glutted by 1600. The new chronicles were often the creation of the printers, who kept supply in close proximity to demand, and whose marketing strategies anticipate the newspapers' appeal to novelty and currency a century and a half later – a resemblance that we shall shortly find to have been hereditary rather than accidental. The production of such

---

[33] On seventeenth-century news and its shaping of perceptions of reality see C. John Sommerville, *The News Revolution in England: cultural dynamics of daily information* (New York, 1996).

[34] *The Great Chronicle of London*, ed. A. H. Thomas and I. D. Thornley (1938), introduction, pp. xli–xlvii, lxv–lxxvi; Robert Fabyan, *New Chronicles of England and France*, ed. Henry Ellis (1811). This was first published by Thomas Pynson in 1516 without Fabyan's name, which first appears in Rastell's 1533 edition.

chronicles began with Caxton's claim that his edition of Higden was a "new chronicle"; it continued with Richard Pynson's retitling of Fabyan's chronicle (originally a "Concordance of Histories") as *New Chronicles*, and with private works, not designed for publication, such as William Latymer's "briefe cronickille" of Anne Boleyn, which is a biography rather than a chronicle.[35] It had almost entirely ceased by the mid-seventeenth century, with some significant exceptions that will be described later.

As late as 1569, the chronicle still seemed to the English writer to be the most appropriate, indeed the only, available vehicle for the written representation of history. Grafton could conclude his *Chronicle at Large* in that year with an apology for his "rude and unlearned woorke, not worthye the name of a Chronicle."[36] The word "chronicle" itself remained in common parlance as a useful generic term for any historical writing, long after the writing of genuine chronicles had ceased. It was possible to use the word in such a way without pejorative associations, for example as the physical embodiment of the collective human memory.

> Let me embrace thee, good old chronicle,
> That hast so long walk'd hand in hand with time.

Thus Hector greets the venerable Nestor in *Troilus and Cressida* (IV, v, 202). Among the men met by a speaker in an anonymous Jacobean dialogue is one "so old that I should have had a Chronicle, to answer him."[37]

At its peak in the later sixteenth century, the chronicle's popularity extended down to the lower levels of the literate. The Devon yeoman Robert Furse, in his family record book, advised his children to read and hear scripture, be familiar with the laws of the realm, and to "have to rede the old crownekeles and shuch like awnshyente hystoryes rememburynge yt ys a commone saynge yt is a shame for a man to be ignorante of that whyche he ofte to knowe."[38] The chronicle provided the most basic kind of record of the past, and it had a divinely inspired archetype in the middle books of the Old Testament, two of which were indeed called "chronicles." Thus when William Fulke described King David to his congregation in 1581 he pointed out that the king's "chronicle" was blotted with sins such as Uriah's death.[39] In addition to recording a man's evil deeds, a chronicle could record his great ones, too, the inclusion of which in a chronicle could guarantee immortality. So Mortimer promises the prospective killer of Piers Gaveston in Marlowe's *Edward II*:

[35] M. Dowling (ed.), "William Latymer's Cronickille of Anne Bulleyne," *Camden Miscellany*, 30 (Camden Soc., 4th series 39, 1990), 23–65.

[36] *Grafton's Chronicle* (2 vols., 1809), II, 567.

[37] Anon., *Choice, chance and change* (1606), sig. D4.

[38] H. J. Carpenter, "Furse of Moreshead: a Family Record of the Sixteenth Century," *Reports and Transactions of the Devonshire Association for the Advancement of Science, Literature and Art*, 26 (1894), 168–84, p. 172.

[39] William Fulke, *A godly and learned sermon* (1581), p. 55.

> And in the chronicle enroll his name
> For purging of the realm of such a plague![40]

The puritan clergyman Stephen Marshall, preaching to the Long Parliament, warned MPs to act so that "the generations to come, and future chroniclers" would look back on their age as one of piety and reformation.[41]

Nor was the distinction between histories on the one hand and chronicles or annals on the other as firm as it might seem, though some historians protested their superiority. Godfrey Goodman refers with reverence to the "chronicle" of Elizabeth's reign by "my most deare and loving schoolemaster, Mr. William Camden, now Clarenceux, the famous and most renowned Antiquarie of our age."[42] In his *A treatise and discourse of the lawes of the forest*, John Manwood uses chronicles frequently as a blanket term for all historical works, though at one point he makes a threefold distinction between "chronicles, histories [and] record."[43] Gervase Markham's encomium on the earls of Southampton, Oxford, and Essex urges the reader to "let their chronicles furnish thy best libraries."[44] Walter Owsolde played upon the association of history with ballads and other types of fiction to distinguish between "histories . . . containing the amorous discourses of young gallants, with the lives of their enamoured mistresses" and "chronicles, declaring the famous and worthy acts of valiant captaines, and famous governers, with the changes and alterations of former times."[45] Here, not for the last time, was new history identified with romance, myth, and imagination, old chronicle with truth and the hard facts of reality.

Many of these comments date from the seventeenth century. By the end of the sixteenth century, however, remarks on the insufficiency of the chronicles, or their lack of style, were becoming modish, particularly among those who believed that they themselves could write with greater eloquence or erudition. Polydore Vergil, the Italian emigré whose *Anglica historia* was the first full-length humanist-style history to be written in England, was no help as a model since he had long been a subject of derision for having raised doubts about the historicity of Brutus the Trojan and the ancient kings described by Geoffrey of Monmouth; most Elizabethans did not, in any case,

---

[40] Marlowe, *Edward II*, scene IV, lines 269–70.

[41] Stephen Marshall, *A sermon preached to the honorable house of Commons*, 26 January 1648 (published 1647/8), pp. 15–16; facsimile in *The English Revolution: Fast Sermons*, ed. R. Jeffs, 30 (1972), p. 110.

[42] Godfrey Goodman, *The fall of man* (1616), p. 366; the first part of Camden's *Annales* had appeared, in Latin, a year earlier.

[43] John Manwood, *A treatise and discourse of the lawes of the forest* (1598), fo. 5v.

[44] Gervase Markham, *Honour in his perfection* (1624), p. 8; cf. Markham and Lewis Machin's play *The dumbe knighte* (1608), where one of the characters refers to the sun, the witness of his deeds, as "Joves great chronicler" (sig. B2) and another boasts that fame will "chronicle mine enterprise" (sig. Hv).

[45] Walter Owsolde, *The varietie of memorable and worthy matters* (1605), "To the curtious reader."

recognize that Vergil's work was not a chronicle at all, since the word was still virtually synonymous with "history." Bishop Francis Godwin proclaimed in 1616 the inadequacies of the *Anglica historia* and his desire for a new national history, something he shared with his contemporary, Francis Bacon.[46] A dozen years later, when Vergil's name was introduced in the House of Commons to support Cambridge's claim to greater antiquity than Oxford, the Oxonian alumnus Edward Littleton showed his contempt for such a witness: "What have we to do with Polydore Vergil? One Vergil was a poet, the other a liar." Edwin Sandys and Dudley Digges both objected to using chronicles as sources for parliamentary speeches (though Digges, for one, seems to have done so quite regularly). Sandys, weighing the respective values of chronicles and law books as sources of precedent, thought "chronicle precedent . . . no better than chronicle law". He was immediately echoed by Digges' declaration "that many things in the chronicles [are] very untrue."[47] Outside Westminster, Edmund Howes, a Welshman who was reluctant to abandon the Galfridian inheritance, thought Vergil had been too critical of the ancient histories, "and himselfe deserveth to bee rejected for his many fabulous narrations"; Henry Peacham repeated the long-standing rumor that Vergil had hoarded and exported out of England many crucial documents, thereby making correction of his errors difficult.[48]

None of this criticism of Polydore Vergil need be taken as an implicit criticism of chronicles as a genre. Howes and Peacham clearly thought they were defending English historical writers against a foreign interloper, while lawyers and parliamentarians such as Digges, Sandys, and Sir Edward Coke wished principally to enforce a distinction between documents with the status of official records and those that had not, a point often overlooked by non-lawyers.[49] Littleton, apparently despising Vergil, had himself announced

---

[46] Francis Godwin, *Annales of England*, trans. Morgan Godwin (1630), sig. A2r; Bacon, *Letters and Life* (7 vols., 1861–74), III, 90–99. For a review of contemporary (and modern) critiques of the chronicles, see Patterson, *Reading Holinshed's Chronicles*, ch. 1. The call for a new national history to replace inadequate, partisan, or outdated ones, including the chronicles, was taken up again in the late seventeenth and early eighteenth centuries by later critics of the chronicles such as Sir William Temple and Laurence Echard, but with no more success: Philip Hicks, *Neoclassical History and English Culture from Clarendon to Hume* (New York, 1996), *passim*; Joseph M. Levine, *The Battle of the Books* (Ithaca, NY, 1991).

[47] *Commons Debates, 1628*, ed. Mary Frear Keeler, Maija Jansson Cole, and William B. Bidwell (New Haven and London, 1977–83), IV, 42 (31 May 1628); *Proceedings in Parliament (House of Commons), 1614*, ed. M. Jansson (Philadelphia, 1988), pp. 356, 358. On the objection of Sir Edward Coke and other lawyers to the use of chronicles as sources of law, see D. R. Woolf, *The Idea of History in Early Stuart England: Erudition, Ideology, and the "Light of Truth" from the Accession of James I to the Civil War* (Toronto, 1990), pp. 27–8.

[48] Henry Peacham, *The Compleat Gentleman*, 3rd edn (1634), p. 51.

[49] Thus the historian and polemicist Peter Heylyn was reminded of the distinctive status of records by one of his correspondents in the 1650s. Herts RO, XII.A.45, Nathan Donbavand to Heylyn, 29 September 1658, specifically cites Coke's argument in the *Institutes*. On the other hand, chronicles provided extremely useful sources of precedent, albeit (as Littleton had

before the Commons barely six weeks earlier that he held Matthew Paris to be "an author of special credit."[50]

More dangerous objections to the chronicle as a form of historical writing would come from other quarters, in particular from humanist-trained Elizabethan and Jacobean historical writers, beginning with Sir Henry Savile's famous blanket denunciation of medieval historiography in the 1590s.[51] Philip Hicks has aptly summarized the humanist position on the chronicle as "a useless jumble of disconnected facts and fictions, written in bad Latin by superstitious monks."[52] The insufficiency of the Elizabethan chronicles offered one of the very few issues on which the classically minded Gabriel Harvey found himself in agreement with his archenemy, Thomas Nashe. Annotating his copy of Livy's *Romanae Historiae Principis*, probably in 1590, Harvey wondered whether a British Livy, Tacitus, or Frontinus would emerge while complaining of the "many asses who dare to compile histories, chronicles, annals, commentaries." These include "Grafton, Stow, Holinshed, and a few others like them who are not cognizant of law or politics, nor of the art of depicting character, nor are they in any way learned."[53] The anonymous author of the continuation of William Martyn's *History of the Kings of England* exploited the annals of John Stow, while attacking chroniclers as a group – "not the learnedst generation among us" – and preferring to any English account of the later sixteenth century the elegant Latin of Jacques-Auguste de Thou's *Historia sui temporis*.[54] The minor verse historian Charles Aleyn, perhaps conscious of the weakness of his own claim to historical veracity, dismissed the chronicle accounts of Henry VII's defeat of the earl of Lincoln's rising as a superficial list of events:

> Chronicles doe it so lamely tell
> As if twere sayd, they came, they fought, they fell.[55]

Most of all, it was easy to poke fun at the reliability of the chronicler by exposing the very disagreement of the sources on which he based his account and his failure to reconcile them. The learned Lord Chancellor Ellesmere refused to cite evidence from Richard II's reign during the debate on the case

pointed out) without standing at law. The genealogical evidences of William Seymour, marquis of Hertford and duke of Somerset in the mid-seventeenth century, including his descent from the family of Grey, contain numerous references to Hall, Fabian, and Holinshed: Hist. MSS Comm., *Bath Longleat MSS*, IV (Seymour papers), 215.

[50] *Commons Debates, 1628*, II, 335 (7 April 1628).
[51] Henry Savile, *Scriptores post Bedam*, preface; BL MS Harl. 6521, fo. 137.
[52] Hicks, *Neoclassical History and English Culture*, p. 24.
[53] Virginia F. Stern, *Gabriel Harvey: his Life, Marginalia and Library* (Oxford, 1979), p. 152. Stern dates this remark to 1580, but Harvey's reference to Camden and Hakluyt in the same passage make the later date more likely.
[54] William Martyn, *The historie of the kings of England since the conquest* (2nd edn, 1638), p. 376.
[55] Charles Aleyn, *The historie of that wise prince, Henrie the seventh* (1638). Aleyn presumably did not include his principal source, Bacon's *Henry the Seventh*, in this number.

of the post-nati in 1608, because "some of our chroniclers doe talke idely [of it] and understand little." And in Jonson's *News from the New World*, already cited, the chronicler despairs of being able to write the truth. "I have been so cheated with false relations in my time, as I have found it a harder thing to correct my book than to collect it."[56] In the Putney debates of October 1647, the Leveller John Wildman, in making his argument that "Our very laws were made by our conquerors," would even turn the traditional charge of excessive inclusivity upside down, into one of class-biased selectivity. "Whereas it's spoken much of chronicles, I conceive there is no credit to be given to any of them; and the reason is because those that were our lords, and made us their vassals, would suffer nothing else to be chronicled."[57]

PARASITE GENRES

Ironically, the very instrument that had given the chronicle its widest readership, the printing press, also contributed in different ways to its "genrecide." By making the chronicle, and with it the facts of the past, a common intellectual currency, the press rendered possible the development of other genres. These clearly derived from the chronicle but were much more able to meet the public demand whether because more readable, cheaper, or more novel. I shall call them, for want of a more accurate phrase, "parasite genres," a term that reflects both their feeding upon a chronicle host and, in the case of one of them – the "chronicle play" – an inability to survive once that host had withered away. The "parasite" historical genres began to flourish from the middle of the sixteenth century, and drew much of their material from the chronicle. They soon proved better able to satisfy public interest in history, with the result that the chronicle itself was soon made redundant.

The functions of any medieval chronicle had variously included the narration of past history, the presentation of information, the communication of news, the commemoration of great events and preservation of documents, and the entertainment of the reader. These functions passed in the Elizabethan and early Stuart period to the newer genres. In short, the chronicle did not so much decay as *dissolve* into a variety of genres such as almanacs (informative); newsbooks, diurnals, and finally newspapers (communicative); antiquarian treatises and classically modeled humanist histories (historical), diaries, biographies and autobiographies (commemorative) and historical drama, verse and prose fiction (entertaining), a process depicted graphically in fig. 1.1.

[56] *Ben Jonson*, VII, 515.
[57] G. E. Aylmer, *The Levellers in the English Revolution* (1975), p. 109.

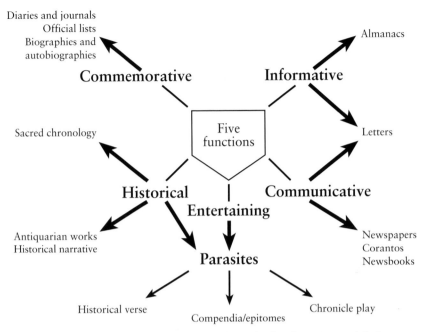

Diaries and journals
Official lists
Biographies and
autobiographies

Almanacs

Commemorative   **Informative**

Sacred chronology

Five
functions

Letters

Historical | **Communicative**

Entertaining

Antiquarian works
Historical narrative

Newspapers
Corantos
Newsbooks

Parasites

Historical verse

Compendia/epitomes

Chronicle play

Figure 1.1   The dissolution of the chronicle: five functions and their
descendent genres.

The most obvious consequence of the advent of print was to rob
the chronicle, now perceived as a public rather than private record of the
past,[58] of its function as the recorder and communicator of recent events, that
is, as a medium of what would soon become the realm of news. Pre-
typographic cultures depend upon a variety of media for the transmission of
events from the human voice to the letter to the manuscript. All are slow in
comparison with print, just as print itself cannot compete with the electronic
media that today have made possible almost instantaneous communication
over thousands of miles. One of the most important changes wrought by
movable type was the speed at which information could be stored, reproduced, and transmitted quickly to a wide audience; the Tudor manipulation
of the press for political purposes shows that contemporaries could exploit
this phenomenon even if they did not yet fully understand its significance. But
this Promethean innovation had one major limitation that has not changed
much in half a millennium: the speed at which a book can be produced

---

[58] The mining of the chronicle for political purposes, and more important the public acknowl-
edgment of this, may be said to have begun with the famous preamble to the 1533 Act of
Appeals, which draws authority from "divers sundry old authentic histories and chronicles."

depends very much on the type of book, its typographical complexity, and its format and size.

The chronicler had never been the primary reporter of news; manuscript newsletters had circulated as early as the twelfth century and, together with oral communication, were certainly more important in this regard. But the chronicle had also enjoyed a special relationship with other forms of news, the newsletter among them, and this relationship had been symbiotic rather than competitive. Readers had included newsletters within the same manuscript volumes as extracts of annals, and chroniclers had themselves borrowed from newsletters and documents supplied by the crown while taking many other facts from the mouths of witnesses deemed reliable: the sharp increase in Scottish material in English chronicles after 1296 almost certainly derives from information supplied by a combination of these sources.[59]

There is a late recognition of the connection between news and the chronicle in John Donne's fourth *Satyre*, whose narrator's strange companion is a conflation of chronicler and gossip monger, connected by their common fixation on the trivial:

> More then ten Hollensheads, or Halls, or Stowes,
> Of triviall houshold trash he knowes; He knowes
> When the Queen frown'd, or smil'd, and he knowes what
> A subtle States-man may gather of that;
> He knowes who loves; whom; and who by poyson
> Hasts to an Offices reversion.[60]

But by the time Donne wrote these lines, a few years before the advent of the 1620s newsbooks, the link between the chronicle and news was already coming apart, something more obvious a few years later in Jonson's very clear distinction between newsman and chronicler in *News from the New World*. The growing detachment of news from history in the half-century leading up to the 1640s thus had a direct impact on at least one of the chronicle's major social functions. In comparison with almanacs, manuscript newsletters, and eventually the printed newspaper, the chronicle was too

[59] D. W. Burton, "1264: Some New Documents," *Historical Research*, 66 (1993), 317–28 includes a contemporary newsletter about the battle of Lewes, in a fourteenth-century volume that also includes William of Malmesbury's *Gesta pontificum*; J. R. Maddicott, "The Mise of Lewes, 1264," *English Historical Review*, 98 (1983), 588–603, especially 592–93, 602–3; C. A. J. Armstrong, "Some Examples of the Distribution of News in England at the Time of the Wars of the Roses," in *Studies in Medieval History Presented to Frederick Maurice Powicke*, ed. R. W. Hunt, W. A. Pantin, and R. W. Southern (Oxford, 1948), pp. 429–54; *The Anonimalle Chronicle, 1333–1381*, ed. V. H. Galbraith (Manchester, 1927), p. xxxiv f.; Lionel Stones, "English Chroniclers and the Affairs of Scotland, 1286–1296," in R. H. C. Davis and J. M. Wallace-Hadrill (eds.), *The Writing of History in the Middle Ages* (Oxford, 1981), pp. 323–48, especially p. 337–39.

[60] Donne, *Satyres*, IV, 97–102, in *The Satires, Epigrams and Verse Letters*, ed. W. Milgate (Oxford, 1967), p. 17. This passage follows by a few lines a similar dismissal as "base, Mechanique, coarse" the man who "keepes the Abbey tombes, / And for his price doth with who ever comes, / Of all our Harries, and our Edwards talke": ibid., lines 75–7.

bulky, too long in the press and too expensive to keep up, either in speed or volume, with the various genres created by print. By the time a chronicler such as Stow had recorded a contemporary event it was already well known; by the time it passed through the press and reached the bookseller it was no longer news but history. And history, as the early Stuart historians well knew, was neither very safely nor truthfully written about contemporary events – as one seventeenth-century commentator would remark in 1648, "Writing your Kings' chronicles in their life time . . . is a doctrine of Devils."[61]

It is thus no accident at all that the virtual end of chronicle publication in England (rare anomalies like Sir Richard Baker's *Chronicle* aside) with the Jacobean and Caroline reprints of Stow, coincided with the first wave of corantos and newsbooks. The chronicler could no longer claim to be the primary or even an effective recorder of the events of the present, since the very notion of the "present" and the universe of literary genres used to represent it had changed. At best he could record the recent past, and that only in year-long periods that were simply too long for a reading culture by now adjusting itself to shorter-term change. Eventually, the weekly newsbook would give way to the dailies for similar reasons. The cavalier poet John Cleveland made the nature of the relationship between newsbook and chronicle explicit in a satire, first printed in 1643, of parliamentary (though not royalist) newsbooks:

A *Diurnall* is a puny chronicle, scarce pin-feather'd with the wings of time. It is an Historie in Sippets [*sic*]; the English *Iliads* in a Nut-shell; the *Apocryphall* Parliaments book of *Maccabees* in single sheets. It would tire a Welch-pedigree, to reckon how many aps [*sic*] 'tis remov'd from an Annall. For it is of that Extract: onely of the younger House, like a Shrimp to a Lobster.[62]

The modern newspaper's distant antecedents are betrayed in the number of newspapers which today call themselves "chronicles," but in the early days of the Restoration newspaper the resemblance lay in more than a name. James Sutherland has remarked on the amount of news about ghosts, storms, fires and floods, monsters and omens that appear in Restoration papers such as Thomas Benskin's *Domestick Intelligence* – the same sorts of information now deemed too trivial for history, and for which the chroniclers had been

---

[61] Anon., *The Kingdomes Briefe Answer, to the Late Declaration of the House of Commons, Feb. 11, 1647* (1648), BL Thomason Tracts E 431 (9), cited in A. J. Bellany, "The Poisoning of Legitimacy? Court Scandal, News Culture and Politics in England" (Ph.D. diss., Princeton University, 1995), 702. On the strictures against "contemporary" history and its eruption after 1640, see Woolf, *Idea of History*, ch. 8.
[62] John Cleveland, *The Character of a London-diurnall* (1647: Wing C4664), p. 1. The manuscript newsletter proved more durable, however, because its recipients liked being part of a select audience and presumed that the sources of their newsletters were often better informed than the public press.

attacked.[63] Even in the 1720s and 1730s, with monsters and prodigies giving way increasingly to scandals and criminals, a sensational element remained that points ahead to the supermarket tabloid. There is a further resemblance between the chronicle and the weekly newsbooks of the Augustan era, and that lies in the manner in which material was frequently digested for the benefit of the reader. Here, the comprehensiveness of the chronicle, with its set of regular year entries, seemed to offer as sensible a solution as any. In the *Grub-Street Journal* of the 1730s, for example, advertisements jostle for place with daily summaries of the previous weeks' news, mainly digested from daily papers, and arranged diurnally in much the same way as a Tudor printer/chronicler like Grafton or Holinshed would have arranged his material under years.[64]

The development of the diary as a popular form of self-expression in the later sixteenth and especially in the seventeenth centuries reflects a parallel adjustment of literary form to temporal perception, once more at the expense of the chronicle. The chronicle had always been in part a record of the writer's personal experience of recent time, and the perception that meaningful events happened on a day-to-day, rather than year-to-year, schedule required the individual to adjust the timetable according to which he recorded those events. Geoffrey le Baker had found he could record contemporary occurrences in the form of a chronicle in the early fourteenth century, as would the master of Peterhouse, John Warkworth, in the late fifteenth century.[65] Seventeenth-century diaries offer a marked contrast. Another cleric, Ralph Josselin, would record on a daily basis the events that affected and afflicted his family, together with news from the wider world. The Berkshire diarist Anthony Blagrave, though he was the cousin of the regicide MP, Daniel, made little reference to political events in his own diary, but he registered his personal affairs, travels, incessant bodily ailments, and even moods with an almost tiresome dailiness.[66]

Insofar as it is a record of unfolding events rather than (as in the case of autobiography) a preorganized retrospective, the diary is, like its public sphere counterpart, the newspaper, simply the chronicle literally "brought up to speed" and turned into a medium for capturing individual perceptions of the flow of events, private, local, or national.[67] The same sorts of entries

---

[63] James Sutherland, *The Restoration Newspaper and its Development* (Cambridge and New York, 1986), pp. 98–99, 122. On the relations between news and history from the 1640s, see Joad Raymond, *The Invention of the Newspaper: English Newsbooks, 1641–1649* (Oxford, 1996), pp. 269–313.   [64] *Grub-Street Journal* (1730), *passim*.

[65] Gransden, *Historical Writing in England*, II, 257–8; *A Chronicle of the First Thirteen Years of the Reign of King Edward the Fourth*, ed. J. O. Halliwell, Camden Soc., o.s. 10 (1839).

[66] Bodl. MS Eng. misc. e. 118 (Blagrave diary, 1650–52), fos. 13v–14r, 16r, 20r, 73v–4, 87r–88r.

[67] On the connection between time consciousness and the diary, especially in the period after the Restoration, see Stuart Sherman, *Telling Time: Clocks, Diaries, and English Diurnal Form 1660–1785* (Chicago, 1996).

that would previously have been recorded annually in chronicles, including prodigies and local or foreign news, religious thoughts and observations on providences and divine judgments, were now entered in diaries along with important personal events.[68] A monstrous mix of the genres can be seen in the sort of "diary/chronicle" composed by the Restoration-era Durham merchant Jacob Bee: "1682. 15 Aug. A blazing stare appeared," a point juxtaposed with local and national affairs, could well be an entry in a medieval chronicle, but the timescale in which it is situated is no longer one of years, but of days.[69] Similarly, the diary of John Ryce of Cheshire, begun in 1686 but containing memoranda back to 1649, arranges its author's historical experience into year-by-year fragments with particular dates given for the major events in his life, such as the flood of 30 January 1662 (the anniversary of the execution of the king) or the earthquake of 7 October 1690.[70] The Essex weaver John Bufton kept, together with his notes on sermons, a diary in his Goldsmith's *Almanack* that also recorded the officers of his trade from year to year.[71] The London turner Nehemiah Wallington packed his diaries with God's judgments and his own familial and personal tribulations.[72]

If the chronicle's functions as newsbearer and preserver of the present were being usurped by the newspaper and the diary, its other principal roles, as narrator of the past and as entertainer or edifier, were at the same time being assumed by a variety of new genres more directly parasitical because concerned with the remote rather than recent past: the humanist or "politic" history; the chapbook "pleasant histories" and broadsheet ballads; almanacs and chronological tables; verse accounts of national history authored by poets such as Drayton, Daniel and a host of lesser names; and the

[68] The other major literary receptacle of personal events, the autobiography, because written retrospectively (like a history) rather than as events unfold, does not appear at first sight to have had as close a connection to the chronicle. Yet there are signs of residual "annalism" in the occasional autobiography, especially lower down the social scale: the Quaker tradesman of Lancaster, William Stout explicitly adopted an annalistic form to write his autobiography, arranging it by calendar year and often beginning years or paragraphs with the typically annalistic incipit "In this year." He records (p. 96) that he read history when a young man; this may have included chronicles, which would have furnished him with an easy organizational principle and removed the need for a more rhetorical shaping of his account into a humanist "life and times." *The Autobiography of William Stout of Lancaster 1665–1752*, ed. J. D. Marshall (Manchester and New York, 1967), *passim*; for a specific example, see p. 91: "This year [1688] must be remarkable for the strong revolution then happening."
[69] *Six North Country Diaries*, ed. J. C. Hodgson, Surtees Soc., 118 (1910), p. 45.
[70] Cheshire RO, DDX 23/2, transcript of diary of John Ryce, pp. 7, 10, 18.
[71] Essex RO, T/A 156, microfilm of the diary of Joseph Bufton of Coggeshall, and Essex RO, D/DBm/Z9, copies of Goldsmith's *Almanack* with interleaved notes. The blurred boundary between the diary as personal record and the chronicle as public history can be seen especially in the writings of a journal keeper like Dr. James Yonge (1647–1721). His journal ends in 1708, but in the next thirteen years he wrote a series of "Plymouth Memoires" that include what amounts to a town chronicle 1439–1715, complete with names of mayors and major events: *The Journal of James Yonge [1647–1721], Plymouth Surgeon*, ed. F. N. L. Poynter (1963), p. 229. For other examples see the last section of this chapter.
[72] Paul Seaver, *Wallington's World* (Stanford, 1985).

Elizabethan–Jacobean history plays. Printers catered to a growing market for
these genres and ensured their permanence, but the deeper origins of their
relatively sudden success lie in the social and cultural changes that England
underwent between the late fifteenth and early seventeenth centuries.[73] Tudor
and Stuart society cannot be easily divided into economic classes, but it was
stratified hierarchically, and by the mid-sixteenth century literary tastes had
themselves altered to reflect this fact. The growth of the parasite genres
suggests that the reasons why an individual might turn to the past, and the
manner in which he might then choose to represent it, varied a great deal up
and down the late Tudor social ladder. Those who read Camden and Sir John
Hayward were unlikely to be more than casual consumers of ballads, almanacs, and of the sort of chapbook histories so well described by Margaret
Spufford, and when they did collect such literature, as both John Selden and
Samuel Pepys would do, they were satisfying other interests than scholarly.[74]
Conversely, the villager listening to or even reading a printed ballad was
extremely unlikely even to have heard of William Camden, let alone to have
read his *Annales*.

The genre that appealed to perhaps the broadest cross-section of Elizabethan society, though one primarily restricted to London, was the history
play. It owed this social inclusivity, which has probably been overstated, to a
preexisting late medieval tradition of popular drama and also to its very close
reliance on the Tudor chronicles for source material. Responsive both to late
Tudor nationalism and to the sixteenth-century demand for visual spectacle,
the plays took events out of the folio pages of the great chronicles, Grafton,
Hall, and Holinshed, and from less voluminous works like Stow's *Summaries*
and *Annales*, and literally brought them to life. The chronicle origin of
particular plays was sometimes explicit, other times not: scholars will probably never sort out entirely Shakespeare's relative debt to Hall or Holinshed,
or their medieval predecessors.[75] Few dramatists made their sources so

---

[73] As Hicks points out, print was a two-edged sword so far as some of these genres were
concerned, nearly overwhelming neoclassical historiography in a sea of epitomes, abridgments and secret histories – in other words, the politic historians fell prey to their *own*
parasites: *Neoclassical History and English Culture*, pp. 41–2; for further discussion of
epitomes see below, chapter 5.

[74] Margaret Spufford, *Small Books and Pleasant Histories* (1981), p. 48 suggests that "the two
cultures," elite and popular, had drawn apart in seventeenth-century England much as they
would do in Scotland in the following century, though of course the barriers were far from
insurmountable, a point reinforced in Tessa Watt's book, *Cheap Print and Popular Piety,
1550–1640* (Cambridge, 1991) and other recent studies, including essays by Jonathan Barry
and Bernard Capp in *Popular Culture in Seventeenth-Century England*, ed. Barry Reay
(London and New York, 1986).

[75] See for instance the long line of older treatments of this issue including G. Bullough, *Narrative
and Dramatic Sources of Shakespeare* (8 vols., London, 1957–75); W. G. Boswell Stone,
Shakespeare's Holinshed (New York, 1896); Lily B. Campbell, *Shakespeare's Histories:
Mirrors of Elizabethan Policy* (San Marino, CA, 1947); E. M. W. Tillyard, *Shakespeare's
History Plays* (1944).

obvious as Thomas Middleton, the dramatist and city chronologer of London. His *Mayor of Queenborough*, set in Arthurian Britain, features a chorus in the person of none other than Ranulf Higden himself:

> What Raynulph, monk of Chester, can
> Raise from his Polychronicon,
> That raiseth him, as works do men,
> To see long-parted light agen.[76]

Sir Thomas Gray of Heton, author of the fourteenth-century *Scalacronica* (and among the earliest lay chroniclers) had once encountered a vision of Ranulf Higden's "spirit" during the Chester monk's own lifetime.[77] A quarter-millennium later, Higden's change in status is remarkable. In Middleton's staging, he has become a dramatic persona embodying *past* knowledge of the past rather than the living beacon of historical commemoration he had provided in Gray's time and, arguably, well into the mid-sixteenth century. Middleton has selected Higden not because of his currency but its opposite: the monk's medievalness, which suits the Arthurian subject matter of the play. By this time, Higden was much more likely to see the light of day as a ghostly figure of prosopopoeia than was his chronicle.

It is impossible to estimate precisely how much larger was the audience for plays than the readership of printed chronicles, but the effect of the chronicle play was probably analogous to that of the film or television dramatization today (hundreds may have seen Kenneth Branagh's *Henry V*, Ian Holm's *King Lear* or Ian McKellen's *Richard III* who have never read a word of Shakespeare). The performance of plays generally preceded their printing – Middleton's was not published until 1661 – but it is the printed ones that outlive the moment, to be read and reperformed in ensuing years. If the proportion of spectators who were sufficiently inspired by a performance to

---

[76] *Works of Thomas Middleton* (7 vols., 1885–86), II, 5. Middleton was appointed "city chronologer" in 1620, the first to hold the office, at an annual stipend of £6 13s 4d, which later that year was increased to £10. He was succeeded in 1620 by Ben Jonson, at a fee of 100 nobles (£33 6s 8d) per annum. In 1633 one Edward Hewes (perhaps Edmund Howes, the continuator of Stow) is listed as having been city chronologer and was given £20 in respect of his age and services. Jonson was succeeded at his death in 1637 by the poet Francis Quarles at the suit of the earl of Dorset (a rival suit on behalf of Thomas May, the future parliamentarian historian, by the earl of Pembroke was unsuccessful). In 1645 the position was given to Walter Frost, again at 100 nobles, but for the first time with the stipulation that he must actually show evidence of his "labours." After a vacancy of several years, the position was awarded at the Restoration to Captain John Burroughs; and in 1668 the city, having decided it was not getting its money's worth, abolished the position and the salary, then being paid to Cornwall Bradshaw, who was given £100 the following year as a settlement for his lost stipend; Bradshaw had held the position since early 1666. On the position and its occupants, see *Analytical Index to the Series of Records Known as the Remembrancia preserved among the Archives of the City of London* (1878), pp. 305–6.

[77] Gransden, *Historical Writing in England*, II, 67. Gray, a soldier and diplomat, was imprisoned by the Scots in 1355, during which time, he tells us, he was inspired to compile his French-language *Scalacronica* ("ladder of chronicles") by a dream in which he met the spirits of a number of chroniclers, including the famous Higden.

read the text in print was small, then the number who went further afield to read the chronicle sources must have been smaller still. The chronicle plays devoted to English history in particular enjoyed a relatively brief vogue between the 1560s and 1620s, their popularity falling off after that, though the explanation for this is not entirely clear. They would enjoy new life but a less heterogeneous audience in the second half of the century, in the tragicomedies of Orrery, Crowne, Tate, and others.[78] In the meantime they had introduced the content of their sources to a much broader audience than had ever been exposed to history before; the price may have been to render those sources themselves virtually unreadable.

The relation to the chronicles of the humanist "politic histories," to use Professor Levy's durable term, of the late Elizabethan and early Stuart period is somewhat different. These departed from the chronicles much more self-consciously than the plays (which as drama rather than prose were not in direct competition), asserting a pedigree from ancient historiography in which certain authors, Polybius, Sallust, and especially Tacitus, figured as paragons of narrative style and political judgment. Moreover, because they existed publicly only in print, they reached a much more select audience, primarily of educated or at least relatively well off gentry and aristocracy. That indeed was part of their *caché*, that they contained worthwhile knowledge, told in an edifying and graceful style better suited to the "compleat gentleman," who was also frequently a courtier and politician. Whether Shakespeare wrote for the masses or reflected a "popular voice" is a question that need not concern us here: it is a certainty that Hayward, Daniel, Godwin, and Bacon, on their own admission, did not. These authors mined from the chronicles the ore that they refined in their own works. They rarely contributed anything like a new interpretation of events, though they often corrected the chroniclers on points of detail or attempted to resolve contradictory reports. Rather, they translated the clipped, rough annals of the past into elegant Latin or vigorous, readable English, sewing their fragmentary sources together into what one of their number, John Clapham, called a "continued historie" and what Bacon designated as "perfect history." They aspired to create unified, vivid characters out of the chroniclers' stylized descriptions and lists of names; to distil moral and political wisdom from the

---

[78] In the view of Phyllis Rackin, *Stages of History: Shakespeare's English chronicles* (Ithaca, NY, 1990), the Elizabethan history plays provided a polyphonic, multivocal staging of the history purveyed hegemonically and univocally in the chronicles, a point explicitly rejected, in connection with Holinshed at least, by Patterson, *Reading Holinshed's Chronicles*, p. 279, n. 10. I would wish to strike a compromise here while raising another issue: the plays certainly exhibit the same Elizabethan and early Stuart tendency to make firmer distinctions between fact and fiction, but polyvocal or not, they also appear to have suffered from the same disintegration of their audience that, I am arguing, occasioned loss of interest in the chronicles on which they were based.

events that the chroniclers merely recorded; and to entertain the elite reader.[79]

In doing all these things, the politic historians, much more clearly than their early Tudor predecessors, drove history further away from its chronicle *sources* in the direction of its classical *models*, even while they claimed to follow the best of those sources unerringly. That was the paradox: the more faithful were the new histories to their sources, the more they contributed to their increasing obscurity by superseding them. They fit very well with the dramatic representations of history being enacted on the stage – much better, in fact, than the original chronicles from which those plays themselves derived. The educated viewer of Shakespeare's *Henry IV* or Ford's *Perkin Warbeck* might well want to satisfy a curiosity about the fifteenth century, but he was more likely to turn to a short general work like Clapham, Martyn, or Daniel, or to a detailed study like Hayward's *Henry IIII* or Bacon's *Henry VII* than to the stream of successive events contained in the chronicles.

The politic history, like the antiquarian treatises and chorographies that were gaining popularity around the end of the century, severely deflated the "top" end of the potential market for chronicles. But what of the lower end? As we saw, the chroniclers and their printers made some attempt in the second half of the sixteenth century to penetrate the bottom end of the market. They might have been successful had not balladeers and almanac writers almost literally taken pages out of their books. Seventeenth-century ballads occasionally borrowed the title of "chronicle," rather as contemporary prose fiction boasted its "true stories," in order to lay claim to feigned historicity and indicate chronological completeness: the Restoration *Wandering Jews Chronicle* is one example. As competitors in the business of communicating factual history, however, almanacs were a more formidable rival. These acquired historical content, in the form of chronologies generally running from the Creation, and a calendar listing the saints' days, late in the Tudor period. Like the lists of fairs and roads that the writers began to include in the 1550s, these historical sections had a practical purpose, since they could help the rural reader with the dating of leases and deeds that frequently employed regnal years.[80] Until late in the sixteenth century, almanac chronologies gave little more information than the number of years elapsed since the Creation or the birth of Christ. But from 1585, when Thomas Porter listed the dates of each "invasion" of England from Brutus to William I, a more detailed

---

[79] Details on these historians may be found in Woolf, *Idea of History*, chs 2 and 5.

[80] Bernard Capp, *Astrology and the Popular Press: English Almanacs, 1500–1800* (1979), p. 62. Works closely related to the almanac and fulfilling some of its functions, such as Dekker's observations on the weather (*The cold year. 1614* [1614]) and the writing tables issued by Frank Adams, Robert Triplet, and, ultimately, by the Company of Stationers itself, provide further examples of the ways in which the many functions of the late medieval chronicle were usurped by newer, more "print-friendly" genres.

chronology quickly became a standard feature, maintained throughout the next century. The prophet-astrologers among the almanac writers, men such as William Lilly and Philip Kynder, inevitably found themselves adding written chronological material to their printed texts to "prove" the correctness of their prognostications; and their readers, too, frequently added marginal additions to the printed entries. Those almanac writers who listed their sources of information relied overwhelmingly on the later Tudor chroniclers, Lanquet-Cooper, Grafton, Holinshed and Stow, supplemented less often by other authors such as Vergil or the German Johannes Sleidan.[81]

Since the almanackers were generally of a higher social and educational background than many of their readers, they provided a valuable service by filtering down the content of the chroniclers, in however adulterated a form, to a geographically dispersed rural audience. Like the history plays in London, but to an even greater degree, the almanac chronologies soon made their own sources of information redundant. At their peak in the mid-seventeenth century, the almanacs, which by then sold for about three or four pence, were published yearly in the hundreds of thousands. The market for these works was not, as Bernard Capp's illuminating study argues, "infinitely expandable," and it was tightly controlled by the same monopoly that regulated the printing of other works, the Stationers' Company. The stationers preferred, instead of introducing new titles, to "keep alive old favorites," much as the printers of Stow and, much later, Richard Baker, kept those works in print after the deaths of their authors.[82] "Brand-name" recognition, the print-era equivalent of ancient authority, was beginning to count for a great deal in the cultural marketplace.

MARKET SATURATION: THE PRESS AND THE PUBLICATION OF CHRONICLES

The fate of the chronicle did not hinge entirely on the emergence of the parasite genres. Even before Shakespeare and Sir John Hayward appeared on the historiographical scene, there are signs that the market for chronicles, especially large and comprehensive ones, was growing soft. This was not evident until relatively late in the reign of Elizabeth, and publications in her sister's reign and the first decade or so of her own suggest the opposite: the

---

[81] Ibid., pp. 215–16. Lilly interleaved the printed copies of his own almanacs with a chronicle-like record of events that vindicated his prognostications: Lilly, *Anglicus, Peace or no Peace, 1645* (1645), Bodl. MS Ashm. 121, between pp. 68–69, 72–73 ("July. many clubmen in Dorset"; Sept. 1, 2, 3 "news montross had taken Edenborough"). Kinder's own collection of his tracts includes "Terminalia," or extracts from various biblical and historical prophets tying virtually every significant event in the history of the world or of England to an earlier prophecy: Bodl. MS Ashm. 788, fos. 4r–102r.

[82] Capp, *Astrology and the Popular Press*, p. 44.

chronicle at first looked rather well-suited to the press. Some of the most prolific historical writers in the period were either printers themselves or had close connections with printers and booksellers: Caxton, Rastell, and Grafton provide good examples. The printer of Cooper's *Epitome of Chronicles* (1559) took an active interest in the work, contributing a brief introductory paragraph before the third book.[83] Holinshed's *Chronicles* is an even better instance. This work was planned by a printer, Reginald or Reyner Wolfe, as a sort of super-chronicle, a universal history and geography on the order of the *Polychronicon*, complete with maps. When Wolfe died his task fell to a publishing syndicate whose members entrusted Raphael Holinshed to complete the job; Holinshed in turn enlisted William Harrison and Richard Stanyhurst to contribute their respective *Descriptions* of England and Ireland. The first edition appeared in 1577. The syndicate then decided that an even larger second edition might prove profitable and took on further partners to share the cost. When Holinshed himself died in 1580, the partners assembled a larger scholarly team that included Francis Thynne, John Stow, and Abraham Fleming, all working under the nominal leadership of John Vowell alias Hooker of Exeter. The result was the huge and rather unwieldy compilation of 1587 that also bears Holinshed's name but with which he had little to do (see plate 1.2).[84]

The sharing of expenses among several publisher-printers, and the corresponding division of scholarly labour was a sign of things to come in major history publishing ventures. By the end of the sixteenth century, printers and booksellers were selling, buying, or exchanging copyrights on certain chronicles, almost certainly in response to their sales. Thomas Marshe exchanged the copyright to Stow's *Summaries* on 31 March 1573 with Henry Binneman or Bynneman for the latter's edition of Terence.[85] The abridgments similarly changed hands a number of times within a few years until finally, in 1607, the Company of Stationers took over their publication. Other publishers were

---

[83] Thomas Lanquet, *Epitome of Chronicles*, ed. Thomas Cooper (1559 edn), fo. 84. The first edition was printed by T. Berthelet in 1549, and Crowley's pirated edition by W. Seres and T. Marshe in 1559. Cooper's own revised editions appeared in 1560 and 1565.

[84] On revisions to Holinshed by Thynne see David Carlson, "The Writings and Manuscript Collections of the Elizabethan Alchemist, Antiquary, and Herald Francis Thynne," *HLQ*, 52 (1989), 203–72, pp. 208ff.; and Patterson, *Reading Holinshed's Chronicles*, pp. 8ff. Patterson's argument about the tendency of humanist historians in the seventeenth century to find the wide range and many authors of Holinshed unsettling is supported in the reaction of the Yarmouth antiquary Henry Manship, who used Holinshed regularly as a source for his *History of Great Yarmouth* but was embarrassed by its verbatim replication of "most unseemly words against the Almighty" uttered by some townsmen, "which, although they be by the said Chronicle, there expressed in the very vile and base terms themselves, yet for my own part, I hold it not meet here to utter, but rather to conceal them." H. Manship, *History of Great Yarmouth*, ed. C. J. Palmer (1854), p. 122.

[85] *A Transcript of the Registers of the Company of Stationers of London, 1554–1640*, ed. Edward Arber (5 vols., 1875), I. 272, 418.

compelled to share larger jobs among them. Grafton had already used other printers in the 1550s and 1560s for his own chronicles while printing for himself his editions of Hardyng and Hall. Archbishop Parker's editions of Asser and of Thomas of Walsingham's *Ypodigma Neustriae* were printed by John Day, the publisher of early editions of Foxe and of two editions of Gildas, but his edition of Walsingham's so-called *Historia Brevis*, which was bound up and sold with these, was printed by Henry Bynneman, who also printed the first edition of Holinshed.[86]

Where simpler works, such as the popular *Breviat cronicle contayning all the kinges from Brute to this daye*, continued to be produced by only one printer at a time (though he might change from edition to edition), collaboration on larger projects was soon almost inescapable. John Speed's *Historie* in 1611 would similarly be a collaborative effort by the author and a quartet of printers and booksellers, in which the efforts of a number of scholars were coordinated by Speed.[87] The late sixteenth-century taste for emblems and other sorts of visual imagery may have increased the attraction of a work like Speed's *Historie*, with its woodcuts, and its companion volume of maps, the *Theatre of the Empire of Great Britain*, but it also drove up considerably their cost of production.[88] Just as some early Tudor chroniclers and their printers had enjoyed special privileges – Pynson, Berthelet, and Grafton had been among the first royal printers – so Speed received financial assistance in the form of a government license to produce the genealogies for inclusion in the Authorized Version of the Bible.[89] These appeared in the same year as his history. Speed also enjoyed the patronage of Sir Robert Cotton and several influential backers who had contributed material, including the then attorney-general, Francis Bacon. The commercial nature of any publishing venture, then as now, meant that money played as great a role in determining the shape and size of a chronicle as considerations of truth or style, and that the

---

[86] Asser, *Aelfredi regis res gestae* (John Day, 1574); *Historia brevis Thomae Walsingham, ab Edwardo primo, ad Henrici quintum* (Henry Binneman, 1574); Walsingham, *Ypodigma Neustriae vel Normanniae . . . ab irruptione Normannorum usq; ad annum 6. regni Henrici Quinti* (John Day, 1574). For Bynneman's privilege to reprint chronicles, granted by patent in 1580, see *Cal. Pat. Rolls Eliz. I*, VII, 540; the privilege is discussed in John Feather, *Publishing, Piracy and Politics* (New York, 1944), p. 13.

[87] The first edition of Speed's *Historie* was printed by W. Hall and A. Beale for the booksellers J. Sudbury and G. Humble. Humble, who published the *Theatre*, received on 29 April 1608 a 21-year privilege to sell it: W. W. Greg, *Companion to Arber* (reprinted Oxford, 1967), p. 154.

[88] Some readers simply chose to borrow copies of larger histories and chronicles and make their own epitomes of them, complete with page references, rather than buy the book: in 1654 Edward Ffloyd drew up such an epitome of Speed: "An epitome of Speeds Historie," MS Rawl. D.139, fos. 1–46.

[89] F. S. Siebert, *Freedom of the Press in England, 1476–1776* (Urbana, 1952, reprinted 1965), pp. 32–33, 39.

Plate 1.2 (*opposite*)   Title page to vol. III of the second edition of Holinshed's *Chronicles* (1587).

printer would have considerable say in the design and production of an historical work for the public consumption, a fact of scholarly life that Drayton complained of bitterly after the publication of his *Poly-olbion* in 1612. In the same year, the penurious virtuoso and intellectual projector Edmund Bolton commented to Sir Robert Cotton of "the conspiracies of booksellers, and printers, to robbe the authors of theyr commoditie."[90]

In *News from the New World*, Jonson was not far from the truth in depicting the chronicler in collusion with the stationer, but he failed to acknowledge a countervailing trend in the publication of historical works: with the exception of occasional giants like Holinshed's and projects that had the assistance of a patron to defray costs, the direction in general was towards smaller, shorter, and cheaper, not longer and heavier. The briefer, the more ephemeral a work – almanacs and calendars were ideal – the more likely it was to sell quickly, and the more easily it could be produced and marketed outside the London booksellers' stalls.[91] John Stow, the most prolific as well as the most able of the late Tudor chroniclers, found this out to his cost. Originally interested in poetry – he built up a substantial collection of Chauceriana and fifteenth-century literature – he tells us that he turned to history around 1564 out of dissatisfaction with recent chronicles. "I seeinge the confused order of our late English chronicles, and the ignorant handling of ancient affairs, consecrated myself to the search of our famous antiquities."[92] In that year he penned his earliest surviving chronicle, an unpublished manuscript, now in the Bodleian, that provides an excellent instance of the transition of the genre from its medieval accretive form to the single-author type characteristic of the smaller chronicles of the print era. In the following year the first octavo edition of Stow's *A Summary of English chronicles* appeared, followed by a second in 1566. He expanded the work with additional research in 1570 and 1575. Meanwhile, he also issued a series of briefer abridgments of the *Summary*, in slightly smaller (sextadecimo) format.[93] The *Summary* kept the traditional form of a city chron-

---

[90] Michael Drayton, *Poly-Olbion* (1612) in *Complete Works of Michael Drayton*, ed. J. W. Hebel, Kathleen Tillotson, and Bernard Newdigate (5 vols., Oxford, 1931–41, reprinted 1961), vol. IV. BL MS Cott. Jul. C.III, fo. 30 (Bolton to Cotton, 16 October 1612).

[91] For one almanac chronology of 1690, see Hist. MSS Comm., *Var. Coll.*, VII (Unwin), pp. 570–73.

[92] John Stow, *Survey of London*, preface. Stow helped with such projects as Speght's edition of Chaucer (1598) and compiled notes on Lydgate (BL MS Harl. 367, fos. 83v, 85; BL MS Stowe 952, fos. 303v–379) and on earlier English poetry. He published *Pithy pleasaunt and profitable workes of maister Skelton* in 1568 and edited *Certaine worthye manuscript poems of great antiquitie* in 1597. Stow's quarrel with Grafton, his principal rival in the chronicle trade in the 1560s and 1570s, sprang in part from Stow's doubting Grafton's claim to have written much of Hall's chronicle before publishing it: BL MS Harl. 367, fos. 1–4, 11. For Stow's work in general see Barrett L. Beer, *Tudor England Observed: the world of John Stow* (Phoenix Mill, UK, 1998).

[93] "A breffe remembraunce of thyngs chaunced with in this realme of England faythefully collected owt of dyvers cronycles . . . [by] John Stowe . . . written with his owne hand"

icle, complete with mayoral years, as did its quarto successor, the *Chronicles of England* (1580). These works were extremely successful; nineteen editions are known and there may have been others. With the quarto *Annales of England* that followed, beginning in 1592, Stow enjoyed similar success.[94] Because he himself both conscientiously corrected each version as it came out and updated it, his *Annales* enjoyed a high level of popularity, sufficient to outlive the author and allow Edmund Howes to reissue them twice, in 1615 and 1631, with his own additions and in an even bulkier folio format.

But Stow himself could not rest satisfied with summarizing earlier chronicles, and like his contemporary, Reyner Wolfe, he appears to have been troubled by the lack of a general chronicle covering the entire island. (This impulse to comprehensive coverage, not well served by any of the parasite genres, would in fact be a recurring theme of seventeenth- and eighteenth-century historiography, though other forms than the chronicle would be used to achieve it.[95]) In the 1605 edition of the *Annales*, the last to appear in Stow's lifetime, he admits to having completed in the 1580s a huge, detailed great chronicle, probably along the lines of Holinshed's tomes. He found to his dismay that no printer would support it, the second edition of Holinshed (in which he was himself involved) then being underway.[96] Even in an age when the number of printers was comparatively small, and publication more strictly controlled, the demand for large, expensive volumes of this kind must never have been great, and two editions of Holinshed would almost certainly have saturated it, at least for a time.[97] The desire for comprehensiveness in recording the past had run up against the need to show a profit in the ledger

(annotation by John Daye, the printer): Bodl. MS Douce 225: this appears to have been one of the items discovered during the search of Stow's study in 1568 (Strype, *Life of Edmund Grindal* [1821], pp. 185, 516). First in the custody of Daye, it passed eventually to Sir James Ware, the Irish antiquary, and then to Henry Hyde, earl of Clarendon. The longer version of Stow's summaries went through seven editions between 1565 and 1590, the shorter through twelve between 1566 and 1618, the last three being edited and continued by Edmund Howes. See the revised *Short-Title Catalogue*, ed. W. A. Jackson, vol. II, items 23319–23340. With twenty-five known editions or reissues of his chronicles, Stow was by far the biggest seller before 1640: see table 1.3 below.

[94] Stow, *Annales of England* (1592). Subsequent editions, each longer than its predecessor, were published in 1600 (to 1600), 1601 (to 1601), 1605 (to 1605), 1615 (to 1614), and 1631 (to 1631); again, the last two were updated by Howes.

[95] Levine, *Battle of the Books*, pp. 277–326; Hicks, *Neoclassical History and English Culture*, p. 29.

[96] Stow, *Annales* (1605), p. 1438; Kingsford, *English Historical Literature*, p. 268. Since the work, if it really was completed, has not survived, there is no way of knowing for certain precisely what shape it took. Under the influence of his younger friend, Camden, Stow may have tinkered with a humanist model, and he refers to the work as a "history of this island" rather than as a chronicle; nevertheless, it is difficult to believe that it would have differed substantially, other than in size, from his earlier works.

[97] John Lewis' *History*, written over a period of years between 1605 and 1615, may not have been published for the same reason, Speed's *Historie* having appeared in 1611. Lewis attempted to gain royal support for his project in a set of proposals, undated, for the printing of a new history of Britain in ten books: BL MS Royal 18.A. xxxvii, fos. 1–20.

book. History was beginning its career as an intellectual commodity, and the conflict of an author's scholarly ambition and a publisher's commercial shrewdness would recur again and again in the ensuing century, and down to our day.[98]

Unless a historical work proved a surprise best-seller (Camden's *Britannia*, even in Latin, began as a small octavo and grew through consistently high sales into the folio of 1607) it was unlikely to go into the reissues or new editions that could offset the initial cost of publication, and few printers were prepared to venture much on the possibility of such success, unless expenses could be offset by assistance from a patron or the work had some endorsement from the government. No one got rich from writing or publishing a history book in Renaissance England, and even shorter works could put an author without a patron into the red: Stow himself had to petition the mayor and aldermen for a pension to offset the costs of printing his *Summaries*, many of which he had born.[99]

Few works were as lavish as the 1570 and 1583 editions of Foxe's *Acts and Monuments*, a work the author of which had himself ruthlessly pillaged the medieval chronicles for tales of martyrdom and persecution.[100] But few appealed so well to national feelings of antipopery. Even so, corners were cut, primarily through the device of using the same engraving to represent a number of different martyrs on different pages. A famous explorer and soldier like Sir Walter Ralegh had high hopes of selling a book like the *History of the World* on the strength of his reputation, even when the government forced the removal of the title page bearing the author's name. Lesser individuals were generally not so fortunate. Edmund Bolton, who was probably interested in securing the post of city chronologer vacated by the death of Thomas Middleton the dramatist in 1627,[101] proposed to the London court of aldermen that they support one of his many pet projects along these lines. This was to be a mammoth new history of London, in Latin and English, complete with maps. In 1632, however, city officials reneged on an earlier promise of assistance when he revealed the true cost of the work – between three and four thousand pounds – much to the anguish of the penniless Bolton, who had already invested considerable time and money in the project. Again there seems to have been room for one such work, but not

---

[98] Aspects of the business of publishing history are dealt with in chapters 5 and 6, below.

[99] BL MS Harl. 367, fo. 8. On 8 March 1604 James I issued a warrant for letters patent to Stow empowering him to collect gratuities and voluntary contributions for defraying his costs.

[100] For an example of Foxe's use of chronicle materials, see BL MS Harl. 424, fo. 62r–v, "The story of King Edward the ij" from the French of "Sir Thomas de la Moore" (actually Geoffrey le Baker). Dr. Thomas Freeman has completed an extensive study of Foxe's use of his sources that was not in print at the time this chapter was completed; I am grateful to him for allowing me to read it in typescript.

[101] *Analytical Index to the Remembrancia*, pp. 305–6.

two, and the aldermen decided instead to accept the offer of Ben Jonson (who in the meantime had been appointed city chronologer in 1628), to present the city with a short chronology of the past four years – a less ambitious project, and one which Jonson was prepared to do for "love" instead of money.[102] The appointment of two dramatists in swift succession to fill a position once occupied informally by urban chroniclers like Robert Fabyan is an interesting demonstration of one genre's colonization of another's turf. It is a nice irony that Bolton himself had only a few years earlier been one of the most vocal critics of the chroniclers in his *Hypercritica, or a Rule of Judgement, for Writing or Reading Our Histories.*[103]

QUANTIFYING THE MARKET

Thus had the printing press brought the Tudor chronicle into the public domain and given it, temporarily, a relatively wide readership while also facilitating the success of its rivals. But the press had another, and malign, effect on the chronicle quite independent of the development of the parasite genres. It eventually forced the cessation of continued chronicle writing in favour of the reedition, summarizing, abridging, or updating of older ones. In the seventeenth century, even the reedition of sixteenth-century favorites like Stow and Rastell gradually proved less attractive to printers, with the result that the chronicles published after 1595 tended to be either unsuccessful, one-edition ventures or scholarly editions of medieval texts.

In order to evaluate this development, we need to turn away from the chronicle's rivals and successors back to the genre itself. Specifically, it is necessary to provide some hard figures on the publication of chronicles throughout the early modern period and, incidentally, to establish empirically the course of the chronicle's decline. Aside from occasional references in documents like the daybook of the Oxford bookseller John Dorne, who sold an unidentified "cronica anglie" for a penny in 1520, we still know all too little about the retail prices of individual titles in early modern England, something to be taken up in more detail later in the present book.[104] So far as

---

[102] BL MS Harl. 6521, fos. 243v, 247–49 (Bolton's notebook and drafts of letters): Bolton noted on 18 October, 1632 that "all the aldermen were against it, though [Sir Hugh] Hamersley and some others spoke for it".

[103] For Bolton's comments see below and Woolf, *Idea of History in Early Stuart England*, pp. 192–93.

[104] F. Madan, "The Day-book of John Dorne," Oxford Historical Society, *Collectanea*, 1 (1885), 71–178, at p. 113 and (for 4d but bound with another book), p. 114; E. Gordon Duff, "A Bookseller's Accounts, *circa* 1510," *The Library*, n.s. 8 (1907), 256–66; W. A. Jackson, "A London Bookseller's Ledger of 1535," *The Colophon*, n.s. 1 (1936), 498–509. As we will see in greater detail in subsequent chapters, private library lists and inventories provide corresponding information about prices from the readership end of the exchange. Sir William More, for instance, paid five shillings for a copy of Fabyan's chronicle and the same

the Tudor chronicles and some other early histories are concerned, the painstaking efforts of bibliographers have provided some help by analyzing the inventories and other surviving records of booksellers and printers. F. R. Johnson and H. S. Bennett, in two articles published a half century ago, estimated that the "average" book retailed, unbound, at about 0.33d per sheet before 1560, and rose with inflation, to about 0.45d from 1560 to the 1630s. These estimates, which probably err on the low side, are at best averages subject to wide variance from case to case. Nevertheless, the correlation of these averages with specific prices for unbound sheets of a large sample of individual titles suggests that the price of *all* history books, chronicles included, increased far beyond the basic rate of inflation.

Table 1.1 summarizes Johnson's and Bennett's findings with respect to historical works. Early and mid-sixteenth century titles retailed at prices significantly lower than the average for all books. From the last quarter of the century, however, nearly all histories (and not merely chronicles) exceeded the average by 20 percent or more; even reprinted works sold to the public at a price higher than the 0.45d average. The sole exception was the first edition of Holinshed – perhaps explaining his publishers' confidence that an expanded edition could still be produced economically. These averages remained fairly constant, even allowing for inflation, from about 1560 to 1635, when book prices began to climb again. It should further be noted that while a work like Holinshed's, through economy of scale and shared responsibility for production, might have a lower per-sheet price than Stow's *Abridgement*, this would be more than compensated for by the large discrepancy in their retail prices, which were also dependent on the number of sheets. This made Stow, though more expensive on a sheet-for-sheet calculation, clearly the cheaper and more vendible, a fact reflected in the actual prices of both books. These findings need not contradict the conventional picture, derived from Louis B. Wright, of the "popularization" of history in Elizabethan England. They may merely show that more people were reading history books of some sort or another despite their relatively higher prices. If so, then we must still ask why the chronicle, almost alone among historical genres, failed to maintain this level of popularity in the following century.[105]

---

for a *Polychronicon*, among the several historical works noted in his account book: J. Evans, "Extracts from the Private Account Book of Sir William More," *Archaeologia*, 36 (1855), 284–310, especially pp. 288–92.

[105] Francis R. Johnson, "Notes on English Retail Book-Prices, 1550–1640," *The Library*, 5th series 5 (1950–51), 83–113; H. S. Bennett, "Notes on English Retail Book-Prices, 1480–1560," *The Library*, 5th series 5 (1950–51), 172–78. In his *English Books and Readers, 1475–1557* (Cambridge, 1952), pp. 224–34, Bennett favors a higher estimate of 0.5d per sheet for the earlier period. If correct, this would make early Tudor chronicles even more clearly underpriced. For a thorough discussion of retail and production costs, see Philip Gaskell, *A New Introduction to Bibliography* (Oxford, 1972), p. 178; M. Plant, *The English Book Trade* (2nd edn, 1965), pp. 35–58, 238–47 also contains useful information.

Table 1.1. *Retail prices of some chronicles and histories, to 1640*

Year	STC no.	Author/title	Price bound	Price unbound	Cost per sheet (unbound)	≥ 20% above/below average cost
1542	10661	Fabyan, *Chronicle*	5s	3s 6d	.20d	–
1542	10662	Same, reissue	5s	3s 6d	.20d	–
1543	12767	Hardyng, *Chronicle*	2s 6d	1s 10d	.23d	–
1550	4626	Carion, *Chronicles*	1s	8d	.10d	–
1550	4626	Same, anr example	—	1s	.16d	–
1552	12723a	Hall, *Union*	12s	9s	.32d	–
1560	19848	Sleidan, *Chronicle*	—	7s 2d	.35d	–
1563	19849	Idem, *Brief Chron.*	—	1s 2d	.48d	av.
1565	15220	Cooper, *Chronicle*	4s 6d	3s 10d	.44d	av.
1575	23325	Stow, *Summary*	4s	3s 8d	.73d	+
1577	13568	Holinshed, *Chronicles*	26s	20s	.45d	av.
1599	12995	Hayward, *Hen. IIII*	—	? 2s	1.20d	+
1613	13000	Hayward, *Lives of III Normans*	—	2s	.60d	+
1618	23332	Stow, *Abridgement*	3s	2s 4d	.71d	+
1622	1159	Bacon, *Henry VII*	7s	4s 6d	.84d	+
1627	5684	Cotton, *Henry III*	1s	6d	1.00d	+
1627	23048	Speed, *Historie*	30s	20s	.69d	+
1633	23345	Stow, *Survey*	—	5s	.73d	+
1638	353	Aleyn, *Henry VII*	1s 8d	1s	1.20d	+

Sources: Francis R. Johnson, "Notes on English Retail Book-Prices, 1550–1640," *The Library*, 5th series 5 (1950–51), 83–112; H. S. Bennett, "Notes on English Retail Book-Prices, 1480–1560," ibid., 172–78. "Average cost" in the right-hand column is calculated as 33d per unbound sheet for publications up to 1559, and 0.45d for publications after 1560.

Despite the relative scarcity of price information about individual sixteenth-century titles, a quantitative examination of publishing trends in the last two centuries of the chronicle's existence may provide at least part of the explanation for its eclipse. I have identified 220 editions or issues (excluding minor variants) of 79 chronicles published between 1475 and 1699. By arranging the items on this list in several ways, we can discover something about the public taste for history and the vendibility of the genre over an extended time.[106] The chronicles can first be broken down according to the

---

[106] This population of 220 was arrived at after an examination of the titles listed in the *Short-Title Catalogue* (STC), the revised *STC*, ed. W. A. Jackson, *et al.* (vol. II), Donald G. Wing, *A Short-Title Catalogue of English Books . . . 1641–1700* (2nd edn, 1972–), the

Table 1.2. The publication of chronicles by fifteen-year periods, 1475–1699

Format	1475–1489	1490–1504	1505–1519	1520–1534	1535–1549	1550–1564	1565–1579	1580–1594	1595–1609	1610–1624	1625–1639	1640–1654	1655–1669	1670–1684	1685–1699	Subtotal	Total
2° O	4	1	2	3	1	1	6	0	3	1	0	3	1	2	3	31	—
2° R	2	6	2	6	5	8	9	2	4	3	3	6	8	7	2	73	104
4° O	0	0	1	0	2	1	3	5	0	1	0	4	0	0	1	18	—
4° R	0	0	0	0	1	2	2	1	2	2	1	1	0	0	0	12	30
8° O	0	0	0	2	3	4	1	2	1	0	0	0	5	3	1	22	—
8° R	0	0	0	0	5	10	10	2	2	4	1	1	2	1	1	39	61
12° O	0	0	0	0	0	0	0	0	0	0	1	0	0	0	1	2	—
12° R	0	0	0	0	0	0	0	0	0	0	4	1	1	1	2	9	11
16° O	0	0	0	0	0	0	2	0	1	0	0	0	0	0	0	3	—
16° R	0	0	0	0	0	0	3	2	3	0	0	0	0	0	0	8	11
Brds O	0	0	0	0	0	0	0	1	0	0	0	1	1	0	0	3	—
Brds R	0	0	0	0	0	0	0	0	0	0	0	0	0	0	0	0	3
Sbtl. O	4	1	3	5	6	6	12	8	5	2	1	8	7	5	6	79	—
Sbtl. R	2	6	2	6	11	20	24	7	11	9	9	9	11	9	5	141	—
Total	6	7	5	11	17	26	36	15	16	11	10	17	18	14	11	220	220

Notes: n = 220; O: original edition; R: reprint or new edition.

format in which they were published. In general those titles listed as "folios" were more expensive than quartos, quartos than octavos, and so forth, all the way down to the single broadsheet.[107] Secondly, one can distinguish, within each chronicle, the first edition from a number (ranging from 0 to n, n > 10) of new editions or reissues of the same text (translations, however, have been indexed as separate "originals," as have abridgments or epitomes of larger works). Finally, the chronicles thus classified by format and edition can be plotted against time from 1475 to 1699. Since there were many years in which no works were published, and short-term fluctuations are not likely to be significant fifteen-year periods have been employed rather than single years. Numbers represented in table 1.2 are fifteen-year cumulative totals, not running averages.[108]

Between 1475 and 1699 there were published 79 "original" chronicles and 141 reeditions. By format, this breaks down into 31 folio, 18 quarto, 22 octavo, 2 duodecimo, 3 sextadecimo, and 3 broadsheet originals, plus 73 folio, 12 quarto, 39 octavo, 9 duodecimo, 8 sextadecimo, and nil broadsheet reeditions. The peak years of the chronicle's visibility on the publishing market (in originals, reeditions, and totals) occurred between 1550 and 1579. This peak is skewed somewhat by the relatively brief popularity of the *Breviat cronicle*, which went through several editions in the 1550s. But even allowing for this it is clear that the chronicle as a published genre was at no time more popular than under the middle Tudors and early in Elizabeth's reign, extending downward in the period 1565–79 to include the sextadecimo format.

National Union Catalogue, and various indices to these works. Titles can often be deceptive, and several items were deleted from the list after inspection. The question what is and what is not a chronicle defies any kind of objective solution, and the decision taken whether to include a particular item may well seem arbitrary in certain cases. In general I have counted all works which either call themselves chronicles, annals, or cognate terms, or which clearly are chronicles despite the lack of such a title. Works published either in England or abroad by English authors are counted, but not editions of English chronicles published by foreigners abroad (for example the collected editions of Jerome Commelyn and André Duchesne). Collections such as Savile, Camden or Twysden have been counted only once when they were bound together but separately if evidence exists (as with Matthew Parker's editions of Walsingham, Asser, and Matthew Paris in the 1570s) that the constituent chronicles were bound or published separately.

107 Leah S. Marcus has recently advanced a similar argument relating to Shakespeare's plays, to the effect that the so-called "bad quarto" version differs from the first folio because the latter's compilers were targeting a more elevated market than that to which the quartos had appealed. "Shopping-Mall Shakespeare: Quartos, Folios, and Social Difference," *HLQ*, 58 (1996), 161–78.

108 These figures were initially calculated in 1985–86 and previously published in my above-cited article "Genre into Artifact." At the time of calculation, neither vols. I (1986) nor III (1991) of the revised *STC* had yet appeared. While newer information in vol. I might add or remove a small number of chronicles from the population, I do not think the picture given in the original analysis would be materially affected, and have not undertaken the lengthy process of recounting them.

Table 1.2 also reveals that the chronicle was primarily issued in folio (104) and octavo (61) format. There were somewhat fewer quartos (30), and only 25 instances of all smaller formats. Again, caution is necessary: these figures are derived from survival rates that are almost certainly distorted in favor of the larger formats. Nevertheless, there can be little doubt that the chronicle remained largely confined to those larger formats and therefore, in all likelihood, to the upper reaches of the literate public. The number of folios peaked at about the same time as the genre as a whole, tailed off sharply in the 1580s and early 1590s, rose slightly from 1595 to 1639 and more steeply from 1640 to the end of the century. Although a few post-1640 titles were inspired in some way by the civil war, the vast majority of later seventeenth-century titles were originals or reeditions of medieval or early Tudor authors.

GENRE INTO ARTIFACT

The relative steadiness of folio sales in comparison with other formats, and the almost complete failure of the chronicle to make a greater impact on the lucrative market for smaller formats (except briefly between 1550 and 1609) indicate that its attraction was less and less attributable to the information it contained and increasingly due to its status as a "collectable" or as a scholarly work of reference in the case of "critical" editions of medieval authors (Selden's *Eadmer*, and the various collections by Savile, Camden, Twysden, Fulman, Gale, and Wharton) rather than as a popular, widely read and commercially volatile form. In modern parlance, the chronicle survived into the seventeenth century primarily as a "coffee-table" book for some and a reference book for others, rather than as a paperback. When Thomas James sent a list of *desiderata* to Sir Thomas Bodley, the latter replied that he would be surprised "if you have not Hall & Fabian," which suggests that these were standard items for any good-sized collection.[109] Similarly, when the anti-quary John Vincent drew up a genealogy for his friend John Withye in 1640, he sought repayment by asking the latter to visit a bookseller in Little Britain and buy him a copy of Hall's *Union*, which Vincent knew to be there. "I pray you buy for me Halls [chronicle] which I looked upon when I went with you & your sonne [to] Londone; the man asked me by 5s for it; it was at the back." That this was no longer a "current" work of history is suggested by Vincent's explanation of the contents of the book to his friend; that its principal value was as a work of reference is indicated by Vincent's remark that the chronicle's primary value lay in its "severall indexes to each kinges raigne."[110] Sir William Twysden, son of the antiquary Sir Roger and himself

---

[109] Bodley, *Letters . . . to Thomas James*, ed. G. W. Wheeler (Oxford, 1926), p. 225.
[110] Bodl. MS Ashm. 798, fo. 7r (Leicestershire colls. of John Vincent, 16 March 1639/40).

a historian *manqué*, wrote to his own son in 1684, buoyed by Bishop Fell's plan to print "some more of those manuscripts as are obscurely buried and lost to public use in private libraries." His interest was manifestly that of a scholar searching for medieval sources rather than a general reader seeking the most current source for a particular fact.[111]

As early as the 1570s, government officials were using chronicles, together with other records, to present briefs to ministers of state. A collection of papers assembled in 1576–77 for Lord Burghley on the development of navigation on the river Lea cited precedents from "the chronicles" as well as examples "recorded by Mr. ffox in his booke of Acts and monuments and by Mr. Hollenshed in his second booke of the discription of Brittaine that the Danes went upon the river with their shipps in the tyme of kinge Alfrede." Over the course of the next century, as it ceased to be the standard form of historical writing, the chronicle paradoxically regained some authority as a primary source of information for administrative and political, as well as historical purposes; this may explain the worries of lawyers like Coke, cited earlier, that the chronicles might become confused with legitimate records. One late Elizabethan or early Jacobean author took every item concerning the liberties and privileges of London that he could find in Holinshed or Foxe and assembled them into a commonplace book of "Remarkables . . . under divers heads," adding from other sources various morsels of historical information that might come in useful, such as historical examples of the troubles caused by bards, prophets, and wizards, the "auncient pestes of England," and proofs of the primacy of the archbishops of York and Canterbury over Scotland and Ireland respectively. When the Restoration Secretary of State, Sir Joseph Williamson, read chronicles at all, it was to ransack them for facts about the history of parliament, the granting of subsidies, or other questions of state, which he extracted "out of Stowe's cronicle" or "out of an unknowne MS but of good credit."[112] Others continued to draw amusement

Because of their close connection to the printing industry, there was some interest in the early eighteenth century in the lives and careers of the early chroniclers, especially among bibliophiles like Joseph Ames: see his letters to John Anstis, John Lewis, and others from 1737 to 1740 in J. Nichols, *Illustrations of the Literary History of the Eighteenth Century* (8 vols., 1817–58), IV, 155–69. Cf. the letters of Ames' associate, the staymaker-turned-scholar George Ballard, who had a particular interest in Richard Grafton: ibid., 217–21 (Ballard to Ames, various letters, 1740–41).

[111] Ibid., IV, 70–71 (W. Twysden to R. Twysden, the younger, 29 September 1684).
[112] Bodl. MS Rawl. Essex 11 (Holman collections), fos. 89rff., dated 1576/7; Bodl. MS Gough London 8, fos. 13v–110r, especially at fos. 55v, 75v–76r, the "Remarkables" taken out of Holinshed and other chroniclers; PRO SP 9/11, fos. 4v, 20v, extracts in Williamson's hand on Edward III's parliaments. Williamson's rival royal official, the licenser Sir Roger L'Estrange, complained, with respect to chronicles, that "'twas a shame to the English Gentry that John Stowe's Chronicle should be the very best History of England yet write in English, who was but a Taylour," as reported by Hearne in *Remarks and Collections* (ed. C. E. Doble, D. W. Rannie, *et al.*, 11 vols., Oxford Hist. Soc., 1885–1921), VII, 280.

from the marvels that could be found in Stow, Holinshed, and Baker and which were increasingly scarce in contemporary historical writing. John Aubrey tells us of a Tamworth physician who, having read in Holinshed of the legendary climactic battle between Hengist and Vortigern by which the Saxons seized Britain, was then informed by a mysterious voice that he would soon see the bones of the men and horses slain. On watching a neighbor's servants dig for marl the next day, he indeed saw bones and potsherds that fitted the description given by Holinshed.[113]

As old books, in print or manuscript, chronicles were also becoming antiquities in their own right, suitable to collect or present as gifts. We know that manuscript copies of the *Brut* continued to circulate through the sixteenth century and into the seventeenth in this manner: among the several fifteenth-century English versions now at the John Rylands Library in Manchester, one was owned successively by Thomas Pawlyn, a London surgeon, and Nicholas Stevenson, a gentleman, and another by several Gray's Inn lawyers before it ended up in the collection of James I's Lord Treasurer, the earl of Marlborough. An even more briskly circulated copy, now at Lincoln College, Oxford, bears the name of several sixteenth-century readers, at least one of whom lived in Street Ashton, Warwickshire.[114] Sir Thomas Fairfax, the civil war general, owned an early fourteenth-century chronicle in manuscript, before it passed to the Leeds antiquary Ralph Thoresby.[115]

The fate of a fifteenth-century manuscript of the chronicle of the archbishops of York, originally compiled by Thomas Stubbs in the 1370s, provides a particularly graphic instance of the process whereby the accretive growth of the chronicle first slowed, then ceased altogether, finally becoming a curiosity passed around among collectors. The manuscript in question, first copied in the fifteenth century, was continued as annals in the early sixteenth century down to Wolsey's time, ending abruptly in the middle of a sentence. Two later hands completed the work with simple lists of the archbishops of York down to the time of Matthew Hutton (consecrated 1596). From there it passed into the hands of James Fayrer, rector of Sulhamsted, Berkshire, who gave it in 1654 to his friend Thomas Barlow (1607–91), a Westmorland collector who was Bodley's librarian from 1653 to 1660, and who left it to the library on his death.[116] By 1605, the year in which the refounded Bodleian acquired the first of several important collections of late medieval Latin chronicles, the genre was already well on its way to becoming a collector's item chiefly valued for its information and quaint style.[117] Meanwhile, pri-

[113] J. Aubrey, *Miscellanies upon Various Subjects* (4th edn, 1857), p. 108.
[114] *MMBL*, III, 416, 418, 422, 642.   [115] *MMBL*, III, 439.
[116] Bodl. MS Barlow 27: Stubbs' text ends at fo. 47v, at which point the first continuation commences, ending in mid-sentence at fo. 60r; the briefer lists appended in the later sixteenth century are at fo. 62v. For description and printed text, see *Historians of the Church of York and its Archbishops*, ed. James Raine (3 vols., RS, 1879–94), III, 388–421; Gransden, *Historical Writing in England*, II, 359.

vate collectors were exchanging manuscripts with what sometimes appears extraordinary volatility. An English illuminated chronicle from Brutus to Henry V, with a Latin continuation in a sixteenth-century hand, was owned by William Waad, clerk of the privy council in 1586; before half a century had elapsed it had found its way successively into the hands of George, Lord Bergavenny, Henry Ferrers the antiquary, and Nicholas Roscarrock the Catholic poet.[118] The antiquary Roger Dodsworth was given a fifteenth-century manuscript of a monastic chronicle by his friend John Stanhope.[119]

The library lists of the learned by the end of the seventeenth century similarly include printed and manuscript chronicles itemized in a way which betrays their datedness. A 1664 list of manuscripts belonging to Archbishop Sheldon contained 151 bound volumes (many of several titles). Of this number at least 60 were historical, including 46 volumes of heraldic and genealogical collections; and among the others were "Caxtons chronicle, old manuscript," Robert of Gloucester's chronicle, "an old manuscript English chronicle called Brute" (two different versions), Asser's life of Alfred in Latin, and, in print, "a very large, but thinne, booke in Spanish contayning a history of Spayne from the Floud."[120]

The sole instance of a highly vendible chronicle after 1640, Sir Richard Baker's *Chronicle of the Kings of England*, offers the proverbial exception that proves the rule. Edited, updated, and revised in later years by gentlemen such as Milton's nephew Edward Phillips, it went through twelve editions and an abridgment before 1700. Updated to the death of George I, it was serialized in 1732.[121] Baker's chronicle was a stock item on the squire's shelf well into the eighteenth century: Addison's Sir Roger de Coverley frequently quoted from the copy in his hall window, and it was also part of the furniture in Sir Thomas Booby's country house in *Joseph Andrews*.[122] As with most

---

[117] Bodl. MS Bodley 101 (four Latin chronicles from the fourteenth and fifteenth century); Bodl. MS Bodley 212 (Camden's gift of a fifteenth-century French MS, formerly in Syon monastery, containing chroniclers such as Henry of Huntingdon); Bodl. MSS Bodley 358 and 359, Sir George More's copy of the Latin text of the *Polychronicon* and Ralph Barlow's gift of a partial text of the same work in 1606.

[118] Bodl. MS Laud misc. 733, fos. 18–169, at fo. 168v.

[119] Bodl. MS Dodsw. 157, fos. 1–5v, the *Historia fundationum diversorum monasteriorum et ecclesiarum per nobilissimam Laceiorum familiam* (chronicle of the monasteries and churches built or endowed by the Lacey family).

[120] Catalog of Sheldon's collection composed by Miles Smith, 31 August 1664, Bodl. MS Tanner 88, fos. 60r–69v.   [121] On serialization, see below, chapter 6.

[122] Sir Roger de Coverley referred to it frequently and used it as a source in his disputes over history with Sir Andrew Freeport: *The Spectator*, 329 (18 March 1712), ed. Donald F. Bond (5 vols., Oxford, 1965), III, 212. Cf. 37 (I, 156) and 269 (II, 551), wherein the remark about Baker and other authors "who always lie in his hall window" is made about Sir Roger. The serialized 1732 version, a reprint in fascicules of the 1730 edition published by Samuel Ballard and a number of associates, is listed in R. M. Wiles' short-title catalog of serialized publications, appendix B in his *Serial Publication in England Before 1750* (Cambridge, 1957), p. 281; Martine Watson Brownley, "Sir Richard Baker's *Chronicle* and Later Seventeenth-Century Historiography," *Huntington Library Quarterly*, 52 (1989), 481–500.

Table 1.3. *The popularity of chroniclers: numbers of editions with intervals between first and last issues, 1475–1699*

2	3	4	5	6	7	8 or more
Arnold 1503–21	Asser 1574–1684	Hall 1542?–52	Bede 1565–1644	Fabyan 1516–59	Commynes 1596–1674	Grafton (9) 1562–72
Florence of Worcester 1590–92	Bale, *Sir John Oldcastle* 1444–48?	Holinshed 1577 (3 distinct issues)–1587	Froissart 1523–1611	Gildas 1525–1691		*Breviat Chronicle* (9) 1551–61
Caradoc of Llancarfan 1584–1697	Codomannus 1590–96	William of Malmesbury 1596–1691	Lanquet/ Cooper 1549–65	Higden 1480–1691		Eusebius (11) 1576/7–1698
Eutychius 1642–54	Monipennie (English edns only) 1612 (3)		"Matthew of Westminster" *Flores Historiarum* 1567–73	Thomas of Walsingham 1574–1603		*Brut* (11) 1480–1528
Hardying 1543 (2)	Ralph de Diceto 1652–91		Matthew Paris 1571–1684			Sleidan (12) 1560–1686
"Ingulf" 1596–1684			Wynkyn de Worde *et al.* (not including the *Brut*) 1515–52			Richard Baker (13) 1643–96
Historia Eliensis 1691 (2)						
Zosimus 1679–84						Stow (25) 1565–1631

Note: Numbers in this table are not directly comparable with those in table 1.2: here, chroniclers have been counted rather than their distinct works, and separate parts of multiauthor editions (e.g. Savile, Camden, Twysden) have been counted individually.

such books, its great virtue was that it provided an elegant summary of all earlier chronicles. Baker himself professed to having compiled it "with so great care and diligence that if all other of our chronicles were lost, this only would be sufficient to inform posterity of all passages memorable, or worthy to be known." And indeed, it frequently turns up as a handy reference source in the notes of Augustan antiquaries: thus in 1712 we find the Braintree, Essex antiquary Dr. Samuel Dale using Baker, among other works, to help him puzzle out the meaning of a church inscription recording a donation by Ethelric and Leofwin to the parish of Bocking. Five years earlier one of the earl of Oxford's correspondents cited a precedent from Baker as if it had status at law, evidently unaware of the objections of common lawyers to this practice in the previous century.[123]

But Baker's *Chronicle* was a throwback, as many readers recognized even in the seventeenth century. Baker himself (1568–1645) was an old man when, as a bankrupt living in the Fleet, he first put pen to paper. He had grown up in the peak years of the chronicle's popularity under Elizabeth, and may have been hearkening back to that time: his chronicle provided so easy a subject of derision for critics like Thomas Blount at least in part because it was an archaism.[124] Half a century after Blount's *Animadversions* on it, Baker's creaky volume was still being reprinted, but it had now moved from object of criticism to victim of satire. Lewis Theobald shrewdly observed that many historians and biographers had retained the annalistic practice of reporting the births of pygmies and giants during the year in which the events they described transpired. This inclusive untidiness and lack of a sense of *gravitas* was in Theobald's mind epitomized in the pages of Baker (conveniently serving here as a link to his Tudor predecessors), "who, with an impartial regard, as far as it lay in his painful powers, has given immortality to princes and tallow-chandlers, heroes and citizens' wives, children that cry'd before they were born, and men that laugh'd all their life time; fools that prophesied in their cradles, and old men that did penance for getting children at one hundred and twenty."[125]

Table 1.3 lists each *chronicler* (rather than his individual works) according to the number of editions or reissues in which his various works appeared, discounting those which appeared only once. It also gives the dates of first and last publication for each author, which reveals something about the market. In general, the most popular chronicles tended to be published in multiple editions over a relatively short period of time: all nine editions of the *Breviat Chronicle* appeared between 1551 and 1561, while Stow (the leader

[123] Essex RO, D/Y/1/1/102 (Dale to William Holman, 18 November 1712); Hist. MSS Comm., *Portland*, VIII, p. 297.
[124] Thomas Blount, *Animadversions upon Sir Richard Baker's Chronicle* (Oxford, 1672).
[125] Lewis Theobald, *The Censor* (3 vols., 1717), II, 130–31.

at 25) peaked in the 1570s and 1580s. Others, such as Eusebius and Sleidan, enjoyed slower but more enduring popularity, which, in the case of those authors, increased in the millennial fervor of the mid-seventeenth century. Those authors who went through fewest editions also tended (not surprisingly) to be published over a short period of time: Arnold's *Chronicle* (*ca.* 1503–21), Hardyng (2 edns, 1543) and "Florence" (now known as John) of Worcester (1590–92) are three examples. On the other hand, a few of these, such as Caradoc of Llancarfan (2 edns, 1584–1697), could turn up again after several decades. The works with the greatest chance of recurring in multiple editions over an extended period of time were mainly by medieval authors (Gildas, Bede, Matthew Paris, Ralph de Diceto, William of Malmesbury, and even Higden) rather than those first written under the Tudors. Again, this reinforces an intuitive feeling about the chronicle as a commodity, that a small but steady market lay in folio collectables or scholarly editions discreetly reissued over a long period, while cheaper formats enjoyed greater popularity at the genre's mid-sixteenth-century peak but did not weather very well its decline in the seventeenth century.

THE CHRONICLE AS EDITORIAL PROJECT

Throughout the Middle Ages chronicles were copied, borrowed, and paraphrased. They often grew more by gradual accretion than by conscious design or systematic composition. Through the erring copyist's hand or the chronicler's personal whim errors were added, details left out, and sometimes wholesale revisions made that have provided a challenge for modern editors. But this was precisely what kept the genre alive, allowing it to grow and change to suit the purposes of generation after generation of writers. As long as historical writing remained confined to the manuscript, any given chronicle would likely differ, even if only on the most trivial textual points, from any other: modern editors must sort out lines of relationship and descent and from those determine the original text of a chronicle as best they can. Print made possible the establishment and reproduction of accurate texts, but it also prohibited further substantive intervention in those texts.[126]

The process that transformed the medieval chronicle into a museum-piece developed slowly through the sixteenth century. Early Tudor printers indeed seemed unconcerned with presenting a text faithful to the original: hence Caxton's and Grafton's attempts to "update" or revise chroniclers such as Higden and Hardyng. At this stage, because of a preoccupation with the relatively recent past, there had yet to develop any real sense of the medieval

---

[126] This is, more or less, what happened to that other post-classical heirloom, medieval Latin, in the hands of humanists who restored it to Ciceronian purity while robbing it of the ability to adapt to change, thereby setting it well on its way to becoming a "dead language."

chroniclers as being not simply earlier historians, but truly remote writers whose works belonged to a different age. Beginning with John Leland, who viewed many of the manuscripts he collected as of "ancient" (that is, more than a century old) origin, English antiquaries acquired a sense of distance both from the periods they studied and from the documents created in those times.

Among the earlier editors, Archbishop Parker's attitude to the chronicles is curious. It is clear that Parker realized them to be texts worthy of study, at least in part for their propaganda value as supports for the antiquity of an independent English church. He employed agents to scour the land for manuscripts. Many of these remain in the Parker collection at Corpus Christi College, Cambridge,[127] including the "Parker" text of the Anglo-Saxon chronicle, and versions of Simeon of Durham and Ralph de Diceto. Parker's correspondents and the prelate himself consistently refer to such works as antiquities; they collected them because they were rare and curious; they studied them because they could throw light on times that seemed increasingly remote but upon which scholars could look back with a genuine enthusiasm. Yet though he had a much greater sense of distance from the chronicles he edited than had Caxton or Grafton, Parker could resist no more than they the temptation of filling in blanks in the manuscripts, "improving" the text with additions written by him or by a talented literary retainer such as John Lyly.[128] As May McKisack once put it, such were the methods of "an age which did not regard the Latin text as sacred and approved the restoration, physically as well as conjecturally, not only of what the author was believed to have written, but of what he might have written had he been in possession of other sources of information."[129] In fact, such enthusiasts *were* getting used to the idea of a Latin text as sacred (even in medieval Latin), but only in the seventeenth century would they put this into practice, and even then with the use of philology to "emend" errors and gaps in ancient authors. Sir Henry Savile's edition of some early medieval chroniclers including William of Malmesbury, Aethelweard, and Roger Hoveden employs Parker's dubious editorial methods. In contrast, Lord William Howard of Naworth deliberately avoided tampering with the text of his "Florence" of Worcester in 1592, though many unconscious errors naturally remained.[130]

Edmund Bolton could agree with Savile (perhaps the most condescending

---

[127] McKisack, *Medieval History in the Tudor Age*, p. 28.
[128] *Correspondence of Matthew Parker*, ed. J. Bruce and T. T. Perowne, Parker Soc. 33 (Cambridge, 1893), pp. 253–54. [129] McKisack, *Medieval History in the Tudor Age*, p. 36.
[130] *Chronicon ex chronicis*, ed. Lord William Howard of Naworth (J. Dawson, 1590; 2nd edn, 1592). "Florence" has now been identified as John of Worcester, in the new edition of *The Chronicle of John of Worcester*, of which vols. II and III have so far been published, ed. R. R. Darlington and P. McGurk, and trans. J. Bray and P. McGurk (Oxford, 1995–99), vol. II, introduction, pp. xvii–xviii.

textual editor that has ever written an introduction) that the monastic chronicle lacked subtlety, vision, eloquence, and even accuracy. He could even accept Savile's airy dismissal of urban chroniclers as, in Bolton's paraphrase, the "dreggs of the baser sort of common people." Nevertheless, Bolton, like Savile himself, was one of a growing number of scholars who realized that detailed research through both the printed and unprinted historical works of the past, "musty rolls . . . dry bloodless chronicles and so many dull and heavy paced Histories," would prove essential to anyone who wished to write a new "universal history for England" in place of the "vast vulgar tomes" produced by the printers.[131] In short, for true history to supplant the recent chronicle, it had to use information from chronicles older still, but seek its literary inspiration elsewhere.

The editors of these works, beginning with Parker, Savile, and Camden, aimed to bring the manuscript chronicles into print, partly for their literary value and partly to suit the developing antiquarian tastes of the wealthy who could afford them, but also in large measure for the politically useful information that they could provide the scholar, antiquary, or historian. They inaugurated a tradition of chronicle editing that continued with Roger Twysden, William Fulman, Thomas Gale, and Henry Wharton in the later seventeenth century,[132] and Thomas Hearne in the early eighteenth.[133] This would climax in the publications in the nineteenth century of the English Historical Society, the Rolls Series and – appropriately given his role in first bringing the *Polychronicon* into print – the Caxton Society.

England's experience was comparable to that of other countries. The work of later Italian Renaissance and post-Tridentine historians like Guicciardini and Sarpi, or of the official historians described by Eric Cochrane encouraged the collection of medieval chronicles as source materials that resulted eventually in the great enterprises of Ludovico Muratori. Despite a rather longer life there, a similar trend in Germany led eventually to the *Monumenta Germaniae historica* and the *Chroniken der Deutschen Städte*. In France, chronicles were published by scholars like André Duchesne, while the Benedictines, who had contributed so much to medieval historical writing, would soon turn to their great project of writing definitive lives of the saints.[134]

---

[131] Bolton, *Hypercritica: or a rule of judgment for the writing of our histories* (written 1621), in *Critical Essays of the Seventeenth Century*, ed. J. Spingarn (3 vols., Oxford, 1908–9), I, 96–97; Patterson, *Reading Holinshed's Chronicles*, p. 5.

[132] Roger Twysden, *Historiae Anglicanae Scriptores X* (1652); William Fulman, *Rerum Anglicarum Scriptorum Veterum* (Oxford, 1684); Thomas Gale, *Historiae Anglicanae scriptores quinque* (Oxford, 1687) and *Historiae Britannicae, Saxonicae, Anglo-danicae, scriptores XV* (Oxford, 1691); Henry Wharton, *Anglia sacra sive collectio historiarum de archiepiscopis et episcopis Angliae ad annum 1540* (2 vols., 1691); Elizabeth C. van Houts, "Camden, Cotton and the Chronicles of the Norman Conquest of England," *British Library Journal*, 18.2 (1992), 148–62; Douglas, *English Scholars*, pp. 156–77.

[133] Thomas Hearne, *Chronica Angliae* (20 vols., Oxford, 1709–35).

Across the channel examples are easy to find in the manuscript collections of the gentry, and English interests in this regard overlapped with continental ones in the world of the Enlightenment republic of letters. There is no need to reproduce these at length, but one instance may serve as illustration. At the beginning of the eighteenth century the Harley family would purchase the so-called "Matthew of Westminster" and several other chronicles or extracts, both printed and manuscript, from the bookseller Christopher Bateman, who was also involved in a project to reprint the "castrated" sheets of Holinshed expurgated under Elizabeth. Through the vigilant eye of its librarian, Humfrey Wanley, the Harleian collection soon rivaled the Cottonian as a center for medieval source material. It was thus among the locations visited in 1725 by Italian scholars searching for material to include in Muratori's great editorial project then underway at Modena.[135]

ORPHANS AND WIDOWS

It is difficult to resist the conclusion that by 1700 the intellectual status of the chronicle amid the many genres that could now be used to represent the past had changed beyond all recognition. Technological and social change had removed its reason for existence, and it ceased to provide an attractive medium for most matters of history, its older examples becoming instead the raw material for modern types of history, which could do that job better themselves. Having lost its home in the now vanished monasteries, and found temporary shelter in the printer's shop, it dwelt principally on the bookshelf, to speak to the general reader only from the footnote. Yet, it would seem, one or two offspring and at least one provincial cousin struggled on.

The period between 1640 and 1699 produced histories, diaries, and a flood of tracts and newsbooks, but only a handful of new printed chron-

---

[134] On these and other activities of the *érudits* from the seventeenth to the nineteenth century, see the papers of Dom. David Knowles, published together as *Great Historical Enterprises* (London and New York, 1963).

[135] *The castrations of the last edition of Holinshead's Chronicle both in the Scotch and English parts, containing forty four sheets; printed with the old types and ligatures, and compared literatim by the original* (1722); Cyndia Susan Clegg, *Press Censorship in Elizabethan England* (Cambridge, 1997), pp. 138–69; Wanley, *Diary*, ed. C. E. Wright and R. C. Wright (2 vols., 1966), II, 258, 284, 336, 355; Nichols *Literary Anecdotes of the Eighteenth Century*, ed. J. Nichols (9 vols. in 10, 1812–16); K. Maslen, "Three Eighteenth-Century Reprints of the Castrated Sheets in Holinshed's Chronicles," *The Library*, 5th series 13 (1958), 120–24; Keith Maslen and John Lancaster, *The Bowyer Ledgers: the Printing Accounts of William Bowyer, Father and Son Reproduced on Microfiche: with a Checklist of Bowyer Printing 1699–1977* (London and New York, 1991), p. 77, no. 968. A parchment folio chronicle of England to 1366 with the succession of popes to Benedict XII ("and some monkish tracts") was sold to Wanley for the library for twenty shillings by Jonah Bowyer the bookseller: Wanley, *Diary*, I, 35 (23 January 1720).

icles.[136] By the Restoration, if not earlier, the very term "chronicle" had lost much of its original meaning, and become a synonym for virtually any record of events past and present. A verse denunciation of Charles II, for instance, was entitled "The chronicle" by its writer. Abraham Cowley's "The Chronicle: a ballad" is a love poem in which the speaker lists various women who have "ruled" him. Its parodying of the contents of real chronicles is obvious:

> Elisa 'till this Hour might raign
> Had she not Evel Counsels ta'ne
> Fundamental Laws she broke,
> And still new Favorites she chose,
> 'Till up in Arms my Passions rose,
> And cast away her yoke.[137]

In the 1740s a whole wave of mock "chronicles," political satires written in the style of the biblical books of chronicles, was inspired by the publication of *The Chronicle of the Kings of England, written in the manner of the ancient Jewish Historians*. This appeared under the name Nathan ben Saddi but was the handiwork of the poet Robert Dodsley. Its accounts of the origins of the curfew bell and of the accomplishments of Geoffrey Chaucer (the latter in mock middle English) demonstrate the situation of the "chronicle" in the age of Pope, Richardson, and Sterne:

> So it was called the Curfew Bell; and at the sound thereof the lights were extinguished, and our fathers slept in the dark . . .
> In these days lived thilk grete poet, hight Geoffery Chaucere, the Fader of Inglis Poesie, whose workis ben ritten in Rime; and imprinted in a Boke, ycleped the Workis of Maister Geoffery Chaucere; and he smothed the Tonge of his contrie, and his Fame is woxen grete in the Land.[138]

But there is little point in satirizing something that is entirely extinct. Just as there are chronicle elements to that most successful of popular literary forms, the almanac, so seventeenth-century writers continued to write "chronologies" or "annals" that were chronicles by a different name, albeit generally without the continuing addition of new events.[139] A few of these

---

[136] See table 1.2 above. Twenty-eight original publications and thirty-five reeditions of works including newly edited chronicles or newly written ones (almost always of recent events like the civil war) exist from the period 1640–99. Of these, a substantial number are editions of medieval works designed for a scholarly readership and frequently in Latin. Of the few genuinely new chronicles, like Baker's atypically popular work, many are really collections of documents that sport the title of "chronicle" or "annals" for rhetorical effect but look very unlike the works of a century earlier.

[137] Bodl. MS Rawl. D. 924, art 55/xi, fos. 316r–318v; Abraham Cowley, "The Chronicle," stanza 3, in *Miscellanies* (1656), *Works*, ed. Grosart, I, 143.

[138] Nathan ben Saddi (alias Robert Dodsley), *The Chronicle of the Kings of England, written in the Manner of the Ancient Jewish Historians* (1740), pp. 11, 34.

[139] Dr. Simon Forman extracted from the Bible an "Account of the years of the wordle [*sic*]" for his own use in 1610, complete with the tabulation – standard in almanacs – of years elapsed *between* events such as the birth of Christ and the reign of Cyrus: Bodl. MS Ashm. 244, art. II, fos. 25–33. The physician-astrologer Philip Kinder kept historical and astrological collections together in a single parchment notebook, which included a chronology of the number

were printed, and sometimes reprinted, like Colonel William Parsons' *Chronological Tables* (plate 1.3). The antiquary John Pointer authored a little two-volume octavo digest of English history, *A Chronological History of England*, published by Bernard Lintot and bearing the imprimatur of Oxford's Vice-Chancellor Bernard Gardiner, the warden of All Souls. Its early years look much like a medieval chronicle, that for 1247 ("Was a great plague in England") being fairly typical. But by the seventeenth century it becomes virtually a diurnal account of events, with entries, suitably accompanied by ideological freight, such as that for 30 January 1648/9. "[King Charles] most barbarously murdered at his own door, about two a clock in the afternoon. The sum of his character given by that noble historian, my Lord Clarendon, is as follows –"; this is then followed by a list of those peers and other worthies who gave their lives in his defense.[140]

The majority of these latter-day chronicles, however, did not reach print, nor were they ever intended to. They exist in unpublished manuscripts, several of which were collected by Richard Rawlinson at the beginning of the eighteenth century, and others of which survive in local repositories. Thomas Wilson, keeper of the state papers under James I, drew up a chronology of memorable events from the Conquest for the benefit of the earl of Somerset in 1614; a contemporary English catholic penned a lengthy history of England in chronicle form a few years later.[141] At about the same time an unknown parliamentarian drew up, again apparently for the press, a chronicle of "memorable accidents" since 1636, while in Berkshire Hannibal Baskervile appended to his account of his own life a short chronicle of such "accidents" in his time.[142] In many instances the retention of the annal format was for sheer convenience, and signified an author's intention to use his chronicle as a source for a more refined book arranged in a different way (plate 1.4). The vast, 427-leaf compilation of the Reverend Samuel Carte, father of the more famous Thomas, was completed about 1700, midway through its author's life. Most of it is arranged in no particular order – it was intended by Carte

---

of generations between Noah, Abraham, David, and Jesus: Bodl. MS Ashm. 429, fos. 46v–47r, 44r (MS reversed); in another volume, Kinder dealt with the problems of rectifying chronology and chronicled the popes and papal institutions from AD 105 to 1626: Bodl. MS Ashm. 788, fos. 132r–133v, 175r, 181r–184v.

[140] John Pointer, *A Chronological History of England* (2 vols., Oxford and London, 1714), I, 36, 186.

[141] Bodl. MS Tanner 302, fos. 69r–86v, 113r–137v; Bodl. MS Rawl. D. 1035, fo. 2 (volume reversed). Other examples include D. R., "A breife discourse of the discents and genealogies of the kings and princes of England from the Conquest unto this daie collected out of the best and approved authors" (dated 1592), Bodl. MS Eng. hist. d. 278, fos. 2r–23v; and Bodl. MS Eng. hist. e. 211, which contains a similar chronology of the 1640s.

[142] Anon. "Certaine memorable accidents which have happened since ye yeere 1636," Bodl. MS Rawl. D. 141. This MS, 90 folios, covers the period from late 1640 to January 1643/4; it attacks institutions such as the Star Chamber and blames the bishops for most of the evils afflicting England; Hannibal Baskervile, "Memorable accidents in London and Westminster in my time," Bodl. MS Rawl. D. 859, fo. 69r.

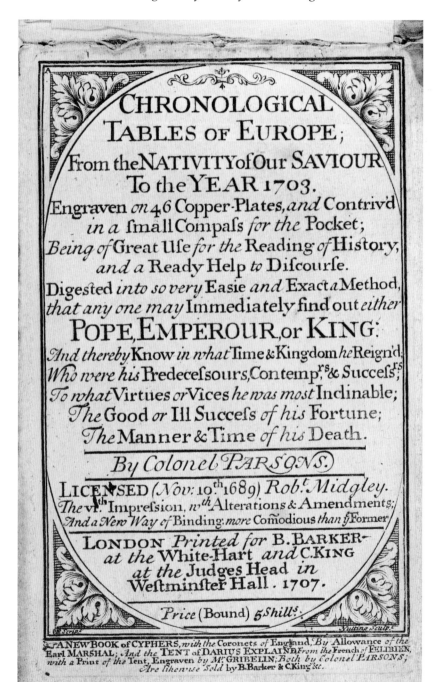

CHRONOLOGICAL
TABLES of EUROPE;
From the NATIVITY of Our SAVIOUR
To the YEAR 1703.
Engraven *on* 46 Copper-Plates, *and* Contriv'd
in a small Compass *for the* Pocket;
Being of Great Use *for the* Reading *of* History,
and a Ready Help *to* Discourse.
Digested *into so very* Easie *and* Exact *a* Method,
that any one may Immediately find out *either*
POPE, EMPEROUR, or KING:
And thereby Know *in what* Time & Kingdom *he* Reign'd,
Who were his Predecessours, Contemp.rs & Success.rs;
To what Virtues *or* Vices *he was most* Inclinable;
The Good *or* Ill Success *of his* Fortune;
The Manner & Time *of his* Death.

By Colonel PARSONS.

LICENSED *(Nov:* 10.th 1689) *Rob.t Midgley.*
The vi.th Impression, *with* Alterations & Amendments;
And a New Way of Binding. *more* Comodious *than y̆* Former

LONDON *Printed for* B. BARKER
at the White-Hart *and* C. KING
at the Judges Head *in*
Westminster Hall. 1707.

Price (Bound) 5 Shill.s

A NEW BOOK of CYPHERS, *with the* Coronets *of* England, *By* Allowance *of the*
Earl MARSHAL; *And the* TENT of DARIUS EXPLAIN'D *From the* French *of* FELIBIEN,
with a Print *of the* Tent, Engraven *by* M.r GRIBELIN; *Both by* Colonel PARSONS;
Are likewise Sold by B. Barker & C King &c.

simply as a sourcebook for better things – but it includes a few sections arranged chronologically. Carte's contemporary, Thomas Tanner, had similar intentions in a quarto volume of his collections for a history of Cambridge, arranging a skeleton history of the university, in Latin and English, as a year-by-year list of events drawn from the archives he had researched.[143]

Perhaps the best example of the last gasp of the chronicle as formal historiography is the huge volume – over 1,000 pages long – written by the obscure Samuel Fleming in the late 1720s. Fleming drew up his "Help to History" in a neat but shaky hand that suggests a limited education, perhaps intending it for publication since the manuscript is complete with running headers and chapter divisions. There is no evidence that it was ever printed, and the reason for this is evident on every page. A giant anachronism, hearkening back to the days of Grafton and Stow, it presents a chronicle of national events from 1603 till the death of George I. Like most chronicles, it is fuller as the writer approached his own time and relied less on other sources; like a chronicle, it gives equal weight to events such as ship launchings and earthquakes, and avoids constructing a continuous narrative.[144]

Among the Barrett papers in the Berkshire record office, one finds several less ambitious efforts at private history writing, including two attempts at writing the history of medieval England.[145] But most interesting is the introduction to the latter of these, "A Chronological History of England to the death of Stephen." This is in fact no chronicle at all, but its authors nevertheless choose to cast their work, "written by two private gentlemen, for their divertisement, without the precarious way of subscriptions" and clearly intended for only private circulation, in the chronicle tradition. They consciously emulate – or mimic – the strong association of author and chronicle, noted in this chapter, by suggesting that since their Christian names begin with T and I respectively, and both their surnames with "B," the reader

---

[143] Bodl. MS Carte 251, Samuel Carte's "Chronological Relation of extraordinary events in all parts of the world from the earliest times to the beginning of 1700, without order"; CUL MS Add. 3824, Tanner collections on Cambridge. For other examples, see: BL MS Add. 5833, fo. (old foliation) 124, William Cole's list of Cambridge mayors 1263–1700 drawn from various sources in 1762, including his own 1747 history of the town; BL MS Sloane 3985, fos. 85–113, anonymous "Chronicle of Remarkable Events, particularly in Church History," from AD 311 to 835.

[144] Samuel Fleming, "A help to history or the Brittish Remembranc[er]," Bodl. MS Rawl. D. 7. This volume, which merits further study, is much fuller from 1679.

[145] Berks RO, Barrett papers (microfiche 3003b) D/EBt Z1 (Stephen to Edward I) and D/EBt Z11 (Caesar to medieval times); these are in different hands and apparently not two parts of the same work.

Plate 1.3 (*opposite*) Printed chronological tables: the title page of *Chronological Tables of Europe*, by Colonel William Parsons, one of several such works popular in the early eighteenth century, adapted from a French work by Guillaume Marcel.

The History of York Minster.

AD. 627. A litle Chappell of wood was erected for the sollemnizing the Baptisme of K. Edwin then newly converted to Christianity by Paulinus and was dedicated to St. Peter. In the same place the said King afterwards laid the Foundation of a larger Church to be built of stone. But not living to finish it, it was built by K Oswald his immediate Successor who dedicated it to St Peter as before.

Dedication. The Feast of the Dedication of this church is on the first day of October which day by a statute of the pte and Chapter 1462. was appointed to be kept as one of the greater Double Festivalls.

AD. 666. The Roof of this Church being fallen, and the walls in many places ruinous. Wilfrid the 1st AB of that name set himself to repair, covering it with Lead, and glazing the Windows &c.

AD. 1066. In the beginning of the Conquerors raigne it was burnt in that great Conflagration occasioned here by the Norman souldiers. But shortly

AD 1068. after viz 1068 Thomas (the first AB of that name) at first to make it serve the turn new corped and repaird it, and afterwards pulling down all the old buildings erected from the very ground a new Cathedrall.

AD. 1277. In the 2d year of King Stephen June 4. The city of York was again almost consumed by Fire whereby this Cathedrall as also St Marys Abbey and 40 other Religious Houses were partly destroyed.

It was a 4th time repaired saith Mr Torr. look for wch he quotes an Indulgence of Joceline Bp. of Sarum placing 40 days penance to all that should contribute to the redifying of it

In the time of K. Henry 2 AB Roger who was Consecrated 1154. new built the Quire and Vaulte under the same as also the ABs Palace.

In the reign of K. Hen: 3 This Church was still in building. for in his 11 year 1227. Walter Gray graunts an Indulgence of 40 days Relaxation from Penance to all such as liberally contributed to the Fabrick thereof

About this time Johannes Romanus the Treasurer of York (not the AB as Godwin mistakes but his Father) at his own charge built the north part of the Crosse-Isle and a goodly steeple in the middle.

The rest of the Fabrick as it now stands was erected as followeth.

AD. 1291. On Friday Aprill. was the Foundation of the nave of the Ch. as it
19. E.1. now stands laid from the west end eastward. the 1st stone being laid (after invocating the Grace of the H Ghost) by Jo: Romanus the AB. vide Stubbs 1727. wth wch agrees a Table hanging up in the vestry, the wch Stubbs says that it was quasi completum infra 40 annos per Willelmum de Melton Archiepiscpm

The Gentry hereabout contributed very much to this structure especially Rob: de Vavasor who gave his Quarry at Tadcaster to find stones for it. And Rob de Percy who graunts free Liberty for the carriage of those stones by land or by water through his grounds lying along the River up to York.

AD 1320. 13. E.2. Wm de Melton graunts an Indulgence of 40 days to all such as contributed to this building

should refer to the work simply as "Tibs Cronicle," which name is set off in bold. They saw their own work as simply another attempt to correct the errors of past chroniclers culminating with Baker. "It is with Cronicles as with Dictionarys," runs the introduction; "every Age produces new writers and every writer new matter and words, raked out of ye old ruines of antiquity."[146]

Because of its familial resemblance to chronology, the chronicle format continued throughout the sixteenth and seventeenth centuries to serve those of a millenarian disposition such as the quaker-turned-Anglican rector, George Keith,[147] those simply concerned with the problem of reconciling biblical events with pagan history, and the godly who found annals the most satisfactory way to record God's actions in recent times. Two early Stuart citizens of Dorchester, William Whiteway and Denis Bond, kept "chronologies" of local/national events in the early seventeenth century, integrating their understanding of history with their perception of news and contemporary events, as David Underdown has recently demonstrated.[148] The notes used by preachers to prepare sermons with historical references are often composed in the form of annals drawn from various historians and chroniclers.[149] A nameless seventeenth-century writer compiled "an index to the holy bible" amounting to a summary history of the world from Creation to Incarnation, complete with days of the week set apart by various religions for worship, and a table of Jewish and Christian months and holidays.[150] Another anonymous writer drew up a similar "Abstract of Chronology" subtitled "A short chronicle from the first memory of things in Europe to the Conquest of Persia by Alexander the Great."[151] A mid-sixteenth century Latin chronicle from the mythical Cymbeline to Edward II survives in the Bodleian, bound together with a contemporary copy of More's *Richard III*, and a late Elizabethan or early Stuart catholic writer's observations on the fall of catholicism in England, the last item cast in the

---

[146] Berks RO, Barrett papers D/EBt Z12 (microfiche 3003b), introduction to D/EBt Z11.
[147] George Keith, *A chronological account of the several ages of the world from Adam to Christ* (New York, 1694); *DNB*, s.v. Keith, George, 1639?–1716. For another example, see the anonymous early seventeenth-century "Chronologia ad Ptolemaei Astronomiam," twenty-five leaves of tables with concordances of years from 800 BC to AD 250: CUL MS Dd. III. 74.
[148] David Underdown, *Fire from Heaven* (New Haven, 1992), p. 46.
[149] Notes of John Lee (alias Warner), archdeacon of Rochester, Bodl. MS Eng. th. e. 176, fo. 17v.   [150] Bodl. MS Eng. th. e. 46, fos. 1, 46v–48.
[151] Bodl. MS Rawl. D. 115: in a hand of the late seventeenth or early eighteenth century, this volume shows much more interest in the problems of mathematical chronology, discussed at that time by Newton and others, than in day-to-day events, yet still appropriates to itself the title of a chronicle; for a similar example, covering dates from AD 200 to 1683 throughout Europe, see Bodl. MS Rawl. Q. e. 23.

Plate 1.4 (*opposite*)   Adaptation of the annalistic format outside the chronicle: a sketch of "The History of York Minster" in Archbishop Sharpe's manuscripts, vol. I, p. 56 (Bishopsthorpe Papers Bp. Div. I).

form of a record of God's judgments and alterations in more remote British and Saxon times.[152]

A complete universal chronicle, remarkably similar to Ralegh's *History of the World* (1614) or an earlier work like the *Magdeburg Centuries*, was composed by the puritan Richard Traves in the early seventeenth century to demonstrate the historical and apocalyptic signs of predestination, election, and judgment, highlighting the sins of the wicked in red ink; at about the same time one Hamond Claxton, living in northern England, drew up in a neat hand his own English summary, in 200 folio pages, of the early chronicle of Eutropius, covering the period from the foundation of Rome to the fourth century AD.[153] In 1644, George Turner of Kilburn completed, in a hand also intended to mimic print, the manuscript of his short chronicle of the world, which included "a breife cronologie to this present yeare 1643, faithfullie collected from many approved authors."[154] The records of the Broadmead chapel in Bristol, a baptist congregation, amount to a chronicle of a specific religious community. Begun by Edward Terrill (1634–85) and then continued by other anonymous members of the congregation, it consciously assumes the annalistic form at points.[155]

A quite different type of survivor was the urban chronicle, somewhat

[152] Anon., "Gods motives to repentance," Bodl. MS Rawl. D. 131 (145 fos.): this last item is the "third part" of a work the remainder of which does not survive – the author's own foliation begins with fo. 233 on the first leaf of the MS.

[153] "Richard Traves his booke," Bodl. MS Ashm. 803 (n.d.), fos. 1–145, especially fos 1r–3r, 86v, 112r; "The Breviarie of Eutropius, abridging the dates of the Romaynes from the fyrst fowndacion of the cytie off Rome untill the thowsand, hundreth and nynth yere of the same," Northumberland RO, ZAL B87/2 (an unfoliated parchment volume, on the last page of which is written "by me Hamond Claxton"); cf. Joseph Bingham (1668–1723), "History of Popish Usurpations and Rebellions from 1512 to 1558," Bodl. MS Eng. hist. f. 13, fos. 1–30, which is also annalistically arranged.

[154] George Turner, "The worlde in a pockett or a little roome," Bodl. MS Rawl. D. 203, fos. 114v–58. The MS, dated (fo. 158v) and signed 12 April 1644, contains much the same information on ancient and modern calendars that one could find in an almanac, as well as an abstract of the ancient kings of Britain, from Samothes. But it is arranged like a chronicle, with year-by-year entries (often in the wrong places) from the birth of Christ (fo. 120v) and includes such details as "Printing invented (1443); Warwick plotteth against Ed. and to draw Clarence to his parte giveth him his daug. in Mariage"; "A greate snow 1615; the K[ing] goeth into Scotland 1617 . . . Sr Walter Rauleigh executed; the last blazing starre 1618" (fos. 147v, 155r).

[155] "Anᵒ. 1658. – Att length, on 3d September, 1658, Oliver Cromwell, that tooke upon himselfe ye place of *Protector* of England, died, and his sonn Richard was proclaimed Protector. Anᵒ. 1659 – And on ye 6 day of ye 3d month, or May, 1659, he was displaced, and ye Commonwealth (or old) Parliament, that Oliver dissolved, Anᵒ. 1653, sate again. Dureing all which time we had peace" (p. 114). External events are also noted, for instance at pp. 181 and 189, an earthquake and a "blazeing starr." *The Records of a Church of Christ in Bristol, 1640–1687,* ed. Roger Hayden, Bristol Rec. Soc., 27 (1974). The pattern of numbering the group's persecutions (127) is also borrowed from medieval chronicles, but via a more recent source like Foxe.

ironically in view of England's relatively weak medieval tradition in this regard. Provincial towns continued to use the chronicle as medium for the keeping of civic records, and for noting important events, long after more sophisticated London audiences had turned to other genres. (The short-lived post of city chronologer in London, held in succession by Middleton, Jonson, and three less notable figures, was abolished in 1670 and its last occupant pensioned off, there being, say the records, "no occasion for this office.")[156] Chronicles of widely varying sophistication and historiographical importance were produced in several towns. Unlike the sixteenth-century London chronicles, which had attempted to adopt a national perspective with disastrous results for their genre, these remained firmly localist in matter and consequently continued to be written in some places into the eighteenth century. The absence of presses outside London and the universities until near the end of the seventeenth century may paradoxically have been a factor in preserving local chronicle writing from any temptation to aspire to a national audience: most of them never had any prospect of being printed. In Bristol, Chester, and Lynn, all towns that acquired presses very late, chronicles, annals, and mayoral calendars remained viable forms, rivaled and often influenced by antiquarian research, for the representation of the civic past.

But an even greater reason lies in the very localism of the town chronicles. A century of humanist historiography had declaimed against the inclusion of the trivial and insignificant in history. Père René Rapin's *Instructions for History*, translated in 1680 by John Davies of Kidwelly, is typical in repeating the Ciceronian injunction that the historian must include only those events or persons that are "great" and that deserve commemoration.[157] National histories that attempted to weave in some of the texture of local life, as Holinshed's writers had done in the 1580s through the inclusion of urban and rural anecdotes, crimes, details of building projects, and grain prices, were no longer possible within the canons of historical writing. This should not surprise us since an analogous process, at work through the seventeenth century, had marginalized local legends and oral traditions in the process of constructing a national memory.[158] Since

---

[156] *Analytical Index to the Remembrancia*, p. 306.
[157] René Rapin, *Instructions for History*, trans. J. Davies (1680), p. 19; Levine, *Battle of the Books*, pp. 268–71. A similar line to Rapin's was taken by the Jesuit Pierre le Moyne in *Of the art both of writing & judging of history: with reflections upon ancient as well as modern historians, shewing through what defects there are so few good, and that it is impossible there should be many so much as tolerable* (1695), p. 132, for whom virtually only the historian Famiano Strada merits comparison with the best of the ancients.
[158] D. R. Woolf, "The 'Common Voice:' History, Folklore and Oral Tradition in Early Modern England," *Past and Present*, 120 (1988), 26–52.

the local and parochial had been so unceremoniously bounced out of national narrative history, where else could it live but in the localities themselves?[159]

Later local chronicles occur in a variety of contexts. Many sorts of civic records, along with the books of particular guilds or crafts, were naturally organized annalistically, with the election of officers (wardens, masters, and aldermen) as the focus for each annal. As the earliest local chronicles had grown out of borough records, so their late descendants continued to develop in this way, the annals becoming a receptacle for information both official and unofficial, local and national.[160] The tanners in Morpeth, Northumberland kept, from 1586 to 1702, a "Bouke of Regestores of the names and sournames of masteres and prentisses," in which the election of quartermasters for each year served much the same function formerly provided, in late medieval urban chronicles, by shrieval and mayoral elections.[161] Not infrequently these annals would fulfill their old function as a peg on which to hang a number of facts relating to the community's more remote past. A seventeenth-century list of ancient British kings (including select events such as the birth of Helena, legendary British mother of the emperor Constantine, and daughter of King Coel) can be found appended to the civic oaths contained in the *Liber*

---

[159] On this matter I concur with the argument of Patterson in *Reading Holinshed's Chronicles*, and in her essay "Foul, his Wife, the Mayor, and Foul's Mare: the Power of Anecdote in Tudor Historiography," in Donald R. Kelley and David H. Sacks (eds.), *The Historical Imagination in Early Modern Britain* (Cambridge, 1997), pp. 159–78. Jonathan Barry establishes the use of historical writing generally as a vehicle of a distinctive urban culture in post-1640 Bristol in his "Provincial Town Culture, 1640–1780: Urbane or Civic?," in Joan H. Pittock and Andrew Wear (eds.), *Interpretation and Cultural History* (Basingstoke, UK, 1991), pp. 198–234.

[160] As G. H. Martin reminds us, even the earliest borough records of the thirteenth century were not exclusively localist in orientation, many using regnal as well as civic calendars, and referring to national or international events: "The Origins of Borough Records," *Journal of the Society of Archivists*, 2.4 (October 1961), 147–53, at p. 151.

[161] Northumberland Record Office, NRO 989/B3. Similar examples can be found in the minute books of the bakers and tanners of Durham and Framwellgate (1656–1721), NRO, ZAN M12/C24 (on deposit from the Society of Antiquaries of Newcastle-upon-Tyne and cited by their kind permission). In contrast, the register book of as central a place as Westminster, from 1595 to 1660 includes the names of burgesses and assistants, and the names of Charles I's children, but records no events, even the regicide: CUL M5 Gg.I.9, fos. 62r–83r. The court books of early Tudor Guildford contain events of local interest including elections of officials and occurrences, like "Also the xxviijth day of July above wreten on John Fyssher late of Westmynster was takyn as a vacabunde at Guldeford above wreten," and the death of one John Irish of Woking, "the wiche John folowyd the kinges Coorte." But although these amount virtually to an informal (albeit inconsistently maintained and incomplete) chronicle, there is no indication that this was the main function of the record, and it should probably not be counted as a legitimate town chronicle. *Guildford Borough Records 1514–1546*, ed. Enid M. Dance, Surrey Record Society, 24 (1958), p. 3.

Juramentorum or Red Parchment Book of the borough of Colchester.[162]
The dispersal of town chronicles through the sixteenth and seventeenth
centuries is indicated in map 1.1.[163] This reveals no striking geographic
pattern, other than a peculiar lack of *town* chronicles in a group of nine
south-central counties (Oxfordshire, Berkshire, Buckinghamshire, Huntingdonshire, Hertfordshire, Bedfordshire, Middlesex, Surrey, and Sussex).[164]
There is no clear explanation for this. It might be suggested that the towns in
these counties fall in close proximity to London, with its earlier chronicle
tradition, or that the impact of the parasite genres and antichronicling
humanist preferences had a greater role. Neither of these explanations is
entirely satisfactory, and neither accounts for the relatively high occurrence
of town chronicles at various times in nearby East Anglia and Kent.

Many of the town chronicles maintained or initiated in the sixteenth and
seventeenth centuries are anonymous in whole or part, but others can be

---

[162] Harrod, *Repertory of the Records and Evidences of the Borough of Colchester* (Colchester,
1865), p. 33, arts. 3 and 4; Essex RO, Chelmsford, T/A 465/123 is a microfilm of the *Liber
Juramentorum*, which, however, lacks the king list, now at the Colchester branch of the
Essex Record Office. I wish to thank the staff of the Essex Record Office, Chelmsford, for
helping me sort through the highly confused pagination of this volume. A very good example
of an urban chronicle initiated as a municipal record and continued over several generations
is the "town ledger" or Black Book of Plymouth, in *Calendar of the Plymouth Municipal
Records*, ed. R. N. Worth (Plymouth, 1893): pp. 15–25 covers the period from 1441
beginning with William Kethricke; "Thys was the First mayre namyd by the Kynge and made
by acte of plyament." It concludes in 1709. Worth has unfortunately extracted only the local
entries, leaving aside references to external events such as the Western rising in Cornwall.
Several entries in the Plymouth chronicle pertaining to the commonwealth period have been
expunged (p. 24).

[163] For a brief but indispensable survey, with a helpful checklist of most local chronicles, to
which I can add only a few specimens on the border of the genre, see A. Dyer, "English Town
Chronicles," *Local Historian*, 12 (1976–7), 285–92; for other instances of town chronicles
see the following: M. M. Rowe, "Some Seventeenth Century Annals," *Devon and Cornwall
Notes and Queries*, 33 (1974), 20–22; A. H. Taylor, "The Municipal Records of Tenterden," *Archaeologia Cantiana*, 32 (1917), 283–302. Tenterden's chronicle, initiated in the
seventeenth century, is contained in a borough custumal (Kent RO, Te/C1, fos. 136v–139). It
begins with "The names of the Bayleifs of the towne and hundred of Tenterden from the
beginning of the liberty begun in the twenty and seaventh yeares of the reigne of Kinge Henry
the sixte"; years in the left margin are regnal only. This chronicle is written in several distinct
hands running up to the late seventeenth century, and Tudor events have been added after the
fact in the occasional informational annal, e.g. fo. 138r, 5 Mary, "This yeare Callis was
loste" or 22 Eliz. (1580), "This yeare was a greate earthquake the 17th day Apr. about 5 or 6
of the clock in the evening." A different hand begins at fo. 139r (1633), at which point years
AD are given as well as regnal yeares, up to 1648 where we read the laconic entry: "Jan. 30th.
The government changed into a commonwealth."

[164] Berkshire had no independent urban chronicles, but Professor Robert Tittler has kindly
informed me that a late Elizabethan reference in the Wallingford borough archives, W/AC1/
1/1 (which I have not personally seen) records payment of a sum to a gentleman of the
Middle Temple to search the town's records, "because we could say nothing thereunto,"
suggesting interest in compiling at least a town history if not a chronicle. A combination
chronicle/minute book of Reading corporation is listed in Hist. MSS Comm., *Eleventh
Report, part VII* (1888), 183–208 and runs from 1622 to 1815.

Map 1.1 Urban chronicles in sixteenth- and seventeenth-century England. Sources: A. Dyer, "English Town Chronicles," *Local Historian*, 12 (1976–77), 291; R. Flenley, *Six Town Chronicles of England* (Oxford, 1911), amended by subsequent additions; C. Gross, *Bibliography of British Municipal History*.

assigned to specific individuals, not all of whom were acting in an official capacity. The Irish physician Thomas Arthur (1619–66) assembled material from Irish archives on the town of Limerick into an entry-book that looks remarkably like a chronicle, with dates AD and mayors on the left side of each page, and select notable events on the right.[165] Others are more clearly the work of an official with regular access to records. Thomas Worswicke, chamberlain of Stafford in the mid-1590s (and its mayor in 1622–23) compiled a chronicle in the form of a catalog of town officers, with sporadic entries for the fifteenth century but more regular ones from 1509 to 1626; it would be continued, with gaps, by other writers up to 1713.[166] An anonymous Suffolk author, perhaps a civic official of Bury St. Edmunds, added to the *Liber de Buria* a volume of town charters, knights' fees and deeds, a brief set of annals *De regibus Anglie*, from the Conquest to Edward III's reign, together with a list of the abbots of Bury; the termination of the annals in the mid-fourteenth century strongly suggests, however, that he simply copied a medieval document and had no interest in bringing it forward to his own time. Richard Girdler, citizen of York, inherited in the mid-seventeenth century an existing chronicle of his city, in the tried and true form of a mayoral and shrieval list, recording events ranging from the death of Chaucer to the creation of the first Lord Mayor. Girdler continued it in his own hand from 1646 to 1664. The events he included ran from the "cruell battell, where the duke of Yorke was slayne" in 1460, to the blowing down of Trinity Steeple in Michaelgate in 1550, the destruction of Ouse Bridge by rising ice in 1564, the price of grain in 1621, and a botched attempt by a disgruntled tailor to assassinate the mayor in 1618. The boundary between events of local and national significance was, as so often, blurred, and single annals often mix the two: thus Girdler's anonymous predecessor wrote of 1464: "This yeare uppon Trinity Sonday kinge Edward the fourth was

---

[165] Dr. Thomas Arthur (1619–66), *Annales magistratum et memorabilium aliquot ad civitatis Lymmeric*, BL MS Add. 31885, fos. 253r–277r. The annalistic form of this is critical, since there also survive numerous town histories that are self-consciously designed to *avoid* looking like chronicles: the unprinted history of Winchester by John Trussell, better known for his printed continuation of Samuel Daniel's *Collection of the Historie of England*, is an example, assembled over a period of twenty years from about 1630 to 1642, yet utterly eschewing any resemblance to a town chronicle. Trussell's "Civitas Winton. Catallogus Benefactorum eiusdem. 1642 opere et industria Johannis Trussel civis et Ald: Ci: predictae collect" is a large parchment volume that includes a variety of humanist verses (on subjects such as the royal donations and concessions to the town) as well as notes on the history of the city, and notes of the various records kept in the council house: Bodl. MS Top. Hants. c. 5.

[166] Staffs. Record Office, D(W) 1721/1/4, fos. 61–178v, Worswicke's "A catalogue of the officers of this town of Stafford"; William Salt Library, Stafford, MS 369, pp. 91–160 (another copy); M. W. Greenslade, *The Staffordshire Historians* (Stafford, 1982), p. 11. Typical entries include: "1576: This yere one George Pedley tylinge of a house, a tyle fell downe, and killed one Dorothy Hendsley" (William Salt Lib. MS 369, p. 130).

crownde at Yorke, and this yeare was the minster at Yorke burned."[167]

Similar examples exist in the manuscript collections of the British Library and the Bodleian, and many more in various local repositories around the country. In some cases, authors would draw their notes from one author only, as one late seventeenth-century note-taker did in closely following "Martin's Chronicle" (which was, strictly speaking, not a chronicle at all, but one of the general regnal histories written under James I).[168] More often, however, a variety of different printed sources appear in such digests. A good example is the anonymously written "A breefe description of England & Wales, with some collections out of the English chronicles," a small octavo volume of 141 leaves composed at the very end of the seventeenth or the beginning of the eighteenth century. The first part of this is written in a deliberate, neat hand, with a running header of "English Chronicle" at the top of each page. It deals with various episodes of English history from Saxon times on and is drawn principally from late Tudor chroniclers like Stow.[169]

We have seen already that Bristol maintained its long-standing chronicle tradition late into the eighteenth century, with annals being kept, in Dr. Barry's words, "by a tobacconist, a peruke-maker, an iron-founder, a wine-cooper and an apothecary" as well as a schoolmaster, a merchant, and several clergymen, "if anything a broader social range than is recorded for earlier chroniclers."[170] Norwich had a similarly long tradition, which also survived. The late fifteenth-century writer Robert Reynys, of Acre in Norfolk, recorded important events from the building of Rome to the battle of Tewkesbury, including both major battles and events in his own family.[171] A more official list of Norwich's mayors and sheriffs from 1403 to 1696

---

[167] Suffolk Record Office (Ipswich), HD1538/162 (*Liber de Buria*, in an anonymous late sixteenth-century hand), fos. 43r–44v, 45r–47v; BL MS Add. 33595, fos. 24r–53v (mayors and sheriffs 1273–1655 AD), especially fos. 35r, 36v, 41v, 42v, 45r; the portion in Girdler's hand begins with 1646 at fo. 52r.

[168] Anon., "Observations out of Martin's Chronicle," BL MS Stowe 1048, fos. 14r–23r. "Martin's chronicle" was William Martyn, *The Historie, and Lives, of Twentie Kings of England*, first published in 1614, and expanded in a third edition of 1638.

[169] BL MS Harl. 27405, fos. 1–57r; the preface to this is by the Georgian antiquary Thomas Martin of Palgrave (1697–1771). From fo. 57 the hand changes, and the MS becomes a set of chapters from a larger work, probably by a different author but written at about the same time, concerned with the reigns of English monarchs from Henry II to Elizabeth.

[170] See above, and Barry, "Provincial Town Culture," p. 213. To the better-known instance of Adams' chronicle could be added the history of Bristol in chronology form contained in a long, narrow volume and covering the period 1245 to 1735, Bristol RO, MS 09594(1), which lists mayors and sheriffs along with local events; a similar example, reaching through several different hands from 1216 to the early nineteenth century, is MS 08159(2), pp. 1–121, "A catalogue of all the mayors, baylifs, prepositors, and sheriffs that have been in the city of Bristol from the first year of the reign of King Henry 3. Anno 1216"; Barry adds several others.

[171] Bodl. MS Tanner 407, fos. 8r (notices of family), 51v–52r. The Tanner catalog ascribes this work to the early sixteenth century.

appears in the mid-seventeenth century, and includes under each annal the remarkable events of the year:

1469. This yeare the kinge came to Norwiche . . .
1515. The duke of Suffolke & the french Quene came to Noweich [*sic*].
1520. This yeare Catheringe Quene of England came to Norwhich.
1534. This yeare the councill chamber built.

Like many medieval town or monastic chronicles, this was the work of more than one hand. The first author, probably the townsman Thomas Chickering, finished writing in 1653. A second, more italicized hand – perhaps that of Chickering's son, also Thomas, a brewer who was mayor in 1676 – continues the chronicle down to 1696, and annotates the annals of the earlier author.[172]

Elsewhere in the east, seventeenth-century Cambridge produced at least one mayoral list, in which the corresponding university vice-chancellors were also recorded. This made reference to both local and national events. There is also an independently written set of extracts from the town's "charter book" arranged in annalistic form.[173] Great Yarmouth had a "chronographical table" that hung in its parish church for over two centuries, where both William Worcestre and William Camden would see it. Eventually it became so fragmentary that it had to be removed from public view into the vestry, where it became part of the borough archives. The Jacobean antiquary Henry Manship consulted it in this new location when preparing his *History of Great Yarmouth*, but he also recalled having previously seen it "more than three score year past . . . hanging on the wall as thou enterest the East Door, usually termed the Marriage Door, which is situate on the south side of the Church aforesd." A new version was prepared at some point in the 1590s, which Thomas Nashe saw in the guildhall. In 1638 Sir John Wentworth of Somerleyton commissioned a third, black-letter version by Richard Rawlyn; the choice of lettering style suggests a conscious attempt to give the new copy the air of antiquity, in contrast to the second version, which Nashe described as being written "in a faire text hand." This last version was still in the guildhall by the early eighteenth century, when the Essex antiquary

---

[172] Bodl. MS Tanner 396, art. 2, fos. 17r–40r, especially 25r, 35r–40r; at fo. 16v the older Chickering records the names of his children; the second hand begins at 35r. On the Chickerings, see Francis Blomefield, *An Essay towards a Topographical History of the County of Norfolk*, 2nd edn, 11 vols. (1805–10), III, 420; IV, 457.
[173] BL MS Harl. 4116, fo. 8 (old: new fo. 10r), "Maiors of Cambridge"; fo. 43 (old: new fos. 49r–51v), "A note of such persons as have bin maiors of Cambridge, and the yeare in which they soe were"; and fos. 614ff. (old: 356v–358r new), "Maiors of Cambridge," a continuation of the previous item (in a similar hand) from 1634 to the reign of Charles II; BL MS Add. 5813, "Extracts from the Mayor's book called ye Charter Book," fos. 112r–118v (new foliation).

William Holman saw and transcribed it, and as late as the nineteenth century was kept in the town's Tolhouse Hall.[174]

Towns in other regions were similarly well-served. Gloucester had Abel Wantner, a citizen who marked the Hanoverian succession with a town history going back through the "antiquities, memoirs and annals of the ancient city" to Geoffrey of Monmouth. Framed as a regnal history for most of its nearly 300 leaves, it nevertheless begins with annals for remote antiquity and concludes with a similarly annalistic chronicle of Queen Anne's reign; Wantner may have found that the chronicle format suited both the sparsity of ancient information and the density of very recent events.[175] In Exeter, alderman Nicholas Izacke drew up memorials of his town, printed in 1724 (nearly sixty years after he completed them), which begin with the Ciceronian "historia est lux veritatis" while asserting the city's great antiquity: "I finde that 'twas builte before London, even at Brutes first landing here by his nephew Corineus, on whom Brute bestowed this west countrey, Anno mundi 2855." Whatever their fate in mainstream humanist historical writing, the ancient Trojans were alive and well in the pages of minor urban chroniclers.[176]

In the north, York found in Christopher Hildyard a writer prepared not only to list all its mayors, bailiffs, and sheriffs but also to publish the work, which in turn would serve as the basis for other antiquaries' collections on the city.[177] An anonymous Beverley author compiled a set of annals for the town, including a list of its mayors, running from the second century to 1724, beginning with the building of a church there at about AD 178 and major events such as the Saxon and Norman invasions before narrowing to such local and county occurrences as the closing of Hull against Charles I in 1642 (here erroneously recorded as 1643), and the renewal of the town charter in

---

[174] Neither of the first two versions of the chronicle survives, though there are late sixteenth-century copies of a synopsis of the second version in BL MSS Add. 12505, fos. 280–81 and Lans. 101, art. 3, fos. 6r–v; Bodl. MS Rawl. Essex 11, fos. 175r–77r, "De Antiquitate et fundatione burgi magnae Jernemuthae," extracted by William Holman from the third version of the chronicle and printed by Thomas Hearne in his edition of Leland's *Collectanea*; *Works of Thomas Nashe*, ed. R. B. McKerrow, 5 vols. (1904–10), IV, 372; Manship, *History of Great Yarmouth*, p. 5; P. Rutledge, "Thomas Damet and the Historiography of Great Yarmouth," *Norfolk Archaeology*, 33, pt. 2 (1963), 119–30, at pp. 124–25.

[175] Bodl. MS Top. Gloucs. c.3, "The History of Gloucester" by Abel Wantner, 1714 (and MS Top. Gloucs. c.2, his collections for this volume).

[176] Devon RO, C1/53, Izacke's "A Memoryall of sundry of the chiefest officers within the cittie of Exeter," dedicated 23 January 1665: fifty-nine leaves of annals, to 1665, are followed (59r–66r) with several pages left blank for future additions, up to 1697.

[177] BL MS Harl. 6115, an interleaved copy of Hildyard's *A List or catalogue of all the mayors and bayliffs, lord mayors, and sheriffs, of the most ancient, honourable, noble, and loyall city of Yorke* (York, 1664), has been annotated extensively by a scholar, more learned than Hildyard himself, who makes reference in his notes to various Anglo-Saxon and Latin charters.

1689.[178] Chester provides several examples of chronicle writing closely re-sembling the Bristol tradition. William Aldersey, an alderman who died in 1616, compiled one set of annals beginning in 1543, which were extended after his death to 1634. At the same time, another chronicle was being compiled, now attributed to Randle Holme I (d. 1655). Holme, the first of four generations of a family of heraldic and genealogical practitioners, was mayor of Chester in 1633–4. Written in the 1620s and covering the period 1300–1620, his chronicle survives in Chester Public Library. Like most of its kind, it offers only brief annals for earlier years, becoming fuller in the sixteenth century and most informative after 1600.[179] Chester had already inspired Archdeacon Robert Rogers and his son to compile a full-scale chronicle of England, focusing on Chester, for which the early material was culled from Holinshed.[180]

Similar examples survive from Southampton, Newcastle-upon-Tyne, Exeter, Okehampton, King's Lynn, and other communities,[181] but these

[178] BL MS Lans. 896 (Warburton collections), fos. 8r–15r, "Annales of Beverley."

[179] Aldersey's Annals, BL MS Add. 39925, fos. 4–29; Chester City RO, Z16, photocopy of original on deposit in Chester Public Library. Once attributed to Edward Whitby (d. 1639), recorder of Chester in 1613, this is now believed to be the work of Randle Holme I, for which attribution I am indebted to the staff of the Chester City Record Office. For two other examples of local historical writing in Chester see "A collection of the maiors who have governed this cittie of Chester and the tyme when they governed," ascribed in a note by Randle Holme II to William Higginson, sheriff of Chester: BL MS Harl. 1989 (Holme MSS), fos. 5r–31r; and, in the same MS, at fo. 32v, a later (*ca.* 1640) account of Chester as "the mother of all other Chesters" (i.e. towns with *chester* or *caster* in their names), interesting as a late survival of local foundation myths.

[180] BL MS Harl. 1948, "A Brevarye [*sic*] or some collectiones of the most anchant & famous cittie of Chester," collected by the Revd. Robert Rogers, BD, the sixteenth-century arch-deacon of Chester and prebendary of Chester Cathedral. The MS itself was, however, "reduced" to its current 150-leaf form by Rogers' son, David, who organized the material into chapters rather than annals early in the seventeenth century; Chester City RO, CX/3, "A Brevary or some Fewe Collections of the Cittie of Chester," was compiled by David Rogers in 1609; cf. A. M. Kennett, *Archives and Records of the City of Chester* (Chester, 1985), p. 75. A later set of Chester collections arranged as annals (and with time marked, almanac style, as "years expired since" an event), BL MS Harl. 2133, fos. 10r–49v (new foliation), may also have been part of the Rogers' collections, and draws its account of the city's history from Holinshed, Foxe, and various medieval chronicles, with complete citations of editions and page numbers. In contrast to these works, assembled as the basis of a town history rather than a history in their own right, compare an earlier Chester chronicle in BL MS Add. 29777. This is a lavishly illustrated roll running from 1326 to 1584, with mayors and sheriffs, the year of the city in the far left margins, and interlined annals written not contemporaneously but in the sixteenth century, e.g. sub 1380: "In this yere wyne and other victualls were verye aboundante," or sub 1543: "In this yeare one Cowley yoman of the garde slewe one Throppe of this cittie of Chester, and for the same was hanged." The annals are thickest in the 1560s and 1570s, falling off thereafter and ending in 1584.

[181] BL MS Add. Egerton 868, fos. 1r–54v, a list of the mayors of Southampton from 1498 to 1671 composed in French, Latin, and English, with town events prominent in the latter part; BL MS Add. Egerton 2425, "A catalogue of all the mayors & sheriffs of . . . Newcastell upon Tyne," running from 1432 to the late eighteenth century and including (fos. 80r–132) various extracts from Froissart: this is a copy of an earlier, seventeenth-century chronicle

official and semiofficial chronicles and chronologies are small in num-ber in comparison with the work of private citizens (a boundary line that is admit-tedly difficult to draw in some cases). The commonplace book of Valentine Bourne of Norwich contains both the names of all the high sheriffs of Norfolk from 1558 and a chronicle of Norwich from 1403 (the year the town received its charter from Henry IV). This chronicle, begun by another hand and continued, perhaps by Bourne, records events such as "a blazing starr" (1471), "a greate sweate called the dead sweate" (1485), and "the good duke of Buckingham beheaded" (1521). It mixes events of national interest such as the Armada with local events: rainy weather that endured all summer in 1426; the building of the water mills in 1429; the death of ten aldermen in 1558; the execution in 1560 of a sixteen-year-old boy for raping a seven-year-old girl; and numerous earthquakes and other prodigies of nature.[182]

Towns have rulers in the same way that countries do, but ones that rotate annually. This helps account not only for the long-standing use of the mayoral year annal as organizing principle, but also for its retention into the seventeenth century. Parishes did not have the corporate identity of towns, but in the course of the later sixteenth and seventeenth centuries they had increasingly become units of civil as well as ecclesiastical adminis-tration, a function initiated with the keeping of parish registers and en-hanced by the annual rotation of minor offices such as churchwardens and overseers of the poor. It is therefore no great surprise that in the seven-teenth century one begins to find such standard documents as churchwar-dens' accounts and memoranda books being adapted into annalistic grids along which to record the parochial past and present. At the turn of the sixteenth century John Paul, vicar of Almondsbury, near Bristol, wrote a list of the parish's vicars that was later copied into a mid-seventeenth-century parish register. This included memoranda of great occurrences from 1483 to his own time. An annal penned by Paul in 1606 integrates local events with national politics: "In the year 1483 (& the first of Richard the usurper) was a wonderfull floud & inundation of the river of Severn";

(referring in the present tense to a visit by Charles I in 1432, fo. 43v) to which later additions have been made; Devon RO, Exeter City Archives, Act Book B 1/4 (1581–88), fos. 1–194 (cf. Hist. MSS Comm., *Exeter*, 313–14): this is a "memorandum book," mainly but not entirely in the hand of John Hooker, arranged chronologically and listing occurrences in the city; Okehampton: Devon RO, 3248A/9/1, unfoliated chronicle copied in 1672 by Richard Shebbeare from "the towne booke of record" and running from 1625 to 1672, with continuations in different hands up to 1698; King's Lynn: BL MS Add. 8937, fos. 2r–15v, from 1517 to 1623 with continuations in at least three distinct hands up to 1673; cf. Tudor version written ca. 1538–42 in Bodl. MS Top. Norfolk c.2.

[182] Bodl. MS Tanner 397. Half of this volume is bound upside down and repaginated from the back cover: foliation is to the reversed sequence: fos. 17r, 22v, 23r–37v. On the Bourne family see Francis Blomefield, *Topographical History of the County of Norfolk*, index (1862), p. 46.

other annals record acts of impiety and the divine judgments upon them.[183]

In 1607, three years after Alexander Strange became vicar of Layston, Hertfordshire, he began a memorandum book with abstracts of charity deeds and wills, notes of subscriptions by parishioners of funds and their disbursements, recording also such events as sermons and remarks on the town bridge. A century later, one of his remote successors in the cure, Thomas Heton (vicar 1703–48) continued the book in this manner, while doing likewise for the parish of Wyddial, where he also served as vicar. Heton used Strange's book to reconstruct the parochial history of Layston, while adding his own remarks, along with a critique of John Selden's *Historie of Tithes*. The Wyddial tithe accounts, commenced by Heton in 1719, also include materials copied from earlier rectors, legal precedents, details of parish boundaries, and various historical and topographical details relevant to the parish, including descriptions of its funeral monuments. Heton's principal contribution to all this was an historical account of the parish beginning with its gift to Hardwin de Scalers by William I, for which he drew on Dugdale's *Baronage*, and Sir Henry Chauncy's *The Historical Antiquities of Hertfordshire*.[184] The Flamstead parish register, initiated in 1598 (with earlier entries copied into it from other sources), is spattered with records of historical events, such as a disastrous flood in 1725.[185]

More formal attempts at the history of a particular church or cathedral which drew largely on chronicles as their sources, were also designed to emulate them. Sometimes arranged annalistically, they occasionally inspired the sort of updating by subsequent generations characteristic of many urban chronicles as well as of earlier medieval monastic ones.[186] The devotion of a layman like Richard Gough to the history of his beloved Myddle about 1700 has a clerical counterpart in "A Rhapsodicall Collection of Various Matters

---

[183] Bristol RO, P/Alm/R/1(a), Almondsbury parish register, 1653, including Paul's list of vicars, written half a century earlier, and copied into this register.

[184] Herts. RO, D/P65 3/3 (Layston parochial accounts); Herts. RO, D/P 127 3/1 (Wyddial parochial accounts). Parish registers often amount to casual chronicles of local events: that for Salehurst, Sussex, which begins in 1575, includes amid the baptisms and burials such items as "Feb. 1578 at this tyme ther was a very great snow"; and "1610. October. Henry Turner a prophane drunkard died excommunicate and was buried in the highe way to the terror [of] drunkards primo die," sandwiched between two baptisms: R. C. Hussey, "Some Entries in Salehurst Parish Books," *Sussex Archaeological Collections*, 25 (1873), 152–62, at pp. 156–7.

[185] Herts. RO, D/P 38 1/1 (film 653), Flamstead parish register 1548–1735, which records the purchase of the book in 1598; D/P 38 1/2, register for 1723–81.

[186] Compare two Lichfield historians of the sixteenth century, William Whitlock (1520–*ca.* 1584), author in 1569 of a "chronicon Lichefeldensis Ecclesie," written at the request of William Walkeden, prebendary of Lichfield; and the anonymous *Historia Ecclesiae Lichfeldensis*, written in 1575, but surviving only in two post-Restoration copies. These works, which I have not seen, are described in M. W. Greenslade, *The Staffordshire Historians*, (1982) p. 9; I am indebted to Mr. Greenslade for a helpful conversation about local history writing in Staffordshire.

relating to the Vicaridge of Wargrave" initiated by William Derham, vicar of Wargrave, in 1690. Like Richard Gough, Derham based his own researches on local manuscripts, as well as oral information and observation (plate 1.5). Unlike Gough, but very much like his medieval monastic predecessors, Derham bequeathed the work to his successors in the vicarage, a number of whom continued to add parochial events as they unfolded.[187]

Our final example in this lengthy account is a chronicle of the kings of England compiled up to 1645 by Thomas Wyatt, rector of Ducklington, Oxfordshire. Wyatt covered events from the Norman Conquest to the death of James I, which he arranged annalistically after the fashion of Stow or Holinshed. Only with the accession of Charles I did he narrow his focus to include local events (including details of troop movements and billeting at Ducklington during the first civil war), and at that point the chronicle virtually becomes a diary. But both the arrangement of material by year and the sort of entry one finds ("A very dry hote summer [1631]"; "A very backward harvest we began to mowe our meadowes August 19 1633"; "A rumour was spred in April 1637 that in a place in Gloucestershire it rained wheate") suggests that for this rural cleric, fifty years of humanist historiography had had very little impact. Judging by the ink and the writing – itself a throwback to Elizabethan hands – Wyatt did precisely as his monkish predecessors of three centuries earlier and more had done: he borrowed heavily from existing works for the period up until his own time, and then scrupulously added events to this in successive years.[188] The comprehensiveness of the medieval and Tudor annals, a continuing goal that lay behind the great number of universal histories and encyclopedias in the late seventeenth and eighteenth centuries, continued to drive individuals to imitate them in defiance of a culture that now privileged style, authorial social status and selectivity over inclusiveness.

By the mid-seventeenth century, the twilight of the chronicle as a published genre was turning to night, and with it was ending the much longer period during which annals had been either the sole or the most important medium for the literary representation of the factual past. The rest of this book will be taken up with many of the same questions that have been addressed, with

---

[187] Berks. RO, D/P 145/28/7, "A Rhapsodicall Collection of Various Matters relating to the Vicaridge of Wargrave in ye Diocess [*sic*] of Sarum: By William Derham late vicar there AD 1690. To be delivered carefully to the Vicar of Wargrave by every person in whose hands this book shall hereafter fall." Cf. D/P 145/3/1, an incomplete nineteenth-century copy.

[188] Bodl. MS Top. Oxon. c. 378, pp. 1–409; the larger part of the chronicle, to the death of James I, ends at p. 233; see especially pp. 234, 269, 281, 283. Pp. 410–94 contain geographical notes on England and Wales and a list of English and Welsh bishops. The entire manuscript is calendared in Hist. MSS Comm., *Eighth Report*, 458b.

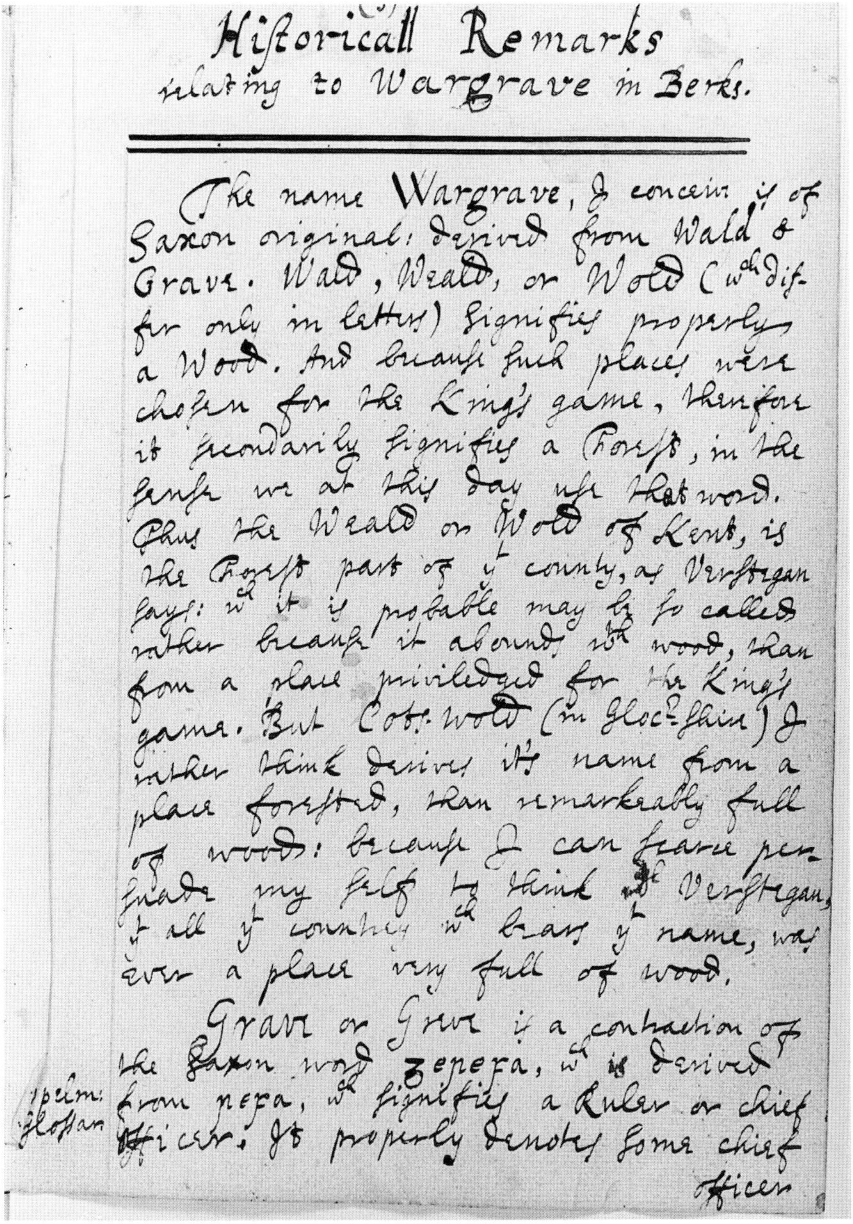

Historicall Remarks
relating to Wargrave in Berks.

The name Wargrave, I conceive is of Saxon original: derived from Wald & Grave. Wald, Weald, or Wold (wch differ only in letters) signifies properly a Wood. And because such places were chosen for the King's game, therefore it secondarily signifies a Forest, in the sense we at this day use that word. Thus the Weald or Wold of Kent, is the Forest part of ye county, as Verstegan says: wch it is probable may be so called rather because it abounds wth wood, than from a place priviledged for the King's game. But Cots: wold (in Gloc: shire) I rather think derives its name from a place forested, than remarkably full of woods: because I can scarce persuade my self to think wth Dr Verstegan, yt all yt country wch bears yt name, was ever a place very full of wood.

Grave or Grve is a contraction of the Saxon word Zerefa, wch is derived from refa, wch signifies a Ruler or chief officer: It properly denotes some chief officer

1 prim: glossar

Plate 1.5 Parochial collections: a page from Berks. RO, D/P 145/28/7, a bound octavo book entitled "A Rhapsodicall Collection of Various Matters relating to the Vicaridge of Wargrave in ye Diocess [sic] of Sarum: By William Derham late vicar there AD 1690."

particular reference to chronicles, in this chapter, including issues of cost, production, and distribution. Before we can evaluate the more economic aspects of the history book's early career, however, some attention needs to be paid to the question of how, and in what contexts, history was being read.

2

The contexts and purposes of history reading

Most discussion of early modern historical writing has, not surprisingly, concentrated on the historians themselves. Yet as Robert Darnton has pointed out, the writers of the texts that turn into physical books are only one part of a complex "communications" circuit in early modern Europe that also includes printers and their workers, publishers, illustrators, booksellers, and readers.[1] Considerable work on the various components of this circuit remains to be done, and it must be done in ways that go beyond traditional intellectual history. It is no longer sufficient to know what was being written and published, nor even how successful a book was in terms of reprinting. We must find out who owned certain books, what value (monetary and intellectual) they placed on them, and how they understood and made use of their contents. This could apply to any division of knowledge, not just history, but much the same sources will tell us both about what sorts of history people were reading, and give us a sense of the relative importance of works about the past compared with works on other matters – religion, natural philosophy, law, politics, music and the arts, and so on.[2] This chapter

---

[1] Robert Darnton, "What is the History of Books?," in *The Kiss of Lamourette: Reflections in Cultural History* (New York and London, 1990), pp. 107–35, and "First Steps Toward a History of Reading," ibid., pp. 154–87. Cf. David D. Hall, "A History of the Book: New Questions? New Answers?," *Journal of Library History*, 21 (1986), 27–38.

[2] The following works, though old, remain useful for the history of reading and of printing in England: H. S. Bennett, *English Books and Readers* (3 vols., Cambridge, 1952–70); M. Plant, *The English Book Trade: an Economic History of the Making and Sale of Books* (1939; 3rd edn 1974), which has been superseded in parts by P. Gaskell, *A New Introduction to Bibliography* (Oxford, 1972); L. Rostenburg, *Literary, Political, Scientific, Religious and Legal Publishing, Printing and Bookselling in England, 1551–1700* (2 vols., New York, 1965). The focus of scholarship has changed substantially since all these works were first published, partly due to the work of pioneering book historians such as Lucien Febvre and Henri-Jean Martin, and partly owing to the influence of Elizabeth Eisenstein's *The Printing Press as an Agent of Change: Communications and Cultural Transformations in Early-Modern Europe* (2 vols., Cambridge, 1979). Among newer works integrating the history of print and publishing with cultural history through a reconfigured *histoire du livre*, see, in addition to Darnton, Robert Scribner, *For the Sake of Simple Folk: Popular Propaganda for the German Reformation* (Cambridge, 1981); Roger Chartier, *The Cultural Uses of Print in Early Modern Europe*, trans. L. Cochrane (Princeton, 1987), especially chs. 5 and 6; Miriam

focuses on the component in the "circuit" about which the least is known, namely the reader, before moving in subsequent chapters through the acquisition of history books and the processes associated with their making and selling. This apparently backwards arc is deliberate, since it is a mistake to regard the reader as simply an "end user," a passive receptacle of historical knowledge imparted to paper by truth-seeking historians and faithfully rendered by their printers and booksellers. Rather, the very nature of historical knowledge was such that it was intended to be socially circulated: once read in a book, it was supposed to be put to practical moral or political use, talked about, shared with friends and family, and interactively revised and reshaped by the reader.[3]

READING ALOUD

A significant amount of history was read aloud, in groups of varying sizes, from the late Middle Ages to the seventeenth century, though it is wrong to think of late medieval reading as exclusively vocal, since silent reading goes back at least to the fourteenth century.[4] This practice continued into the nineteenth century and beyond, as we know from innumerable references in novels, letters, and diaries, but with some very important differences. From the Restoration onward, there were many more printed history books from which to choose, and there were incomparably more literate readers, so that books read aloud were also available to be read silently at a later time by the more interested among their auditors, which had not generally been the case

---

U. Chrisman, *Lay Culture, Learned Culture: Books and Social Change in Strasbourg, 1480–1599* (New Haven and London, 1982); most recently see an important collection of essays, *Printing the Written Word: The Social History of Books, circa 1450–1520*, ed. Sandra L. Hindman (Ithaca, NY, 1991) that, though it deals with the period prior to mine, nevertheless has useful things to say about early modern books in general. The process of moving the history of reading, and of books, in England, from its former bibliographic focus into the European historiographic stream has only recently got underway with such projects as the History of the Book in Britain. Two useful, recent essays that point to ways in which reading habits can be reconstructed are Anthony Grafton and Lisa Jardine, "'Studied for Action': How Gabriel Harvey Read his Livy," *Past and Present* 129 (1990), 30–78; Lorna Hutson, "Fortunate Travelers: Reading for the Plot in Sixteenth-Century England," *Representations*, 41 (1993), 83–103. Although I cannot agree in all respects with their interpretation of both the motives and manner of early modern history reading, I have profited from both of these essays. Most recently, the "physiology" of reading has been examined by Adrian Johns in *The Nature of the Book: Print and Knowledge in the Making* (Chicago and London, 1998), pp. 380–443.
[3] For the concept of the social circulation of historical knowledge see my book in progress, tentatively entitled *The Social Circulation of the Past: English Historical Culture, 1500–1730*.
[4] Materials from this section previously appeared in my article, "Speech, Text, and Time: The Sense of Hearing and the Sense of the Past in Renaissance England," *Albion*, 18 (1986), 159–93. For medieval examples, see Joyce Coleman, *Public Reading and the Reading Public in Late Medieval England and France* (Cambridge, 1996), especially pp. 117–21.

in earlier times.[5] Furthermore, the setting of vocal reading itself shifted decisively over three centuries, moving out of the court, great household, marketplace, or institutional forum, and into the more intimate setting of the private home, as a direct consequence of greater literacy and more numerous books. Finally, it is also difficult to estimate the number of occasions on which an historical work was read aloud, particularly in a formal setting, since late medieval and Renaissance England had not developed a culture of courtly public reading to the degree that was true across the channel and in Italy, under regimes that placed a high degree of stress on official historiography.[6] For all these reasons, a straightforward comparison of the history readers of early Tudor England with their Augustan successors of two centuries later would be rather meaningless.

The language of many early modern histories does, however, betray a continued orientation to aurality in the face of an ever-increasing density of printed materials. Midway through his account of the reign of King Edward III, the Jacobean historian John Speed paused to remind his readers of what had gone before, an account of Edward's wars in France, by way of leading into his next subject, the king's godliness. "You have heard a part of great king Edwards victorious fortunes in battle, both by land and sea; be not ignorant of his pietie."[7] Speed's choice of language is striking: "You have heard." Many early modern authors employed this same style of reference. In 1600, Thomas Danett commenced a chapter of his *A continuation of the history of France* with the sentence, "You have heard how a truce for five years was concluded betweene the kings of Fraunce and Spaine."[8] To justify the printing of a quotation from a medieval manuscript, William Camden urged his reader to "heare the verie words out of that private historie."[9] Richard Verstegan directed the reader to "heer the testimony of sundry ancient and approved authors."[10] The anonymous author of *The historie of*

---

[5] Paul Saenger, "Silent Reading: Its Impact on Late Medieval Script and Society," *Viator*, 13 (1982), 367–414; Paul Saenger, *Space Between Words: The Origins of Silent Reading* (Stanford, 1997).

[6] Saenger, *Space Between Words*, pp. 128–30; Andrew Taylor, "Into His Secret Chamber: Reading and Privacy in Late Medieval England," in James Raven, Helen Small, and Naomi Tadmor (eds.), *The Practice and Representation of Reading in England* (Cambridge, 1996), pp. 41–61; N. Tadmor, " 'In the Even my Wife Read to Me': Women, Reading and Household Life in the Eighteenth Century," in Raven, Small, and Tadmor (eds.), *Practice and Representation*, pp. 162–74; Roger Chartier, "Leisure and Sociability: Reading Aloud in Early Modern Europe," in *Urban Life in the Renaissance*, ed. Susan Zimmerman and Ronald F. E. Weisman (Newark, DE, London, and Toronto, 1989), pp. 103–20.

[7] John Speed, *The historie of Great Britaine* (1623), p. 699.

[8] Thomas Danett, *A continuation of the history of France* (1600), p. 132. Danett also uses the phrasing, "upon this occasion which you shall now heare."

[9] William Camden, *Britain*, trans. Philemon Holland (1610), p. 402; cf. William Somner's use of the phrase "as I told you" in *The antiquities of Canterbury* (1640), p. 242.

[10] Richard Verstegan (alias Rowlands), *A restitution of decayed intelligence* (Antwerp and London, 1605), p. 50.

Mervine, a chivalric romance, reminded the reader of an earlier event with the remark: "the childe (as you have heard) was baptized."[11]

As historians, we have all had occasion to refer the reader back to earlier points in our articles, theses and books, the present one included. As a rule, such passages begin with a phrase like "we have seen," or "it has been shown," not "you have heard." In general, we do not address the reader in the vocative case (though it might be said that in writing these words I am implicitly addressing you, the person now reading them, while my footnotes tell you to "see" other people's works). Nor do we usually regard what we have written as being audible unless we have specifically designed it to be so-delivered, as in the case of public lectures and conference papers. The much greater frequency of metaphors of sound rather than sight in Renaissance texts suggests that the writers who employed it thought of their works not as silent artifacts to be studied exclusively with the eye, but as instruments for the conveyance of their authorial voice to a public which in turn was conceived of as a virtual audience.

This vocal conception of the intercourse between an absent author, living or dead, and his or her reader shows up most clearly in Tudor historical writing, particularly in the widespread practice of inventing speeches for historical characters, which dates back to Thucydides. With a few exceptions, most Elizabethan and early Stuart historians continued to use this device freely, for such speeches could illustrate the character of an historical personage far more effectively and immediately than could straightforward narrative. But there was more to the custom than this: Renaissance historians derived from the rhetorical tradition within which they worked an oratorical conception of their art which they were not ready to abandon. A history was *itself* more an extended speech than a visualized text. Herodotus and other ancient historians had read their works aloud to audiences. John Speed may have been so influenced by the prose of the Authorized Version (which was itself "appointed to be read in churches"), for which he composed the genealogies, that he wrote his *Historie* to be read aloud. Given the gargantuan proportions of Speed's book, and of others such as Foxe's *Acts and Monuments,* it seems likely that many contemporary historians intended their works to be heard, that is, read aloud to an audience, as well as read silently. This in turn helps explain their frequent habit, shared with other prose writers, of addressing their imagined audience in the vocative case. They framed their narratives as verbal utterances on two levels: on a literal level, from speaker to audience, and on a figurative level, from the writer to the private reader. On the other hand, an increasing sophistication in index-

[11] J. M., *The history of Mervine* (1612), p. 5.

ing (plate 2.6) and tabular display (plate 2.7) is evident in histories and chronicles toward the end of the sixteenth century; this tendency reached maturity in the seventeenth, suggesting that their authors (or at least their printers) also had a developing sense of the history book as a repository of information that could be consulted as well as read. This provides a caution against overemphasizing the oratorical aspect of history.

It is probably safe to say that prior to 1600, and perhaps even a century later, most people would have heard their history in one form or another long before they read it, if they ever read it at all. A significant amount of book-based historical education still consisted of a master reading to his pupils from select texts, among them historical. Sir James Whitelocke's undergraduate education in the 1580s, at the hands of Rowland Searchfield, in large measure involved the latter reading to his charges from religion, Hebrew, Greek, and history, "in whiche I toke great delite, and especially in Titus Livius." An MP speaking on the succession issue in 1566 believed that his fellow members had either "read or heard" of the unfortunate events occasioned by Henry IV's usurpation in 1399. Roger Ascham, refuting the argument that ignorance of God is more desirable than knowledge of his doctrine, claimed that he had "never hard or red, that any auncyent father of the primitive chirch, either thought or wrote so." Richard Senhouse, bishop of Carlisle, commented that his contemporaries talked freely of the mythical past. They might "speake of Aeneas and Rutulus" or "hear of wounded Achilles," though they paid, he thought, less attention to sacred history. "Hast thou not heard of the foolish marriage that Emperor Heliogabalus made?" asks one character in Brian Melbancke's *Philotimus*.[12] Preachers frequently made use of historical examples, and many parishioners undoubtedly acquired their first and perhaps only awareness of an extended past through listening to the episodes from biblical and classical history that enlivened the Sunday sermon. This, indeed, was one of the arguments adduced by Thomas Starkey in favor of vernacular services, which would allow common people to

hearken the stories of the Bible commonly rehearsed, which are rehearsed only for this cause – that the people hearing them may be the rather stirred to follow the

[12] *Liber Famelicus of Sir James Whitelocke, a Judge of the Court of King's Bench, in the Reigns of James I and Charles I*, ed. J. Bruce, Camden Soc., o.s. 70 (1858), p. 13; *Proceedings in the Parliaments of Elizabeth I*, ed. T. Hartley (1981–), I, 131; Roger Ascham, *English Works, Toxophilus, Report of the Affaires and State of Germany, The Scholemaster* (Cambridge, 1904), p. 210; cf. p. 11, where he writes that the use of the longbow in English history is a fact of which "both oulde men and chronicles doe tell"; Richard Senhouse, *Foure sermons* (1627), p. 65; Melbancke, *Philotimus* (1582), sig. S. ii. Richard Bancroft introduced an historical quotation with an injunction to the reader to "heare the historie": *A survey of the pretended holy discipline* (1593), p. 186.

THE
INDEX.

N. B. *K.* ſtands for King, *Kᵐ* for Kingdom, the Letter (*n.*) before the Number of the Page, means the Note at the Bottom of the Page.

A

ADELARD *K. of* Weſſex, 211

Adelfrid *K. of* Northumberlaud, 160 *maſſacres the Monks of* Bangor, ibid. *is ſlain in Battle,* 164

Adelwach *K. of* Suiſex *dethroned by the K. of* Mercia, 202 *is reſtored and ſlain in Battle,* ibid.

Adelwalt *K. of* Eaſt-Anglia, 192

Adrian *(the Emperour) comes into* Britain, 60. *is ſtilled the Reſtorer of* Britain, ibid.

Agricola *(* Julius*) ſent into* Britain *by* Veſpaſian, 54. *his ſeven Campaigns,* 55——57. *brings the* Britons *to conform to the* Roman *Cuſtoms,* 55. *is recalled and poiſoned by* Demitian, 59

Alban ; *(St.) his Converſion,* 86. *firſt Martyr in* England, ibid. *his Relicks,* 188

Albion, *whence ſo called,* 13

Alcred *K. of* Northumberland *depoſed,* 179

Alcuinus ; *an Account of him and his Work, n.* 292

Aldrick *K. of* Kent *vanquiſhed by* Offa, *the laſt of the Race of* Hengiſt, 200

Aldroen *K. of* Armorica *ſends the* Britons *Aid,* 101

Alulph *K. of* Eaſt-Anglia, 192

Alfred *K. of* Northumberland, 176

Alfred VIth Saxon *K. ſent to* Rome *at five Years old,* 308. *anointed by the Pope,* ibid, *defeated by the* Danes, 324. *his Wars with the* Danes, 328, 330. *reduced*

example of the old fathers and holy men whose virtues are celebrate in our temples and churches. For what availeth else this rehearsing of these legends and loud singing thereof now, in a strange tongue as they be rehearsed?[13]

A century after Starkey, in a much-cited remark, John Aubrey remembered that his nurse had "the history of England from the conquest down to Charles I in ballad." Ambrose Barnes, the Restoration alderman of Newcastle was "furnisht for all manner of conversation in history" according to his biographer. "He entertained men to admiration by reciting the times, places, occasions and precise actions, as if he had seen them." George Puttenham offers a particularly vivid picture of ballad singers and blind harpers performing for "boys or countrey fellowes that passe by them in the streete." He notes that their subject was "for the most part stories of old time," by which he means the romances, "made purposely for recreation of the common people at Christmasse diners and brideales, and in taverns and alehouses and such other places of base resort."[14]

The phrase "history doth mention" is commonplace.[15] Samuel Daniel begins his verse history of the Wars of the Roses with an epic convention: "I sing the civil wars." When Shakespeare's Richard II sits upon the ground, it is to tell sad stories of the deaths of kings, not to read about them.[16] Puttenham, discussing historical poesy, felt that the past was lost to the senses, partly because "historicall reportes" were not sung as often as they had been in ancient times. He himself wrote a "historicall ditty in the English tong of the Isle of great Britaine." This was not intended for private reading but, like the old chivalric romances, was "to be more commodiously sung to the harpe in place of assembly, where the company shalbe desirous to heare of old adventures and valiaunces of noble knights in times past, as are those of King Arthur and his knights of the round table, Sir Bevis of Southampton, Guy of Warwicke and others like."[17] Thomas Hobbes, a few decades later, asserted in the preface to his translation of Thucydides that the peculiarly pithy style

---

[13] Thomas Starkey, *A dialogue between Reginald Pole and Thomas Lupset*, ed. Kathleen M. Burton (1948), p. 189.

[14] M. R., *Memoirs of the Life of Mr. Ambrose Barnes*, Surtees Soc. 50 (1866), p. 151; John Aubrey, *Brief Lives*, ed. O. L. Dick (1972), p. 29; George Puttenham, *The arte of English poesie*, ed. Gladys Doidge Willcock and Alice Walker (Cambridge, 1936), pp. 83–84.

[15] For example, Thomas Nabbes, *Hannibal and Scipio* (1637), V, ii, sig. Kv.

[16] Samuel Daniel, *The Civil Wars* (1595–1609), ed. Laurence Michel (New Haven, CT, 1958), p. 71; *Richard II*, III, ii, 155–60.   [17] Puttenham, *Arte of English Poesie*, p. 42.

Plate 2.6 (*opposite*) Indexing history: indexes became increasingly important to readers wishing to "look up" particular facts in the late sixteenth and seventeenth century. By the early eighteenth century, indexes had become a standard feature of most historical works. Here indexing is illustrated in vol. I of Rapin-Thoyras' *History* translated by Nicholas Tindal (1728–32).

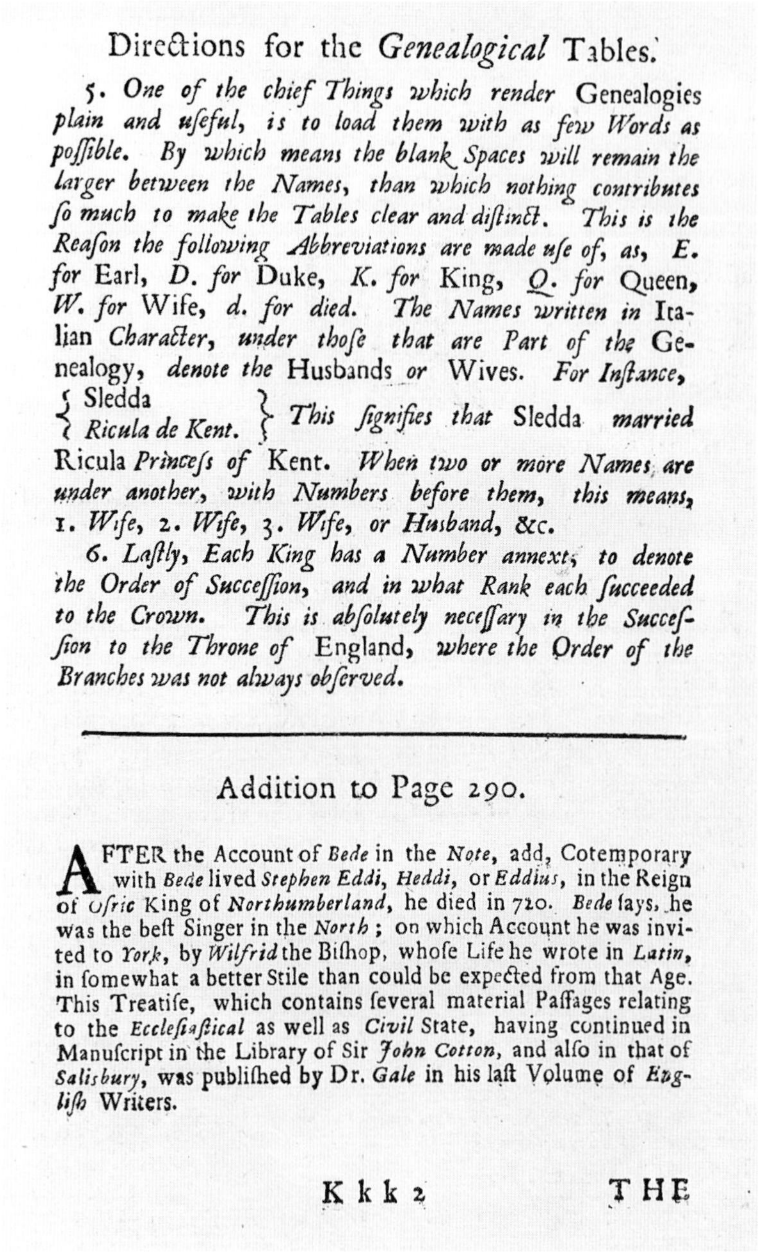

Directions for the *Genealogical* Tables.

5. *One of the chief Things which render* Genealogies *plain and useful, is to load them with as few Words as possible.* By *which means the blank Spaces will remain the larger between the Names, than which nothing contributes so much to make the Tables clear and distinct.* This is *the Reason the following Abbreviations are made use of, as,* E. *for Earl,* D. *for Duke,* K. *for King,* Q. *for Queen,* W. *for Wife,* d. *for died.* The *Names written in Italian Character, under those that are Part of the Genealogy, denote the* Husbands *or* Wives. *For Instance,*

{ Sledda
{ *Ricula de Kent.* } This *signifies that* Sledda *married* Ricula *Princess of* Kent. When *two or more Names are under another, with Numbers before them, this means,* 1. *Wife,* 2. *Wife,* 3. *Wife, or Husband, &c.*

6. *Lastly, Each King has a Number annext, to denote the Order of Succession, and in what Rank each succeeded to the Crown.* This is *absolutely necessary in the Succession to the Throne of* England, *where the Order of the Branches was not always observed.*

Addition to Page 290.

AFTER the Account of *Bede* in the *Note*, add, Cotemporary with *Bede* lived *Stephen Eddi, Heddi,* or *Eddius,* in the Reign of *Osric* King of *Northumberland,* he died in 720. *Bede* says, he was the best Singer in the *North* ; on which Account he was invited to *York,* by *Wilfrid* the Bishop, whose Life he wrote in *Latin,* in somewhat a better Stile than could be expected from that Age. This Treatise, which contains several material Passages relating to the *Ecclesiastical* as well as *Civil* State, having continued in Manuscript in the Library of Sir *John Cotton,* and also in that of *Salisbury,* was published by Dr. *Gale* in his last Volume of *English* Writers.

Plate 2.7   The visual culture of the history book, in directions for using the genealogical tables to the revised edition of Francis Sandford's *Genealogical History*, revised by S. Stebbing (1707), sig. Kkk2.

of the Athenian is "rather to be read, then heard" – hardly a necessary caveat if histories were not also being heard.[18]

SOURCES FOR THE STUDY OF HISTORY READING

The records dealing with readings in a formal public setting are on the whole rather scarce. Happily, this is not at all the case with the history of reading as a whole, and particularly not with private readers alone with their books, or perhaps in the company of a small circle. So far as the reading of history is concerned, jottings in and from history books are among the best sorts of evidence, since they not only tell us when, and how frequently, a book was read, but often what the reader made of it. Early readers frequently added their own comments and glosses to their history books, as they did to Bibles and practical treatises (see plate 2.8). An annotated copy of the 1667 edition of George Cavendish's *Life of Wolsey* in the Bodleian Library is one example.[19] Another, somewhat later, is provided by the Kentish antiquary Sir Roger Twysden's Latin and Italian annotations, added over several years, in two distinct copies of Paolo Sarpi's *History of the Council of Trent*. These refer to many books printed as late as the 1650s.[20] Twysden underlined occasional passages in red, and gave cross-references in the margins to earlier and later passages, and to other books. He also wrote textual pointers in the margin ("Leo X" at page 3 signifying that pope, for instance) designed to make the volume easier for him to refer to on future consultations. And he added information to authorial assertions: where Sarpi discusses papal/ imperial relations in the late twelfth century, Twysden responds in the margin with a precise page reference to the medieval chronicler Orderic Vitalis. Sarpi's reference to Adam occasions the Twysden gloss "Genes.

---

[18] Thomas Hobbes, "Of the Life and History of Thucydides," in *Eight bookes of the Peloponnesian warre written by Thucydides* (2nd edn, 1634), sig. (b).

[19] Bodl. MS Gough Oxfordshire 22. It was common practice to have printed books interleaved to permit more extensive annotations: John Tanner (brother of the more famous Thomas) annotated an interleaved copy of John Kirby's *The Suffolk Traveller* (Ipswich, 1735), a successful travel book with antiquarian information: Suffolk RO, HD 1538/66. For a good example of the circulation of a printed historical book just after its publication, with the express view to its revision, see the letter to the Revd. George Plaxton, chief steward of Lord Gower's estates, from F[rancis] Skrimsher of Forton, 23 February 1713/14: Staffs RO, D593/K/1/1/7: "I'll send you my Erdswick to correct & insert what you have collected in the History of my Lord's Staffordshire Estate" (Skrimsher was helping Plaxton with his history of the Gower estates in Staffordshire and Shropshire).

[20] Folger STC 21760, copy 2. This is the 1619 Italian-language edition of Sarpi's *Historia del concilio tridentino* (London: Giovanni Billio, i.e. John Bill, 1619, folio), with annotations by Twysden. Compare the annotations in his hand on a duplicate of this book, now BL C.55.k.6 (microfilm copy in Folger Film acc.426.1), which includes some identical but also several different references.

XVIII.21."; and when Sarpi discusses the brief pontificate of Dedel (1522), Twysden thickens it with a citation from Guicciardini.[21]

Like Twysden with his Sarpi, the herald John Gibbon wrote notes into his copy of Stow's *Survey of London* (1598) near the end of the seventeenth century. The front of the volume is interleaved with remarks like "In Watling Street my father livd & dyde," that connect the text to his own family heritage, together with injunctions to himself to investigate matters he did not understand: a note to "Quaere where this Cassibelans Towne was" follows Stow's account of this lost town, west of London. Gibbon even supplies his own pen and ink doodles and pictorial symbols for various structures – bridges, chapels, castles, and gates – mentioned by Stow, and reminds himself in places to "Note this well." Throughout we can observe Gibbon making sense of what he read by turning it into his own prose and by connecting it with what he knew independently through remarks like "Joan of the Tower Queene of Scotts was borne in the Tower = daughter of Edw.2" or "I John Gibbon have observed the Armes on the east end of St. Dunstans church" of Sir John Oldcastle and his wife (under Stow's account of Aldgate ward). There is even the proud annotation next to the name of a fifteenth-century mayor that "from this Sir William [Crowmer] doe I Johan Gibbon Blewmantle duely descend." The reading process included the correction of what he read by what he had discovered on voyages through other texts: "Stow forgot Sr Henry Weever kt of the Bath sub Edwdo 4o, but not forgott

---

[21] Folger STC 21760, pp. 9, 10, 19. In almost every case Twysden's gloss is written in the language of the other book cited. The following works are cited in the Folger copy. For the sake of space I shall give only abbreviated references here and in other lists: Orderic Vitalis; Guicciardini, *Historia d'italia*; Matthew Paris, *Historia maiorem* (1571 edn); Matthew Paris, *Historia abbatum* (1639 edn); Socrates, *Ecclesiastica Historia*; "Matthew Westminster" (the *Flores Historiarum*); William of Newburgh; Bellarmine; Evagrius; Spelman's *Concilia*; Eadmer, *Historia novorum*, ed. Selden; Selden, *De jure naturalis et gentium*; Scaliger, *De emendatione temporum* (1629 edn); Bede; Florence of Worcester; Francis Godwin, *De praesulibus angliae*; J. Pitseus, *De scriptoribus Angliae in vita cardinalis Poli*; J.-A. De Thou, *Historia sui temporum* (Geneva 1620 edn), with a side reference to Camden, *Britannia* (1607 edn): "Sic Camdenus in Agro Warwicensi pag. 424 et Thuan. lib. 20 propr finem, pag. 623" (Sarpi, p. 393); Paolo Giovio, *Historiarum sui temporis* (Florence, 1551–53 edn); an unidentified *Historia Venetiana* glossed "Mauroceni" but perhaps that by Giovanni Nicolo Doglioni published at Venice in 1598; Girolamo Franchi di Conestaggio's *Historia delle guerre della Germania inferiore* (1634 edn); La Popelinière's *L'histoire de france* (probably 1582 edn); Nicephorus (= Nicephorus Callistus' *Ecclesiasticae historiae libri xviii*); Platina, *Lives of the popes*; Niccolo Orlandini, *Historia Societatis Iesu* (1615); Abraham Bucholzer, *Chronologia* (here used at p. 41 of Sarpi to provide an exact date not given in Sarpi's text); Polydore Vergil, *Anglica Historia*, again used to supply a death date of a mentioned person, Giovanni Colletto, "obiit anno domini 1519. huius laudes vide apud Polidorum Virgilium in fine lib.26 Hist. Ang." (Sarpi, p. 56); an unspecified history of Rome in Italian; the third volume of Baronius' *Annales Ecclesiastici*; Roger Hoveden's *Annalivm pars prior & posterior* (1596); a 1559 edn of Remigio Nannini's annotations on the chronicler Giovanni Villani; the *Historia Ecclesiastica tripartita* by Sozomen; Eusebius *Ecclesiastical History*; and William of Malmesbury, *Historia novella*. Several authors are referred to many times, for instance Baronius and Matthew Paris. References are precise in nearly every case, and even the *tavola* (index) is annotated.

TO
THE HONEST AND
VNDERSTANDING
READER.

TO giue thee good content, and to delight thy successors with the plaine knowledge of the occurrents in generall, which hapned in the daies of their fore-fathers. I haue vsed my best diligence and industry: and if in reading the same, it may please thee but to vse the tenth part of that patience, which in the collection thereof I haue endured, thou shalt doe thy selfe a great pleasure and me a high fauor. What I might say more, and that very iustly I now forbeare, hauing spoken somewhat to that purpose in the Epistle Dedicatorie of my abridgement: which for a generall answer vnto all scandalls, calumny, and malicious obiections against me, I haue annexed it at the end of this booke. If these my tedious labours of impartiall truth, be kindly accepted and honestly construed: then perhaps some other in time to come may be encouraged to enterprize the like. Expect no filed phrases, Inke-horne termes, vnquoth words, nor phantastique speaches, but good plaine English, without affectation, rightly befitting Chronologie: If Cicero's eloquence, Plato's Oratorie, or Virgils lofty verse, be thy chiefe desire: Pauls churh-yard is now plentiously furnished to satisfie thee: yea, and that so excellently well written in thy mother-tongue, as no forraigne Nation may compare with thee: no, not the Germans, of whom it hath beene said, to haue all Stories, Arts and Sciences in their vulgar language.

Doe not backbite me for my good meaning, nor play the Momus when thou hearest truth. It is extreme basenesse to abuse him, that in all his endeauors seekes to loue and honour thee. Read vnderstandingly, and iudge indifferently.

The ancient Britaines amongst many their ancient Prouerbs, say: it is the least requitall of honest courtesies, to accept them kindly, and it is the smallest frendship that may be, to giue good words of the absent. But if neither desire, nor desert may gaine thy fauour, it shall euer remaine as much thy fault as my hard hap. Therefore freely vse thy speach and wit as thy own pleasure for laughing toungs, and vile encounters of the ignorant, proud, and enuious, haue so tyred me, that henceforth I will rest sans feare or care of their braine-sick imitations. But to generous spirits, honorable mindes, learned heads, and vnderstanding hearts, I humbly prostrate my life and labours at their reuerend feete:

knowing

Plate 2.8 From Stow's *Annales*, 1631, continued by Edmund Howes, sig. ¶, "To the honest and understanding reader," a page showing marginal annotations by an anonymous seventeenth-century hand.

by Weaver's funerall monuments p. 393."[22] A reader with somewhat different interests, John Thomas, interleaved and thickly annotated his copy of the 1610 English translation of Camden's *Britannia*; adding his own comments, together with poetry and extracts from other histories he had read, he provided himself with page references to passages elsewhere in *Britannia* itself, to other works of relevance to Camden's topics, and to manuscripts in his own possession. What had been a large and expensive book became virtually the skeleton of an historical commonplace book.[23] Like Gibbon and Twysden, Thomas' study habits provide compelling evidence that early modern readers were not passive receptacles but rather active directors of a dialogue involving both the text at hand and the many other authors to which it could be related. Printed marginal notes (plate 2.9) and, slightly later, footnotes, were just beginning their long life in the scholarly apparatus.[24] They were not simply supports produced by authors, however, but invitations to readers to bring their own textual "guests" to the table.

The manner in which many historical works were studied also speaks to the endurance of the annal, observed in the previous chapter, as a unit for digesting history into usable chunks. Where Twysden chose to annotate his two copies of Sarpi's *History of the Council of Trent*, another reader chose instead to abstract its major events into annals for easy reference.[25] A copy of Christopher Helwig or Helvicus' much-cited world chronology, interleaved at front and back, contains such entries as "1671. Dutchess of York died Mar. 31. Interred April 5. A fire in Oxford consuming 50 dwelling houses Apr. 25. K. of France comes to Dunkirke 18th, 2800 men . . . The crown stole out of the Tower May 9." In the text of the book itself, the owner annotated more sparingly, focusing on Helvicus' tables of the various European dynasties, to which he or she added Latin notes on martyrs taken from Foxe's *Acts and Monuments*.[26] In the 1690s and early 1700s a reader

---

[22] Folger printed books STC 23341 copy 2, pp. 2, 26, 41, 173, 236.
[23] Bodl. MS Top. gen. c.36, John Thomas' copy of *Britannia*.
[24] Anthony Grafton, *The Footnote: A Curious History* (Cambridge, MA, 1997).
[25] Lambeth Palace MS 2656, "A Summarie of the History of ye Councel of Trent (Conteining Eight bookes), collected by me, G L., 1629." The second edition of Nathaniel Brent's translation of Sarpi appeared in 1629 and is most likely the edition to which the reader referred.
[26] Christopher Helwig or Helvicus, *Theatrum historicum et chronologicum* (6th edn, Oxford 1662). Folger shelfmark H1413, front and p. 147. For another example, see the annotations at the start of a copy of Thomas Uvedale's translation of *The Memoirs of Philip de Comines* (1712), a few notes on flyleaves of each of the two volumes, like "the superstition of Lewis 11th. 361", "the cruel usurpation of ye Princes of Italy 501": copy no. 2 in the Queen Anne collection at University of Texas, Austin, HRC, shelfmark DC 106.9 C723 1712 HRC/QUA.

Plate 2.9 (*opposite*)   Printed marginal notes and page layout illustrated; in Holinshed's *Chronicles*, 1587. Note the use of distinctive fonts in the glosses to separate citations of sources from subject pointers.

Scala temporum.

marks was trulie repaid againe in the next yeare following. ¶ Also this yeare on Whitsundaie li. Edward the fourth created the lord Berkeleie, vicount Berkeleie, at Gréenewich. ¶ In this yeare also an house on London bridge called the common siege, or priuie, fell downe into the Thames, where thorough it fiue persons were drowned. ¶ This yeare the king with his quéene kept a roiall Christmas at Windsor.

The king fea-steth the ma-ior and alder-men.

Also this yeare was one Richard Chawrie maior of London, whome king Edward so greatlie fauoured, that he tooke him (with certeine of his bre-then the aldermen, & commons of the citie of Lon-don) into the forrest of Waltham, where was ordei-ned for them a pleasant lodge of gréene boughs, in which lodge they dined with great chéere; & the king would not go to dinner vntill he saw them serued. Moreouer he caused the lord chamberlaine, with o-ther lords, to chéere the said maior and his companie sundrie times whilest they were at dinner. After din-ner they went a hunting with the king, and flue ma-nie deare, as well red as fallow, whereof the king gaue vnto the maior and his companie good plentie, and sent vnto the ladie maires and hir sisters the al-dermens wiues, two harts, sir bucks, and a tun of wine to make them merrie with, which was eaten in the drapers hall. The cause of which bountie thus

Fabian pag. 511.

shewed by the king, was (as most men did take) for that the maior was a merchant of wonderous ad-uentures into manie and sundrie countries. By rea-son whereof, the king had yearelie of him notable summes of monie for, his customes, beside other plea-sures that he had shewed vnto the king before times. ¶ This yeare the Scots began to stir, against whom the king sent the duke of Glocester & manie others, which returned againe without any notable battell.]

Imbassadors south of Scotland.

In this verie season James the third of that name king of Scots sent into England a solemne ambas-sage for to haue the ladie Cicilie, king Edwards se-cond daughter, to be married to his eldest sonne James, prince of Scotland, duke of Rothsaie, and earle of Caricke. King Edward and his councell, perceiuing that this affinitie should be both honou-rable and profitable to the realme, did not onelie grant to his desire; but also before hand disbursed cer-teine summes of monie, to the onelie intent that the marriage hereafter should neither be hindered nor broken. With this condition, that if the said mariage by anie accidentall meane should in time to come take none effect; or that king Edward would notifie to the king of Scots, or his councell, that his plea-sure was determined to haue the said marriage dis-solued: then the prouost and merchants of the towne of Edenburgh, (should be bound for) repaiment of the said summes againe. All which things were with great deliberation concluded, passed, and sealed, in hope of continuall peace and indissoluble amitie.

But king James was knowne to be a man so wedded to his owne opinion, that he could not aduise them that would speake contrarie to his fansie: by meanes whereof, he was altogither led by the coun-sell and aduise of men of base linage, whome for their flatterie he had promoted vnto great dignities and honourable offices. By which persons diuerse of the nobilitie of his realme were greatlie misused and put to trouble, both with imprisonment, exactions, & death; insomuch that some of them went into volun-tarie exile. Amongst whome Alexander duke of Al-banie, brother to king James, being exiled into France, & passing through England, taried with K. Edward : and vpon occasion moued him to make warre against his brother, the said king James, for that he forgetting his oth, promise, and affinitie con-cluded with king Edward, caused his subiects to make roads and forraies into the English borders,

spoiling, burning, and killing king Edwards liege people.

King Edward, not a little displeased with this vn-princelie doing, prouoked and set on also by the duke of Albanie, determined to inuade Scotland with an armie, as well to reuenge his owne iniuries recei-ued at the hands of king James, as to helpe to re-store the duke of Albanie vnto his countrie and pos-sessions againe. Hereupon all the Winter season he mustered his men, prepared his ordinance, rigged his ships, and left nothing vnprouided for such a iour-nie: so that in the beginning of the yeare, all things apperteining to the warre, and necessarie for his voi-age, were in a readinesse. To be the chéefteine of his hoast, and lieutenant generall, Richard duke of Glo-cester was appointed by his brother king Edward, and with him were adioined as associats, Henrie the fourth earle of Northumberland, Thomas lord Stanleie lord steward of the kings house, the lord Louell, the lord Greiestocke, and diuerse other no-ble men and woorthie knights.

Preparation for warre a-gainst Scot-land.

1482 Anno Reg.22. An armie sent into Scot-land.

These valiant captens came to Alnewike in Nor-thumberland, about the beginning of Julie, where they first incamped themselues, & marshalled their hoast. The fore-ward was led by the earle of Nor-thumberland, vnder whose standard were the lord Scroope of Bolton, sir John Middleton, sir John Dichfield, and diuerse other knights, esquiers,& soul-diers, to the number of sir thousand and seauen hun-dred. In the midle-ward was the duke of Glocester, and with him the duke of Albanie, the lord Louell, the lord Greiestocke, sir Edward Wodwille, and o-ther, to the number of fiue thousand & eight hundred men. The lord Neuill was appointed to follow, ac-companied with thrée thousand. The lord Stanleie led the wing on the right hand of the dukes battell with foure thousand men of Lancashire & Cheshire. The lord Fitz Hugh, sir William a Parre, sir James Harrington, with the number of two thou-sand souldiers, guided the left wing. And beside all these, there were one thousand appointed to giue their attendance on the ordinance.

Abr. Fl. ex I.S. pag.749. Creplegate builded.

¶ In this yeare Edmund Shaw goldsmith and ma-ior of London newlie builded Creplegate from the foundation, which gate in old time had bene a prison, whereunto such citizens and other as were arrested for debt (or like trespasses) were committed, as they be now to the counters, as maie appeare by a writ of king Edward the second, in these words: *Rex vic London salutem. Ex graui querela capti & detenti in prisona nostra de Creplegate, pro x. li. quas coram Radulpho Sandwi-co,tunc custode ciuitatis nostræ London, & I. de Blackewell custode recognit. debitorum,&c.* King Edward held his Christmas at Eltham, and kept his estate all the whole feast in his great chamber; and the quéene in hir chamber, where were dailie more than two thou-sand persons. The same yeare on Candlemas day, he with his quéene went on procession from saint Ste-phans chappell into Westminster hall, accompanied with the earle of Angus, the lord Greie, & sir James Liddall, ambassadors from Scotland. And at his pro-céeding out of his chamber he made sir John Wod-vnder-treasuror of England, & sir William Cates-bie one of the iustices of the demonplées, knights.]

Records.

But to returne to the kings affaires concerning Scotland. The roiall armie aforesaid, not intending to lose time, came soddenlie by the water side to the towne of Berwike, and there (that with force, and that with feare of so great an armie)tooke and ente-red the towne: but the earle of Bothwell, being cap-teine of the castell, would in no wise deliuer it; where-fore the capteins, vpon good and deliberate aduise, planted a strong siege round about it. When this siege was laid, the two dukes and all the other soul-diers

Anno reg.23. 1483

Berwike woone by the Englishmen.

interleaved and annotated with thick marginalia his copy of the 1622 edition of Ralph Brooke's *Catalogue and Succession of the Kings . . . of this Realme.* Frequently the annotations consist of emendations from a more recent work, Francis Sandford's *A Genealogical History of the Kings of England* (1677), as well as older historians like Speed and Stow. On William I the reader writes, "In his 7th year he forced Malcolm K[ing] of Scotland to be his Homager, in his 13 he constrained ye princes of Wales to do him fealty: Sandford, p. 2 to p. 18." The reader has even added a set of pedigrees of kings and nobles on the interleaves, annals of various reigns mentioned in the Brooke text, and marginal details about various persons mentioned, like "He built a church for Fryers at his manor of Langley where the soul of Pieres de Gaveston should be prayed for." Throughout, the annotator used his or her notes to add details that are not contained in the book itself. A cross in the printed text signals a marginal note about Edward II's gaolers, "who stifled him in his bed with heavy bolsters & after through a pipe thrust a red hot iron into his fundament that no marks of violence might be seen." A Brooke reference to Eleanor Cobham inspires the reader to write of the duchess of Gloucester that "She had unlawfull Familiarity with him before marriage"; a note on the brief reign of Edward V refers its author, and subsequent readers of the volume, to a seal printed in John Speed's *Historie of Great Britain*.[27]

An even more compelling example of the tendency of readers not simply to absorb their texts but to emend and interpret them by addition or correction has recently been provided by John Morrill, who has illuminated the mentality of the puritan iconoclast William Dowsing through a reconstruction of his library, which included an extensive section of historical titles – Plutarch, Livy, Josephus, Bacon's *Henry VII*, Hayward's *Edward VI* and Foxe's *Acts and Monuments* among them – and an examination of his copious annotations. Dowsing had a compulsion to gloss various of his books thickly with references to John Foxe, of whose *Acts and Monuments* he appears to have

---

[27] Folger MS G.b. 15, especially pp. 25, 95 and interleaved fos. 73, 75v, 89, 109. Readers frequently acquired similar sorts of books, in sheets, and then bound them together. See, e.g. Folger MS 170–496.39, a collection of printed octavos, mainly about Bohemia, with extensive notes in closely-written Latin. On the spine are, in a seventeenth-century hand, titles such as "Varii tractatus de rebus Bohemicis; *Icones regum Galliae*; La chronique des favoris." The works include *Aeneae Silvii Senensis de Bohemorum origine ac gestis historia* (Cologne, 1523); Aubertus Miraeus or Le Mire, *De rebus bohemicis liber singularis* (Leiden, 1621); Aubertus Miraeus or Le Mire, *De bello bohemico Ferdinandi II, Caesaris . . . commentarius* (Cologne, 1622). Bound in between these last two items are sixteen blank leaves, the first ten of which are full of very closely written Latin extracts headed "Ex chronicis Borekij"; then two more works by Le Mire (Miraeus). Several works on French history are bound at the back, such as an anonymous *Epitome chronicorum regum Galliae à Pharamondo ad Carolum eius hominis nonum* (Paris, 1566) complete with woodcuts of French kings; and finally, the very cheaply printed *La chronique des favoris* (actually by F. Fancan, though no author or printer appears on the title page).

owned three editions.[28] Nor was Dowsing unique. William Whiteway of Dorchester took copious notes on Herodotus, Livy, and Procopius. He owned copies of Josephus, Froissart, Buchanan's *History of Scotland*, Speed's *History of Great Britain*, Bacon's *Henry VII*, Camden's *Britannia*, and both Stow's and Holinshed's *Chronicles*. Moreover, he is known to have read Guicciardini's *History of Italy*, various modern histories of Spain, the Netherlands, Venice, and France. The French Huguenot Théodore Agrippa d'Aubigné's *Histoire universelle* (on the wars of religion from 1560 to 1598) was of such interest that Whiteway translated it into English, while collecting materials for his own projected history of the reigns of Kings James and Charles.[29] Another early Stuart reader of books on history and policy digested his reading into a colorful illuminated vellum roll giving a kind of flow chart of historical examples, perhaps for posting on a wall, on the tactics to be followed by a ruler in governing subjects and utilizing the resources of his kingdom.[30]

Scraps of paper with notes interleaved between books, or tucked into boxes of family accounts, are also common, and can range widely in subject, as the reader drew disparate sources together, often for the solution of a practical problem concerning estates, pedigrees, or local political matters.[31] Joseph Bufton, a Coggeshall, Essex weaver, took notes on historical and biographical works, together with his notes of funeral sermons, in ephemeral books ranging from his *British Merlin* and Goldsmith's *Almanack* to a copy of *The Compleat Tradesman*.[32] Any student of Tudor and Stuart antiquarianism will be familiar with the vast collections of transcripts from central and local documents that can be found not only in the archives of published

---

[28] John Morrill, "William Dowsing, the Bureaucratic Puritan," in *Public Duty and Private Conscience in Seventeenth-Century England*, ed. J. Morrill, P. Slack and D. Woolf (Oxford, 1993), pp. 173–203, especially pp. 180, 182.

[29] For the reading of Whiteway and his Dorchester fellow-townsman, Denis Bond (both of whom kept personal "chronologies" and made inventories of their libraries), see David Underdown, *Fire from Heaven* (New Haven, 1992), pp. 55–56.

[30] Anon., "The mappe, or survey of a kingdome," Folger MS L.b. 625. This is subdivided in Ramist form to give various options, with examples, as under the category of whom a prince should use as soldiers, one option being "Use in warre the gentlemen only, disarminge the common people, as Lewys the eleaventh did in Fraunce" and the alternative being to "Arme the common people forbiddinge by lawes the gentlemen to handle armes, as the popular commonwealths." Another copy of this roll, on sixteen pages, appears to be that described in Hist. MSS Comm., *Second Report*, II, 85.

[31] E.g. Devon RO, 189M add3/F5/6, a collection of small slips of notes, made in the seventeenth century in Latin, on Roman history, especially the Caesars; Cheshire RO, D4434/1, a late seventeenth-century book of transcripts by an anonymous antiquary from books including Camden's *Remains*, various works on legal cases and on Cheshire history, a passage from John Evelyn's *Silva* and an account of the death and burial of Charles II.

[32] Essex RO, D/DBm/Z9, papers of Joseph Bufton, notes on funeral sermons 1663–77 and remarks on an abridgment of *The History of Mr. Baxter's Life and Times*, the latter contained in a copy of N. H., *The Compleat Tradesman: or, the exact daily companion* (1684), inscribed "Joseph Bufton his booke 1685."

historians like Foxe and Stow, but also in the state papers of officers of the realm, and scattered about the kingdom in family muniments, where they offered a support for land claims or genealogical pretensions.[33] Readers were also – to the horror of modern librarians and bibliophiles – much less squeamish about cutting up their books in order to rearrange them for readier access in appropriate commonplace books and collections. In an age before photocopying and with only rudimentary indexing, this was less sin than necessity, though it is still surprising how often costly books, such as Camden's *Britannia*, were put to the knife. An anonymous mid-seventeenth century collector cut out the section on Devon in the 1610 English edition of *Britannia*; John Warburton, a Cheshire antiquary who lived nearly a century later, included in his collections on Cheshire antiquities and churches pages and illustrations from the very expensive 1695 English edition and revision of *Britannia*, as well as such equally formidable books as Dugdale's *Monasticon*, Fuller's *Worthies*, Drayton's *Poly-Olbion*, and the more popular digest chorography, also entitled *Britannia*, by Richard Blome.[34]

Diaries and journals are also useful, in a different way, because of what they reveal about a writer's reading habits, his or her reactions to particular works and, by the placing of remarks, the early modern thought processes that lead the pen sideways from one subject to the next. Richard Stonley, a teller in the Receipt of Exchequer during the reign of Elizabeth, lived in St. Botolph's parish, London, but also owned land in Essex. He kept a diary that survives for three short periods in the 1580s and 1590s, and which gives some indication as to his reading habits, for instance "This day after morning prayer I kept home at my books with thanks to God at nyght." Although Stonley, in contrast to some later diarists, is unhelpful as to specific titles read, biblical stories featured prominently. A rhymed extract from the biblical "history" of Judith and Holofernes heads his daily entries at one point, and figures from ancient history with biblical associations, such as Artaxerxes (Esther's Ahasuerus), also intrude.[35]

John Locke's various journals and notebooks, written nearly 100 years later, are more informative, containing a miscellany of information on weather, medical matters, and personal affairs, complete with detailed extracts from his reading: here a lengthy extract from Rushworth's *Historical Collections* on the Second Bishops' War; there some remarks on particular

[33] E.g., an eighty-page volume containing a transcript of the Domesday Book, on Cheshire, from the tally-office at Westminster, done at the request of the Arderne family of Cheshire in the later seventeenth century: Cheshire RO, DAR/I/46 (Arderne papers); Twysden's notebook on Tudor history (1620–30) in Folger G.b. 7 R (historical collections *ca.* 1620–30).

[34] Devon RO, 903Z/Z23, pp. 199–208; Cheshire RO, D4489 (Warburton collections).

[35] Folger MS V.a. 459, 60, 61, diary of Richard Stonley for 1581–82, 1593–94 and 1597–98: entry for 3 October 1582, diary vol. I (V.a. 459), fo. 79r; cf. entries at fo. 95v (20 Dec. 1582); MS 60, fo. 9v (17 June 1593), and elsewhere. The purchase of particular books such as Hooker's *Laws* is occasionally mentioned but no histories are listed.

historians. These comments are sometimes ordered in ways that seem peculiar to modern eyes. A disquisition on the subject of Greenland, for instance, is interrupted by the digression (apparently excited by the association of Greenland and Lapland with surviving paganism), that "Herodotus [is] the first credible historian we have of the heathens" and praise of "Thucydides that excellent ancient historian," before the Greenland material continues. Elsewhere Locke copies, for reasons unclear from the context, a passage from Burnet's *Reflections on Mr. Varillas' History* that praises the impartiality of Camden's *Annales*.[36] A large notebook that Locke began to compile in 1667 contains the names of several historians on one side and extracts in Latin and English from various critics and commentators on them, intended as a quick guide to the best writers on particular historical subjects. Commynes is "All good but espetially ye life of Lewis the eleventh"; Hegesippus is "a grave church writer of prime antiquity"; and one may find in Guicciardini "the interest of all ye states and princes of Europe."[37]

The many slots into which historical facts and trivia could be plugged, and the contrasting landscapes of different readers' mental villages, with history variously neighbored by philosophy, religion, law, fiction, and humor can be found represented in other cases less famous than Locke's. Changing tastes within the same collection can be found by comparing the reading of Sir Richard Berkeley of Stoke Gifford and Rendcombe (*ca.* 1531–1604), a prominent Gloucestershire politician and soldier, with the collections of his grandson, Richard Berkeley, Esq., who shared his grandfather's protestant piety and classical training, but had also acquired an interest in more modern periods of history, represented in printed leaves taken from Commynes' *Memoires* in French, and Berkeley's translation, as a present for his own son, John (a soldier killed in the Thirty Years' War) of the *Commentaires* of Blaise de Monluc.[38]

---

[36] Bodl. MS Locke f. 7, pp. 97–8, 101; all of this, including the Greenland material, is part of a set of notes on his reading of vol. I of Moses Pitt's *The English Atlas* (2 vols., Oxford, 1680–82); cf. Bodl. MS Locke f. 8, p. 26.

[37] Bodl. MS Locke f. 14, e.g., pp. 6, 17. For another example see Houghton Lib. MS Eng. 1091, fos. 1–29, a duodecimo notebook "On the earl of Straffords tryal and death." This begins with an ode to "Great Strafford" by "Sir John Denham" (perhaps actually by Sidney Godolphin); it is partly a series of historical notes on books like Rushworth's *Historical Collections* and partly a set of ruminations and meditations on Strafford's fate.

[38] Sears McGee, "Sir Richard Berkeley: Jester, Philosopher and Politician in Elizabethan Gloucestershire," unpublished essay, in which are discussed the Berkeley papers in the Gloucestershire Record Office, FmS/C 3/5 (Commynes); FmS/C 3/3 (Monluc). I am indebted to Sears McGee for providing me with a copy of his paper, to Mrs. Margaret Richards for furnishing me with a handlist of the archive, and to His Grace the Duke of Beaufort for permission to cite from the latter. The opinions expressed regarding the differing interests of the two Richard Berkeleys are my own and I thank Professor McGee for confirming them, though this picture may have to be revised when he concludes his study of the Berkeleys' commonplace books.

Commonplace books are an especially rich source for the history of reading. That of Thomas Pennington, written over a period between 1665 and the beginning of the eighteenth century (and added to by at least one other contributor) contains, sprinkled about with miscellaneous information such as directions for casting and hanging church bells, nuggets of historical information like "Potatoes were first brought to Europe by Sr. Francis Drake in his return from his expedition to the Spanish West Indies in 1586"; a slightly later hand adds "King Bladud was the discoverer of the Bath springs," giving as the source a book called the "Young Lady's Geography."[39] John Jackson devoted a commonplace book from 1663 to 1694 to his reading in "severall histories both divine and hystorical." This contained extracts from specific works like Ralegh's *History of the World*, and topically arranged notes on various historical questions such as "when England was first devided into parishes?" An anonymous commonplace book compiled during the 1670s is full of topics such as "chancellors of England," "the names of the five members that were questioned by K. Charles," "the names of 11 members that the army charged anno 1647."[40] The collections of William Jackson, the Yarmouth customs-master, are part chronicle, with lists of the town's bailiffs from the early fifteenth to the late seventeenth century, with notes on its coats of arms, and part miscellaneous notes derived from books like James Howell's *Londinopolis*, which had itself been largely an adaptation of Stow's *Survey of London*. Jackson included similar information on Norwich officers, remarks on medieval kings, records of local and national events, and notes on seventeenth-century worthies, including the entire text of the earl of Essex's scaffold speech in 1601. Virtually the whole volume derived from Howell, Peter Heylyn's *Cosmography*, Thomas Fuller's *Church-history*, and Gabriel Richardson's 1627 work *Of the state of Europe*, which Jackson called a "Hystory of Europe."[41] All of these books were by his time several decades old: for the casual reader, even more than the learned antiquary, long-since published digests and epitomes often had a much longer "shelf-life" than they do today.

An early commonplace book of William Whiston, the Augustan divine and chronologer, is similarly full of references to historical works arranged under titles like "death," "conversion," "churches," and "proverbs [&] wise sayings"; here, the author most often cited is Stow, whose *Annales* had last been reprinted in 1631.[42] As a chronologer himself, Whiston was naturally con-

---

[39] Folger MS V.a. 423, fos. 24r–45r, especially fos. 29r, 45r.

[40] CUL MS Gg.2.25, fos. 14r–40v (extracts from Ralegh), 41r; CUL MS Dd.2.62, fos. 97r and 213, for a story from Fynes Moryson about the countess of Holland and her 365 children born under a curse.

[41] CUL MS Oo. VI.115, Jackson collections, fos. 14r, 44, 48, 49–53, 56, 67–70, 119–124v, 131–135v, 148, 151.

[42] Bodl. MS Eng. misc. d.297, Whiston commonplace book, *passim*. Though undated, the work contains references (pp. 414–15) to books left to Whiston by his father, placing it relatively

cerned with such things, but it is important to note the degree to which ordinary readers, who might themselves have only a passing interest in a subject, would make similar notes. Historical collections initiated as students could be continued into middle age by the nation's future clerics and statesmen. Sir John Lowther (1655–1700), the future Viscount Lonsdale, began to keep such a book in 1686, at the age of thirty-one. This includes notes on a 1654 edition of Madeleine de Scudéry's popular historical romance, *Artamenes* (often known as *Le Grand Cyrus*), on Sir Edwin Sandys' so-called "History of the Western Churches" (*A relation of the state of religion*, first published in 1605, when it was publicly burned, but reprinted several times since); Peter Heylyn's *Cosmography*; Cornelius Nepos' *Miltiades* (one of that author's lives of illustrious men); and miscellaneous remarks and collections about the kings of England from William I to Charles II.[43] Richard Coffin, an enthusiastic Devon squire whose collecting activities will be examined in more detail in chapter 3 below, processed some of his voracious reading into a "messelany" of historical notes on such matters as the names of the Anglo-Saxon kings (drawing here principally from Camden's *Remains*), and the names of local families, for which he was also dependent on local informants.[44]

Further examples are easy to find, such as an anonymous English commonplace book of the late seventeenth and early eighteenth century, probably kept by a clergyman. On a topic like "bishops" this author writes, from "Comber p. 184" (perhaps Thomas Comber's *An Historical Vindication of the Divine Right of tithes*, 1682) the following: "At first the sole charge of every citty & the adjacent parts lay upon the bishop till by the increase of the faithfull it became necessary for him to take unto himself certain . . . deputies, to whom he committed the office of instructing, reserving to himself the rights of government and superiority (as is excellently proved by some of our own authours)." Other snippets from historical and antiquarian reading are decidedly unhistorical: "Mr. Carew in his survey of Cornwall assures us upon his own knowledg that to live till 90 years of age is ordinary in every place and in most persons accompanyed with an able use of the body and their senses." Amid several jokes and epigrams, an extract from Guicciardini on Cesare Borgia leads the author to reflect not on the military career of the latter but on the salacious life of his father. "He was base sonne

---

early in his long career. A comparable manuscript, Bodl. MS Carte 20, especially fos. 33, 41v, 82v, 124v–125v, jointly compiled by John and Thomas Carte, over the first twenty years of the eighteenth century, is written in Greek, Latin, and English and ranges from theology and classical literature to history, considering subjects like Irish bards, Phoenicians, and the role of the oak tree in pagan religions; it also includes notes on specific books such as White Kennett's *Parochial Antiquities* and a kind of working chronological list of extant English historians.   [43] Cumbria RO, D/Lons/W.1/32.

[44] Devon RO, Z19/31/2, "A Messelany of hystoricall ffragments." This is a 260-page compilation principally devoted to tracing certain family names back beyond the Conquest.

to Rhoderick Borgia otherwise called Pope Alexander the sixth. This Alexander was the first of the popes that openly owned his bastards."[45] The miscellany compiled by John Collet (b. 1633) is a similarly mixed bag of remarks on kings and popes, biblical history, jokes, and witticisms by or about ancient and medieval figures, and short disquisitions on matters as diverse as the history of St. Paul's Cathedral, the popular canonization of Henry VI, the tale of Jack of Newbury and his 100 looms, and various examples of extremely aged men like Old Parr, dwarfs, and human "giants" such as William Evans, the porter to Charles I.[46] An anonymous commonplace book of the early seventeenth century, now at the Newberry Library, shows an interest not simply in history but in historiography: it includes a heading for "historica" and a list of "Romayne writers of other [i.e. other nations'] historyes," along with considerations of genre and method influenced by recent continental *artes historicae* such as Reinerus Reineccius' brief *Oratio de historia* (Frankfurt, 1580) and Marc Antoine Muret's commentaries on Tacitus.[47]

The commonplace book of Henry Oxenden, alphabetically indexed by its author, is especially useful in relating his reading to his life and his world view. Inscribed on its inside cover is his judgment that among histories "The Bible is more antient then any authentique stories of the heathen by 3000 yeares," followed by his own version of the rise and fall of the four world monarchies, Assyrian, Persian, Greek, and Roman. Interspersed with the reading are notes of the births of his various ancestors, his children and himself. "I Henrie Oxinden eldest sonne of the said Richard was borne at Canterburie. Jan 18 1608./Tho. Oxinden borne at Barham Feb. 11 1633." Most interesting are his various extracts from assorted books, including a lengthy one from Sir Anthony Weldon's notorious libel of James I and his times, *The Court and Character of King James*, against which Oxenden has added the epigram *qui nescit dissimulare nescit regnare*, implicitly accepting Weldon's portrait of James as a corrupt modern Tiberius. But many of the facts are more miscellaneous, the sort of "trivia" or remarkable events and even jokes involving the famous, useful for the gentleman to be able to recall in conversation, and some of a sexual and romantic tone: "Cardan was 40 yeares old when hee began to studie"; "Philip King of Macedon was a cuckold, & his wife thrust him out of doores; yet hee made a jest of it sayth Nevesanus"; and "The world never produced two such men as the 2 Scalagers [*sic*]: they were of the ancientest knowne familie in Xtendome." Else-

---

[45] Houghton Lib. MS Eng. 586, pp. 22, 343. A prayer on p. 290 is dated 29 June 1714, but much of the volume seems earlier.

[46] Bodl. MS Sloane 3890, fos. 26r, 39v, 51r, 57v, 58r–v, 64r–68v; some of these are extracted in *Anecdotes and Traditions illustrative of early English history*, ed. W. J. Thoms, Camden Society, o.s. 5 (1839).   [47] Newberry Library Case MS A15.179, fo. 5r.

where, the entries become more narrow, turning decidedly historical. Here is an extract from "Josephus his account of Jesus Christ," the title given in red in the margin, followed by an extract in English. There, we find remarks that were probably culled from an *ars historica* as much as from direct reading on particular historians' qualities: "Dionysius Halicarnassus is the truest historie that wee have of the Greekes; hee had libertie to go the records of the Romans & wrot nothing but what he found there"; or "The records of the Persians are extant, those of the Egiptians & Caldeans are lost"; or "Tacitus was an excellent politician"; and "Joseph Scaligers book De Emendatione temporum is excellent." But even these are interspersed with twenty or so one-line remarks on everything from the falsity of the Hermetic texts to the properties of opium. A whole page is devoted to a few short lines extracted from Bacon. These are headed "The History & Reign of Hen. 7th written by Francis Lord Verulam Viscount St. Alban 1622," whereafter Oxenden's reading of that book follows:

Although Richard the third were a Prince in militar vertue approved, jealous of the honour of the English nation, & likewise a good Law maker, for the ease & solace of the common people: yet his cruelties, & parricides in the opinion of all men weighed down his vertues & merits; & in the opinion of wise men, even those vertues themselves were conceived to be rather fained, than true Qualities ingenerate in his judgement or nature. p. 2.[48]

Oxenden's notes have a counterpart in the summaries of various printed English histories that Abraham Wright (father of James, the future antiquary) wrote out for himself while a student, probably from books that he did not own. Some even appear to be notes taken with a view to annotating a copy of the book at some future time. The books digested include William Martyn's *History of the Lives of the Kings of England*, Speed's *History of Great Britain*, Francis Godwin's *Annals* of the early Tudors and Camden's *Annales* (in the 1630 Robert Norton translation), and the notes on each book are subdivided under headings like "Out of K. Rich: ye first." The order of extracts suggests that Wright was reading chronologically both within each book and through all the books, proceeding year by year so as to construct his personal history of the realm from four different authors. He included precise page references, and unlike some of our other examples, the pattern of references indicates a slow and deliberate, page-by-page reading and

[48] Folger MS V.b. 110, commonplace book of Henry Oxenden *ca.* 1642–1700. The MS includes a longer extract (p. 177) from Edward Stillingfleet's *Origines sacrae* (1662), and some remarks on the uncertainty of ancient histories, especially because of calendar variations. At p. 278 is a brief extract attacking Marchamont Nedham, "vid. a brief chronicle of the intestine war in the 3 kingdoms. By Hol. p. 278" actually a work by James Heath. Oxenden kept other books with such materials, as is evident in his own cross-reference of a full page of extracts from Job chs. 21 and 24 (on the subject of atheism) to writings elsewhere: "see concerning this in my large paper booke, & my little booke."

rereading of each text, on the model recently proposed by Professors Grafton and Jardine, rather than indiscriminate consultation or perusal.[49]

Some readers even went so far as to digest their reading for the benefit of children or kin into unpublished histories. Sarah Cowper, mother of the Augustan earl and judge, William, Earl Cowper, kept both a diary and an extensive series of commonplace books, filled with historical and exemplary anecdotes from her reading and conversation, and at one point went to the trouble of digesting William Howell's *An Institution of General History* as a means to make peace with her daughter-in-law, Judith, whom she disliked.[50] An anonymous Restoration father penned a "Cinnus historicus" for his son, a 440-page octavo manuscript that begins with a brief summary of world history from Roman times and continues with a summary of European and English history, throughout which he constantly digresses to make comparisons between an historical episode and more recent events or persons, a good example of the enduring perception of the past as principally a font of analogies with the present.[51] At about 1669, another nameless reader of works on ancient Britain, who was well-versed in ecclesiastical history and had some knowledge of Old English, penned his own incomplete history of Britain, apparently inspired by a desire to repudiate the criticism in Selden and other antiquaries of the Galfridian legends, and to establish to his own satisfaction that popular assemblies had met since pre-Roman times, and that the Commons had been part of parliament since at least the ninth century.[52] The author of a Latin history of Britain, *ca.* 1660, pasted in woodcut likenesses of the kings (many of which did not in the least resemble

---

[49] BL MS Add. 22608, described as "comments on books and plays read by a student at one of the universities" and entitled (page v) "Excerpta quaedam par AW adolescentem": microfilm copy in Folger Film Acc.356.2. Wright's reading included printed copies of plays by Shakespeare and Jonson in addition to the historical titles. Extracts from "ffrancis B. of Hereford," i.e. Bishop Francis Godwin's *Annals* of the early Tudor monarchs (42r), then at fo. 43 "Out of ye History of Queene Elizabeth written by Mr. Camden (translated by R. N.: edit. 1630)." Regnal years are given in the left margin and Wright noted details to be added into books at a later time, e.g. p. 65, "Things to bee inserted in ye raigne of Henry ye 7th." Not every such compendium was arranged annalistically, since some readers preferred to write continuous prose: for an example of a nonannalistic compendium see the Latin epitome of Roman and European history, written *ca.* 1700, in Newberry Library, Case MS 6A.66, fos. 1–50v.

[50] William Howell, *An Institution of General History* (1661 and several subsequent editions); Hertfordshire RO, Panshanger MSS, D/EP F.41 (Sarah Cowper MSS). This MS consists of 755 closely written quarto pages, beginning with the Flood and ending, somewhat more summarily, with the previous two centuries. According to an autograph inscription at the front of the MS, it was abstracted from Howell's *Institution* (which is not mentioned) by Sarah Cowper in 1686 (the year in which the account concludes), when she was forty-three. I owe the identification of its source as Howell to Dr. Anne Kugler, who is completing a study of Dame Sarah's life and writings.

[51] Anon., "Cinnus Historicus," CUL MS Add. 3454, fos. 1–27 *et passim*.

[52] Anon., "De Synedriis Britanicis" (written *ca.* 1669), Northumberland RO, ZAN M13.D8, pp. 1–141, especially at pp. 2, 68, 140–41; property of the Society of Antiquaries of Newcastle-upon-Tyne and cited with their kind permission.

known images) he had snipped from various historical books, adding his own clumsy ink drawings of coins from certain reigns, as if imitating the layout of Speed's *History of Great Britain*. Unlike most of these do-it-yourself historians, he included references to his reading in Polydore Vergil and William of Malmesbury, and recent works like the earl of Monmouth's translation of Biondi's *An History of the Civill Warres of England* (1645).[53] Foreign works were also boiled down, as in a 76-page "abstract of Mazery" (François de Mézeray) from Pharamond to the assassination of Henri IV.[54]

The contexts of history reading are nearly as variable as the number of readers. Further down the social ladder, the Lancaster Quaker William Stout, who was born in the year of the Great Plague, tells us that while a new journeyman in the ironmongering trade he passed his evenings and other times "out of busnes" reading not only religious books but "history, geography, surveying or other mathematical sciences." This was apparently a lifelong habit, since in the 1740s, when he was in his late seventies – semiretired and reliant on spectacles – he passed his days reading the Bible together with Echard's *History of England*, and Foxe's *Acts and Monuments*.[55] Where the Elizabethan gentleman John Newdigate read Foxe to find examples of the evils of drunkenness, half a century later the Lancashire apprentice and nonconformist Roger Lowe spent a morning reading the Book of Martyrs as a palliative to tippling, in the home of James Woods, a nonconformist preacher from whom he regularly borrowed books. Both men were nursing a hangover from having been "a litle mery the other day."[56] Reading and drinking or eating are in fact two activities that went together more frequently than the sober and serious studies of early modern scholars would have us believe, in contrast to the fierce strictures against taking one's sandwiches into the Bodleian or Library of Congress to which modern scholars are used. Henry Prescott, the Anglican deputy registrar of the diocese of Chester, almost invariably combined the library and the libation, as we shall see in greater detail further on. Samuel Pepys read *Fuller's Church History* and *Worthies* after going to Michell's pub to drink; he had his own

[53] Houghton Lib. MS Eng. 1709, "Anglicanae Historiae Spicilegia Aliquot," (written *ca.* 1660), especially p. 106. The work is far from complete; frequently there are pages designated for certain kings and sometimes with pictures, but no text, as if the author divided the book first into kings and then started writing reign-by-reign as fancy took him, ending with a paean to the "martyr" Charles I. Biondi's history concerns the fifteenth-century civil wars.

[54] Herts. RO, VIII. B.55. This has been misdated to *ca.* 1600, far too early given that it derives from a mid-seventeenth-century French author.

[55] *The Autobiography of William Stout of Lancaster 1665–1752*, ed. J. D. Marshall (Manchester and New York, 1967), pp. 96, 232–33.

[56] Vivienne Larminie, *Wealth, Kinship and Culture: The Seventeenth-Century Newdigates of Arbury and their World* (1995), p. 149; *The Diary of Roger Lowe of Ashton-in-Makerfield, Lancashire, 1663–74*, ed. W. L. Sachse (New Haven, 1938), pp. 15, 98, 114 (1 March 1663, 8 March 1666, 17 May 1667). Lowe's literacy had made him a kind of unofficial notary in his community.

collections on the history of the Navy read aloud to him at supper.[57] The connection between harder narcotics and historical imagination that Bonnie G. Smith has recently noted of Germaine de Staël in the early nineteenth century is anticipated by a century in the Jacobite John Byrum's fatal treatment of his sister Ellen with laudanum after her reading of Clarendon "disturbed" her.[58]

Diaries such as Pepys' or Lowe's have one advantage over commonplace books in that they sometimes illustrate the physical contexts of reading: not just what was read, but how often, when, where, and under what circumstances. Unlike Lowe, casually tripping over the pages of Foxe's entertaining stories while his head throbbed, fourteen-year-old Thomas Isham (whose overbearing father obliged him to keep a Latin diary) was obliged to pass one wintry day, a heavy snow falling outside, in a tutorial lesson on Caesar's *Commentaries*.[59] Ralph Thoresby took Samuel Clarke's *Historian's Guide* (an almanac of seventeenth-century English historical events) on his antiquarian strolls.[60] Pepys, who was even fonder of books than he was of sex, read at home, at his office, and, like a modern suburban commuter, in various locations in between, taking a "little history of England" with him on the barge to Deptford.[61] Nicholas Blundell of Little Crosby, Lancashire, who was less inclined to either activity, nonetheless records reading the occasional history. Although it was not his major form of leisure, he dipped into the second volume of Jean Crasset's *Histoire de l'église du Japon*. It was not uncommon for him, and other readers, to have more than one book on the go: Blundell writes on 18 and 19 November 1715 of "making an end" of Richard Head's four-volume *English Rogue: A History of the most Eminent Cheats of Both Sexes* (1666–80; complete

---

[57] Pepys, *Diary*, VIII, 94 (3 March 1667); IX, 506 (2 April 1669); *The Diary of Henry Prescott, LL.B., Deputy Registrar of Chester Diocese*, ed. J. M. Addy, 3 vols., Rec. Soc. of Lancs and Ches., 127 (1987–97), I and II *passim*, for which see discussion below in this chapter.

[58] *The Private Journal and Literary Remains of John Byrom*, ed. R. Parkinson (2 vols. in 4), Manchester, 1854–57), I, 46–48, cited by Johns, *Nature of the Book*, p. 383; Bonnie G. Smith, *The Gender of History: Men, Women and Historical Practice* (Cambridge, MA, 1998).

[59] *The Diary of Thomas Isham of Lamport (1658–81) kept by him in Latin from 1671 to 1673 at his Father's command*, trans. Norman Marlow (Farnborough UK: Gregg International, 1971), 61 (9 November 1671). Sir John Perceval, reading Caesar for two hours every afternoon at university, remarked that he was enjoying the experience much more than a year earlier, when he had been obliged to study the same text in school. Hist. MSS Comm., *Egmont*, II, 190, 192 (Perceval to Sir Robert Southwell, 23 November 1699).

[60] *The Diary of Ralph Thoresby*, ed. J. Hunter (2 vols., 1830), I, 446.

[61] Pepys, *Diary*, IV, 175 (5 June 1663). Another context within which Pepys read his histories was as a guide to the same matter done dramatically. Prior to seeing a revival of Heywood's *If you know not me, you know nobody*, a play about Queen Elizabeth's life and troubles (and one he would dislike), he brushed up on his late Tudor history by reading in Speed about the Spanish Armada. *Diary*, VIII, 387 (16 August 1667).

edition 1688), and of another book of what we would now consider light reading.[62]

Diurnal reading information from the likes of Blundell and Pepys is not uncommon; that from the Roger Lowes and William Stouts of the world is harder to find. A good instance of a history reader from the middling strata of society who kept a reasonably detailed record both of his book-buying activities and of his reactions to what he read is Edmund Harrold, a Manchester wig-maker during the reign of Queen Anne.[63] From his manuscript diary we learn, for instance, that on 1 August 1712 Harrold (a kind and sensitive man judging by the diary's familial entries) read "ye History of ye principality of Orange and how it has been harrased by Lewis 14 and how he's persecuted of protestants," and, more interestingly, that "it just made my heart ake to hear of his Actions to them."[64] The diary is especially useful in conveying the manner in which a perpetually impecunious tradesman kept up his interests and reconciled them with work. On 15 August 1712, he finished a wig, and then "went to Hardick [Ardwick], cut off 2 heads hair for Mr. Jo: Dickenson a wig; then we swapt for 28 books, and I'm to give him 2s to boot and Spark's *Feasts and Fasts* for ym. Then I smoked a pipe and drank I bottle of drink; then I bought of Mrs. Brown 6 books for 3s. bound; I'm to pay both at Michaelmas next without fail." A few days later he was in Ardwick again and bought four more books for 3s 10d from Dickenson, who was "steward" to Mrs. Brown, a local book-dealer. On 27 November Harrold swapped his copy of Dean Comber's *On Church Liturgies* with Dickenson for "Roberts on bible in folio 12d to boot."[65] On 1 December he made a further trade, this time exchanging Spark's *Feasts and Fasts* for "19 pamphletts & bks." In the last few days of the year, after working hard for several days, he rewarded himself by exchanging more books with John Heywood, getting "Knowles History on ye Turk: & went to Jo Hewoods H[o]us[e] with Sam: Oaks & saw his bks."[66] And the year – a bad one, financially and personally (his beloved wife Sarah died on 18 December) – ended with Harrold passing the nights of 27–30 December "auctioning," finding himself "in sobriety & bks, only I'm ill set for money, very dull

---

[62] *The great diurnal of Nicholas Blundell of Little Crosby, Lancashire*, ed. Frank Tyrer, Record Society of Lancashire and Cheshire, vol. 110, 112, 114 (1968–72), I, 181; II, 152. Blundell also made a point of visiting the study of the Bollandists in Antwerp, "where they are writing the Lives of all the canonized saints" (II, 176). Jean Crasset's book was *The History of the Church of Japan*, trans. N. N. (London, 1705–7), first published in French (Paris, 1689).

[63] Chetham's Library, MS A.2.137, diary of Edmund Harrold, wig-maker of Manchester, 1712–16, fos. 92ff.; I have used this in preference to the anonymously edited *Diary of a Manchester Wig Maker*, Chetham Society 68 (1866), pp. 172–208, which is so selectively and inaccurately transcribed as to be virtually worthless; I have, however, provided cross-references to the printed text in certain instances.

[64] Harrold diary, 1 August 1712 (cf. printed edn, p. 181).   [65] Cf. printed edition, p. 183.

[66] Not in printed edition.

business, also much indisposed in body, & sometimes wandring thots comes on me with melancholy a great rent and little trade so that I'm in a great straite what to do."[67] Harrold, who cited the church fathers a good deal, found that by 1714 he was having to sell many of his books by auction; his case provides a powerful reminder that reading invariably took place within a specific set of social and economic circumstances that, for all but the wealthiest collector, often constrained and dictated what was read, for how long, and to what end.

WHY READ HISTORY?

The familiar Ciceronian and Renaissance injunctions to read the past for examples and cautionary tales, repeated by seventeenth-century historiographers like Degory Wheare, are apt to seem a bit cold and impersonal, and there is no doubt that history reading could be approached with a dispassionate interest in the acquisition of such lessons. On the other hand, it could also be an intensely personal experience, as Edmund Harrold's reaction to the trials of the Huguenots suggests. We know from remarks on other recent histories, such as Foxe's *Acts and Monuments* or the various *Lives* of pious individuals that readers, male and female, often had strong reactions to what they read, and that the emotive as much as the intellectual experience became increasingly important to historians over the next two centuries as the history faced strong competition from the romance and eventually the novel, culminating in David Hume's famous statements about the duty of the historian to stir as much as to inform. [68] The reactions of Mary Rich, countess of Warwick, for instance, demonstrate that the unnamed "histories" she read as a duty to her husband in the 1660s had little impact on her. In contrast, when reading Foxe, privately and with others, she "found my heart mightily affected with ye great courage w[hi]ch those blessed martyrs suffer'd."[69] Sarah Savage, early in the eighteenth century, commented with regard to reading history and biography, "What does it avail to hear, & read,

---

[67] This is mistranscribed, p. 202, leaving out, for instance, the crucial words "& bks."

[68] "Of the Study of History," in *The Philosophical Works of David Hume* (4 vols., New York and Edinburgh, 1854), 508–13; Hume to Mure, October 1754, in *The Letters of David Hume*, ed. J. Y. T. Greig (2 vols., Oxford, 1932), I, 210; Hume to William Robertson, April 1759, in *New Letters of David Hume*, ed. R. Klibansky and E. C. Mossner (Oxford, 1954), p. 48; Mark Salber Phillips, "If Mrs. Mure be not Sorry for Poor King Charles': History, the Novel, and the Sentimental Reader," *History Workshop Journal*, 43 (1997), 11–31. A revised version of this essay is incorporated in Professor Phillips' book *Society and Sentiment: Genres of Historical Writing in Britain, 1740–1820* (Princeton, 2000), which appeared as the present work was being copy-edited.

[69] BL MS Add. 27358 (miscellaneous collections from the diary of Mary Rich), fo. 42r (26 May 1670).

& approve the lives of holy men, if I be not in some measure provoked thereby to imitation?"[70]

What one read of the historical past could also be used to give order and meaning to personal autobiography and to put it in a wider context, as illustrated in the memoirs of the puritan divine John Shawe (d. 1672), written for the benefit of his son. Shawe describes the suppression of the Feoffees for impropriations, "whose names and qualitys you may read in Mr. Fuller's 'Church History,' book xi. p. 136." He summarizes the Long Parliament's long history by saying "the history whereof you may read in our chronicles with dry eyes, which others did with wet." After a very quick summary of the highlights of the civil war down to the execution of Charles I, he says, "But these you may read (without danger) in our chronicles, to which I remit you."[71] Further on, Shawe shifts tactic to use history for a different end, a comparison of names. In telling the story of his own conflicts with the baptist, John Canne, Shawe draws an analogy for his son between Canne, who had "troubled both England and Scotland," and a more distant John. "Our chronicles tel of one John, that lived in the reign of King Richd. 2d, anno 1384, who had been lord mayor of London, who was commonly called John Combertowne, because of his fury and sedition he combred every place where he came."[72] Shawe's enemies were able to play this game as well: when appointed a royal chaplain by Charles II at the king's coronation, his royalist foes at Hull appointed a minister in his place who delivered a sermon in which, the sensitive Shawe thought, "it is supposed he doth gird and glance at me covertly, in mentioning Dr. Shawe, in King Richard 3d's time, that countenanced and furthered Richard 3d to get the kingdome." In response, he warned his son against the folly of penalizing those who have the same name as notorious persons mentioned in history.

Dr. Goddard preached at St. Paul's Crosse against k. Edwd. 4th, as well as Dr. Shaw there did for Ricd. 3d. Are Goddards worse? So bishop Stillington much furthered the coronation of Richard 3d; are Stillingtons now the worse? Was Judas the good Apostle that wrote the epistle of Jude, any whit the worse because he was of the same name with Judas the traitor? . . . Is the name of Goodwin worse because of wicked

---

[70] Bodl. MS Eng. misc. e. 331, p. 77 (commonplace book of Sarah Savage), 1 January 1716. For physical reactions to reading, especially among women, see Johns, *Nature of the Book*, pp. 413–14 and, in briefer form, Adrian Johns, "The Physiology of Reading in Restoration England," in Raven, Small, and Tadmor (eds.), *Practice and Representation*, pp. 138–61.

[71] *Memoirs of Master John Shawe, sometime vicar of Rotherham . . . 1663–4*, ed. J. R. Boyle (Hull, 1882), pp. 12, 19, 23. This is an excellent illustration of how the nonclassical history had become a standard piece of intellectual furniture and a discursive reference point by the Restoration, offering to writers and readers a source, external to the self depicted in autobiography, against which facts and perceptions could be measured.

[72] Ibid. pp. 44–45. Shawe's description of himself having preached before Cromwell with the same candor as "old Latimer" (p. 53) would similarly appear to be a clear borrowing from his reading of John Foxe's description of Hugh Latimer's preachings before Henry VIII.

Earl Goodwin in k. Edwd. the Confessor's time, or loyal Barzillai the worse for being of the same name with him mentioned 2 Sam.: 21.8?[73]

Shawe's play with names (and his injunction against overliteral use of such play), as much as his ability to seize upon and dissect an episode from the past – something preachers were trained to do in constructing sermons on Scripture – points to the continuing tendency of many early modern readers to read their histories for the example, the isolated episode, the portable anecdote, rather than end to end for a complete sense of the work. This approach to reading helps to explain the increasing vogue for the tersely quotable Tacitus over the languorous periods of Livy at the end of the sixteenth century. The same habit of thought that arranged knowledge into commonplace books actually approached the reading of the texts from which those commonplaces were drawn with this in mind rather than, to borrow a phrase from Lorna Hutson, "reading for the plot." An especially good example occurs in an anonymous set of notes written in the 1690s on a variety of histories that had been mined by their reader for the memorable and the lurid: "I remember a merry story in Giraldus Cambrensis (Itinerar: L:2: c.13)" the reader notes, "& out of him related by Mr. Camden in his *Britannia* p. 604." These tales, the humor of which has not always traveled well across 300 years, involve a Jew traveling to Shrewsbury with the archdeacon of Malpas (Cheshire), whose name was Peach or Peche, and a dean named Devill. The remarks consist almost entirely of a series of puns on their names.[74] Elsewhere his "notes out of [Richard] Graftons abridgm[en]t" consist entirely of the parentage of Brutus the Trojan and his arrival, fixing it at Year 2855 of the world and 1108 before Christ, along with the story of Brutus' landing at Totnes and the foundation of London as Troy-novant. The "logic" of selection is likely to elude the modern reader, though some anecdotes had clear contemporary resonance. The tale of John of Gaunt not

---

[73] Ibid., pp. 63–65.

[74] Various extracts from Harrington's political treatise, *Oceana*, are followed by the note that

> James Howell tells us touching the earle of Strafford that tho hee were a man full of abillity eloquution and confidence & very well understood ye lawes of England, yet hee had heard there were two things wherein his wisdom was questioned. First that having a charge ready against his cheefest accusers, yet hee suffred them to have ye priority of suite, which if hee had got, hee had thereby made them partyes and so incapable of being produced against him. Secondly that during the time of his tryall hee applied not himselfe with that complyancie to his jury as hee did to his judges, being observed to comply only with the Lords and not with the House of Comons. Folger MS V.b.300, anonymous extracts from English books, c. 1690–96, fo. 32v.

> Although not specified, the Howell book mentioned is certainly the second (1649) instalment of his *Dodona's grove*, an allegory of the history of the 1630s and early 1640s. At fo. 34r are notes on Thomas Smith, ed., *V. Cl. Gulielmi Camdeni, et illustrium virorum ad G. Camdenum epistolae* (1691), the published letters of William Camden, butting up against "Some notes out of Bedes eccles hist. of ye church of England. Hee was an English man & lived about 724. translated by Stapleton: 4[ie quarto]: 1564."

being a real son of Edward III but instead a changeling for a female child resembles the baby-in-the-bedpan story involving the birth of a prince to James II's queen in 1688, only a few years earlier.[75]

This pattern of reading for incident, example, and analogy changed slowly in the course of the later seventeenth and eighteenth centuries as a number of tightly structured narrative political histories appeared, from Clarendon through Goldsmith, Hume, and Gibbon, appealing to the same interest in connected episodes and short-term development that could be found developing, on the fictional side of the personal library, in the Georgian novel. And even Clarendon's famous work may well be an exception that proves the endurance of an older practice, a narrative history that could still be broken down into topics and episodes for easier memorization. Not every reader saw it as an intricate Thucydidean masterpiece of connected historical storytelling. In dedicating a work to William Bateman, the translator and author John Ozell reminded his patron of his father's historical reading activities. "Every body knows, that as Sir James Bateman had a good title to the rich man's distemper, so he had a full share of it; but every body does not know, that in those frequent and painful recesses occasion'd by the gout, he would spend five or six hours together upon some good English historian; which, by diverting his mind, afforded him more relief than was in the power of art to give." But this "five or six hours" need not imply the sort of consecutive page-turning a modern reader might apply to a can't-put-it-down thriller or a popular history. In Bateman's case, his faculties diminishing in old age, it appears to have meant rather persistent rereading of the same episodes so as to commit them to memory.

I learnt this from himself; as likewise, that his memory growing every day less retentive, he was more delighted with memoirs and short minutes, wherein there was an agreeable variety of facts and remarks, than with a long discourse chain'd together according to the rules of history; for this reason, I suppose it was, he had read my Lord Clarendon over ten times; his work being rather memoirs for a history, than a history itself.[76]

---

[75] Fos. 52, 59r. Another anecdote lifted from Grafton (54r) involves a peripheral figure connected with Henry VIII's amicable grant.

[76] François or Francis Misson, *M. Misson's Memoirs and Observations in his Travels over England*, trans. John Ozell (1719), dedication by Ozell, p. iv. Another example of frequent rereading can be found in the catholic writer and former royalist officer William Blundell (1620–98), who was much impressed with the prodigious learning of a young Pole he had met at a Dieppe inn in 1660. Blundell confesses "I could scarcely mention anything, even out of those Latin books which I had studied and pored on with endless repetitions, but he had it almost by heart; or else knew the substance thereof much better than myself. Especially Barclay's 'Argenis,' the historical part of which I had read over no fewer than eight times." William Blundell, *Crosby Records: A Cavalier's Note Book*, ed. T. E. Gibson (1880), p. 279. Blundell, too, could recall particular episodes in other history books that he had reread, referring to an episode he had encountered in the fifteenth book of Davila's history of the French religious wars: ibid., p. 220.

Clarendon might not have been pleased with this assessment of the literary
merits of his work.

This point about history reading (and perhaps about reading in general) can
be illustrated at length in the miscellaneous notebooks – sometimes collectively called a "diary" though they follow no diurnal pattern – of John Ward
(*ca.* 1629–81), amateur physician and, from 1661 until his death, the vicar of
Stratford-upon-Avon. These contain, amid proverbs, recipes, medical notes,
and astrological comments, abundant references to historical episodes about
which he had read, episodes which took his pen in surprising directions.[77]

History, thought Ward, "delivers to posterity an inventory of men's virtues." Throughout his volumes are scattered the traditional humanist injunctions about the gravity and seriousness of history, the need for truthfulness
and the historian's duty to impartiality. He repeats pieties about the limits of
historical knowledge and the distinction between the fictions of poets and the
verities recorded by historians. "Good schollars seldome take things upon
trust; particularly see two noble exhortations to trial of what wee receive for
truth; the one in the preface to Selden's 'Historie of Tithes,' the other in the
preface to Harvey of 'Generation.'" Ward trumpeted his faith in the existence of certain indisputable, irreducible historical facts and a limited form of
skepticism. "Believing is but opinion, if the evidence bee but probable, but if
itt bee such that cannot be questioned, then tis as certaine as knowledge; for
wee are no less certaine that there is a great towne called Constantinople,
than that there is one called London; wee as little doubt that Queen Elizabeth
once reigned, as that King Charles now reigns."[78] But his practice in extract-

---

[77] Folger MS V.a. 284–99, Ward notebooks, fifteen volumes; only a small section of this was
printed by C. Severn in his 1839 edition, entitled *Diary of the Rev. John Ward, A.M., Vicar of
Stratford-upon-Avon* (1839); for Ward's career and the "diaries" see Robert G. Frank, Jr.,
"The John Ward Diaries: Mirror of Seventeenth-Century Science and Medicine," *Journal of
the History of Medicine and Allied Sciences*, 29 (1974), 147–79, which article does not,
however, discuss other subjects than medicine, save noting a decline in Ward's medical
interests after 1670, in the direction of history. Severn's edition consists of extracts, randomly
selected, and is therefore of no help in determining what Ward read and in what order.

[78] Folger MS V.a. 284, p. 19; V.a. 288, fos. 106, 205. See also V.a. 288, fos. 56v–57r for the
stock citation about history being *magistra vitae*, from Cicero's *de Oratore*, immediately
followed by notes that "4 hundreds are now in Warwickshire. Kineton, Knightlow, Borlick-
way, and Hemlingford" (fo. 57r) and several pages on local place names and their literary
sources. Cf. Severn edn, pp. 196, 205, and the following: "A true historian should bee neither
party, advocate, nor judg, but a bare witnes"; "In auncient historie, if wee will have anything
of truth, wee must have something of falsehood; itt is as impossible to find antiquitie without
fables, as an old face without wrinkles" (Severn edn, pp. 115, 216). We do not know exactly
which books Ward owned. In V.a. 288, fo. 32 he wrote the heading for "An Account of all the
Books in my studie and household stuffe in my house taken about Michaelmas: 1667" but did
not continue it.

ing materials from history was quite at odds with such dicta, and with the *gravitas* of humanist historiography in general, which we have previously seen directed against the inclusiveness of Tudor chronicles. Ward regularly blended the serious with the trivial, and conflated written sources with "facts" he had heard casually in conversation. In other words, while he chanted the Ciceronian conventions of history's truth and dignity, picked up from the prefaces to the books he had read, Ward's wider usable past was much less orderly and homogeneous. It embraced biblical, classical, medieval, and modern history, the low and humorous as well as the high matters of state and war to which historians were supposed to confine themselves. A series of extracts from a set of books on a particular subject typically includes Ward's efforts to digest his reading into at least one concise table or summary: several pages concerning ancient and biblical history, for instance, include a catalog of all the kings of the twelve tribes of Israel as listed in the Bible, as if to save him the trouble of having to keep the other books close at hand.[79]

Some particularly dense volumes of historical notes written between 1658 and 1665 range through medieval and recent history, as Ward made observations on persons and events, noted remarkable or interesting facts, and frequently issued himself earnest injunctions to look for further information on the matter read, or on some other subject that has sprung to mind, or to buy copies of particular books.[80] "Remember that I buy some particular histories of the Gothes and Vandales as Jornandes or some other: and to see whether Sr. Walter Rawleigh is long on that subject." This is shortly followed by "Remember when I goe to London to buy Gusman and Jacobus de Voragine and some other such merrie authors: to peruse in winter nights." Discussion of matters gothic continues twenty-four leaves further on with a note that "Olaus Magnus archbishop of Upsal hath written a historie of the Gothes, and Vandals, as allso Jornandes, and Grotius."

Isolated and apparently unconnected facts were placed in the notebooks as reminders to allow Ward to make sense of other historical episodes. "King James during his reigne in Scotland was heavily pestered with the presby-

---

[79] V.a. 284. The frequency with which accessible but mnemonically difficult lists were recopied into commonplace books opens up the question of whether, as has been suggested, most readers did in fact work with several books in front of them, in the fashion of Gabriel Harvey: Jardine and Grafton, "Studied for Action," 30ff. The practice of many of the readers discussed in the present chapter, particularly toward the latter part of the period, seems to have been quite different: *seriatim* readings and rereadings of texts, sometimes with references from one to another but also considerable time spent on copying precisely to avoid such back and forth book-flitting. Most readers here, too, seem to have been much less deliberate, and they were open to serendipitous discovery and rediscovery of authors in a manner that is playful, rather than serious and calculated.

[80] V.a. 287, fo. 10v, where a disquisition on Henry IV and the duchy of Lancaster (fo. 10v) is interrupted with notes to "Remember to inquire" into a medical topic and to buy a book.

terians" is a sentence that most likely arose from Ward thinking about the presbyterians of his own time while reading about the Scottish Calvinists of the late sixteenth century. The remark "Hermolaus Barbarus was a Venetian and made official at Rome in his Embassie; before that he was patriarch of Aquileia" follows a note on the fall of Constantinople and precedes one on Dutch wedding customs. "Charles the 5th had a base daughter called Margaret who was governess of Low-Countries and married to Octavian, prince of Parma as well as a base sonn called Don John of Austria" ends a line, on the next which follows "Cardinal Baronius was one of the first of the order of the Oratorians." In some cases, Ward's pen betrays lapses of memory or slips of expression. "I hear that Dugdale is making additions to Spelmans glossaria, and explaining words as he does; Spelman goes but to L [i.e., the letter *L*], as I think: remember the next time I goe to London that I view all Mr. Seldens [*sic*] works, and particularly his Villare anglicanum." In this case he wrote Selden when he clearly meant "Dugdale," the author of that work and the subject of the sentence.[81]

Other volumes of Ward's notebooks reveal the same approach to reading, the same impulsive urge to follow something up when time and travels allowed. "Remember to inquire more particularly into the Bizantine historians the number of the volumes and the price to bee paid for them: and the names of the Authors and whether Budeus was a Translator or author of any thing there." A reminder "to peruse [John] Stow's Survey of London" is followed by the fact that a royal palace mentioned earlier in the notes "was burnt downe by fire accidentally in King Henry the 8th time . . . see Bakers chronicle."[82] Famous "firsts," a well-known feature of published almanac

[81] V.a. 287, fos. 22v, 76r, 77v, 83r, and 109r (Goths), 108r, 136r. For further examples of orphan facts, see throughout V.a. 288, e.g. fo. 78v: "Catesby seemed to be the first who propounded the gunpowder treason" and "Henry the 3d was killed at St. Cloud, where the Council for the massacre was held." "Dr. Lightfoot thinks that a close comment on the Chronicles would contribute much light to other scriptures" i.e. the Book of Chronicles in the Bible, this amid pages of notes on the origins and history of the Quakers (fo. 108r). "The conference at Hampton Court was in the year 1604" is followed on a new line by "The vandals a wild and savage people who have left such a name in the world for their actions" (fo. 132v). Many of these remarks are memoranda, the equivalent of today's apparently useless sports statistics, to be dragged out in conversation to impress an audience, for instance "The first emperor that was according to historians excommunicated by the pope was Henry the 4th" (fo. 98v) and "Sarah is the only woman whose age is recorded in scripture." On the use of historical memoranda see D. R. Woolf, "Memory and Historical Culture in Early Modern England," *Journal of the Canadian Historical Association*, n.s. 2 (1991), 283–308.

[82] V.a. 293 (*ca.* 1663–65), fos. 7r, 8v, 13r, 65r, 76r; "when I goe to London remember the Centuriators," fo. 25; cf. a note to buy "the historie of gavelkind by Silas Taylor" (fo. 73v); on fo. 38v is a reminder to himself to index his "character books"; at fo. 68v is a note that "those that put out the Magdeburg Centuries were fflacius Illyricus, Johannes Wigandus, Mathias Juden, Basilius ffaber," and that "Edmund Earl of Derby who died in Queen Elizabeths days was famous for Chyrurgerie and bonesetting and hospitalitie: Bakers Chronicle p. 371." At fo. 144v Ward records that "The Kings of England usualy make choise of some man of eminencie to write their historie who commonly was of St. Albans near London source of news and books: Matthew Paris was an Englishman borne in Cambridgeshire."

chronologies, also interested Ward and were duly extracted, along with other memorabilia, from Baker and his other books. "Richardus Anglicus our first physitian flourisht about 70 years 1230" appears in a passage of notes written up in chronicle form. "An ounce of silver in King Johns time was valued but at twenty pence. Sir Rich. Baker relates that in K. Henry the 3ds time a child was borne in Kent that at 2 years old cured all diseases . . ." "There are 745 parks in England: King Henry the first made the first park for inclosing deer at Woodstock." Among other things, this pattern of references strongly suggests that Ward had recently acquired a copy of Baker's *Chronicle* to go along with Stow, and that he was comparing details between the two.[83]

Yet if Ward's reading was not tightly structured and devoted to a particular end, neither was it frivolous and chaotic. Present concerns, the matter of daily life, naturally weighed into his decision to pause over a particular passage in his reading. As a local physician, he read his histories with an eye to past cases of disease, leading at one point to a discussion of the leprosy of "Hugh de Orwal," William the Conqueror's archbishop of Canterbury. The parochial cleric's concern with monetary inflation arises from a casual remark in one of his books. "Godwin of Bishops: p: 234: there says that 5 shillings hath now scarce so much silver in it, as 5 groates had formerly; no wonder then if things have treble the prices they were 300 years agoe." The subject of episcopal freedom to top up the stipends of underpaid vicars and curates from their rectors' funds emerges from a reading of Dugdale, which leads in turn to a curiosity about Dugdale's own cited authority, "one Dr. Rives a learned civilian who wrote on this subject. Remember to buy him." A similar preoccupation inspired him to "Remember most strictly to inquire how it came about that so much church land was alienated in the days of Edward the 6th and Queen Elizabeth."[84] Most of these plans for further research, urgent as they sound, were stillborn since they do not appear to have been pursued elsewhere in the notebooks. "Remember to search out the extent of the jurisdiction of our peculiar at Strat[ford] and that out of the auncient grant in K. Edward the 6ths time. Routing up the papers in the chamber and likewise searching in the Roles for the original graunt for it is graunted to us as the colledges had it, but the maine question is how it was graunted us the colledge at first, and whether it may not bee probable that it is wholy exempt even from the Bishop himself . . ."[85] On occasion, he lingered for some time, even days, on a particular volume, such as Dugdale's *Antiquities of Warwickshire*, glossing his notes from the main author with references to other historical works, many of which were actually given in the printed marginal notes of the book he was reading.

Ward's paging through Foxe's Book of Martyrs certainly occurred in at

---

[83] V.a. 295 (date *ca.* 1666–69), fos. 10r, 41v–42r, 69r.
[84] Ibid., 88r, 89r; V.a. 288, fo. 58r; V.a. 292, fo. 156r.   [85] V.a. 293, fo. 130v.

least one patch of several consecutive readings as he pillaged the *Acts and Monuments* for material on English secular as well as religious history. In this case, Ward uncharacteristically read the book in chronological order.[86] Blips of episodes from Foxe, and Foxe's sources, are sprinkled about, commencing with the heading "ex lib: martyr: begins with the apostolic martyrs; 6–8 list of the successive persecutions." Foxe's comparison of himself with Livy is repeated in Ward's notes, and Ward largely adopts Foxe's periodization of church history into ages or periods in organizing his remarks.[87] Arrival at the section of Foxe's text dealing with William the Conqueror creates a space in the notebook for a host of related facts peripherally connected with that king. "King William the Conqueror died about the same time as did pope Hildebrand or Gregory the 7th the great sorceror. It is reported of William the Conqueror that he left but one bishop that was in before the land and that was Wolstan bishop of Worcester."[88] Ward's shadowing of the text in his recording of it includes not only the chronology, but Foxe's own comparisons, for instance the martyrologist's use of the quasi-miraculous survival of Huldrych Zwingli's heart after his body had been burnt to foreshadow a similar occurrence in the case of Archbishop Cranmer. "Zwinglius slain amongst his citizens the Zuirickmen the enemies burn his bodie: his friends came the next day to see whether any part of him was remaining, where they found his heart in the ashes whole and unburnt, as is allso credibly reported of the heart of Cranmer." Even the banderoles on Foxe's woodcuts, with their terse, godly declarations uttered amid the flames, were transferred holus-bolus into Ward's notes. "Mr. Rogers the 1st martyr in queen maries days . . . Mr. Saunders took up the stake and kissd it saying welcome the cross of X: welcome everlasting life."[89] And where Foxe resorts to dramatic dialogues in representing scenes between persecutors and martyrs, Ward follows suit. The notes on Foxe end abruptly, as Ward slides into a series of remarks on Roman history from a variety of authors. "Nero never gave more than an hour for one to prepare for his mortal blow."[90]

---

[86] V.a. 289, fo. 130v. This was written no later than 1661, since it refers to Cardinal Mazarin as still living.

[87] V.a. 289, fo. 20r (the "2nd intervall" of the church). Cf. fo. 21r for a lapse into the apparently trivial and jocular. "It is historied of John Patriarch of Alexandria who was a niggardly man that as hee was att praier there appeard to him a comly virgin having on her head a garland of olive leavs, and prayinge her self mercy. This damsell told John that if hee would take her to wife hee should profitt well. [query] Whether this bee true or faind for a morality"; this is accompanied by a page reference to Foxe. On fo. 24r Ward records how "the Danes put to death King Edmund" and the story of King Alfred, who also "had great scufflings with the Danes."   [88] Ibid., fos. 27r, 28r.   [89] Ibid., fo. 43r.

[90] Ibid., fos. 57v, 73v–74r; although he was almost certainly reading it in Tacitus, Ward replaces the story of the rape of Sejanus' adolescent daughter before her execution with a sanitized and incomplete anecdote that leaves out the full horror of the tale. "There was a daughter of Sejanus so young, and of so litle understanding, that shee going to execution cried out what have I done, whither will they lead mee? If I may bee forgiven I will doe bad noe more: there needs nothing but a rod to correct mee."

The apparent randomness to all this is more easily explained if one accepts a playful dimension to reading and acknowledges that much of early modern literacy consisted in browsing of a much less systematic sort than is practiced now. If we accept that not everyone read in the highly structured, purposeful way that did a paid professional like Gabriel Harvey, or a focused antiquary like Roger Twysden, then a joke about the past like "Gustavus and Augustus, are the same names only with a transposition of letters: Scanderbeg is as much as Alexander the Great" begins to make sense, juxtaposed with serious discussions of war and policy.[91] History, it seems, could free the mind to wander as much as fixing it upon important tasks; and the factual past, as much as the fictions and romances decried by moralists as frivolous time-wasters, could transport the reader of Foxe, Livy, or Froissart into an imaginative landscape where his or her imagination could perambulate freely. The more traditional Renaissance manner of lifting episodes from out of their contexts for didactic purpose, in the manner of Machiavelli, is here being challenged by a more holistic, leisurely experience of the historical text, in which pleasure is reconciled to virtue.

READING PATTERNS AND THE POPULARITY OF HISTORY: TWO CASE STUDIES

Two further and more detailed examples of history reading, both from northern England (and thus well removed from the somewhat distorting effect of the London and Oxbridge booksellers and presses), are provided by the diaries of Christopher Parkes, a minister at Haughton, Durham, in the second half of the seventeenth century, and (over a shorter period) Henry Prescott, the Anglican deputy registrar of the diocese of Chester. Neither offers the rich evidence of quirks of thought that occurs in John Ward's multivolumed miscellany, with all its instances of abrupt turns down mental side-roads. Instead, these documents give us a more detailed and ordered – and to some degree quantifiable – picture of the place of history reading among intellectual and social activities.

Parkes, about whom little is known,[92] was the author of a manuscript that is more than a commonplace book but less than a full diary, giving much information as to how he acquired and read or, as he invariably put it, "perused" historical and other books, over a period of five decades. Next to

---

[91] V.a. 293, fo. 127v.
[92] Folger MS V.a. 95, "commonplace book" (so-titled in catalog) from 1651 to 1700. Parkes does not appear to have been a rector at Haughton. He may be the same as the Christopher Parkes who was admitted pensioner to St. John's College, Cambridge in 1660, then already vicar of Catterick near Richmond: *Alum. Cant.*, part 1, vol. III, p. 309. Parkes was perform- ing clerical duties in 1662, suggesting that he had taken the oath of allegiance, though he held no living. I thank Laetitia Yeandle for help with identifying Parkes and other information about his writing.

the 1587 book of common prayer that he had stitched into the larger manuscript volume, Parkes reminded himself, on an unknown day, to "buy these books of Mr. Birckbek" (a local bookseller), the titles specified being, as befit a cleric, mainly religious but also including "that History of Britt. under ye Rom: Saxons &c with lives of Conq. & other kings."[93] A note on the very next page refers to some books "left with Mr. Birckbek," implying either that they are ones that Parkes had decided to sell (and deposited for appraisal) or, more likely since Parkes includes prices, unbound sheets he had purchased and left with the bookseller to arrange for binding. These include "Lavator on Chronicles" (5s) and an Anglo-Saxon Old Testament (2s 6d). A list of "choice bookes" is, again, principally religious, but also includes a work on sacred history, Lightfoot's "harmony of chronicles" (the *Centuria Chronographica*), and a recent life of the Quaker James Nayler.[94]

Like John Ward, Parkes was not content with simply buying books. His own record of his intellectual activities reveals him to have been a systematic searcher out of works in libraries. On 20 August 1653 Parkes drew up a catalog of the books in his hands at Haughton, some of which may have been borrowed. It includes most of the early seventeenth-century items that one might expect to find: a two-volume annotated Tacitus in octavo format, Livy, the *Historia Augusta*, Nepos, Justin, and Thomas Godwin's *Moses and Aaron* (a book often known, like its ancient progenitor Josephus, as the *Jewish Antiquities*), and Degory Wheare's *Relectiones* [sic], the Latin version of a popular early Stuart manual on history reading. The list was evidently augmented subsequently since it also includes some later works: William Cave's *Ancient Church Government*, an antiquarian title by J. G. Gronovius on coinage, and *Theologo-historicus*, the life of Peter Heylyn by his son-in-law, John Barnard. Also listed are Gilbert Burnet's brief pamphlet *The life of William Bedell* (the early Stuart scholar and bishop of Kilmore) and another edition of Tacitus.[95]

More interesting than the list itself, however, is Parkes' decision at two points in his career, the 1650s and again from 1689 to 1700, to record the books that he perused, month by month. This record includes a regular diet of historical and antiquarian texts, a few of which he would reread. The first of these records his reading since entering the ministry in the 1650s.[96] In it

---

[93] I have been unable to identify the history to which he refers, though Speed's *Historie of Great Britain* (1611), reprinted in 1650, is a possible candidate.

[94] Folger MS V.a. 95, unpaginated (following Book of Common Prayer).

[95] Ibid., p. 46. An undated but later catalog of Parkes' personal books includes many items neither in the 1653 catalog nor in the record of "books perused" in the 1650s and 1690s, such as Fuller's *Church-history*, the "life of Ussher" (by Richard Parr) and *The Historical and Chronological theatre of Christopher Helvicus*, which appeared in English in 1687, half a century after its first publication in Latin.

[96] V.a. 95, unpaginated.

Table 2.4. *Christopher Parkes' reading matter, 1655–1663, by principal subject*

Year	Historical-biographical	Religious	Other	Total for year
1655	3	36	8	47
1656	0	29	1	30
1657	6	29	5	40
1658	3	33	4	40
1659	2	37	1	40
1660	5	20	2	27
1661	0	12	0	12
1662	1	25	3	29
1663	1	12	0	13

Parkes first records 110 titles, without times of reading, since he took up his cure: they include Camden's *Annales*; an unspecified "Annals of some of English kings" (perhaps Stow); "History of Brittaine from Jul. Caesar to K. Stephen" (perhaps Samuel Daniel's *First Part of the History of England*, which covers exactly that time span); an ecclesiastical history by "Sympson" (Edward Simson's *Chronicon historiam Catholicam complectens*, 1652); and various works of Samuel Clark including his *The Lives of Sundry Eminent Persons* (1683). Between items 111 and 390, however, Parkes broke down according to year his reading of books he either borrowed or owned and those he came across elsewhere. The complete picture is represented in table 2.4,[97] giving the proportions of historical/biographical, religious, and other books perused.[98]

[97] Ibid. The distribution of item numbers is as follows: Jan. 1655–Jan. 1656 (nos. 111–58); Jan. 1656–Jan. 1657 (nos. 159–88); Jan. 1657–Jan. 1658 (nos. 189–228); Jan. 1658–Jan. 1659 (nos. 229–68); Jan. 1659–Jan. 1660 (nos. 269–308); Jan. 1660–Jan. 1661 (nos. 309–36); Jan. 1661–Jan. 1662 (nos. 337–48); Jan. 1662–Jan. 1663 (nos. 349–77); Jan. 1663–Jan. 1664 (nos. 378–90).

[98] Notable history titles read include the old and the recent: Charles Cornwallis, *The life and death of our late most incomparable and heroique prince, Henry, prince of Wales* (1641); Thomas Fuller, *The Church-History of Britain* (1655) and *The appeal of iniured innocence, unto the religious learned and ingenuous reader* (1659); Cresacre More, *The Life and Death of Sir Thomas More* (1631); Sir William Dugdale, *Monasticon Anglicanum* (vol. I, 1661); John Spottiswood, *The History of the Church of Scotland* (1655); an unidentified life of Oliver Cromwell; Shakespeare's *Richard III*; a set of "Secret Lives from Constantine the Great to O. Protector" (unidentified, 1658); Prynne's introduction to the "history" of Laud's trial (i.e., the work usually known as *Canterburie's Doome* [1646], though 1659 is the date given here); Bishop Fell's *The life and death of that reverend divine, and excellent historian, Doctor Thomas Fuller* (1662); Francis Osborne, *Historical memoires on the Reigns of Queen Elizabeth and King James* (1658); Isaac Basire, *The Ancient Liberty of the Britannick Church* (1661); James Heath's *Flagellum or the Life . . . of Cromwell* (1662); and Nathaniel Bacon's *The history of Athanasius* (1664 [1663 in MS]).

Parkes also consulted some manuscript works, including a register of institutions by the Archdeaconry of Richmond 1418–42, and a folio manuscript of ecclesiastical causes and precedents that he "borrowed of the Registrar of Richmond." Perhaps searching for the choicest books to buy, he looked over the bookseller William London's published *Catalogue of the Most Vendible Books* in 1659. The account is silent as to Parkes' readings, and his other activities, for a quarter-century, but it resumes in 1689, when he was an old man, and continues to September 1700. This second list is less neat and not so consistently informative as to time, but it contains a slightly higher proportion of historical works.[99]

Henry Prescott's diary, unlike Parkes', covers a relatively short period, but it was kept much more systematically (virtually every day for a period of fifteen years, except for a gap of nearly a year throughout 1713) and is hence fuller with regard to his reading and other antiquarian activities. It is sufficiently detailed so as to tell us from day to day – and not merely year to year – which books Prescott read and the proportion of them that was historical. Unlike Parkes or John Ward, Prescott was a layman, albeit one who earned his living working, in a rather leisurely fashion, on behalf of the diocese. A prominent local figure whose favorite and most regular activities were walks on the Roodee and nightly pints of beer and claret, Prescott's historical interests were also diverse, ranging from chronology to modern history and biography, to classical antiquities. Interestingly, he had little taste for medieval authors, though Roger Twysden's edition of chronicles appears in his reading occasionally, he preferred the works of Elizabethan and Jacobean historians like Stow, Camden, and Speed.[100]

---

[99] An initial set of 174 items is followed at p. 54 by a more careful account, mimicking that of the 1650s, of "Books begun to be perused since year 89": these include Peter Heylyn's *Cosmography*, various works on religion and geography; Thomas Fuller's *Church-History* (MS p. 55 in July); Samuel Daniel's *Collection of the Historie of England*, with its continuation by John Trussell (ibid.; also read in July); Paul Rycaut's *Turkish History* (MS p. 56); Thomas Burnet's *Theory of the earth* (7 February 1693/94, MS p. 58); Arthur Wilson's *Life of King James*, for which no date of reading is given; William Wotton's *Reflections on Ancient and Modern Learning* (August 1694, MS p. 60); and an unidentified "History of Religion" (September 1694, ibid.). From January 1694/95 the list becomes more detailed, or the reading level increases (MS p. 60). January reading includes "Sir Wm Temples Introduction to a history of Engl." and several religious books. Readings for the month of May include only two books (most months have five or six), of which one is historical, *Burnet's Memoirs of Q. Mary*; June's list includes "Coats Life of 4 Kgs" (perhaps a mistake for Nathaniel Crouch's *The Secret history of the four last monarchs of Great Britain* [1691]), MS p. 62. In July 1696 he was reading Michael Geddes' newly published *The Church-History of Ethiopia* and six other religious books, including John Toland's *Christianity not mysterious* (pp. 64–65 of MS). His reading for 1697–98 includes John Selden's *Historie of tithes* along with Thomas Comber's *Historical Vindication* in response (February and March). The total of all books perused from January 1689 to September 1700 comes to 402 (not counting books reread, which are only occasionally mentioned).

[100] E.g., *Diary of Henry Prescott*, II, 481 (Kennett's *History of England*, containing many of the Jacobean hisorians); 554 (Stow's *Annales*).

Prescott regularly lent and borrowed books, especially on history, and was not always a timely returner of them; he borrowed *A Memorial of the Church of England* (a set of political and ecclesiastical pamphlets that included a "vindication of the apostles") from a Mr. Maul on 21 July 1705, read it in two sittings over the next few days, and returned it to its owner on 24 July. On the other hand, he had to be reminded by the chancellor of the diocese, while the two were drinking at the Fountain, his favorite pub, of "a book long ago lent, Bronchursts Centuriae, with reflections on borrowing books and not returning them."[101] On 22 November 1706 Prescott lent Calvisius' *Chronicles* to his friend Mr. Davies, another local antiquary. It was from Davies that he attempted to obtain a copy of the new edition of John Leland's *Itineraries* (published by Thomas Hearne at Oxford in nine volumes from 1710 to 1712), finally buying it by subscription. Prescott also either owned or borrowed a manuscript of the additions to Bishop Francis Godwin's century-old *Catalogue of Bishops*.[102] He was not sentimentally attached to his books, unlike his treasured and much-displayed set of Roman coins, and even on those rare occasions when he enthused about a book, such as Milton's *Paradise Lost* (an interesting choice for a Jacobite sympathizer who liked to mark the birthday of the Old Pretender), he might eventually sell it to a friend.[103]

Prescott also bought books, as he did coins and other artifacts, in moderate quantities, though less often than he read them. To the probable annoyance of a series of booksellers, all men of substance in Chester (including the mayor, Joseph Hodgson or Hodson), he tended to loiter about the shops "diverting" himself in their books, often only buying a work *after* he had read it, as in the case of Pufendorf's *Introduction to the History of Europe, Asia &c.*[104] Through the winter of 1705/6 he was helping the earl of Derby to "procure the library at Knowsley," buoyed by the news from an informant that the library was "great and noble, of most of the Fathers entire. History especially French, constituted of Folios above the proporcion of the other volumes, he reckons the whole 2900."[105] When his brother-in-law, a clergyman, died, Prescott and his son Jack were soon on site putting together a rudimentary catalog of the library, and paying the widow, Henry's sister, for

---

[101] Ibid., I, 49, 62, 86; the *Memorial* was published in several parts from 1703 to 1708. For a further sharp reminder from his bishop about an overdue book in the middle of December, 1704, see ibid., p. 82.

[102] Ibid., 125, 131, 298. Calvisius' work is one of several editions of Seth Calvisius (1556–1615), *Chronologia, ex autoritate potissimum Sacrae Scripturae, et historicorum fide dignissimorum* (Leipzig, 1605, and several updated versions throughout the seventeenth century).

[103] Ibid., II, 331, 332, 513 (James III's birthday); having sold his Milton in 1711 he appears not to have worried, on picking up *Paradise Regained* five years later (II, 507) that he did not have a matching set.   [104] Ibid., II, 319, 323, 536.

[105] Ibid., I, 81, 113, 115. He was unsuccessful in acquiring the library and the books were sold to Michael Johnson, the prominent Lichfield bookseller.

several titles, including an edition of Eusebius. On another occasion he wrote "I chuse out some of Mr. Price's library to the value of 2 guineas and give direction to write to the present owner about them." In 1710 he noted his having bought "Dr. Bingham's Antiquities of the Christian Church 2 vol., for 9s and Brett LL.D. his Account of Church Government for 5s." And he kept his ear to the ground for news of forthcoming and recently published works; while drinking with his friend Dr. Entwhistle he secured the promise of a copy of Clarendon's *History of the Rebellion*, published three years earlier.[106] Plot's *Natural History of Oxfordshire* cost him eleven shillings in 1712, along with 4s 3d for a much older chorography, Lambarde's *Perambulation of Kent*, though neither features prominently in his reading. In May 1719, only a fortnight or so before his own death, he paid £1 2s 6d for Echard's *Roman History*, but spent most of the day immersed in *Robinson Crusoe* (borrowed from a bookseller), which he initially took to be a real history rather than fiction, though suspecting its authenticity. There is a hint of self-reproach in his admission, in 1717, that he had paid a shilling for a copy of Zosimus, not merely a "Heathen Historian" but a notorious antichristian writer of the eastern empire.[107]

Such diurnal notes of books borrowed or bought are not rare for the Augustan era; what is less common is the sort of systematic record of books, or parts of books, read over an extended period, that Prescott provides. He gave his reading, a good third of which was historical or biographical, extraordinary prominence in his diary entries, telling us not just what he read, but in many cases the number of times he returned to the same book, and the conditions under which he read it. On 10 December 1705 for instance, he gives us an account of the weather, his morning exercise, and his letter-writing, concluding with "I fall into Salusts Bellum Iugurthinum in-gaga read it over." The following day ends with the brusque note "I turn Florus," and five days later Prescott, feeling a bit feverish, was "turning" yet another book, on Roman sepulchral urns. This "turning," like Parkes' or Ward's "perusals," suggests a casual and desultory rather than an intense style of reading.[108] The words he most often uses to describe his reading activities are "apply to" and "divert in," and it is apparent that he meant to make a distinction between two styles of reading. On the one hand, he sometimes undertook a concentrated and intensive reading, generally in order from beginning to end (as in his careful and chronological reading of the various components of Kennett's *History of England* in 1715, or his parallel reading of Stow's and Camden's accounts of Queen Elizabeth's reign two years later). On the other hand, there are frequent instances of a very different sort of reading, a much more haphazard perusal of works in no

---

106 Ibid., I, 92, 102, 134, 174, 280.   107 Ibid., II, 350, 353, 601, 695.
108 Ibid., I, 81, 181.

particular order.[109] An unusually busy day on 18 July 1708 (I, 181) concluded in a more leisurely manner as Prescott "read Heylin's introduction to the Life of Archbishop Laud and with my coz. Kendrick, recreate in my domestic pint." Some works he would read over a period of days or weeks (presumably those he had borrowed from friends or booksellers); others he would pick up and put down at infrequent intervals over a number of years, for instance Camden's *Britannia*, which he began (perhaps not for the first time) in 1714 but only got down to seriously a year later, or Heylyn's life of Laud, *Cyprianus Anglicus*, read first in 1708 and then again seven years later.[110] Other books appear sporadically, presumably plucked off the shelf with a full stomach and an aching head as his fancy took him: he "dipped" in Thucydides with his domestic pint late one hot evening in 1711, but would finish it, in greater sobriety and during the day, over the course of the following week.[111]

Figure 2.2 breaks down Prescott's reading, as recorded in his diary beginning in 1704. The entries continue, with some interruptions, to 1719, stopping a few weeks before his death from years of alcoholic abuse. In contrast to Christopher Parkes, for whom history was a minor interest, historical and antiquarian works account for nearly half of the titles that Prescott read in whole or in part, 125 in all, with religion and philosophy (principally works of contemporary theology and polemic, and ancient philosophical classics such as Cicero and Seneca) a close second at 101, many of which titles he must have read in connection with his work as deputy registrar. Politics and law account for only 44 titles, literature 47, and science, medicine or geography combined only 15. One can also analyze the reading by the period of author, where known. "Contemporary" authors, those writing from 1660 to his own time, comprise over a third, at 135, with works written from 1500 to 1659 also a solid third at 115. Only six medieval authors are specifically mentioned (among them Twysden's edition of chronicles); on the other hand, Prescott remained a keen reader of classical literature, which at 76 titles amounts to half the contemporary numbers.[112] It is worth remarking, too,

---

[109] Ibid., II, 480–81 (Kennett); II, 561 (Stow and Camden). Prescott himself very clearly distinguished serious study of books from their more leisurely pursuit: "After dinner rather seeking for Books in my Library than reading," ibid., II, 407 (27 September 1714); "I rather divert in than apply to Books," ibid., II, 604 (15 November 1717).

[110] Ibid., I, 181; II, 451, 452, 454.   [111] Ibid., II, 313–14.

[112] Henry Prescott's reactions to his histories are rather flat in comparison with an earlier diarist, Pepys, who frequently tells us not just what he read but what he thought of it: Davila's *Storia delle guerre civile di Francia*, which Pepys perused in his home in 1666, struck him as "a most excellent history as ever I read." Pepys, *Diary*, VII, 206 (14 July 1666). Reading Fuller's *Church history*, one of his favorite books and one he would reread periodically, Pepys fell upon "Cranmers letter to Queen Elizabeth, which pleases me mightily for his zeal, obedience and boldness in a cause of religion." His enthusiasm led him to confuse Cranmer with Archbishop Grindal: IV, 329–30 (11 October 1663).

Individual titles counted only once even if read over several days or years; authors such as Cicero have been tabulated by distinct works, for example *De Oratore* and *Orator* counted separately.

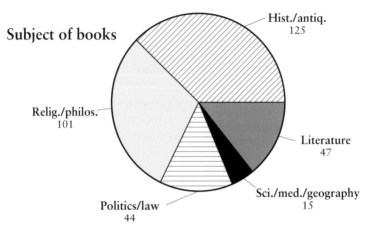

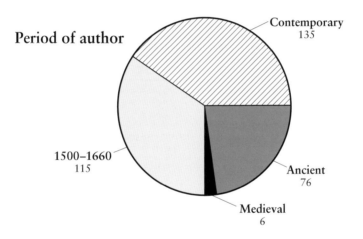

Figure 2.2 Henry Prescott's reading, 1704–19. Source: *Diary of Henry Prescott*, vols. I and II, ed. J. M. Addy and P. McNiven, Record Society of Lancashire and Cheshire, 127 (1987) and 132 (1994).

that a significant number of the works here counted as "literary" were historical plays and verse, in particular those of Shakespeare and Drayton, and that one should not assume the literary reading to have been casual or frivolous and the historical reading serious and focused. On the contrary,

Prescott's reading of *King Lear* – again over a pint – was accompanied by an effort to verify what we would call the "facts" of Lear's reign in an historical handbook, Matthias Prideaux's *Easie and compendious introduction for reading . . . histories*, several editions of which had been published since 1648.[113]

Prescott's reading was sometimes dictated by the occasion. A thorough Tory who regularly marked anniversaries such as 30 January (the execution of Charles I) and 29 May (the Restoration of Charles II), he saw to it that he read appropriate matter on such days. He generally kept 30 January with a sermon in the morning, while in the afternoon he "applied" himself to the "history of the day," including readings of *Eikon Basilike*.[114] There is no sense of his looking to these works for specific lessons or morals; they are selected purely because they seem to suit the occasion and can make him mindful of the event. Prescott and his son would celebrate 29 May 1718, Restoration Day, by having the latter read "proper parts" of Clarendon's *History of the Rebellion* over a pint and a meal. On the same anniversary a year earlier he had marked the day by paying eighteen shillings for a copy of John Walker's *Sufferings of the Clergy*.[115] Some of this reading was private, the solace of a man easily bored and frequently indisposed by his overindulgent drinking. But reading, and the exchange of knowledge, were also a major part of Restoration and Augustan sociability, and much of Prescott's was semipublic, as when he entertained a visitor in his study with his coins and books, and in particular with his *Memoirs* of the earls of Derby, or when he and several friends enjoyed "a great course of learning and antiquity" over four talboys at the Swan, one of his haunts. The topics of these discussions were not always to Prescott's taste: although he was the last to leave a successful dinner party at Sir William Meredith's, "detaind by Discourse of Loyalty, Hereditary succession and History," even Prescott thought a visitor from Manchester had grown "historical and tedious" over a bottle of wine.[116]

As Prescott aged, the regular walks declined in frequency and the drinking increased. So did the link between the drinking and the reading. It is a rare occasion in the later years of the diary when the old man did not have one hand on his favorite "pint of Dyson" while turning the pages of a learned book with another. One can now imagine more cheery and amusing fare for convivial reading than Caesar's *Commentaries*, Weever's *Ancient Funerall Monuments*, Camden's *Britannia*, Heylyn's *Cyprianus Anglicus*, Hobbes'

---

[113] *Diary of Henry Prescott*, II, 407.   [114] Ibid., II, 343, 374, 380, 489.

[115] Ibid., II, 636 (29 May 1718); an earlier reading by his son had occurred on 1 March in the same year, II, 621; ibid., II, 579 (29 May 1717).

[116] Ibid., II, 341, 469, 477, 613, 639, 687; on reading and sociability, versus "bookishness," see Johns, *Nature of the Book*, p. 470.

A list of some of the ~~Lordes~~ Lords
treasurers of Eng
=land.

Geffrey de Clinton was
Ld Treasurer of Eng
land under K: Henry
ye first.
John Ruthall was Lord
Treasurer to Henry 3th
Eustace de Falconbrig
Bishop of London was
Ld Treasurer also to
K: Henry ye 3d.
Hugh Pateshull was
Ld Treasurer ye 18
of K: Hen: ye 3d.
Tho: unmundham was Ld
Treasurer yes th of Hen 3
Joseph Chancy prior of
St Johns was Ld Treasurer
2[?]8 of 6 to Edw: 1 me

Sr walter Norwellury
Ld Treasurer of England
under Edward ye 2d
Robert woodhouse was
Ld Treasurer of England
ye fourth yeare of Edmund
ye 3d.
Sr Rich: scroope L h Bolton
was Treasurer of England
the 46 th of Edw: ye 3d &
then gave way to Sr Rob
Aston.

Robert Hales cheif prior
of ye Kts of St John of the
Jerusalem was Treasurer
of England ye 4 th of Ri
chard ye 2d
Hugh Segrano was Ld
Treasurer of England
ye fifth of Rich: ye 2d
Robert walden was Ld
Treasurer of England
ye 12 th of Richard ye 2d
will: Scroope Earl of Wilts

Plate 2.10 Compiling usable lists from historical works exemplified in "a list of some of the Lords Treasurers of England," from Bodl. MS Rawl. D. 969, art. iv, fos. 56v–59r, an undated and anonymous historical notebook, principally relating to Kent, from the middle to late seventeenth century.

Behemoth, or the will of Henry VIII. Even Drayton's *Polyolbion* (rather lighter fare, despite Selden's erudite "illustrations" in which Prescott took a particular interest) seems like heavy going, verse or not.[117] But history, a major pastime of the elite in the eighteenth century and after, could be read in many ways. Prescott's experience suggests that the study of the past was already well on its way to being a leisurely recreation rather than the highly focused study practiced by Anthony Grafton and Lisa Jardine's Gabriel Harvey, or by William Sherman's John Dee,[118] and by many other readers of a century earlier.

DUDLEY RYDER AND THE SOCIAL USES OF HISTORY READING

As has been seen above, early modern readers preserved copious notes from historical works that they had bought or borrowed in commonplace books and sometimes in notebooks specifically devoted to historical matters; useful facts or quotations for memorization or writing could then be looked up, complete with chapter-and-verse references to an array of authors (plate 2.10). Some of this did indeed have practical purpose, but not necessarily the sort envisaged by a Dee or Harvey. A case in point, from much nearer the end of our period than the humanist Harvey, is that of the young law student Dudley Ryder, future Chief Justice of the King's Bench and peer of the realm (the latter for the briefest of moments, since he died of apoplexy in 1756 on learning of his advancement). The son of a Dissenting draper, Ryder was himself a nonconformist and whig who was obliged to seek his education at Edinburgh University. He kept a diary in 1715 and 1716, one of the explicit purposes of which was to record what he read every day and his moods on that day, so that he could review it later and "know what best suits my own temper." Most of all it would help him to remember what he read. The diary covers a much shorter span than Prescott's or Pepys', and is less fully packed with book titles, but it gives us a very good sense of what a young, ambitious law student thought he should read and how best to do so. An added benefit accrues from the fact that, like Pepys half a century earlier, Ryder wrote in shorthand, sharing with the Restoration diarist both a strong libido and a proclivity for hanging about with whores – though in Ryder's case a bit more nervously and confused by his infatuation for a tailor's daughter, Sally Marshall.[119] Again like Pepys, young Dudley read in a variety of contexts, at his lodgings, at booksellers' stands, and while traveling from place to place,

[117] *Diary of Henry Prescott*, II, 341, 377, 409, 419, 452, 454, 456, 476, 477, 536.

[118] William H. Sherman, *John Dee: The Politics of Reading and Writing in the English Renaissance* (Amherst, MA, 1995); cf Kevin Sharpe, *Reading Revolutions* (New Haven, 2000), which offers an extended study of another reader, Sir William Drake.

[119] *The Diary of Dudley Ryder 1715–1716*, ed. W. Matthews (1939), pp. 29 (n.d. 1715), 72 (8–9 August 1715), and 211 (3 April 1716).

taking Sallust's *Conspiracy of Catiline* – a topical book in the year of the Fifteen – to dinner one day, dipping back into it after practicing his viol another. Feeling ill after a bad night's sleep, he consoled himself by reading in both the poet Virgil and the modern *Universal History* by Perizonius.[120]

It is very tempting to see Dudley Ryder's repeated reading of Sallust as a later example of Harvey's serial glossing of Livy, and he admitted that he had no time for other pursuits, such as mathematics, because "reading the ancients" was of "more immediate service for me in my character of a lawyer."[121] Yet the circumstances and purposes of his reading were entirely different. Ryder was no Elizabethan humanist, Cambridge educated, devoted to making the lessons of history applicable to contemporary politics, whatever his interest in the law. His interest in reading in general, and history in particular, derived entirely from social concerns. Above all, the compulsively shy Dudley saw history as a great way to meet women. Anxious that he might not mate – "the having children is a kind of continuance and prolonging life into future ages and generations" – the young man was regrettably ill at ease around others, especially the female sex. Repeatedly lamenting his tongue-tiedness and inability to entertain women in his acquaintance, he resolved on an extensive reading programme to broaden his font of *bons mots*. This was Erasmus' notion of *copia* truly turned to the pursuit of Folly, and her ally History knocked down from the noble heights of the *magistra vitae* – or at least it was to give the term "mistress" a different meaning than either Cicero or Erasmus had intended.[122] Sometimes Ryder's tactics may not have worked: he read Burnet's *History of the Reformation* to the women at his lodging-house, though privately admitting that he found the bishop's style "too stiff and formal." At other times he resorted to spouting romance or to self-help books like the *Art of Pleasing Conversation*, in which he found a chapter "about the method of flattery and the manner of introducing and using it among the ladies." A pleasant walk with some ladies along the marsh at Hackney turned Ryder's conversation to love, his thoughts to "gallantry and knight-errantry and enchanted castles and cruel giants who barbarously treated the Fair," and his eyes away from Coke or Sallust in the direction of *The Adventures of Lindamira, a Lady of Quality*.[123] Above all, what he craved was *stories*, true or false, to be able to haul out of his mental bag of tricks at a moment's notice; his colorless and sketchy memories of a trip to

[120] Ibid., pp. 67 (3 August 1715), 70 (6 August 1715), 130 (3 November 1715, for his reading at the booksellers), 171 (23 January 1716). Sallust was a favorite of Ryder's; the next month he continued with the *Jugurthine War*: ibid., p. 92 (8 September 1715).

[121] Ibid., p. 150 (16 December 1715).

[122] Ibid., p. 92 (8 September 1715); p. 224 (20 April 1716).

[123] Ibid., p. 337 (27 September 1716), for his reading of De la Rivière Manley's *The Secret History of Queen Zarah and the Zarazians* (1705); ibid., pp. 209–10 (31 March and 1 and 2 April 1716); ibid., p. 357 (1 November 1716) for the *Art*.

Paris proving unequal to a witty conversation about France, for instance, he decided to refresh them by reading someone else's published travel accounts.[124]

Reading periodicals and his lawbooks helped somewhat, but the latter were dull and the former, especially his favorites, Addison and Steele, too familiar in his circles to impress anyone. Jealous of the local female mania for the charismatic Hackney preacher John Barker, Ryder went into London in April 1716, where the solution to his social angst finally hit him: it was history, ancient and modern that appeared to offer him the greatest chance at cultural literacy, an avenue to acquired civility that would produce promotion, honour, and, more urgently, sex. "I have a mind to read over the best classics and also gain a good knowledge of the history of England." That, plus a healthy dose of "our most polite authors" would improve his verbal and written style and give him much more to say in gentle company. He fretted that the demands of reading law reports, the overboiled veggies of his literary diet, would leave little time for the historical and literary dessert, but he finally managed to divide his day between morning pursuits of *lex angliae* and post-prandial perusals of lighter fare – in fact, the later in the day the lighter. "For reading the Roman authors I think the best time will be from about an hour after dinner till 5 or 6 o'clock" he thought, "and from that time till bed for English history and polite authors in English, because they are most proper to keep me awake, such as plays, romances, poetry, essays, anything of wit or humour or imagination." A few months later, his plan was not very far along – reading all those books could be difficult – and he sought a shortcut, or at least a head start. As luck would have it, he opened his closet and happened to see therein a copy of Samuel Pufendorf's *An introduction to the history of the principal kingdoms and states of Europe* (trans. 1695) and "it came into my head to make myself master of his account of England as a kind of an introduction into the study of our history. Began to read it." [125] Ryder never landed the fetching tailor's daughter, but he prospered as a lawyer and judge, and eventually married, producing a son and future earl. One likes to think that he ruled many a conversation in history along the way.

CHANGING NOTIONS OF THE USES OF HISTORY

There was a growing number of readers, like Dudley Ryder, for whom the acquisition of historical knowledge for its own sake (or for personal or social

---

[124] Ibid., p. 282 (23 July 1716); p. 297 (16 August 1716).

[125] Ibid., p. 219 (13 April 1716); p. 298 (18 August 1716). On 5 September 1716 (ibid., p. 313) he also started reading Rushworth's *Historical Collections*, but principally as a source for the legal case against ship money rather than for social intercourse.

utility) transcended any high moral purpose. This was especially true among the antiquaries, who were increasingly seeing their researches as an end in themselves, unlike their medieval and Renaissance predecessors. William Smith, for example, apologized for criticizing some of his friend John Strype's work, but added that this was necessary:

For I think one end of writing history as well as reading it, is to advance mens facultys, & to gain experience by their travells in this kind. And it is a difficult if not impossible attainment to improve in any kind of learning without casting an eye back & makeing some observations, where in they were formerly defective.[126]

This emphasis on "improving" historical learning is what seems most appealing to modern scholars interested in the origins of disciplines like history *as* disciplines. But even as late as 1700, this was still only a minority's sense as to what was truly important in writing or reading about the past. This chapter has suggested that the ways in which history was read, how it was selected, and the purposes behind its study could vary considerably, from an occasional activity of leisure to one of deep learning, from entertainment and social promotion to self-improvement. John Strype, like William Cave and Samuel Clark before him, would build his career on biographies of Tudor prelates, balancing recreation and duty in his judgment that "The reading the lives of eminent men is both pleasant and useful."[127]

By 1700 there are some subtle changes in the ways in which history is being conceptualized, or simply thought about, on a day-to-day basis. Although the past was by then still being turned to for didactic reasons, its examples are now figures and episodes *in* rather than *from* history; there is an awareness of different historical contexts, and a sense that the present comes from, rather than replicates, the past. This is best illustrated in the use of the word *history* as virtually a synonym for the past – as opposed to being a mere collective for "historians"; this usage becomes increasingly frequent in the second half of the seventeenth century, and by the early eighteenth it is commonplace.[128]

As a single example of this shift in attitude, we can offer one of the most prolific and articulate of literary figures in the Augustan age, Jonathan Swift. The one-time secretary to another genteel amateur history writer, Sir William Temple, Swift wrote an unfinished sequel to his master's *Introduction to the History of England*, getting as far as 1155 before other matters distracted

---

[126] CUL MS Mm.VI.49, fo. 23, Smith to Strype, 15 May 1701.
[127] *Letters of eminent men, addressed to Ralph Thoresby*, 2 vols. (1832), II, 77 (Strype to Thoresby, 4 November 1707).
[128] In his unpublished *Aretology*, written in the mid–1640s, Robert Boyle wrote that "History" (rather than historians or histories) bore witness to examples of heroic virtue long before the existence of books of ethics: *The Early Essays and Ethics of Robert Boyle*, ed. John T. Harwood (Carbondale and Edwardsville, IL, 1991), p. 54.

him.[129] Between 1710 and 1714, however, he coveted the post of Historiographer Royal. This was not an unrealistic hope, given that its first incumbents, James Howell, John Dryden, and Thomas Shadwell, had weak claims to the title of historian; only since 1690, with the appointment of the naturalist-topographer Robert Plot and then the antiquary Thomas Rymer, had the Crown seen fit to bestow the office on the basis of erudition.[130] It was, regrettably for Swift, about to stay in scholarly hands with the appointment of the eminent legal antiquary, Thomas Madox, and in any case Swift had a formidable, almost desperate, rival in the Harleian librarian and former draper's apprentice, Humfrey Wanley,[131] a brilliant palaeographer who may have lost out because of his low social origins and the waning fortunes of his patron, the earl of Oxford, at the end of the reign of Anne.

Although the Dean of St. Patrick's, Dublin, as Swift became in 1713, gave up his own plans to make himself the new Camden who would write of the glorious reign of Queen Anne (settling for just her last four years),[132] he continued through the rest of his career to read widely and to comment on matters historical, making him pretty typical of the well-educated, civilized reader with a strong interest in the past but little inclination to pursue its close study.[133] Swift consistently makes reference to historical persons and episodes in his prose writings, and frequently uses the word *History*, with a capital *H*. Take, for instance, his satirical treatment of political dissimulation in the *Examiner* in 1710:

Who first reduced *Lying* into an Art, and adapted it to *Politicks*, is not so clear from History; although I have made some diligent Enquiries: I shall therefore consider it

---

[129] Robert C. Steensma, "'So Ancient and Noble a Nation': Sir William Temple's History of England," *Neuphilologische Mitteilungen*, 77 (1976), 95–107; J. R. Moore, "Swift as Historian," *Studies in Philology*, 49 (1952), 583–604.

[130] D. R. Woolf, "Narrative Historiography in Restoration England: A Preliminary Survey," in W. G. Marshall (ed.), *The Restoration Mind* (Newark, DE, 1997), pp. 207–51; W. Maurer, "Dryden's Knowledge of Historians, Ancient and Modern," *Notes and Queries*, n.s. 6 (1959), 264–66, which article overrates Dryden's depth of historical learning.

[131] *Letters of Humfrey Wanley*, ed. P. L. Heyworth (Oxford, 1989), pp. 284, 286 (Wanley to Harley, 15 and 17 December 1713). The second, and angry, letter reveals that this was certainly Wanley's perception of his impending loss to some "man of great estate."

[132] Moore, "Swift as Historian," pp. 586–87; Harold Williams, "Jonathan Swift and *The Four Last Years of the Queen*," *The Library*, 4th series, 16 (1936), 61–90; J. W. Johnson, "Swift's Historical Outlook," *Journal of British Studies*, 4 (1965), 52–77. Swift's library also demonstrates a broad interest in history: W. LeFanu (ed.), *A Catalogue of Books Belonging to Dr. Jonathan Swift, Dean of St. Patrick's, Dublin, Aug. 19, 1715* (Cambridge, 1988) is a facsimile of Swift's collection just after he failed to become Historiographer Royal. It can be compared with the auction sale catalog of the dean's books assembled after his death to show that he continued to purchase histories on a variety of topics; this is in H. Williams (ed.), *Dean Swift's Library* (Cambridge, 1932).

[133] Johnson, "Swift's Historical Outlook," is the best attempt at a reconstruction of Swift's historical thought from a wide range of his writings.

only according to the modern System, as it hath been cultivated these twenty Years past in the Southern Part of our own Island.[134]

This is not a particularly imaginative, clever, or unusual passage. Indeed, one could almost open any book of Augustan prose polemic, or political poetry, or sermons, and pick a page at random with a reasonable prospect of finding something similar – Defoe's "History of Projects" beginning with Noah's ark and the Tower of Babel, for instance.[135] It is also a satirical passage, meant to make people laugh, and mocking those who study the past for the origins of the present rather than imitating them. But one or two significant things are going on in these lines, and elsewhere in the historicizing mind of the Augustans, that did not go on in the heads of their Renaissance predecessors. First, History is conceived as a whole, a font of information which needs to be read at length in order to be able to speak authoritatively on such an issue as "the origins of lying"; it is not sufficient to extract a few cautionary examples as illustrations of past liars. Secondly, it is the history of lying itself that is the theme of the passage, not "ye evyll fates of those who tell lyes" – Swift is not out simply to criticize the vice of lying as such. Indeed he continues in another paragraph by providing Lying with the paper authority that was by then *de rigeur* for any claim to antiquity, a genealogy.[136] Finally, having decided that the remoter reaches of the past are either obscure or too difficult to search over thoroughly, he departs from historical tradition altogether to consider lying in its "modern system," bespeaking a sense of period that may not be profound, but is certainly clear; it is the same sense that Sir Joshua Reynolds would make more explicit half a century later when he urged painters of scenes from antiquity not to introduce into their work anything that might "remind us of modern times."[137]

In another issue of the *Examiner*, published a week later, Swift describes how he goes about getting his information – where the apposite examples or "parallels" can be drawn, and what certain terms mean. Here, he cites the practice adopted by satirical writers of describing living people in an unlibelous fashion by referring to them as historical characters whom they may resemble in personality or deed. Swift calls this "looking into History for some Character bearing a Resemblance to the Person we would describe," and he cites a bad example, of a newspaper writer referring so vaguely to an English political figure as the "Constable of France" that Swift, the reader, cannot deduce whom is meant. In order to avoid replicating the error, Swift

---

[134] *The Examiner*, 14 (9 November 1710), in *The Prose Works of Jonathan Swift*, vol. III, ed. H. Davis (Oxford, 1940), iv, p. 9.

[135] Defoe, "The History of Projects," in *The Earlier Life and the Chief Earlier Works of Daniel Defoe*, ed. H. Morley (1889), p. 38.   [136] Ibid.

[137] "The mind is thrown back into antiquity, and nothing ought to be introduced that may tend to awaken it from the illusion." Joshua Reynolds, *Seven Discourses Delivered in the Royal Academy by the President* (1778), p. 182.

resolves to study history intensely for his parallels, but he soon discovers that the historians of the past, much less the characters, are not always willing to come when called.

> I have been for some Time consulting *Livy* and *Tacitus*, to find out the Character of a *Princeps Senatus*, a *Praetor Urbanus*, a *Quaestor Aerarius*, a *Caesari ab Epistolis*, and a *Proconsul*. But among the worst of them, I cannot discover One from whence to draw a Parallel, without doing Injury to a Roman Memory.[138]

Swift does make use of his reading: he describes in a line or two the career of Verres, the corrupt governor of Sicily, while meaning in fact the earl (later marquis) of Wharton, whig politician and lord-lieutenant of Ireland, who had once refused Swift the office of chaplain in his household. But he also recognizes that this type of historical personation, which is accompanied by the tantalizing "absolute Power of altering, adding or suppressing what Circumstances we please" so as to ease the fit of historical to contemporary,[139] does violence to both past and present. Elsewhere, Swift makes explicit comparisons between the 1711 attempt on the life of Sir Robert Harley, Tory Chancellor of the Exchequer, and various other historical assassinations from Julius Caesar to Henry III of France and the duke of Buckingham. Here, however, the lack of complete congruence between the present and the past is more helpful, for it allows Swift to dismiss his own examples as faulty, and thereby to demonstrate that the recent crime is "not to be paralleled by any of the like kind we meet with in History."[140] This is the same sort of hyperbole that, in a popular form, now attaches to the commonplace use of words like *classic* and *historic* to set things apart from events that have gone before, not to show their similarities.

The knowledge that the square peg of historical examples does not quite fit the round hole of present circumstances unless we shave a bit off the edges and use a cudgel to drive it home did not deter Swift or any other satirist from such carpentry: classical and historical comparisons with the present continue, inevitably, to pop into educated conversation to this day. But again it bespeaks an uneasy awareness of artifice and even dissimulation, a sense that no matter how true a history might be, it will lose its relevance the moment its subjects are brought into direct comparison with the present. This is the negative, skeptical side of the awakening sense of historical individuality, of the incommensurability of historical eras, that is most often associated with historicism, and there are hints of it much earlier than Vico and Herder. Francesco Guicciardini, for instance, had grasped the nettle at the very

---

[138] *The Examiner*, 17 (17 November 1710), in Swift, *Prose Works*, iv, pp. 26–27. [139] Ibid.
[140] *The Examiner*, 32 (15 March 1710/11), in Swift, *Prose Works*, iv, pp. 106–7. Cf. Swift's reactions, and references to Tacitus, in *The Correspondence of Jonathan Swift*, ed. H. Williams (5 vols., Oxford, 1963–65), I, 213, 219–20 (Swift to Archbishop William King, 8 March and 10 April 1711).

beginning of the sixteenth century. In his now familiar critique of Machiavelli's usage of *exempla*, Guicciardini owned up to worrying that the contingencies in one situation made it of limited applicability to the present or future. Nearly two centuries later, this was certainly the view of the young Robert Boyle, grandson of Guicciardini's Elizabethan translator Sir Geoffrey Fenton. Boyle thought that while princes might profit from reading the histories of neighboring states, ordinary men ought to study "cheeflyest their owne actions," there being the greatest conformity in that domain between past and future actions . He specifically repudiated reliance on history as a guide "because of the disparity both betwixt times and persons" and because "the omissions of hystory" have concealed many material circumstances surrounding actions, which one "must not be a Macchiavel that ignores."[141]

Guicciardini aside, the overwhelming majority of Renaissance writers of history used the past for contemporary commentary with few such reservations. England was no different in this respect than the continent. A narrative about the past could be used implicitly to criticize or praise the present, as in Bacon's *Henry VII*, with its extended analogy to James I, or Sir Robert Cotton's *Bildungsroman* on the reign of Henry III, which thoroughly twists the facts of that king's reign so as to offer mild criticism of the Buckingham influence at court. Another strategy involved extending the classical trope of prosopopoeia (literally "mask-making") and making the dead speak: the *Mirror for Magistrates* did this, harmlessly, in the mid-Tudor period, and a protestant polemicist such as Thomas Scott gave the device a political edge in the 1620s, as he resuscitated the ghosts of heroic Elizabethans to discuss among themselves the failure of James I's pacifist policies.[142]

Whatever the endurance of this literary tactic, it was certainly at its fag-end by the early eighteenth century, at which time we find it doubled, and satirized in this doubling, by the likes of Addison and Steele's Isaac Bickerstaff. In an issue of the *Tatler*, Bickerstaff records a dream – the unreality of the encounter with the past thus made explicit – wherein the heroes of the past are conducted to a hall of fame. They are led not by their own deeds but by the equally dead historians who have written about them; and the scene is amusing in another way as well, since Alexander the Great is nearly lured by Quintus Curtius into an apartment of "fabulous heroes" before he and his

---

[141] Guicciardini, *Maxims and Reflections of a Renaissance Statesman (Ricordi)*, trans. Mario Domandi (New York, 1965), pp. 39, 69, 71, 77; *The Early Essays and Ethics of Robert Boyle*, ed. John T. Harwood (Carbondale and Edwardsville, IL, 1991), p. 207. The partial catalog of Boyle's books that Harwood includes as an appendix, with only a dozen works of history in 699 items (and those mainly to do with religious or ecclesiastical history) suggests that Boyle's interest in reading history did not increase as he aged: ibid., pp. 249–81.

[142] For Scott, see my "Two Elizabeths? James I and the Late Queen's Famous Memory," *Canadian Journal of History*, 20 (1985), 167–91; for Cotton, see Kevin Sharpe, *Sir Robert Cotton, 1586–1631: History and Politics in Early Modern England* (Oxford, 1979).

honor, in the form of a jeopardized historicity, are rescued by some "real" historians" headed by the worthy figure of Arrian.[143]

The reading of history took place in a wide variety of contexts, and for all the classical rhetoric surrounding its dignity and moral effectiveness, those contexts were not uniformly serious. The Tudor chroniclers, as we saw in the previous chapter, stressed the usefulness of the information they purveyed to readers, but much of this did not meet with the approval of the humanist historians and critics – Edmund Bolton, Henry Savile, and Degory Wheare – who succeeded them. In the seventeenth century, especially after 1640, the types of history broadened considerably, with the most dignified translation of Thucydides and the most light-hearted romance or chapbook equally laying claim to the title of "history." This has often been seen as simple generic confusion, or as an instance of the determination of fiction writers to have their works treated with the same gravity as the historians, a trend that continued with the novel in the eighteenth century. But perhaps the distinction between fiction and history, between entertainment and "serious" writing is itself a false polarity. The examples of reading in this chapter demonstrate that it is not always possible to put history in the "serious" category, as something studied in pious silence for uplifting purposes, regardless of the Ciceronian commonplaces that continued to be repeated. Perhaps what is most noticeable is that historical discourse was increasingly a key part of sociable relations, including casual conversation, playfulness and courtship, human interactions that run a gamut of feeling from the sublime to the ridiculous, and which embrace an even wider range of conversational contexts from the political and economic to the sexual and drunken. The eighteenth century would see history assume an increasingly important role in the socialization of both young men and young women. The gendered character of this phenomenon is much too complex to be dealt with in passing here,[144] though the end of the process is readily visible in early nineteenth-century novels such as Elizabeth Hamilton's *Memoirs of Modern Philosophers* and, more famously, Jane Austen's *Northanger Abbey*. In 1730 most of that lay ahead, and beyond the chronological scope of this study, which must now venture in a different direction. Having now sketched the "how" and "why" of history reading, we return in the next two chapters to the matter of *what* histories people had available to them and how many of them ended up, read or unread, on the shelves of private and institutional libraries.

---

[143] Steele and Addison as Bickerstaff, in *The Tatler*, 81 (15 October 1709), ed. George Aitken (4 vols., 1898–9), II, 227–231.

[144] I have addressed the subject at length in my essay, "A Feminine Past? Gender, Genre, and Historical Knowledge in England, 1500–1800," *American Historical Review*, 102.3 (June 1997), 645–79.

3

The ownership of historical works

Having asked how early modern people were reading their history books, we are faced with a further question: how widely diffused was historical knowledge in printed form? The prima facie answer would appear to be "not very" in 1500, "rather more" a century later, and "a great deal" a hundred years later still. Evaluating the spread of historical knowledge through print is a tricky matter, compounded by the wide range of sources available, not all of which are equally suited to every purpose. It would be helpful, however, to know more precisely what sort of works came into private hands, how they moved in and out of circulation through lending, purchase, and inheritance, and – of no small consequence – how much they cost. The questions of acquisition, storage, circulation, distribution, and price will be handled in subsequent chapters; the present addresses itself specifically to the ownership of books by individuals.

HISTORY BOOK OWNERSHIP: THE EVIDENCE OF WILLS AND INVENTORIES

Two obvious but hitherto underexploited sources for evaluating the historical content in the parlors and closets of the literate Tudor and Stuart man or woman are wills, together with the inventories that often survive with them, and private library lists or catalogs. Wills and inventories are more difficult to use, because although a vast number survive, the great majority offer no specific information on book titles owned. Random samplings of wills, while immensely useful to the historian of material culture interested in the objects people owned, tend to be a frustrating exercise in haystack searching for those interested in finding particular sorts of items, books included; the needles are scarcer still if one is hunting for particular types of book. In one study, Peter Clark examined 2,771 Kentish wills from Canterbury, Faversham, and Maidstone and found evidence of book ownership in general rising above 40 percent in all three towns, with two of every three gentlemen owning a book of some sort in the last twenty years before the civil war.

References to specific titles other than the Bible were considerably less common (only about a quarter of the whole sample). Nevertheless Clark was still able to categorize the more complete references, finding the Bible and other religious works near the top, several instances of Foxe's *Acts and Monuments* close behind, but other history books, chronicles included, "many furlongs behind."[1]

On the other hand, thanks to the indexing performed by many local record offices and major research libraries, it is often possible to find particular wills and inventories that mention books by title. Bibliographical scholars such as Dr. Elisabeth Leedham-Green have gathered together the wills and inventories administered by the institutions, such as Cambridge University, where large concentrations of books are more likely to be found.[2] Even outside such a rich vein as the university, wills alone can tell us to whom a book was left, and sometimes whence the owner acquired it. The promising young medieval scholar Henry Wharton, who died at the age of thirty in 1695, left his large collection of printed books to his father, Edmund, also a clergyman, for the duration of the older man's life, after which they were to pass to Gonville and Caius College, Cambridge; Wharton excepted from this provision the books that he had received as a gift from his father in the first place. Like most wills wherein books are mentioned generically, Wharton's tells us something about the nature of the collection and where it probably ended up, while giving little specific detail on the type of books, though in Wharton's case – he was a prolific author and editor of medieval texts – we can infer that a significant number pertained to ecclesiastical history.[3] Reference in a will to a particular book can indicate a special interest in it on the part of either donor or heir. In 1599 Richard Roberts of Sheffield gave "the booke of Chronicles which he haith of myne" to a friend, who had borrowed it previously.[4] William Fyshe, merchant, of Scarborough, left his own Holinshed's *Chronicles* to his son Robert while dividing all his other books among his several

---

[1] Peter Clark, "The Ownership of Books in England, 1560–1640: the Example of some Kentish Townsfolk," in *Schooling and Society*, ed L. Stone (Baltimore, 1976), pp. 95–111, quotation at p. 103. A similar survey for the end of the seventeenth century by Ian Maxted, based on a much smaller sample of Devon inventories, found that the proportion of book-owning households was approaching 50 percent by 1700: I. Maxted, " '4 Rotten Cornbags and Some Old Books': the Impact of the Printed Word in Devon," in Robin Myers and Michael Harris (eds.), *Sale and Distribution of Books from 1700* (Oxford, 1982), pp. 37–76, at p. 57.

[2] E. Leedham-Green, *Books in Cambridge Inventories: Book-lists from Vice-Chancellor's Court Probate Inventories in the Tudor and Stuart Periods* (2 vols., Cambridge, 1986), hereafter referred to as *BICI*.

[3] CKS, Maidstone, PRC 32/56/351, will of Henry Wharton. The books did not, in the end, get to the college; I am grateful to Mr. Gordon Hunt, sublibrarian of Gonville and Caius College, for searching the college records on my behalf for evidence of the bequest.

[4] Borth. Register of wills, York Diocese, 1598–99, 27B, fo. 631v (Richard Roberts, proved 10 July 1599).

sons.[5] Thomas Hall, clerk, of Langtoft, gave several books to his heirs, including the "Book of Martyrs" bestowed on his son Ralph.[6]

Probate inventories are more helpful as to the composition of libraries, though they frequently will say only that "books" were among a decedent's goods, and estimate their value, not always very carefully. Even where a more precise notation is made of the books in a study or closet, there remain problems of identification. Nevertheless, many inventories do exist that give sufficient detail on books to allow some preliminary generalizations to be made, at least concerning the top 10 percent of society. The extensive work done by historians of material culture and the growth of a consumer economy in the latter part of the early modern period can provide some background, though it is normally not genre-specific.[7] Richard Harrison of Lichfield, "clerk" (d. 1676) owned £160 of furnishings in an inventory the total worth of which was £400: his study held books valued at £50, and in his hall he had "A Bible and stand and Booke of Martyrs" together worth fourteen shillings.[8] Insofar as they were luxuries in any form, books were less socially specific than other nonessentials, in the sense that they can be found in inventories at virtually all social levels.[9] Once one discriminates among subjects and even formats (folios versus duodecimos or chapbooks, for example) then a good deal more social differentiation is to be expected.

Although there are exceptions in both periods, the average size of the historical component in private libraries represented in inventories was much more extensive in the seventeenth century than in the sixteenth.[10] The over-

---

[5] Borth. Wills P.25B, fos. 813, 815r (William Fyshe, proved 9 March 1592).

[6] Borth. Dean and Chapter of York wills, 1557–1638, vol. V, fo. 246v (Thomas Hall, proved July 1620).

[7] Lorna Weatherill, *Consumer Behaviour and Material Culture in Britain, 1660–1760* (London and New York, 1988), pp. 43, 50. In Weatherill's analysis of several thousand inventories, books were three times as common in London as in northeast of England. London ranked fourth in book ownership in the late seventeenth century, but was "clearly ahead" by 1705. Sorting by occupation, books appeared as frequently in rural as in urban *trade* inventories, p. 79.

[8] Ibid., p. 181. Lower levels of books in inventories in 1720s Worcestershire than in 1669–70 suggests not that consumption had dropped but that the source, inventories, began to account for books under the more general rubric of household items. Carole Shammas has rightly cautioned against overgeneralizing about regional and chronological changes at the present, since statistically insignificant numbers can often mask wider book ownership than appears in the documents: *The Preindustrial Consumer in England and America* (Oxford, 1990), p. 111.

[9] This was David Levine and Keith Wrightson's finding in their study of Whickham: books are only in one-sixth of all inventories, but at all social levels. *The Making of an Industrial Society* (Oxford, 1991), p. 235.

[10] My conclusions are reinforced by the library lists being published in Professor R. J. Fehrenbach's and Dr. Elisabeth Leedham-Green's series Private Libraries in Renaissance England (hereafter PLRE). I am very grateful to Dr. Leedham-Green for information on the project, and to Professor Fehrenbach for providing me with a machine-readable chronological list of several catalogs not yet in print at the time of writing, such as those of Bishop Richard Cox and Sir Edward Dering, with historical items separated out.

whelming majority of books in early Tudor wills are religious,[11] except in concentrated scholarly communities such as Oxford and Cambridge, and within the professions, especially lawyers and physicians. The inventory of books belonging to Thomas Goldstone, prior of Christchurch, Canterbury, during the reign of Henry VII, contained seventeen volumes, which were almost exclusively religious together with a few rhetorical works.[12] The 36-volume collection of the Leicestershire lawyer Sir Roger Townshend (d. 1500) is exceptional in that it included at least two medieval chronicles (one of these in manuscript), an Alexander romance, and a number of religious biographies and hagiographies.[13] In contrast, the Tudor Cambridge inventories assembled by Dr. Leedham-Green reveal a high number of historical works, preponderantly by classical authors. Later in the sixteenth century the identifiable book references in wills are easier to find, even in more remote locations. John Auston (d. 1574), the minister of Addington, left fifty-eight books dispersed through his hall and several other rooms, but the historical content was small: one unspecified "historia scholastica," probably the medieval text on biblical history and genealogy by Peter Comestor, and a "historia ecclesiastica" (most likely Eusebius), valued at 6d.[14] Similarly, the twenty books of John Mulcaster, a borderer who died in 1594, included "1 booke intituled Polidorus Virgilius in Latten." References by author alone are problematic and in this case, the low valuation of 8d makes it very likely that the work referred to was not the *Anglica historia* but Vergil's much better known, and cheaper, *De rerum inventoribus*.[15]

By the mid-1600s, in comparison, most middling to large collections of books (a mid-sized collection being taken in this study as 500 to 2,000 titles, and a large one anything above that) would have somewhere between 8 and 10 percent historical works, excluding fictional works and romances entitled

[11] Ida Darlington (ed.), *London Consistory Court Wills, 1492–1547* (London Rec. Soc., 1967), *passim*. Compare the history-less inventories of the Tudor and Jacobean Worcestershire gentry with the inventories of Thomas Vernon Esq. of Hanbury Hall (1708 and 1721) and Nicholas Lord Lechmere of Evesham at Hanley Castle (1727). The Vernon 1708 list contains 122 volumes of which 26 (13 distinct single or multivolume works) are histories. The Lechmere list has 154 volumes of which 35 titles (several in more than one volume) are histories ranging from Camden's *Britannia* (1610) and other Jacobean works to the *Acts and Monuments* (1684 edn) and a few later works. *Inventories of Worcestershire Landed Gentry 1537–1786*, ed. Malcolm Wankyn, Worcestershire Hist. Soc., n.s. 16 (1998), pp. 321, 334, 416–19.   [12] Hist. MSS Comm., *Var. Coll.*, I, pp. 224–25.

[13] C. E. Moreton, "The 'Library' of a Late-Fifteenth-Century Lawyer," *The Library*, 6th series 13 (1991), 338–46. The chronicles, identified tentatively by Moreton, are Werner Rolewinck's *Fasciculus temporum*, a world chronicle from Creation to the 1470s, and a manuscript of Trivet's *Annales*, listed as "a rede boke of cronycles of kyng Edward le fyste."

[14] Cumbria RO, P.1574 (Auston), will and inventory of John Auston. It is clear from the disposition of the books in the house, and not altogether surprising since he was a cleric, that Auston kept his religious books close at hand, in his chamber, while the few nonreligious items, including the ecclesiastical history, were demoted to the hall and, one presumes, less constant use.   [15] Cumbria RO, P.1594 (Mulcaster).

"histories." Like most averages, this is of limited use and at best provisional. The variance on either side could be considerable, and even the exclusion of fiction from the count is problematic given the reluctance of some owners to make such a distinction themselves.[16] When the third earl of Essex died in 1646, for instance, his library of 155 print or manuscript volumes contained ten works entitled "histories," all in English, of which three were fictions – Huon of Bordeaux, Palmerin of England, and Amadis of Gaul. These were listed together (an indication of the survival of chivalric interests, at least in the case of this old civil war general) with Eusebius, Tacitus' *Histories*, Louis Turquet de Mayerne's *General History of Spain*, Polybius, Ammianus Marcellinus, Jean de Serres' *History of France*, and Richard Verstegan's *Restitution of Decayed Intelligence*.[17]

A survey of a number of small libraries (or subsets of libraries, since many owners kept books in more than one residence) provides a better illustration of the diffusion of history books than can an arithmetic mean, and more clues to the particular tastes of the owner. Of the small collection of sixty-four books that Sir George Etherege the dramatist is known to have read while in diplomatic exile in Ratisbon in the 1680s, eleven were historical, the largest category other than plays and literature.[18] The personal library of Lady Margaret Heath, wife of Sir Robert, the Caroline judge, was kept in her closet and included eighty-three titles. These were principally religious and herbal works in folio or quarto, but she also owned an octavo "History of the latter times of the Jewes" (Josippon's *The Wonderful and Most Deplorable history of the latter times of the Jews*), a quarto *Short History of the Anabaptists* (the brief work first published anonymously in London in 1642), *Dodona's Grove*, James Howell's historical allegory of the years leading up to the civil war; and Thomas Heywood's biography of *England's Elizabeth*.[19]

---

[16] This figure is based on my assessment of approximately 100 manuscript library lists and probate inventories containing itemized books, in the second half of the seventeenth and early eighteenth century. The figure is for the moment provisional, and should not be taken as more than a crude estimate, subject to wide variation. A library list that I have not personally surveyed but that nevertheless comes in with a similar percentage of histories is that of John Bowes, the Durham cleric, whose 46 books on history and politics amount to 8.3b percent of his total of 535 books: see David Pearson, "The Library of John Bowes of Durham," *Book Collector* 35 (1986), 475–93. It should be pointed out that some major libraries could come in well below that figure: John Locke's library of 3,641 volumes, on one count, contained only 127 titles in history and biography, or 5.1% percent but precise comparisons between studies are difficult since its editors do not include antiquarian works under "history" (a further twenty-five titles are indexed as "antiquities," like Budé's *De asse* [Lyon, 1550] or Jean Poldo d'Albenas' *Discours historial de l'antique et illustre cité de Nismes* [Lyon, 1559]): John Harrison and Peter Laslett, *The Library of John Locke* (2nd edn, Oxford, 1971), pp. 18–19 and appendix V, pp. 292–308.

[17] BL MS Add. 46189, fos. 155v–158, inventory of goods of Robert, earl of Essex.

[18] See P. Beal, " 'The Most Constant and Best Entertainment': Sir George Etherege's Reading in Ratisbon", *The Library*, 6th series, 10 (1988), 122–44.

[19] BL MS Add. Egert. 2983, fo. 79.

John Nidd, a fellow of Trinity College, Cambridge was principally interested in medical and alchemical subjects, yet the 287 books in a catalog which he himself compiled shortly before his death in 1659 include ten historical items, mainly in Latin or English.[20] When Charles Squire was ejected from Peterhouse for scandalous conduct in 1699, he took much of the college plate with him but left behind ten shillings worth of books, twenty items in all. These included John Selden's *Analecton Anglo-Britannicon libro duo* and Edward Cooke's *History of the Succession of the Kings of England*.[21] The forty-three titled books of the Durham scholar and musician Marmaduke Peart (d. 1658) included only a quarto "Ecclesiasticall History" and a set of lives of the primitive fathers, both probably works by Samuel Clarke.[22] The sixty-seven books of Thomas Harneis, listed in the memorandum book of his friend, Robert Sampson, rector of Cuxwold, included Fuller's *Church-history of Britain*, "The history of England by Foxe" (undated, and, probably an abridgment of the *Acts and Monuments*), and "an hystorical description of the island of Britain."[23]

Given the increasing involvement of the clergy in historical and especially antiquarian research in the second half of the seventeenth century, it is surprising how often clerical collections show little sign of history book ownership. The Reverend Robert Lowther of Carlisle, who died in 1670, possessed no historical books among the nine personal and several borrowed volumes found by his executors. Similarly, the will of Hugh Halswell, rector of Cheriton, proved in 1671, bequeathed to several friends in Somerset and Hampshire his few books, specified in a codicil, all of which were on theological or religious subjects.[24] The very small personal library of Edward Platt, a clergyman in the parish of Graveney, Kent, who died in late 1659 or early 1660, contained only forty-nine books, according to its inventory, of which the sole historical items (in addition to some books of statutes) were a copy of Suetonius and a by-then very old work, Bishop Cooper's edition of Thomas Lanquet's chronicle. Since Lanquet and Cooper's chronicle had not been reprinted since 1565, we can infer that Platt, who was plainly no collector of antiquarian books, had received his copy as a gift, or perhaps

---

[20] The historical items include Ammianus Marcellinus, Johann Carion's *Chronicle*, Guicciardini's *La Historia d'Italia*, Lucan's *Pharsalia*, Francis Godwin's *A catalogve of the bishops of England*, Jean Bodin's *Methodus*, Diogenes Laerius' *De vitis philosophorum*, selections from Machiavelli, Johann Alsted's *Thesaurus chronologiae*, and (in English) Herbert of Cherbury's *The life and raigne of King Henry the Eighth*. These were all in the selection of his books that Nidd bequeathed to his friend William Lynnett, a fellow of Trinity: *BICI*, I, no. 195.
[21] *BICI*, I, no. 197.
[22] Durham UL, Durham Probate Records, Marmaduke Peart, Inventory 1658: Peart also had "a hundred twenty small bookes" valued at £1 10s, but given his occupation these may have been music books.   [23] BL MS Add. 4348, fos. 22v–23v, dated *ca.* 1703–17.
[24] Cumbria RO, P.1670/Robert Lowther; Hants. RO, 103M 87/1, will of Hugh Halswell, 14 February 1671.

inherited it.[25] The smallness of Platt's library contrasts strikingly with the collection assembled in the early eighteenth century by John Lister (1660–1735), the pluralist rector of Rochford and vicar of Carewdon. The 715 works he purchased for his own use from the London printer, William Bowyer (presumably not the only books he owned) were overwhelmingly religious, but one can also count twenty historical items among them. These, too, tended to be on sacred or ecclesiastical history, though there were some more exotic titles, such as a 1716 *Catalogue of Medals from Julius Caesar to the Emperor Heraclius*, Nathaniel Salmon's *Roman Stations in Britain* (1726) and David Durand's French *Histoire du seizième siècle* (1725–26), in serialized numbers. As Maslen has pointed out in analyzing Lister's library, the parson was "creating an instrument of work, not a collection of best books."[26]

As clerical libraries were biased in the direction of religious, theological, and controversial materials, so lawyers' libraries were preponderantly filled with legal texts. An inventory of the goods of Lord Chief Justice Sir Henry Pollexfen, compiled on his death in 1691, included 326 books. Again, however, there was also a solid core of historical works, twenty-one in all, the largest category of works other than law.[27] An inventory taken in 1658 of the twenty-seven books in the possession of Sir Edmund Bacon also included a significant number of legal texts, two bibles, and three histories: Bacon's *Henry VII*, an octavo *History of France*, and an edition of Plutarch, as well as some other works touching on history, such as Henry Peacham's *Compleat Gentleman*, with its chapters on history and antiquities, "Speed's maps" (either Speed's *Theater of the Empire of Great Britain* or his *A prospect of the most famous parts of the world*) and "two bookes of the histories of kalenders."[28]

[25] CKS, Maidstone, PRC 11/22/53, inventory of Edward Platt of Graveney, 30 January 1659/60.

[26] Keith Maslen and John Lancaster, *The Bowyer Ledgers: the Printing Accounts of William Bowyer, Father and Son Reproduced on Microfiche: with a Checklist of Bowyer Printing 1699–1977* (London and New York, 1991), app. 2, pp. 411–46; K. Maslen, "Parson Lister's Library," *Transactions of the Cambridge Bibliographical Society*, 9 (1987), 155–73, quotation at p. 160.

[27] Devon RO, 346M/F495, pp. 17–26. The twenty-one historical items listed, without information on value or date of edition, were: John Selden, *The History of Tithes*; an unidentified volume of "Secrett historyes"; Foxe's *Acts and Monuments* in 3 vols. (probably the widely used 1641 edition); two copies of Machiavelli's *History of Florence*, one specified as being in Latin and one in either Italian or English (unspecified); Rushworth's *Historical Collections* (vols. I and II only); Rycaut's *History of the Turks*; the second part of Burnet's *History of the Reformation*; Knolles' *General History of the Turks*; Thomas Hobbes' translation of Thucydides; Nathaniel Brent's English translation of Sarpi's *History of the Council of Trent*; a history of the civil wars of France (probably Davila); Peter Heylyn's *Ecclesia restavrata, or, the History of the Reformation of the Church of England* and *Cyprianus Anglicus* (his life of Archbishop Laud); Tacitus' *Germania*; Bodin's *Six Books of a Common weal*, in Richard Knolles' translation; James Howell's *Lustra Ludovici*, or life of Louis XIII; an unspecified history of the Low Countries; and Camden's *Britannia*.   [28] BL MS 39244, fos. 24v–25r.

A more systematic analysis of a number of Cambridge inventories, mainly from the sixteenth and early seventeenth centuries, will provide a solid baseline against which to evaluate shifts in interest over the hundred or so years thereafter. Inventories of any kind must be used with caution in almost any circumstances.[29] When one is studying them for the purpose of evaluating personal libraries, this is especially true. Even assuming that most appraisers took some care in writing down their sums (and we know from simple addition that many did not), books are not staples, and appraisers who were cavalier when estimating the worth of commonplace items like bedsheets and clothing could be notoriously so when dealing with an unfamiliar volume. This risk increases when one is dealing with Latin, Greek, or foreign works whose value would simply be beyond the powers of many appraisers to estimate with any reasonable accuracy.

Such problems are mitigated, if not altogether eliminated, in the extensive run of inventories presented in the Vice-Chancellor's probate court from the 1520s until the early seventeenth century. These documents list the goods of deceased members of the university (including servants, also under the "privilege" of the university) and offer a good indication of the breadth of university reading in the sixteenth century.[30] Because the appraisers were most often booksellers themselves, and because the same appraisers were used time and again, often for a period of several years, four of them for two decades each, some greater faith can be placed in their estimates of an individual's library than would usually be the case.

A little later in this chapter, we will use the inventories to construct a profile of the popularity of particular historical authors, especially classical ones, in the sixteenth and early seventeenth centuries. For now, it is worth

[29] Leedham-Green, *BICI*, index. Dr. Leedham-Green's own subject index follows Gesner's sixteenth-century topics, and is not mutually exclusive (that is, the same title may be in more than one heading). Although I have not used it in determining categories in my own analysis of the data, it is interesting that 352 names fall under history (some under generic titles like "Chronicles" or "Spain"). There are more under history than law, grammar, rhetoric, poetry or politics, but less than in medicine, philosophy, and especially theology (by far the biggest category at about 1,200 authors). One or two points about the lists and assumptions made in analyzing them should be made here: the inventories contained in *BICI* were compiled mainly by stationers and booksellers; and very few libraries had any significant number of books in manuscript, though there are exceptions. Many books were clearly second-hand and show up in more than one inventory: some sold from one seller to another. Others were bequeathed from one owner to the next – a warning against equating the number of mentions of a title with the availability within the areas of multiple copies at the same time. Booksellers, several of whose inventories are included here, sold used copies as well as new ones; the occurrence of multiple copies in tutors' libraries suggests they were lent out to students. Age differences appear to matter a great deal in size and content of libraries. Some history authors, such as Livy, Caesar, and Thucydides, were primarily used for teaching rhetoric. There is also, interestingly, no evidence that antiquarian, as opposed to narrative history, books were shelved differently, in contrast to the very clear distinction between history and antiquities that had been made from as early as the mid-Elizabethan era.

[30] Although the latest inventory is from 1760, very few date from after 1610, the Vice-Chancellor's probate court having been used less and less after that date.

examining the inventories themselves to see what information can be gleaned about the place of history in the Tudor scholar's library. Some qualifications of this exercise are in order. First, the court's jurisdiction was never universal (increasingly less so from late in the 1500s), and the surviving inventories are patchy from decade to decade. They become highly sporadic after 1600, with few surviving beyond that date. So we shall have to look elsewhere for the seventeenth and early eighteenth centuries, and should not assume that even the relative fullness of lists for a decade like the 1550s offers an accurate *upper* number of the ownership of historical works. Secondly, several individual inventories are faulty in some particular aspect. Those with a large number of prices missing have therefore not been used to calculate decadal values (though they can be used for other purposes, such as estimating the popularity of individual authors). Those inventories that have been identified as pertaining to deceased booksellers have also been discounted, so far as book totals are concerned (but not, again, in dealing with the ownership of particular historical authors). Booksellers' stocks, while far from immune from changing tastes, were nevertheless dictated by other than pedagogical concerns. Thirdly, the size of libraries, and the format and value of individual books in each library, varies to such a degree that any attempt at working out an "average" book price would almost certainly be meaningless; some attempt is made instead to gauge the size and value of libraries as a whole, and to give a *range* of prices, high and low, assigned to particular books. Finally, it would be unwise to leap from evidence of the inventories to conclusions about the personal preferences of individuals, especially where other sources are available. The inventory of John Caius, whose interest in the age and antiquities of Cambridge erupted into a controversy with the same-named Thomas Caius (or Key) of Oxford, lists only two works, neither of which is historical, but that is in large measure because Caius left Cambridge a year before his death in 1573, taking the vast majority of his books with him; it is certainly not because he had no interest in history.

With such limitations and cautions in mind, we can confine ourselves to an analysis of the inventories in terms of the number of historical (here including biographical and antiquarian works) listed, the total number of works listed, and the percentage of works that are histories, totaling each figure for every decade from 1530 to 1609.

The sharp rise in total values in the 1580s is largely illusory, for in 1589 there died Andrew Perne, master of Peterhouse and dean of Ely, the owner of one of the largest libraries of his time. Perne had some 2,585 titles valued at £352 3s 4d, of which 282 (11 percent) were histories of various sorts, from the commonplace Caesar, Aelian, and Suetonius to more recent items like the expensive *Magdeburg Centuries*, worth some £3. Perne owned a copy (and

Table 3.5. *Value (by decade) of books in Cambridge inventories*

Decade	Number of inventories in decade	Value of history titles £ s d	Value of all books in decade inventories £ s d	Value of history to all books as percentage
1530–39	5	4-6-0	41-16-2	10
1540–49	37	9-7-8	138-10-8	7
1550–59	64	24-12-6	355-12-7	7
1560–69	24	18-8-0	256-17-8	7
1570–79	9	3-3-4	60-6-5	5
1580–89	16	51-4-9	554-14-4	9
1590–99	9	6-14-5	143-14-4	5
1600–9	9	1-19-9	72-11-5	1

sometimes more than one) of a good third of all the titles mentioned in the Cambridge inventories. Yet his library, if it distorts the totals for the 1580s, does not much change the proportional value of histories for that decade. Outsized as Perne's library may have been, his near 11 percent historical holdings is not wildly out of proportion with the other inventories of the 1580s, a decade in which historical interest at Cambridge is known from qualitative evidence to have increased, hand in hand with the popularity of foreign manuals like Jean Bodin's *Methodus*, of which Perne appears to have owned two copies, one quarto and one octavo.

Table 3.5 well reveals the limitations of the evidence, most strikingly the great variation from decade to decade in the number of inventories. The most interesting pattern suggested here is a rather unexpected *decline* in the relative value of history books as compared with all others, and their proportion to all books, in the 1590s and 1600s. Table 3.6 gives, without monetary value, the proportion of each decade's collective inventories (again excluding flawed items and booksellers' inventories) that consists of historical titles. This table more or less confirms the picture given in table 3.5, complete with the decline in percentages (of books this time, not money values) after 1589.

We cannot really ask whether Tudor Cantabrigians were *buying* more or less history since ownership does not equate with purchase: many items in one inventory appear later on in other inventories, the same copy of a book often reaching successive owners through bequest rather than purchased new or even second-hand. But does this mean that individuals on the whole owned fewer, rather than more, historical titles than in the middle years of the sixteenth century? Qualitative evidence suggests otherwise: the 1580s was the decade of Camden and the enlarged edition of Holinshed, a decade

Table 3.6. *History books in the Cambridge inventories; histories and other titles*

Decade	Number books	Number of histories	Percentage of histories
1530–39	529	37	7
1540–49	2575	137	5
1550–59	3359	229	7
1560–69	1149	121	11
1570–79	317	25	8
1580–89	4532	334	7
1590–99	1484	69	5
1600–9	617	23	4

just before the advent of the Shakespearian history plays and of the "parasite genres" discussed in chapter 1. We therefore must consider other explanations – beyond the obvious one that the inventories themselves are too patchy for the later decades to bear much weight as evidence of historical tastes.[31] The first is simply that there were now so many copies circulating in a relatively closed environment such as Cambridge, and especially in college libraries (which do not feature here), that individual *ownership* of texts of all kinds, not just histories, was declining. Yet the reverse of this is also true, that many owners had two or more copies, often of different editions, of the same title, lending them out to pupils if they were teaching fellows. Better explanations can be found. Certain of the ancient historians – Sallust, Livy, Caesar, Quintus Curtius – were now so familiar within the curriculum that they may have eluded valuers; while classical historians of more recent popularity, for instance Tacitus, had not yet made their way into cheap editions widely distributed. This explanation is confirmed by a glance at the popularity of individual authors in the inventories: there is only one copy of any work of Tacitus listed before the late 1580s (in an anonymous inventory dating before 1558), while occurrences of Caesar's *Commentaries*, immensely commonplace before 1589, decline thereafter.

What we *can* see in the Cambridge inventories is that at the university writings on medieval and modern history steadily increased in popularity in the second half of the sixteenth century and into the seventeenth. This is in part in response to the increased production of such works – the previously discussed "boom" in the production of English chronicles from the 1550s to the 1580s. But the influence from writer to reader was not in one direction,

---

[31] The relative scarcity of inventories from the 1570s, 1590s, and 1600s, in comparison with the cornucopia of the 1550s and 1580s, suggests the need for extreme caution here.

and the production of more, or fewer, titles in a genre was dictated by readers' interests at least as much as the other way around.

If the inventories are a reliable index, then the size and composition of Cambridge libraries could vary enormously according to profession, wealth and, in the case of teaching fellows, pedagogical responsibilities. The first inventory to include "historiographi" as a separate item was that of Edward Moore (d. 1539), fellow of St. Catherine's College, but his inventory is unusual for the degree to which it is arranged in categories, rather than by size; Moore's historians included Livy, Sallust, Diodorus Siculus, Suetonius, and a "fragmentum commentariorum Cesaris."[32] Eleven items out of his total of just over 100 are historical, including some not counted under "historiographi." That is a respectable proportion at this early date, but not very surprising in view of the prominence of historians as texts for the teaching of grammar and rhetoric. Another early case, that of the Yorkshire-man Geoffrey Blythe, includes twenty-seven historical titles out of 191 listed items. But most owners had fewer histories and a great many had none: isolated copies of Lucius Florus or Sallust dot early lists dominated by theological and grammatical works. Alice Edwards, widow, one of the few women whose goods were surveyed by the Vice-Chancellor's court, left fifteen named titles (plus some "olde bookes in the stodye") in 1546, inherited from her husband, David, an MD and fellow of Corpus, who had predeceased her in 1542; these were primarily works of grammar and religion, and there is not a single item of history.[33]

In the mid-1540s there appear the first signs of interest in post-classical history, with editions of Higden's *Polychronicon* and – soon to be an ubiquitous favorite – Johannes Carion's *Chronicle*. But the first really substantial private collection in Cambridge of English historical books, or even works about English history written in Latin (from Bede to Polydore Vergil) appears to have been that of the erstwhile heretic turned conservative bishop, Nicholas Shaxton. At his death in 1556, Shaxton left (in addition to Latin authors such as Eusebius), copies of then more exotic fare: Hector Boece's *Cronica Skotorum* and "a lytle inglysshe cronicle" valued at only a penny. Much more substantial collections of English, and European, materials lay ahead, and a significant proportion of all works owned originated in continental rather than English presses. John Bateman's inventory of 1559 includes only fourteen historical works out of 424 titles, a relatively low percentage, but a significant number of these were, along with standards like

[32] The source for the next paragraph is *BICI*, vol. I; since the inventories are alphabetized, there is no need to give page numbers for each reference.
[33] For evidence of female ownership of history books see, however, D. R. Woolf, "A Feminine Past? Gender, Genre, and Historical Knowledge in England, 1500–1800," *American Historical Review*, 102 (1997), 645–79.

Sallust and Lucan, largely nonclassical. Over and above early medieval works like Eusebius, we find in his library Ranulf Higden's *Polychronicon*, a "Cronicon diversorum authorum," and, again, Carion. The last mentioned, available in relatively cheap editions worth a few pennies (compared to the more formidable *Magdeburg Centuries*, which retailed in folio for well over one pound), enjoyed an enormous vogue in the middle to late part of the century. John Welles' library, inventoried in 1570, included amongst a preponderance of theological and literary works, Guicciardini, Polydore Vergil, a "Cronica melanctonis" (actually another edition of Carion's *Chronicle*) and several classical historians, in all fourteen historical works out of sixty named items, or a startling 23 percent. The moderately large library of John Hatcher, MD, who died in 1587, was overwhelmingly medical, but included some historical matter, such as Stow's *Summary of Chronicles*. Most of these had probably been inherited from his son, Thomas, the antiquary, who had predeceased his father in 1585.

The question of the price of various histories in early modern England, particularly for the seventeenth and early eighteenth centuries, will be dealt with in greater detail in chapter 5 and appendix A, but it is worthwhile treating it here more briefly, to get some sense of the value of the history books listed in the Cambridge inventories. Here, too, there was enormous range, and two copies of the same work, valued in the same year, could have widely divergent values. The copy of Polydore Vergil's *Anglica Historia* owned by Robert Beaumont, master of Trinity, was valued on his death in 1567 at 3s 4d, the precise sum assigned to the same copy two years previously when Beaumont had inherited it from his brother John. In 1569, however, William Lyffe, who had nine historical works, and Martin Parkinson, who owned eleven (in the case of the latter, with a tendency toward expensive chronicles in folio), each died possessed of a copy of Vergil: Lyffe's, in three volumes, was valued at four shillings – not a great amount for a work of that size – while Parkinson's, the format of which is not given, was valued at six shillings.

The wide discrepancy in prices for works such as Polydore Vergil's, and for even more vendible titles like Carion and the classical historians, because it is combined frequently with scanty information as to the precise date of edition, means that any attempt at the construction of serial price data for individual authors is doomed before it begins. This need not stop us, however, from noting the *range* within which historical authors sold. Tables 3.7–10 break down the inventories according to individual authors: ancient, medieval, modern foreign, and modern British. From left to right the columns represent author; title; date of the first inventory in which the work appears and of the last; number of inventories in which the work occurs; number of inventories in which more than one copy of the work occurs; and

Table 3.7. *Ownership of ancient historians in Cambridge, 1535–1609*

Author	Title	First	Last	No.	> 1	High price £ s d	Low price £ s d
Aelian[a]	*Opera/Varia Historia*	1556	1592	11	1	0-5-0	0-0-3
Appian	*De bellis . . .*	1546	1605	15	2	0-3-0	0-0-6
Arrianus	*Exp. Alex.*	1539	1589	6	1	0-4-0	0-0-6
Caesar	*Commentarii*	1537	1608	58	6	0-2-4	0-0-2
Q. Curtius	*Alexander*	1537	1605	25	1	0-1-4	0-0-2
Diodorus Siculus	*Bibliothecae historiae*	1537	1589	13	1	0-1-8	0-0-2
Diogenes Laertius	*De vitis philos.*	1535	1605	28	3	0-3-0	0-0-4
Dio Cass.	*Hist. Romanae*	1569	1598	6	1	0-3-6	< 10d
Dionysius Halicarn.	*Opera/Antiq. Romanorum*	1560	1591	8	1	0-13-0	0-0-3
L. Florus	*Gesta/Epitome*	1541	1591	15	0	0-3-0	0-0-1
Heliodorus	*Ethiop. Hist.*	1539	1593	9	0	0-1-4	0-0-3
Herodian	*Historiarum libri viii*	1537	1592	32	4	0-1-8	0-0-2
Herodotus	*Opera*	1537	1609	23	3	0-6-0	0-0-3
Josephus	*Opera*	1538	1598	31	3	0-15-0	0-0-10
Justinus	*Hist. exordium*	1537	1598	42	5	0-1-3	0-0-2
Livy	*Historical works*	1537	1593	47	7	0-10-0	0-0-4
Lucan	*Pharsalia*	1539	1605	24	4	0-2-0	0-0-2
Plutarch	*Opera/Vitae/ Epitome*	1535	1601	40	7	0-13-4	0-0-3
Polybius	*Historia*	1537	1592	6	0	0-1-4	0-0-2
Sallust	*Var. Works*	1537	1593	57	10	0-2-0	0-0-1
Suetonius	*Vitae*	1537	1607	40	5	0-6-8	0-0-4
Tacitus	*Var. Works*	< 1558	1607	6	1	0-3-4	0-1-0
Thucydides	*Histories*	1545	1601	12	1	0-5-0	0-0-6
Xenophon	*Var. Works*	1537	1609	30	4	0-8-0	0-0-2

[a]Much of Aelian's work is concerned with natural history, especially animals, the *Varia historia*, however, deals with people and with human history.

highest and lowest prices given for a title (regardless of format, which is not always obvious from the inventories). Where lowest price is given for an item bundled together with other titles it has been signified by a < (less than); highest prices are derived exclusively from items valued singly. The few inventories later than 1609 have been omitted. Booksellers' inventories *have been included* in this count. Items that appeared only once (for example, Matthew Paris' *Historia maior* and Saxo Grammaticus' *Danorum regum*

Table 3.8. *Ownership of medieval historians in Tudor Cambridge*[a]

Author	Title	First	Last	No.	> 1	High price £ s d	Low price £ s d
Bede	*Eccles. Hist.*	1543	1591	4	1	0-1-6	0-0-4
Caradoc of Llancarfan	*Hist. of Cambria*	1588	1589	2	0	0-16-0	0-2-0[b]
Cassiodorus	*Historia tripartita*	1541	1589	5	0	0-3-4	0-0-6
Philippe de Commynes	*De rebus gestis Gallorum Historia*	1565	1590	6	1	0-1-4	0-0-5
Eusebius	*Chronicon*	1538	1591	10	0	0-2-8	0-0-8
Eusebius	*Hist. eccles.*	1537	1608	46	7	0-15-0	0-0-4
Eutropius	*Hist. Romanae*	1559	1589	4	1	0-2-8	0-0-6
R. Fabyan	*Chronicles*	*ca.* 1588	1589	2	0	0-4-0	0-2-6
Geoffrey of Monmouth	*Britannia . . . regum origo*	1537	1591	5	1	0-5-0	0-0-2
R. Higden	*Polychronicon*	1546	1589	4	0	0-2-0	0-1-8
"Matthew of Westminster"	*Flores historiae*	1588	1589	2	0	0-5-0	0-3-4
Nicephorus Callistus	*Ecclesiasticae historiae*	1556	1608	8	0	0-13-4	0-2-3
Nicephorus Chartophylax	*Chronologia*	1589	1592	3	1	0-5-0	0-4-6[c]
Otto of Freising	*Chronicon and Rerum gestarum*	1542	1559	2	0	0-2-6	0-2-0
Paulus Diaconus	*Hist. Lombards*	1545	1593	3	0	0-0-6	0-0-4
Petrus Comestor	*Historia scholastica*	1537	1586	11	1	0-1-4	0-0-4
T. Walsingham	*Historia and Ypodigma*	1588	1589	3	1	0-6-0	0-3-4
Zonaras	*Compendium hist.*	1576	1589	3	0	0-8-0	0-5-0

[a]Criteria as in table 3.7.
[b]Parchment copy.
[c]Both high- and low-priced copies belonged to Perne, and are priced together with two and four other books respectively.

heroumque historiae) are not represented here. The popularity of some historians is not difficult to fathom. Eusebius remained throughout our period the preeminent work on early Christian history; Perne had six different editions of his *History*. The wide price ranges reflect the number of different editions of certain authors: those set with expensive Greek lettering, or Greek and Latin, usually lie at the upper end of the price range.

When compared with the preceding table, it is clear that medieval historians were considerably less in evidence in Tudor Cambridge than the ancient historians. This is not at all surprising given that there were as yet few medieval western or Byzantine historians in print, compared to the ancients. In comparison, post-medieval historians, especially those with a Reformation connection (Carion and the *Magdeburg Centuries*) and those about ancient subjects, such as Budé's *De asse* (on Roman coinage) were more common (table 3.9). But contemporary British authors, most of whom would at this stage have been chroniclers, were least popular, in contrast to the appetite for their works that we have shown developing elsewhere in the country at the same time. Price, judging by the range of costs, seems to have little effect on taste: one could find historical works of all kinds at various prices, but the longevity of the ancients and their popularity as set texts meant the availability of more editions in various formats.

CHANGING RECOMMENDATIONS FOR THE ACQUISITION OF HISTORY BOOKS

History books on a variety of subjects competed increasingly for space on the shelves of learned libraries, though the Tudor Cantabrigians' preference for ancient historians, who had lost little of their authority despite two centuries of philology and numismatics, remained strong right through the eighteenth century. Dr. Thomas Barlow (1607–91), Bodley's librarian during the civil wars and interregnum, and subsequently a bishop, wrote a short tract for a young friend in the 1640s, advising him which books to put in a new library, "for Historians they will be of infinite use for your library & learning." The list includes Herodotus and various other classics, especially those treated by the Dutch historian Gerhard Vossius in his *De historicis graecis* and *De historicis latinis*, "incomparably the best most learned & most usefull for this purpose," that purpose being to have "an exact enumeracion both of greeke & latine historians." Barlow also recommended various works on ancient chronology, such as those by Joseph Scaliger, and suggested that his friend might want to have at hand a dictionary and glossaries to help deal with "barbarous" (that is, medieval Latin and vernacular) words. But the list does not include a single modern history, or even a medieval chronicle.[34]

Such snubbing of the moderns, and lack of interest in British or even modern history, was less and less the rule as the seventeenth century wore on, without interest in or dependence upon ancient historians at all declining. The historical bookshelf was not a pie whose redivision was a zero-sum gain for one subject or another; rather, the pie itself was expanding. Barlow's classically minded recommendations might be contrasted with those of his much younger contemporary, the northern knight and future peer, Sir John

[34] Thomas Barlow, "To a friend who desired the names of some bookes," Bodl. MS Tanner 301, fos. 100r–v, 107r.

Table 3.9. *Ownership of modern foreign historians in Tudor Cambridge*[a]

Author	Title	First	Last	No.	> 1	High price £ s d	Low price £ s d
"Berosus"	*De Antiquitatibus*	1559	1589	3	0	0-1-4	0-0-8
"Berosus"	*Antiq. Italiae*	1559	1589	3	0	0-1-4	0-1-0
Flavio Biondo	*De Roma inst.*	1542	1589	5	0	0-5-0	0-0-6
Jean Bodin	*Methodus*	1586	1592	7	2	0-10-0[b]	0-0-6
G. Budé	*De asse*	1539	1591	11	2	0-3-0	0-0-2
J. Carion	*Chronicon*	1546	1591	24	2	0-5-0	0-0-1
D. Chytraeus	*Chronologia*	1588	1589	4	2	0-2-0	0-1-0
P. Emili	*De rebus gestis*	1542	1589	4	0	0-5-0	0-1-0
M. Flacius	*Magd.Cents.*	1567	1608	8	1	3-0-0	0-3-4
J. Foresti (alias Bergomensis)	*Nov. Hist. & supp. chron.*	1546	1589	5	0	0-3-0	0-0-6
Johann Funk	*Chronologia*	1569	1608	4	0	0-6-0	0-0-6[c]
Ach. Gasser	*Hist. mundi*	1541	1589	5	0	0-0-6	0-0-1
Paolo Giovio	*Hist.sui temp.*	1569	1589	3	0	0-3-4	0-3-0
Guicciardini	*Hist. Italy*	1569	1589	2	0	0-8-0	0-2-0
Olaus Magnus	*Hist . . . septen.*	1589	1601	4	1	0-3-4	0-0-6
Papire Masson	*Annalium libri quatuor*	1578	1589	2	0	0-1-8	0-1-8
J. Nauclerus	*Chronicon*	1569	1589	2	0	0-10-0	0-5-0
H. Pantaleon	*Chronographia*	1569	1593	6	1	0-3-4	0-0-6
Platina	*Lives of popes*	1537	1608	18	2	0-4-6	0-0-6
Carlo Sigonio	*Various works*[d]	1569	1592	18	3	0-8-6	0-0-10
C. Stephanus	*Dictionarium historicum*	1578	1608	4	0	0-5-0	0-1-4
Trithemius	*Chron. monast. Hirsaugiensis*	1567	1589	3	1	0-5-0[e]	0-3-4

[a]Criteria as in table 3.7. It might be noted that the humanist historians of Europe are less in evidence here than medieval authors, indigenous authors, and original classics; the major exceptions are the Italians Paolo Giovo and Paulo Emili.
[b]Perhaps a mistake for 10d, given the other prices.
[c]Value suspect, since one of two books for this price.
[d]Here no distinction is made among at least six different Sigonio titles dealing with various aspects of ancient and biblical history.
[e]One of three books amounting to this value.

Lowther (1655–1700, from 1696 Viscount Lonsdale). In a memorandum that he composed in the 1680s on the books "such as in my poor opinion everie gentleman should have," Lowther included, together with titles in divinity, grammar, and poetry, nearly 100 historical works (over half the entire list), from Thucydides and Livy to Ralegh, Camden and, more

Table 3.10. *Ownership of modern British historians in Cambridge*[a]

Author	Title	First	Last	No.	> 1	High price £ s d	Low price £ s d
John Bale	*Chronicle of J. Oldcastle*	1550	1567	2	0	0-1-8	0-1-4
J. Bale	*Catalogus script. Brit.*	1552	1589	5	0	0-5-0	0-0-8
G. Buchanan	*Hist. Scot.*	1588	1589	5	2	0-6-0	0-2-8
J. Caius	*De antiq. Cant. & Hist. Cant.*	1587	1608	9	1[b]	0-1-4	0-0-4
W. Camden	*Britannia*	1589	1605	4	0	0-2-6	0-0-8
Maurice Chauncy	*Historia . . . martyrum*	1546	1589	2	0	0-0-10	0-0-2
Chronicles, unspecified	—	1542	1598	15	2	0-15-0	0-0-1
John Foxe	*Acts & Monuments (Eng. & Latin)*	1586	1589	4	1	1-10-0	0-5-0[c]
Ric. Grafton	*Chronicles*	1583	1589	3	0	0-0-10	0-0-4
R. Holinshed	*Chronicles* (1577)	1583	1583	1	0	0-4-0	0-4-0
R. Holinshed	*Chronicles* (1587)	1589	1589	2	1	1-13-4	0-16-0
Tho. Lanquet	*Epitome of chronicles*	1550	1596	4	0	0-3-0	0-2-0
Geo. Lily	*Chronicon*	1589	1605	2	0	0-0-6	0-0-2
Joh. Major	*Hist. Brit.*	< 1558	1589	3	0	0-0-8	0-0-6
Alexander Neville	*De furoribus*	1578	1592	4	0	0-1-6	0-1-0
J. Stow	*Chronicles*	1587	1598	4	0	0-1-0	0-0-8

[a]Criteria as in table 3.7. Note that the author category "Chronicles, unspecified" includes the Leedham-Green heading "Chronicles" and "England, appendix: 'the Chronicles of England,'" *BICI*, II, 203, 301, all of which are post-medieval. This does *not* include those under the heading "Histories of Britain," several unidentified works which may be either medieval or Renaissance in origin (*BICI*, II, 428), among which are "20 History bookes" in the 1596 inventory of Benedict Thorowgood. Nor does it include assorted unidentified chronicles of France (*BICI*, II, 355) for which neither the language nor the time of writing is clear. It is interesting to note the surprising unpopularity of a much read Elizabethan text, the *Mirror for Magistrates*, which only occurs complete in the inventory of Denys in 1578 (one of two books valued at 2s 4d). It should also be observed that, in contrast to classical authors, very few modern historical authors occur more than once per inventory, a fact explicable in terms of the still principally rhetorical use of the classics.

[b]Perne owned five of the nine copies of Caius' works, not including the single copy of the *Historia Cantabrigiensis academiae* (published 1574).

[c]Other copies just miss the 1609 cut-off; the lowest price is one of two Perne books valued together at 5s.

recently, Burnet.[35] The reading recommendations of the Augustan bookseller and autobiographer John Dunton, who had a good sense of the preferences of readers, included an extensive historical rubric of sixty-one titles, including some moderns who here assume equal status with their ancient predecessors as desiderata: Camden's *Britannia*; Burnet's *History of the Reformation*; William Cave's *Antiquitates Apostolici* and *Apostolici* (collected lives of the apostles and fathers respectively); Sir Paul Rycaut's *History of the Turks* (available by this time in several different editions); John Rushworth's *Historical Collections* ("all the parts"); Bishop Spottiswood's *History of the Church of Scotland*; Sir Walter Ralegh's *History of the World*; Bacon's *Henry VII*; Lord Herbert's *Henry VIII*; Samuel Daniel's *Collection of the Historie of England*; Degory Wheare's *Method and Order of Reading both civil and ecclesiastical Histories*; and Baker's *Chronicle*, plus many others, compared with only sixteen classical historians.[36]

This promotion of modern historians into the ranks of the "must-read" category is supported by many other book-acquisition recommendations. A list of "the choysest bookes of severall artes & sciences" compiled in the commonplace book of the mathematician and traveler John Greaves (1602–52) contains a separate page of "historici" that include Ralegh's *History of the World* and "Knolles his English history" [*sic*].[37] The notebook of Anthony Dopping, future bishop of Meath, contains a 1660 memorandum of advice for studies from Jeremy Taylor, bishop of Down, with specific recommendations for reading in church history stretching beyond Eusebius and the earliest church historians.

It were as well also if you would a litle looke into the Ecclesiasticall history to which purpose procure Eusebius with Scaligers admirable animadversions upon it; the Tripartite history; Calvisius his chronology; Dr. Mountagues history of the church; Casaubons exercitacions in Baronius' annals, and then you may bee set to read Baronius his annals without danger . . . In the reading these authors I have recom-

---

[35] Cumbria RO, D. Lons./L2/6, pp. 79–83.

[36] John Dunton, *The Young-Students-Library* (1692), p. vi. On Dunton's historical publishing activities see Joseph M. Levine, *The Battle of the Books* (Ithaca, NY, 1992), pp. 303–5; for his career and publications, Stephen Parks, *John Dunton and the English Book Trade: a Study of his Career with a Checklist of his Publications* (New York and London, 1976). Despite his active involvement in the selling of several Augustan histories, Dunton does not appear elsewhere to have valued history very highly. In a short list of the "best of books" (*Life and Errors* [1705], p. 61) that he recommended to apprentices for leisure reading, history came right at the end, and with the rather unenthusiastic remark that "After all, if the work I have cut out ben't enough to employ my Time, I'd venture upon Mr. Tyrrel's *History of England*, for 'tis really a shame that a man should be altogether a novice in the history of his own nation." As preparation for continental travels he suggests (p. 391), "The last preparation I'd make . . . shou'd be as perfect a knowledge as I cou'd get of my own native country, our civil constitution, and the history of the kings and queens of England."

[37] Bodl. MS Lat. misc. e.115, commonplace book of John Greaves; the Knolles book is probably a mistake for Richard Knolles' *History of the Turks*, written in English, which continued to be reprinted into the late seventeenth century.

mended to you, pray, observe what quotacions they have that thereby you may perceive what authors they make use of & espetially read: for 'tis likely they are the best books; many books are not usefull.[38]

In contrast, the cleric Dr. John Conant drew up, at a young friend's request, a catalog of the minimum number of books he should expect to study and, preferably, own, which veers sharply back to the ancients. Like most clerical lists, divinity figures prominently, but history is among the first, rather than last, topics discussed, with Conant recommending in chronological order the usual ancients (Herodotus, Xenophon, Thucydides, Polybius, Diodorus Siculus, Dio Cassius, Dionysius of Halicarnassus, Plutarch, Livy, Tacitus, Suetonius, Ammianus Marcellinus, Sulpicius Severus, Herodian, and "all ye scriptores hist. Augusta"), with Degory Wheare's *Method and Order* serving as a guidebook through them.[39]

PRIVATE LIBRARIES AND THEIR CATALOGS

Fortunately, we have a more accurate source than off-the-top-of-the-head recommendations to assess what was really in the collections of the nobility, gentry and well-off members of the urban middling sort. Private library lists and formal catalogs, increasing in number during the Renaissance and almost commonplace in the later seventeenth and eighteenth centuries, are even more helpful than inventories on some aspects of book ownership. Although they cover a very small segment of the literate population, and do not for the most part include useful data such as prices, catalogs confirm more or less the same pattern revealed by inventories and suggestions for reading: the later in the period that we look, the more likely we are to find a higher proportion of historical works per library, and a more significant number of works by post-classical historians. As with the inventories, this is certainly not an absolute rule. Even early and mid-Tudor lists and catalogs sometimes contain significant numbers of historical titles. A list of the bedding and hangings belonging to Edward Seymour, the future Protector Somerset, in 1539 also includes two books: one was the Bible and the other the "Crownacle of Frossert," as one might expect of a man then making his name in Henry VIII's military service.[40] The anonymous library recently attributed to Bishop Cuthbert Tunstall contained sixty-nine historical works, overwhelmingly classical but with a few modern humanist histories, out of 483 titles.[41] The books of Henry, Lord Stafford, cataloged in 1556, included

---

[38] CUL MS Add. 711, fos. 5v–10v, especially fos. 9v–10r.
[39] Chetham's Library, Manchester, Mun A.2.21, fos. 3r, 6r–6v. Perhaps most interesting is Conant's suggestion that his friend pick "the best editions, for you'le find infinit benefit by that both by the goodnes of their print and the incorruptnes of the text."
[40] Hist. MSS Comm., *Bath Longleat*, IV (Seymour papers), 120 for Seymour inventory.
[41] BL MS 40676, edited in W. H. Herendeen and K. R. Bartlett, "The Library of Cuthbert

a great deal of law (canon and civil), grammar, theology and agriculture, but also a whole page of "historiographorum libri"; containing fifty-one items.[42]

Moving ahead chronologically to the late Elizabethan and Jacobean era, there are signs not of exorbitant growth, but at least of ownership more than keeping pace with the production of historical books in different genres. The great Elizabethan scholar John Dee even made history one of the major catalogs of his library of 2,292 printed books, in which could be found 18 titles in British history, biography, or antiquities, and 109 of all other kinds.[43] The library of John, Lord Lumley, which was built up from an initial acquisition of the confiscated books of Archbishop Cranmer, would come to the Crown in 1609, forming the beginnings of the Royal Library. Lumley's collection was even more historically oriented, with "historici" the second largest category, after theology; most of the historical titles were added by Lumley himself in the last years of the sixteenth century. Excluding strictly topographical works and fiction shelved with histories, and including historical works that Lumley, like many other owners, classified with "Theologi," he had 484 books or manuscripts dealing with historical, antiquarian, chorographic, or biographical subjects, of which 103, nearly a quarter, concerned British history. This included probably the most substantial collection of medieval manuscript chronicles and Tudor printed chronicles yet formed, with Hall, Stow, Holinshed, and Lanquet represented, though not Richard

---

Tunstall, Bishop of Durham," *Papers of the Bibliographical Society of America*, 85 (1991), 235–96.

[42] "Catalogus omnium singulorum librorum apud caston Stafford," Staffordshire RO, D(W) 1721/1/10 (letter book of Henry, Lord Stafford). Stafford had copies of the 1519 Basel edition of Eusebius, *Caesar* (Basel, 1532); Froben's *Historia Ecclesiastica* (4 vols., Basel, 1549); Jacobo Filippo Foresti da Bergamo's *Supplementum chronicarum* (Paris, 1535); Carion's *Chronicle* (1539); the *Pastyme of People* by John Rastell; and "the cronicles of England and other realmes" (perhaps Froissart or Fabyan). A supplementary catalog of 1565 appended adds more chronological titles as well as one or two unidentifiable "chronicles" and an edition of Diodorus Siculus.

[43] *John Dee's Library Catalogue*, ed. J. Roberts and A. G. Watson (1990), a facsimile of the 1583 manuscript catalog. Titles include Carion, Arrian, and other ancient historians, but is not preponderantly classical; it includes several of the sixteenth-century *artes historicae* by Sebastian Fox-Morcillo, François Baudouin, Jean Bodin, and the collection edited by Johann Wolf, *Artis historicae penus octodecim scriptorum*, 2 vols. (Basel, 1579); several English chronicles, mainly kept together, including Holinshed (1577 edn), Hardyng (1543), Cooper/Lanquet (1565), Richard Arnold's chronicle (Antwerp, 1503 or London, ca. 1521) and several successive editions of Stow. This suggests that Dee was as interested in the continuations and updates on the recent past as in the treatments of more remote periods. There is also in the collection a great deal of foreign history, on Spain and the Americas, in keeping with Dee's imperial vision; and, finally, select medieval chroniclers like Thomas Walsingham and Gildas. Dee's manuscripts, 199 in total, also include nine historical texts, of which the most interesting is the *Polychronicon* but also an unknown "Historia anglica eiusdem anonymi papyri," no. 150, probably the MS of the *Brut* chronicle now in the Cottonian collection of the British Library. On Dee's historical reading, see the valuable discussion in William H. Sherman, *John Dee: the Politics of Reading and Writing in the English Renaissance* (Amherst, MA, 1995), especially pp. 90–94.

Grafton. And aside from the classical authors, in original and English translation, Lumley's holdings in continental works included very new titles like
Baronius' *Annales*, relatively commonplace summaries like Carion's *Chronicle*, and Renaissance Italian humanist historians such as Pietro Bembo,
Marco Antonio Sabellico, and Paolo Giovio.[44]

Lumley and Dee were exceptional bibliophiles, each with stronger than
normal antiquarian interests, and it is best not to take them as typical. Other,
smaller, collections throughout the two centuries reveal somewhat different
levels of historical interest and different choices among historical genres. The
library assembled by Sir Thomas Roe, the early seventeenth-century diplomat, bequeathed to Sir Maurice Berkeley (the son of Roe's stepbrother
Richard Berkeley) was cataloged in 1647 and includes several histories of
specific interest to an ambassador, such as Turquet de Mayerne's *Generall
Historie of Spaine*, Pasquier's *Recherches de la France*, the *Memoirs* of du
Bellay, de Thou's *Historia sui temporis* and several works on the history and
geography of Bohemia and other European states; Roe's classical histories
were principally those like Caesar, Sallust, and Polybius, mainly concerned
with war and peace, as were his medieval selections such as Commynes.[45] We
should not be surprised to find very different selections elsewhere, and later,
as well as some items that seem to fall into the realm of the more
commonplace, like the editions of Caesar's *Commentaries* possessed at one
time or another by virtually any university student or graduate: John and
Richard Newdigate, for instance, had several of the ancient historians between them, along with a few less commonplace items, such as Camden's
Britannia and Samuel Daniel's *Collection of the Historie of England*.[46]

Jumping ahead a century we find evidence both of more histories in
libraries, in terms of proportion, and also – more significantly – more

---

[44] *The Lumley Library: the Catalogue of 1609*, ed. S. Jayne and F. R. Johnson (London, 1956).
My count has, as usual, ignored the contemporary classifications, according to which books
that might seem quite historical were shelved with different subjects (one copy of Bede, for
instance, under *Theologi*, along with Alan Cope's attack on Foxe and other protestant
historians). It is interesting to note, however, that the library contained the *Historia fabulosa*
of Palmerin, shelved between two learned Latin items, an edition of Paolo Giovio's *Vitae
illustrium virorum*, and a copy of Johann Sleidan's edition of Commynes. Lumley, notorious
for his fascination with his own ancestry, did not carry this love of the old into his collection
of books: he owned very few manuscripts, only a hundred incunabula (mainly inherited from
the Cranmer and Arundel collections that formed the root of his own library), and he
preferred later editions to earlier ones: Jayne and Johnson, introduction, p. 11.

[45] Gloucs RO, FmS/D 3/2/8 (formerly 504 M14 31 (33)), catalog of books in Roe's bequest to
Sir Maurice Berkeley, 1647. I am indebted to Sears McGee for lending me his photocopy of
this, to Mrs. Margaret Richards for furnishing me with a handlist of the archive, and His
Grace the Duke of Beaufort for permission to cite from it.

[46] Vivienne Larminie (ed.), "The Undergraduate Account Book of John and Richard Newdigate, 1618–21," *Camden Miscellany*, 30 (Camden 4th series 39, 1990), pp. 149–269; I am
grateful to Dr. Larminie for discussing John Newdigate's historical interests with me prior to
the publication of this volume.

libraries at different social levels having at least some histories in them. Among the aristocracy and wealthiest gentry, it is not surprising to find a high proportion of historical works of various sorts. A list of the books belonging to Anthony Grey, earl of Kent included by 1698 seventy-seven volumes (several of which were manuscript), of which thirty (39 percent) were historical, including a large number of chronicles (*Polychronicon*, the *Brut*, Sprott and Trivet) along with more modern works (Cotton's *A Short View of the Long Life and Raigne of Henry the Third*, Selden's *Privileges of the Baronage*) and many volumes of genealogical or heraldic writing.[47] The "Booke of Writeings" concerning his estates in Westminster and Yorkshire surveys the library of Thomas Tufton, sixth earl of Thanet in a catalog compiled at various times between 1684 and 1729. Thanet kept 120 of his books in the "evidence house," or muniments, at his Appleby home, including an unnamed heraldic book "commencing from William Duke of Normandy the Conqueror"; a single volume of Holinshed's *Chronicles* (1577 edition), and a variety of classical and modern historians.[48] While a cross marks Spottiswood's *History of the Church of Scotland* as the only historical item among several books to be given away, Thanet's list also marks with an *o* each item removed by the earl to his London residence. The history books were disproportionately high among those selected to accompany him, including his copy of *Britannia* and the regnal histories by Habington, Bacon, and Herbert of Cherbury that combined into a complete narrative of the Yorkist and early Tudor era.[49] The MP and Admiralty commissioner Sir

[47] Bodl. MS Rawl. D.888, fos. 6r–8r.
[48] Bodl. MS Don. e 85, pp. 5–10, listing fifty-five folio volumes of all subjects, historical and nonhistorical (including several romance "histories" in large format). Quartos include *The Mirror for magistrates*; Godwin's *Catalogue of Bishops*; "A very old history of the Picts & Scotts"; a history of the annexation of Portugal by Spain; Sir Roger Williams' *Actions of the low countries* (with a preface by the Jacobean historian Sir John Hayward); and an unspecified history of King Arthur and the round table. Total = 30 quartos in all subjects and 6 histories. There are thirty-five octavos in all subjects, with no histories (suggesting Thanet's historical collections ran to the more expensive). Other historical titles include: Justin in a folio edition, North's translation of *The lives of Epaminondas, of Philip of Macedon, of Dionysius the Elder, and of Octavius Caesar Augustus*; Thucydides; Camden's *Britannia*; Spottiswood's *History of the Church of Scotland*; "A chronicle to King James' Reign"; William Habington's *Edward IV*; the English translation of Francis Godwin's *Annales of England*; Arthur Wilson's *History of Great Britain* (despite its title, essentially an account of James I's reign only), an edition of Commynes; Bacon's *Henry VII*; Herbert of Cherbury's *Henry VIII* and several other modern works the identities of which are ambiguous, such as a catalog of the kings of England and another of nobility and heraldry (perhaps those early seventeenth-century works by Augustine Vincent and Ralph Brooke, or Thomas Milles).
[49] A second Thanet list in the same MS, pp. 139–43 gives Thanet's 101 books of various sizes left at Hothfield, Kent, in October 1687, and probably includes items already mentioned in the previous list. The historical items in this list are as follows: John Guillim's *Display of heraldry* (both the 2nd edn of 1632 and the 4th edn of 1660); Commynes (1614); several French books in quarto and octavo or smaller: Caesar's *Commentaries* (1658); Jean Baptiste du Tertre's *Histoire générale des isles . . . dans l'Amérique* (1654); Jean de Serres' *Inventaire général de l'histoire de France* (1653); Pierre Dupuy's *Histoire des plvs illvstres favoris anciens et modernes* (1659 and 1661 editions); Famiano Strada's *Histoire de la guerre de*

John Lowther (1642–1706, a cousin of the above-mentioned John Lowther, Viscount Lonsdale) compiled a lengthy and detailed catalog of his own books in April 1698, listing 818 books (many in several volumes) arranged by size, language, and subject. Of these, 242 were historical (29.6 percent), ranging from editions of medieval and modern historical chronicles to foreign histories, antiquarian and heraldic works, and biographies. In 1701 he compiled a further list of books brought from the closet of his London house, forty-four in all (excluding smaller pamphlets), of which nine were historical.[50]

By the early eighteenth century, history had established a place for itself in the private libraries of persons well below the level of either noblemen such as Lords Thanet and Kent, or even the *nouveau riche* Lowthers. The 110 books kept in the parlor (as of 8 September 1712) of the Bancroft family home at Browsholme included twenty-one historical items, overwhelmingly modern.[51] The 116 folio or quarto, and 349 smaller-format books that George Hudson, vicar of Great Stanmore, Middlesex, listed in his account book include twenty-five historical titles, a large number in Italian and French.[52]

Flandre (1675); Eutropius' *Breviarium historiae romanae* (1621); and a French life of St. Mary Magdalen de Pazzi (1676). Finally, there are some undated English books: *Memorials of the English Affairs* (i.e., Bulstrode Whitelocke, 1682); Sleidan's *History of the Reformation*; and Rushworth's *Historical collections of private passages of state, weighty matters in law, remarkable proceedings in five parliaments* (1659–1701).

50 Cumbria RO, D. Lons./L2/6, pp. 34–68. The 1701 list is at pp. 71–72. Compare Lowther's list with an earlier manuscript list, from about 1610, contained in a book that may have belonged to one of his ancestors: John Willis, *The art of stenographie* (1602), Folger printed books STC 25744a, "A note of what books I left at Lowther" *ca.* 1610; this contains twenty-five volumes, including the Willis title itself and an edition of Aesop's fables, but no historical works.

51 Lancs. RO, D DB 64/17. This includes neither prices nor the format of the books. The items include: Anthony Weldon, *The court and character of King James*; *England's Worthies* (not Fuller's famous collection of biographical sketches, but rather one of the works by that title written respectively by William Winstanley and John Vicars); a history of the reign of Charles I; a "Survey" of Turkey (Knolles or Rycaut?); Virgilio Malvezzi's *Romulus and Tarquin*, trans. Henry Carey; Fulke Greville's *Life of Sir Philip Sidney*; Thomas Gumble's *Life of General Monk*; a "Portugal chronicle"; "Lyvis History" (an edition of Livy); Cornelius Nepos' *Life and Death of Pomponius Atticus*; Alessandro Giraffi's *An Exact Historie Of The Late Revolutions in Naples*, translated and continued in a second part by James Howell; the "State of Venice" (either James Howell's *S.P.Q.V.* or, less likely, the much earlier study by Gasparo Contarini translated in the sixteenth century); Dio's Roman history in Latin; Sallust's *Conspiracy of Catiline*; Montrose's "History," in Latin (that is, Bishop George Wishart's *I[acobus] G[raemus]. De rebvs avspiciis serenissimi, et potentissimi Caroli dei gratia Magnae Britanniae regis*); and a work simply noted as "Events of ye Spanish monarchy."

52 Devon RO, 3177 Add. B/F1/1, account book of George Hudson, *ca.* 1710. Histories listed as in his library include: Thomas Godwyn's "Antiquities" (i.e., *Romanae historiae anthologia recognita & aucta*, 1689); Guicciardini, *Storia d'Italia* (Venice, 1623); Sarpi, *Historia del Concilio Tridentino* (2nd edn, 1629); three unidentified histories with Italian imprints; Quintus Curtius (1696); an edition of Lucius Florus (Amsterdam, 1692); Laurence Echard, *Roman History* (1696[–98]); Aelian, *Variae historiae libri xiiii* (1701); Luc Courchetet Desnans, *The History of the treaty at Nimueguen* (English trans., London, 1681); Philippe Briet, *Annales mundi*, 2 vols. (Paris, 1662–63); William Wotton, *The History of Rome*

We know from an autograph list that in 1720 the deist and freethinker John Toland had 155 books in his room "at Mr. Hinton's a carpenter in Putney," and that this was more books than he had space to shelve: several had to be piled, sixteen or more high, on a number of chairs, including Edward Lhwyd's *Archaeologia Britannica,* and Hugh MacCurtin's *A Brief Discourse In Vindication Of The Antiquity Of Ireland Collected Out Of Many Authentick Irish Histories And Chronicles* (1717).[53] Gerald Salvin, squire of Seaton Carew near Hartlepool, County Durham, drew up a list of his personal books at the family home, Owton, about 1700 in which history was particularly prominent: of the seventy-eight titles (which also include many law books and volumes on nature and geography), twenty-four are historical and biographical, and these heavily favor recent English history, especially the civil wars, rather than the classics: there is more of Rushworth and Heylyn than Caesar and Plutarch.[54] In contrast, the much larger library of John Belson of Brill, Buckinghamshire, a Roman Catholic notable for his historical interests, contained a surprisingly small number of history books, principally classical historians and a few older European titles such as Stow's *Chronicles,* Camden's *Remains,* Commynes, and Sarpi's *Council of Trent.* The sixty-six historical works listed herein, a large assortment by the standards of a century or so earlier, works out to only 6 percent of the approximately 1,000 books listed, a nearly invisible shrub in a forest dominated by catholic controversial literature (four copies of Robert Parsons' *Three Conversions of England,* for instance) and numerous romances like Amadis of Gaul.[55]

The historical component of any private library must be taken in perspective, since in most small and middle-sized personal collections religious titles

(1701); Samuel Pufendorf, *An Introduction To The History Of The Principal Kingdoms And States Of Europe* (2nd edn, 1697); C. *Cornelii Taciti opera* (Leiden, 1687); Abbé de Fourcroy, *A new and easy method to understand the Roman history,* trans. T. Brown (1696 [*sic:* actually 1695]); Gilbert Burnet's *Life and Death of Sir Matthew Hale* (1683 [*sic:* 1681 or 1682]); Louis le Gendre, *The History Of The Reign Of Lewis The Great Till The General Peace Concluded At Reswick In The Year 1697* (1699); "Le Mesne" [*sic:* i.e. Pierre Le Moyne], *Of the art both of writing & judging of history* (1695); Paul Pellisson-Fontainier, *Histoire de l'Académie françoise* (The Hague, 1788 [*sic* in MS = 1688]; Michele Agnolo Florio, *Historia de la vita e de la morte de l'illustriss. signora Giovanna Graia* [i.e. Jane Grey] (Middleburgh, 1607).

[53] BL MS Add. 4295, fos. 41–43. Of 121 listed books (which does not match Toland's own total, fo. 41, of 155, suggesting that the list is not complete), eight were historical titles. Cf. the list of books in Folger STC 22214, copy 1 of *The workes of Lucius Annaeus Seneca,* trans. T. Lodge (1614), the flyleaf of which has two names on it, "Mrs. Catherine Hughes her booke" and Thomas Eyton; the back flyleaf has the later name of John Hughes, possibly the Augustan poet and history editor: the "note of all my books wch are wth mee"[1625] is by Eyton and is pasted inside the front cover. Its forty-five items including Tacitus in English, Justin, Sallust, Valerius Maximus, Diogenes Laertius' lives of the philosophers in English and Latin, the balance being mainly religious works and some poetry.

[54] Durham County Record Office, D/Sa/E.784.

[55] Newberry Lib. Case MS 6A19, catalog of books in the study of John Belson, 1729; *DNB,* sub Belson, John.

predominated throughout the sixteenth and early seventeenth centuries. As one modern author has put it, in commenting on the growth of personal libraries in early New England, "The book most commonly found in early private libraries was, of course, The Book."[56] It is neither accurate nor necessary to the argument of the present study to suggest that history was evolving into *the* most important subject in most Tudor and early Stuart libraries: there was still not enough of it around, even if readers had shown such inclinations. Even in 1700, when the titles available had expanded enormously, most catalogs would contain no more than a fifth-part historical matter, and generally somewhere in the range of 10 to 15 percent.

On the other hand, it is also clear that the likelihood of finding some historical titles in any library is vastly greater the closer we get to 1700: the gradual increase in historical readership during the later sixteenth century became, if not quite a flood, at least a more rapidly rising, bubbly flow. This is a more meaningful measure of the dispersal of history in print. When compared with either the lists of the later seventeenth century and later, or with the inventories generated by an atypical community like the university, the probability of identifying any sort of historical work in most small libraries prior to the reign of Charles I is considerably reduced, as a few further examples suggest. The only historical work to appear in an anonymous list of twenty-two books "received" from one Richard Wrigley, dating from about 1620, is Bishop Godwin's *Catalogue of Bishops*. A note of the eleven Latin and two English books owned by one George Shirle or Shirley, about 1600, contains Valerius Maximus, which has historical elements but was chiefly a text studied for moral philosophy. An anonymous list made in 1595 by a book owner (probably a university student or young fellow) covers 204 titles, overwhelmingly in octavo and smaller formats; its four histories were the stock undergraduate classical authors Sallust, Herodian, Plutarch, and Justin.[57]

Against these one can contrast the library of Robert Middleton, vicar of

---

[56] J. W. Kraus, "Private Libraries in Colonial America," *Journal of Library History*, 9 (1974), 31–53. Nonetheless, it is worth noting that the soldier Miles Standish's collection, at his death in 1656, included Caesar's *Commentaries* and an account of the campaigns of Gustavus Adolphus, while perhaps the earliest documented New England library, that of William Bradford, who sailed on the *Mayflower*, included Guicciardini's *History of Florence*: ibid., 34–35. George K. Smart's figures for Virginia, compiled over sixty years ago, may be in need of revision, but show a slight growth from 12 percent to 15 percent in the number of history books in a sample of seventeenth- and eighteenth-century libraries: G. K. Smart, "Private Libraries in Colonial Virginia," *American Literature*, 10 (1938), 24–52.

[57] Folger STC 24119 note of books received bound in William Tooker, *Duellum sive singulare certamen cum Martino Becano Jesuita* (1611); Folger printed books, 220–6089, note of books belonging to George Shirle[y] *ca.* 1600, at back of copy of D. *Erasmi Roterodami opus de conscribendis epistolis* (Basel, 1522). The book also bears in at least two places the name of Henry Shirley, and was originally bound in a medieval manuscript; Houghton Lib. f. MS Eng. 788, unfoliated.

Cuckfield in Sussex from 1690 to 1712, who left his nearly 700 books, including a wide variety of histories and antiquarian texts, to Simon Patrick, a young law student at the Middle Temple (and son of a dead friend of Middleton, Simon Patrick the elder, bishop of Ely); this gift came, however, with the condition that young Patrick become a cleric himself when he achieved his majority, and abandon the law.[58] On a smaller scale, one can compare Elizabethan and early Stuart lists with the fifty-eight titled books and numerous pamphlets of Jonathan Roddam, merchant and alderman of Newcastle, whose library included Ralegh's *History of the World*, Guillim's *Display of Heraldry*, Lodge's translation of Josephus, Sleidan's "Key to History," Kennett's *Roman Antiquities*, and Burnet's *History of the Reformation*.[59] The list of a private library at Redland, Gloucestershire, in 1717,

---

[58] W. Sussex RO, Add. MS 29144. This catalog was compiled, in a big parchment book dated "16 May," after Middleton's death according to a term in his will of 18 March 1711/12, and was not completed for twenty years, during much of which time the books were in the hands of Anne Patrick, the will's executor. Edition details are given, but without valuation. The catalog consists of 691 named books (excluding pamphlets, many of which were of a marginally historical nature, e.g. "A vindication of King Charles the martyr," 1693; the "Historical monthly mercury" for November 1701). They break down into the following sizes and languages: 64 English folios, 60 English quartos, 212 English octavos plus 9 in a different category; 40 English duodecimo or smaller format; 65 Latin/Greek folios; 63 Latin/Greek quartos; 57 Latin/Greek octavos; 93 Latin/Greek books in smaller formats. Historical titles include: Henry Spelman's *Glossarium archaiologicum* (1687); William Cave's *Scriptorum ecclesiasticorum historia literaria* (1688), *Antiquitates apostolicae, or, The history of the lives, acts and martyrdoms of the holy apostles of Our Saviour, and the two evangelists, SS. Mark and Luke* (1677), and *Apostolici: or, the history of the lives, acts, death and martyrdoms of those who were contemporary with, or immediately succeeded the apostles* (1677); Samuel Cradock, *The history of the Old Testament methodiz'd according to the order and series of time wherein the several things therein mentioned were transacted* (1683); François Eudes de Mézeray, *A General Chronological History of France*, trans. John Bulteel (3 vols., 1683); Robert Knox, *An Historical relation of the island of Ceylon* (1681); "Baker's Chronicles Imperfect" (1674); Tacitus, *Annales*, in English (4th edn, 1612); Peter Heylyn, *Cosmographie* (1670); Foxe, *Acts and Monuments* (3 vols., 1641); Rushworth, *Historical Collections* (1659–81); Edward Stillingfleet, *Origines Britannicae: or, the antiquities of the British churches* (1685); Camden's *Britannia* (1695); Thomas Burnet, *Archaeologiae philosophicae: sive Doctrina antiqua de rervm originibvs* (1692); William Beveridge, *Institutionum chronologicarum libri II* (1669); Pierre Danet, *A complete dictionary of the Greek and Roman antiquities* (1700); William Whiston, *A short view of the chronology of the Old Testament* (Cambridge, 1702); Whiston, *A new theory of the earth* (1708); Livy, *History*, vol. III only (Elzevier edn, Leiden, 1653); Livy, 2 vols. (1702); Michael Geddes, *The history of the Church of Malabar* (1694); John Woodward, *An essay toward a natural history of the earth* (1695); Jacques Abbadie, *The history of the late conspiracy against the king and the nation* (1696); John Potter, *Archaeologica graeca, or, the antiquities of Greece*, vol. I of 2 (1703); 2 vols. of a 3-volume life of William III (perhaps P. A. Samson, *Histoire de Guillaume III* [The Hague, 1703]); one of Edmund Howes' continuations of John Stow's *Annales* or *Abridgement of the English chronicle*; Thomas Long, *The History of the Donatists* (1677); and Stow's *Chronicles* (1598). As in so many libraries, there are several unmatched sets (for instance, the Livian history in 3 volumes from different editions), and the library is further interesting for the high proportion of books printed in England or by English authors. Most books were of relatively recent origins, though clearly some were second-hand and some very old.

divided by size, includes thirty-five folios, of which twenty-one were historical, seventy-four quartos (containing eight histories), sixty-two octavos (sixteen histories), and twenty-five unsized books (six histories). A further collection in the house's Chamber consisted of fifteen books, including a history of
Turkey in large folio, the second volume of Edmund Ludlow's *Memoirs*, the
first volume of Rushworth's *Historical collections*, and folio histories of
France and of Venice. In all, the library consisted of 196 books, of which
fifty-one (26 percent) were historical, antiquarian, or biographical works,
with the folio format heavily favored.[60]

To some extent this is a matter of which catalog one happens to find, and
other variants than period must of course be weighed in, such as the social
status and age of the library owner when he or she ceased to collect (often
but not always the time of death). One is more likely to find extensive
historical titles in the catalog, or inventory, of an older person than a
younger, just as the older will have acquired more books of every kind.
Student lists, such as that of John and Richard Newdigate, cited above, or
that of Daniel Malden, studying at Cambridge in 1657, frequently have very
few histories, and those most often the prescribed Greek and Latin texts
such as Caesar, Sallust, Livy, Florus, and the like.[61] When Henry Herbert
went up to Oxford in January 1670, he was sent with seventy-two books,
including several standard classical historians, Caesar's *Commentaries*
(along with Suetonius, perhaps the most commonplace classical work in
private libraries, and among the first works of history owned by any student), Florus' *Epitome* of Roman history, an unspecified work of Tacitus,
Quintus Curtius' *Life of Alexander*, and Justin's *History*. In addition, he
owned a copy of Thomas Godwyn's *Romanae historiae anthologia recognita et acta* (despite its Latin title, a highly successful English-language manual of Roman antiquities), first published at Oxford in 1614 and reprinted
many times before 1700.[62] None of the ancient historians would have been
out of place half a century earlier. Even if the number of persons owning
history books and the size of private libraries had grown, reading tastes

---

[59] Durham UL, Durham Probate Records, Jonathan Roddam, 1712, inventory.

[60] BL MS Add. 36651, fos. 40–43: among the most interesting historical titles are a large
number of histories of foreign realms (Turkey by Rycaut, Spain by Mariana, France by
Mézeray), a single volume of "Chronicles of England &c," (almost certainly Holinshed),
Ralegh's *History of the world*, Samuel Daniel's *Collection of the historie of England*, a
number of more recent works including Winston Churchill's *Divi Britannici* and Ludlow's
Memoirs, and a variety of classical historians. It is worth noting the low percentage of
historical works in quarto; this fits the pattern already discerned for the publication of
chronicles, and which is reinforced by the stockbook extracted in appendix A below.

[61] CUL MS Dd. VI.82, fos. 83v–81r (vol. reversed); Malden's *catalogus librorum* lists 105 titles,
of which only two are histories, a Greek folio edition of Herodian and an unspecified "church
historie," perhaps but by no means certainly the recently published *Church-history* by Fuller
(1655).   [62] BL MS Add. 37157, fo. 69r–v.

among the undergraduate audience remained relatively unchanged.

Within the broad category of history, there are many different divisions, and a person's place and status could determine the shape and tone of a particular collection: one might reasonably expect the libraries of parochial clergy, for example, to contain a greater number of works of divinity, and of ecclesiastical history, than those of the nearby gentry. This is not always the case. Tucked away amid the tithing records in the personal accounts of the rector of Sulhamstead Abbots is a list of the 231 books he owned in 1724 (including several added to the list later, in the 1730s and later), and a further account of 153 books that he inherited from his deceased brother in 1728. Together with the preponderance of devotional texts, the first list includes oddities like a number of novels and romances, and forty-four historical works (including various parts of the serialized *Modern History*). Among these it is scarcely surprising to find works like John Hacket's life of Archbishop Williams, the 1693 *Scrinia reserata*, nor the large number of classical histories (Xenophon, Livy, Tacitus, Florus, and the like); and of course there are works that straddle history and divinity like Thomas Burnet's *Sacred Theory of the Earth* and Bishop Nicolson's *English Historical Library*, the very popular Augustan guide to historical literature. But the list also includes Anthony Wood's 1674 *Historia et antiquitates universitatis Oxoniensis*, Clarendon's *History of the Rebellion*, Buchanan's *History of Scotland*, Voltaire's *History of Charles XII*, a life of Oliver Cromwell, and several works by Sir William Temple. The 1728 list contains a similar range of subjects, but only nine historical works, some of which duplicated those already in the rector's possession, though one, Echard's *Roman History*, was a new addition.[63] As a library, this is not remarkably different in subject coverage from the ninety-one books of John Percival in the early 1680s, a collection principally devoted to religion, grammar, medicine, and poetry, but one that also included Burnet's *History of the Reformation* in two volumes, Izaak Walton's *Life of Bishop Sanderson*, and William Cave's *Lives of the Fathers*, all three of which were by now standard items in clerical libraries.[64]

THE HISTORICAL CONTENT OF TWO LARGE LIBRARIES: ROBERT BURTON (1640) AND THOMAS BAKER (1740)

A final dramatic demonstration of the relative "gains" made by historical subjects as a whole, and individually, in their appeal to the learned can be

---

[63] Berks. RO, D/P124/3/2, Sulhamstead Abbots rector's accounts. In my count of the 1724 list I have not included an added page of twenty-nine volumes that clearly comes from a later period (it lists, for instance, Archibald Bower's *History of the Popes* [1748–66]); several items are smudged, making a precise count impossible.

[64] BL MS Add. 47024, fos. 81v–83v (vol. reversed).

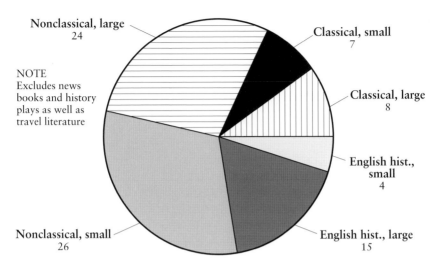

Total = 84 titles (4.8% of 1,740 titles in library)

Figure 3.3   Subjects of history books in Robert Burton's library, 1640. Source: Nicholas K. Kiessling, *The Library of Robert Burton* (Oxford, 1988).

had by the comparison of two large and well-known private libraries, collected a century apart. The first, and smaller, was that of Robert Burton, the Oxford polymath and author of the *Anatomy of Melancholy*, a book which demonstrates the enormous breadth of his interests, which included the historical (fig. 3.3). Of the 1,740 titles in Burton's collection, eighty-four were on historical subjects (4.8 percent). Of these, broken down by format (folios and quartos taken together as large size, octavos grouped with the smaller formats), nonclassical works (medieval or modern and not pertaining to British or Irish history) predominate in both sizes, with classical historians forming the smallest category. British history and antiquities are represented in such works as William Burton's *The Description of Leicester Shire*, Richard Carew's *Survey of Cornwall*, Holinshed's *Chronicles* (in the first edition of 1577), John Hayward's *First part of the Life and Raigne of King Henrie the IIII*, and John Twyne's *De Rebus Albionicis, Britannicis atque Anglicis, commentarium libri duo*; together they account for fifteen large and four small items. The surprisingly small number of classical historians is easily explained when one realizes that there was a finite number of classical titles, even when, as so often, more than one copy might be owned. But it is also an indication of the increase in book-buying of modern titles, both new historical/antiquarian works and editions of medieval works, since

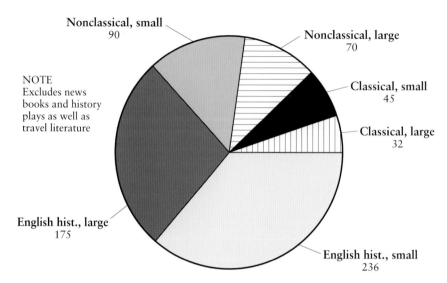

Total = 648 titles (15.1% of 4,290 titles in library)

Figure 3.4   Subjects of history books in Thomas Baker's library, 1740. Source: Frans
  Korsten, *A Catalogue of the Library of Thomas Baker* (Cambridge, 1990).

the period of the Cambridge probate inventories discussed earlier in this
chapter.[65] Seventeenth-century book buyers, especially the most devoted,
were not, apparently, content with simply collecting the oldest texts available, nor the oldest authors, and for all the dominance of ancient historians
over early modern historical writing, they were quickly outnumbered by
their Renaissance and seventeenth-century successors.

   That this trend would continue on a rising curve is demonstrated by the
second list, that of Thomas Baker, the Cambridge antiquary and bibliographer who died in 1740, just after the end of our period. Baker's was a much
larger library, at 4,290 titles, than Burton's, and a full 15.1 percent (648
titles) in it were historical. While the increased percentage of histories can be
partly attributed to Baker's somewhat more highly focused interests, that in
itself is a mark of the degree to which history had assumed a position of
increased prominence on Augustan bookshelves. Classical historians shrink
even further in proportion, the seventy-seven in this list amounting to less
than 2 percent of the total (fig. 3.4). The most remarkable change is the
prominence of titles devoted to British history, antiquities, and historical

   [65] Nicholas K. Kiessling, *The Library of Robert Burton* (Oxford, 1988).

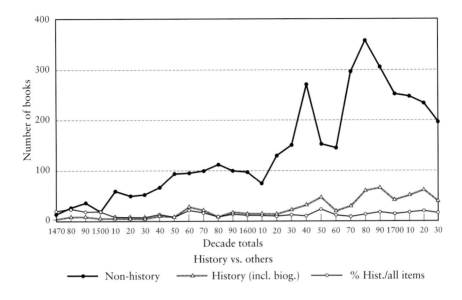

Figure 3.5   Decade of publication of books in Thomas Baker's library. Source: Frans Korsten, *A Catalogue of the Library of Thomas Baker* (Cambridge, 1990).

philology (as with Burton's list, history plays, historical romances, and travel literature have been discounted). Fully 411 books in large and small size, or 9.5 percent, deal with matters British or Irish. Perhaps most striking of all, the publication dates, by decade, of the books in Baker's library (fig. 3.5) suggest a strong market for relatively recent works, even allowing for a down-turn in Baker's book buying in the last years of his life.[66]

ASSEMBLING THE ENGLISH HISTORICAL LIBRARY: THE CASE OF
PORTLEDGE, DEVON

We have seen several examples of readers recommending this or that selection of history books to their friends, pupils, and relations; the seventeenth century also saw the transformation of the Renaissance *ars historica* – a tradition stretching from Bodin and Keckermann to Degory Wheare – into critical treatises on the merits of particular historians by the likes of René Rapin, Pierre Le Moyne, Nicolas Lenglet du Fresnoy, and their English translators and imitators, of which the most successful Augustan survey was

[66] Frans Korsten, *A Catalogue of the Library of Thomas Baker* (Cambridge, 1990).

Bishop Nicolson's *English Historical Library*. It is therefore fitting to close this chapter with an illustration of such recommendations being put into practice.

In 1683 or shortly thereafter, Richard Coffin of Portledge near Bideford (1622–98) in Devon drew up a shelf-by-shelf list of his books that included (leaving aside smaller pamphlets and tracts kept in drawers) 1,075 separate items, of which eighty-three (7.7 percent) were historical.[67] But this was not enough. With some time and considerable money, he aspired to fill the holes in his collection, and to this end he hired a London agent to buy books for him, and to keep him informed about political developments in the capital. The extensive correspondence from the mid-1680s to the late 1690s (between Coffin, who would serve as sheriff of Devon in 1685, the year of the Bloody Assizes), and the agent, a professional newsletter writer named Richard Lapthorne, survives together with Coffin's family correspondence in four folio volumes in the Devon record office.[68] This is worth examining here in some detail, since it gives some indication both of the breadth of one provincial worthy's library and the lengths he was prepared to go to in order to obtain particular items.

The letters from Lapthorne to Coffin, without the latter's responses and requests, give us only half a picture of their relationship, but it is still possible to read from them both the nature of the relationship between provincial collector and London agent, and what sort of books caught a buyer's fancy. If Lapthorne heard of a particularly interesting library coming on the market, he would inform Coffin in Devon. When Lapthorne's London neighbor, one Dr. Merret, whom the book dealer thought "the oldest physician in England," decided to retire to the countryside in 1695, he approached Lapthorne about selling his library, and the latter informed Coffin that an entire collection might be had without going through the auction.[69] Lapthorne took

---

[67] Devon RO, Z19/8/5 Portledge library catalog; cf. the April 1682 letters to Coffin from Walter Dight regarding the purchase of several of John Selden's books: Z19/40/8b, folder 8, arts. 62, 63, 64.

[68] Devon RO, Z19/40/3,4,5,6 (Portledge Library Letter Books A–D), which includes original and modern transcriptions: further references will identify individual correspondence by the date on the original letter. Many of the letters are printed in *The Portledge Papers, being Extracts from the Letters of Richard Lapthorne, Gent., of Hatton Garden London, to Richard Coffin Esq. of Portledge, Bideford, Devon*, ed. Russell J. Kerr and Ida Coffin Duncan (1928); the idiosyncratic method of "extraction" used in this edition has compelled me to cite the original manuscripts instead. For a recent account, see M. Treadwell, "Richard Lapthorne and the London Retail Book Trade, 1683–1697," in Arnold Hunt, Giles Mandelbrote and Alison Shell (eds.), *The Book Trade and its Customers, 1450–1900: Historical Essays for Robin Myers* (Winchester, UK, 1997), pp. 205–22. The library itself remained intact for a century after Coffin's death, and was dispersed in 1801, at which time it amounted to over 4,000 items. I am grateful to the late Professor Michael Treadwell for exchanging information with me concerning Lapthorne, whose correspondence with Coffin he was editing at the time of his sadly premature death in April 1999.

[69] Devon RO, Z19/40/5, Lapthorne to Coffin, 25 May 1695.

orders from Coffin, as he presumably did from several other clients, and he also regularly sent him, in advance, copies of published auction sale catalogs, inviting Coffin to mark the items he wished the agent to pursue, and to give some indication of the money he was willing to pay, and offering him first refusal of a title. On some occasions, Lapthorne purchased items that Coffin then refused, and was obliged to sell them elsewhere, sometimes to those whom he had outbid at the auction. In at least one instance, a strain developed in the relationship, when Coffin apparently accused his agent of delaying sending him an auction catalog in order to get a better price from another client, a charge that a hurt Lapthorne vigorously denied.[70] On another occasion, Coffin sent his agent on a wild goose chase in search of a survey of Hertfordshire by one "Sir Hardress." Lapthorne eventually realized that Coffin meant Sir Henry Chauncy, who indeed had his survey of the antiquities of Hertfordshire close to completion. On 2 January 1697, Lapthorne was able to report that plans to publish the work were going ahead and that subscriptions were being taken. Proposals for the book were printed and a copy was sent to Coffin, who duly signed up for the book, through Lapthorne. But Chauncy's work would not appear until 1700, too late for Coffin, who had died at Christmas 1698.[71]

It is difficult through much of this to avoid the conclusion that Lapthorne felt a degree of urbane disdain for his provincial client, whom he may have viewed, ex-sheriff or not, as an undiscriminating dilettante with money to burn. On one occasion, for example, he warned Coffin not to sink money into a work by Nathaniel Crouch:

I shall take care to send the bookes you write for. But I am apt to think you are mistaken in your choyce of Crouches bookes for they are generally but trifles & not much regarded by the skilfull in learning being collections jumbled togeather & exposed to make a present penny & fit only for the purchase of ordinary people but however unless you contradict your order they shall be sent.[72]

Lapthorne could lead Coffin on, persuading him that he was trying to secure him the best possible value. "Those books that goe at reasonable rates I buy; others that run too high I let slip till better opportunities," Lapthorne wrote on 4 March 1688, advising his impatient customer that the auction had not

---

[70] Devon RO, Z19/40/3 (Lapthorne to Coffin, 10 December 1687). A later auction, one of a series held to liquidate the library of Thomas Rawlinson, saw 4,000 lots sold over twenty-six nights at St. Paul's coffeehouse: see discussion in chapter 5, below, and B. J. Enright, "The Later Auction Sales of Thomas Rawlinson's Library, 1727–34," *The Library*, 5th series, 11 (1956), 23–40, 103–13, at p. 39.

[71] Devon RO, Z19/40/6, letters from Lapthorne dated 5 September, 26 September and 7 December 1696, and 2 January, 16 January and 3 April 1697. Coffin's name is also on the published subscription list for Robert Plot's *Natural History of Stafford-shire* (1686).

[72] Lapthorne to Coffin, 27 March 1697, Devon RO, Z19/40/6 (Portledge Library, Letter Book D), unfoliated.

yet come to a coveted copy of Philostratus.[73] On another occasion he spoke of his great labors in visiting twenty booksellers to secure Coffin a cheap copy of "Philpot" (probably John Philipot, the Caroline herald and author or editor of a variety of antiquarian works), only finding one valued at 10s, which he refused to pay knowing that "within 2 or 3 yeares they were cheaper." At various times Lapthorne found Coffin a copy of Daniel King's *Vale royal of England* (a chorography of Cheshire) for 5s 6d, a discourse on British history by Roger Gale for 20s, and Spelman's *Concilia*; a Bede for 7s, Ashmole's *Order of the Garter* for £1 5s ("very dear"); and the new edition of *Camden's Britannia* in 1695 for £1 17s.[74] Since any receipts Lapthorne may have sent to Coffin have not survived, and we have only his letters and the occasional statement of account, it is difficult to know whether Coffin was really getting value from his indefatigable agent who, after all, was out to make a profit.

But if Lapthorne was attempting to fiddle his client, he had underestimated Coffin's own ability to drive a bargain. Throughout most of 1688, while the realm was preoccupied with the Seven Bishops' Case, the birth of a prince, and the possible invasion by William of Orange, Lapthorne was principally engaged in scouring London booksellers' stalls for histories for Coffin, and above all a copy of one of the best-known of medieval works, Higden's *Polychronicon*. As the 1683 list shows, Coffin already owned some early medieval chronicles, including Bede, and he had copies of several Tudor annalists, including Lanquet, Stow, Holinshed, in addition to European works by Sleidan and Carion. But many more were available, and Coffin plainly felt there was a gap in his holdings – room certainly for the famous Higden. Writing to his ardent employer in January 1688, Lapthorne indicated that "Mr. Millington lately told mee hee had a policronicon & would use mee kinde for it. I intend to see it." Alas, the Higden was not to be had, at any price. By August, Lapthorne had almost despaired of finding one until, by sheer accident, a copy came to light at a bookseller while Lapthorne was looking for another work for himself. There followed tortuous negotiations as the agent attempted (or so he wished to persuade Coffin) to get his client a good price. "The bookseller tho' an old and cuning artist it fell out was ignorant of the author," and Lapthorne was able to secure it for eight shillings.

Lapthorne also had other clients to serve, as he often reminded Coffin. Dangling the bait before his vexed correspondent, Lapthorne speculated that he might himself "have twenty shillings of a bookseller for my bargain,"

[73] Devon RO, Z19/40/4 (Portledge Library Letter Books), 4 March 1688 and 2 January 1692.
[74] See Lapthorne's letters of 24 March 1688 (King) in Devon RO, Z19/40/3, and the following in Z19/40/4: 13 June 1691 (Gale and Spelman), 17 December 1692 (Bede), 4 August 1694 (Ashmole) and 1 April 1695 (Camden). Lapthorne also billed Coffin for charges incurred in carrying away bundles from auctions, and binding and gilding unbound works or those smaller items that could be bound several together.

pointing out that the volume was in good shape, except for a damaged binding, which he suggested Coffin let alone "because of its antiquity & not new binde it." Lapthorne may have been bluffing, for by November, Coffin, a shrewder judge than his agent credited, had still not committed himself to buying the volume. Lapthorne sent a reminder that "the policronicon I have in my custody & its yours as safe as if you had it." Still no response came: even a year later, on 16 November 1689, the newly parsimonious Coffin had not paid. Lapthorne now drew his attention to the interesting manuscript notes in the margins of the book, and even offered a hook: he would hire an amanuensis to make some notes out of it for Coffin's perusal (not an uncommon practice), though he warned of the "unreasonable" prices such scribes charged. Finally, a month later, the exasperated agent, balancing his need to sell an expensive book with his relations with a valuable client, let Coffin know that he had found an old "imperfect" English translation of the *Polychronicon* and had given the bookseller Coffin's name. Once burnt, Lapthorne was clearly not about to buy a second copy on Coffin's behalf. The seller wanted a mere six shillings for it which, with a touch of disdain for his client's sudden turn of thrift, Lapthorne advised Coffin to accept.[75]

The negotiations between Lapthorne and Coffin are a good illustration of one way in which a library of historical material could be built up over a period of a few years, even without the resources of the Harleys and the perspicacity of a Humfrey Wanley. Yet it also reminds us that the desire for knowledge, or even the desire to collect, is subject to economic and physical restrictions. In subsequent chapters, the cost and means of purchasing such books will be addressed at greater length. Before we can study that matter, however, we should recall that there was another way in which a history book could be acquired, albeit only temporarily: it could be borrowed.

[75] Devon RO, Z19/40/3 (Portledge Library Letter Books), letters from Lapthorne to Coffin dated 21 January 1688, 28 July 1688, 25 August 1688, 17 November 1688, 16 November 1689 and 15 December 1689.

4

Borrowing and lending

The history of libraries, public and private, is an especially active branch of intellectual and cultural history at the present time. In addition to the work done for France by a number of scholars, in particular Roger Chartier, serious study of British and colonial American libraries is well underway.[1] Lists of small collections are gradually finding their way into print in such volumes as the *Private Libraries in Renaissance England* series, and we know from these as well as from the larger catalogs of major collectors that the possession of a personal library was rapidly becoming a mark of prosperity. By 1700 it had become one of the principal indicators of educated civility. As we saw in the previous chapter, history books were increasingly well represented in personal libraries of all sizes. This chapter continues that discussion but focuses it in a slightly different direction, on the role of the library – not just of a collection of books but of the physical space of their storage – in disseminating historical knowledge.[2]

INFORMAL BORROWING AND LENDING: BENEFITS AND CONSTRAINTS

Before we pass on to libraries proper, the place of informal borrowing networks in the exchange and discussion of historical titles deserves some attention, since these were both far more numerous and more socially inclusive, at least within roughly equal social ranks. Virtually every literate person in England, from an urbane bibliophile like Pepys or Evelyn down to

---

[1] R. Chartier, *The Order of Books: Readers, Authors and Libraries in Europe Between the Fourteenth and Eighteenth Centuries*, trans. Lydia G. Cochrane (Oxford, 1994); cf. Clive Wainwright, "The Library as Living Room," in Robin Myers and Michael Harris (eds.), *Property of a Gentleman: the Formation, Organisation and Dispersal of the Private Library 1620–1920* (Winchester, UK, 1991), pp. 15–24.

[2] In this chapter, as elsewhere in the present study, the word *library* is generally intended to denote a collection of books, regardless of where they were kept. The design of private houses to include a large room dedicated specifically to the housing of books in such a manner as to promote both study and sociability was in fact quite rare before the late seventeenth century, famous exceptions such as Montaigne's aside: Mark Girouard, *Life in the English Country House: a Social and Architectural History* (New Haven and London, 1978), p. 169.

the apprentice Roger Lowe, could magnify his or her access to books by borrowing or lending as opposed to buying, and the effects of this were doubtless most telling among the poorer sort of aspiring reader such as Lowe.[3] Among the wealthier, price was less the problem than access to rare or even proscribed books, and Anne Goldgar has pointed out that members of the early eighteenth century republic of letters were as often praised for acts of generosity in assisting their colleagues as for anything they had actually written.[4]

Obvious advantages of economy were offset by certain disadvantages, less likely to be tolerated in those with greater disposable wealth. A book borrowed could not be marked up by the borrower; it was not always available for easy verification of material; and it incurred expense and risk in transportation if borrowed from any great distance. There were also attendant problems in getting books back (one recalls Henry Prescott being reprimanded by a superior for failure to return a borrowed book), and to a private owner the disappearance of even a single volume could represent a considerable loss of movable property. Elizabeth Josselyn, the wife of a London stationer, lent several of her small collection of books to John Felton, the future assassin of the duke of Buckingham, noting that the only one he did not return was her "History of the Queen of Scots." It was small wonder that Elizabeth later recalled Felton as an unpleasant and melancholic character, "much given to reading of books, and of very few words."[5] As John Locke's correspondence with his Cambridge friend John Covel indicates, there was always the chance that a borrowed book might not be returned, especially if the borrower died without making adequate arrangements.

I received the booke you sent me safe entituled the acts of English votarys written by Johan Bale. I mention the title so particularly that if I should dye before I restore it again you may demand it of my executor for though it be but a little booke yet possibly it is not every day to be met with & tis fit you should have your own again & not loose by the favour you have done me in lending it me.[6]

---

[3] *The Diary of Roger Lowe of Ashton-in-Makerfield, Lancashire, 1663–74*, ed. William L. Sachse (New Haven, 1938), pp. 15, 54.

[4] Anne Goldgar, *Impolite Learning: Conduct and Community in the Republic of Letters 1680–1750* (New Haven and London, 1995), pp. 17, 153.

[5] *CSPD, 1628–29*, p. 343, examination of Elizabeth Josselyn, 3 October 1628. A late eighteenth-century example from Scotland involved a "history of Alnwick castle" lent by Sir John Stewart to the duke of Atholl. Stewart, on poor terms with Atholl, requested its return together with some other items lent five years previously on 29 November 1786. The duke responded that he had taken the book and other items as gifts rather than loans, since he had not requested them, and could not recall if the history of Alnwick was among them, since he had not personally read it: Hist. MSS Comm., *Var. Coll.*, V, p. 268.

[6] CUL MS Mm.6.50, fo. 209, Locke to Covel, 1 July 1698. Cf. Locke's library papers, 1675–1704, containing bills of sale and notes about books, many historical works included, lent to friends like the historian James Tyrrell: Bodl. MS Locke b2; John Harrison and Peter Laslett, *The Library of John Locke* (2nd edn, Oxford, 1971) for Locke's own collection.

Despite such risks, the borrowing and lending of books of all kinds went on continuously and thereby exended the social circulation of any single copy of a work, compensating for the relatively small edition size of most titles. Some individuals even grouped together to establish libraries in common, with all members contributing and the books residing at one member's house.[7] The extensive diary of Humphrey Mildmay of Danbury, Essex (grandson of the more famous Sir Walter), kept through the 1630s, contains several references to books lent, Mildmay being a frequent bedtime reader as well as a compulsive playgoer.[8] On the last day of a five-week trip to London during which he purchased many books, he set out for home, "my cart heavy laden," having first "lent to Mrs. James 2 booke thone Cornelius Tacitus & thother Mr. Sandis his Ovids Mettamorphosis by Jone her mayde delivered to her eod. die." In May 1640, after a visit to church and dinner with friends, he lent "Hollinsheads Cronicle to Will: Hothersall, B[ishop]: Hall to Mrs. Thistle: & Brooke Herralde to him [i.e. to Hothersall]."[9] Richard Furney, a Gloucestershire archdeacon of the first half of the eighteenth century, made use of his friend's volumes when compiling collections for a history of the county.[10] We know from the diary of William Westmacott at about the same time that he regularly lent his books to neighbors and friends, and that historical works were among those that circulated most frequently. Born in 1650, Westmacott, the son of an ejected minister and schoolmaster, eventually settled in Newcastle-under-Lyme, Staffordshire, where he lent money as well as books. Recorded in an old man's shaky hand, the volumes loaned include, other than religious works, a number of biographies, especially of the godly, and among his borrowers were several local widows.[11]

One should not, of course, underestimate the difficulties facing readers with a particular question or problem. Henry Manship, the Yarmouth antiquary who was writing a history of his town in the 1610s, went to the considerable trouble of riding fourteen miles "to see and read" a copy of

---

[7] For an example of this see the arrangements for collective ownership of books, mainly legal, in 1633 by John Derkin, who describes himself as "servus" to Stephen Pott, Laurence Sadler, and Francis Hill, all common lawyers: CUL MS Dd. V.44, fos. 1r–40r.

[8] Folger MS W.b. 600 Diary of H. Mildmay, 1633–47 (typescript transcription of BL MS Harl. 454): e.g. p. 9 (11 March 1634), "this day I sente or lente: 5: bookes to Dr. Osbolston, whoe wente home to Parenden, I lente Rudl: 10:s"; ibid., p. 64, "I have lent my booke called Hooker Eccles: History to my brother Anth": 6 April 1637. The reference to Hooker's *Laws* as a history, repeated in a marginal gloss, is an interesting example of the imprecise use of terms like *history* by readers, as opposed to more genre-conscious authors.

[9] Mildmay diary, pp. 101–2 (30 May 1639); ibid., p. 142 (30 May 1640).

[10] Folger MS W.b. 581–88, Historical collections on Gloucestershire by Richard Furney *ca.* 1695–1753, written *ca.* 1713–30. On the flyleaf of vol. 582 (a set of extracts from a vellum MS of Winchcomb Abbey, temp. Ed. III) is the note "Lent me by Sr. John cope Baronet of Bramwell in the parish of Eversleigh in the county of Southampton, July 1730; returned to him Aug. 4th following."   [11] Folger MS V.a. 441.

Speed's *Theatre of the Empire of Great Britain* on hearing of its publication, since he did not wish to rely on "a Yermouth record only." The Georgian Anglo-Saxon scholar Elizabeth Elstob, doomed to provincial exile after the early death of her older brother William, would lament in 1735 that her attempts to procure a copy of William Somner's Anglo-Saxon dictionary (1659) had come to nought. "Antiquaries in these parts are so scarce that I cannot hear of one of whom I can borrow it."[12] William Stratford had promised a friend that he would use his influence to obtain on loan the earl of Oxford's copy of Rymer's *Foedera*, but found this more difficult than he had anticipated.[13]

The reasonably prosperous reader would often compensate for difficulties in borrowing a particular item by having copies drawn up in manuscript, which conferred the additional benefit of making them exclusive owners of a distinctive copy. This practice applied both to existing manuscript works and sometimes to books already in print but hard to come by. Lord Burghley, for instance, was the recipient at about 1575 of a chronicle of England from Norman times down to Richard II.[14] As Harold Love has shown, the claim of the manuscript as a socially privileged medium for particular literary works was far from extinct as late as the Restoration; and even if it was ultimately fighting a losing battle against the already swelling host of printed materials, the number of available historical manuscripts in circulation was large.[15] Readers would frequently transcribe, or have copied for them, entire works from a borrowed book if they could not find or could not afford a copy of their own, and other works circulated in manuscript well before they were printed.[16] Amid miscellaneous extracts of poetry and literature in the collections of Sir John Newdigate, first baronet, is one of the many manuscripts of Sir Francis Hubert's verse *Life of Edward II*, widely circulated in the 1620s before its publication.[17] Copying went on from better-known printed books also. In 1646 one reader, possibly the Edward Shepley whose name appears at the top of the manuscript, copied from start to finish Peter Heylyn's

---

[12] Henry Manship, *The History of Great Yarmouth*, ed. C. J. Palmer (1854), p. 6; CUL MS Add. 4481, fo. 3r (Ellis transcripts of Elstob correspondence), Elizabeth Elstob to George Ballard, 29 August 1735 (written as 1795). For the ruin of some of Ralph Thoresby's books, soaked while being carried back from one borrower, see *Letters of Eminent Men, addressed to Ralph Thoresby, FRS* (2 vols., 1832), II, 155 (Dr. John Smith to Thoresby, 15 April 1709).

[13] Hist. MSS Comm. *Portland*, VII, 52, 53 (Stratford to Edward Harley, 1 September 1711).

[14] Folger MS V.b. 196, signed "William Cecil" on p. 1; for early Tudor manuscript presentation, see D. R. Carlson, *English Humanist Books* (Toronto, 1993).

[15] Harold Love, *Scribal Publication in Seventeenth-Century England* (Oxford, 1993).

[16] H. R. Woudhuysen, *Sir Philip Sidney and the Circulation of Manuscripts, 1558–1640* (Oxford, 1996), pp. 116–33.

[17] Bodl. MS Eng. poet. e. 112, fos. 1–73v. I owe this reference to Dr. Vivienne Larminie; cf. Vivienne Larminie, *Wealth, Kinship and Culture: the Seventeenth-Century Newdigates of Arbury and their World* (1995), pp. 112, 113, 159 for Newdigate's historical reading.

A Help to English History, of which there were already two published editions.[18]

It was the custom of many seventeenth-century historians, including Bacon, Herbert of Cherbury, and Gilbert Burnet, to have collections made for them from relevant manuscripts and printed works rather than doing the "research" themselves; nor were many local antiquaries strangers to this practice.[19] Richard Andrews, a friend of the Essex antiquary William Holman, apologized for not returning a book belonging to Holman, and for not sending him a long-promised manuscript genealogy. He nevertheless begged the favor of a transcript from one of Holman's as yet unprinted works.[20] Transcription was sometimes done by the owner, but more often by a secretary or a copyist hired at the recipient's expense. John Locke was a lifelong borrower of books who only enjoyed the benefits of his own extensive library late in life, following his return from exile. Even then, he still needed hard-to-get volumes from friends such as the bibliophile Covel, and a transcribed passage was often easier than sending the whole book. Wanting to check a passage pertaining to monsters in the Italian historian Benedetto Varchi, Locke asked Covel to have his servant transcribe it, "because it is a book I know not where to meet with & I shall have occasion to make use of the story."[21] When he could not find a copy of the printed book anywhere, Locke had made for his own use a fair copy of Thomas May's fifty-year-old poem *The victorious reigne of Kinge Edward the third*.[22] The costs of such exercises could mount quickly, and simply getting them done at all was not a given, but dependent on the goodwill of the owner or custodian of a book or manuscript. Sir Robert Cotton was famous for allowing open access to his library of manuscripts in the early seventeenth century, but a hundred years later Humfrey Wanley was not nearly as accommodating. He was known to begrudge providing transcripts from Harleian items, snippily refusing even the bishop of Chester's request that he consult some papers in his master's library.[23]

[18] Bodl. MS Carte 248, fos. 1–64, at fo. 2r.

[19] Folger MS G.a. 6, the Gilbert Burnet collections on the civil war is an octavo book of some 200 leaves with extracts, mainly from Nalson's *Impartial collections*, made for Burnet rather than by him and bearing his bookplate; cf. Hist. MSS Comm., *Thirteenth Report*, part 1, pp. 279–331. For Bacon and Herbert's use of copyists, see D. R. Woolf, *The Idea of History in Early Stuart England* (Toronto, 1990), p. 137; D. R. Woolf, "John Selden, John Borough, and Francis Bacon's *History of Henry VII*," *Huntington Library Quarterly*, 47 (1984), 47–53. For the relation of amanuenses to the printing of books, see chapter 5 below.

[20] Essex RO, D/Y/1/1/11, Andrews to Holman, 4 November [1723].

[21] CUL MS Mm.6.50 (Covel letters), fo. 210, Locke to Covel, 1 July 1698; Harrison and Laslett, *The Library of John Locke*, p. 11.

[22] Bodl. MS Locke c. 46; this is not an entirely accurate transcription of May's 1635 book.

[23] Hist. MSS Comm., *Portland*, VII, 238, William Stratford to Edward Harley, 15 June 1718.

THE ARRANGEMENT OF KNOWLEDGE

Various problems, both intellectual and physical, were created by the flood of books into English libraries. The sheer difficulties of shelving and retrieving, as information overflowed its medieval and Renaissance classificatory boundaries, can be seen especially in larger and middle-sized collections, the physical evidence of such problems visible in some cases through shelfmarks, bindings, and groupings together of different titles within a single cover or in close proximity; it is also visible in surviving catalogs and from external documentary evidence of various sorts.

By the later seventeenth century it was no longer possible simply to put books on a shelf without thought as to both their ease of retrieval and the aesthetic appearance of fully laden presses. We know, for instance, that Archbishop William Wake spent several days in 1705 in the task of setting his books up on shelves.[24] Samuel Pepys' repeated fussing over his shelving in the 1660s is a recurring theme of his diary. Manuals on how better to classify and arrange knowledge according to what amount to disciplines and subdisciplines appeared from British and continental writers such as John Dury and Gabriel Naudé.[25] These manuals were not always helpful to private owners, some of whom, like John Locke, preferred to develop elaborate reference systems of their own in order quickly to track down not only books but particular passages. Locke did not buy a copy of one book that might have provided a suitable model, the *Catalogus Impressorum Librorum bibliothecae Bodlejanae in Academia Oxoniensi* when it appeared in 1674. Pepys had read Naudé's work and found it interesting but ill-suited to a library of his size.[26] In some instances, classification could be determined in part by the needs of users or even the workers who shelved them. The ingenious system of diagonal lines and dots on the fore-edges of books in the Ipswich town library in the mid-seventeenth century was designed by its librarian Cave Beck to help his illiterate assistant reshelve the books, fitting them into their proper sequence by matching the patterns.[27]

[24] Lambeth Palace Lib. MS 1770 (diary of William Wake), fos. 20–21. On the redesign of gentry homes since the mid-sixteenth century to make allowance for studies, see Felicity Heal and Clive Holmes, *The Gentry in England and Wales, 1500–1700* (1994), pp. 278–80.

[25] John Dury, *The Reformed Librarie-Keeper* (1650); Gabriel Naudé, *Advis pour dresser une bibliothèque* (Paris 1627), translated (with revisions) into English by John Evelyn as *Instructions concerning Erecting of a Library* (1661); Sidney L. Jackson, *Libraries and Librarianship in the West: a Brief History* (New York, 1974), pp. 166–71; Jack A. Clarke, *Gabriel Naudé 1600–1653* (Hamden, CT, 1970), pp. 17–31; Paul Nelles, "The Library as an Instrument of Discovery: Gabriel Naudé and the Uses of History," in Donald R. Kelley (ed.), *History and the Disciplines: the Reclassification of Knowledge in Early Modern Europe* (Rochester, 1997).

[26] Harrison and Laslett, *Library of John Locke*, introduction, pp. 30–42; Pepys, *Diary*, VI, 252 (5 October 1665).

[27] John Blatchly, *The Town Library of Ipswich* (Woodbridge, UK, 1989), p. 33.

Yet if the immediate impact of bibliographic guides and model catalogs is ambiguous, their long-term influence on the classification of knowledge is beyond doubt. The seventeenth century witnessed what amounted to a classificatory revolution. This involved the reshaping of knowledge and its containers, away from older schemes built on the conservation of independent spheres of study, best retrieved by private readers mnemonically or through the aid of the topoi in commonplace books. In its place, librarians, bibliographers and encyclopedists began to conceive of fields of knowledge (not quite yet modern disciplines) as both interdependent and public, and worked toward the organization of information retrieval through cataloging; at the same time, they began to conceive of the library itself as not merely a vessel for the containment of old wisdom, but as a site for the generation of new knowledge.[28] The line between the privately idiosyncratic and the publicly logical was not a clear one, and traces of older systems often endured in newer ones: the imperial pressmark associated with the catalog of Sir Robert Cotton's manuscripts in the British Museum is in itself a relic of Cotton's own use of a mnemonic cue, the placement of busts of various Roman emperors atop the several cases in which his treasures had been kept over a century earlier.

The arrangement of books by faculties (arts, theology, law, medicine) in college libraries was in itself not well suited either to smaller, private libraries or for large, heterogeneous collections such as those of the universities, which by 1700 were acquiring materials rapidly and comprehensively.[29] Sir Thomas Bodley, whose own educational tastes were conservatively humanist, could not possibly have envisaged the vortex of learning into which his refoundation would evolve within half a century of his death, but even he anticipated some of the coming problems. Bodley's design for the refounded Oxford library supplemented the "stall-system" long used by many of the colleges (including his own, Merton), which did not allow for sizes smaller than folio, with wall shelving for smaller formats, previously stored in

---

[28] For knowledge classification in the sixteenth to eighteenth centuries see Rudolf Blum, *Bibliographia: an Inquiry into its Definition and Designations*, trans. Mathilde V. Rovelstad (Folkestone, UK, 1980), pp. 35–67; Luigi Balsamo, *Bibliography: History of a Tradition*, trans. William A. Pettas (Berkeley, CA, 1990), pp. 60–97; Helmut Zedelmaier, *Bibliotheca Universalis und Bibliotheca Selecta: Das Problem der Ordnung des gelehrten Wissens in der frühen Neuzeit* (Cologne, Weimar, and Vienna, 1992), especially pp. 225–49. The broader brush used in Michel Foucault's classic *The Order of Things* (New York, 1971) remains illuminating. Michael Hobart and Zachary S. Schiffman, *Information Ages* (Baltimore, 1998) offer the most insightful analysis of the effects of knowledge containers on the knowledge contained from antiquity to the computer age; I am indebted to the authors for allowing me to read their book in advance of publication.

[29] J. N. L. Myres, "Oxford Libraries in the Seventeenth and Eighteenth Centuries," in Francis Wormald and C. E. Wright (eds.), *The English Library Before 1700* (1958); N. R. Ker, "Oxford College Libraries in the Sixteenth Century," *Bodleian Library Record*, 6.3 (January 1959), 507–8.

cupboards.[30] The Bodleian's shelfmark system, which assigned a new acquisition a permanent location in a particular physical place, has mystified many a North American accustomed to Dewey or Library of Congress cataloging. It was, however, an ingenious seventeenth-century solution to the problem of metastasizing knowledge, a scheme that has worn rather well nearly four centuries later, since it provides room for expansion without the continuous moving of every old item as new books are added. It was no accident that Humfrey Wanley advised the designers of the new library at St. Paul's, completed in 1710, to follow the organizational blueprint laid down by his former place of work above the Oxford Divinity School.[31]

The logic of classification was naturally affected by external factors, size of book within subject being the most obvious. The special requirements of donors were among these influences, and are a boon to the modern scholar interested in studying complete, stand-alone collections, but were frequently a thorn in the side of those who had to house such bequests. Some were simply unwilling to do so: the Inner Temple lost its claim to a large share of John Selden's books when it refused to provide a separate space to shelve them together, as required in Selden's will (a service which the Bodleian, however, was happy to provide in what is now "Selden End"). When the books of the Jacobean biblical scholar John Duport eventually came to Trinity College, Cambridge after the Restoration, they represented a vast increase in the college's holdings with which it was ill-equipped to deal. John Laughton complained that he had "our whole library to set in order, and to make new catalogues for it."[32]

History books were among the collections in private and public libraries from very early in our period, and by 1700 they were creating problems of classification in their own right, even among middling-sized collections of 2,000 books or less (plate 4.11).[33] The days of the lonely copy of Higden's *Polychronicon* or even Stow's *Annales*, keeping close company with works on piety, household economy, and horsemanship, were effectively over by 1600, and it was already questionable whether Caesar and Livy should be

---

[30] Anthony Hobson, "English Library Buildings of the Seventeenth and Eighteenth Century," in Paul Raabe (ed.), *Öffentliche und Private Bibliotheken im 17. und 18. Jahrhundert: Raritänkammern Forschungsinstrumente oder Bildungsstätten?* (Bremen and Wolfenbüttel, 1977), pp. 63–74, a brief but useful overview of changes in physical space and design of libraries.

[31] *The Letters of Humfrey Wanley*, ed. P. L. Heyworth (Oxford, 1989), pp. 258–62 (Wanley to unknown recipient, 16 September 1710).

[32] J. Nichols, *Illustrations of the Literary History of the Eighteenth Century*, 8 vols. (1817–58), IV, 81 (John Laughton to John Nalson, 2 August 1681).

[33] John Locke's library, at over 3,500 volumes, was a large one by contemporary standards, though small when compared to the collections of a Sunderland, Sloane, or Harley. The famous "noble" collections were much larger still, but for that reason do not set a fair standard of "largeness"; for definitions of small, medium, and large within the present study, see chapter 3 above.

Historians

D: Josephi vita Historia   Fr. 5. 13.

vita di Esopo.   Fr. 5. 18.

Mores et Leges Gentium Jo: Boemi. Fr. 5. 28.

vida y cartas de Marco Aurelio. Fr. 6. 3.

Historia Ethiopique de Heliodorus. Fr. 6. 6

Computus Ecclesiasticus Clavij. Fr. 6. 17.

Le Theatre du Monde. Fr. 6. 25.

Roma Ricercata dal Martinelli. Fr. 6. 31.

Julian the Apostate.   Fr. 7. 3.

The History of France under Mazarine. Fr. 7. 7.

Mercurius Gallo-Belgicus Tom. 1. Fr. 8. 2 6½. 81

Tom. 2.   Fr. 8. 3.

Tom. 3.   Fr. 8. 4

Tom. 4.   Fr. 8. 5.

Tom: 5.   Fr. 8. 6.

Tom. 6.   Fr. 8. 7.

Tom: 7.   Fr. 8. 8.

Rich: Lassels Voyage of Italy. Fr. 8. 10.

Selecta Delicia P: Suavij. Fr. 8. 11. 6½. 14½

Of the River Nile.   Fr. 9. 15.

Bacons History of the Winds. Fr. 10. 4.

unhappy Prosperity. Fr. 10. 6.

Memoires de M. D. L. R. Fr. 10. 19

Hollinsheds Chronicle. A. 11. 2.

Polidorus virgilius de rebq Ang: A. 11. 4.

Origines Judiciales by Dugdale. A. 11. 7.

The Journal of S. Amour   A. 11. 8.

The History of Draining by Dugdale A. 11. 9.

Historical Antiquities of Cheshire A. 11. 12.

R: Hacklint of English voyages. A. 12. 5.

The vale Royal by D. King. A. 12. 6.

The History of Philip de Comines. A. 12. 9.

kept together with classical rhetoric or combined with modern history, many owners increasingly choosing the latter course. The book owner now had to puzzle a bit longer about where to shelve certain genres, such as biography, antiquarianism, or chronology. Some older habits die hard: one might now incline to put a work like Foxe's *Acts and Monuments* in with Camden and Holinshed under "history"; most seventeenth- and early eighteenth-century owners continued to keep Foxe, along with other ecclesiastical historians such as Eusebius, under "divinity," thereby maintaining the long-standing division of histories into the two grand categories, sacred and profane.[34]

INSTITUTIONAL LIBRARIES

In our assessment of the circulation of historical reading matter and its availability it is important that the role of *institutional* (a more accurate term than *public*) libraries not be neglected. History was not a major subject of study in the Middle Ages, and the number of manuscripts of chronicles known to have existed in the libraries of monasteries, cathedrals, colleges, and chapels is quite small in comparison to works in the core religious and moral curriculum, books of statutes and the like, a picture confirmed by the studies of the late N. R. Ker. Nevertheless, histories could be found there, with Higden and Geoffrey of Monmouth especially prominent; the numbers swell somewhat if one includes among the historical such genres as hagiography and martyrology in addition to chronicles-proper. The records of St. George's chapel, Windsor list the acquisition, for twenty-eight shillings four pence, of a "Martyrology" in 1400.[35] Not all the cathedrals had equally strong collections, the nine secular cathedrals of the pre-Henrician period being less well-endowed than those attached to religious houses.[36] Moreover, the holdings of the great medieval libraries were substantially disrupted by the Reformation, even in the cases of those abbeys that survived the

---

[34] Most modern libraries have continued to keep Foxe with the divinity books: under the "BR"s rather than the "DA"s, for instance, in the Library of Congress system. The categorical ambiguity raises problems of nomenclature for us, too. As elsewhere in the present work, I will use the phrases *history book(s)* or *historical book(s)* interchangeably, and have defined them broadly to include both traditional narrative histories and chronicles, but also antiquarian works, historical philology, sacred genealogy and history, and biography or autobiography. Unless otherwise noted, I do not include fictional or romance *histories* under this rubric.

[35] Hist. MSS Comm., *Var. Coll.*, VII, p. 32.

[36] The nine being in the dioceses of Lincoln, York, London, Exeter, Salisbury, Chichester, Lichfield, Wells, and Hereford, in contrast to the "monastic" cathedrals, Durham, Norwich, Rochester, Canterbury, Worcester, Winchester, Coventry, and Carlisle. I am grateful to Richard Sharpe for drawing my attention to the differences in bibliographic holdings.

Plate 4.11 (*opposite*) Page from a contemporary catalog of the library of the Towneley family, Chetham's Library, Manchester, Mun. A.2.67.

dissolution as cathedrals: the revived cathedral libraries of the later seventeenth century owed their strengths to the efforts of contemporary and recent canons, deans, and bishops, rather than to a continuous tradition from the Middle Ages.

The importance of the great college and university libraries at Oxford and Cambridge (the university collections being largely the creations of the seventeenth century), and of the smaller collections at other educational foundations such as Eton and Winchester Colleges, hardly needs to be restated here. From a very early date they included, quite apart from their great collections of manuscripts and other medieval documents, significant holdings in printed histories. Eton College's library had, at the death in 1623 of one of its greatest provosts, Sir Henry Savile, over 1,000 volumes of which a number were historical.[37] An early list of the Bodleian's printed books and manuscripts drawn up in 1603–4, before the permanent separation of the manuscripts, shows history as a small but not insignificant subject area, with authors including Herodotus, Thucydides, Eutropius, Sozomenus, Einhard, Henry of Huntingdon, Roger Hoveden, Commynes, Sabellico, Gaguin, and du Haillan. Modern chronicles, such as Holinshed and Grafton, are conspicuously absent, betraying the preferences of Sir Thomas Bodley himself, who was not alone in favoring the old and especially the classical.[38]

The early records of the Bodleian provide much incidental information on the costs of particular items, their transport, and incidental costs like binding and chaining,[39] and for the copying out of catalogs. Bills amounting to £3 8s 8d from three different Oxford sellers for binding several books were paid by the librarian, Thomas James, on 7 September 1613. The receipt of moneys paid to Josias Guy, one of two regular carriers between Oxford and London, cover "carriage of books at diverse times as it appeareth by bill." In 1634–35 the library paid £1 9s 11d to Thomas Edgerlie or Eadgerly for bringing "Sir Kenelme Digbies bookes from London." These were in fact the books left to Digby in 1632 by his former tutor, Thomas Allen, the *eminence grise* of Gloucester Hall. On the advice of Sir Robert Cotton and Archbishop Laud,

---

[37] Robert Birley, "The History of Eton College Library," *The Library*, 5th series, 11 (1956), 231–61, at p. 245.

[38] Bodl. MS Bodley 763, fos. 62r–190v; Jackson, *Libraries and Librarianship in the West* pp. 145–49. But one also recalls Bodley's view, expressed to Thomas James, that Hall and Fabian were standard items for a collection: above, chapter 1 and Bodley, *Letters . . . to Thomas James*, ed. with an introduction by G. W. Wheeler (Oxford, 1926), p. 225.

[39] For the cost of chains at Wells Cathedral in 1735, see Hist. MSS Comm. *Dean and Chapter of Wells*, II, 527; on chains at Winchester Cathedral library during and after the civil war period, see *Winchester Cathedral Documents, AD 1636–1683*, vol. II, ed. W. R. W. Stephens and F. T. Madge (Hampshire Rec. Soc. (1897), p. xxv; Walter Oakeshott, "Winchester College Library before 1750," *The Library*, 5th series 9 (1954), 1–16, and Winchester Cathedral archive, Chapter Order Book, 1661 and 1662, modern transcript, items 21, 22. I am indebted to Miss C. J. Humphreys of the Hampshire Record Office for drawing my attention to this document and for supplying a photocopy.

Digby passed them on to the Bodleian, but the library had to bear the transportation costs, which included a further three shillings to an unnamed person for fetching the books from the carriers, who had only conveyed the books as far as the town limits, and two shillings to porters "for carrying them to the Librarie." A similar bequest from Laud himself in 1635–36 also came with a price: the carrier received £2 5s 2d "for bringing my Lord of Canterbury his bookes [and] coynes" among other items.[40] The Bodleian records show books being bought both "here and there in London" and as far away as the Frankfurt book fair, and still others being bequeathed from far afield.[41] John Rous or Rouse, Thomas James' successor as Bodley's librarian (not to be confused with his same-named contemporary, the Cambridge diarist), often bought the books himself and was subsequently reimbursed by the library, to which perhaps we owe the good fortune of such precise accounts. At one time Rouse paid an unspecified sum to "Badgers wife" (the spouse of Richard Badger, beadle of the Stationers' company) for "an old chronicle of St. Alban."[42]

The early acquisitions of the Bodleian included a number of histories beyond the standard classics, though theology and logic were at this stage far more important areas of collection in part because relatively few new historical and antiquarian books, English or otherwise, had been published in comparison with the boom in the later seventeenth century. Even before it became a deposit library, along with the Royal Library and the University Library at Cambridge, through the 1662 Press Act (a measure reiterated in the Copyright Act of 1710),[43] the Bodleian had already worked out an arrangement with the Stationers' Company regarding new books, and in any case many authors saw merit in having a copy of their work in the great library: the early Jacobean historian John Clapham even provided funds for

---

[40] *The Bodleian Library Account Book, 1613–1646*, ed. Gwen Hampshire (Oxford, 1983), pp. 6, 10, 99, 105. Further costs were incurred in keeping tidy the reading-room above the divinity school (the "Arts End," added in 1610); at various times in the mid–1640s, during the royalist use of Oxford as the king's headquarters, locals such as "Goodwife Carpenter a poore woman and two of her daughters" were paid 18s for helping the porter to sweep the library and closets weekly, and they were paid 8d for helping, along with several "poore schollars" (who collectively got 1s) "for helping to tie, brush bookes and shelves against the Visitation of the Librarye": ibid., pp. 144, 150–51. For comparable records of expenses for upkeep at Eton College Library, see Birley, "The History of Eton College Library," 238.

[41] Hampshire, ed., *The Bodleian Library Account Book*, pp. 49, 84.

[42] Ibid., pp. 59, 64; this chronicle has been identified by Hampshire as Bodl. MS e. Mus. 42, an English version of Rogerus Albanus, *Progenies regum Britanniae*, written *ca.* 1461 and now in a seventeenth-century binding.

[43] The deposit rights granted in the 1662 Press Act and most of its successors, including the 1710 Copyright Act, were unhelpful, however, on the precise mechanism whereby libraries were to receive their free copies; as a result, in the course of the eighteenth century the statutory privilege would become an empty, unenforceable shell, most libraries failing to receive very much by this method: John Feather, *Publishing, Piracy and Politics: an Historical Study of Copyright in Britain* (1994), p. 100.

the library to buy his own history of England in 1606.[44] Others were bought at the instigation of the librarians. The earliest extant book bills, from the period of Thomas James' librarianship, include a copy of Thucydides in Greek purchased in 1615 for 3s 6d; the 1562 Graeco-Latin edition of the Byzantine historian Nicephorus Gregoras (15s); and a history of England in French (£1 10s).[45]

Owing in large measure to its founder and the efforts of Thomas James and his seventeenth-century successors, the Bodleian occupied an almost unique position throughout most of the seventeenth century as an unofficial national library, as Humfrey Wanley noted during the 1690s.[46] Yet the genuine article, an official or at least royally sponsored library intended to serve the reading interests of the realm's intellectual elite, was much slower in coming. The Tudors and early Stuarts ignored several different proposals from scholars such as Leland, John Dee, and Sir Robert Cotton for the establishment of a national library of books and manuscripts, a decision that led to some of the literary wealth of the dissolved monastic libraries being irrevocably lost, though much of it ended up, like monastic property, in private hands.[47] Genuinely public libraries of the sort that would eventually be found in boroughs throughout Britain appeared in the seventeenth century for the first time, but they grew much more slowly than private collections. Even London had no truly public library until the very end of the seventeenth century, as distinguishable from the private, and usually socially exclusive, collections of Sir Hans Sloane and the Harleys. This was a less agreeable facet of London life observed by the Huguenot emigré Francis Misson.[48] John Evelyn considered it a "greate reproch" to the city and strongly supported Thomas Tenison's project to establish a public library in the 1690s.[49] Even in 1705,

[44] W. Dunn Macray, *Annals of the Bodleian Library*, 2nd edn (1890), p. 28.

[45] Ibid., pp. 160–61. This bill includes such titles as Gonçalo de Illescas, *De la Historia Pontifical* (part 2, Bruges, 1578) and Henry Haestens, *Memorabile histoire du siège d'Ostende* (Leiden, 1615). A 1645 bill includes 5s 6d for Henricus Guthberletus (Hendrik Gutberleth), *Chronologia* (Amsterdam, 1639): ibid., pp. 176–77.

[46] BL MS Harl. 7055, fos. 42r–44r, now printed in S. G. Gillam and R. W. Hunt, "The Curators of the Library and Humphrey [*sic*] Wanley," *Bodleian Library Record*, 5.2 (October 1954), 85–98, at p. 88.

[47] R. H. Fritze, "'Truth hath lacked witnesse, tyme wanted light': the Dispersal of the English Monastic Libraries and Protestant Efforts at Preservation, *ca.* 1535–1625," *Journal of Library History*, 18 (1983), 274–91; I. R. Willison, "The Development of the British Museum Library to 1857 in its European Context: a tour d'horizon," in Raabe, *Öffentliche und Private Bibliotheken*, pp. 33–61.

[48] François or Francis M. *Misson's Memoirs and Observations in his Travels over England*, trans. John Ozell (1719), pp. 174–75, 195 comments on the Tenison foundation and on the scarcity of libraries throughout the kingdom, though conceding that "There are a great many noblemen [i.e., peers and gentry] in England that love books, and have good collections of them."

[49] *Remarks and Collections of Thomas Hearne*, ed. C. E. Doble, D. W. Rannie, *et al.* (11 vols., Oxford Historical Society, 1885–1921), I, 60.

Dr. Thomas Smith, custodian of the Cottonian collection, would complain to his friend Thomas Hearne of the dearth of libraries in the City.[50] In 1697 Richard Bentley pointed to the decaying condition of the once-great Royal Library of James I, of which he had been appointed keeper in 1694. In 1697 Bentley presented a detailed proposal for the statutory establishment of a national library in a new building. It would take over another half-century, a further serious blow in the Cottonian fire of 1731, the political connections of the energetic Sloane, and the offer of the latter's own books to the nation, before the new library was finally established at Montagu House, as part of the British Museum, bringing together the Sloane, Harleian, and Cottonian collections, with the Royal Library to be merged by gift of George II in 1757. And even then, it was eighty more years until the library acquired its famous domed reading-room (just abandoned for St. Pancras as this chapter was written), together with some measure of independence from the museum, Sloane himself having envisaged his books and manuscripts as a mere appendage to his equally remarkable collection of natural curiosities.[51]

During the middle and later eighteenth century, and beyond the boundaries of this study, the situation would improve considerably both within and outside the metropolis, as the larger cities and provincial towns developed two other types of library, from which, more importantly, books could be borrowed rather than merely consulted *in situ*.[52] The "circulating" library arose as a device by booksellers to market some of their unsellable stock – a concession to the fact that many readers wanted to read certain books rather than own them; customers would pay a "rental" fee for the use of a title, and/or an annual subscription fee, practices already used by coffeehouses during the late seventeenth century. A rental would often be the first step toward a purchase: Francis Sitwell, for instance, paid seven shillings to a bookseller in January 1731 "for six plays & reading the Roman history."[53] The earliest such library appears to have begun in Huntingdon in 1718; they were well established exactly a century later when, at the conclusion of *Mansfield Park*, Jane Austen's Fanny Price selected a number of histories and

---

[50] *The Diary of John Evelyn* (6 vols., Oxford, 1955), IV, 368 (13 February 1684). For a scheme to assemble a public library at Boston (New England) in the 1720s, see J. Nichols, *Illustrations of the literary History of the Eighteenth Century*, (8 vols. 1817–58), IV, 270 (Timothy Cutler to Zachary Grey, 2 April 1725).

[51] Willison, "The Development of the British Museum Library," p. 48.

[52] Hilda Hamlyn, "Eighteenth-Century Circulating Libraries in England," *The Library*, 5th series 1 (1947), 197–222; James Raven, "From Promotion to Proscription: Arrangements for Reading and Eighteenth-Century Libraries," in James Raven, Helen Small, and Naomi Tadmor (eds.), *The Practice and Representation of Reading in England* (Cambridge, 1996), pp. 175–201, principally concerned with the period from 1740 onward.

[53] Paul Kaufman, "Coffee Houses as Reading Centres," *Libraries and their Users* (1969), pp. 115–27 and "The Community Library: a Chapter in English Social History," ibid., pp. 188–222, at p. 191.

biographies from a circulating library. The "subscription" library, which originated in Augustan book clubs and reading societies was much less widespread and developed fully later still. Of more immediate relevance here, though even more restrictive in its readership, is a third category, sometimes called the "appurtenant" library, a library attached to a society or body that existed for reasons other than simply to have a library – the Society of Antiquaries or the Royal Society, for instance. Many of these arose in the later seventeenth century and some still exist; the Gentleman's Society founded at Peterborough in 1722 required its new members each to present a volume "either in history, antiquities, philosophy &c" to a collection intended ultimately for public use in Peterborough Cathedral.[54]

Within the larger category of institutional libraries, however, a more important development for the circulation of history books was the growth of what might be called the "community" library. This in itself is a somewhat elastic term that covers a variety of different sorts of public and semipublic (in the sense of being commonly owned) repositories, the purposes of which were often quite different. The three most common sorts were the parochial library, the school library and, of much later and slower growth, the town or borough public library.[55] Though these could scarcely hope to compete with the wealth of the great university and private libraries, they were ultimately of greater importance in bringing rural society into a national historical culture, since they contained a supply of historical reading matter that was accessible, if not borrowable, by a broader constituency than the gentry.[56] We know from the diarist, William Whiteway, that puritan Dorchester had a library of its own before the civil wars; and even a small town like Totnes in Devon was possessed, by the end of the century, of "a pretty small library of old books."[57] As Paul Kaufman has shown, the prominence of political

[54] Nichols, *Illustrations of the Literary History of the Eighteenth Century*, IV, 357 (Robert Smyth to Zachary Grey, n.d. 1745, re. Grey's membership in the Society). For the various types of eighteenth-century library, see P. Sturges, "The Place of Libraries in the English Urban Renaissance of the Eighteenth Century," *Libraries and Culture*, 24 (1989), 57–68.

[55] Kaufman, "The Community Library"; Thomas Kelly, *Early Public Libraries: a History of Public Libraries in Great Britain Before 1850* (1966).

[56] The dissenting academies of the post-Restoration era, in contrast to the universities and to Anglican parishes, did not develop a library system until the mid-eighteenth century; though about fifty of these had been founded by 1730, it was not until that year that the first institutional library attached to an academy was established. As D. L. Ferch explains, this was in spite of the enormous importance placed by dissenters on reading, and is at least partially explained by a greater reliance on private libraries because of the fear of persecution and its frequent consequence, book confiscation, which destroyed more than one private collection between 1663 and the accession of George I and probably encouraged self-imposed limits on private libraries: Ferch, " 'Good books are a very great mercy to the world': Persecution, Private Libraries, and the Printed Word in the Early Development of the Dissenting Academies, 1663–1730," *Journal of Library History*, 21 (1986), 350–61.

[57] David Underdown, *Fire from Heaven: Life in an English Town in the Seventeenth Century* (New Haven, 1992), pp. 55–56; *The Journal of James Yonge [1647–1721], Plymouth Surgeon*, ed. F. N. L. Poynter (1963), p. 148.

history, biography, and memoirs in the holdings of such libraries would increase quite sharply in the eighteenth century: By 1798 the prospectus of one circulating library's holdings shows history and travel taking up 75 percent of the titles, while religion has shrunk to 1 percent; Hume and Gibbon, wrote one wit, "Take the air in a coach, or sedan every day."[58]

Although school and parochial libraries were more widespread than borough libraries, they were also more limited in their contents, though this, too, could vary according to the initial benefaction. The eminent preacher Thomas Plume (1630–1704), vicar of Greenwich for nearly half a century and eventually archdeacon of Rochester, endowed a library in his home town of Maldon, Essex, to be placed in the free school he had founded a few years earlier. He left the town some property to provide capital, all his own books – some 7,000 to 8,000 titles – and some very specific terms for the library's administration. Plume's librarian had to be in orders, and preferably "a scholar that knows books." He would have to post a £200 bond as surety against stealing any of Plume's books, and he was to be present at least four hours a day, six days a week, to permit access.[59]

Many of these "libraries" are perhaps too grandly titled. In most instances they were small collections, often housed in existing rooms and corners of old buildings scarcely designed for the purpose and sometimes dangerously unsuitable. Indeed, this was sometimes true of larger libraries as well – a maltster who had been keeping his wares in the fratry at Carlisle Cathedral was ordered to remove them in April 1704 because the mouse population was wreaking havoc on the library below – but more concerted efforts were made by many cathedrals toward the end of the seventeenth century to preserve against both the environment and theft.[60] Fire was a constant risk, and there was little security for books, though churchwardens' accounts from the sixteenth century on frequently list specific titles – mainly Bibles and sometimes a copy of Foxe – as part of the church inventory. Most smaller parochial libraries were in the charge of their incumbents, who sometimes had their own volumes. Many would donate some or all of their own volumes to the parish on their death or departure. Thomas Townsend, rector of Codlingstock, died in 1702 leaving all his printed books to his successor.

---

[58] Kaufman, "The Community Library," pp. 189, 197–8.
[59] S. G. Deed and J. Francis, *Catalogue of the Plume Library at Maldon, Essex* (Maldon: Plume Library Trustees, 1959); Frank Herrmann, "The Emergence of the Book Auctioneer as a Professional," in Robin Myers and Michael Harris (eds.), *Property of a Gentleman: the Formation, Organisation and Dispersal of the Private Library, 1620–1920* (Winchester, UK, 1991), pp. 1–14, at pp. 2–3.
[60] Cumbria RO, D/MH, Cathedral Leasebook 1672–1707, p. 107 (28 April). Worcester, for instance, moved its books from the nave to the chapterhouse in the 1680s, where they remained for nearly two centuries. This did not of itself add to the security of either books or manuscripts, which continued to stray: I. Atkins and N. R. Ker, introduction to their edition of Patrick Young, *Catalogus Librorum manuscriptorum bibliothecae Wigorniensis* (Cambridge, 1944), p. 26.

The shelf list of these books show 59 folio volumes, 69 quartos, 89 octavos (including three stray volumes appended at the end), and 188 titles in smaller format. The vast majority of his books were religious or moral, but Townsend also owned 22 historical works (mainly folios and quartos), and these included both classical texts and select modern works, many of which were not concerned with church history.[61] Eighteen years later, Robert Turie, assistant minister of Sheffield, left to the curates of Bradfield the use of his similarly sized collection. This bequest was largely religious, but again included a wide assortment of historical, antiquarian, or geographical works. Some of these, too, were on ecclesiastical topics (Cave's *Lives* and Michael Geddes' *Church-history of Ethiopia*), but others were not: Turie had owned Peter Heylyn's *Cosmographie*, Richard Baker's *Chronicle*, Geoffrey Fenton's Elizabethan translation of Guicciardini's *History of Italy*, Bishop Nicolson's *Scottish Historical Library*, an English translation of Vertot's *The history of the revolutions in Sweden*, and Aylett Sammes' *Britannia antiqua illustrata*.[62] The incumbents' library at Basingstoke, cataloged in 1728 as part of an inventory of church goods, similarly included seventy-three books, of which seventeen were historical.[63]

Like Townsend and Turie, Richard Forster, rector of Crundale, bequeathed his substantial collection of books to the parish, to be administered by successive incumbents and by the living's patron, Sir Edward Filmer of East Sutton. In 1734 Filmer instructed Silas Drayton, the new rector, to copy out in fair hand Forster's original catalog and to have it bound, together with a blank quire at the end for recording future benefactions. "I intended to have wrote it at leisure-hours according to your first-mention'd indulgence to me, but shall now make it the sole business of the day." Once finished this

---

[61] Borthwick Inst., Bp. C and P I/24. The historical works included Funk's *Chronology*, Josephus' *Antiquities*, Olaus Magnus' *History of the Goths*, William Martyn's *Historie, and Lives, of the Kings of England*, Cave's *Antiquitates Apostolicae*, Heylyn's *Ecclesia Restaurata, Help to English History*, and *Cyprianus Anglicus*, Platina's *Vitae pontificorum* in Latin, Cosin's *Scholastic History of the Canon of Scripture* and *Historia transubstantionis papalis*, Tillesley's *Animadversions* on Selden's *History of Tithes*, Carion's *Chronicle*, the epitome of Roman histories by Lucius Florus, and Suetonius' *Lives*. There is no space in an already long book to list every historical item contained in each library; throughout the rest of this chapter, the historical contents of libraries are, with few exceptions, summarized numerically or illustrated with select titles.

[62] Turie's library list of 1720, more fully recorded since it includes dates of editions, has a similar distribution of subject areas to that in Townsend's, but the selection of histories is quite different: Borthwick Inst. Bp. C and P II/18.

[63] Hants. RO, 35 M48/16/17–20: items include Eusebius; Scaliger's *De emendatione temporum*; Ussher's *Annales*; Livy; Sallust; Caesar's *Commentaries*; Quintus Curtius; Florus; Velleius Paterculus; Lucan; William Lloyd's *Series chronologica*; William Whiston's *Short view of the Chronology of the Old Testament*; and the first (1659) volume of John Rushworth's *Historical Collections*. The Rushworth title was given by James Rolstone, citizen of London, but most of the rest (including all the other histories) by the vicar, Dr. George Wheeler.

book was to be held and maintained by the incumbents; future ministers were to sign the original in Filmer's hands at East-Sutton.[64] The latest parochial catalog in our selection, it contains an extensive collection of history ranging well beyond matters of the church, select titles of which are reproduced in table 4.11, together with their estimated values.

Forster had clearly been an avid bibliophile. He owned a high proportion of religious works, including books of "popish controversy" and collections of sermons, and his will leaves the volumes, together with a collection of chronological tables he had acquired, "as a parochial library . . . for the use of all succeeding rectors."[65] Yet the number of secular histories, including very recent works, is unusual for a parochial library – certainly when compared to the "standard issue" of seventy or so titles of some described below. This suggests that its founder and patron envisaged it less as an exclusive armory for incumbents writing sermons or combating atheism and immorality than as a general reference library for the parish elite. The high proportion of English and Irish history in the catalog is also of interest, in comparison with the classical bias of most cleric's libraries even half a century earlier. There were also a few treasures, works that elsewhere might have fitted into the nascent "rare book" category, like a copy of the 1549 prayer book, here valued at a mere four shillings, or an unvalued copy of the first edition of Camden's *Remains* (1605).[66] The presence of such an extensive library in the parish may also owe something to the support of the patron, Filmer, a book collector in his own right, though it would be unwise to assume that gentry reading interests were always more secular than those of their clerical counterparts. A list of gifts to the Sutton Courtenay parish library about 1720 consists largely of works on church history donated both by local gentlemen and neighboring clergy.[67]

---

[64] Houghton Lib. MS f. Eng. 789, "A copy of a catalogue of books, left by the Reverend Richard Forster, MA, rector of Crundale, to his successors in the said living, for ever; taken and presented to Sr. Edward Filmer of East-Sutton, Bart. Patron of the said living, by me Silas Drayton rector of Crundale AD 1734." Fos. 1–41, quarto vol., complete with valuations; this includes a letter dated 15 October 1734 from Silas Drayton to Filmer.

[65] Ibid., fo. 38v.

[66] Houghton Lib. MS Eng. 790 is an autograph catalog of the books in Edward Filmer's study taken by him in November 1708. Its books are arranged under the usual categories – divinity, philosophy, poetry, and so on – but have the added interesting feature of a catalog numbering system showing the title's proper place on its shelf, individual volumes in a multivolumed set having individual numbers. This strongly suggests a personal library from which persons other than the owner were expected to borrow. The total number of books, not including pamphlets, is 498, of which historical works account for forty-five, slightly under 10 percent.

[67] Berks RO, D/P 128/25/1 (microfilm 452), list of donors of books in Sutton Courtenay parish library, *ca.* 1720. Donations include Foxe in three volumes (by Doctor Charles Tucker), Heylyn's *Aerius Redivus or the History of the Presbyterians* (by Robert Hill, former minister at Drayton); Josephus' works, including the *Jewish Antiquities* (by Mr. Francis Justice of Sutton Courtenay); and Jeremy Collier's edition of Louis Moréri's *The great historical, geographical, genealogical and poetical dictionary* in 2 vols. (by Mr. James Justice).

Table 4.11. Histories in the Crundale library (1734) and their valuation in £ s d (selected titles only)

Folio

Anthony Wood, *Athenae Oxonienses* 1691/2	1-5-6
William Camden, *Britannia* 1695	no price; annotation says "a present"
White Kennett et al., *Complete History of England*, 2nd edn, 1719	3-10-0
Edward Hyde, earl of Clarendon, *History of the Rebellion* 1702–4, 3 vols.	3-17-0
Josephus, *Opera* (Oxford, 1700), Greek and Latin	0-10-6
Richard Knolles, *The history of the Turkish Empire* (continued by Rycaut), 3 vols., 1687	3-0-0
Serenus Cressy, *Church history of Brittany* (annotated "popish"), 1668	0-10-0
Paolo Sarpi, *History of the Council of Trent*, trans. N. Brent, 1629	0-5-6
Henry Wharton, *Anglia sacra*, 2 vols, 1691	1-12-0
John Nalson, *An impartial collection of the great affairs of state* (undated: 1682–83)	2-0-0
James Ussher, *Britannicarum ecclesiarum antiquitates*, 1687	1-0-0
Christoph Helvicus, *Theatrvm historicvm et chronologicvm* (interleaved) (Oxford), 1662	0-12-0
Peter Leycester, *Historical Antiquities*, 1673	0-5-6
John Pettus, *Fodinae regales, or, The history, laws and places of the chief mines and mineral works in England, Wales, and the English Pale in Ireland*, 1670	0-2-6
John Lewis, *The history and antiquities, ecclesiastical and civil, of the Isle of Tenet [sic] in Kent*, 1723	endorsed "donum authoris"
John Lewis, *The History and Antiquities of the Abbey and Church of Favresham*, 1727	"donum authoris", no value assigned
John Foxe, *Acts and Monuments*, 3 vols, 1632	

Quarto

Louis de Maimbourg, *The history of the crusade*, trans. John Nalson	0-11-6
Bartolomeo Sacci (Platina), *The lives of the popes*, trans. and continued by Paul Rycaut, 1685	0-16-6
Joshua Barnes, *The history of that most victorious monarch Edward III*, Cambridge, 1688	0-15-0
Richard Baker, *Chronicle*, 1674 edn	0-0-0 [sic]
John Morton, *The Natural History of Northampton-shire with some account of the antiquities*, 1712	1-3-6
Robert Thoroton, *Antiquities of Nottinghamshire*, 1712	0-7-6
John Evelyn, *Numismata: a discourse of medals, antient and modern*, 1697	0-15-0

Title	Value
Robert Cary, *Palaeologia chronica: A chronological account of ancient time in three parts*, 1677	£2 combined
William Cave, *Antiquitates Christianae*, including Jeremy Taylor's *Life of Christ* (9th edn of 1703?)	
Gilbert Burnet, *History of the Reformation*, 3 vols., 1681, 1683, 1715	2-7-0
John Strype, *Memorials of Thomas Cranmer, Archbishop of Canterbury*, 1694	no value assigned
John Strype, *The life and acts of Matthew Parker*, 1711	4-5-0
John Strype, *Annals of the Reformation*, vol. I, 1709	1-13-6
John Strype, *The history of the life and acts of . . . Edmund Grindal*, 1710	1-13-6
John Strype, *The life and acts of . . . John Whitgift, DD*, 1718 (bound together with preceding item)	0-18-0
Wm. Somner, *Antiquities of Canterbury* (including Nicholas Batteley, *Cantuaria Sacra*), 1703	no value assigned
John Marsham, *Chronicus canon aegyptiacus ebraicus graecus et disquisitiones*, 1672	no value assigned
Philippus van Limborch, *Historia inquisitionis*, Amsterdam, 1692	5-7-0
Louis Ellies Dupin, *A new history of ecclesiastical writers . . . epitomised in English*, trans. W. Wotton, 5 vols., 1692–1703	no value assigned
Isaac [i.e. Jacob] Spon, *The history of the city and state of Geneva*, 1687	0-4-6
Edward Stillingfleet, *Origines Britannicae or, the antiquities of the British churches*, 1685	0-11-5
Robert Plot, *The natural history of Oxford-shire*, 1677 (entitled simply "History of Oxfordshire" in MS)	0-10-0
John Harris, *The History of Kent*, 1719	no value assigned
William Dugdale, *Antiquities of Warwickshire*, 1656	0-16-6
Octavo[a]	
Henry Guthry, *Memoirs of Henry Guthry, late Bishop of Dunkel [sic], in Scotland*, 1702	0-3-6
Edward Wells, *An historical geography of the Old and New Testament*, 4 vols., 1711	1-1-0
Thomas Tanner, *Notitia monastica, or, A short history of the religious houses in England and Wales*, Oxford, 1695	0-4-6
William Wotton, *Reflections on ancient and modern learning*, 1697	0-6-0

Total all books = 850 volumes

---

[a]The collection also includes a number of duodecimo and smaller-sized volumes, and tracts and pamphlets bound together.

The generosity of departing ministers like Forster and Thomas Plume was essential to the establishment of parochial libraries that would, like magnets, attract future donations. But the administration and upkeep of the endowments were not always straightforward. The occasional incumbent could not resist helping himself to parochial volumes that had been left in his charge. Some parishes solved the problem by making ministers agree to articles on the use and maintenance of libraries, as seen above in the case of Plume's collection at Malden, and at the very end of the seventeenth century Dr. Thomas Bray (1656–1730), an enthusiast for the equipping of ministers in far-off America,[68] developed a scheme to erect libraries in every deanery or large parish in England. With the backing of the church, and eventually of the Society for the Promotion of Christian Knowledge (est. 1699), Bray also succeeded in pushing through parliament an act for the "better preservation of parochial libraries"; his work was carried on after his death by an admiring group of "Associates" assembled in 1723.[69] The rules established by the Bray-inspired statute, copies of which are often included with extant parochial library catalogs, obliged rectors and vicars to make and sign a catalog for deposit with the diocesan consistory court, mandated the keeping of a donors' book, and enjoined churchwardens to lock up the library on the death of the incumbent and keep it shut till a new minister was appointed; penalties for embezzling books were laid out; most interestingly, incumbents were forbidden to lend the books.[70]

The Bray-created parochial libraries were centrally organized, individual libraries being assigned a number, and incumbents were instructed to draw up catalogs and have them printed. Some parishes went beyond the minimum requirements: Wigton enforced on its vicars a covenant whereby they promised not to remove any books from the library at any time.[71] Henry

---

[68] B. C. Steiner, "Rev. Thomas Bray and his American Libraries," *American Historical Review*, 2 (1895–96), 59–75.

[69] *Bibliotheca parochialis, or, A scheme of such theological heads both general and particular, as are more peculiarly requisite to be well studied by every pastor of a parish: together with a catalogue of books which may be read upon each of those points* (1697); considerably expanded in second edition of 1707, in which Bray envisaged a pyramidal system of libraries with parochial, lending libraries at the bottom and decanal and general libraries above. At one point Bray drew up a list of the places supplied with libraries, arranged by diocese, county, and town. Not surprisingly, a survey of some of the listed catalogs shows the books to be overwhelmingly religious and polemical, even the history books.

[70] Folger MS W.b. 595, unfoliated, preface to a register of Feltham, Middlesex, parish library, probably the address given at its foundation, *ca.* 1725. The library was founded by Sir Nathan Decker and this volume was intended as the register of the books but (unfortunately for us) was never used as such. It includes the printed text of the act for preserving parochial libraries: this library was to be divided into theoretico-practical works, didactical tracts on Christian doctrine (including historical works and philology), and pastoral books.

[71] Cumbria RO, PR/36/40–42, articles of agreement sealed 22 October 1687 between Thomas Tullie, chancellor of the diocese of Carlisle, Henry Geddes, vicar of Wigton, and several churchwardens. Item 42 in the bundle is a catalog of the Wigton library from the early

Walmsley, curate of the parish of St. Leonard, New Malton in Yorkshire was directed in 1721 by the lawyer for Thomas Wentworth, Esq., the principal patron of the parish's new library, to sign receipts on the catalog he received along with the books, in the presence of churchwardens "or other principal inhabitants" and send one copy to the archbishop of York and the other to the London lawyer, Henry Newman of the Middle Temple: the receipt itself is endorsed by Walmsley, the two churchwardens, and three parishioners. This might seem a great trouble over a tiny library of four shelves and seventy-one volumes; the total value of the books, less £1 6s for the bookcase and £1 5s packing and shipping was only £20 18s 3d. But it bespeaks the serious determination of ecclesiastical authorities and lay patrons alike to ensure that their endowments were administered in a safe and orderly fashion.[72]

The larger college and cathedral libraries had in fact anticipated or even surpassed parochial measures several decades earlier, with Bishop Cosin's library at Durham (1669) a pace-setter on such matters as the use of wall shelving, which aided accessibility, and, in darker buildings, improved visibility.[73] The chapter order book of Winchester Cathedral for 1669 ordered the compilation of a catalog of the cathedral's books – an earlier list of the muniments and charters had been drawn up in 1646 after the second overrunning of the library by troops in October of that year. The 1669 order forbade anyone who was not a prebendary from having a key to the library. A 1676 order repeated this need for a catalog and allotted funds for chains to bind the books, and the will of the diocese's bishop, George Morley (1597–1684) dictated restricted but regular opening hours tied to the seasons to maximize the use of natural light.[74]

Not surprisingly, most parochial libraries (both locally founded ones and

---

eighteenth century, and a handwritten copy of Bray's statutory *Rules*. Some of the parish's books, acquired in 1687, came from a bequest by a Huntingdonshire minister, including a copy of Izaak Walton's *Lives*.

[72] Borth. Inst. Bp. C and P II/20, and appended catalog of parochial library no. 62. Cf. another example of similar size, the first item of which was Eusebius, *Ecclesiastical History*, parochial library no. 18, for Marske, in the North Riding of Yorkshire, receipted by the vicar, churchwardens, and three parishioners in 1712: Borth. Inst. Bp. C and P I/38.

[73] D. Pearson, "Elias Smith, Durham Cathedral Librarian, 1633–1676," *Library History*, 8 (1989), 65–73; Hobson, "English Library Buildings," p. 68. Durham was also the first cathedral library to have a thorough modern catalog of its manuscript holdings drawn up, Thomas Rud's *Codicum manuscriptorum Ecclesiae Cathedralis Dunelmensis catalogus classicus*, though this was not published until 1825.

[74] Hants RO, Winchester cathedral transcripts, graciously provided by Miss C. J. Humphreys of the Hampshire Record Office. John Chase, chapter clerk of the cathedral, drew up a catalog of the library's printed and manuscript holdings, a transcript of which is in the cathedral library: *Winchester Cathedral Documents, AD 1636–1683*, ed. W. R. W. Stephens and F. R. Madge (Winchester, Hampshire Rec. Soc., 1897), introduction, items 21–24. I am again grateful to Miss Humphreys and to her colleague Sarah Lewin for the above references and informative correspondence.

the smaller number of Bray-created libraries of the Augustan era) were devoted primarily to religious works, and although ecclesiastical history and antiquities constituted a major category of divine learning, by no means all parishes included any sort of history, ecclesiastical or otherwise. On the whole, however, the likelihood of finding historical works increases as one moves forward in time. The thirteen titles listed in the Stevenage vestry minutes for 1575, for instance, included Erasmus' *Paraphrases*, Bishop Jewel's attack on the catholic Thomas Harding, ecclesiastical injunctions and forms of prayer but nothing that could really be deemed primarily historical.[75] In contrast the Bray-created Wigton library, according to an early eighteenth-century catalog and valuation, comprised seventy-six volumes. Though these were also overwhelmingly theological (including the commonplace Eusebius, *Ecclesiastical History*, valued at one pound), Wigton also had a five-shilling copy of Burnet's *History of the Reformation*.[76]

It is not true, contrary to a much-repeated error, that every parish church in the land was required by parliamentary statute to possess John Foxe's *Acts and Monuments* – the 1570 order mandating this emanated from the Convocation of the southern province, and applied only to cathedral churches. Nevertheless, the Book of Martyrs is by far the most common historical item in small church collections up to the late seventeenth century, when upstart newcomers like Burnet began to be acquired in addition. In 1577 a parishioner found guilty of sexual misconduct was ordered by the church courts to buy for his parish of St. Andrew's, Hornchurch, Essex a copy of the Bible and "Mr. Foxe's last book of monuments," both to be fastened by lock and chains on a desk within the church.[77] Foxe would sometimes be accompanied by late antique historical works with a similarly religious spin, such as Josephus or Eusebius, and by modern authors such as Ussher and Stillingfleet. The Wantage churchwardens' accounts of 1629 inventoried all church goods and noted all the parochial books, including a brand new addition to the collection, a "booke of the Jewish history given by Mr. ffrauncis Slade vicar." Later wardens grew familiar enough with that volume to list it simply as "Josephus" in subsequent accounts, and in 1638 the parish acquired "a booke of Martyrs in two volumes," almost certainly the 1583, 1610 or 1632 edition of the *Acts and Monuments*.[78]

[75] Herts RO, D/P 105/8/1, Stevenage vestry minutes.
[76] Cumbria RO, PR 36/42, "A Catalogue of the Parochial Library at Wigton in Cumberland, contained in a Case marked number 35." Cf. the very similar parish library at Oldbury, Shropshire, which included a Eusebius (also valued at £1), an abridged version of Burnet's *History of the Reformation* (five shillings): Bodl. MS Rawl. D.834, fos. 9–12, 24r–v, 27r–30, 59r–v.
[77] Marjorie Keniston McIntosh, *A Community Transformed: the Manor and Liberty of Havering, 1500–1620* (Cambridge, 1991), pp. 195, 227, 272.
[78] Bodl. MS Top. Berks. c.44 (Wantage churchwardens' accounts), fos. 94v, 106v, 116r.

The other local institution that was amassing collections of books was the school. If parish libraries stressed religious and moral works, the catalogs of schools similarly emphasize the rhetorical, grammatical, and practical. History was not a distinct subject in the scholastic curriculum before the late eighteenth century, and where ancient historians were read it was almost always with a view to teaching pupils Latin and Greek. We should not, therefore, look for a significant change in historical content in the school lists of the later sixteenth and seventeenth centuries. Nonetheless, historical items, including some nonclassical ones, occasionally turn up, reflecting the wishes of founders or patrons. By 1640 the extensive school library at Tonbridge, Kent held, in addition to Foxe, Camden's *Britannia*, Selden's *Titles of Honor*, and Speed's *History*.[79] When Sir John Lowther established a grammar school in the 1690s, he expressed the wish that pupils not waste their time on "poetry or fiction," but devote their attention to "studies such as every man that bears a character in the world must know." Although he thought some attention ought to be paid to religion and morality through classical writers, he was specific in desiring pupils to learn "geography & the general scheme of history and chronology," along with mathematics for the more able.[80] A catalog of the library at St. Bees school, Cumberland, in 1693 includes 427 books – a sizeable collection for a small northern school – of which fifteen were historical.[81] John Strype's note on the books on which the upper forms at St. Paul's School were examined in 1710 included four or five titles per class, including a historical work in most cases (Quintus Curtius for the fifth form, book 9 of Eutropius for the sixth form, and book 6 of Livy for the eighth form). The 1720 catalog of the Penrith grammar school, founded

---

[79] Peter Clark, "The Ownership of Books in England, 1560–1640: the Example of some Kentish Townsfolk," in *Schooling and Society*, ed L. Stone (Baltimore, 1976), pp. 95–111, at p. 96.

[80] Lambeth Palace MS 1742 (Gibson papers, part 2), fo. 77.

[81] Cumbria RO, DRC/0/St. Bees/Misc.; a partial catalog for the same school is in Lambeth Palace Lib. MS 3094 (library catalogs), fo. 195. Items include: Lancelot Addison, "History of the Jews" (= *The Present state of the Jews*), 8vo; Jean Bodin, *République*; *Chronicon Carionis*, 24mo; Jean de Bussières, *Flosculi historici delibati nunc delibatiores redditi*; Thomas Fuller, *The history of the holy war*, fo; Thomas Godwyn, *Romanae historiae anthologia recognita et avcta*, 4to; Herodian, *Historia*, 8vo; *Historia Augusta* (one volume only), 8vo; Justin, *Historia*, 8vo; Lucan, *Pharsalia* in both 24mo and 8vo editions; Thomas Milles, *The Catalogue of Honour*, fo; Plutarch's *Vitae* (Latin), 8vo and *Lives* (English), fo; a fragment of a Latin edition of Sallust, 8vo; Thucydides in Latin 4to. In the same decade, the rules drawn up at the Carlisle grammar school specified twenty-nine titles for the improvement of languages, manners, and religion, including seven historians, all classical: Suetonius, Florus, Eutropius, Lucan, Justin, Caesar, and Xenophon: Cumbria RO, bound photocopies, "Notitia schola liberae grammaticalis Carliol." In comparison, the prescriptions in the register book of the Free School at Penrith in the early eighteenth century (Cumbria RO, DEC 2/2) assign much more modern texts, albeit on classical subjects: in place of Thomas Godwyn's old pot-boiler, it prescribes John Potter's *Archaeologia Graeca: or, The antiquities of Greece*, Laurence Echard's *Roman history*, and Basil Kennett's *Romae antiquae notitia*, along with Claudian and Herodian.

by Queen Elizabeth, conveniently includes prices paid for each volume (excluding those donated). It comprised forty-nine volumes, valued at £5 9s, and including such titles as a 1697 edition of Sallust (2s 6d), Xenophon's works in Greek (Florence, 1526) (5s), an undated edition of Tacitus' *Annals, Agricola,* and *Germania* (2s 6d), an undated edition of Livy (1s 6d). It also contained several nonclassical items, such as Sebastian Munster's *Cosmographiae Universalis,* a popular sixteenth-century continental work of geography and history (6s 6d), Abraham Bucholzer's *Chronologia* (Frankfurt, 1612) (1s), and two Tudor titles, Alexander Neville's "Kettus" (*Norfolk's Furies*), bound with Christopher Ocland's *Anglorum praelia* (1582) (6d).[82]

The distribution of books in a small selection of early school and parochial libraries (with one exception, Kington, all in the north), divided according to major areas of study, is shown in table 4.12. Several of these were Bray libraries, incorporating what amounted to a set of standard texts, of which the few historical works were invariably church history or godly lives. Flookburgh, for instance, had in common with other parochial libraries its copy of Eusebius' *Ecclesiastical History,* Burnet's *History of the Reformation* (abridged version), and one biography, *The exemplary life and character of James Bonnell, Esq., late accomptant general of Ireland* by William Hamilton, archdeacon of Armagh, together with lives of bishops and the godly. St. Leonard's in New Malton, Yorkshire had virtually the same proportions of books, but instead of Burnet's history, substituted Louis Ellies Dupin's *History of the Church,* translated by Thomas Fenton. Bradfield and Codlingstock do not follow the pattern, but the sources used are not, in these instances, numbered Bray catalogs but rather lists of founding donations made by generous incumbents. They show that a considerably broader range of historical works was available locally, and are deliberately included in the table to illustrate the point that the Bray libraries cannot be taken as a complete measure of the breadth of parochial libraries.

GIVING HISTORY

Donations to local libraries are informative less because they suggest an increasing historical content from the mid-seventeenth century on, than because the documents recording benefactions often say something about the donors themselves. A list of donors to the parish library of Bury St. Edmunds from 1595 to 1599 already includes a good number of historical works, by no means all of them classical. Of forty-one donors identified by Dr. John Craig, most but not all were gentlemen. Of the histories given to the library,

---

[82] BL MS Lans. 1197 (Strype collections), fo. 103r; Cumbria RO, DEC 2/2, "An account of the books, bought for the use of the school, with the price of each book," 1720, with additions to 1723.

Table 4.12. *Distribution of books by major category in select parochial and school libraries, 1687–1720*

Multivolume sets counted as one title, distinct titles counted separately even if bound together, parish registers, often included in printed lists, excluded from count

Parish or school location	Date of list	History/ geography	Classical literature and philosophy[b]	Grammar/ rhetoric/ language/ poetry	Religion theology and mortality
Kington schl	1700[a]	7	21	34	27
Penrith schl	1720	8	8	19	11
Bradfield (bequest)[c]	1720	22	5	7	140
Codlingstock (bequest)[d]	1702	31	27	27	240
Wigton	1687	3	0	0	72
Marske	1712	3	0	0	75
Flookburgh	1725	5	0	0	71
St. Leonard	1721	4	0	0	66

[a]Approximate date at which books inventoried in modern times were known to be in the library.
[b]Does not include ancient historians, historical poets (e.g. Lucan), or contemporary works about them; these are grouped under history.
[c]Several items outside these categories excluded from table: e.g. "The Present State of England," that is, Chamberlayne's *Anglia Notitia* (London, 1682), and Grotius' *De Jure Bello & pacis* (The Hague, 1680), and several works on medicine and law.
[d]As with Bradfield, but a wider range of "others" including works of political thought by Hobbes and Lipsius.
Sources: Kington: P. E. Morgan, "The Library of Lady Hawkins' School, Kington, Herefordshire," *National Library of Wales Journal*, 24 (1985), 46–62, at p. 53; Penrith: Cumbria RO (Carlisle), DEC 2/2; Bradfield: Borthwick Inst. Bp C and P II/18; Codlingstock: Borthwick Inst. Bp. C and P I/24; Wigton: Cumbria RO, PR 36/42; Marske: Borthwick Inst. Bp C and P I/38; Flookburgh (Cartmel parish, Lancs.): Lambeth Palace Lib. MS 3094, fos. 99–100; St. Leonard (printed cat.): Borthwick Inst. Bp. C and P II/20.

Thomas Baist, a Thetford grocer, presented a copy of Nicephorus Callistus, *Scriptoris vere Catholici ecclesiasticae historiae* (Frankfurt, 1588) in 1596; John Brounwyn, a Bury townsman probably also of gentry status, endorsed the copy of Dionysius of Halicarnassus, *Scripta quae exstant omnia et historica* (Frankfurt, 1586). William Jermyn, a gentleman who at the time was quarreling vigorously with the episcopal authorities, gave many books, including several expensive multivolume titles, among which were Josephus' *Opera* (Geneva, 1584) and the *Magdeburg Centuries* (that is, *Ecclesiastica historia*, 8 vols., Basel, 1560–74). In 1595, Augustine Styward (d. 1597) of Lakenheath, Suffolk, a lawyer of the Inner Temple, bestowed a manuscript copy of Bede's *Ecclesiastical History and commentary on the Acts and Epistles*, which had once belonged to the Brigittine nuns at Syon. A further title, Nicetas Acominatos' *Historia* (Geneva, 1593) cost 4d, according to a note in this still-extant volume, and was acquired in about 1610 in exchange for an illustrated volume simply listed as "Plantarum icones." The exchange was made at the request and by the advice of the churchwardens "and other chief inhabitants of this parish." Thus as early as 1610 the community leaders had collectively decided to give up a book with illustrations for a rather more esoteric Byzantine history.[83]

The town library founded at Ipswich in the 1590s tells a similar story. The original endowment for this had included Bede's *History* and Higden's *Polychronicon*. Before long it acquired "Speed's chronicle" (the 1611 edition of Speed's *Historie of Great Britain* given by Bezaleel Sherman, a grocer of St. Laurence parish who died in 1618). In 1628 the vintner John Catcher donated Sir Walter Ralegh's *History of the World*. Similar donations trickled in throughout the century, as the library acquired Silas Taylor's *History of Gavelkind* from its author in 1668, and an ex-officer named Captain Devereux Edgar donated the 1695 *Camden's Britannia*, edited by Edmund Gibson. Perhaps the most substantial single donation of history books came in 1680, when Dr. John Knight, surgeon to Charles II, left his manuscripts and two volumes of Dugdale's *Baronage* to Gonville and Caius College, but bestowed most of his remaining books on the Ipswich library. These included a virtually complete set of works on historical antiquities and topography: the three-volume Dugdale *Monasticon*, Dugdale's *Warwickshire*, William Burton's *Leicestershire*, Robert Thoroton's *Nottinghamshire*, Richard Carew's *Cornwall*, William Lambarde and John Philipot's antiquarian surveys of Kent, William Smith and William Webb's similar work on Cheshire (published by Daniel King in 1656 as *The Vale-royall of England*), and several works on heraldry and genealogy.[84] Gloucester Cathedral Library

---

[83] John Craig, "Reformation, Politics and Polemics in Sixteenth-Century East Anglia Market Towns," Ph.D thesis, University of Cambridge, 1992, app. V, pp. 189–93 (I am indebted to Dr. Craig for providing me with a copy of this appendix). The 1599 catalog of this library, most of the 133 items in which have been provisionally identified by Craig (app. IV, pp. 179–88), includes eighteen historical titles, among them a significant number of foreign imprints.

[84] Blatchly, *The Town Library of Ipswich*, pp. 22, 28, 38, 39, 41. The other works in the Knight bequest included Elias Ashmole's *The institution, laws & ceremonies of the most noble Order of the Garter*; Peter Leycester's *Historical Antiquities* (principally about Cheshire); William Burton, *A commentary on Antoninus, his Itinerary, or journies of the Romane empire*; Christopher Helvicus or Helwig, *Theatrum historicum et chronologicum* (many editions possible); an unspecified work of Beroaldus; Thomas Milles, *Catalogue of Honour* (incorporating earlier work by the herald Robert Glover); and Robert Plot, *The Natural history of Oxford-shire*. By the end of the seventeenth century, the Ipswich library had about 700 printed books, of which ninety-nine can be positively identified as historical works. In

received a similarly large donation of 206 volumes from the library of John Selden at the instance of his executor, Chief Justice Sir Matthew Hale. Given Selden's interests, it is not surprising that these included a high proportion of historical, philological, and antiquarian works.[85] Of the 294 books left to Cartmel Priory church by Thomas Preston of Holker Hall, Lancashire, in 1697, twenty-seven were historical, a number that included sizes ranging from duodecimo to folio, and titles from the ancients to Peter Heylyn's *Help to English History*, Matthias Prideaux's 1650 guide to reading histories, Stow's *Survey of London*, Camden's *Britannia* (1590 edn), *Carionis chronica* (1594), Lambarde's *Perambulation of Kent* (1596), the 1610 edition of Foxe's Book of Martyrs and Jacques-Auguste de Thou's *Historia sui temporis* (1630).[86] Such large benefactions often came, as we have seen, attached to expensive and entangling strings, or conversely were left to the discretion, honesty, and perhaps inaction of immediate beneficiaries. When Sir John Crewe of Utkinton died in 1711, he left his books to found a public library at Chester. But until one was set up, and had already acquired another founding donation of books, Crewe's remained in his study at Utkinton Hall for the use of his immediate heirs, the Arderne family; the books ultimately reached the Chester library only in 1753.[87]

The donor book of the Coventry grammar school for the period 1622–75, and a 1697 catalog of its library, also reveal much about both its contents and patrons. Henry Bressey, gentleman, donated Holinshed's *Chronicles*, Sleidan's edition of Froissart and Commynes, and the second volume of a "history of the martyrs in french." Henry Billingham, clerk, donated Josephus' *Antiquities* in Latin, an expensive folio in six volumes; one John Barker gave a two-volume copy of Johannes Nauclerus' *Cronica*. A major benefaction came in June 1676 from Dr. Ralph Bathurst, the Vice-Chancellor of Oxford University: eleven books, including the folio edition of Anthony Wood's recently published *Historia et antiquitates universitatis Oxoniensis*. Samuel Clarke gave a copy of his own *A General*

addition to the works already listed, these included the 1610 edition of Foxe, most of the major sixteenth- and seventeenth-century English historians and antiquaries, numerous works on chronology and church history (for instance Baronius' *Annales Ecclesiastici*, the *Magdeburg Centuries*, Johan Funck's *Chronologia*, Nicephorus Callistus' *Ecclesiastical History*) and a great number of medieval chronicles in the early seventeenth-century editions by Sir Henry Savile and William Camden, as well as some more popular works, such as the 1665 edition of Baker's *Chronicle*. This was a library intended to appeal to a wide range of reader, judging by the mix of English and Latin or foreign-language books.

[85] Bodl MS Lat. Misc. c. 47 (modern transcription), mentioning the following items (among others) in sizes ranging from folio to octavo: the medieval chronicle *Flores historiarum*; Henry Savile's edition of chronicles, the *Rerum scriptores*; Spelman, *Glossarium*; Selden's own *Marmora arundeliana, Jani anglorum facies altera*; G. J. Vossius' *De historicis Graecis*; Camden's *Remaines*; John Norden's *Specvlvm Britanniae. The first parte. An historicall, & chorographicall discription of Middlesex*; Johann Alsted's *Thesaurus chronologiae in quo universa temporum & historiarum series ponitur*; and a copy of the ubiquitous Lucius Florus.

[86] Chetham's Lib., Manchester, Mun. A.2. 9 (nineteenth-century transcription).

[87] Cheshire RO, DAR/H/10.

Martyrologie (1652). Christopher Davenport, a former student of the school, and his son Henry donated at different times two antiquarian texts, Giacomo Lauro's *Antiquae urbis splendor* (4 vols., Rome, 1637) and John Weever's *Ancient funerall monuments* (1631). Another family donation came from William and Walsingham Gresley, gentlemen, and included an early seventeenth-century edition of Camden's *Britannia*. The mayor, William Hancocke, donated a copy of Foxe's Book of Martyrs. Perhaps most interesting is the donation by the widow, Margaret Porteman, of Sir Walter Ralegh's *Historie of the World*, since it is the only item bestowed by a woman. Lest we take this as evidence of female interest in history, one should quickly add that a donation, especially by a widow, may just as likely suggest that she did not share her husband's interest in the volume.[88] This was probably also true of Margaret Shallcross, widow of Edward, rector of Stockport, who gave her husband's books to the vicar of Leek, along with twenty shillings to repair them.[89] It was almost certainly the case with Helena Sandys, widow of Edwin, archdeacon of Wells and canon residentiary, who passed on to Wells Cathedral the manuscript history of it that her husband had inherited from its lay author, Nathaniel Chyles.[90]

---

[88] CUL MS Add. 4467 (donor book) and 4468 (catalog). Other donors include: John Hales (Herodotus and Thucydides); Matthew Hulme (two books including *Cronicon Carionis*); Thomas Holbach, gentleman (Scaliger, *De emendatione temporum*); Thomas Hobson, citizen (*Munsteri cosmographia*); Philemon Holland, the Coventry doctor and translator of Camden (whose donations ironically included no historical works); the bookseller Henry Holland, listed simply as "citizen of London" (his own *Herwlogia*); John Kimberley, vicar of Holy Trinity Church in Coventry (two books including Edward Lhwyd's *Archaeologia Britannica*); Henry Leigh, gentleman (eleven books, all authored by his father Edward, including the biblical study *Critica sacra* and of *Observations on the First twelve Caesars*); Gabriel Miles, citizen of London (Sarpi's *History of the Council of Trent*); William Massam, merchant (2 vols. of Eusebius' *Opera Graeca*, including his ecclesiastical history); Thomas Potter (the English translation of Pierre Gassendi's *The mirrour of true nobility and gentility* [a biography of the French virtuoso and antiquary, Nicolas Fabri de Peiresc]; William Rogerson, barrister (Herodotus' works in Greek and Latin); Thomas Saunders, J. P. (Caesar's *Commentaries* in English); John Sandbrooke, London citizen (a "Turkarii historia" in one volume); Clement Throckmorton, knight (Livy's histories in English, in an early seventeenth-century edition); John Wightwick, citizen (Sleidan, *Commentaries*, in English); Thomas Wheate of Glympton, Esq. (five books including Spelman's *Glossarium*); John Wright, a six clerk of Chancery and former scholar (the *Chronicon Saxonicum*, edited by Edmund Gibson in 1692); and the school's most illustrious former pupil, Humfrey Wanley (thirty-two books); cf. *Letters of Humfrey Wanley*, ed. P. L. Heyworth (Oxford, 1989), p. 42 (Wanley to Edward Owen, 17 October 1696).

[89] A 1711 catalog by the then vicar of Leek, James Osbourne, lists forty-four folio, sixty-seven quarto and seventeen octavo volumes, and the next eleven vicars added thirty-four more volumes: the collection was broken up later in the eighteenth century but the catalog is part of the Leek parish muniments, and is being transcribed by Mr. M. W. Greenslade of the William Salt Library, Stafford, to whom I owe this reference and a helpful discussion of Staffordshire libraries.

[90] Hist. MSS Comm., *Dean and Chapter of Wells*, II, 491; see p. 514 for another donation in 1726.

TAKING HISTORY HOME

This chapter began with informal borrowing and lending of history books and concludes with the beginnings of more formal circulation from institutional libraries. How easy it was to borrow books from these is unclear. Not every library was as restrictive in its loan practices as the Bodleian, whose keeper John Rouse famously refused the loan of Théodore Agrippa d'Aubigné's *Histoire universelle* to Charles I during the civil war. The practice of chaining books, which began to disappear in the first third of the eighteenth century, was standard in most open-access libraries before then, the books placed with their spines inward. This was not always sufficient protection, since the books could be and were removed by borrowers. At Winchester College in 1660 (the library of which had been spared the depredations inflicted on Winchester Cathedral's muniments during the civil war), the warden was able to have a copy of Davila's *Historie of the civil warres of France* unchained and removed for his own use. Sir Thomas Bodley recognized the risk of "embezeling" but was reluctant to take the further precautions urged on him by his librarian, preferring to trust in "mens othes, and consciences."[91]

Theft was very clearly a problem, and chaining remained commonplace in institutional libraries throughout the seventeenth century since corporations could ill afford the loss of expensive volumes. In one of the earliest borough libraries, that founded at Leicester in the 1630s, the books were kept chained, and moneys had to be allotted for chains and staples periodically.[92] Any modern librarian charged with protecting her or his holdings from rapacious or simply forgetful scholars will sympathize with John Parker, the oldest son of Archbishop Matthew Parker. The register in Corpus Christi College, Cambridge, where the archbishop's collection of books and manuscripts reposes, contains a note by his son to the effect that several listed books were already missing, "either lent or embeceled."[93] By the end of the seventeenth century, many libraries had begun to require borrowers to leave promissory notes, and in some instances to provide bonds for the return of volumes.[94] At the Plume Library in Maldon, those readers who were not

---

[91] Oakeshott, "Winchester College Library," pp. 5, 16; *Letters of Sir Thomas Bodley to Thomas James*, ed. G. K. Wheeler (Oxford, 1926), pp. 25, 28.

[92] *Records of the Borough of Leicester*, ed. Helen Stocks (Cambridge, 1923), pp. 270, 549.

[93] Corpus Christi College, Cambridge, MS 575, p. 12, reproduced in R. I. Page, *Matthew Parker and his Books* (Kalamazoo, MI, 1993), plate 2. The elder Parker's habit of keeping borrowed manuscripts himself makes the comment especially poignant: Birley, "History of Eton College Library," p. 239.

[94] See Humfrey Wanley's observation to Thomas Hearne that "Those that borrow books out of Libraries here, are very glad, if they can gett them by their bare Notes. I have been often put to the Charge of Bonds." *Letters of Wanley*, p. 309 (Wanley to Hearne, 9 November 1714).

"strangers" could borrow books on leaving a *vadimonium* (that is, a chit promising to bring them back).[95] Parochial libraries were at first intended by Thomas Bray to be for reference only, and principally for the resident clergy, but by the time of his 1697 *Essay towards Promoting all necessary and useful knowledge, both divine and human* he had reversed himself, and from the very beginning the libraries founded on his scheme were patronized by local gentry, who were permitted to take volumes home.[96]

This in turn influenced the older, independently established libraries eventually to give over the practice of chaining, except for more expensive (and in any case less easily borrowed) folios. The first book of 511 lent from the parochial collection of St. George's, Doncaster, was borrowed by Dr. Roger Perkins, a layman, in December 1726. The work was Rollin's *History*, and it would be the most frequently borrowed book during the next half-century of a set of records that ends in 1776 with the return of Rapin-Thoyras' *History of England*.[97] There is nothing like a regular run of circulation lists to compare with those available to modern library historians, but occasional sources give a sense of the flow of books, and sometimes manuscripts, in and out of libraries. The evidence is very scanty, but some cathedrals and monasteries were lending historical books in the late Middle Ages: a memorandum of loan dated 7 June 1392 from a canon of Exeter Cathedral authorized the loan of a copy of Higden's *Polychronicon* to John Schepways, the chancellor of the diocese, on pain of paying 20 marks if he failed to return it by Michaelmas (it was returned on 15 October); Winchester Cathedral had a small lending library even earlier.[98] For the seventeenth century, the more limited lending records of a private library such as Sir Robert Cotton's can provide similar information.[99]

For the eighteenth century, the library registers or "borrowers' books" of several cathedrals show historical works circulating for periods ranging from days to several years. Paul Kaufman demonstrated many years ago, from the registers of Canterbury, Carlisle, Durham, Gloucester, Winchester, York, Exeter, and St. Paul's, that a wide range of materials circulated during the eighteenth century, that many works were lent repeatedly (Durham having the highest rate of circulation, between 1711 and 1801: 6,364 loans to

---

[95] S. G. Deed and J. Francis, *Catalogue of the Plume Library at Maldon, Essex* (Maldon: Plume Library Trustees, 1959).

[96] Bray, *An essay towards promoting all necessary and useful knowledge, both divine and human: in all parts of His Majesty's dominions, both at home and abroad* (1697); Steiner, "Rev. Thomas Bray and his American Libraries," p. 63.

[97] Paul Kaufman, "New Light from Parochial Libraries," in his *Libraries and their Users*, pp. 93–101, at p. 94.

[98] Hist. MSS Comm., *Var. Coll.*, IV, p. 268; *MMBL*, II, 817; A. B. Emden, *A Biographical Register of the University of Oxford to AD 1500*, 3 vols. (Oxford, 1957–59), III, 1689; Oakeshott, "Winchester College Library," p. 8.

[99] BL MS Harl. 6018, Cotton's book-lending list for 1621.

borrowers of 1,419 identifiable books lent). Not all of these are useful for our period, and most of the records pertain to years after 1730; the registers of Canterbury, Gloucester, Exeter, and St. Paul's lie entirely beyond that year. Nevertheless, the trend that they show for the later eighteenth century casts light on developing patterns of the early 1700s: of 2,708 books lent in Kaufman's sample, divinity (including ecclesiastical history) led at 703 (with the Bible and biblical texts and commentaries running to 224). Two separate categories, "History and Antiquities" (426) and "Biography and Memoirs" (169), followed, with "Voyages and Travels" (including topography) at 153, and other subjects, from philosophy (91) to music (20), language and dictionaries (109), physic and anatomy (17), and so on. Without knowing precisely which titles Kaufman placed in which category, it would be unwise simply to add his groupings together into the broader category of "history books" as used in the present study, but the extraordinary prominence of works dealing with aspects of the past is clear enough.[100]

Among the eight registers used by Kaufman, the first few years of that at York Minster (1716–1820) provide an illustration of the books borrowed and range of borrowers, represented in table 4.13. Borrowers were not only local scholars and church officials, but sometimes visitors from as far afield as Cambridge, albeit with local connections. The novelist Laurence Sterne, while prebendary of the minster from 1741–1754 (and nephew of its precentor, Jacques), would remove to his vicarage at Sutton some twenty titles, including three volumes of Bayle's *Historical and Critical Dictionary*, five volumes of the gargantuan *An Universal History from the Earliest Account of Time*, and two early seventeenth-century "classics," Speed's *History of Great Britain* and Sarpi's *History of the Council of Trent*.[101]

As indicated in this selection from a much longer record, borrowers were either closely associated with the minster (for instance the dean and precentor), or were local gentlemen of some note; this opening of the collection to the laity revised the library's seventeenth-century policy, which had restricted borrowing to minster clergy.[102] Lesser clergy and laity, even if from prominent families, needed special permission and the vouching of a prebendary, as did the young Francis Drake, physician and future historian of York (and himself the son and namesake of a local antiquary). What is more

---

[100] Paul Kaufman, "Reading Trends at Cathedral Libraries," in his *Libraries and their Users*, pp. 76–92.

[101] Paul Kaufman, "Mr. Yorick in the Minster Library," in his *Libraries and their Users*, pp. 90–92; Elizabeth Brunskill, *Eighteenth-century Reading: Some Notes on the People who Frequented the Library of York Minster in the Eighteenth Century, and on the Books they Borrowed*, York Georgian Society Occasional Paper 6 (York, 1950), pp. 7–31. Analysis of the MS is my own, but I have used Brunskill as my principal authority for the identity of borrowers.

[102] Brunskill, *Eighteenth-century Reading*, p. 7.

Table 4.13. *Historical works circulating from York Minster Library, 1717–1743*

Title of work	Borrower(s)	Date lent[a]	Date returned (if known)
L. Moréri, *Great Hist. and Geog. Dict.*	Mr. John Audley (twice)	1717?[a]	2 May 1720
		30 July 1722	13 Aug. 1724
W. Dugdale, *Monasticon Anglicanum*	Mr. John Richardson	17 June 1717	12 Sept. 1718
	John Audley	19 May 1724	20 Oct. 1725
	Martin Brathwait		3 Sept. 1727
	Rev'd Thomas Lamplugh[b] (3 vols.)	20 Sept. 1728	26 April 1729 (vols. II, III only)
	idem, vol. I only	23 June 1730	27 Aug. 1730 (vol. I)
"Scriptores Historiae Dunelmensis"[e]	John Hildyard,[c] for Bielby Thompson, Esq.[d]	23 Nov. 1742	
B. Twine, *Antiquitates Oxonienses*	Dr. Thomas Mangey[f]	28 Aug. 1723	10 July 1728
[J. Brunet], *Histoire du droit canonique*	John Audley	18 July 1721	n.d.
R. Twysden, *Decem Scriptores Rerum . . .*	John Audley	18 July 1721	n.d.
	John Audley	19 May 1724	n.d.
	Dr. Martin Brathwait	24 Sept. 1728	2 July 1729
	[Francis] Drake (of St. John's College, Cambridge)	n.d.	18 Sept. 1731
Eadmer, *Historia novorum*	R[ichard] Osbaldeston[g]	24 Nov. 1731	n.d.
Hist. Romanae Scriptores	Francis Drake	6 Nov. 1729	18 Sept. 1731
	Francis Drake	6 Nov. 1729	18 Sept. 1731[h]
	Dean of York [R. Osbaldeston]		12 Feb. 1731/2
Rymer, *Foedera*, vol. II *idem*, vol. I and II	Dean of York [R. Osbaldeston]	12 Feb. 1730/31	12 Feb. 1731/2
J. Selden, *Opera omnia*, ed. Wilkins, vol. I	Dean of York [R. Osbaldeston]	n.d.	12 Feb. 1731/2

C. Baronius, *Annales*, vol. I	Richard Wainhouse	28 Dec. 1732	n.d.
[Hiob or Job] Ludolf, *Historia* [*Aethiopica*]ⁱ	Richard Wainhouse	25 Oct. 1734?	n.d.

ᵃ? indicates obscurity or illegibility in MS.

ᵇPrebendary of Knaresborough and canon residentiary; grandson of Archbishop Thomas Lamplugh of York (d. 1691).

ᶜA York bookseller.

ᵈOf Escrick Park.

ᵉManuscript: now York Minster Library MS XVI.I.12, described in N. R. Ker and A. J. Piper, *Medieval Manuscripts in British Libraries* (4 vols., Oxford, 1969–92), IV, 720–22. This was probably first acquired in the early seventeenth century through Archbishop Tobie Matthew; also described as items 44–45 in Edward Bernard, *Catalogi librorum manuscriptorum Angliae et Hiberniae in unum collecti* (Oxford, 1697), part 2, pp. 1–2. I am grateful to Mr. C. B. L. Barr, sublibrarian at York Minster, for informative correspondence on this and other items.

ᶠSee *DNB*: Mangey, who was a prebendary of Durham, was married to a daughter of Archbishop Sharp of York. Mangey also borrowed from the Durham library: Kaufman, "Reading Trends," p. 83.

ᵍRichard Osbaldeston, dean of York and future bishop of Carlisle and London: *DNB*, sub "Osbaldeston, Richard."

ʰDrake's books were taken out "by order of Mr. Lamplugh," suggesting Drake had leave to borrow, for nearly two years, several books that he then returned at the same time.

ⁱJob Ludolf, *Historia Aethiopica* (Frankfurt, 1681), now York Minster Library shelfmark IV.E.14; this appears in the library's catalog as early as 1687, for which information I am again grateful to Mr. C. B. L. Barr.

Source: York Minster Lib. Acc. 1988/22/4.

surprising is the degree of latitude in the length of loan of some very expensive books and even manuscripts, which in turn suggests that many of the books were being read over extended periods, and not merely consulted on particular points. Most of the books that circulated pertained in some way to ecclesiastical history, or to regional history and antiquities, with Dugdale's *Monasticon Anglicanum* and Roger Twysden's edition of medieval chronicles, the *Historiae anglicanae scriptores X* being the most borrowed items.

The presence of history books in libraries, whether or not they were physically lent, represents one major way in which historical knowledge in written and printed form increased its prominence on the intellectual horizons of the literate population in town and country during the seventeenth century. The impact of this should not be overstated in view of some of the restrictions we have noted, and in view of the still relatively narrow selection of works available in many of the libraries. And, as noted earlier, to borrow is not the same as to possess. Previous chapters have demonstrated the conspicuous and increasing presence of historical books in private houses. The final two chapters of this study will investigate the equally important questions of how they got there, and at what cost.

$$\text{——} \twoheadleftarrow 5 \twoheadrightarrow \text{——}$$

Clio unbound and bound

If the readers of history have been neglected in comparison with its writers, the same is true of the economic transistors in the "communications circuit," the printers, publishers, booksellers, and auctioneers who produced, distributed, and sold historical works among their other wares. From the days of the Renaissance scholar-printer to the era of Augustan bookseller-cum-bibliophiles like John Dunton and John Bagford, those who made or sold books played a crucial role in the dissemination of historical knowledge. Although much of this continued to circulate informally through oral information and manuscript, the emergence of a modern historical culture in England would not have occurred but for the involvement of enterprising, risk-taking businessmen, many of whom were themselves interested in historical matters, and others who simply saw the way to a profit. In the next chapter, the process of marketing, selling, and buying history books will be our concern. In the present chapter, matters of production, copyright, and especially pricing are foregrounded.

CONDITIONS OF PUBLICATION: CENSORSHIP, LICENSING, AND PRINTING

Throughout the period of late Tudor and early Stuart regulation, the Stationers' Company – chartered by Mary I in 1557 and dominated by the booksellers from the middle of Elizabeth's reign – had a virtual monopoly on the registration of new titles, on the transfer of rights to existing titles, and over the regulation of apprenticeship in the printing industry. The internal system of regulation and licensing that it developed over the next three decades was tightened up in a Star Chamber decree of 1586, and reconfirmed in a proclamation of 1623. After several decades of wrangling within the Company about monopolies on certain titles, it was in 1603 granted a royal patent to establish an "English Stock" of well-selling titles that could be republished at intervals by its shareholders, a subsection of wealthier members of the Company. The English Stock included several important

Elizabethan and early Stuart historical works, such as Foxe's *Acts and Monuments*, Daniel's *Collection of the History of England*, various versions of Stow's *Chronicles*, and John Speed's *Genealogies* for the Bible.[1] Proof of ownership of the "copy" of any work outside the English Stock (which subsumed earlier Tudor patents), and not specifically protected in a subsequent letter patent from the Crown – the "privilege" by which some books were issued – depended entirely on entrance in the "register" or "hall book" of the Stationers' Company; we will analyse this for its historical contents further along.[2]

Over and above the Company's control over "propriety," which was enforced internally through its own court, a Star Chamber decree of 1586 required certain categories of books (principally but not exclusively religious), to be submitted to a clerical licenser for inspection; all "political" searches for illegal books became properly the domain of the court of High Commission early in James I's reign. This, too, was far from all-encompassing, and it has been plausibly suggested that it was never intended to catch every possible expression of opposition to the Crown. The absence of any controls over the importation of paper from abroad provides one suggestive clue, the considerably greater concern with popish or heretical material imported from abroad another.[3] Many titles either evaded censorship altogether or slipped past inattentive licensers to become controversial after the fact. John Hayward's *First part of the Life and Reign of King Henry IIII*, the most notorious history published in Elizabeth I's reign, is a telling example. Its carelessly granted imprimatur very nearly wrecked the clerical career of one future prelate, Samuel Harsnett, but only because Hayward

[1] Cyprian Blagden, "The English Stock of the Stationers' Company," *The Library*, 3rd series, 10 (1955), 163–87 and *The Stationers' Company: a History, 1403–1959* (1960), pp. 92–105; G. Pollard, "The English Market for Printed Books," *Publishing History*, 4 (1978), 7–48, at p. 24; Adrian Johns, *The Nature of the Book: Print and Knowledge in the Making* (Chicago and London, 1998), pp. 230, 259. A Latin Stock was established in 1616 and an Irish Stock (essentially a monopoly on the export of materials to Ireland as well as printing within the island): M. Pollard, *Dublin's Trade in Books 1550–1800* (Oxford, 1989), p. 36.

[2] Arnold Hunt, "Book Trade Patents, 1603–1640," in Arnold Hunt, Giles Mandelbrote, and Alison Shell, *The Book Trade and its Customers 1450–1900: Historical Essays for Robin Myers* (Winchester, UK and New Castle, DE, 1997), pp. 27–54. Having a patent or privilege for printing a book did not necessarily preclude it also being entered on the register. Most though not all patents were in fact in the hands of members of the Stationers' Company. Hunt's list of books printed by patent or privileged in the early seventeenth century includes a significant number of historical works, such as translations of Caesar's *Commentaries*, Justin's *Histories*, and Leonardo Bruni's *History Concerning the Wars of the Goths in Italy*, granted for seven years, to Thomas Wilson, Esq. of London and Percival Golding, Gent, son of the deceased translator, Arthur Golding, for works translated by Golding and by Wilson. Samuel Daniel published his *Collection of the historie of England* (1618) under a ten-year privilege.

[3] Johns, *Nature of the Book*, pp. 190, 230; Cyndia Susan Clegg, *Press Censorship in Elizabethan England* (Cambridge, 1997), pp. 3–76; Sheila Lambert, "State Control of the Press in Theory and Practice: the Role of the Stationers' Company before 1640," in Robin Myers and Michael Harris (eds.), *Censorship and Control of Print in England and France, 1600–1910* (Winchester, UK, 1992), pp. 1–32.

had the bad luck (or bad judgment) of dedicating it to the earl of Essex.[4]

During the civil war and through the first part of the interregnum, censorship all but ceased and publication, as is well known, substantially increased for nearly a decade; this occurred in spite of parliament's assumption of regulation of the trade in the absence of the king.[5] Reimposition of restrictions by parliamentary ordinances of 1643 and 1647 and by statute from 1649 to 1651 and 1653 to 1659 foreshadowed the more thorough removal of the Stationers' control over the output of the press that commenced with the 1662 Press Act. This statute placed the licensing of most categories of books in the hands of a government-appointed Surveyor of the Press, Sir Roger L'Estrange. Except for a period of lapse during the Popish Plot and Exclusion Crisis, the act and its successor statutes continued in force until 1695. In that year, it finally expired and the bill designed to replace it failed to pass. There then ensued, for fifteen years, what amounted to a publishing "state of nature." After several abortive attempts at a regulatory bill (the last, in 1707, assisted by then-Secretary Robert Harley and his client, Daniel Defoe), vigorous pressure from the printers and booksellers finally resulted in An Act for the Encouragement of Learning (1710), usually known as the Copyright Act though it also dealt with other book-trade matters. This law restored some degree of order by granting a 21-year copyright to the authors of existing books and one of fourteen years (renewable for a second term) to authors of new books. It rather feebly allowed for complaints against any traders who advertised or sold books at a "high or unreasonable" rate (a virtually unenforceable measure repealed in 1745 without ever having been put to the test). Finally, extending a measure first introduced in 1662, it established nine deposit libraries that were to receive copies of all new books and new editions of old ones.[6] The act did not restore licensing, but neither did it permit a "free" press since matters of sedition and libel could still be dealt with by the courts and by parliament, and economic controls on the flow of newspapers and pamphlets that most concerned successive ministries soon resulted from the 1712 Stamp Act.[7]

[4] W. W. Greg, "Samuel Harsnett and Hayward's *Henry IV*," *The Library*, 5th series, 11 (1956), 1–10 and *Some Aspects and Problems of London Publishing Between 1550 and 1650* (Oxford, 1956), p. 61; *The First and Second Parts of John Hayward's the Life and Raigne of King Henrie IIII*, ed. J. J. Manning, Camden Soc., 4th series 42 (1991), p. 18.

[5] Lambert, "State Control of the Press," 23. Dr. Lambert's very useful article, which corrects the older account of Siebert, *Freedom of the Press in England, 1476–1776* (Urbana, 1952) on many points, seems to me to underestimate the post–1640 increase, even if it was not the atomic explosion once imagined.   [6] Johns, *Nature of the Book*, p. 199 n. 33.

[7] The Copyright Act also excluded from its coverage any foreign-printed book in Greek, Latin, or foreign languages, and it exempted the universities from its provisions for any copies that they owned. John Feather, "The Book Trade in Politics: the Making of the Copyright Act of 1710," *Publishing History*, 8 (1980), 19–44 and *Publishing, Piracy and Politics: an Historical Study of Copyright in Britain* (1994), pp. 50–64; R. Astbury, "The Renewal of the Licensing Act in 1693 and its lapse in 1695," *The Library*, 5th series, 33 (1978), 296–322; on the Stamp Duty see J. A. Downie, *Robert Harley and the Press: Propaganda and Public Opinion in the*

In the two decades leading up to the Copyright Act, a group of London booksellers had imposed controls of their own making by combining into a series of "congers" that from 1695 oligopolized the production and distribution of English books by controlling sales to retailers and to provincial sellers, and sharing desirable titles, effectively creating for themselves a collective copyright by selling off rights only within their select group. It was out of this system that great publishing dynasties like the Tonsons would emerge to dominate publishing in the eighteenth century.[8] The end of licensing also meant the rapid expansion of the provincial press. By 1730 there were over seventy presses in London, and most large towns had a printer and a newspaper. Smaller communities would have either a permanent bookshop or a stallholder acting as an employee or agent of a bigger bookseller, who might have several shops or stalls in different towns.[9]

COSTS

A variety of expenses were incurred in printing a book. These included labor (for the compositors, devils, proofreaders, and other printing workers), capital investment and the depreciation of presses, the replacement of aging fonts, ink, and other supplies, and, of course, whatever funds were to be paid to an author, if that author were not himself paying for the privilege of publication.[10] Marketing, our topic in the next chapter, was also a concern, increasingly so in the more competitive later seventeenth century, though this was no longer a matter that much affected printers. Their craft had by this time become separated from that of the booksellers who would sell the finished book and, often, a separate "undertaker," a publisher or syndicate of publishers (who were themselves usually booksellers) who would coordinate production or even commission a work.[11]

Age of Swift and Defoe (Cambridge, 1979), pp. 149–61. The history of licensing measures throughout the entire period is concisely summarized in Johns, *Nature of the Book*, pp. 239ff.

[8] Johns, *Nature of the Book*, p. 151; John Feather, *The Provincial Book Trade in Eighteenth-Century England* (Cambridge, 1985), p. 3; Kathleen M. Lynch, *Jacob Tonson, Kit-Cat Publisher* (Knoxville, TN, 1971). One definition of a conger, from the *Dictionary of the canting crew* (1700), is "a set or knot of topping book-sellers of London who agree . . . that whoever of them buys a good copy, the rest are to take off such a particular number . . . in quires, on easy terms."

[9] Feather, *Provincial Book Trade*, p. 13; Johns, *Nature of the Book*, p. 72.

[10] On the size and organization of printers' houses, see Johns, *Nature of the Book*, pp. 72ff.

[11] The most detailed description of the printing trade and its practices is that of a contemporary, Joseph Moxon, *Mechanick Exercises on the Whole Art of Printing* (first published 1683–84), ed. Herbert Davis and Harry Carter (1958). There were exceptions to this separation even in the eighteenth century. The printer William Bowyer the elder, who did virtually no retail, nevertheless acted in such a role for John Lister, an obscure Essex clergyman, providing him with 737 titles (including several intended for one of Lister's friends, a Mr. Tyrell), among which were several historical and antiquarian works, and copies of periodicals, like Lintot's *Monthly Catalogues*, from which Lister clearly ordered further works through Bowyer: Keith

By far the largest cost in the conversion of an author's text into a reader's book was the paper, which could vary considerably in quality and was as a rule more expensive in England than on the continent, from which it had to be imported owing to the near complete absence of an indigenous paper-making trade.[12] Individual book owners sometimes took the step of ordering special copies on superior paper, while some printers were conversely known to cut costs on expensive books by not printing them on the paper they deserved. There were many complaints about the paper in the expensive 1695 edition of *Camden's Britannia*, and when, only a dozen years later, another edition was contemplated, one reader was hopeful that this would be produced "on better paper than the last, which was so wretched that it displeased every body," though he expressed concern that the buyers of the original book would object to having "that costly edition trumped upon and set aside."[13] As a rule, the booksellers undertaking a work – or authors themselves where a work was self-published – supplied printers with paper in advance, though sometimes the printer would provide this and build it into his charges.[14]

Certain economies of scale could be achieved for works with a mass market that could be cheaply printed, but larger works, especially the expensive folios and quartos that were amassed by historically minded biblio-philes, were unlikely to pay for themselves, particularly given the greater traffic in used books compared to the present. Edition sizes all across Europe had grown substantially between the beginning of the print era, when runs of 200 to 300 were common, to a standard of 1,000 to 1,500 by the start of the sixteenth century, a figure that did not increase thereafter until the eighteenth century. One reason for this is that the economies realized at about 1,500 copies diminished after 2,000, which soon became the uppermost limit for a single edition. In England, there was the further limitation by decree, from

Maslen and John Lancaster, *The Bowyer Ledgers: the Printing Accounts of William Bowyer, Father and Son Reproduced on Microfiche: with a checklist of Bowyer printing 1699–1977* (London and New York, 1991), appendix 2, pp. 411–46; Keith Maslen, "Parson Lister's Library," *Trans. Cambridge Bibliographical Soc.*, 9 (1987), 155–73.

[12] A paper mill was set up at Stevenage in the 1490s by a London mercer, but the trade remained overwhelmingly dependent on foreign supply: C. P. Christianson, *Memorials of the Book Trade in Medieval London: the Archives of Old London Bridge* (Cambridge, 1987), p. 30.

[13] *Letters of Eminent Men, addressed to Ralph Thoresby, FRS* (2 vols. 1832), II, 80, Nathan Drake, vicar of Sheffield and prebendary in church of York, to Thoresby, 27 November 1707. For Thomas Hearne's more serious objections to the errors in the 1695 *Britannia*, see his letter to Thoresby of 27 December 1708, ibid., II, 137. According to Edward Lhwyd, Henry Clements of Oxford was underselling the London undertakers of the 1695 *Britannia* "out of spight" at a rate of thirty-six shillings bound, but soon had to raise his price to thirty-eight: R. T. Gunther, *Early Science in Oxford*, vol. XIV, *Life and Letters of Edward Lhwyd* (Oxford, 1945), p. 259.

[14] This is well illustrated in the ledgers of the Bowyers in the first two-thirds of the eighteenth century: Maslen and Lancaster, *The Bowyer Ledgers*, introductory commentary, p. xxxii.

1586 to 1637, on behalf of journeymen compositors who naturally preferred smaller runs and potential recompositions: in those years, runs were limited to 1,500 copies for all books except those in small type or very small format, such as primers.[15] Other sorts of savings were possible, for instance in the casting of fonts, and as a rule the mass-produced books of the post-1640 era were more cheaply printed than their Renaissance predecessors.

The decision to illustrate or not, with how many pictures, and whether to engrave (as most higher-cost antiquarian works did) or to use instead the cheaper medium of woodcuts, also played a part in determining production cost. By the late seventeenth century, the quality and number of illustrations was rivaling the type of paper as a measure of the value of the book: as historical and especially antiquarian knowledge increased, readers and authors demanded increasing accuracy from representations of coins, altars, and other archaeological finds, as well as aesthetically pleasing frontispieces. Just as sixteenth-century printers had repeatedly used old devices and wood-cuts, so their seventeenth-century successors would borrow ready-made engravings from other books. Thomas Baker boasted to Ralph Thoresby that one illustration of the tomb of his college's foundress "cost me nothing, being the same with that in [Francis] Sandford's *Genealogical History*, which was made use of by my bookseller's contrivance," though he added that "the College arms was new, and is pretty fair, clean cut."[16]

As noted in chapter 1 above, the "average" book price, working from unbound sheets rather than bound pages, has been estimated by H. S. Bennett and F. R. Johnson at between 0.33d to 0.5d a sheet up to 1640, and was certainly rising above that as we move into the later seventeenth century.[17] Production costs in 1598 have been assessed at about 0.15 to 0.25d per sheet, including the paper itself, and the Stationers' Company laid down a maximum retail price for ordinary books of 0.5d a sheet (pica or English type) and 0.67d for brevier and long primer type. In the sixteenth century, retail prices may have been up to three times the cost of production, but that profit margin had been reduced considerably by 1700. By the first decades of the eighteenth century, retail prices had increased to about 2.5d a sheet on average. Although the cheapest popular books could sell for as little as 0.67d a sheet at this time, a really expensive luxury book, complete with illustrations, engravings, and maps might go for as much as four pennies a sheet.[18]

[15] Cyprian Blagden, "The Distribution of Almanacks in the Second Half of the Seventeenth Century," *Studies in Bibliography*, 11 (1958); Philip Gaskell, *A New Introduction to Bibliography* (Oxford, 1972), pp. 160–70.

[16] *Thoresby Letters*, II, 259, Baker to Thoresby, 29 June 1710.

[17] Francis R. Johnson, "Notes on English Retail Book-Prices, 1550–1640," *The Library*, 5th series 5 (1950), 83–113; H. S. Bennett, 'Notes on English Retail Book-Prices, 1480–1560," ibid., 172–78. H. S. Bennett, *English Books and Readers, 1475–1557* (Cambridge, 1952), pp. 224–34.

The retention of amanuenses both for the copying of scholarly materials (for instance, extracts from other books and manuscripts) or, more routinely, for the provision of a printer's copy from the author's original manuscript was a further expense: Bishop Fell and the delegates of Oxford University Press allowed the scholar Edward Bernard twenty pounds per annum for an amanuensis to assist in preparing an edition of the works of Josephus that was, in fact, never completed.[19] Authors of very expensive books were often expected to provide a fair copy themselves under terms agreed in advance with the publisher or bookseller.[20] Compositors, who set the type for sheets, were expected to set anywhere between 1,000 and 1,200 characters an hour, which required that they work with considerable speed; contemporary commentators such as Joseph Moxon insisted that they should also have some scholarly qualifications, which suggests that they may have mediated creatively between author and final text, especially if a manuscript were unclear; certainly they had greater freedom to revise than modern typesetters.[21] They were sometimes paid with a copy of the book, and, increasingly from the Restoration on, in cash either by the week or per set of signatures. In addition, other perquisites accrued to print-workers by tradition, for instance the drink and tobacco given to Oxford pressmen when printing actually began: Hearne paid 3s 7½d for drink and tobacco in January 1730 to the pressmen when his edition of *Thomae Caii Vindiciae Antiquitatis Academiae Oxoniensis* began to roll off the press, and an additional shilling six weeks later when the "O" signature in the first alphabet was reached.[22]

Correction or proofreading was an additional expense, and by the end of the seventeenth century it had become increasingly common to farm this out to a person other than the author himself as a second pair of eyes.[23] The proofreader Thomas Ruddiman was paid £3 for his correction of Sir Robert Sibbald's *Introductio ad Historiam rerum a Romanis Gestarum in ea*

---

[18] Gaskell, *A New Introduction to Bibliography*, p. 178, on which most of this prefatory account is based; cf. M. Plant, *The English Book Trade* (2nd edn, 1965). The business of the company can be followed in *Records of the Court of the Stationers' Company, 1576–1602*, ed. W. W. Greg and E. Boswell (1930); *Records of the Court of the Stationers' Company, 1602–1640*, ed. W. A. Jackson (1957).

[19] Percy Simpson, *Proof-Reading in the Sixteenth, Seventeenth, and Eighteenth Centuries* (1935, reprinted 1970), p. 40; for an interesting account of the copying of the manuscript of Clarendon's *History of the Rebellion*, the press copies of which are now Bodl. MSS Clarendon 114–20, see Simpson, *Proof-Reading*, pp. 90–92.

[20] Simpson, *Proof-Reading*, p. 141, for the example of Ezechiel Spanheim's contract with Richard Smith, the London bookseller, for a new edition of a major antiquarian text, Spanheim's *Dissertationes de praestantia et usu numismatum antiquorum* (2 vols., 1706–17). For an illuminating discussion of the preparation of manuscripts for the press (as distinct from presentation copies), see H. R. Woudhuysen, *Sir Philip Sidney and the Circulation of Manuscripts, 1558–1640* (Oxford, 1996), pp. 109–15.

[21] Johns, *Nature of the Book*, pp. 87, 105–106.   [22] Ibid., p. 153.

[23] Moxon, *Mechanick Exercises*, pp. 233–39, 246–50.

Borealis Britanniae parte quae ultra murum Picticum est (1706).[24] Correctors had, potentially, even greater powers to alter an authorial text than did compositors, and were more likely to be educated. Indeed, when the corrector claimed scholarly abilities equal to the author, the result could be conflict: Henry Wharton, employed by Richard Chiswell to proofread one of John Strype's books, refused to turn his corrections over to Strype for fear that the historian would undo or ignore some of them. With correctors allowed, even tacitly, such interventionist powers, the reader of any historical text could thus not be certain that the book he or she read was absolutely as the author had left it.[25] (A sense that the book was already the product of several hands may in turn help explain readers' willingness, noted in chapter 2 above, to add their own comments to texts; in effect they became simply the most recent revisor of a page already once-removed from its author). The expenses accruing to correction could be especially great when the work involved learned languages and required the services of a trained scholar of Wharton's calibre: the antiquary Hearne subsisted in large part on his correction work for the Clarendon and Sheldonian presses at Oxford. One estimate of the cost of book correction in the eighteenth century places it at between 1s 6d and 7s 6d per sheet of scholarly text. The correction of the proofs for the second, octavo edition of Clarendon's *History of the Rebellion* (1706) cost seven shillings a sheet; two years later the correction of all three volumes of the second folio edition (3 volumes in 466 sheets) cost £58 5s in total, or 2s 6d per sheet, considerably less than the octavo.[26]

Value was added with every step, and the final product, if sold over the counter by a bookseller with no discount (as sometimes was allowed with special customers, principally other booksellers) might sell for 20 to 30 percent more than the discounted or wholesale price, which itself would already have a smaller profit margin added. Retail book prices therefore varied with the size of the book in numbers of sheets, its format, the complexity of the composition, and whether it was then sold bound or unbound (either in sheets or, in some cases, with the quires stitched together). The purchase of unbound volumes was quite common since wealthier consumers often preferred to display their tomes in a uniform or at least similar binding, sometimes stamped with a crest or coat of arms. The cost of binding, if the work was sold unbound, was itself not inconsequential. We know that Dr. Claver Morris paid 4s 3d to bind a copy of Richard Knolles' *Generall History of the Turks*, though his accounts specify neither the

[24] Ibid., pp. 49–54 (for authorial proofreading), 158.
[25] The point, and the Strype example, derive from Johns, *Nature of the Book*, pp. 103–4.
[26] Simpson, *Proof-Reading*, pp. 113, 198–202, 210–12; cf. discussion of comparable European prices in Anne Goldgar, *Impolite Learning: Conduct and Community in the Republic of Letters 1680–1750* (New Haven and London, 1995), p. 43.

edition involved nor the price of the unbound book.[27] Booksellers would bid for the commission to furnish great collectors with their books, and bookbinders to have the job of binding items that came in loose sheets or that required rebinding for the purpose of uniformity and aesthetic appearance. Thomas Elliot, the regular binder to the earl of Oxford, was frequently in ill grace with the earl's bulldog, Humfrey Wanley, for tardy service, while Christopher Chapman, the earl's other regular binder, was threatened by Wanley in 1722 with the loss of their business if he did not get on with his work.[28]

Less wealthy bibliophiles than the earl of Oxford often had to shop for themselves in the booksellers' stalls, but they too arranged for special bindings. Prospective buyers would visit shops and purchase a particular volume, leaving it to be bound and collected at another time. Thus Pepys negotiated with a bookseller in 1668 for a copy of Foxe's *Acts and Monuments*, which was delivered bound to his home on 12 October.[29] In 1666 he would negotiate with a binder to gild the backs of all his books "to make them handsome."[30] He could not restrain himself from rising early to walk to St. Paul's Churchyard one morning to see two of his histories the moment they were ready, Anthony Weldon's *Court of King James* and Sir Edward Peyton's *The divine catastrophe of the kingly family of the house of Stuarts*. He was much pleased with how they adorned his study, "it being methinks a beautiful sight." The anti-Stuart sentiments of both these titles did not detract from his delight, an indication that some readers did not judge a cover by its book.[31] On the other hand, Pepys watched his editions to make certain that

---

[27] E. Hobhouse, "The Library of a Physician *circa* 1700," *The Library*, 4th series, 13 (1932–33), 89–96, at p. 94.

[28] *The Diary of Humfrey Wanley, 1715–1720*, ed. C. E. Wright and Ruth C. Wright (2 vols., 1966), I, 74, 136; II, 275; *Letters of Humfrey Wanley*, ed. P. L. Heyworth (Oxford, 1989), p. 443 (Wanley to Edward Harley, 8 May 1722).

[29] Pepys, *Diary*, IX, 284 (21 August 1668); IX, 327 (12 October 1668). In later years Pepys would also buy the ninth (1684) edition of Foxe's book, in 3 vols., probably intending it as a gift: this copy is now at the Houghton Library of Harvard University (location f*EC65.P3988.Zz684f) and each volume, bearing Pepys' bookplate, is inscribed "For my Worthy Friend Major John Ayres Anno Dom. 1700. S. Pepys." Pepys similarly "bespoke" a copy in quires of Sprat's *History of the Royal Society* when it appeared in 1667. He had learned of the publication of the book while hanging about the booksellers' for news a week earlier: *Diary*, VIII, 387 (16 August 1667); VIII, 380 (10 August 1667).

[30] Ibid., VII, 243 (13 August, 1666). He was able to bespeak Rushworth's *Historical Collections* in 1663, despite a vow to himself swearing off such lavish purchases for a while, by the casuistry of charging it to the king and keeping it at his office: IV, 395 (23 November 1663). This was not entirely disingenuous, since he at one point (VI, 10 [15 January 1665]) found himself having to cram, from Rushworth's account of the impeachment of Buckingham in 1626, in order to prepare himself for a meeting with the king involving naval policy.

[31] Pepys, *Diary*, VI, 33 (9 February 1665). Pepys of course bought used books also, and sometimes was able to acquire them unbound, or have them rebound. On visiting the chambers of the lawyer Henry Moore, he agreed to buy Moore's "old Cambdens *Brittania*," and immediately took it away to his bookseller to be rebound to match his other volumes. Ibid., II, 21 (21 November 1661).

he had the finest, or at least the most authentic, version of any text. When James Howell published his edition of John Selden's *Mare Clausum*, previously issued during the interregnum with a preface by Marchamont Nedham, Pepys cannot have been the only owner of the Nedham edition who, rather than buy a whole new edition, simply purchased a separately printed copy of the 1663 frontispiece to paste into the book in place of the corresponding and offensive republican page.[32]

PRICE INFORMATION AND ITS SOURCES

Catalogs and probate inventories of the type that we have hitherto analyzed primarily for title-contents can also provide ample, if not completely reliable, evidence of the prices of particular books. The library of a Cambridge physician, enumerated by its owner in 1595, consists of mainly religion and surgery, but also contains a list of history books, arranged by size, and including their prices.[33] When Edward Bernard, the astronomer and future Savilian professor, became a fellow of St. John's College, Oxford in 1658, he listed some 135 of his own books including a Livy worth 4s, Caesar's *Commentaries* (1s 6d), an unspecified work of Tacitus (1s), a Eusebius and a Suetonius (1s 6d each), and six-penny copies of Aelian's *Varia historia* and Dictys of Crete's pseudohistorical *De bello Troiano*.[34] Anthony Wood bought Edward Larkin's *The true effigies or portraicture of the chief philosophers, historians, etc.*(1659) for two shillings, in sheets, in August 1662; two more shillings got him three other books, including a *Life of Sir Thomas More*, perhaps that published by Cresacre More in 1642. Wood also paid 4d for a copy of Edward Alleyn's *A Catalogue of the Noblemen and Peers of the Kingdom of England* (1662), as he noted on its title page.[35]

---

[32] Pepys, *Diary*, IV, 105 (17 April 1663); cf. Stat. Reg. II, 322. Pepys also had it ruled with red ink, "which, with the new Orthodox title, makes it now very handsome," ibid., IV, 107 (21 April 1663); Esther Potter, "To Paul's Churchyard to treat with a Bookbinder," in Robin Myers and Michael Harris (eds.), *Property of a Gentleman: the Formation, Organisation and Dispersal of the Private Library 1620–1920* (Winchester, UK, 1991), pp. 25–41.

[33] Bodl. MS Rawl. D.213, fos. 4v–5r: Plutarch's *Lives* in English (14s), folio; Sallust (12d), 16mo; Camden *Britannia* (5s), 8vo; Alexander Neville, *De furoribus Norfolciensium* (1s), 8vo; John Caius, *De antiquitate Cantabrigiensis Academiae libri duo* (18s), no size given; Dio Cassius (3s), 8vo; Herodotus in French: (2s), no size given. The author groups many items under the rubric "History bookes and poets," including many that are neither. In the entire list (fos. 2v–5v) there are 258 items in formats from folio down to pamphlet, and on subjects including medicine, religion, and philosophy. Only a dozen items can really be considered historical or antiquarian, and he had multiple copies of some authors, like Quintus Curtius or Plutarch, in different sizes.

[34] Bodl. MS Lat. misc. f. 11, fos. 13v–17v, headed "the names of my bookes taken June 17 1658." The list also included a more expensive work, Herodotus' *Histories*, worth 12s.

[35] Wood's *Life and Times*, I, 454, 466; Bodl. Lib. shelfmark Wood 289 (6), and Wood 276.A. no. 92.

It is difficult to move from the different sorts of evidence of the cost of particular books to generalizations about averages and trends, though a provisional attempt will be made to do this in appendix A below. The inventories discussed in chapter 3 above give some sense, but the values assigned by an appraiser, even if he was himself a bookseller, need not reflect actual sums paid for a book. The fact that books very rarely before the mid-seventeenth century and only inconsistently thereafter contain a printed price indicates that a good deal of bartering went on at the retail level between buyer and seller, and it is no wonder that the most successful booksellers found themselves more attracted to large-scale wholesaling. John Dunton observed that if he could have lived his life over he would have chosen to work on subscription and wholesale trade rather than run a shop, since "unless a man can haggle half an hour for a farthing, be dishonest, and tell lies, he may starve behind his ship-board for want of subsistence."[36]

The contents of a private library depended, as we have seen, not only on intellectual interest and position, but on money. John Ward envied the happy condition of a university scholar like John Prideaux (of whom it was said that he once bought books by the bushel from a bookseller in Oxford). He himself was less fortunate, and an elderly divine had told him it would cost a minimum of £700 to furnish an adequate study for himself, a figure which far exceeds the value of most personal libraries below the level of the aristocracy throughout the seventeenth century.[37] Manuscript catalogs and book lists, including the scattered references to book-buying in private account books, are of use in estimating the size and worth of libraries, along with their contents. The information can be patchy: all we know of the "history of Scanderbeg" listed in the Willoughby family accounts for 1572 is that it was purchased for thirteen pence.[38] The papers of several members of the Manners family, earls of Rutland, are more helpful. Margaret, countess of Rutland's household expenses for 1550 include, on one day, 6s 8d "for a cronicle of the [sic] Thucides" and 14s 8d for Hall's *Chronicle*.[39] Various accounts of the Manners family expenses, taken by its long-time servant, Thomas Scriven or Screven, show a consistent effort to acquire history books, both new and

---

[36] John Dunton, *Life and Errors* (1705), p. 87. The relation of "wholesale" to retail prices is illustrated in the Folger Shakespeare Library bookseller's stockbook abstracted in appendix A below.

[37] *Diary of the Rev. John Ward*, ed. C. Severn (1839), pp. 184–86.

[38] Probably Marin Barleti, *Historia de vita et gestis Scanderbegi Epirotarum principis* (Rome, 1520?).

[39] Hist. MSS Comm., *The Manuscripts of His Grace the Duke of Rutland, GCB, Preserved at Belvoir Castle*, 4 vols. (1888–1905), IV, 369. The "merry tales" was *A Hundred Mery Talys* (1526).

old.[40] On 7 May 1586, for instance, Scriven recorded five shillings spent "for K[ing] Arthure booke for my Lady" and two and sixpence for the brand new *Britannia* by Camden. On 15 August of the same year, he paid eighteen shillings for "Sansovino, his Univerall history written by Ph.Bergamo."[41] Two weeks later he paid one pound for a two-volume history of France in folio.[42] And later in the year Scriven acquired for 3s 6d a Latin version of Pandolfo's history of Naples, the *Compendio delle historie del regno di Napoli, composto de M. Pandolfo Collenuccio* (Venice 1539 or 1541), as well as John Ferne's new book of heraldry, *The Blazon of Gentrie* for 5s.

Scriven apparently had a brief to collect anything either new and interesting or old and exotic, much as Humfrey Wanley would enjoy, in a very different intellectual environment, a century and a quarter later. On 4 November 1586 Scriven paid 2s 6d for Machiavelli's *Discourses* in French (together with another book); elsewhere on the same day he acquired a two-volume edition of Livy in French, together with the chronicles of Thomas Walsingham and Matthew Paris, and "Polidor Virgill's history of England," all for four pounds and five shillings. The Matthew Paris would certainly have been Archbishop Parker's 1571 edition of the work usually known as the *Historia majora* and the Walsingham Parker's 1574 edition of the *Ypodigma Neustriae* and *Historia brevis*. Again on the same day, Scriven paid 8d for "a little French booke of the Inquisicion of Spaine" (probably the *Histoire de l'Inquisition d'Espagne, exposée par exemples* [Geneva, 1568], taken from the Latin of R. Gonsalvius Montanus). And on 16 November he paid ten shillings for a much older book, Fabyan's *Chronicle*, together with seven shillings for Laurentius Surius' *Commentarius brevis rerum in orbe gestarum ab anno Salutis MD usque in annum MDLXXIII* (Cologne, 1586). In 1612, Scriven undertook a similar spate of book-buying for Francis, the sixth earl, whose historical tastes also ran to foreign works, but with a preference for translations. Scriven's purchases in this year list, in addition to some literary and religious works, Louis Turquet de Mayerne's *The Generall Historie of Spaine*, newly translated by Edward Grimeston (1612) for one pound; the similarly new translation by William Shute of Thomas de Fougasses' *The Generall Historie of Venice* (1612) for fifteen shillings; and another edition of Camden's *Britannia* for thirty shillings, probably the 1610 Philemon Holland translation.

Similar stories are told in other aristocratic houses, but tastes could vary considerably. The accounts of Lord Hastings for the period 1638–40 show

---

[40] Hist. MSS Comm., *Rutland*, IV, 388–91, 490–91, from which all the following information on Scriven's purchases derives.

[41] *Sopplimento delle Croniche universali del Mondo* (2 vols., Venice, 1581).

[42] Probably Belleforest's *Les grandes annales et histoires generales de France* (2 vols., Paris, 1579).

his household acquiring historical works of a mainly military and chivalric flavor, such as Charles Aleyn's verse *Historie of . . . Henrie . . . the Seventh* and John Beaumont's poem *Bosworth Field* at a shilling each, and Sir Thomas Hawkins' translation of Giovanni Baptista Manzini's *Politicall observations upon the fall of Sejanus* at 2s 6d.[43] Only a few years later, in 1646, during a time of heightened millenarian interest at the end of the first civil war, Algernon Cecil bought several volumes of a chronological flavor, including Johann Alsted's *Chronology* (5s), Degory Wheare's *De ratione legendi historias* (1s 6d); Johann Sleidan's *De quatuor summis imperis* (1s 6d), and David Chytreus' *Chronologia historiae Herodoti et Thvcydidis* (1s 6d).[44]

References in memorandum books, almanacs, and loose accounts further reinforce the impression that history was an increasingly prominent subject in the luxury purchasing of the better-off gentry and aristocracy during the seventeenth and early eighteenth centuries. John Coke, the son of Charles I's Secretary of State, Sir John, spent 1s 4d on a copy of "Sleidan's chronicle" at Cambridge in Michaelmas term 1626, together with a more expensive edition of Diogenes Laertius (four and sixpence) and, for a shilling, the arms of the two universities.[45] The Restoration MP Sir John Nicholas, son of another Secretary of State, did little reading to judge from his diary (mastiffs being his preferred recreation), but he still managed to spend fifteen shillings in 1668 on a copy of Sarpi's *History of the Council of Trent* in English along with five shillings on a Book of Common Prayer for his wife.[46] The accounts of Sir John Crewe in the early 1690s include invoices from his bookseller making mention of many theological and practical works, but also historical and heraldic items like "1 sh. of heraldry 1s 0d"; "1 hist. presbyt. 6d." In January 1691 he purchased the brand new work by "R.B." (Richard Burton, the pseudonym of Nathaniel Crouch), *The Secret history of the four last monarchs of Great Britain, viz., James I, Charles I, Charles II, James II* for a shilling, the only historical work among twenty-eight bought, while a few months later he spent £1 on a "historical account of English government" and 6s on Edward Cooke's *The history of the successions of the kings of England*.[47] The accounts of Richard Norton of Hampshire for "books and

---

[43] Hist. MSS Comm., *Report on the manuscripts of the late Reginald Rawdon Hastings, Esq.* (4 vols., 1928–47), I, 390.

[44] Another bill has other, more commonplace titles including Caesar's *Commentaries* for 2s 9d, and Quintus Curtius for 2s: Hist. MSS Comm., *Calendar of the manuscripts of the Most Honourable the Marquess of Salisbury . . . preserved at Hatfield House, Hertfordshire* (24 vols., 1883–1976), XXII, 388, 391.

[45] Hist. MSS Comm., *The manuscripts of the Earl Cowper, K.G., preserved at Melbourne Hall, Derbyshire* (3 vols., 1888–89), I, 284.

[46] Folger MS V.a. 419–20, diary and account book of Sir John Nicholas 1668, 1674, written in copies of Thomas Gallen's *Almanac* for 1668 and 1674.

[47] Cheshire RO, DAR/A/59 (Crewe accounts, loose slips).

plays" between 1709 and 1714 are similarly informative, including 5s 6d paid for "the peerage of England," 1s 6d for a play on Jane Shore, and an unknown sum for a "history of the peace with France."[48]

Lesser gentry, members of the professions, and, in particular, merchants, were equally inclined to keep such records – we have the Jacobean letter writer William Trumbull's several notes of sums spent for histories such as a French edition of Josephus' *Jewish Wars* and English editions of Sallust and Pedro Mexia, as well as a recent book like Richard Knolles' *General History of the Turks*.[49] John Neale, a merchant living in Alborough Hatch, near Colchester, kept a meticulous set of business accounts from 1680 to 1686, which includes the titles and prices of the books he purchased. These include an abridged version of Burnet's *History of the Reformation*, purchased in November 1682 for six shillings. In July 1683 he paid £1 to "Mr. Perrot," the local bookseller, toward the total cost of the new edition of Foxe's Book of Martyrs, unbound (and in advance, since the book did not appear until the following year). On a trip to London in December 1684 he took his unbound sheets of Foxe back to London (where they had originated) and had them bound in vellum at the cost of eight shillings.[50]

The roughly contemporaneous account book of Arthur Brooke of Oakley Magna, Northamptonshire, recorded between 1678 and the mid-1690s, is only slightly less informative. Brooke was a casual but regular buyer of books, in small numbers, mainly at fairs. On most occasions he does not oblige us with the title of the work bought, betraying a certain indifference, or an attraction to the look rather than the content of a volume he spied. He laid out £2 2s for unspecified books in March 1679, and the following July a further sum of 18s 6d, on a trip to London, for "Hylin" (perhaps a work by Peter Heylyn), along with various legal works, a dictionary, George Meriton's *Anglorum gesta, or, A brief history of England* (2s 2d) and the blank account book itself.[51] Claver Morris, a West Country physician, paid 2s 6d in 1694 for "Cardinal Wolsey" (presumably Cavendish's *Life*).[52]

---

[48] Hants. RO, 5M50/814; cf. Bishop Nicolson's purchase (2 November 1704) of Serenus Cressy's (Hugh Paulin) *Church History of Brittany* (Rouen, 1668) for 7s 6d, from among the "old books in Moor-fields" while in London for parliament, *The London Diaries of William Nicolson*, ed. C. Jones and G. Holmes (Oxford, 1985), p. 219.

[49] Hist. MSS Comm., *Report on the manuscripts of the Marquess of Downshire, preserved at Easthampstead Park, Berks.* (4 vols. in 5, 1924–40), II, 139, 182–83.

[50] Bodl. MS Top. Essex f. 1 (account book of John Neale), fos. 21v, 29r, 34v, 36v, 65v.

[51] Folger MS V.a. 440 (unfoliated account book of Arthur Brooke): at Michaelmas 1678 he bought three further books, none of which was historical, at "Harborrow fair." On 18 July 1680 he bought two books, one of which was a history of the "Counsell of Trent," probably Sarpi's since it is referred to in English, but possibly the later (and untranslated) *Istoria del Concilio di Trento* by Sforza Pallavicino in 2 vols. (Rome, 1656–57).

[52] *The Diary of a West Country Physician, AD 1684–1726*, ed. Edmund Hobhouse (1934), p. 149 (16 November 1694). Morris was a greater lover of music than history, and did not enjoy historical drama; he records watching strolling players and musicians and was dragged

There is as yet no general database of prices known to have been paid for particular books of various sorts during the early modern period. A useful list of prices once assembled by H. G. Wheatley is now a century old, often anecdotal in evidence, and in serious need of updating.[53] The customs and excise sources so useful for eighteenth-century book historians as to gross quantities and their values are of little help as to specific titles.[54] So far as domestically printed titles, the closest thing to a trade-wide contemporary record assigning specific prices to books are the so-called *Term Catalogues* that run from 1668 to 1711. These are disappointingly patchy, especially at the upper end, and are less reliable than actual bills and accounts, since the prices are often hedged with a proximizing "about." Their usefulness is further vitiated by the decision of the seventeenth-century publishers John Starkey and Robert Clavell to exclude cheap books and to charge a fee for inclusion, something recognized by other members of the book trade as early as 1669 in supporting rival listings.[55] Similar problems apply to other sorts of source. Because of the immense variation in size and edition (rarely given outside library catalogs and inventories), availability, and unknowns like binding (or the lack of binding), no meaningful "average" price of historical works can therefore be constructed at the present time. Even where we know the prices of two copies of the same edition of a book, sold a few years apart, the discrepancies are greater than can be accounted for by mere inflation. As we saw above, John Neale paid £2 in two instalments, plus eight more shillings for binding his copy of the 1684 edition of Foxe when it came out, having subscribed in advance. Six years later, the nonconformist John Pinney would pay £2 12s for the same edition.[56]

reluctantly to a performance of "the tragedy of Jane Shore" by a friend named Mr. Haynes, for whose benefit it was staged: ibid., p. 121 (2 August 1725). Cf. CUL MS Dd.10.64, fos. 68–72, an anonymous library catalog from the late seventeenth century, bound together with an early seventeenth-century Italian translation of Tacitus, but in a different hand, including what are probably the sums paid for the books, most of which were expensive: Matthew of Westminster (5s); Olaus Wormius' *Fasti danici* (8s); Helvicus' *Theatrvm historicvm et chronologicvm* (3s); Ammianus Marcellinus (£1); William Burton's *A commentary on Antoninus, his Itinerary, or journies of the Romane empire, so far as it concerneth Britain* (5s); Anthony Wood's *Historia et antiquitates Universitatis oxoniensis* (£1 18s); Selden, *De anno civili veterum Iudaeorum*, including "Aser" (that is, Ussher's appended *De Macedonum et Asianorum anno solari*) at 2s 6d; Seth Calvisius' *Opus chronologicum* (8s); and Henry Spelman's *Glossarium* (16s). Of the 266 titles, in varying sizes but without dates of editions, and incompletely listed, only nine can be positively identified as historical.

[53] H. B. Wheatley, *Prices of Books: an Inquiry into the Changes in the Price of Books which have Occurred in England at Different Periods* (1898). Wheatley's estimate (p. 97) of "ordinary" prices of octavos at "five or six shillings" in the early eighteenth century is an unstatistical and impressionistic figure best belied by the evidence in appendix A below; the variation on either side of that figure is far too great for it to stand as meaningful.

[54] Pollard, *Dublin's Trade in Books*, pp. 39–42 provides one example of the use of such data for the late seventeenth century.   [55] See Edward Arber's cautionary preface to *TC*, I, pp. x–xvi.

[56] *Letters of John Pinney 1679–1699*, ed. G. F. Nuttall (1939), app. vii, no page; account book of John Neale, Bodl. MS Top. Essex f. 1, fos. 21v, 29r, 34v, 36v, 65v.

Bookseller's bills and accounts, receipts and invoices in private papers, and scattered references in diaries and account books to titles purchased or ordered can all provide reasonably reliable information as to the price paid for individual books at a particular time. Among these sources, actual bills and receipts issued by booksellers and stationers are especially fruitful and are best cited here individually, in connection with their purchasers. We might begin at the top, with William Cecil. The future Lord Burghley, who had pronounced tastes even as a younger man for the antiquarian and historical, purchased seventy-two books (some of which were duplicate copies) listed in seven distinct booksellers' bills between 1554 and 1556. Historical works included a Greek Herodotus (6d), a history of Portugal (1s 2d), a history, also written in Portuguese, of the Indies (3s 6d), and a work listed simply as "Monumenta antiquat.," in quarto (3d).[57] "Wholesale" prices (a somewhat anachronistic term applicable principally to trade between booksellers) can also be gleaned from bills. A set of bills from Thomas Chard or Chere of London to a Cambridge stationer to whom he supplied books for sale in the university, includes a number of specially ordered historical works amid the diet of textbooks conveyed by the famous carrier Hobson and generally in multiple copies. One bill lists a single copy of a book called the "Queen of Scottes" (8d). A second list has books for delivery to "my lord chancellors son and his kinsman," among which are mainly literary titles like Lyly's *Euphues*, *Palmerin of England*, and two copies of Aesop in Greek and Latin, in sextedecimo. A third undated bill, somewhat longer, includes two "tragicall historyes" (10d); two *historia populi dei* (6d); Bevis of Hampton (9d); a "Chronikle of emperors" in quarto (probably the 1571 quarto edition of Pedro Mexia's *The foreste; or, Collection of histories* (2s 4d); a version of Guy of Warwick (4d); and Justin's epitome of Trogus Pompeius (1s 4d).[58]

Nearly a century later, extant bills show an overall slight rise in prices. This is owed not only to general inflation but also to the increasing gravi-

---

[57] Folger MS PR 1405 B88. A similar set of bills copied into a copy of Roger Ascham's *Disertissimi viri Rogeri Aschami Angli* includes Caesar's *Commentaries*, *Antiquitates galloises*, Carion's *Chronicle*, Lucan, "Crispin" [i.e. Jean Crespin's French martyrology]: thirty-one books in all. Folger printed books, STC 828 (London, 1581), copy 1, list of books at end of printed book (volume reversed). This also lists the colors (green and red) in which these should be bound.

[58] Folger MS X.d. 168 (1–3) set of book bills from Thomas Chard or Chere (1583–84) to Thomas Bradshaw, Cambridge stationer, and William Knowsley (Chard's one-time apprentice and by then Bradshaw's). The lists are incomplete owing to cropped sides and top; they are discussed in R. Jahn, "Letters and Booklists of Thomas Chard (or Chare) of London, 1583–84," *The Library*, 4th series 4 (1923–24), 219–37, which article does not identify all the books; and D. Paige, "An Additional Letter and Booklist of Thomas Chard, Stationer of London," *The Library*, 4th series 21 (1940–41), 26–43. On Chard, who operated in London till *ca.* 1618, see below, p. 231 and Plomer, i, 65.

tation of history books purchased by the moderately to very wealthy – who were more likely to have running accounts such as this – into larger formats intended for reading in private libraries rather than carrying abroad. A single receipt issued to the great scholar John Selden by Cornelius Bee for a total of fifty-two books purchased from Bee in 1648 and 1649, includes several very expensive historical works: a Greek and Latin edition of Xenophon's works (£2), a Dionysius of Halicarnassus (£4), a six-volume edition of Baronius' *Annales Ecclesiastici* (£6), a Greek Diodorus Siculus (£1), the *Annalivm ecclesiasticorvm Veteris Testamenti epitome* by Jacques Salian, and an unpriced chronicle by Matthew Paris.[59] Selden's tastes were more exotic than most. Other bibliophiles of similar voraciousness collected books at a more moderate price: a bill forwarded to John Moore, bishop of Norwich by his friend, Dr. John Postlethayt lists eight unbound books that the doctor had received on behalf of the prelate, among which were Cornelius Nepos (3s), Dionysius Halicarnassus (4s) and John Potter's *Archaeologica graeca* (5s 3d).[60]

This picture of modest inflation up to about 1700 is reinforced by a more inclusive set of bills, principally for less expensive titles than Selden collected, from the last quarter of the seventeenth century. These were sent by the bookseller Francis Tyton to a provincial client, Sir John Wittewronge, for the stationery, gazettes, newsletters, and books with which Tyton had supplied that Hertfordshire baronet between 1675 and 1682. These include bills in 1675 for a history of The Netherlands (10s) and an unspecified history in German (3s). More precise titles are more helpful in assigning value to a work. In 1679–80 Tyton invoiced Wittewronge for "1 history of ye plott" (3s 6d); a copy of Baker's *Chronicle* (£1 1s), Richard Baxter's *Church-history of the government of bishops and their councils abbreviated* (7s), and "Straffords trial" (17s), the last item probably the newly published eighth volume of Rushworth's *Historical Collections*, devoted to the fall of Charles I's minister in 1641.[61]

---

[59] Lambeth Palace Library, Fairhurst MSS, 3513, fos. 21r–v, invoice from Bee to Selden, 1 October 1649.
[60] Folger MS X.d. 476: undated (1697) letter, Postlethayt (in London) to Moore. John Moore was one of the greatest of Restoration bibliophiles, leaving 29,000 books and 1,790 MSS; his library sold in 1714 to George I for 6,000 guineas; the king then gave it to Cambridge University: *DNB*, sub "Moore, John" and Seymour De Ricci, *English Collectors of Books and Manuscripts (1530–1930) and their Marks of Ownership* (Bloomington, IN, 1960), pp. 34–35. The other works include a Russian grammar, two books of logic, and two poets, Pindar and Homer, the total bill coming to £2 10s 4d. The histories occupy the middle range of the prices, well above the logics and grammar, but less than the Pindar, which was "of the best paper" and worth £1 10s on its own.
[61] Herts. RO, D/ELw.F16.

The book trade bills kept by certain larger libraries established in the seventeenth and eighteenth centuries further support this impression of greater inflation at the upper end of the book market. Dr. Pearson has examined and transcribed the bills and vouchers in the Durham Dean and Chapter Library from 1635 to 1740. The bills begin with a list (in the hand of Bishop John Cosin) of books purchased from Richard Whitaker of London in 1635 and resume with bills from 1680. Table 5.14 notes the historical works acquired, their price, the date at which they were acquired, and the bookseller who sold them.

PURCHASING HABITS

Keeping up with Clio's acolytes was not cheap. By the last quarter of the seventeenth century, an extremely expensive book like the second edition of Dugdale's *Origines Juridicales, or historical memorials of the English laws* (1676), might retail for several pounds – the copy belonging to the Northampton topographer and Lincoln's Inn bencher John Bridges (1666–1724) sold at the auction of his books in February 1726 for £7, fifty years after its publication.[63] In the late 1680s, the Somerset presbyterian John Pinney cataloged his 266 books, listing their prices. These include several histories, the above-mentioned 1684 edition of Foxe (£2 12s 0d), Fuller's *Church-History* (£1 7s 6d) and a "History of anabaptists" (4d). Except for the last item, the histories are among the most expensive books.[64]

This does not, however, mean that no history could be read at all without the expenditure of large sums, only that the "latest" and most luxurious works, or books whose value was enhanced by the fame of their author (Clarendon or Bacon, for instance) were priced at the higher end. Against this there was also available, at the lower end of the price range, a vast and growing assortment of epitomes, abridgments, digests, and even extracted

---

[62] Bills with no historical works and no books at all (e.g. bills for stationery) are omitted. Book identifications are by the present author, aided by the staff of Durham Dean and Chapter Library, and are not provided by Pearson's transcript, which is free of blame for any errors arising herein. Among the other details these bills give us are the cost of binding various books: the *Camden's Britannia* purchased from William Werdon in 1695 (the Gibson edition published that year) was bound with lettering and marbling in the following spring for 6s 6d. It may be added that this set of bills also provides much evidence that the history of English reading habits cannot be told from the *Short-Title Catalogue* and its successors alone: many of the books purchased bore foreign imprints.

[63] *A Catalogue of the Library of Thomas Baker*, ed. Frans Korsten (Cambridge, 1990), item 2164.

[64] *Letters of John Pinney, 1679–1699*, ed. Geoffrey F. Nuttall (London and New York, 1939), app. vii, no page. The anabaptist work might be Richard Blome, *The fanatick history, or, An exact relation and account of the old Anabaptists and new Quakers* (1660) or, more likely given the very low cost, a pamphlet such as Anon., *A Short history of the Anabaptists of high and low Germany* (1642).

sections of longer books, printed on cheaper paper, without bindings and often though not always in small format; and bargains could even be had occasionally on books that one might expect to have cost more.

This can be seen best in the accounts of a well-educated but financially stretched group such as the rural clergy, many of whom simply entered books with the rest of their parish expenses and revenues. Those without scholarly pretensions were more likely to buy historical works at the lower end of the price range, Giles Moore being a good example. The rector of Horsted Keynes, Sussex, Moore died in 1679, having kept a detailed record of his book purchases for much of the preceding quarter-century. Although these were primarily religious, he also acquired several historical works, paying a shilling for Nicholas Bernard's *The life & death of . . . Dr. James Usher* (1656) in 1657, £1 14s for a second-hand copy of Camden's *Britannia* in 1658 (adding to it, the following year, a separate map of Worcestershire, "to starch to Cambdens Britannia," for 6d). Aside from occasional lavish indulgences such as the Camden, most of Moore's acquisitions fell at the lower end of the price range, some costing only a few pennies, such as Lambert van den Bos' *The life and raigne of King Charles* at 8d (1659) or "The history of Portugall" (*The History of Portugal*, 1662, by "a person of quality"), picked up for 8d while on a visit to London. In 1660 Moore paid a few pennies each for several almanacs, but 2s 6d for Richard Verstegan's *Restitution of Decayed Intelligence*, a work first published in 1605 but reprinted as recently as 1655. His purchases continued slowly but steadily: in 1661, a copy of Peter Heylyn's *Historia Quinque Articularis* (3s); in 1663 a copy of Fuller's *Worthies* for 18s and, more economically, 1s 4d on the vehemently royalist James Heath's biography of Cromwell, *Flagellum* and ten shillings for a book that was probably Heath's newly published *A brief chronicle of the late intestine war in the three kingdoms of England, Scotland and Ireland.*[65]

Sometimes Moore bought his works from, or through, visiting chapmen, sending the 4s cost of his copy of John Selden's *De dis syris*, "by J. Wood, Tanner"; Wood, a regular provisioner of Moore's, probably also delivered the book. Trips to London afforded the more direct pleasures of the bookstalls at St. Paul's Churchyard, long the site of the most prosperous of the London booksellers, and in October 1663 Moore bought from Philemon Stevens at the Gilded Lyon a six-shilling "chronicle of the warres of England"; a trip just over a year later took him to Mistress Mosely's bookshop, where for ten shillings he acquired a copy of John *Weever's Ancient Funerall monuments*. Moore's regular bookseller in London, however, was William

---

[65] *The Journal of Giles Moore*, ed. Ruth Bird, Sussex Record Soc. 68 (Lewes, 1971), pp. 116–20, 180–92.

Table 5.14. Historical works acquired by Durham Cathedral Library, 1635–1730, and their costs

Doc. date	Bookseller	Total books	Author	Title and edition date	Price £ s d
1635	Whitaker, Richard	27	Scaliger, J.	Opus de emendatione temporum, 1629	1-3-0
			Flavius Lucius Dexter (in fact a forgery by J. Roman de la Higuera)	Chronicon omnimodae historiae, 1627	0-12-0
			anon.	Antiquitatum Romanorum Hispanarumque in nummis veterum dialogi XI, 1617	0-17-4
1680	Hutchinson, Jonathan	7	Cluverius, P.	Germaniae antiquae libri tres, 1631	1-8-0
			Sandford, Francis	Genealogical History of the kings of England, 1677	2-2-6
			Dugdale, Wm	A short view of the late troubles in England, 1681	0-16-0
1691 (March)	Werdon, William	3	Cox, Richard	Hibernia Anglicana: or, the history of Ireland, 2 vols., 1689–90	1-6-6
1691 (Dec.)	Werdon, William	8	Camden, William (ed. T. Smith)	Epistolae, 1691	0-8-6
1692 (Oct.)	Werdon, William	8	Rushworth, John	Historical Collections, 1659 et seq[a]	2-6-0
			Wood, A.	Historia et antiquitates Universitatis Oxoniensis, 1674	1-10-0
			Seckendorf, Veit Ludwig von	Commentarius Historicus et apologeticus de Lutheranismo, 2 vols., 1692	1-16-0
1693–94	Werdon, William	10	Benoist, Elie	History of the . . . Edict of Nantes, 1694	0-10-6
			Strype, John	Memorials of Thomas Cranmer, 1694	1-4-0
			Geddes, Michael	History of the Church of Malabar, 1694	0-5-4
1694–95	Werdon, William	2	Wharton, Henry (editor)	History of the troubles and tryal of . . . William Laud, 2 vols., 1695[–1700]	1-0-0
1723	Innys, William and John (London)	16	Camden, William	Britannia, 1695	1-12-0
			Hélyot, Pierre	Histoire des ordres monastiques, 8 vols., 1714–19	8-0-0
			Chevillier, André and Jean de la Caille	L'origine de l'Imprimerie de Paris, 1694 and Histoire de l'imprimerie et de la librairie, 1689	1-5-0

Year			Author	Title	Price
			Dupin, Louis	De antiqua ecclesiae disciplina dissertationes historicae, 1686	0-9-0
1727	Waghorn, John	3	Newton, Isaac	Chronology of ancient kingdoms amended, 1728	0-16-0
1728	Woodman, James and Lyon, David or Daniel	5	Mabillon, Jean	Vetera analecta, 1723	1-4-0
1729	Waghorn, John[a]	45	Selden, John	Eutychii Aegyptii, Patriarchae orthodoxorum . . ., 1642	0-1-6
			Selden, J. and Pococke, Edward	Contextio gemmarum, sive Eutychii . . . Annales, 1656	1-1-0
			Heidegger, Johann Heinrich	De historia sacra patriarcharum exercitationes selectae, 2 vols., 1667–71	0-7-0
			Burnet, Gilbert	History of his own time, 2 vols., 1724[–34]	0-15-0
1730	Waghorn, John	6	Kennett, White	Register and chronicle ecclesiastical and civil, 1728	1-16-0
			Lucan (F. Oudendorp, ed.)	Pharsalia, 1728	1-4-0
			Willis, Browne	Survey of the Cathedrals, 2 vols., 1727	1-8-6
			Eusebius (W. Reading, ed.)	Historiae Ecclesiasticae, 3 vols., 1720	3-0-0

[a] Seven volumes of an edition of Rushworth are currently in the Durham Dean and Chapter Library, shelfmark I.II.27–33.

[b] Sale of private library of the Revd. John Allason (1667–1728), rector of Middleton-in-Teesdale, through Waghorn, to Dean and Chapter Library.

Source: David Pearson, "Book Trade Bills and Vouchers from Durham Cathedral Library, 1634–1740;" History of the Book Trade in the North, *Working Papers*, 45 (Sept. 1986). I wish to express my gratitude to Mr. Roger Norris, deputy librarian, Durham Cathedral, Dean and Chapter Library, for his help in identifying precisely the works mentioned in Pearson's transcript among current library holdings.

Grantham of the Bear, and it was to Grantham that Moore paid ten shillings for four books in 1666, including the 1663 translation of *The history of Henry IV. surnamed the Great, King of France and Navarre* by Hardouin de Beaumont de Péréfixe, bishop of Rhodes and archbishop of Paris.[66]

A clerically authored source of a very different kind, and the work of a much more active book collector than Giles Moore, is the enormous manuscript "catalogus librorum" compiled by the Reverend James Allgood of Nunwich. A member of a prosperous Northumberland family, Allgood was a keen follower of book auctions. This catalog is not a description of his actual collection, which must have been considerably smaller,[67] but a compilation from several auction sales in the 1680s and after, for example that of the library of Richard Smith, the Little Moorfields bibliophile and Secondary of the Poultry Compter, who died in 1675. Smith's large collection, many of the rarer books in which had come from the earlier collection of the Jacobean notary Humphrey Dyson, was auctioned on behalf of Smith's daughter Martha Hacker by the bookseller Richard Chigwell or Chiswell in May 1682. The sale of the "libri Historici Philologici &c.," 2,491 lots in all, took a total of eight days. Unlike most of the printed sale catalogs, Allgood's manuscript record of the sale actually includes prices for most items and generally gives the year of the edition.[68] The Allgood list is too long to be reproduced in full here, but some of the best-known historical works from the 1682 Smith auction, all in folio format, and their prices are laid out in table 5.15.

THE SECOND-HAND MARKET

Allgood's list, if we assume that he recorded the prices accurately, reveals that an old book was not necessarily more expensive than a more recent title. What appears to be the 1493 *Nuremberg Chronicle* sold for a mere 15s, and Caxton's chronicle for 8s 4d. In contrast, the 1597 reprint of Foxe's *Acts and Monuments* is priced at £2, and a much-used reference work, Dugdale's *Monasticon*, at over £5. Size and subject still counted as much as antiquity in determining the price of any book, and histories were no exception. Giles Moore's above-mentioned purchases of some older titles inexpensively also

---

[66] Ibid., pp. 188, 190, 192. His other purchases included Bishop Cosin's *The history of Popish transubstantiation* (one of two books together costing 18s 6d): ibid., pp. 117–18.

[67] Northumberland RO, ZAL/21/8, Allgood's will and testament of 1744 makes no reference to an extensive library; I am grateful to Mrs. S. Wood, senior archivist, for correspondence on this matter.

[68] Northumberland RO, ZAL/85/1 (Allgood papers), fos. 1–301v; for Allgood and his family, see Northumberland County History Committee, *A history of Northumberland* (London and Newcastle-upon-Tyne, 1893–1940), XV, 200; a catalog by Smith of his own books is BL MS Add. 21096; for Smith and Dyson see E. G. Duff, "The Library of Richard Smith," *The Library*, 2nd series 8 (1907), 113–33; for Chiswell's sale, see Wheatley, *Prices of Books*, pp. 113–16.

suggests this, and other examples can be mentioned. John Bagford, who as both bookseller and print-history enthusiast knew the value of his own goods, offered Thomas Baker the century-old historical poem by William Slatyer, *Palae-Albion: the historie of Great Britanie to this present day* (by no means an outstanding specimen of Jacobean verse, much less of historiography) for a mere two shillings.[69]

A general upward inflation of book prices thus made historical and antiquarian works (except the Crouch-type potboilers, and cheaper still chapbooks and broadsheets) more costly at the same time that the numbers of them increased – a situation depressingly familiar at the end of the twentieth century. In response, many buyers became hard-nosed bargain hunters. Samuel Hartlib reported to John Worthington in 1659 that a new edition of Joseph Scaliger's chronology, the *Thesaurus temporum*, could now be had from an Amsterdam press for "half the price" of earlier editions, which had sold for twelve rix dollars a copy.[70] Worthington himself had never heard of Joshua Childrey, an author whose popularization of works on antiquities and topography, the *Britannia Baconica*, would appear in 1660, but he remarked that "if the book be worthy, as it is cheap . . . it is then a greater charity to the public."[71] Samuel Pepys, so often given to spendthrift enthusiasm, periodically tried to hold the line on costs, making choices between history and lighter fare such as plays or French romances. Shopping for this Navy Board functionary was often a matter less of looking for a particular title than of having to control the urge to spend up to several pounds on books. His decisions were often reached after much agonizing deliberation. In 1663 he spent an afternoon at his booksellers with some extra money, "and found myself at a great loss where to choose." He confessed that he "could not tell whether to lay out my money for books of pleasure, as plays, which my nature was most earnest in; but at last, after seeing Chaucer – Dugdales *History of Pauls*, Stow's *[Survey of] London*, Gesner, [Sarpi's] *History of Trent*, besides Shakespeare, Johnson, and Beaumont's plays, I at last chose Dr. Fuller's *worthys, the Cabbala or collections of Letters of State* . . . with another little book or two."[72]

Scarce books could occasion joy at a bargain snapped up or frustration at

[69] Korsten, *Catalogue of the Library of Thomas Baker*, item 1176, citing an undated letter from Bagford to Baker in Bodl. MS Rawl. D. 375, fos. 177–78; M. M. Gatch, "John Bagford, Bookseller and Antiquary," *British Library Journal*, 12 (1986), 150–71; T. A. Birrell, "Anthony Wood, John Bagford and Thomas Hearne as Bibliographers," in R. Myers and M. Harris (eds.), *Pioneers in Bibliography* (Winchester, UK, 1988), pp. 25–39.

[70] *The Diary and Correspondence of Dr. John Worthington*, ed. James Crossley (Chetham Soc., o.s. 13 1847), I, 146–47.

[71] Ibid., p. 237. Worthington also noted, in comparison, that a recent work, the *Bibliotheca Criticorum*, on the Bible, had sold bound "no less than 15£ and I doubt fewer will therefore purchase it."

[72] In fact, Pepys would return to buy all those mentioned above except the Gesner; they remain in the Pepys Library at Magdalen College, Cambridge. *Diary*, IV, 410 (10 December 1663).

Table 5.15. *Select history titles from James Allgood's catalog of the Smith library*

Author	Short title of work	Date of edn	Price £ s d
C. Baronius	*Annales*, 12 vols.	1609	5-6-6
J. Scaliger	*Chronicon*	1658	1-7-0
M. Parker	*De antiq. eccles. Brit.*	1605	0-16-0
M.Flacius *et al.*	*Magdeburg Centuries*, 7 vols.	1564	2-19-0
H. Savile (ed.)	*Anglorum rerum scriptores post Bedam*	1652	2-17-0
Eadmer	*Historia novorum* (ed. Selden)	1623	0-16-0
W. Dugdale	*Monasticon Anglicanum*, 3 vols.	1655–73	5-1-6
Bede	*Historia Ecclesia anglicana et leges anglo-saxonicae*	1644	1-5-2
[H. Schedel, *Nuremberg Chronicle*]	*Chronicon chronicorum ab initio mundi*	1493	0-15-0
J.-A. de Thou	*Historia sui temporum*, 5 vols.	1620	4-5-0
H. Spelman	*Glossarium*, "opt ed." with MS notes by Smith	1664	0-15-0
G. Burnet	*History of Reformation*, 2 vols.	1682	1-18-8
W. Caxton	*Caxton's Chronicle*	1498	0-8-4[a]
W. Camden	*Britannia* (English), 2 vols. including maps	1610	2-10-0
W. Camden	*History of Q. Elizabeth*, trans. Norton	1630	0-7-6
J. Foxe	*Acts and Monuments*, 2 vols.	1597	2-0-0
R. Fabyan	*Chronicle*	1559	0-11-8
T. Fuller	*Church-History* and *The appeal of injured innocence*	1655–59	1-10-0
E. Hall	*Hall's Chronicle*	1550	0-6-10
J. Heath	*Chronicle of Civil Wars*	1676	0-11-0
S. Daniel	*Collection of historie of England*, cont. by J. Trussell, 2 vols.	1641	0-12-6
G. Buck	*History of Richard III*	1646	0-6-0
W. Habingron	*History of Edward IV*	1640	0-7-0

W. Martyn	Lives of Kings of England	1615	0-8-2
A. Wilson	History of Britain	1653	0-9-6
Josephus	Histories, trans. Lodge	1620	0-16-0
R. Higden	Polychronicon	1527	1-8-2
J. Speed	Historie of Great Britain, large paper	1627	1-14-0
A. Sammes	Britannia antiqua illustrata	1676	0-9-6
J. Stow	Annales	1615	0-12-6
J. Weever	Ancient Funeral Monuments	1631	0-11-0
J. Taylor	Life of Jesus Christ	1657	0-15-0
H. Townshend	Historical Collections	1653	0-7-6
J. Rushworth	Historical collections, 3 vols.	1659–80	2-10-0
J. Froissart	Chronicles, trans. Berners	1525	0-10-0

[a]Eleven Caxton books sold at the Smith auction for £3 4s 2d in total; but thirteen Caxtons from the library of Dr. Francis Bernard, former physician to James II, sold for the significantly lower price of two guineas altogether in 1698: Wheatley, *Price of Books*, pp. 115, 121.

an extortionate price. William Stratford wrote enthusiastically to inform his friend and fellow bibliophile Edward, Lord Harley that he had just acquired, after a long search, a *second* copy of Sprat's *History of the Royal Society*.[73] In contrast, the antiquary Thomas Baker crankily noted on his copy of Sir Edward Peyton's *Divine catastrophe of the kingly family of the house of Stuarts* (a work with which the nonjuring Baker, like the royalist Pepys fifty years earlier, had no sympathy) that "this book, tho' a libel, yet is very scarce & hard to be met with, & cost me more then it is worth."[74] Henry Gyles indicated to Ralph Thoresby a willingness to part with his copy of Dugdale's *History of St. Paul's* for 30s, it being "a scarce book" that now sold for that price, but bluntly pointed out that he had another potential buyer.[75]

Second-hand books had been readily available since the early seventeenth century, and as early as 1628 the warden of the Stationers' Company compiled a list of booksellers who specialized in the dispersal of old libraries and in the importation of continental used books, principally from fairs at Frankfurt and Leipzig.[76] The extent to which ordinary book owners relied on the second-hand market can be illustrated from one unusual autograph book catalog, that of the Dissenter Simon Browne (1680–1732), who was successively a congregationalist minister at Portsmouth and at the Old Jewry, London. Compiled on the back pages of a letter book in March 1709, Browne's catalog lists the titles of works, the number of volumes, whether they were acquired new or used, and at what price. Of the 169 items in the catalog, and forty-four others listed as acquired subsequently, 111 (52 percent) were new, one or two were "new bound" or "mixt" (an old book bound in with a new one), and the rest were second-hand. Among the historical works owned by Browne, the division was slightly in favor of the used book: thirteen new and fifteen used or mixed, with recent titles tending to be acquired new, and older works having for the most part been previously owned, including classical historians (but not modern works on classical antiquities, such as those by John Potter and Basil Kennett), and early and mid-seventeenth-century English histories such as Fuller's *Church-history*.[77]

---

[73] Hist. MSS Comm., *The manuscripts of His Grace the Duke of Portland preserved at Welbeck Abbey*, (10 vols., 1891–1919), VII, 29, 169 (Stratford to Harley, 12 April 1711).

[74] Baker bought it at an auction for five shillings. Korsten, *Catalogue of the Library of Thomas Baker*, item 1826.

[75] *Letters of Eminent Men, addressed to Ralph Thoresby, FRS*, II, 79, Henry Gyles to Thoresby, 25 November 1707.

[76] Frank Herrmann, "The Emergence of the Book Auctioneer as a Professional," in Robin Myers and Michael Harris (eds.), *Property of a Gentleman: the Formation, Organisation and Dispersal of the Private Library 1620–1920* (Winchester, UK, 1991), pp. 1–14; J. Lawler, *Book Auctions in England in the Seventeenth Century (1676–1700)* (1898).

[77] BL MS Add. 4367, fos. 34v, 35v, 37–40: "A catalogue of my books taken March 16th 1708." I have not followed Browne's own page totals of his books, which count individual tomes in multivolume sets separately.

Table 5.16. *An early eighteenth-century cleric's book acquisitions, new
and used*

Work	Status	Price £ s d
Charles Estienne, *Dictionarium historicum ac poeticum*	used	0-2-6
Friedrich Spanheim, *Summa historiae ecclesiasticae*	new	0-16-0
Enrico Noris, *Historia pelagiana*	new (1708?)	0-5-0
S. Grynaeus (ed. and trans.), *Eusebii Pamphili, Ruffini, Socratis, Theodoriti, Sozomeni, Theodori, Evagrii, et Dorothei Ecclesiastica historia*	new-bound	0-6-0
J. Potter, *Archaeologia graeca*	new (1706?)	0-11-0
T. Fuller, *Church-history of Britain*	used	0-7-0
Xenophon, *Opera*, Greek and Latin	used	1-0-6
B. Kennett, *Romae antiquae notitia*	new (1704?)	0-4-6
J. Rushworth, *Mr. Rushworth's historical collections abridg'd amd improv'd*	new (6 vols., 1703–8)	0-5-0
Clarendon, *The History of the Rebellion and Civil Wars . . . Faithfuly Abridg'd*	new (5 vols., 1703)	0-4-0
E. Calamy (ed.), *An abridgment of Mr. Baxter's history of his life and times*	new	0-6-0
"History of Europe since Nijmeguen"[a]	new	0-6-0
G. Burnet, *The Abridgement of the History of the Reformation of the Church of England*	new (4th edn, 1705?)	0-5-0
D. Petavius, *Rationarium temporum*	used	0-2-4
A. Strauch, *Breviarium chronologicum*	new (1699?)	0-5-0
Caesar, *Opera omnia*	used (1697?)	0-2-6
Historiae Romanae Epitomae	used[b]	0-0-6
Machiavelli, *Historie fiorentine di Niccolo Machiavelli*	used	0-1-6

[a]Unidentified: possibly Anon., *History of the Peace with France and War with
Holland in the Year 1672 & seq.* (1712), though this seems doubtful.
[b]A collection, published in Amsterdam in 1647 and including a number of historical
epitomes of the late antique and early medieval era: Lucius Florus, C. Velleius
Paterculus, Sextus Aurelius Victor, Paulus Diaconus, Cassiodorus, Eutropius, Sextus
Aurelius Victor, Sextus Rufus Festus, Messala Corvinus, and Jordanes.

Browne's books are provisionally identified, with conjectural editions in
parentheses for the items denoted as "new," in Table 5.16.

With the exception of Xenophon, this list of historical titles is in the low
end of the market: there were few fancy illustrated folios or subscribed copies
in this collection, and the owner appears to have had an eye for a bargain,

judging by the selection of used books: the abridged Clarendon served his purposes just as well as the handsome but expensive full-length Oxford edition. Browne's library looks very much like a minimal attempt to buy just what was necessary to keep up with fashion combined with the flexibility to buy used older works, like an Italian edition of Machiavelli's *Florentine History*, when they became available.

In addition to the market for second-hand books, which from the 1670s were increasingly sold through auction, it should be noted that there was always a small but steady supply of stolen books in circulation, especially in the London area, with historical titles figuring regularly in charges, since they were often among the most valuable. On 28 February 1581 a Chelsea laborer named Croxton Jenkyn burgled the home of George White, Esquire, stealing a carpet worth 20s and a French book entitled "Le historie des gueres d'Italie" (perhaps an edition of Guicciardini) valued at 16d; the felon was sentenced to hang but later released.[78] A gang of thieves was prosecuted in London in May 1592 for stealing several books, including two by Quintus Curtius worth three shillings. In 1599 a widow of Gray's Inn Lane was charged with stealing a copy of Fitzherbert's *Abridgement* from the Society's library.[79] A book recorded simply as "A Historie Bible," perhaps Eusebius Pagitt's *History of the Bible*, a popular question-and-answer guide to Scripture, was among several books, mainly religious, stolen from the London home of John Drawater in 1615, and valued at 8s, neither the cheapest nor the most expensive item taken.[80] On Christmas Day 1626, one Richard Yonge burgled Robert Wilson's lodgings in High Holborn, stealing several books including some expensive legal texts and a *Henry the Fourth*, worth 12d (perhaps Shakespeare's play rather than Sir John Hayward's prose history), "a quadregesimo of Edward the third" (1s) and "The first parte of Edward the third" (1s).[81] A labourer was prosecuted in 1682 for stealing, among other items, several books, including Burnet's *Some Passages in the Life and Death of John, earl of Rochester* (2s 6d) and a *Life of Richard the Second* (2s).[82] Civil actions to recover lost books were also not unknown: ownership of a "History of the French troubles" by the French historian la Popelinière was contested before the Court of Requests in 1589 between an

[78] *Calendar of Assize Records: Essex Indictments, Elizabeth I*, ed. J. S. Cockburn (HMSO, 1978), nos. 1212, 1326, pp. 211, 228.

[79] *Middlesex County Records*, ed. J. C. Jeaffreson, o.s. 1 (1886, reprinted 1972), pp. 206, 255. In each of these cases the accused was literate, pleading clergy and being branded, suggesting that they were not in entire ignorance as to the subjects of stolen books.

[80] Ibid., 2 (1887, reprinted 1974), p. 109. For an incident of books being stolen from a school on a Sunday in February 1710, see the diary of Claver Morris (1659–1727), *The Diary of a West Country Physician*, p. 61.

[81] *Middlesex County Records*, ed. J. C. Jeaffreson, o.s. 3 (1888, reprinted 1974), p. 13.

[82] Ibid., 4 (1892, reprinted 1975), p. 152.

Anglesey gentleman named Richard Griffith and the London bookseller Thomas Chard.[83]

The scholarly "half-life" of many history books – the period of time over which they continued to retain high vendibility either through their author's fame or their informational content – was considerably longer in the early modern era than it is today. This was obviously more true of some branches of history than others. Just as rewriting the narratives of Livy and Tacitus remained till the time of Gibbon a forbidding task, so too, superseding the great antiquarian and narrative histories of the sixteenth and early seventeenth centuries proved difficult. It was far easier to replace one duodecimo chronology or octavo epitome of world history with another than it was to supplant Camden's *Annales*, far simpler to revise and republish the *Britannia* than to start from scratch – hence Gibson's reworking of the trusty chorography in 1695 and Richard Gough's more thorough revision less than a century later. Writing a more magisterial survey of English history than one's predecessor seemed an especially Icaran ambition, though a string of historians from Samuel Daniel, Robert Brady, and Sir William Temple in the seventeenth century, to Laurence Echard, Paul de Rapin-Thoyras, John Oldmixon, and David Hume in the eighteenth successively aspired to do just this.[84]

In spite of the much more rapid increase in new titles from 1640 onward, one consequence of this longevity was that would-be historians and antiquaries had to face competition not only from each other but also from their illustrious predecessors. In addition to the steady market for classical historians, either in reprinted older editions or new philological texts by continental scholars like G. J. Vossius, J. G. Graevius, and J. F. Gronovius, the home-grown historical works published in the late sixteenth and seventeenth centuries proved remarkably durable, their ownership trafficked in long after they were being actively reprinted.

In the sixteenth century certain printers had been given occasional rights or "privileges" to reprint certain specified books, and occasionally even

---

[83] PRO REQ 2/74/34; the book in question would have been either la Popelinière's *La vraye et entière histoire des troubles et choses memorables . . . depuis l'an 1562* (La Rochelle, 1573), or its English translation, *The historie of France: the foure first bookes* (1595). For an example of books as part of a disputed bequest, *ca.* 1710, see *The Diary of Henry Prescott, LLB, Deputy Registrar of Chester Diocese*, ed. J. M. Addy, 3 vols., Rec. Soc. of Lancs. and Cheshire, 127 (1987–97), I, 121.

[84] Philip Hicks, *Neoclassical History and English Culture from Clarendon to Hume* (New York, 1996), pp. 143–209.

entire genres, Richard Tottel's Marian-granted monopoly on legal printing being an early example. The first instance of a history being so disposed is Elizabeth I's 1580 grant to Henry Bynneman of the exclusive "privilege," for twenty-one years, to reprint Thomas Cooper's continuation of Lanquet's *Chronicle*. This was a nugatory right in itself, since the work was never, in fact, reprinted, but it carried the potentially more important freedom to reprint all chronicles.[85] Over the next century, publishers frequently considered it worth their while to acquire the "copy" or propriety of both proven sellers and works in which an interest might revive.[86] A shortage of supplies of second-hand copies, on the auction market or elsewhere, might eventually make it productive to republish even an old, and rather undistinguished, Jacobean history like William Martyn's *The historie, and lives, of the kings of England*.[87] A catalog of the books registered by Humphrey Moseley, one of the most prolific mid-seventeenth-century publishers of historical works (active 1630–61), shows rights to a selection of them being reassigned to two stationers, Thomas Cockerill and Dorman Newman. Cockerill's share would in turn be reassigned to Jacob Tonson in 1718. This particular list is of interest because although it does not represent all of Moseley's printing interests, it does contain a high proportion of historical works, mostly printed in the 1650s. These include history plays, romances, and ballads, with a "history" title, and a number of works for the learned, such as George Buck's 1646 edition of his uncle and namesake Sir George's revisionist *The history of the life and reigne of Richard the Third*, Famiano Strada's *De Bello belgico* (1650), as well as some slightly older titles such as Christopher Lever's *History of the Defendors of the Catholique faith* (1627).[88]

---

[85] Feather, *Publishing, Piracy and Politics*, p. 13. This grant carried with it the more important privilege to reprint *all* dictionaries and chronicles, which helps to explain the prominence of Bynneman as a chronicle printer, but in fact a variety of late Tudor chronicles were produced by other printers, and Bynneman, who printed the first edition of Holinshed's *Chronicles*, was not involved in the second edition of Holinshed in 1587.

[86] For the notion of copy, and a persuasive argument that it should not be confused with the authorially defined "literary property" of the eighteenth century, see Johns, *Nature of the Book*, pp. 105, 187; copies were traded in fractions of a half, a third, or even less among booksellers: for the case of one bookseller's copies, see Giles Mandelbrote, "Richard Bentley's Copies: the Ownership of Copyrights in the Late Seventeenth Century," in Hunt, Mandelbrote, and Shell, *The Book Trade and its Customers*, pp. 55–94.

[87] Old editions of Sarpi's *History of the Council of Trent* (1st edn 1619) and *The History of the Ottoman Empire* (1st edn 1679) by Paul Rycaut were still in demand, though difficult to get, in 1765: see Hist. MSS Comm., *Report on manuscripts in various collections* (8 vols., 1901–14), VI, 440.

[88] Bodl. MS Eng. misc. d. 493, indexed at fos. 37–40, no date. Other history titles included Procopius (1652), Herbert of Cherbury's account of Buckingham's military expedition to the Isle of Rhé (1655), Samson Lennard's translation of Scipione Mazzella's *Parthenopoeia, or, The history of the most noble and renowned kingdom of Naples*, William Sanderson's *A compleat history of the life and raigne of King Charles, from his cradle to his grave* (1656), an

In the autumn of 1709, less than three months before the copyright bill received its first reading (on 11 January 1710), Jacob Tonson II (nephew of the first Jacob Tonson),[89] paid £100 to George Wells of London and his sister Mary for their shares in and, in some instances, the full copy of 311 books of all sorts, including Shakespeare's plays. Many of the sixteen historical works (5 percent) included were Restoration books such as Sprat's *History of the Royal Society* and several works by Dugdale, the *Monasticon* (itself abridged in 1693 by James Wright), *Baronage*, and *Origines Juridicales*. Also included was a half-share of a steady-seller, Camden's *Britannia* in Latin, the fourth and eighth parts of the same book in English, and a share in an "epitome" of Camden. Some older titles were included in the deal, all from the first four decades of the seventeenth century, for instance a half-share in Francis Godwin's 1616 *De praesulibus Angliae commentarius* or *Catalogue of Bishops*, a new edition of which was underway in 1710, and a quarter-share in the same author's *Annales of England*, a Jacobean-era history of the reigns of Henry VIII, Edward VI, and Mary I.[90]

Augustan booksellers were not above colluding to fix the price of some high-demand titles, though we are apt to overrate the extent of this practice by listening exclusively to the complaints of librarians like Humfrey Wanley and private collectors such as Thomas Baker. Certainly there is evidence of inflation in a hot market, such as that of the early eighteenth century, when the number of collectors was a great deal higher than a century earlier but the size of editions had not yet risen substantially. Wanley was probably right in believing that "the current prices of books are much advanced during these late years." He was therefore pleased when, at the 1721 auction of the stock of Robert Fairbairn (a Scottish Jacobite bookseller who had fled the realm), the major buyers, all booksellers, had colluded to keep the books to a low or "vile" rate.

This plot was nearly undone, however, after a few Latin and Greek

English translation of Sallust by William Cross (1658), 2 vols. (1657, 1660) of Thomas Stanley's four-volume *The History of philosophy*, and the 1659 edition of Agrippa d'Aubigné's *Histoire universelle*.

[89] Plomer, iii, 291–92.

[90] Folger MS S.a. 160, single parchment sheet folded, dated 22 October 1709. Godwin's work was under revision as recently as 1705 by Dr. Matthew Hutton, rector of Aynho: *The London Diaries of William Nicolson*, p. 310 (26 November 1705). Other early works included: the half-part of an old chronological work, Thomas Lydiat's *Defensio Tractatvs de variis annorvm formis antiquissima & optima contra Iosephi Scaligeri obtrectationem*, a fifth of "Mathew Paris's history," a third-share and quarter-share of "Martins chronicle" (*The historie and lives of the kings of England* along with the copyright to this work), half of a life of Mary, Queen of Scots, John Selden's *Titles of Honor*, and Richard Verstegan's *Restitution of Decayed Intelligence*. The Camden title referred to might be the recent two-volume *Camden's Britannia abridg'd* published by Joseph Wild in 1701, but is more likely the work published by John Bill in 1626 (STC 4527), which would be more consistent with the other Jacobean works in the list.

manuscripts of late medieval date went for a high price to Paul Vaillant the émigré Huguenot bookseller. Vaillant showed no restraint in bidding because he himself had an "unlimited" commission from the enthusiastic but undiscriminating whig minister, Charles Spencer, earl of Sunderland, to buy the books at any cost, which led to "unaccountably high prices."[91] Even so, Vaillant managed to strike a good bargain on certain lots thanks to the silence of his fellow-bidders; he was so pleased at the purchase of a 1472 printed edition of Virgil's *Opera* for £46, "that he huzza'd out aloud, & threw-up his hat for joy, that he had bought it so cheap." Wanley learned that as a result of this auction the major booksellers had also collectively agreed to put up the cost of first-edition philological texts, "and indeed of all old editions accordingly." Sunderland, once again, had apparently agreed to pay £50 per book for six printed titles, further fueling this mini price rise. Within a few months, Wanley was quietly rejoicing at Sunderland's demise, by which "some benefit may accrue to this library, even in case his relations will part with none of his books. I mean, by his raising the price of books no higher now; so that, in probability, this commodity may fall in the market; and any gentleman be permitted to buy an uncommon old book for less than fourty or fifty pounds."[92]

The fate of the Rawlinson library, one of the greatest privately assembled collections of the early eighteenth century, tells a similar story. Thomas Rawlinson, Addison's "Tom Folio," had, like Sunderland, been active in attending sales and giving commissions for purchases – so active that he too "strangely advanced the price of books," in the words of his friend, Thomas Hearne. He was unable to resist buying multiple copies of the same books or even the same editions. It all proved too much when Rawlinson's fortunes collapsed with the South Sea Bubble, and he was obliged to sell many of his duplicates. The impregnation of his servant Amy Frewen – a gin-sodden coffeehouse harlot if we believe the scurrilous accounts of his friends – forced Rawlinson into a financially disastrous marriage soon after. This quickly finished him with his creditors, hastening his death in 1725 at the age of

---

[91] Sunderland's enthusiasm for "the expensive humour of purchaseing old editions of books at extravagant rates" was ridiculed by Richard Bentley in a conversation with William Nicolson. *The London Diaries of William Nicolson*, p. 199 (6 February 1703); he died in debt to a number of booksellers. On occasion, overextended aristocrats were obliged to put their libraries on the market before they died: this happened to Henry Hyde, second earl of Clarendon (1638–1709), between 1700 and 1703: *Letters of Wanley*, p. 201 and editor's note (Wanley to Arthur Charlett, 2 January 1703).

[92] *Diary of Wanley*, I, 125, 139; he similarly objected in 1726 when the barrister John Bridges auctioned his books at Lincoln's Inn, and bade for them himself "merely to enhance their price": ibid., II, 405–6. Collusive manipulation of auctions by groups of booksellers acting in concert to depress prices is discussed in Katherine Swift, "Dutch Penetration of the London Market for Books, c. 1690–1730," in G. Berkvens-Stevelinck *et al.* (eds.), *Le Magasin de l'univers: the Dutch Republic as the Centre of the European Book Trade* (Leiden, New York, and Copenhagen, 1992), pp. 265–79, at pp. 265–67.

forty-four. To add insult to injury, when Rawlinson's much younger brother, the antiquary Richard, returned from his European travels expecting to find the estate that had been entailed on him, he was sorely disappointed. Richard learned that a death-bed will and fictitious suit had succeeded in breaking the entail, placing all the books on the auctioneers' block, leaving the despised widow an annuity and paying the debts, but utterly cutting Richard out. He spent the next ten years in the agonizing process of arranging a series of auctions of the once-magnificent library, watching collectors like Lord Coleraine descend like vultures on its carcass. It was of no comfort that the flooding of the marketplace with Rawlinson's rare books, many of them in multiple copies and badly bound, caused the market for incunabula, and for heraldic and genealogical works, to deflate as quickly as the Bubble itself.[93]

Aside from the sporadic intervention of big spenders like Rawlinson and Sunderland, other, extraneous factors could drive up the price of individual books, and older books in general inflated sharply during the 1710s and 1720s.[94] Sheer rarity was of course among these influences, though the evidence from James Allgood's earlier purchases from the auction of Richard Smith's library, discussed above, suggests that there is no necessary correlation between a book's antiquity and its cost: fifteen shillings for a 1493 edition of the *Nuremberg Chronicle* seems a small sum even for the less inflationary late seventeenth century.[95] Political or economic disturbances could have sudden if often short-term effects. The second Dutch war drove up sales of Fulke Greville's *Life of Sidney* in the last days of 1667, Pepys' bookseller selling four copies within a week or two, after having sold none in his entire previous career.[96] In the previous year, the Great Fire had all but destroyed in sheets several major works by authors such as Dugdale and Spelman. The losses of some booksellers were enormous and some were wiped out completely: Joseph Kirton of St. Paul's Churchyard was ruined and died of grief, so his customer Pepys thought, barely a year later. Clarendon recorded that the Stationers' Company alone suffered £200,000 in losses.[97] The immediate result was that the cost of some books inflated

---

[93] B. J. Enright, "The Later Auction Sales of Thomas Rawlinson's Library, 1727–34," *The Library*, 5th series, 11 (1956), 23–40, 103–13. When the Harleian library sold in 1742 for £13,000 to the bookseller Thomas Osborne, he was accused of setting prices too high, but this appears not to have been the case: Wheatley, *Prices of Books*, p. 32.

[94] Swift, "Dutch Penetration of the London Market," p. 278.

[95] Duff, "The Library of Richard Smith," p. 122. [96] Pepys, *Diary*, IX, 6 (2 January 1668).

[97] Ibid., VIII, 526 (12 November 1667); *The Life of Edward, Earl of Clarendon* (2 vols., Oxford, 1857), I, 293–94. The first (1666) edition of Dugdale's *Origines Juridiciales, or historical memorials of the English Laws* was largely destroyed save for a few copies in the Great Fire, though Pepys managed to pick one up in 1667: *Diary*, VII, 297 (26 September 1666) and VIII, 168 (15 April 1667). A fire at the printer William Bowyer's on 29/30 January 1713 similarly destroyed fifty sheets of Ralph Thoresby's *Ducatus Leodensis* and much of the first edition of Sir Robert Atkyns the younger's *Ancient and present state of Glostershire* (1712): Maslen and Lancaster, *The Bowyer Ledgers*, p. 13, no. 170; I. Gray, *Antiquities of*

virtually overnight. Pepys' new bookseller, John Starkey of Fleet Street, near Middle Temple Gate, offered him the diplomat Sir Paul Rycaut's *The Present State of the Ottoman Empire* for fifty-five shillings, which Pepys ruefully records "was sold plain before the late fire for 8s, and bound and colored as this is for 20." We need not feel too sorry for him since this purchase put him in a very exclusive club: his coloured edition was one of a limited run of six, four of which went to the king, Lord Arlington, and the dukes of York and Monmouth.[98]

RATES OF PUBLICATION

How much history was being turned out by the printers of early modern England? The obvious answer is "more and more." Thomas Tanner, the Augustan bishop and manuscript collector drew up a list of materials available on English history alone,[99] including sources in print, and found no less than 368 distinct titles; even discounting reprints and reeditions, this was surely an underestimate. Fig. 5.6 breaks down Tanner's list according to subject and genre, and reveals that from Tanner's perspective, the number of medieval and modern chronicles (excluding medieval histories of the church like Bede) still available in print was substantial, outdistancing even medieval ecclesiastical history and relatively new genres like chorography. What Tanner's list does not show, except by silence, is the almost complete disappearance of new chronicles and the rapid growth of humanist political histories of England, as well as of antiquarian studies, in the seventeenth century; nor does it show the degree to which the "modern ecclesiastical history" category was largely a product of the religious disputes of the middle and later decades of the seventeenth century.

Tanner's list is the estimate of an intelligent bibliographer whose researches would later be published posthumously as the *Bibliotheca Britannico-Hibernica* (1748). Thorough as he was, his survey should be supplemented by other, more objective measures. The meticulous ledger-

---

Gloucestershire and Bristol (Gloucester, UK, 1981), p. 51; Brian S. Smith, "Sir Robert Atkyns," in J. Simmons (ed.), *English County Historians, First Series* (Wakefield, UK, 1978), p. 71.

[98] Pepys, *Diary*, VIII, 156 (8 April 1667). Pepys may have been in error as to the pre-fire price, since the first edition of Rycaut's (1628–1700) *The Present State of the Ottoman Empire* did not appear till 1667, though a price may have been set in advance of publication and prior to the Great Fire. Rycaut's later work, *The History of the Turkish Empire* (1680 [actually published late in 1679]) was among the most successful of Restoration histories, and he was knighted soon after its publication. Written by England's consul at Smyrna, it was initially intended to begin in 1640, but its author was persuaded at the last minute to push it back to 1623, the date at which Knolles' early Jacobean account of the Ottomans had stopped. S. P. Anderson, *An English Consul in Turkey: Paul Rycaut at Smyrna, 1667–1678* (Oxford, 1989), p. 229.   [99] Bodl. MS Tanner 88, fos. 76r–92r.

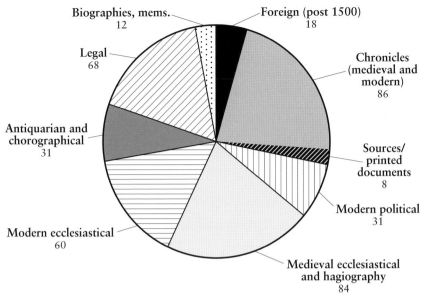

Figure 5.6 Historical writings by subject: a late seventeenth-century estimate. Thomas Tanner's list of printed materials on English history. Source: Bodl. MS Tanner 88, fos. 76r–92r.

keeping of the printer William Bowyer the elder at the beginning of the eighteenth century shows, for instance, that of the 1,610 items issued by his presses from 1710 to the end of 1730, eighty-eight were of a historical nature.[100] Another useful source, albeit an imperfect one, is the Stationers' Register, which from about 1580 records all titles entered for publication and reassignment of rights; the 1662 Press Act made such recording statutory by turning the register into a record of licenses, and it is therefore more reliable as to total output, though by no means foolproof, after that date. Nevertheless, it reveals the degree to which historical titles constituted part of the company's business.[101] Fig. 5.7 displays the movement in *entries* of

[100] The 5.5 percent figure that this yields rises considerably if one discounts the many Bowyer items that were specimens or single sheets rather than complete books. Figures derived from Maslen and Lancaster, *The Bowyer Ledgers*, checklist, pp. 1–128.

[101] In this count, unlike others in the present work, I have included the historical drama and verse that were a formidable part of the Elizabethan and early Stuart population's sense of history. For a similar usage of the register to trace movements in religious books during the earlier part of this period, see Tessa Watt, *Cheap Print and Popular Piety* (Cambridge, 1991), p. 45. The registers only record perhaps half of the books printed and do not account for illegally or surreptitiously printed works; nor, as noted above, do they include a great many works published by patent or privilege. The figures from the register used in figure 5.7 were derived using the following protocol: "British" (including Scottish, Irish, and Welsh)

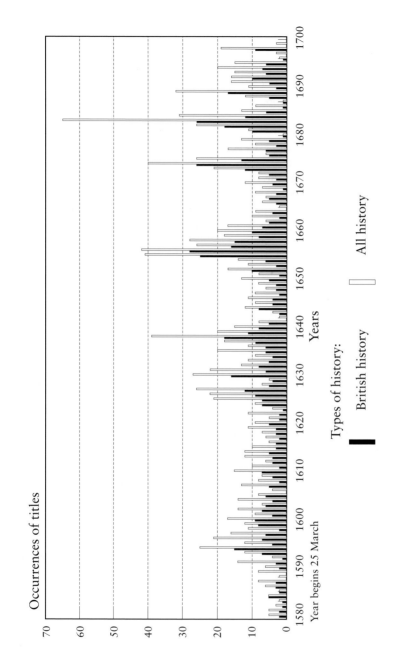

Figure 5.7 History in the Stationers' Register, 1580–1700, including fictional "histories," verse, and historical drama.

historical titles – which cannot be equated with publication rates – and also those dealing specifically with British history (a much smaller number) and shows some quite pronounced jumps in particular years. The most significant fluctuations occur in the early 1590s, 1640s, the late 1650s, and the early 1680s. The coincidence of these as periods of great political turmoil offers a tempting explanation, but one that may be too facile: weakened censorship in the 1640s and 1650s, and again after 1679 must surely account for an overall increase in printing of many sorts of book, not all of which appear in the register. Nevertheless, even if one discounts some of the sharper movements (further explicable by the individual tallying of occasional "package" entries that included several discrete titles), it is clear that the numbers for the second part of the period are higher in both general and British categories for nearly all years; the low point in the mid-1640s may simply be a consequence of many more printers and publishers sidestepping registration. In short, there is an overall upward trend in historical titles, and the peaks get steadily higher, but there is no straight and steady line that would confirm a continuous increase. This should not, indeed, be very surprising: we know there to have been a particular spurt of historical prose and verse in the 1590s, Shakespeare's history plays and Samuel Daniel's *Civil Wars* being among the products; other years produced large numbers of reprints or new editions of fictional "histories," chivalric romances, and stories of artisanal heroes like Jack of Newberry.

Although not strictly comparable as a source, the listings of books in early eighteenth-century bibliographic periodicals (a tradition beginning with Andrew Maunsell in the 1590s and continuing with William London in the 1650s and the *Term Catalogues* from 1668 to 1709) provide evidence for the rate of history publication at the very end of our period.[102] The above-noted weaknesses of the *Term Catalogues* are reflected in these publications, but there is still some useful information to be had. In particular, the *Monthly Catalogue* put out by John Wilford between 1723 and 1730 offers a glimpse not only of yearly but seasonal publication shifts in history, and the enhance-

---

history comprises all prose, verse, and drama, including ballads and chivalric romances listed as "histories," and those works on antiquarian or chorographic topics. The year here begins on 25 March, in keeping with the Company's practice in keeping the register (though not with its practice of starting masters' and wardens' terms of office on 1 July). Assigned rights are tabulated as well as new entries, meaning that this is an index of *transactions* rather than a measure of individual titles, much less of total printed output. Biographies or "lives" are, as usual, included. Works with key words like "historical" are included in the title unless clearly unhistorical: natural history is thus excluded, but Robin Hood ballads included. Separately entered woodcuts and plates with historical images are also counted.

[102] Andrew Maunsell, *The first part of the catalogue of English printed bookes* (1595); William London, *A catalogue of the most vendible books in England, orderly and alphabetically digested* (1657); *TC*.

ment of its position relative to other subjects since the 1660s.[103] It is clear from the total publications in the seven years covered that historical works, in all genres, occupied a significant proportion of all new books (fig. 5.8). The largest category, including what we would now call "professional" (medical, legal, educational, and instructional) titles, accounted for 29.5 percent; religion, morality, and theology (excluding separately published sermons not included among books, and also excluding works of biblical chronology or ecclesiastical history), only 23.3 percent, and literature and language, including fiction, a mere 21.3 percent. History, in contrast, amounted to 25.9 percent, split almost evenly between British or Irish history, and the history of other parts of the world. Even if one takes Wilford's selection as being incomplete, and the overall numbers as somewhat low, they are still far beyond any reasonable guess at the subject distribution of a century earlier, when historical works were a much smaller part of the total output of printing presses. The story is roughly the same for reprints (fig. 5.8), with religious works counting for slightly more (26.3 percent) and history a bit less at 19.9 percent – a fifth as opposed to the quarter of new books. This means that among all books (completely new, new editions, and reprints) whose recent or impending printing was announced in Wilford's pages, something like 22 percent were in some way or other devoted to history.

Breaking the genres down further, and according to date of publication, provides other information (figs. 5.9a–b). The book trade in all subjects was prone to seasonal fluctuations: August and September were slow months, and Wilford sometimes issued only one catalog covering both months. The busiest months were generally, though not invariably, in the first half of the year. On the whole, the peaks rise toward the end of the decade, very likely reflecting a general increase in printing rather than an improvement in Wilford's inclusiveness (if anything, he was suffering from the rivalry of other publications by the late 1720s, and his publication was swallowed up by these after February 1730). The slightly greater number of books published in the winter months, and the usual late summer slump, is mirrored in the books advertised in the first (1731) volume of the *Gentleman's Magazine*

---

[103] J. Wilford, *The Monthly Catalogues* (1723–30; reprinted, 2 vols., 1964). This periodical was a revival of the earlier catalog put out from May 1714 to March 1717 by Bernard Lintot, which in turn was a continuation of the series of *Works of the Learned, or an Historical Account and Impartial Judgment of Books newly Printed, both Foreign and Domestick* (1691–92) and of the earlier *Term Catalogues*: see G. Pollard and A. Ehrman, *The Distribution of Books by Catalogue from the Invention of Printing to AD 1800* (Cambridge, 1965), pp. 133–34. I have chosen Wilford's catalog both because it runs right to the end of the chronological period of this study, and because Wilford was more systematic than his predecessors in keeping books separate from pamphlets, periodicals, and sermons, which have not been counted in the totals here (though it should be noted that serialized history books, for example Rapin-Thoyras, are listed under periodicals and thus do not figure).

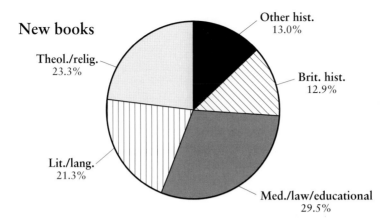

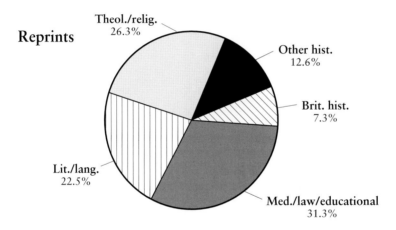

Figure 5.8   History publication in the 1720s: total figures from Wilford's *Monthly Catalogues*.

(see fig. 6.10 at p. 266 below). Although classical histories maintained the prominence they had enjoyed in previous decades, they were rivaled by British and European works ranging from the various learned editions of chronicles published by Hearne, to Strype's ecclesiastical biographies, to assorted antiquarian and heraldic works. The proportions are similar, but the numbers larger, for reprinted works (fig. 5.9b), which in virtually every genre outnumber the new books.

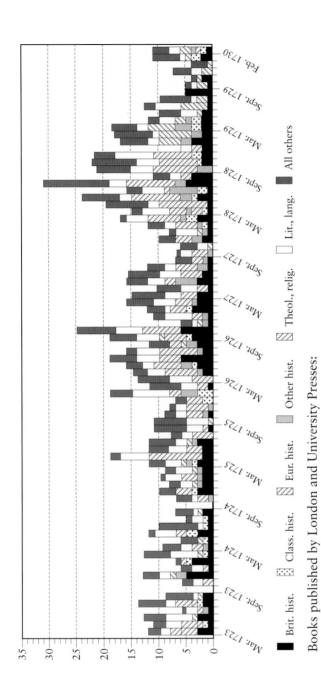

Books published by London and University Presses:

■ Brit. hist. ▦ Class. hist. ▨ Eur. hist. ▨ Other hist.

■ Theol., relig. ▨ □ Lit., lang. ■ All others

Note
Excludes foreign imprints, pamphlets, serials, and tracts

Figure 5.9a The publication of history in the 1720s: Wilford's "monthly catalogues," 1723–30: new editions.

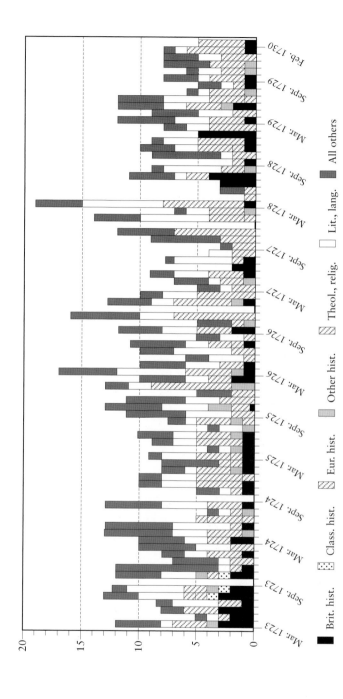

Books published by London and University Presses:

■ Brit. hist.   ⬚ Class. hist.   ▨ Eur. hist.   ▨ Other hist.

▨ Theol., relig.   ☐ Lit., lang.   ■ All others

Note
Excludes foreign imprints, pamphlets, serials, and tracts

Figure 5.9b   The publication of history in the 1720s: Wilford's "monthly catalogues," 1723–30: reprints.

CAMDEN's
BRITANNIA
ABRIDG'D;
WITH

IMPROVEMENTS, and CONTINUATIONS, to this present Time.

To which are added,

Exact LISTS of the Present Nobility of *England*, *Scotland*, and *Ireland* :

Also a Valuation of all

Ecclesiastical Preferments
At the End of each County.

With many other Useful Additions.

The whole Carefully Perform'd, and Illustrated with above Sixty Maps Exactly Engraven.

VOL. II.

London, Printed by *J. B.* for *Joseph Wild*, at the *Elephant* at *Charing-Cross*. 1701.

Plate 5.12   A major work abridged for a wider market: the 1701 version, revised and much reduced, of Edmund Gibson's earlier edition of *Camden's Britannia*, 1695, itself one of the major historical publications of the end of the seventeenth century.

PUBLISHERS AND AUTHORS

Faced with rising costs, greater competition from foreign (especially Dutch) booksellers and a growing provincial book trade,[104] publishers and booksellers used a variety of strategies, including serial publication and advance subscription (both of which are discussed in chapter 6 below) to ensure that their products got out and to avoid the specter of loss of capital. Piracy was neither universal nor the tactic of a rare unscrupulous few, but rather a blurry area into which normally conscientious printers and publishers might occasionally slip, since the line between the reprint and the pirated edition was itself fuzzy.[105] There was no strict ownership of titles, as such, before 1710, at which time the Copyright Act placed intellectual property somewhat timidly in the hands of authors, thereby generating a half-century's worth of legal contention over the interpretation of the act.[106]

Even where entire editions were not pillaged by rival printers, enterprising popularizers like the notorious Nathaniel Crouch, alias Richard Burton, could quickly boil down a number of original historical books into a cheaper octavo or duodecimo and turn a profit.[107] Camden's *Britannia*, for instance – already abridged as early as 1626 by John Bill – was epitomized anew by Joseph Wild in 1701, barely six years after Gibson's edition (plate 5.12). One recalls Richard Lapthorne's warnings to his client Richard Coffin about wasting his money on such fare, the alleged low character or inferior rank of the abridgers being as much an indictment of their books as the lack of authenticity of their contents. This added to the comparable denigration of Tudor chroniclers, a century earlier, for lack of style and vulgar origins a new charge, that of greed and outright dishonesty. The most respectable of historical works was vulnerable to abridgment into cheaper editions, or it could be "abstracted," perhaps with the meat of other works into an epitome, as Alexander Ross did, quite successfully, with Ralegh's *History of the World* in his *Marrow of Historie* in 1650. The last case of piracy handled

---

[104] Swift, "Dutch Penetration of the London Market," pp. 265–79. For an incomplete list of English local sellers see Arber, *Stat. Reg.*, V, p. lii; cf. D. Palliser and D. G. Selwyn, "The Stock of a York Stationer, 1538," *The Library*, 5th series 27 (1972), 207–19.

[105] Michael Harris, "Paper Pirates: the Alternative Book Trade in Mid-Eighteenth-Century London," in R. Myers and M. Harris (eds.), *Fakes and Frauds: Varieties of Deception in Print and Manuscript* (Winchester, UK, and Detroit, 1989), pp. 47–69; John Feather, "English Books in the Netherlands in the Eighteenth Century: Reprints or Piracies?," in C. Berkvens-Stevelinck *et al.* (eds.), *Le Magasin de l'univers: the Dutch Republic as the Centre of the European Book Trade* (Leiden and New York, 1992), pp. 143–54. I thank Fiona Black for this last reference.

[106] Mark Rose, *Authors and Owners: the Invention of Copyright* (Cambridge, MA, 1993); Feather, *Publishing, Piracy and Politics*, pp. 64–96.

[107] On Crouch's "commodification" of history see Robert Mayer, "Nathaniel Crouch, Bookseller and Historian: Popular Historiography and Cultural Power in Late Seventeenth-Century England," *Eighteenth-Century Studies*, 27 (1993–94), 391–419.

internally by the Stationers' Company, in 1722, dealt with an "abstract or abridgment" in two volumes of Joseph Bingham's *Origines ecclesiasticae or, The antiquities of the Christian church* (10 vols., 1710–22), together with parts of Laurence Echard's *History of England*. The Stationers, whose master that year was the bookseller Robert Knaplock, compared the books and found, not surprisingly, that Francis Fayrer and the conger that had printed this work had violated the copy of Knaplock himself in the Bingham work and of Jacob Tonson in the Echard.[108] The enterprising and astute London stationer Timothy Childe conceived of a scheme to have Thomas Hearne abstract Clarendon's *History of the Rebellion* even as the last volume of the first (1702–4) edition was in press at the Sheldonian in Oxford (plate 5.13). Hearne was ideally suited to the task, since he was then in straitened circumstances that had already obliged him to take on the job of indexing the *History* for the university press. Childe hoped that Hearne could get at the printed sheets at the university press by bribing "a workman concerned in it" and that he would thereby be able to add material by other authors such as Rushworth into the projected epitome and beat the third Oxford volume to the bookstalls. Childe evidently had a few qualms about all this. Hearne's half of the correspondence does not survive, so we do not know what he thought, though his profitable self-publication of his own editions of chronicles somewhat later suggests both that he too had a sense of pounds and pennies, and that he did not entirely trust publishers. Childe had some standards: he insisted on "other authors" being consulted, "because we must not call it an abridgment of Clarendon lest the family and the University be offended." He eventually abandoned the scheme entirely, not least because an abridged version of the *History* (a copy of which we have seen in the hands of the congregationalist minister, Simon Browne) was produced by John Nutt in 1703.[109]

---

[108] Johns, *Nature of the Book*, p. 512 n. 137. Doing an abridgment was an easy way around a patent. About 1624 one Gilbert Diglen, who says he was a student of mathematics and former servant to Prince Henry, applied for a 21-year patent for "a smale booke, being the epitomy of Mr. Camdens Britannia." The patent was never enrolled, but Dr. Hunt, who cites the example, identifies it with STC 4527, *The Abridgment of Camden's Britannia with the maps* published by John Bill in 1626; presumably Diglen sold to Bill his sheets and his privilege. Hunt cites a similar example, never printed, of a 1621 attempt to abridge Foxe's book of martyrs by patent. Hunt, "Book Trade Patents," pp. 30ff.

[109] Simpson, *Proof-Reading*, p. 202; I. G. Philip, "The Genesis of Thomas Hearne's *Ductor Historicus*," *Bodleian Library Record*, 7.5 (July 1966), 251–64 reproduces this correspondence from Bodl. MS Rawl. lett. 14, fos. 377–90 and Rawl. lett. 4, fos. 484–85, which papers I have not personally examined. The letters from Childe run from 2 November 1702 to 26 October 1704, a period unfortunately before the beginning of Hearne's *Remarks and Collections* in 1705.

Plate 5.13 (*opposite*)   Title page of volume III of the first edition of Clarendon's *History of the Rebellion* (CUL), a copy whose last private owner was the philosopher Bertrand Russell.

THE

HISTORY

OF THE

REBELLION and CIVIL WARS

IN

ENGLAND,

Begun in the Year 1641.

With the precedent Paſſages, and Actions, that contributed
thereunto, and the happy End, and Concluſion thereof
by the KING's bleſſed RESTORATION, and
RETURN upon the 29th of *May*, in the Year 1660.

Written by the Right Honourable

EDWARD Earl of CLARENDON,

Late Lord High Chancellor of *England*, Privy Counſellor
in the Reigns of King CHARLES the Firſt and the Second.

Κ'ημα ἐς ἀεί. *Thucyd.*

Ne quid Falſi dicere audeat, ne quid Veri non audeat. Cicero.

VOLUME THE THIRD.

O X F O R D,
Printed at the THEATER, *An. Dom.* MDCCIV.

Collaboration within publishing syndicates for more expensive books, to distribute the costs of printing, became more frequent in the second half of the seventeenth century.[110] There were certainly precedents for this in the sixteenth century – Holinshed's *Chronicles* most famously – but what had then been a rare and risky exception had now become common practice.[111] The 1695 edition of Camden's *Britannia* was the result of some complex negotiations among two enterprising publishers, Abel Swalle and Awnsham Churchill, and the young cleric Edmund Gibson, who in turn enlisted the assistance of several other authors.[112] So was the White Kennett/John Hughes production of *A Complete History of England* in 1706, and, somewhat later, the most ambitious project of the middle decades of the century, the gigantic *Universal History* launched in 1729 and published between 1736 and 1765.[113] But this sort of transaction also occurred on a smaller scale, a good example being the Halsted, Essex antiquary William Holman, who left his vast collections in manuscript form to his son with specific instructions on what to do with them. The younger Holman entered into a contract with the rector of Great Waltham, the prolific translator Nicholas Tindal, whereby the latter agreed "to digest, improve, and make what additions he can to the said materials, and prepare them for the press" (plate 5.14). Once complete, the elder Holman's life's work was to be printed "at the joint cost and charges of the said Mr. Holman and Mr. Tindal," both of whom were to share profits and ownership of the copyright.[114]

---

[110] Gaskell, *New Introduction to Bibliography*, p. 180.

[111] One aspect of publication that had changed little since the time of Holinshed was that authors themselves were often expected to underwrite the cost of an expensive book that they wished to see published, a factor that should not be undervalued in explaining a quite separate increase in collaborations among authors toward the end of the seventeenth century; the experience of William Dugdale and Roger Dodsworth in getting the *Monasticon Anglicanum* to press beginning in the early 1650s is an excellent example.

[112] Much detail on the making of the 1695 *Britannia* can be gleaned from the correspondence of one of its most important contributors, Edward Lhuyd or Lhwyd, who complained that thrifty Swalle and Churchill expected him to produce his thorough revisions of the Welsh sections of *Britannia* using only materials available in Oxford: R. T. Gunther, *Early Science in Oxford*, vol. XIV, *Life and Letters of Edward Lhwyd* (Oxford, 1945), pp. 188–90, 197–98, 244–46, 259–60; G. Walters and F. Emery, "Edward Lhuyd, Edmund Gibson and the Printing of Camden's *Britannia*, 1695," *The Library*, 5th series 32 (1977), 109–37.

[113] Joseph M. Levine, *The Battle of the Books: History and Literature in the Augustan Age* (Ithaca, NY, 1991), pp. 306–19, 327–36; Guido Abbattista, "The Business of Paternoster Row: Towards a Publishing History of the *Universal History* (1736–65)," trans. Elizabeth P. Danieli, in *Publishing History*, 17 (1985), 5–50.

[114] Essex RO, T/A 497, contract dated 2 February 1731/32, in the hand of the eighteenth-century Essex antiquary Philip Morant, who witnessed it; the Knaptons' 1732 project to publish a quarto *History of Essex* compiled by Tindal from materials assembled by Holman resulted in an abortive serialization, for which see the next chapter and R. M. Wiles, *Serial Publication in England Before 1750* (Cambridge, 1957), p. 120. There are other examples of publishing projects being passed from father to son: Thomas Philipot published under his own name the antiquarian study of Kent, *Villare Cantianum*, by his father John, the herald. The edition of Bede published by George Smith of Burnhall in the early eighteenth century

John Strype, whose career was well-served by partisan patronage and the possession of a sinecure rectory at West Tarring, nevertheless relied for some of his income upon contractual arrangements with publishers. In the case of his new edition of Stow's *Survey of London*, the articles agreed between Strype and a coterie of publishers headed by Richard Chiswell make clear the degree to which the production of historical texts had become a commercial as much as an intellectual undertaking. Strype was to receive a limited sum for expenses (including "gifts" to clerks and servants, presumably for copying documents), and a flat payment of £103 payable in instalments. In addition he was to receive the equivalent of the modern author-discounted copies, "6 copies wel bound in Calves leather, lettered on the back"; an additional copy was to be "very wel & decently bound" for presentation to the Lord Mayor and court of aldermen, to whom the work was to be dedicated. For his part, Strype's expenses included 3s for an order from the aldermanic court for a search of the city's books; 2s 6d gratuity to the court's door-keeper and 10s 9d payment to the deputy keeper of the Tower records; a further half-crown to the town clerk's servant for writing out names of wards and their aldermen, and 5s for a list of all London's mayors and sheriffs; 1s for a copy of the arms of the London livery companies; and 2s 6d "for an old Stow's survey" in folio.[115]

We are at the mercy of surviving correspondence and business records, which are incomparably fuller for the last third of our period than earlier, where there is no golden source such as Philip Henslowe's diary provides for Elizabethan drama. It is clear nonetheless that the conditions of publishing books of any kind, histories among them, had changed unrecognizably in the seven decades that separated the death of William Camden in 1623 from the publication of Gibson's reedition of Camden's *Britannia*. Yet the conditions in which Camden had written in the 1580s were themselves quite different, in turn, from those that had pertained in the immediately preceding decades. At the beginning of the sixteenth century, historical books had been principally the work of the publishers, as printers such as Caxton and his early Tudor successors such as Wynkyn de Worde, John Rastell, and Richard Grafton took the initiative in bringing old works like the *Polychronicon* to press, and in Rastell and Grafton's cases writing new ones.

The entry into historical authorship of the courtiers, gentry, and nobles near the end of the Elizabethan period had reversed this relationship. With

had in fact been prepared by Smith's recently deceased father: *Thoresby Letters*, II, 320, Smith to Thoresby, 12 November 1715. Although Thoresby had requested a picture of the elder Smith in front of the book, his son chose instead to use a frontispiece designed by his father, partly because "we have no likeness of him but what was drawn when he was a young man, which was not like him when altered with age": *Thoresby Letters*, II, 343, same to same, 18 February [1715/16].

[115] BL MS Lans. 1197, fo. 14r, Strype articles of agreement.

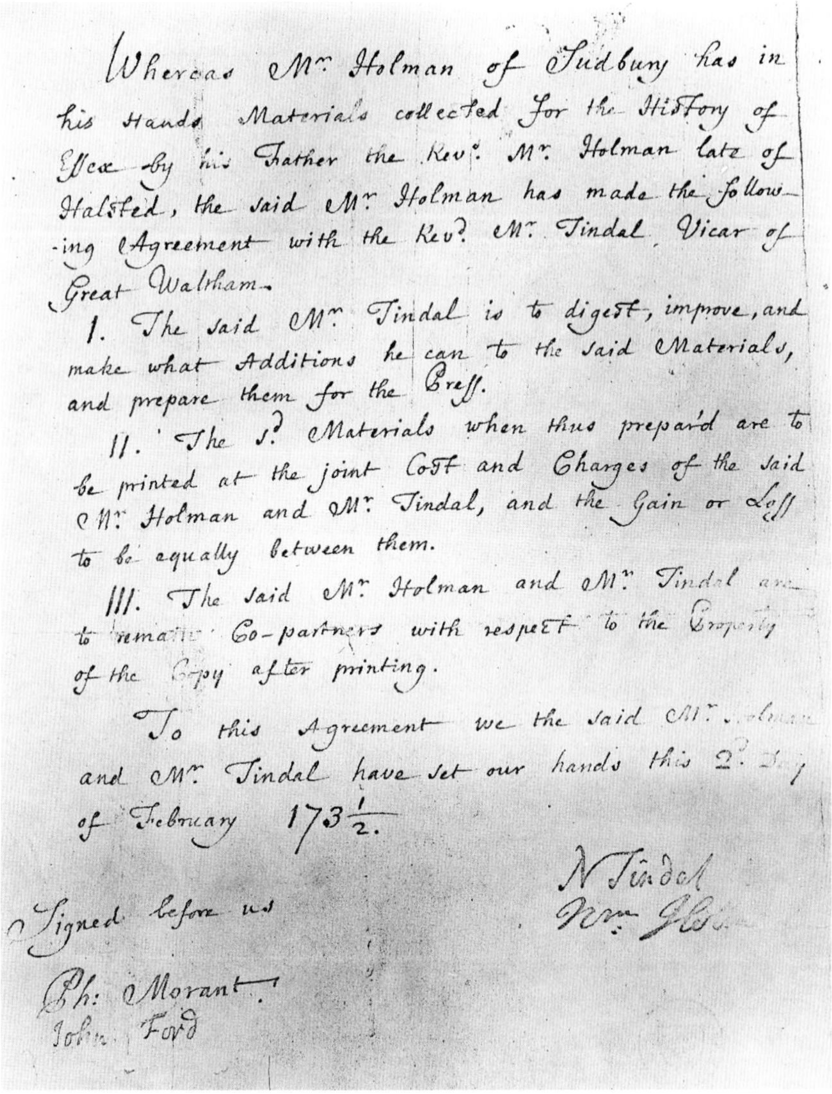

Whereas Mr. Holman of Sudbury has in his Hands Materials collected for the History of Essex by his Father the Revd. Mr. Holman late of Halsted, the said Mr. Holman has made the following Agreement with the Revd. Mr. Tindal, Vicar of Great Waltham.

1. The said Mr. Tindal is to digest, improve, and make what Additions he can to the said Materials, and prepare them for the Press.

II. The sd. Materials when thus prepar'd are to be printed at the joint Cost and Charges of the said Mr. Holman and Mr. Tindal, and the Gain or Loss to be equally between them.

III. The said Mr. Holman and Mr. Tindal are to remain Co-partners with respect to the Property of the Copy after printing.

To this Agreement we the said Mr. Holman and Mr. Tindal have set our hands this 2d. day of February 173½.

N Tindal
Wm Ho[lman]

Signed before us

Ph: Morant
John Ford

Plate 5.14   A contract to write a history from preexisting collections. An agreement between William Holman the younger and the translator-historian Nicholas Tindal to turn the collections of the Revd William Holman the elder into a history of Essex, witnessed by the future historian of Essex, Philip Morant, and in his hand. The intent of these articles is both to authorize Tindal to use the materials and to assign copyright jointly to him and to the younger Holman, while also dividing the expenses of publication. Essex Record Office, Chelmsford, T/A 497.

notable exceptions such as the publisher-organized Holinshed's *Chronicles*, the period from 1575 till the middle of the seventeenth century had established the priority of the historian, rather than the printer, publisher or bookseller, as identifiable, public maker of his history. This, of course, was how "names" such as Camden, Bacon, Herbert of Cherbury and later Clarendon, among historians of the recent past, came to be marketing tools in their own right. Business concerns were certainly important – recall the precipitous decline of the chronicle before the civil war – but were offset by the peak in independent patronage, the Renaissance equivalent of corporate sponsorship.[116] Under the pressure of increasing demand for historical works of all sorts after 1640, the author/publisher priority began to shift, if not back to the Caxton era, then at least to a sort of market-driven equilibrium, with printers, stationers, and booksellers engaged in a symbiotic relation with both established and neophyte historians and antiquaries to produce works that would both sell and do their authors credit.

A compelling example with which to close this chapter comes from a series of letters between Thomas Hearne, then a 24-year-old MA of St. Edmund Hall, Oxford and the London stationer Timothy Childe over the design of a new manual on the reading of history.[117] We have already met this pair in the context of Childe's scheme to bring out a potted version of Clarendon's *History*. And an odd couple they were indeed: at one end, the impecunious scholar, mired in texts and manuscripts at the Bodleian, taking on publishing and research jobs to make a living while planning the more serious classical editions that would really advance his career; at the other, the knowledgeable but mercenary publishing projector acting as a sort of early literary agent, and interposing himself between a potential author and the printers and booksellers who would eventually produce and sell the work. Then again, perhaps the combination is not odd at all. It resembles very closely the condition of any recent history Ph.D, still unemployed, and told his or her scholarly book is too narrow and unappealing to publish, who is encouraged into writing a textbook or doing an edition of gobbets for A-level revision as

---

[116] In an interesting essay that appeared after this chapter was completed, Paul J. Voss suggests a decline in patronage as early as the 1590s, and the beginnings of what would amount to publisher promotion and advertising through colophons and title pages. "Books for Sale: Advertising and Patronage in Late Elizabethan England," *Sixteenth Century Journal*, 29 (1998), 733–56. For more on advertising, in its more mature, post-1640 phase, see the following chapter.

[117] Philip, "Genesis of Hearne's *Ductor Historicus*." My account of the facts and correspondence of the relationship derives wholly from Philip's article, though my interpretation of the matter departs from his at some points. Levine, *Battle of the Books*, p. 287 and elsewhere discusses the *Ductor* and cites Philip's article, but strangely overlooks Childe's role in the process, thereby leaving the impression that solely intellectual considerations – the tastes of gentry readers (who were not in any case Childe's targeted market) were involved in the fashioning of Hearne's version of the work.

a means of getting her or his name out into the public domain at Dillon's, if not into that higher commonwealth of learning whose gates are kept by the *Times Literary Supplement*.

In 1698 there had appeared at London, in a single volume issued by Childe at the White Hart in St. Paul's Churchyard, the *Ductor historicus or a short system of universal history*. This was translated in part out of Pierre de Lorrain, abbé de Vallemont's *Eléments de l'histoire*, by Abel Boyer and John Savage, but "chiefly composed anew" by W. J., M. A., a man still erroneously supposed by the *English Short-Title Catalogue* to have been Hearne, who was not yet on the scene.[118] The *Ductor* provided a handy guide to ancient history *ab orbe condita* to Christ's birth. By 1702, Childe realized he had a potential money-maker on his hands, if not quite a golden goose. He made plans to extend the *Ductor* into a second volume covering the modern era. As luck would have it, Childe's wife was the daughter of John Crosley, an Oxford bookseller, and Crosley in turn knew Hearne. The latter was then busily assisting in the preparation of an edition of Greek geographers, but already hatching plots of his own. Hearne had conceived the idea of a "chronological enchiridion" or guidebook to history, along with an added two-volume history of England. On the first proposal Childe was keen, since, as he told Hearne "your thoughts having already lain that way it will be more easyly as well as more accurately performed by you than another"; he was prepared to pay fifteen shillings a sheet to his hired pen, or £22 10s for the entire second volume. This was rather less than the £2 per sheet he had paid another young scholar, John Potter (a future archbishop of Canterbury, no less) for what proved to be the enormously successful *Archaeologia Graeca*, in 1697–98; but then the print was smaller for Potter's volumes, permitting more "matter" on a sheet; and, he reminded Hearne, "you will readily grant that was a work of as much difficulty as this."

Childe was no fool. He was well read and knew the books from which Hearne could draw, including rival chronologies like Giles Strauch or Aegidius Strauchius. But at heart he was, like most publishers, looking to the bottom line as much as the title page. He was therefore not inclined to give Hearne *carte blanche* in either revising the 1698 *Ductor* or writing his second volume. He insisted on his own scheme rather than Hearne's project for a rather more learned enchiridion, which Childe thought a work "cheifly usefull at the Universitys and therefore more proper to be undertaken by the Oxford booksellers than the London ones" (translation: this will not sell). Diplomatically honey-tonguing Hearne as "a gentleman not capable of letting any thing unaccurate pass his hands," he also reminded the eager author of some facts of scholarly life:

[118] Philip, "Genesis of Hearne's Ductor Historicus," p. 252.

But herein I must admonish you that bookselling is a trade and we are obliged to have the greatest regard to the book that sells most, which too often are the foolishest. Wherefore learned books unless upon a popular subject do seldom yeild us near so much profitt as a brisk essay or a pert poem . . . So you must consider that this book is for but a few people's use and so no great number can be sold.[119]

Childe needed to cajole Hearne into doing the best job possible on a more modest scale that more closely resembled the original *Ductor*, promising him that a good performance would lead to the enhancement of Hearne's reputation as a scholar. Despite the editorial praise, Childe had no intention of allowing Hearne to have his head, given the latter's youth and ambitions. Doubtless Childe knew also the tendency of recent graduates to stray down the seductive garden paths of learning, footnoted boughs thickly foliated with the fruits of erudition, but productive of somnolent readers and poor publishers. He therefore conceded Hearne's better qualifications to select material with one breath but set down limitations and requirements with the next, insisting on the inclusion of a summary of laws in England, discussions in the introduction on topics like the "origine of all notable customes" such as parliaments, jury trials, and town customs noted by previous authors such as Camden. These were to be mentioned "without fail," a clear sign that Childe was aiming at an urban readership. He left it to Hearne to decide whether or not to include the by now suspected pseudo-Berosus at the beginning of the revised volume one, but was insistent that in treating the Yorkist–Lancastrian succession wars "'tis necessary to be a little particular in the genealogy because the stress of the contest lay upon it." Childe would eventually even dictate that in Hearne's revision of volume one he adopt the period of 3,950 years between the Creation and the birth of Christ, simply because "that is followed by most chronologers," politely referring the younger man to William Howell's major summing up of early seventeenth-century chronology, the 1661 *Institution of General History*, and offering to provide him with a copy of two earlier continental chronologies by Denis Petau and Hendrik Gutberleth, as well as the recent chronological digest by Strauch, which book he proposed Hearne take as his base, since it was widely used by readers.

Throughout all this Childe kept hammering away at one particular nail: the key to success was to pitch the book so that it could appeal to two different sorts of reader: the learned whom Hearne needed to impress with his knowledge, and the greater number of "vulgar" whom Childe badly needed to buy the book *en masse*. There was thus a delicate balance to be set between ponderous erudition and lightweight oversimplification, and Childe was probably sincere in fearing the latter as much as the former.

[119] Ibid, p. 256, quoting Bodl. MS Rawl. lett. 14, fo. 379 (Childe to Hearne, 24 November 1702).

You know already my intention, viz., that the English History be handsomely told in short, in such stile as to please as well as instruct the vulgar, and at the same time by quotations for every passage not only justify what you say but also inform a learned reader where he may find the matter more at large. But in the case of difference between authors, I must desire you not to break the thread of discourse too much in discussing it, but rather to do it in a note at bottom, for those learned disputes tho' necessary to be mentioned are tedious to most readers.[120]

We need not follow the transactions further to get the general picture, though one could add to this sort of pre-authorship negotiation innumerable early eighteenth-century examples of frosty correspondence between authors and publishers about late payments, hold-ups at press, and printers' errors. The circulation of historical knowledge had become, by 1700, as much a matter for businessmen as for scholars and statesmen, with individual scholarly patrons now much less likely to sustain the loss margin of an entire learned book than they had been in the later sixteenth century. Publishers knew very well by now exactly what sorts of books would sell, and they knew how the books would be put to use by their readers. The communications circuit, publishers, booksellers, printers, readers, and authors generated historical knowledge in response to economic realities as much as cultural practices. Clio was in business to make money.

---

[120] Ibid, pp. 258–59, quoting Bodl. MS Rawl. lett. 14, fo. 383 (same to same, 10 May 1703).

6

Marketing history

"I went to Warrington and sold Josephus, a booke soe cald Concerneing Jewish Warrs"   *Diary of Roger Lowe*, 17 May 1667[1]

As the fretting of booksellers like Timothy Childe reminds us, economic considerations could have a good deal to do with the decision to buy a book; varying types of interest ranging from genuine intellectual curiosity to sheer acquisitiveness had an equal impact on the separate decision actually to read it. John Worthington put it succinctly when congratulating his friend John Lightfoot on the publication of his *Centuria Chronographica*. "Though books sell but little, those that are able to buy, less mind books; and those that would buy, are less able, having little to spare from what is necessary for their families."[2] In the previous chapter, the cost of both producing and purchasing history books was our principal concern. In this final chapter we will examine the ways in which cost, among other factors, determined the means by which history books were acquired, and how it drove creative booksellers – and a few authors – into the commercial strategies that helped to make the intellectual marketplace of the eighteenth century a very different one from that of the previous period.

Booksellers were not, of course, simply remote correspondents. Their stocks occupied a physical, visitable space and overlap, in that sense, with the function of the library. Just as not all books were read after purchase, some could be read before they were bought by desultory browsers. As active a bibliophile as Thomas Hearne confessed to Ralph Thoresby that he knew of a letter published by Thoresby in the *Philosophical Transactions of the Royal Society*, concerning recent Yorkshire numismatic discoveries, purely from having "looked on it in the bookseller's shop." The notes of John Ward, whose wide-ranging reading has already been discussed, are peppered with references to books perused only at booksellers, in libraries, or at friends'

---

[1] *The Diary of Roger Lowe of Ashton-in-Makerfield, Lancashire, 1663–74*, ed. W. L. Sachse (New Haven, 1938), p. 115.
[2] John Worthington to Dr. John Lightfoot, 13 February 1666: BL MS Lans. 1055 (Lightfoot papers), fo. 64r.

255

homes.[3] Other readers pillaged the bookstalls with the voraciousness of descending locusts. While many Londoners were entertaining themselves watching criminal trials in the winter of 1700/1, the fourteen-year-old William Stukeley, who had been brought to the city by his father, found himself with time and money on his hands, a dangerous combination. The future antiquary soon happened upon the booksellers' stalls at St. Paul's and in Westminster, where for several days he loitered, filling his pockets with books (as well as an assortment of compasses, microscopes, and other scientific instruments), prompting his father to chide him for profligate spending.[4]

Among the seventeenth century's most famous browsers was Samuel Pepys, whose diary gives plenty of examples of books – histories prominent among them – read only in part and in passing. Having, for instance, taken the cleric and historian Thomas Fuller to an alehouse, in 1661, Pepys learned of Fuller's forthcoming *History of the Worthies of England* (a "history of all the families of England," as Pepys put it). Its author boasted he could tell Pepys more about his own family than he knew himself. But Pepys, as we have seen, could be a careful buyer, and when he first encountered the published *Worthies* at the booksellers he proceeded to spend several hours reading it on the spot without, for the moment, buying it; he would still be disappointed, for the book contained no mention of his family at all.[5] Pepys closely inspected Peter Heylyn's newly published biography of Archbishop Laud, *Cyprianus Anglicus*, at Starkey's the bookseller in 1668, before he bought it.[6] Half a century later, Henry Prescott was an inveterate browser, as we saw in chapter 2 above, familiar to the Chester booksellers. As deputy registrar, it was his responsibility to prove wills, and he may have had something to do with the appointment of Joseph Hodgson in 1711 to appraise the books in the goods of Robert Booth, Esq., a prosperous Chester citizen with a modest library who had died late that year.[7] Prescott's own

---

[3] *Letters of Eminent Men, addressed to Ralph Thoresby, F.R.S.*, 2 vols. (1832), II, 121 (Hearne to Thoresby, 24 October 1708); Folger MS V.a. 293, notebooks of John Ward, *ca.* 1663–65, for a fuller analysis of which see above, chapter 2. For another example, notes taken from a volume of Livy, see Herts RO, D/EX471.Z4.

[4] Bodl. MS Eng. misc. c. 533, fo. 12r (Stukeley papers).

[5] Pepys, *Diary*, II, 21 (22 January 1661); III, 26 (10 February 1662). Despite this disappointment, he would eventually buy the book and it would provide comfort to him on his twenty-ninth birthday, when suffering from a cold: III, 34 (23 February 1662). He and his wife Elizabeth read it at various points in the *Diary*.

[6] Ibid., IX, 291 (28 August 1668).

[7] Cheshire RO, Wills WS/1711 (Robert Booth of Chester, Esq., will made 21 November 1711; inventory made 17 December 1711 and signed by Prescott as deputy registrar). The books, individually appraised by Hodgson, include histories altogether worth £2 2s, several titles being estimated very low, a further caution against using inventory data for the price of books, even where booksellers were involved. They include Richard Verstegan, *Restitution of Decayed Intelligence* (9d); an unidentified history of Charles II (1d); *Chronologie Veneta* (3d

dealings with the booksellers were far from smooth. He had regularly purchased books from Randle Minshull of Chester,[8] but Prescott's habit of borrowing the books so as to read them extensively before deciding to purchase led to a nasty argument between him and the bookseller in 1712, when Minshull not unreasonably refused to oblige him with another short-term loan. According to Prescott, who had spent some time in Minshull's shop a few days earlier, looking over some folio titles that the bookseller had acquired at auction, Minshull fell on "rude answers, that hee knew how to manage his shop & books and car'd not whether any body woud buy Books of him or not." Prescott in turn "told him hee was a saucy and extravagant fellow in talking so slightily of his customers" and retreated, as was his wont, to a pub to soothe his nerves. Thenceforth Prescott conducted his business exclusively in the shop of Hodgson, Minshull's rival – where he soon resumed his old habits.[9] It was in part to deal profitably with this sort of problem that circulating libraries would be developed only a few decades later, permitting the curious but cautious reader to take a work home, for a fee, with a later option to buy.

MEANS OF ACQUISITION

Throughout the sixteenth century and much of the seventeenth, printing was restricted to London, the two universities, and, later, the archiepiscopal seat of York. Although surreptitious books were printed elsewhere in the king-

---

[MS blurred]); a history of Cardinal Mazarin in French, perhaps Galeazzo, conte Gualdo Priorato, *Histoire du ministere du cardinal Jules Mazarin, premier ministre de la couronne de France* (Amsterdam, 1671 [2d]); a history of the Count-Duke of Olivares (possibly the compilation entitled *The Rise & fall of the late eminent and powerful favorite of Spain, the Count Olivares*, translated by Edward Chamberlayne and first printed in 1652 [3d]); Platina's *Lives of the Popes*, continued by Sir Paul Rycaut (1685) (5s); Sir Peter Leycester's *Historical antiquities* (3s); Spelman's *Glossarium Archaiologicum* (7s); an unidentified *History of Venice*, perhaps that by Fougasses, in the English translation of 1612, or alternatively that by Paolo Paruta translated in 1658 (2s 6d); a "siege of Breda," which is probably Herman Hugo, *The siege of Breda*, translated by "C. H. G." (Ghent?, 1627) (1s); *Cottoni posthuma*, ed. James Howell (9d); John Potter's *Archaeologia Graeca, or the Antiquities of Greece* (5s); "a booke of cutts Skenkins discription of Rome" (5s); Basil Kennett's *Romae antiquae notitia or the Antiquities of Rome* (1st edn 1696 and much reprinted) (1s); an unidentified *Antiquities of Rome* in two volumes, perhaps the classical history by Dionysius of Halicarnassus (9s); and John Woodward's *An Essay Toward a Natural History of the Earth* (1695) (1s). The list includes a wide range of materials including "high-end" titles, expensive antiquarian works with engravings, as well as the sort of cheaper potted biographies and narrative histories that went for a shilling or less.

[8] The son of the bookseller John Minshull, d. 1712, on whom see Plomer, iii, 208 and H. R. Plomer, "A Chester Bookseller, 1667–1700: Some of his Customers and the Books he Sold Them," *The Library*, n.s. 4 (1903), 373–83.

[9] *The Diary of Henry Prescott LLB, Deputy Registrar of Chester Diocese*, ed. J. M. Addy, 3 vols., Red. Soc. of Lancs. and Cheshire, 127 (1987–97), II, 346–47, 425, 615.

dom (and often given foreign or mythical imprints to disguise their origins), this regulation of the industry placed some limits on the availability of printed material, over and above any separate governmental censorship of particular titles or genres. The absence through most of our period of a provincial press was partially compensated for by the development of a network of London booksellers, urban hawkers and "mercuries," provincial carriers, and rural chapmen who could take cheap print, as they did news, into the countryside.[10] History books were not ideally suited to this type of carriage since they were generally too bulky for most chapmen, whose principal market lay in any case below the social elite. Histories could, however, be ordered from London, or sold through provincial booksellers and local agents, who begin to appear in greater numbers from as early as the 1590s.[11]

In London and the larger cities, including the university towns, large-stock booksellers running shops of varying degrees of permanence catered to a market of visiting buyers from the gentry, citizenry, and clergy, men like Daniel Fleming. That northern antiquary bought, for three and six shillings respectively, Selden's *Titles of Honor* and Camden's *Annales* in English on the same trip in the winter of 1654/55, during which he also paid a pound for the copying out of his pedigree.[12] Out in the provinces, books were sold door to door as well as through agents, by catalog, and through local booksellers. Nicholas Blundell of Little Crosby, Lancashire, reports the arrival at his home of one James Steward, "with some books to sell."[13] By the beginning of the eighteenth century, most provincial towns had one or more booksellers, and occasionally also a printer.[14] Information on the provincial booksellers is less easy to come by than that for their London counterparts. Complete booksellers' catalogs of the size of the Folger manuscript analyzed in appendix A below are comparatively rare before the later seventeenth century. For the earlier period, probate inventories can once again fill the void, though only a handful survive for provincial booksellers outside London, Oxford, and Cambridge before 1700.[15] In this connection, the inventory of Michael

[10] Tessa Watt, *Cheap Print and Popular Piety, 1550–1640* (Cambridge, 1991); for hawkers and mercuries see Adrian Johns, *The Nature of the Book: Print and Knowledge in the Making* (Chicago and London, 1998), p. 156.

[11] Marjorie Plant, *The English Book Trade* (3rd edn, 1974), p. 253 records examples of local booksellers as early as the late fifteenth century, but these were few and far between.

[12] Hist. MSS Comm., *The manuscripts of S. H. Le Fleming, Esq., of Rydal Hall* (Twelfth Report, appendix vii [1890]), p. 21.

[13] *The Great Diurnal of Nicholas Blundell of Little Crosby, Lancashire*, ed. Frank Tyrer and J. J. Bagley (3 vols., Rec. Soc. of Lancs. and Cheshire, 1968–72), II, 1.

[14] John Feather, *The Provincial Book Trade in Eighteenth-Century England* (Cambridge, 1985); T. Belanger, "Publishers and Writers in Eighteenth Century England," in I. Rivers (ed.), *Books and Their Readers in Eighteenth-Century England* (Leicester, UK, 1984), pp. 5–26.

[15] Ian Maxted, "A Common Culture? The Inventory of Michael Harte, Bookseller of Exeter,

Harte, an Exeter bookseller who died in 1615, includes several named books from what clearly was a much larger stock. Among thirty-seven named or partly named, one can identify with reasonable certainty two copies of a history of Spain (perhaps that of Juan de Mariana, since Edward Grimeston's translation of Turquet de Mayerne's Spanish history had only appeared in 1612), Thomas de Fougasses' *General History of Venice* (1612), and Hoby's translation of la Popelinière's *History of France* (1595).[16] Harte's is a substantive inventory for its time – about 4,558 volumes between hall and warehouse – and the histories it includes reflect the early seventeenth-century interest in the history of foreign places, derived mainly through English translations; we can only guess at the books, not in his possession when he died, that had actually been bought.

Harte had begun his career as a London apprentice, and throughout the seventeenth century London exerted considerable influence on the provincial trade. Both before and after 1700 the London booksellers would make regular trips into the counties, especially in the southeast, to cement connections with clients who might become more than simply associates to a series of transactions. Richard Wilkins or Wilkin, traveling from his London shop to visit his several Sussex clients, breakfasted one morning at Thomas Marchant's house in Hurst.[17] The less substantial Thomas Minsheu or Minshew had inherited his father's books along with numerous debts. By the 1620s he lived in Fetter Lane, London and made his living "by the sale of bookes"; on one occasion, he left London on a Tuesday, riding a bay nag, "and spent his tyme this weeke in ridinge up and downe to gentlemen's houses to sell bookes," only to find himself mistakenly arrested on suspicion of highway robbery.[18]

Book owners also acquired their titles for themselves in a variety of ways: on trips to larger centers, through the assistance of friends and private agents,

1615," *Devon Documents in honour of Mrs. Margery Rowe*, ed. Todd Gray (Devon and Cornwall Notes and Queries, 1996), pp. 119–28. Other types of inventory than probate exist, for instance those taken where books were involved in legal disputes: the Chancery action by his creditors against John Benson, son of the Quaker grocer and bookseller Robert Benson (who had fled to Pennsylvania to avoid his debts in 1699) is a case in point, contained in PRO, C5 259/9, and printed in P. Isaac, "An Inventory of Books sold by a Seventeenth-Century Penrith Grocer," History of the Book Trade in the North, PH 53 (December 1989), which lists 332 titles in 1,111 volumes, valued at nearly seventy-five pounds; only eleven of these titles are historical and there are, in comparison to other booksellers' stocks, very few foreign-imprint books. Neither fact is surprising in view of the fact that Benson was almost certainly servicing a market for schoolbooks rather than the tastes of private collectors.

[16] Devon RO, Exeter Court of Orphans Records, DRO/ECA/ Book 144, pp. 129–34, inventory of Michael Harte. I am indebted to Ian Maxted for lending me a copy of this inventory and his transcription of it prior to publication as Maxted, "A Common Culture?"

[17] E. Turner, ed., "The Marchant Diary," *Sussex Archaeological Collections*, 25 (1873), 163–203, at p. 183.

[18] *Reading Records. Diary of the Corporation, 1431–1654*, ed. J. M. Guilding (4 vols., London and Oxford, 1892–96), III, 147–48.

and even directly from the author himself: John Hervey, earl of Bristol, purchased David Scott's *History of Scotland* for £1 6s direct from its author in 1732 (it had been published by subscription in 1727), and he rather grudgingly gave his kinsman William Bond £21, "as a present, upon his dedicating Buchanans History to me, tho' against my consent."[19] It was increasingly common practice, at least among those of moderate affluence, to establish a regular relationship with a well-connected bookseller who could keep his clients' different interests and desired items in mind when acquiring stock. Sir Thomas Browne conceived a passionate admiration for Sir Paul Rycaut's *History of the Turkish Empire* (though he conceived that it did not, quite, supplant the Jacobean book by Richard Knolles to which it was a sequel); he had his daughter Betty read selections to the family and believed that combined with Knolles, it "will then make one of the best histories wee have in English." Browne was so enthusiastic about the book that he wanted his son Edward to have a copy of his own. "I would not have you borrowe it, because you may have it allwayes by you." But the elder Browne lived in Norwich, which, while not an impossible distance from London, where Edward dwelled, meant either buying a copy for him and risking it with the common carrier, or building on his relations with the local bookseller. At last he wrote to Edward that "I have found out a way how you shall receave Ricauts historie without sending it by the carts." This involved Browne's Norwich bookseller, George Rose, sending an order to his correspondent, Robert Clavell (who would in fact copublish the second edition in 1687), who would then release a copy to Edward. Aside from the complexity of the arrangement, it is plain that Browne trusted his local bookseller rather more than Rose's London counterpart, since he did not plan to pay up until he learned from Rose that Edward had indeed received the book in London.[20]

The personal papers of George Plaxton, rector of Barwick-in-Elmet, Yorkshire, but resident at the Staffordshire estates of Lord Gower (for whom he was estate steward) in the early 1710s, include bills from Michael Johnson, a prosperous Lichfield bookseller who was also a friend of Plaxton, whom he had assisted in some genealogical inquiries. Among Plaxton's responsibilities was the buying of books for Gower. In 1714 Johnson sent him Jeremy Collier's *An ecclesiastical history of Great Britain, chiefly of England* (the second volume of which had just been published). In 1722 he presented two bills for Plaxton's attention, including Thomas Salmon's *A review of the history of England, as far as it relates to the titles and pretensions of our*

[19] *The Diary of John Hervey, First Earl of Bristol, with Extracts from his Book of Expenses, 1688–1742* (Wells, Somers., England, 1894), expenses, pp. 93, 95.

[20] *Works of Sir Thomas Browne*, ed. G. L. Keynes (2nd edn, 4 vols, Chicago, 1964), IV, 145, 148, 149 (Browne to Edward Browne, 22 December 1679; 5 January 1680; 19 January 1680).

several kings, and their respective characters from the Conquest to the Revolution, Camden's *Britannia*, and John Lowthorp's abridgment of the *Philosophical transactions of the Royal Society*.[21] Plaxton's purchases on behalf of his patron are a further reminder that the great and powerful, who might own extraordinary libraries, frequently counted on learned servants or clients to make their selections for them: the pairing of the Harleys' money and Humfrey Wanley's talents was simply the same phenomenon on a grander scale. Many of the books that John Locke bought in the early 1680s (including William Howell's *Institution of general history*, John Marsham's *Chronicus canon*, William Drummond's *History of Scotland*, and Redman Westcot's 1682 translation of John Selden's *Jani anglorum facies altera*) were purchased for his patron, the earl of Shaftesbury.[22]

Like Browne, Plaxton, and Locke, many readers solved their ordering problems simply by setting up an account for books and stationery supplies with a provincial and sometimes also a London bookseller, often sticking with the same vendor for an extended period. Daniel Fleming, for instance, was not content to rely on the occasional visit to London, and his accounts show him ordering, usually through a local Westmorland bookseller, works such as James Heath's *Brief Chronicle of the late intestine wars*. He paid a Kendal merchant 14s 6d for Dugdale's *History of St. Pauls Cathedral* and 4s 6d for the *Life of the . . . Duke of Newcastle* by his widow (the celebrated duchess), prices which specifically included the cost of delivery.[23] The Lon-

---

[21] Staffs RO, D593/K/1/1/6, Johnson to Plaxton, 19 February 1713/14 and 26 July and 4 October 1722. For Johnson, whose stock sold as far away from Lichfield as Birmingham and Uttoxeter, see Feather, *The Provincial Book Trade*, 13.

[22] Bodl. MS Locke f. 5 (1681), pp. 2, 90, 125–26; MS Locke f. 6 (1682), p. 62; MS Locke f. 7 (1683), p. 77. None of these titles occurs in John Harrison and Peter Laslett's listing of *The Library of John Locke* (2nd edn, Oxford, 1971). Other historical works acquired at this time, however, do appear later in Locke's library, including (nos. 1830, 2526; pp. 180, 224) Gabriel Sagard's *Histoire du Canada*, and Job Ludolphus' *Historia Aethiopica*, mentioned specifically as "for my Ld," suggesting that some of Locke's own books may have been originally purchased for Shaftesbury. It was also extremely common for those going to a larger center like London to buy books on behalf of their friends. Ralph Thoresby did much buying for the Yorkshire antiquarian community while in London supervising the printing of his own book. *Thoresby Letters*, II, 384 (Revd Joseph Cookson, vicar of Leeds, to Thoresby, 20 May 1723).

[23] Hist. MSS Comm., *Le Fleming*, 372, 377 (1665 and 1667). Fleming also sent James Banks to pay James Cock for Sprat's *History of the Royal Society*, at seven shillings, and several other cheaper books, the combined carriage charge from London to Westmorland was only sixpence: ibid., 377 (24 December 1667). Buyers do not seem to have consolidated orders from London to save transport costs: barely two weeks later Fleming dispatched Banks with 22s for Cock to provide a copy of Dugdale's *Origines Juridiciales*: ibid., 378. The 14s 6d paid by Fleming for Dugdale's *St. Paul's* is close enough to the fifteen shillings paid by Sir William Clarke to John Playford for the same book in 1661 (Hist. MSS Comm., *Report on the manuscripts of F. W. Leyborne-Popham, Esq., Littlecote, Co. Wilts.*, [1899], p. 188), part of a larger purchase worth over £5, to suggest some degree of price standardization setting in. There were, of course, exceptions such as the 1684 edition of Foxe's *Acts and Monuments* discussed above.

don bookseller Richard Wilkin wrote to the vicar of Walton on Trent, John Frewen, in 1729, to inform him of his retirement from business and referring Frewen to William Parker, his journeyman of nine years, to whom Wilkin had sold the business, complete with its client list.[24] The transactions of Robert Gosling, a major bookseller and London alderman of the same era, provide a further example, especially useful because of his familiarity among antiquarian and scholarly circles.[25] A major publisher of historical works in his own right, Gosling sold books from a shop at the Mitre, against St. Dunstan's Church, Fleet Street, and his ledger book survives for the years 1730 to 1740. Although tantalizingly incomplete on such matters as the location and status of many of his clients, it does provide a sense of his inventory and its movement. Gosling's business was surprisingly uneven, with good years (1731, 1736 and 1739–40) sometimes being followed by bad ones, but history books remained more or less constant sellers throughout: in only one year, 1738, did Gosling have healthy sales for his general stock and poor sales for historical titles. On the whole, the percentage of historical titles for which debits are recorded ranges between 10 and 20 percent (somewhat higher in 1732 to 1735, years of generally slower sales), with the lowest point being about 6 percent of total books in 1738.[26]

[24] E. Sussex RO (Lewes), FRE 1179, Wilkin to Frewen, 30 January 1728/29.

[25] On Gosling see Plomer, iii, 130; Gosling's stock, one of the largest in London, had been valued at £2,218 at the time it was sold in a 1743 trade sale: T. Belanger, "Booksellers' Trade Sales, 1718–1768," *The Library*, 5th series, 30 (1975), 281–302, at p. 300.

[26] Bodl. MS Eng. misc. c. 296, fos. 1–113. The surviving ledger is clearly a continuation of an earlier book, and starts only in late 1730. For this reason, 1730 totals have been lumped in with 1731. The credit side is usually on the recto, till half-way through the manuscript. Each client's account is kept on the debit side, often carried over from a previous or to a later ledger, with accounts settled periodically. Prices are unfortunately not always given for individual books if the client bought several items together. This, combined with the large disparity in format from obvious expensive folios (for instance, an old edition of Camden's *Britannia* and Rushworth's *Historical Collections*), to small books for school and even things like "heads of kings," make it impossible to establish an average price, or even to determine with any accuracy the percentage of revenue deriving from histories. Annual totals for all books and for histories take 1 January as the start of the year, though Gosling in fact used both 1 January and 25 March. Multiple copies of certain works explain sudden leaps in sales. Like many booksellers, Gosling dealt a great deal in schoolbooks and legal texts, and was always selling historical authors like Nepos and Florus (along with commonplace items like the Book of Common Prayer, Bibles and grammars) in large numbers, often to schoolmasters as well as pupils. Multiple copies have been counted individually, but not several volumes of a work such as Rushworth, listed in one copy. Magazines and newspapers are not counted (for instance, the *Spectator*, *Craftsman*, *Gentleman's Magazine*), but serially published books are, such as Rapin-Thoyras' *History*. This last title was very popular in the list and sold in sequential numbers (for discussion of which see further below in this chapter): thus six numbers of Rapin-Thoyras sold to a single client counts as six histories because (unlike a multivolume work like Rushworth), they represent separate ledger transactions, though not, of course, six distinct decisions on the part of the client to purchase the title. Statutes and legal books are counted in the total, but stationery supplies such as paper are excluded. Books are counted if mentioned as having been sent for binding on behalf of a customer and not mentioned elsewhere, but are not double-counted (some he sold bound; others Gosling

In one way, however, there was no substitute for an actual visit to a bookseller, and not simply because of the attraction of browsing without commitment. Booksellers' premises were social spaces that, much like coffee-houses and clubs, had a place in the creation of a "public sphere" of English intellectual life; their proprietors often took an interest in the nurturing of civilized discourse that went beyond their economic motivation. Bookshops became convenient meeting places for groups of visiting scholars and gentle-men – John, Lord Ashburnham recounts one such gathering at George Grafton's Fleet Street shop in January 1687; the notorious pirate Edmund Curll (famous as the nemesis of Alexander Pope) established his own "litera-tory" in his Bow Street, Covent Garden house, as a center for antiquarian scholarship.[27] Booksellers also served as a depository for privately owned books (as well as those being sold), manuscripts, letters, and packages, and even staging posts: One of Anthony Wood's favored booksellers, Francis Bowman of Oxford, provided the young Thomas Isham and his party with shelter and dry clothes when they arrived in town wet and muddy from a summer storm.[28] Even the larger booksellers who were also publishers, preoccupied with the bottom line, picked up historical interests themselves and aided their clients and friends in a variety of ways: we have seen that the mercenary Timothy Childe was very well-informed as to what a vendible manual like the *Ductor historicus* ought to contain. Strype's life of Bishop Aylmer was actually printed by a man named Aylmer who took a personal interest in the project because, Strype noted, he "derives himself in a direct line from him."[29] William Stukeley, a regular bookhound, was lent a large vellum roll of the late fifteenth century by "Mr. Hopkinson the bookseller"; another bookseller, William Cowper, began in 1676 the first catalog of the manuscript holdings of Sir Hans Sloane.[30] And with excusable commercial self-interest in mind, a publisher like Jacob Tonson might even write individ-ual letters to a well-known scholar to put the word out about an impending publication.[31]

Marketing in the sixteenth century had generally been a matter of word of

apparently received from customers who may have bought them elsewhere and given them to him to have bound).

[27] E. Sussex RO (Lewes), MS Ash. 932 (diary of John Ashburnham), vol. II, fo. 33; Johns, *Nature of the Book*, pp. 120–24.

[28] For papers and MSS changing hands via bookseller as intermediary, see Francis Atterbury to George Hicks (2 April 1700?), Hist. MSS Comm., *Calendar of the manuscripts of the Marquis of Bath, preserved at Longleat, Wiltshire* (5 vols., 1904–80), II, 177; *The Diary of Thomas Isham of Lamport (1658–81)*, p. 221 (9 July 1672).

[29] *Thoresby Letters*, II, 248 (Strype to Thoresby, 23 May [1710]).

[30] SAL MS 264, fo. 37v, note by Stukeley, 21 June 1735; ibid., fo. 63v–64v, transcript by Stukeley.

[31] "Jacob Tonson sends word that a copy of that author [Sallust] is now come to the press, done by a gentleman who has spent two years in that work." *Thoresby Letters*, II, 82 (Revd George Plaxton to Thoresby, 23 December 1707).

mouth and communication between bookseller and reader (and, of course, patron and paid writer). It became much more systematic in the seventeenth century, with advertisements for new books carried on blank pages at the ends of other books offered by the same sellers. In the eighteenth century periodicals, published prospectuses, newspapers, and publishers' catalogs would significantly extend the advertising possibilities. Book catalogs appear for the first time in the late sixteenth century – Andrew Maunsell issued such a list in 1595, and William London, a bookseller in Newcastle-upon-Tyne, issued in 1657 a general *Catalogue of the most vendible books in England*, all of which he claimed to have in stock.[32] Catalogs issued by publishers of their own books alone were more rare before the mid-eighteenth century, but also enjoyed some success: when Henry Dodwell, the Camden professor at Oxford, sent a catalog of the books being published from the Sheldonian Theatre in 1694, his Irish correspondent enthusiastically ordered several of them and passed the catalog on to his friends.[33] By the middle of the seventeenth century regular trade announcements were made, of which the most important were the so-called *Term Catalogues* that ran from 1668 to 1711. Other tactics included the posting of title pages as advertisements, and, from the 1650s, the printing of sellers' lists in books or, from 1685, their insertion at the end of a book.[34]

An examination of these advertisements reveals a significant presence of historical works (plate 6.15). In the little less than four years that the *Spectator* carried notices of books "this day published," 361 titles were listed, including twenty-eight historical and biographical works (plays included), or, about 7.7 percent.[35] Other periodicals reveal similar proportions. Historical and parahistorical books advertised in the first volume (1731) of the *Gentleman's Magazine*, here represented in fig. 6.10 included many current fact sheets with "history" in the title, such as *The History of Executions*, together with serialized English and French editions of Paul de Rapin-Thoyras' *History of England*, and some older works such as an edition of Tacitus, and John Trenchard's *A short history of standing armies in England*, a brief political tract first published in 1698. Also included were a healthy assortment of critiques of and polemics against recently published works, and responses to those critiques, for instance *A letter to the reverend subscribers to a late voluminous libel, entitled, The History of England, during*

[32] G. Pollard and A. Ehrman, *The Distribution of Books by Catalogue from the Invention of Printing to AD 1800* (Cambridge, 1965), pp. 125–28.
[33] Bodl. MS Eng. lett. c. 29, fo. 22.
[34] P. Gaskell, *New Introduction to Bibliography* (Oxford, 1972), pp. 182–83; Pollard and Ehrman, *Distribution of Books by Catalogue*, pp. 147–74.
[35] *The Spectator*, ed. Donald F. Bond (5 vols., Oxford, 1965), V, appendix III, pp. 205–24.

ADVERTISEMENTS.

To be Lett,
(To be enter'd upon at Michaelmass next)
A House at Temple-Mills, Hackney-Marsh, lately a Callicoe Prin-ter's; with Coppers, and other Conveniencies standing; also Ground and Water sufficient, fit for the said Business, a Distiller, Brewer, Whitster, or Dyer. Enquire at the said House, or of Mr. *John Middleton* at the General Post-Office, Lombard-street, and know further.

This Day is published,
Number II. *containing 20 Sheets in Folio, Price 3 s. 6 d.* of
AN Universal History, from the earliest Account of Time to the present: Which comprizes not only the General History of the World, but that of every particular Empire, Kingdom, and State, from its first Foundation to its Dissolution, or to our own Time; with an exact Account of the Migration, and Conquests of every People, the Successions and Reigns of their respective Princes, their Religion, Government, Customs, Learning, &c. The whole immediately extracted from the original Authors, and illustrated with necessary Maps, Cuts, Chronological and other Tables.
To be continued Monthly.
Printed for J. Batley in Pater-Noster Row, E. Symon in Cornhill, N. Prevost against Southampton-Street in the Strand, T. Osborne in Gray's-Inn, and J. Crokatt near St. Dunstan's Church in Fleet-Street; and sold by T. Payne at the Crown in Ivy Lane, near Pater-Noster Row; of whom may be had Numb I.
N. B. Number III. is in the Press, and will be speedily publish'd.

On Monday next will be published,
THE Life of *MAHOMET.* Translated from the French Ori-ginal written by the Count of Boulainvilliers, Author of *the Pre-sent State of France,* and of the *Historical Memoirs* thereto subjoined.
'Tis true, Composing is the Nobler Part,
But good Translation is no easy Art.   Roscommon.
Printed for W. Hinchliffe, at Dryden's Head under the Royal-Ex-change.

This Day is published,
(*Written originally for the Entertainment of the King by the celebrated Madam de Gomez,*)
SECRET MEMOIRS of the COURT of PERSIA. Printed for Weaver Bickerton, in Devereux-Court, near the Middle-Temple. Price 5 s.   *Of whom may be had,*
I. The *Curious and Profitable Gardener;* with a Description of the *Great Aloe* and *Torch Thistles.* By Mr. COWELL of Hoxton.
II. Dr. Wood's Anatomy of the Heart, and Origin and Circulation of the BLOOD.
III. A View of the present Affairs of IRELAND; containing a List of ABSENTEES, and Modest Proposal. By Dr. SWIFT.

and Carriers; with an Account of all the Fairs and Market Towns in England. Price 1 s.

This Day is published,
AN APPEAL to the genuine RECORDS and TESTIMONIES of Heathen and Jewish Writers; being full EVIDENCE for the Truth of the Christian Religion, and its primitive Doctrines. In se-veral Conferences. Part I.
The Truth of the Bottom is plainly this: All the great Things that modern Deists affect to say of Right Reason, as to its Sufficiency in discovering the Obligations and Motives of Morality, is only a Pretence to be made use of, when they are opposing Christianity.
Dr. Clarke in his Boyle's Lecture.
Refrain not to speak when there is Occasion to do Good: Strive for the Truth up to Death, and the Lord shall fight for thee.
Ecclus. iv. 23. 28.
Printed for L. GILLIVER at Homer's Head against St. Dunstan's Church, Fleet-street. Price 1 s. 6 d.
Where may be had, just publish'd,
An Essay, founded upon Arguments Natural and Moral proving the Immortality of the Soul. Translated from the original MSS. of the Archbishop of Cambray. Price 1 s.

BOOKS printed for JOHN BROTHERTON, at the Bible next the Fleece Tavern in Cornhill.

Cambden's Britannia	Blair's Sermons, 5 Vol.
Burkit on the New Testament	Life of Oliver Cromwel
L'Estrange's Josephus	Gordon's Geog. Grammar
Tillotson's Works, 3 Vols.	Boileau Oevre poetique
Bacon's Works, 4 Vols,	Pilgrim's Progress
Lock's Works, 3 Vol.	Tales of the Fairies, 3 Vol.
Oldenburgh of Exchanges	English Tutor
Addison's Works, 4 Vols. 4to	Musical Dictionary
Puffendorf's Law of Nature	Shakespear's Plays
Bailey's Dictionary, fol.	Congreve's Works
Wood's Institutes, fol.	Garth's Ovid
Carckas's Rates, fol.	Boyer's Telemachus
Stevens's Spanish Dictionary	Meige's State of Britain.

With Variety of single Plays and Pamphlets.

This Day is published,
Numb. IV. of
Historia Literaria: Or, an exact and early Account of the most valuable Books published in the several parts of Europe.
Floriferis ut apes in saltibus omnia libant
Omnia nos itidem.———— Lucret.
To which is added, The present State of Learning, Ex-tracts of several Letters from Helmstadt, Hamburgh, Bour-deaux, Paris, Amsterdam, London, and a Catalogue of new Books imported during the Month of August, by N. Pre-vost and Comp.
Printed and sold by the said N. Prevost, over against Southampton-street in the Strand, and E. Symon in Cornhill, and to be had at J. Batley's in Pater-noster Row, J. Crokatt and L. Gilliver in Fleet-street, T. Osborn in Grays-Inn, and T. Payne in Ivy-lane, 8vo, London, 1730.
Where may be had, Number I. II. and III.

Plate 6.15 The advertisement of historical works, illustrated from the final page of *Grub Street Journal*, 37 (1730).

the Reigns of the royal house of Stuart.[36] By the beginning of the eighteenth century, a reader could open a periodical such as the *History of the Works of the Learned* and not only learn of the publication of a book, but read a review of it as well (plate 6.16).

Another obvious way in which history books were circulated, without booksellers being involved, was through gifts and bequests. The attraction of

[36] *Gentleman's Magazine*, 1, 455 (October 1731). So common is the word *history* in newsbooks and gazeteers that it appears to have become a codeword for any "factual" or truthful report of recent events, for instance in regular issues of Salmon's *Modern History*, or Earbery's *Occasional Historian*. For the early relations of history and the periodical press in Europe see Harcourt Brown, "History and the Learned Journal," *Journal of the History of Ideas*, 33 (1972), 365–78.

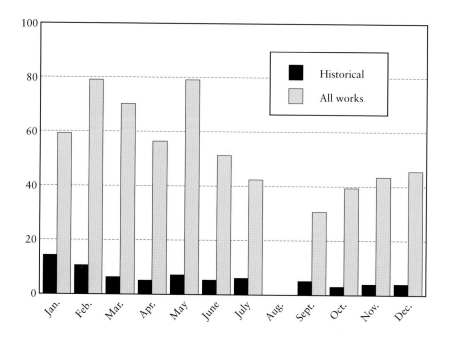

Figure 6.10   Publication of historical matter: notices in *Gentleman's Magazine*, 1 (1731). Booklist for August is absent.

the book as physical artifact, regardless of its intellectual contents, to which many owners may have been indifferent, has on the whole been underrated, though some attention has been paid to the use of books as gifts to cement or repair social and familial relations.[37] Because historical and antiquarian books were often especially valuable, they circulated in no small numbers in this fashion: when William Elstob went to call on Bishop Nicolson in 1711 he brought with him a gift copy of his sister Elizabeth's celebrated edition of the *English Saxon Homily*.[38] On the occasion of his election to the Royal

[37] Natalie Zemon Davis, "Beyond the Market: Books as Gifts in Sixteenth-century France," *Trans. Royal Hist. Soc.*, 5th series 33 (1983); Anne Goldgar, *Impolite Learning: Conduct and Community in the Republic of Letters, 1680–1750* (New Haven and London, 1995), pp. 19–20; Johns, *Nature of the Book*, p. 482; on the enduring "magical" or superstitious qualities attached to certain books, see David Cressy, "Books as Totems in Seventeenth-Century England and New England," *Journal of Library History*, 21 (1986), 92–106.
[38] *The London Diaries of William Nicolson*, ed. C. Jones and G. Holmes (Oxford, 1985), p. 531 (9 January 1711).

Plate 6.16 (*opposite*)   A page from the *History of the Works of the Learned*, vol. III (January 1701), p. 18, an early example of a critical review of a history book.

18   **The Works of the** L E A R N E D,

Unienda ergo in Patre Tuo Augusto & Te
Omnium Majorum Gloria
Ut in vobis olim revivifcat

L E O P O L D U S,

Omnium priorum Cæfarum Compendium
Omnium futurorum Exemplar,
Cujus laudum capax non eft orbis, licet fit plenus.

Hiftoire du Regne de Louis XIII. *i. e.* The Hiftory of the Reign
of *Louis* XIII, King of *France* and *Navarre*. Tome II. Part I.
Containing the moft remarkable Occurrences in *France* and
Europe, from the Meeting of the States General, till the Mar-
riage of the King. Part II. Containing the Hiftory from the
King's Marriage, till the removal of the Queen Mother.
Printed at *Amfterdam*, 1701. 12°. Part I. Pages 378. Part II.
Pages 434. By *Michel le Vafor.*

IT fuffices in general, to obferve, That in refpect of the Method, this fecond Volume is every way like the firft. Here
our Author makes ufe of the fame Liberty, the fame fort of Reflections, and purfues the fame general Defign, and he ufes the
fame Digreffions, with relation to the Hiftory of the other States
of *Europe :* Nay, perhaps his Reflections are more in Number,
and he takes more Liberty than in the firft Volume. He makes
an Apology for himfelf as to two Things, in a fhort Advertife-
ment, at the end of this fecond Volume. The firft is, that it it
is larger than the former, tho' it contains but the Hiftory of a-
bout three Years. He fuppofes that indifferent Perfons will par-
don him this, Prolixity, when they reflect upon the great Intrigues,
which he came to difcover, and on the confiderable Affairs which
he gives an Account of·
The Particulars of what paffed in the Affembly of the States
General of the Kingdom, a great Conteft between the King's
Council and the Parliament of *Paris*, concerning the lawful Authority of that ancient Court, their Remonftrances againft the
Diforders of the Government ; their Inftances for the Reformation of the State ; two Civil Wars ; the famous Conference
of

Society in 1702, Dr. James Yonge, a Plymouth surgeon and budding tory who had acquired some high connections, was rewarded for a spirited defense of the memory of the earl of Clarendon by the historian's son, Laurence Hyde, earl of Rochester, who presented Yonge with a copy of his father's *History of the Rebellion*, the first part of which had just been published.[39] Sir William Trumbull was similarly favored by the historian's older son, Henry, the second earl of Clarendon, who sent him both volumes I and II as they appeared.[40] Sir John Reresby's friend and patron the duke of Newcastle presented him with a copy of Robert Thoroton's *Antiquities of Nottinghamshire*, which pleased the vain Reresby no end since "he often takes notice of my family."[41] When Alice Berrie, a widow of Beccles, died in October 1619 she left to her friend Mr. Thomas Rose "the Book of Acts & Monuments of Mr. Fox," to be delivered by her kinsman Thomas Harris.[42] Claver Morris, like James Yonge a West Country physician, recorded only two history books in his diary, one of which, "the New History of the Kings of England (suppos'd to be written by Dr. Welwood) in 2 volumes in 8vo," he gave his niece.[43] The earl of Bristol bought a number of major historical works from booksellers like Jacob Tonson and Paul Vaillant between 1690 and 1735; the last of these was a nine-volume history by Charles Rollin, purchased for his daughter.[44] Among the 176 principally religious books that William Whiston inherited from his father was a copy of Baker's *Chronicle*, Camden's *Remains*, and an unspecified "historia latina."[45]

---

[39] *The Journal of James Yonge [1647–1721] Plymouth Surgeon*, ed. F. N. L. Poynter (1963), p. 214.

[40] Hist. MSS Comm., *Report on the manuscripts of the Marquess of Downshire, preserved at Easthampstead Park, Berks.*, 4 vols. in 5 (1924–40), I, part 2, p. 862, Clarendon to Trumbull, 23 October 1703. Trumbull had already received, in 1696, a copy of Pierre Bayle's *Dictionnaire* from the author himself: ibid., pp. 647, 699.

[41] *The Memoirs of Sir John Reresby of Thrybergh, Bart., MP for York, &c. 1634–1689*, ed. J. J. Cartwright (1875), p. 217 (19 August 1681).

[42] *Wills of the Archdeaconry of Suffolk 1620–1624*, ed. M. E. Allen, Suffolk Rec. Soc., 31 (1989), no. 150, p. 88. This was one of the very few named books to be left in a Suffolk will between 1619 and 1624.

[43] James Welwood (1652–1727), physician and whig supporter of William III, and author of the much reprinted *Memoirs of the most material transactions in England for the last hundred years preceding the Revolution in 1688* (1700); *The Diary of a West Country Physician, AD 1684–1726*, ed. Edmund Hobhouse (1934), p. 54. The other mentioned book was an epitome of Josephus.

[44] *The Diary of John Hervey*, expenses, p. 94.

[45] Bodl. MS Eng. misc. d. 297, pp. 39, 41, 42–43, 414–15, commonplace book of William Whiston. William Stratford, having heard his friend Edward Harley complain at Bath of being unable to find a particular volume of the "Magdeburgenses" (i.e. the *Magdeburg Centuries*), anxiously enquired as to which volume, so that he could verify that his own set, inherited from his father, was complete: Hist. MSS Comm., *The manuscripts of His Grace the Duke of Portland, preserved at Welbeck Abbey* (10 vols., 1891–1900), VII, 239.

FOREIGN HISTORIES

A more informal network of correspondence that far exceeded the book-sellers' client lists started in the mid-sixteenth century and grew within less than a century to embrace rural readers, London and university scholars, churchmen, and booksellers at home and abroad, many of whom traveled annually to bring back foreign books from continental book fairs. The biggest of these was the Frankfurt *Buchmesse*, which dated from the late Middle Ages and had expanded enormously in the second half of the six-teenth century.[46]

A vigorous market for foreign books existed from virtually the start of printing, and by the eighteenth century a regular series of customs ledgers recording imports and exports was being kept.[47] Those who wished to be conversant with the latest work of French, German, or Dutch historical scholarship could hardly be bound by the horizons of English printers and authors. Aside from the trade in proscribed foreign titles (for instance by the Elizabethan printer John Wolf, who was frequently in trouble for importing unlicensed Italian books in the 1590s[48]), many booksellers made a point of adding foreign titles, often acquired at the Frankfurt fair, to their lists. This saved clients the bother of having continental correspondents do their buying for them. Henry Fetherstone's *Catalogus Librorum in diversis locis Italiae emptorum, anno 1628* and its sequel (1636) included a variety of foreign historical and antiquarian books, including several in manuscript.[49] Some booksellers even specialized in foreign works. James Allestry or Allestree, who provided the Royal Society members with their tomes, had a particu-larly good stock of French and foreign books, according to Pepys, who elsewhere refers to spending time in Paul's Churchyard, "at the forreigne booksellers, looking over some Spanish books."[50] Half of a century later, the earl of Bristol obtained his history books from a variety of dealers (getting

---

[46] "If any of the English booksellers come to Francfort fair, you may tell them to enquire of the Geneva booksellers whether they have anything for them": James Petiver to J. Constant at Lausanne, 19 March 1713, BL MS Sloane 3339, fo. 14v. On the Frankfurt fair, see Mathilde Rovelstad, "The Frankfurt Book Fair," *Journal of Library History*, 8 (1973), 113–23.

[47] G. Barber, "Book Imports and Exports in the Eighteenth Century," in Robin Myers and Michael Harris (eds.), *Sale and Distribution of Books from 1700* (Oxford, 1982), pp. 77–105; these records are not specific as to titles and have therefore not been used in the present study.

[48] On John Wolf (fl. 1579–1601), and surreptitious printing in general, see D. B. Woodfield, *Surreptitious Printing in England 1550–1640* (New York, 1973), pp. 5–33.

[49] F. J. Levy, "How Information Spread Among the Gentry, 1550–1640," *Journal of British Studies*, 21 (1982), 11–34, at p. 16; for an earlier catalog see Pollard and Ehrman, *Distribu-tion of Books by Catalogue*, pp. 124–39.

[50] *Diary*, VIII, 521 (6 November 1667); IV, 87 (27 March 1663). The bookseller Sheeres sent him a two-volume edition of Mariana's *Historia general de Espana*, unsolicited but nonethe-less to Pepys' delight; IX, 537 (28 April 1669).

Echard's *History of England* from Jacob Tonson, for instance); but he looked especially to Paul Vaillant for titles such as Montfaucon's *L'antiquité expliquée et representée en figures*, for which he had subscribed in advance in 1723, and for Joseph-Nicolas Charenton's French translation of Juan de Mariana's history of Spain.[51]

The increasing flow of travel abroad in the seventeenth century allowed individual tourists to pick up bibliographic gems at booksellers in Rome, Venice, Amsterdam, and Paris, together with the medals, coins, and paintings that were so important a part of the memorabilia from the Grand Tour. On his own tour in 1700–2, Martin Bowes of Suffolk kept a careful account of his acquisitions in books and art, and of their cost. One list of the books he purchased at Rome in 1701 includes 112 items, of which twenty-six fall into a category of "Roman antiquitys and curiositys." The historical books, nearly all by classical and foreign authors, include several narrative histories and works on inscriptions, coins, and medals, and the lists indicate their prices, converted to sterling. In Paris, Bowes acquired forty-eight more books, again including several historical works. In both lists, with virtually no exceptions, the historical and antiquarian titles were among the most expensive items purchased, including maps and pictures.[52]

As with domestic volumes, books could be ordered from abroad as well as purchased in person, through a friend, agent, or foreign bookseller. Thomas Coke, vice-chamberlain to George I, asked Michael Kinkaid, in Paris, to find a book of French royal medals, but the only bookseller who had it in stock, one Mariette, wanted fifteen pounds, an exorbitant sum, leading Kinkaid instead to commission two other booksellers to find a cheaper copy.[53] John Locke received several Dutch, Italian, and French books, mainly octavo and duodecimo volumes, from a Mr. Brisbon, who brought them from France.[54]

---

[51] *Diary of John Hervey*, expenses, pp. 93–94. When Vaillant passed his business on to Nicholas Prevost, Bristol later bought Vertot's *History of the Knights of Malta* and Rapin-Thoyras' *History of England*.

[52] Suffolk RO (Ipswich), HA93/9/24. The historical works, as conjecturally identified by the present author from author and short title, include Suetonius (3s); *La science des medailles* (3s); Davila, *Historia delle guerre civili di Francia* (£1); Battista Nani, *Historia della republica Veneta* (£2 5s); Guido Bentivoglio, *Historia della guerra di Fiandra* (£2); Sarpi, *Council of Trent* (8s); Guicciardini, *Storia d'Italia* (n.p.); Fedele Onofri, *Cronologia Veneta* (2s).

[53] Hist. MSS Comm., *The manuscripts of the Earl Cowper, K.G., preserved at Melbourne Hall, Derbyshire*, (3 vols., 1888–89), III, 120.

[54] Bodl. MS Locke f. 4 (Journals, 1680), pp. 141–42. The books included Mézeray's *Histoire de France*, a life of Cesare Borgia in two volumes (perhaps Tomaso Tomasi's *La vita di Cesare Borgia detto poi il duca Valentino* [Monte Chiaro, 1671, but published in one volume]), Abraham Nicolas Amelot de la Houssaye's *Histoire du gouvernement de Venise* (Paris, 1677), a translation of Xenophon, a history of Henri III (probably the four-volume *Recueil de diverses pièces servant a l'histoire de Henry III, roy de France et de Pologne* [Cologne, 1663]), and five volumes of the *Journal des Sçavants*. For another example, involving G. Marcel's *Tablets chronologiques* then available only in Paris, see the request of Sir Richard Bulstrode (then in Brussels) to Sir William Trumbull – September (n.d.) 1686: Hist. MSS Comm., *Downshire*, I, part i, 221.

One must sympathize with travelers obliged through friendship or patronage to carry with them books intended for others. The problems of domestic distribution, already mentioned, were here compounded by matters of exchange, sea carriage, and even language. Complaints about carriers are about as common as those muttered against booksellers. Theodore Janssen, a Ghent scholar and correspondent of Dr. Thomas Smith, undertook to send the latter a book in 1695; when after some time it had not arrived Janssen was obliged to make excuses, adducing this as evidence of the laziness and corruption of sailors and booksellers alike.[55] "I have at last got my cargoe of books from France," reported Dr. George Clark to his friend Arthur Charlett, on receiving a tardy shipment that included Montfaucon's great illustrated work on antiquities, "some of which I payd for last September was 12 month."[56] The correspondence of the divine and philologist Henry Dodwell (1641–1711) relates worse tales than this. In 1703 William Percivale wrote to Dodwell from Cashel about the "miscarriage" of several books and of the perils of using middlemen, in this instance a buyer named Pulteney, who lived at a bookseller's in Utrecht and had been contracted to send them. Bishop Fell informed Dodwell one October that the newly printed sheets of Dodwell's *Dissertationes Cyprianicae* (1682), supposed to be carried by the Oxford bargemen from the university press had been held up by works on the river and the repair of turnpikes.[57]

The extent of the trade in foreign books, historical and otherwise, at the end of the seventeenth century is illustrated especially well in the accounts of one publisher and bookseller, Thomas Bennet of Oxford, and his successor Henry Clements, who belonged to a powerful "knot" or conger and between them ran an import/export trade in books between Oxford and the continent, in particular to The Netherlands, from the 1680s and 1719.[58] Much of their trade consisted of foreign books, particularly Dutch- and French-printed volumes. So dominant had Dutch philology proved through most of the seventeenth century, the golden age of Vossius, Grotius, and Gronovius (and of great scholarly publishing houses such as the Elzeviers), that England was a heavy importer of such works.[59] Trade both ways was overwhelmingly

[55] Bodl. MS Smith 46, fos. 59–60; cf. ibid., fos. 69–72 for further communications breakdowns.
[56] Bodl. MS Ballard 20 (Charlett letters), fo. 151r–v, Clark to Charlett, 10 May 1720.
[57] Bodl. MS Eng. lett. c. 28, fo. 64r; MS c. 29, fos. 2r, 69r.
[58] Norma Hodgson and Cyprian Blagden, *The Notebook of Thomas Bennet and Henry Clements (1686–1719)*, Oxford Bibliog. Soc., n.s. 6 (1953). Appendix 5, which lists alphabetically all the books bought by Bennet (1664–1706) and his apprentice and eventual successor after 1706, Clements (1686–1719). Bennet was the printer of Wood's *Athenae Oxonienses* (2 vols., 1691–92), over which there arose a libel suit when Wood charged that Bennet had changed the text (see *The Life and Times of Anthony Wood, antiquary, of Oxford, 1632–1695*, ed. A. Clark (5 vols., Oxford Hist. Soc., 1891–1900), IV, 18).
[59] Bennet's records give only his out-going correspondence to his continental contacts. For the reverse side, letters from various continental publishers to an English distributor, see the correspondence, mainly in Latin, of Samuel Smith (printer to the Royal Society), in Bodl. Rawl. lett. 114, on which see Marja Smolenaars and Ann Veenhoff, "Samuel Smith, 'an

in unbound books, which wealthier buyers preferred because they could have them bound to taste.[60] Bound volumes were also less easily packaged and bore higher duties, though occasionally they too were exported or imported. Bennet apologized to the Leipzig merchants George Weidman and J. L. Gleditsch for having to send bound copies of John Speed's *Historie of Great Britaine*, Elias Ashmole's *The institution, laws & ceremonies of the most noble Order of the Garter*, and others because they had not been available in sheets for many years: they were, as we would say, out of print.[61] The items traded included a large number of classical texts, as one might expect in a university town, such as the six copies each of Nepos and Quintus Curtius that Bennet received from the Waesberghes of Amsterdam and Danzig in 1686, along with what looks very much like a "special order," a three-volume folio set of Eusebius' works. Some items crossed the channel more than once: unsold copies of a number of books, including Louis Moréri's *Great Historical, Geographical and Poetical Dictionary*, were returned to continental dealers for refund in the 1690s.

Bennet kept his contacts informed of English books that they might be interested in adding to their lists, advising Weidman and Gleditsch in July 1706 of the imminent publication of *A complete history of England*.[62] Matters of readership tastes emerge as well from Bennet's letters. "I will have also some more of ye Hofmanni Lexicon, and Antiq: Romanorum," Bennet wrote to the Leiden publisher Pieter van der Aa in 1699, adding the postscript that "Gronovii Antiquit: Graec: is not well liked in England yet."[63] His

Honest Enough Man, for a Bookseller,'" *Antiquarian Book Monthly* (February 1997), 36–39. Smith ran an even larger operation than Bennet, and would commission foreign booksellers to look for copies, sometimes multiple, of books for which he thought there was demand, or he would buy new books, sometimes in large quantities. Books from the continent were often cheaper because paper was expensive in England. For instance, the Booksellers' Guild of Amsterdam fixed rates for up to 100 copies of Leclerc's *Dictionnaire historique*, quoted to Smith by his Dutch contact Pieter van der Aa of Leiden; sometimes price was quoted per sheet. In turn, judging by Bennet's letters, Dutch sellers were often offered English stock at below the trade price to English sellers: see remarks by Hodgson and Blagden in *Notebook of Thomas Bennet and Henry Clements*, pp. 16–17.

[60] Thus William Stratford, at Christ Church, wrote to Edward Lord Harley on 15 December 1714 to ask him to make enquiries at Cambridge as to Joshua Barnes' *History of Edward III*, a work sold only by the author in his lifetime, and specifically requesting a copy in sheets while willing, if necessary, to accept it bound: Hist. MSS Comm., *Portland*, VII, 210–11. For Barnes' earlier misadventures with this book, see below, p. 292.

[61] *Notebook of Thomas Bennet and Henry Clements*, p. 24.

[62] Ibid., p. 46; cf. notice of this publication in *TC*, III, 513.

[63] *Notebook of Thomas Bennet and Henry Clements*, p. 48 (Bennet to Pieter van der Aa, Leiden, 7 February 1698/99); P. G. Hoftijzer, "The Leiden Bookseller Pieter van der Aa (1659–1733) and the International Book Trade," in C. Berkvens-Stevelinck, *et al.* (eds.), *Le Magasin de l'univers: the Dutch Republic as the Centre of the European Book Trade* (Leiden and New York, 1992), pp. 169–84. In 1713 van der Aa would become the principal successor to the old Elzevier scholarly publishing empire by buying up a significant amount of its stock from the widow of Abraham Elzevier, who died in 1712.

lukewarm reaction to Gronovius' important book may have been a negotiat-
ing ploy, since on 28 July 1699 Bennet requested two sets of Graevius'
Thesaurus Romanorum Antiquitatum, and asked van der Aa for a price on
the Gronovius. Graevius was apparently selling reasonably well, and on 22
August Bennet put in a request for the *Thesaurus* on large paper. He was
reasonably optimistic that once Gronovius' book, the twelfth and final
volume of which had yet to be printed, was complete, he would be able to sell
the volumes he had on hand, ordering two copies from van der Aa on 2
January 1701/2.[64] The correspondence also reminds us that because English
booksellers were net importers, there were inevitable complaints of trade
surpluses. Bennet was obliged to issue frequent nagging reminders to van der
Aa that the Leiden publisher had agreed to spend at least half as much in
buying English books from Bennet as the Englishman spent in importing
from van der Aa.[65] Some of the books Bennet proved successful in selling
abroad included the 1695 edition of *Camden's Britannia*, Thomas Smith's
edition of Camden's *Epistolae*, and Wood's *Athenae Oxonienses*, of which
Bennet was also the publisher.[66]

"THIS BOOK SHOULD BE IN EVERY ENGLISHMAN'S HAND": SERIAL PUBLICATION

It is easy, in the era of Visa and American Express cards, and seductive
running accounts at Blackwell's, to spend large sums of money for dozens of
books at a time without worrying especially about paying for them for a
while. This was also true for much of the readership of history books in the
seventeenth century, since lines of credit with booksellers permitted more
affluent readers from Pepys to Robert Harley to settle accounts at half-yearly

---

[64] *Notebook of Thomas Bennet and Henry Clements*, pp. 49, 59. On 22 August 1699 Bennet
expressed concern to van der Aa that he would be unable to sell the *Thesaurus Antiquitatum
Graecum*, but was willing to try for two or three months and then either send the books back
or the money if sold. See also same to same 23 February 1699/1700, p. 54.

[65] Ibid., p. 62. Hodgson and Blagden's appendix gives three prices for books listed: the price
paid by Bennet; the trade price (to other English sellers) and the advertised retail price. Books
were sometimes bartered between the printers and publishers, but for a higher price than in
cash. Retail price in Bennet's trade was up to a third again as much as the trade price. The
overall value of book imports and exports, estimated by Hodgson and Blagden (based on
ledgers of the inspector general of customs in the PRO and excluding maps, prints and any
trade with Turkey), from Michaelmas 1696 to Christmas 1704, and Christmas 1705 to
Christmas 1706 suggest imports from all countries totaled £1237 15s 8d (Michaelmas
1696–Michaelmas 1697), and £2041 3s. 10d. (Michaelmas 1697–Michaelmas 1698), a
pattern which continued. Samuel Smith was also, heavily, a net importer of books from van
der Aa: Hoftijzer, "Pieter van der Aa," p. 176, further evidence that the trade in upper-end
Latin scholarly books (both antiquarian/philological, and scientific) was still dependent on
foreign printers.

[66] Among books Bennet ordered (5 April 1700) was Camden's edition of medieval chronicles,
the *Anglica, Normanica, Hibernica, Cambrica, a veteribus scripta* (Frankfurt, 1603).

or yearly intervals. This was less likely to assist with the dissemination of books further down the economic and social ladder, where a book bought often meant foregoing something more urgent. Since authors and publishers were anxious to promote their intellectual wares to as wide a paying audience as possible, there was need of some strategy to make books available to a less prosperous clientele. Abridgments and epitomes, as we have seen in previous chapters, had long been one approach used to get around this problem. Stow's Elizabethan *Chronicles* and *Annales* existed in versions of differing lengths, and various summaries or compendia of successful but expensive works such as Foxe's *Acts and Monuments* and Ralegh's *History of the World* had also appeared from time to time. This did not answer the problem of how to get the "real thing," the full-scale, lengthy history or antiquarian work, on to the shelves of those too poor to buy them outright.

In 1678 an anticatholic propagandist named Henry Care published a weekly journal entitled *The Weekly Pacquet of Advice from Rome*, which, with some interruptions prompted by its often inflammatory contents, continued until 1683. This was virtually the first example of a book broken down into separate, numbered fascicules designed to be sold cheaply and collected in volumes by readers, thereby inaugurating the serially published book. This marketing tactic had a bright future in the eighteenth and nineteenth centuries, when publishers of a succession of novelists from Fielding to Dickens and Trollope would make use of it. What is often overlooked, and was even unrecognized in R. M. Wiles' still-indispensable account of early serial publication, is that Care's antipapal polemic, subtitled *The History of Popery*, was in fact a history book, deliberately broken down into instalments to give it a mass circulation and only afterwards collected together into book form. As Care himself put it, "most of these successive sheets have fallen into many thousand hands, who were never like to meet with the elaborate volumes of better authors, nor would otherwise have had so full a prospect of popery."[67] Care's experiment immediately produced an imitator in a 1680 work entitled *The Weekly Pacquet of Advice from Germany: or, The History of the Reformation of Religion There*. There were only two more serial publications before the end of the century, and a few more in the reign of Anne. But the trick worked, and near the end of George I's reign, it really began to take off as a marketing and distribution ploy. Together with abridgments, compendia, and almanacs, the serial publication method

---

[67] Henry Care, *The Weekly Pacquet*, 3 vols. (1682), III, sig. b (preface to vol. III). I am indebted to Lois G. Schwoerer to drawing my attention to Care's book and for sharing some of the results of her research on him prior to publication; in the meantime, see James Sutherland, *The Restoration Newspaper and its Development* (Cambridge and New York, 1986), pp. 85, 190, 193, 204.

played an important part in getting history into the hands of most of the reading public.[68]

What publishers and booksellers soon discovered was that as effective a tool as serialization was for religious works, poetry, romances, plays, and eventually novels, it was almost ideally suited to the history book. Or perhaps more accurately, the history book was ideally suited to serial publication, since the need to fill weeklies with enough material to keep them above the cut-off length of the first (1712–25) Stamp Duty in itself generated a paper vacuum that required filling with more than advertisements. Even after the revised, 1725 duty forced a change of format with some loss of space, readers were by now used to something more than news and announcements, and history, along with poetry, essays, and fiction fitted the bill – it was for this purpose that James Read would print snippets of Burnet's *History of his Own Time* in his *Weekly Journal* in 1734. The principal rivals to the weekly journals, the newer periodicals of the 1730s like the *Gentleman's Magazine*, which eluded the 1725 duty, would follow suit.[69]

Historical titles of various kinds – grand surveys of national history, newer genres like the historical atlas, ambitious universal histories, collective or individual biographies, and even some county antiquarian works – would all be serialized between 1678 and 1739. Even if one counts the histories conservatively and discounts parahistorical works like Batty Langley's *Ancient Masonry, both in Theory and Practice* (1733), history dominates the early list of number books: of the 211 published from 1678 to 1739 inclusive, eighty-nine were historical.[70] And this figure does not take into account the inclusion of sheets of serialized history in newspapers and pamphlets, which were not designed to be kept and bound into volumes but which nevertheless provided another conduit of historical knowledge into private households. As Eustace Budgell, editor of *The Bee*, correctly predicted in commenting on the release of Voltaire's *Charles XII*, in Saturday instalments, that it would be only a matter of time before the same treatment was given to Rapin-Thoyras, Josephus, Ralegh, Plutarch, and Bayle.[71] And, as another writer remarked in the *London Journal* in criticizing the reprinting of extracts of Vertot's *Revolutions of Portugal* in the pages of *Fog's Weekly Journal* (in an

---

[68] Serial publication only really begins to take off in 1724–25 and even more strongly after 1732. Most of the works so published thus fall outside the chronological boundaries of the study. The indispensable but aging work on the subject is R. M. Wiles, *Serial Publication in England Before 1750* (Cambridge, 1957), from which this section is largely drawn. Wiles of course recognized the *fact* that Care's book was a history but he makes little comment throughout his book on the dominance of history among works published serially.

[69] Sutherland, *The Restoration Newspaper*, p. 35; J. A. Downie, *Robert Harley and the Press: Propaganda and Public Opinion in the Age of Swift and Defoe* (Cambridge, 1979), pp. 149–61.

[70] Figures derived from Wiles, *Serial Publication*, appendix B, pp. 267–320.

[71] Eustace Budgell, *The Bee: or Universal Weekly Pamphlet* (February 1733), 29.

apparent parabolic incitement to rebellion against the Excise Tax), "these Weekly Journals are not wrote merely to Retail old History; no, the Weapons of their Warfare are Allegories, Fables, Parables, Hieroglyphicks, and parallel history."[72] The use of history as political parable by Bacon, Cotton, and others a century before was alive and well and living in a different media universe.

There were some limitations on the application of serialization to the history book. It required an even greater investment of funds by a publisher up front, despite the prospect of greater sales. In addition to paying an author or translator, money had to be spent on illustrations, on proposals to print, and on announcements in newspapers and other types of advertising. The case of Dennis de Coetlogon may serve as illustration. De Coetlogon, a foreigner who billed himself as "Chevalier," was imprisoned for several weeks in Newgate in 1737. Anxious to avoid returning there as a debtor, he sought a "royal license" for the publication of his very expensive *Universal History of Arts and Sciences*, which, when granted, allowed him to bill the book as published "By His Majesty's Command"; at the same time, he had each weekly number of this work, which appeared over six years, entered in the Stationers' Register. This double safeguard was essential given his having spent "upwards of one thousand pounds" on assembling, printing, and advertising the book. Such licenses, advertised in newspapers and reprinted in some of the numbers, prohibited abridgments and unapproved reprints for fourteen years and signaled royal protection of the compilation from piracy.

The same was true with another serialized work, the hugely ambitious *An Universal History, from the Earliest Account of Time to the Present* published in twenty volumes in the middle years of the eighteenth century. Initiated in 1729 with a proposal printed in the *Monthly Chronicle*, it was collected from "the best authors" by several contributors, including George Sale, John Campbell, and the notorious charlatan known as George Psalmanazar. Its first number appeared in May 1730, three months behind schedule, with five of the original eight proprietors having withdrawn even before then, and Sale having been ousted from the project by the booksellers. The first full volume was complete only five years later, in twelve numbers. The shares in the project would continue to change hands. James Crokatt, who may have been the originator and was certainly the director of the first volumes, stayed on for twelve years before he found that his shaky business could no longer sustain the project; he withdrew in 1742. This massive series would also be protected by a royal license granted in 1739, but while that was a guard against piracy it helped neither production nor distribution. In fact, it had little effect on the pirates either – two octavo editions appeared in

[72] Remarks from the *London Gazette*, reprinted in Budgell, *The Bee* (February 1733), 109.

Dublin in 1744 and 1745 respectively, and it took a response in the form of a cheap octavo to preserve the market for the English syndicate. As we will see, this episode also tells us something about the other major marketing tactic of the period, subscription.[73]

Another limitation on serialization is suggested both by the titles chosen and by the frequent phrase "compiled from the best authors." It was not the tactic of choice for new works, for which subscription was more dependable, but mainly a way of republishing older titles for a newer, less wealthy audience who might be familiar with the name of a book by reputation. Clarendon's *History of the Rebellion*, as it appeared in 1702–4, might have been a good candidate but was not serialized, perhaps because the topic and the author were so marketable as to make the extra investment on advertising unnecessary, or because of the 1703 publication of John Nutt's abridged edition in London. Instead, among historical works (and most other kinds also), three sorts of book tended to be serialized: translations of foreign and especially French histories (many of these by the Reverend Nicholas Tindal), including works by Augustin Calmet (1724), Claude Fleury (1726), Antonio de Herrera y Tordesillas (1725), François Catrou and Pierre Julien Rouille (1725), Jacques Lenfant, (1728), Jacques-Auguste de Thou (1728), and Pierre Bayle (1733); reprints or new editions of old reliable domestically authored histories from the Elizabethan and early Stuart period such as Foxe's *Acts and Monuments* (1733), Herbert of Cherbury's *Henry VIII* (1740), Ralegh's *History of the World* (1735), Camden's *Britannia* (1733), and the Undead of seventeenth-century historiography, Baker's *Chronicle* – on its way to being a fossilized fixture in Squire Western's rustic library – and, finally, a few more recent titles like Burnet's *History of the Reformation* (1733). Some of these were so successful that they were reissued in new series – Care's original 1678 *Weekly Pacquet* reappeared in threepenny numbers as *The History of Popery* in 1735, and Ralegh's may have been redone as a supplement to the *Hereford Journal* in 1739. Many of the compilations were little better than the older abridgments and compendia. Tobias Smollett, most famously, was paid three guineas a sheet for writing the 332 sheets (eleven volumes) of his *History of England*, published by James Rivington and James Fletcher in 1758; in addition he received £500 for revisions and corrections, and the publishers also had to spend £300 on advertising and a further £200 on printing proposals.[74]

The translations were difficult to control since the copyright act was ambiguous on that subject, permitting one publisher to commission what

[73] Guido Abbattista, "The Business of Paternoster Row: Towards a Publishing History of the *Universal History* (1736–65)," trans. Elizabeth P. Danieli, in *Publishing History*, 17 (1985), 5–50. [74] Wiles, *Serial Publication*, pp. 5–6.

THE
HISTORY
OF
ENGLAND,
AS WELL
Ecclesiastical as Civil.

BY
Mr. De Rapin Thoyras.

VOL. I.

CONTAINING

I. The PREFACE, with a brief Account of the Author's Life, and a DISSERTATION concerning the
Origin and Nature of the ENGLISH CONSTITUTION.
II. A short INTRODUCTION concerning the Manners,
Customs, Government, and Religion of the antient Britons, with the Origin of the Picts and Scots, and
the Time of their Settlement in Britain.
III. The History of ENGLAND from the Invasion
of the Romans to the End of the Reign of Edward the Martyr, in four Books.

Done into ENGLISH from the FRENCH, with
large and useful NOTES mark'd with an *, by
N. TINDAL, A. M. Vicar of Great-
Waltham in Essex.

LONDON:

Printed for JAMES and JOHN KNAPTON at
the Crown in St. Paul's Church-Yard. M DCC XXVII.

Facing the Title.

Mr. DE RAPIN THOYRAS

Vertue sculp.

Plate 6.17   The first version of a successful serialized work of history, Paul de Rapin-Thoyras' *The history of England, as well ecclesiastical as civil*, translated by Nicholas Tindal, 15 vols. (1728–32), vol. I.

amounted to a countertranslation of a foreign history already in progress elsewhere. In 1725, for instance, rival translations of Catrou and Rouille's *Histoire romaine, depuis la fondation de Rome* into English, by Richard Bundy and John Ozell respectively, appeared from two different publishing syndicates.[75] The same fate awaited Pierre Bayle's celebrated *Historical and Critical Dictionary* in 1733. Between 1728 and 1732, the most popular *History of England* of the first third of the eighteenth century appeared, that by Paul de Rapin-Thoyras (plate 6.17), translated by Nicholas Tindal, rector of Great Waltham and master of the Royal Free School at Chelmsford. James and John Knapton had finished the publication of Tindal's version of Rapin-Thoyras in monthly octavo numbers, bound in fifteen volumes, when trouble struck. The appearance in weekly sixpenny numbers of a rival translation by one John Kelly of the Inner Temple, from a printer named James Mechell, threatened to destroy their market. They responded with a folio version of Tindal's translation, to be issued in weekly fascicules and to amount eventually to two folio volumes of 400 sheets, worth £2 2s. Despite their rival's head start, they were able to win the war on the basis of advertising and the generally more favorable reviews of Tindal's version, of which one reviewer commented in the *London Journal*, "This Book should be in every Englishman's Hand."[76] The success inspired the Knaptons to commission a continuation by Tindal, again issued serially beginning in 1736. In such a way did the single most commercially successful history mentioned in the present work reach, if not *every* Englishman's hands, at least many more than nearly all its predecessors; it would take no less a talent than David Hume to knock Rapin-Thoyras off his pedestal.[77]

Religious history was also successfully serialized. Foxe's *Acts and Monuments* already had a very long life as the vehicle of Elizabethan and early Stuart protestant consciousness, initially directed primarily against Rome and Madrid. Influential in the lower-literacy climate of the pre-civil war era through its woodcuts, it probably would not have needed serialization to ensure continued life in the eighteenth century, since the new enemy, France, had similar catholic associations, now overlaid with newer fears of Jacobite subversion and universal monarchy. Nevertheless late in 1732 it began to appear in threepenny instalments, which readers could order by subscription.[78] The blurb published by a Smithfield printer expresses as powerfully as

[75] Ibid., pp. 98, 106.
[76] Plomer, iv, 166; *London Journal*, 696 (8 October 1732), cited in Wiles, *Serial Publication*, p. 108.
[77] Hugh Trevor-Roper, "A Huguenot Historian: Paul Rapin," in Irene Scouloudi (ed.), *Huguenots in Britain and their French Background, 1550–1800* (1987), pp. 3–19.
[78] Margaret Aston and Elizabeth Ingram, "The Iconography of the *Acts and Monuments*," in David Loades (ed.), *John Foxe and the English Reformation* (Aldershot, 1997), pp. 66–142. For the career of Foxe's book in the eighteenth century, see Eirwen Nicholson, "Eighteenth-

the reviews of Rapin-Thoyras the aim of getting the work into as many, and poorer, hands as possible. "The purchase of so voluminous a work cannot be reached by everyone's purse at once; and therefore this expedient was resolved on, of publishing a certain number of sheets weekly, by subscription, that the common people might be also enabled by degrees to procure it."[79] A competitor assembled by one Harry Lyndar of the Inner Temple under the title *A Book of Martyrs the Best Preservative against Popery* also appeared at the same time. Older works of sacred history, such as those of Josephus, appeared in serial form, as did newer ones like Gilbert Burnet's *History of the Reformation*, Thomas Stackhouse's *History of the Bible*, and Strype's *Annals of the Reformation of the Church of England*.[80]

Finally, antiquarian works were also serially issued, though with somewhat less success than political histories. In 1711, Herman Moll's 1708 *Atlas Geographus* was issued as numbers in five volumes, with a one-volume supplement on British geography and historical topography by the Revd Anthony Hall of Queen's College, Oxford and a printer named Thomas Cox. The supplement soon outgrew its home, overwhelmed by communications from local gentry providing information about their counties. The *Magna Britannia*, as this work became known, ended up as a separate serial in its own right. It was a kind of super-Camden for the early eighteenth-century reader, adding to the 1695 Gibson edition of *Britannia* (itself to be serialized later, in 1733, as a supplement to the *British Observator*) in "a more large History, not only of the Cities, Boroughs, Towns, and Parishes, mentioned by them, but also of many other Places of Note, and Antiquities since discovered." It would also stretch to include a complete chronology of events under Britons, Romans, Saxons, Danes, and Normans, the lives of bishops and martyrs, parliamentary acts, and the "pedigrees of all our noble families and gentry." All this was to come from "the best Relations extant," collected by the "impartial hand" of Anthony Hall. It was indeed another compilation, not an original work of scholarship, but in terms of the dissemination of historical learning, that is not the point. Buy this, its lengthy subtitle implies, and you will need no other work on such matters.

Even county antiquarian studies could be produced serially, though they are not as prominent as political and religious histories. Nathaniel Salmon, who had already unsuccessfully serialized *The Lives of the English Bishops, from the Restauration to the Revolution* in 1731, ventured a *History and Antiquities of Essex* in 1739–40, but this failed to complete its projected

---

Century Foxe: Evidence for the Impact of the *Acts and Monuments* in the 'Long Eighteenth Century,'" ibid., pp. 143–77.

[79] Listed in *Gentleman's Magazine* (January 1733); printer's remark quoted in Linda Colley, *Britons* (New Haven and London, 1992), pp. 25–26.

[80] Wiles, *Serial Publication*, pp. 109–13, 129, 157–58, 291.

twenty-one one-shilling numbers when its author discovered he could not cover the entire county in that space; it did not help, as the Essex antiquary Philip Morant commented to Richard Gough, that his transcriptions of source material were inaccurate.[81] Nicholas Tindal, whose previous experiences with writing history for serialization had prospered, misfired when he, too, attempted a *History of Essex* in 1732, again at the instigation of the Knaptons, and using the papers given him by the son of the now-dead antiquary William Holman, as noted in the previous chapter. The book, intended to fill three volumes, was to be sold in seven-sheet quarto numbers priced at 1s 6d a number; it was advertised as available not only in London, from the Knaptons, but also from booksellers in Chelmsford, Norwich, Bury St. Edmunds, Halsted, Ipswich, Saffron Walden, Braintree, Colchester, and "the rest of the towns of Essex." In the end, only two numbers appeared. Francis Blomefield fared slightly better in initiating his own *Essay towards a Topographical History of the County of Norfolk* in 1736, but he died in 1752 before the last volume was complete.[82]

HISTORY BY SUBSCRIPTION

Although examples occur much earlier in the seventeenth century, it was late in the Restoration that authors, faced with increasingly cost-conscious printers and booksellers, first began regularly to issue "proposals" in advance of the publication of works, inviting prospective buyers to sign up for their copies early, and thereby guarantee jittery publishers a minimum level of sales, or alternatively bypass them altogether.[83] By 1701, about thirty-five books had been issued by subscription, and numbers rose rapidly thereafter; in the 1720s alone, 222 books were so published. Historical and antiquarian works were among the earliest books offered by subscription. In 1673, for instance, Aylett Sammes advertised his *Britannia Antiqua Illustrata* in the *Term Catalogues* as "ready for the press." The book came out three years later, sold initially by the author himself and then by the bookseller Robert Clavell, who picked up the unsold copies and issued them at £1 6s bound.[84] Sammes was followed very quickly by the herald Francis Sandford in 1677, with his *Genealogical History of the Kings and Queens of England* (1677, and eventually reissued by subscription in Samuel Stebbing's 1707 revision) (plate 6.18) and a few years later by William Howell; the third and fourth volumes of the second edition of Howell's *Institution of General History*

[81] Ibid., p. 93; John Nichols (ed.), *Literary Anecdotes of the Eighteenth Century* (9 vols., 1812) II, 706.   [82] Wiles, *Serial Publication*, pp. 93, 119–20, 233, 286, 319.
[83] E.g., proposals for printing the history, re. Sir Henry Chauncy's *Historical Antiquities of Hertfordshire* (1700; Wing C3742), which involved five booksellers at the subscription stage.
[84] TC, I, 159, 235, 264.

The NAMES of the SUBSCRIBERS to this Edition of the Genealogical Hiſtory of the Kings and Queens of *England*, to the Year 1707.

The PATRONS of the New CUTS.

THE Moſt Illuſtrious Princeſs, the Princeſs *Sophia* Electoreſs and Dutcheſs-Dowager of *Brunſwick-Lunenburgh* ; the Mauſoleum of King *James* the Firſt.

The Moſt Serene Prince, *George-Auguſt* Prince-Electoral of *Brunſwick-Lunenburgh* ; the Plate of Medals of the Moſt Serene Electoral Family.

The Moſt Reverend Father in God, *Thomas* Lord Arch-Biſhop of *Canterbury* ; the Mauſoleum Plate of Queen *Mary* the Second.

The Right Honourable the Earl of *Godolphin* Lord High-Treaſurer of *England* ; the Mauſoleum Plate of *Mary* Queen of *England*, Wiſe of King *Charles* the Firſt.

The Right Honourable the Earl of *Nottingham* ; the Great-Seal of King *Charles* the Second.

The Right Honourable the Lord *Guilford* ; the Great-Seal of King *James* the Second.

The Right Honourable the Lord *Somers* ; the Great-Seal of King *William* and Queen *Mary*.

The Right Honourable Sir *Nathan Wright* Kt. ſometime Lord Keeper of the Great-Seal of *England* ; the Great-Seal of King *William* the Third.

The Right Honourable the Earl of *Marchmont* ; the Great-Seal of Queen *Anne*, before the Union of the Two Kingdoms.

The Right Honourable the Lord *Cowper*, Lord High-Chancellor of *Great Britain* ; Her Majeſty's Great-Seal, as Queen of *Great Britain*.

Private PLATES.

Her Grace the Dutcheſs-Dowager of *Beaufort* ; the Plate of His Grace the late Duke of *Beaufort*'s Monument at *Windſor*.

The Reverend and Honourable *Robert-Lumley Lloyd*, Clerk ; the Plate of the Monument of *John* Lord *Lumley*.

Chriſtopher Rawlinſon Eſq; the Plate of the Monument of Mr. Searj. *Rawlinſon*.

A.

HIS Grace the Duke of St. *Albans*.
Edward Alexander, of *Doctors Commons*, *Lond*. Gent.
The Reverend Mr. *Richard Allen*, Fellow of *Sidny-College* in *Cambridge*.
Mr. *William Allingham*, Teacher of the Mathematicks.
Joſeph Aſton Eſq;
Mr. *James Anderſon*, Writer to Her Majeſty's Signet in *Scotland*.
Edward Arblaſter of *Lyzedgein Longdon* in Com. *Staff*. Eſq;
John Atherton of *Totneſs* in Com. *Devon*, Gent.
Mr. *Maurice Atkins*, Bookſeller.

B.

The Moſt Noble *Henry* Duke of *Beaufort* ; Four Royal Books.
The Moſt Noble *Wriotheſly* Duke of *Bedford* ; One Royal Book.
The Right Honourable the Lord *Bruce*, Son and Heir-Apparent to the Earl of *Ailesbury*.
The Right Honourable *Charles* Earl of *Berkeley* ; Two Royal Books.
Sir *Edward Bagot* of *Blithfield*, *Staffordſhire*, Bar. One Royal Book, and One of the Small Paper.
John Baſſet of *Umberleigh* and *Heanton-Court*, *Devonſh*. Eſq;
Mr. *John Barnes*, Bookſeller.
Allen Bathurſt of *Battleſden* in *Bedfordſhire*, Eſq;
Mr. *Benj. Barker*, Bookſeller.
Robert Baylis of *London*, Gent.
Robert Bellaſis Eſq;
Robert Baker of *Doctors Commens*, *Lond*. Gent.
Bryan Bentham of *Chatham* in *Kent*, Gent.
Jeremiah Bentham of *London*, Gent.
Thomas Bernard of the *Inner Temple*, *Lond*. Gent.
John Bardardiſton of *London*, Gent.
Mr. *Phil Biſhop*, Bookſeller in *Exeter*.
Edward Blount Eſq;

Mr. *Bettely* of *Lewiſham*, *Kent*.
Samuel Bohume of *Doctors-Commons*, *Lond*. Gent.
Mr. *Jonah Bowyer*, Bookſeller.
Mr. *Daniel Brown*, Bookſeller.
Rupert Browne of *Doctors-Commons*, *Lond*. Gent.
Charles Battely Eſq;
John Burton of *London*, Gent.
Mr. *John Buſhel*, Grocer.

C.

The Right Honourable *Hugh* Lord *Clifford* of *Chudleigh* in *Devonſhire*.
The Right Honourable the Lord *Coningsby*.
Sir *Henry Carew* of *Haccomb* in *Devonſhire*, Bar.
Mr. *Thomas Chapman*, Bookſeller.
Col. *Robert Child* of *Lincolns-Inn-Fields*.
Alex. Choke of the City of *Weſtm*. Gent.
James Cholmley Eſq;
Thomas Clowne Eſq;
Aunſham Churchill Eſq;
Mr. *Robert Clavel*, Bookſeller.
Mr. *Henry Clements*, Bookſeller in *Oxon*.
Mr. *Francis Coggan*, Bookſeller.
Sir *John Cooke* Kt. Dean of the *Arches-Court* of *Canterbury*, and Clerk of the *Pipe*.
John Cottle of *Doctors-Commons*, *Lond*. Gent.
Mr. *Samuel Crouch*, Bookſeller.
Richard Curtis of *Eltham* in *Kent*, Gent.

D.

The Right Honourable the Lady *Mary* Counteſs of *Derwentwater*.
Mr. *Thomas Davis*.
Simon Deg of *Derby* Town in Com. *Derb*. Gent.
John Diſney Eſq;
Richard Duck Gent.

E.

The Right Honourable the Earl of *Eſſex*.
Devereux Edgar of *Ipſwich* in *Suffolk*, Eſq; Juſtice of Peace;
John Edgcomb of *Aveton-Gifford* in Com. *Devon*, A. M.
Everard Exton of *Doctors-Commons*, *Lond*. Eſq;
Charles Eyſton Eſq; at *Eaſt-Hendred* in *Berks*.

F.

The Rt. Hon. *Robert* Lord *Ferrers* ; One Royal Book.
William Fowler of *St. Thomas* in *Staffordſh*. Eſq;
Mr. *William Freeman*, Bookſeller.
Rowland Fryth of *Thornes* near *Lichfield* in *Staffordſh*, Eſq;
Mowbray Herald of Arms Extraordinary.

G.

The Right Noble *Henry Grey* Marquis of *Kent*, Ld. Chamberlain of Her Majeſty's Houſhold , a Royal Book.
The Right Honourable *John* Lord *Granvile*, Baron of *Potheridge* ; a Royal Book.
Thomas Gardiner Gent. Keeper of Her Majeſty's Small Guns within the Tower of *London*.
The Honourable Sir *Gilbert Gerard* Bar.
The Reverend *John Gery* D.D. of *Sweepſton*, *Leiceſterſh*.
Thomas Giles of the *Prerogative-Office*, *Lond*. Gent.
Geffrey Glaſier of *Doctors Commons*, *Lond*. Gent.
Mr. *Timothy Goodwin*, Bookſeller.
The Reverend *William Grahme* Dean of *Wells*, Clerk of the Cloſet in Ordinary to Her Majeſty.
The Honourable Major *Granville*.
Mr. *Robert Goſling*, Bookſeller.
Mr. *John Gouge*, Bookſeller.
William Le Grand Eſq;
Mr. *George Grafton* Bookſeller.
Thomas Green of *Weſtminſter*, Eſq; One Royal Book;
Thomas Greenhil of *Kingſtreet*, *Bloomsbury*, Gent.
John Greve of *Romley* in Com. *Stafford*, Gent.
Sir *John Guiſe* of *Rancomb* in Com. *Gloceſter*, Bar.

H.

The Right Honourable *Theophilus* Earl of *Huntingdon* ; one Royal Book.
The Rt. Hon. *Charles* Lord *Halifax* ; one Royal Book.
The Rt. Hon. the Lord *George Howard*,

were printed for his widow, who issued the proposals two years after Howell's death, in 1683.[85]

Subscribers included booksellers, corporations, or private individuals who agreed to take several copies and act as distributors in their locality, while the gentry and nobility whose names dominate the subscription lists of most books generally received unbound or temporarily wrapped sheets that were then given to a binder and often stamped with familial arms or interleaved to allow the owner to annotate the work. When the Society of Antiquaries received its subscribed copy of Strype's new (1720) edition of Stow's *Survey of London* in 1721, the six-guinea price made it among the most expensive of antiquarian works recently printed. The society's treasurer was ordered to have it bound in four volumes with interleaved pages to allow fellows to make corrections and additions, providing another illustration of the continued active involvement of readers in the refashioning and improvement of the texts they read.[86] Charles Leigh urged a provincial bookseller to send him any subscriptions to his *Natural History of Lancashire, Cheshire, Derbyshire*, together with "the coats of arms of the gentlemen that have subscribed," so that Leigh could forward them to his printer in Oxford, where the work was about to go to press.[87] Topographical and geographical works were frequently given custom-designed illustrations of the subscriber's castles or houses, as well as their arms, for instance in Thomas Brodrick's two-volume *A Compleat History of the Late War in the Netherlands* (1713), where the names of special subscribers were marked by a dagger.[88] On occasion, individual engravings within a book could be dedicated to a particular subscriber in exchange for an extra contribution; Richard Rawlinson advised Thomas Hearne that he could increase the profit margin on his editions of antiquarian works "by tying every subscriber to a cutt each besides subscription money."[89]

In addition to issuing separately printed proposals for circulation, would-be authors and publishers made use of the advertising medium provided by

---

[85] *TC*, I, 461; Sarah L. C. Clapp, "Subscription Publishers Prior to Jacob Tonson," *The Library*, 4th series, 13 (1932–33), 158–83, at p. 167.   [86] SAL, Minute Book 1718–32, pp. 40–41.
[87] Bodl. MS Don. d. 89, fo. 19, Charles Leigh, in London, to a Mr. Whitworth, Leeds bookseller, 21 May 1700; this is perhaps the John Whitworth active in Manchester 1697–1727: Plomer, iii, p. 311.
[88] P. J. Wallis, "Book Subscription Lists," *The Library*, 5th series 29 (1974), 255–86, at p. 258; F. G. Robinson and P. J. Wallis, *Book Subscription Lists: a Revised Guide* (1975).
[89] Rawlinson, quoted in Pollard and Ehrman, *Distribution of Books by Catalogue*, p. 186.

Plate 6.18 (*opposite*) Subscription list to Samuel Stebbing's revised edition of Francis Sandford, *Genealogical History of the Kings of England* (1707); the first edition of Sandford's work (1677) was among the earliest historical works published by subscription.

catalogs and periodicals. The catalogs put out by John Wilford in the 1720s, discussed in chapter 5 above, frequently contained proposals for new books amid the list of just printed and anticipated works. In October 1729, for instance, the *Monthly Catalogue* and *Monthly Chronicle* carried the first extensive proposals for the *Universal History*, a project that typifies both the development of historical interests to this point and the encyclopedic trend of publishing in the early eighteenth century, manifested in volumes such as Kennett's *Complete History of England* and the various dictionaries of history that had appeared in the previous three or four decades.

It hath been justly complain'd, that though the World abounds with books, which pass for *General Histories*, a *General History* is a thing still wanting: for either they do not descend low enough, which is the defect of Sir Walter Raleigh's; or if they do, they seldom go further than the European nations, which is the fault of Dr. Howel's, the most general history extant in English; not to mention several other imperfections in them, for want of the discoveries and improvements which have been made in history, chronology, and geography since their time.

The projectors of this work, oddly anticipating the postmodern sensitivity to eurocentrism, aimed to give the history of every nation separately, "by which means the lesser monarchies and states will be freed from the historical bondage of the greater." They promised to correct errors of chronology and geography, and to give greater credit to "an author who writes the history of the age he lived in, than to one who wrote in the following . . . making an allowance for the partiality of authors, where it may apparently be presumed." Despite their recognition of partiality in their sources, they promised themselves to avoid controversy. A detailed "plan of the universal history" was included in the next, November issue of the *Monthly Catalogue*. The promises of method and scope, beginning with the Flood and proceeding geographically through all the regions of the world, were jauntily optimistic in their aims, though in strictly intellectual terms neither realistic nor especially new. There had been similar calls for "perfect" history going back, via Francis Bacon, to the French Renaissance. By the time the seventh volume of the first part of the *History*, that dealing with antiquity, appeared in 1744, the plan to include previously neglected peoples had been largely abandoned, or at least postponed to the "modern" volumes, some years away from publication. In other respects, this looks like the sort of large-scale project we saw in the heyday of the Elizabethan chronicle, with Holinshed and his associates, now on a grander scale; it is as if Wren or Vanbrugh were closely following the model of a Tudor manor house.

What had changed since the late Renaissance days of Holinshed, la Popelinière, and Bacon is the systematic use of the press deliberately to construct a market for yet another "new, improved" history (plate 6.19), exploiting such recent developments as the establishment of the Regius chairs of history to magnify demand. The initial proposals provided much detail – misleading as it turned out – on the contents of the proposed work and its publication schedule, and they show subscription and serialization working together. Because of the enormous expense involved in producing and buying such a large, multivolume work, the initiating booksellers (a consortium of eight led by James Crokatt and Robert Gosling) intended to ration their buyers to monthly numbers of twenty sheets, trusting in the public to demonstrate an interest, and in the "several gentlemen of figure and learning" who had set the work in motion, to drum up business. Each set of twenty sheets was to retail at three shillings and sixpence; the whole first part, in seven volumes, would sell bound for fourteen guineas, well beyond the pockets of the vast majority. As Guido Abbattista's definitive study of the project shows, the decision to launch a cheaper, octavo version at six guineas for the set, however, significantly expanded the market for the work in the 1740s by appealing to a very different social set.[90]

The *Universal History* is exceptional only in its size and length of time in production. Historical works of considerably less ambition appear with disproportionate prominence in the list of all works for which subscriptions are known to have been taken up to 1730. By that year, 388 works in all subjects had been so printed, if one counts the multiple lists for successive editions of certain works, and of these 128 were works about history, ancient, medieval, or modern, or concerned with antiquities, historical philology, or chorography. This amounts to some 32 percent of all subscribed works and reinforces one recurring theme of the present book, that history was becoming a socially differentiated subject, with overlapping but distinct elite and middling-sort audiences.[91]

Obtaining sufficient subscriptions was especially important in the case of bulky folios, whether completely new titles like Robert Cary's *Paleologia chronica: a Chronological account of ancient time* (1677) or Richard Blome's *Britannia* (1673), an abridgment and synthesis of Camden and other topographical writers. It was also of use in the case of older works where demand for a new edition needed to be tested. The 1684 edition of Foxe's

---

[90] J. Wilford, *The monthly catalogues* (Oct.–Nov. 1729; reprinted, 2 vols., 1964), II 120–24, 135–40; Abbattista, "The Business of Paternoster Row," 7–17. For a rural rector's violent opposition to the universal history see Thomas Allen (rector of Kettering) to the earl and countess of Huntingdon, 14 July 1742: Hist. MSS Comm., *Report on the manuscripts of the late Reginald Rawdon Hastings, Esq.*, 4 vols. (1928–47), III, 35.

[91] Figures derived from F. J. G. Robinson and P. J. Wallis, *Book Subscription Lists: a Revised Guide* (Newcastle-upon-Tyne, 1975); figures are based on a simple count of listed titles and do not include natural history (except works with substantial antiquarian sections, like Plot's *Natural History of Oxfordshire*), nor, insofar as they occur, fictional history and romance (for instance the edition of Don Quixote that had twenty-two "encouragers" in 1700 [Robinson/Wallis, *Subscription Lists*, no. 700MOT]). The count does not include subscription lists disovered by Dr. P. J. Wallis and the PHIBB subsequent to 1975; works on Scottish history are, however, included.

> TO THE
>
> # R E A D E R.
>
> THE Firſt Edition of this GENEALOGICAL HISTORY, was compiled by the Direction and Encouragement of His late Majeſty King *Charles* the Second, of Bleſſed Memory, who very largely Contributed towards the Compleating thereof; and was ſo well Satisfy'd with the Uſefulneſs of the Work, as well as with the Author's Performance, that he graciouſly permitted it the Honour of his Royal Patronage.
>
> The Approbation and Succeſs the Book met with after its Publication, occaſion'd the whole Impreſſion to be ſoon diſpos'd of: And as it has been for ſome Years very Scarce, and much Enquir'd for; ſo, it is preſum'd, an Improv'd Edition will be Acceptable to the Publick. The *Reader* will therefore find a Continuation of the Lives and Reigns of our ſeveral Monarchs from King *Charles* the Second to the preſent Time, and alſo the Genealogies of the Royal Family, and of other Illuſtrious and Noble Families, Deſcended from any of the Royal Branches, according to the beſt Account that could be obtain'd from the ſeveral Noble Perſons concern'd; and where ſuch Accounts could not be procur'd from the preſent Heirs, (which will not appear in above two or three Inſtances) the Deſcents of thoſe Noble Perſons are left (altogether, or much) in the ſame manner, as they were Printed in the former Edition; it being thought more Adviſeable ſo to do, than to infert the Continuation of any Noble Family either Erroneous or Imperfect.
>
> If it be conceiv'd, that the Hiſtorical Relation of the Four laſt Reigns is too Particular, and not exactly agreeable with the Method purſu'd by Mr. *Sandford*: It is anſwer'd, That when the moſt Remarkable Occurrences and Tranſactions, which have happen'd within the laſt Fifty Years, came to be Conſider'd, they appear'd to be more Numerous, and contain'd more Matter, than what paſs'd in a Century before; ſo that it was preſum'd, many of them were too Conſiderable, to be unobſerv'd, and has much Encreas'd the Number of Sheets, above what was deſign'd, when the *Propoſals* were firſt Publiſh'd, for which no further Conſideration can now be expected; and therefore it is humbly hop'd, that this Extraordinary Charge, together with the Difficulties and Delays met with in procuring the Continuation of ſeveral of the Deſcents, will make the SUBSCRIBERS ſome Amends for the ſeeming Tediouſneſs of its Publication.
>
> a　　　　　　　　Whereas

Plate 6.19 (*above and opposite*)　　Justification for a new and "improved" edition of a subscription work, in Samuel Stebbing's edition of Francis Sandford's *Genealogical History* (1707).

Acts and Monuments was heralded by such proposals, as was a new edition of Richard Knolles' *General history of the Turks* updated by Rycaut, and the 1695 Gibson edition of *Camden's Britannia*.[92] An author unwilling to issue proposals for an expensive work was at considerable risk, as Roger Gale warned Ralph Thoresby, who was considering sidestepping the normal

---

[92] *Proposals for subscribing the famous history of the Turks* (1687, Wing K.701); this was followed later that year by a three-volume folio edition produced by four different publishers: TC, II, 210 (Wing K.702, 703, 703A and 703B); *New proposals for printing by subscription, Cambden's Britannia, English: newly translated, with large additions* (1693, Wing C.373).

To the READER.

Whereas it may be Objected by fome, That the Sculptures in this Edition cannot be fo good as thofe in the former : To Satisfie therefore the Curious in this Matter ; All the Old Plates were carefully Revis'd, before they were now Printed ; and where any Defect appear'd, it has been Supplied by the beft Hands.

In this Edition are Added Fourteen New Plates, all well Grav'd, and anfwerable to the others, *viz.* Three Maufoleum's, Six Great-Seals, Three Monuments, One Plate of Medals of the Moft Illuftrious Family of *Brunfwick-Lunenburgh*, and One fmall Plate of the Effigies of Our Late Sovereigns, and of Her Prefent Majefty, which were not in the Firft Edition ; fo that the whole Number of Sculps in this Volume amount to an Hundred and five.

All due Care has been taken in Printing off the feveral Sheets and Cuts, yet fome of them have not pafs'd free from Miftakes ; and therefore fuch as have been made by the Prefs, the *Reader* is Defir'd to Amend by the *Addenda & Corrigenda* at the End of the Book, and likewife any other that may have been Over-look'd or cafually Omitted.

The

---

process of publication and printing his *Ducatus Leodiensis* at his own expense.

I can by no means, however, advise you to run the hazard of printing this work at your own charges; for besides the demand of a great sum of money for paper, printing, &c., which you must part with long before you can hope for any return of advantage, if your book should chance to sell slowly, you would be a very great loser by it. This, indeed, might be obviated by publishing proposals for a subscription, one of which should be, that half the money should be paid down at the time of subscription: and I should not think it very difficult for your friends to procure a sufficient number to set the press at work, and buy paper too. A specimen and proposals might be printed off, and some bookseller at London entrusted with it, to disperse it to Oxford, Cambridge, and other places, where encouragement might be expected. By that means you would see in a little time if you had encouragement enough to go on with it that way: and, if it failed, you might then think of selling the copy to some bookseller, though it would be certainly to great disadvantage. Therefore, I should think the best way would be, to try first what the booksellers would give for it; and, if you thought their proposals worth their acceptance, to close with them without undergoing any further trouble or hazard.[93]

John Strype, who had considerable experience in dealing with booksellers and publishers, not all of it pleasant, offered Thoresby similar advice, suggesting that 500 subscribed copies marked a break point below which most booksellers were unlikely to undertake the printing of a volume.

I know not what method to propose to you in your dealing with a bookseller, for I am not very crafty in it myself. They commonly consider the number of sheets, and thereby compute the charge in paper and printing; and then expect competent gain for their own pains, and offer their reward to the author for his copy proportionable. Some are so honest as to tell you particularly the expenses; and then leave it to the owner of the copy to make his demands. If they have the encouragement of 100 or 150 subscriptions, they will venture to print. If they foresee they may vend 750, they will advance the author's reward. But in printing but 500 they say they make but little advantage. Some authors will be at the whole charge themselves, and allow a bookseller a consideration for selling them. I mention these things; but the best way is to talk with them yourself.[94]

The reception of proposals can give us hints as to the popularity of a genre, or even the reputation of an author. In the case of history, some proposed titles would be lapped up by a thirsty aristocratic or gentry audience, either before or after publication. The collecting activities of Richard Coffin, described in a previous chapter, offer one example. Another is the young Sussex peer John Lord Ashburnham (b. 1687), later first earl, whose cash book for 1711 contains a payment, in the hand of his secretary, to "Mr. Walter" on subscription for a proposal to print "the armes of the baronage of England."[95] In such a case, it is difficult to judge whether the purchase was a mark of real interest or merely the conspicuous expenditure and *noblesse oblige* of a young man who had come into his title only a year previously. Some works would sell so well before and after publication that the publisher would intervene to encourage the preparation of a second edition: this happened in the case of one Augustan "best-seller," Bishop Nicolson's *English Historical Library*.[96]

There is plenty of evidence to indicate that many historical works met with

---

[93] *Thoresby Letters*, II, 254 (Gale to Thoresby, 13 June 1710). Gale proved correct: for Thoresby's bitter complaints about the booksellers' treatment of him, see unpublished letter to Gale, Borthwick Inst. MD 144, unfoliated letter (23 May 1720).

[94] *Thoresby Letters*, II, 271–72 (Strype to Thoresby, 15 September 1710). An undated but preliminary manuscript subscription list for Strype's life of Archbishop Grindal includes only twenty-nine names, each for a single copy: BL MS Lans. 1197 (Strype collections), fo. 16r.

[95] E. Sussex RO (Lewes), Ashburnham MSS, 3000, fo. 16r, 2 June 1711.

[96] *Thoresby Letters*, II, 275 (Nicolson to Thoresby, 9 October 1710).

less enthusiastic responses, though the complaints of authors about publishers, then as now, are often notoriously exaggerated. Browne Willis would complain to his friend Thomas Hearne in 1715 of sluggish sales of the latter's edition of the early Tudor antiquary John Leland's *Collectanea*. Willis, who had signed up for twelve sets of this multivolume work, was now trying to unload them, with the help of his own bookseller, at £3 a set, a relatively expensive book by contemporary standards. His failure to sell them speedily caused him to lament the tastes of the country squire. On 21 July, Willis reported that sales had picked up, and asked Hearne to ensure that the copies were bound before sending them to him, or at least put in paste or parchment wrappers, or else "our country gent. will find it difficult to gett them here bound up." Five days later, however, he wrote back to Hearne in despair, fearing that his market was close to saturation. "I hope to dispose of the 3 I had of you but when I can't tell for I have had one of them turned back on my hands & am only paid for one & that I beleive not so contently. Learning is at a very low ebb amongst our country squires who are not very conversable except att horses & doggs."[97]

Willis' gloom was understandable, and his was far from the only instance of turgid sales of an expensive volume with a limited market, though Hearne's many self-published editions of medieval chronicles sold by subscription in very small print runs did quite well, showing that the publishers were not quite indispensable. John Ogilby, who died just before subscription became a serious option, was less fortunate. Having flirted with economic ruin on a number of occasions, he had often distributed his books through a lottery system. He seemed to have turned the financial corner when, late in life, he was appointed the "King's Cosmographer and Geographic Printer" by Charles II. In 1669 he issued proposals for a new "English Atlas," and in 1675, a year before his death, Ogilby produced this under the title *Britannia*. Despite sharing a name with Camden's more famous work – a marketing ploy that may have backfired – the book proved a commercial disaster, and copies had to be disposed of in yet another lottery after Ogilby's death.[98]

The subscription system alone did not offer salvation. Joseph Morgan, author of a two-volume *Complete History of Algiers* (1728–29) would meet a fate similar to Ogilby's half a century later. Morgan was so distressed at his lack of success in raising subscriptions, and at the failure of several subscribers actually to come up with their funds – only 113 of 266 subscribers had actually paid by the time the first volume was published – that he

[97] Bodl. MS Rawl. lett. 27A, fos. 31r, 34r-v (Willis to Hearne, 21 and 26 July 1715).
[98] "Ogilby's Heir," in *John Ogilby, Cosmographer Royal: Catalogue of a Commemorative Exhibition held at Guildhall Art Gallery* (1976); H. G. Fordham, "John Ogilby (1600–1676), his *Britannia*, and the British Itineraries of the Eighteenth Century," *The Library*, 4th series 6 (1925–26), 157–78; Katherine S. Van Eerde, *John Ogilby and the Taste of his Times* (Folkestone, Kent, 1976), 79–94 on his publishing activities.

included a bitter invective against the whole system of "subscription hunting" in which he lamented that he was "one dwindled to accost, cap in hand, under the scandalous pitiful and contemptible character of subscription hunter. An abject vocation." Although Morgan vowed he would rather be a "hackney horse" than solicit further, he did in fact pursue further subscriptions for the second volume. And pity the case of the Scotsman John Mack Gregory, would-be antiquary and topographer, his career ruined by the subscription system. For some years Gregory had been following his "profession of geography & history & the languages, printing at my own charge a small book of sepulchres, & endeavouring to print by subscription a great book of Turkey." He had given copies of the small book to all the bishops and many other persons of note in England as a way of getting them to subscribe to the book on Turkey. Many of them did, but the price proved too high, and the production too slow, and at the death of the queen in 1714 a flurry of political activity caused his buyers lost interest, driving him back to Edinburgh in poverty, and then to Cambridge, where he pathetically petitioned John Covel for some work.[99] Public preoccupation with politics had previously harmed the subscription plans of Edward Lhwyd around the time of Queen Anne's succession. Bishop William Nicolson's complaint to Ralph Thoresby of slow subscriptions to proposals by Lhwyd seem only too reminiscent of the Renaissance and modern topos of public indifference to higher learning. "By the attempt I have made for subscriptions, I have reason to fear that the encouragement his work meets with will be somewhat cool. The nation is distracted with politics and intrigue; and every thing that looks towards the advancement of learning droops and is out of countenance," Nicolson observed pessimistically. "This honest man must be supported some way or other; and pains we must take to serve him."[100]

John Strype was similarly skittish about the prospects of his own *Annals of the Reformation and Establishment of Religion*. "It will make about one hundred and fifty sheets in folio; so that the bookseller is loth to venture upon it without a subscription." He asked Thoresby, whose letters and diary are a cornucopia of information on contemporary scholarly publishing, to drum up potential subscribers among "the learned in your parts." The Leeds antiquary obliged by subscribing for two sets of the *Annals* himself, and by pressing some of his own friends, such as George Plaxton, who rather grudgingly agreed to subscribe to the *Annals*, "though his [Strype's] last was a very dry book, and wants both moisture and seasoning."[101] Similar prob-

---

[99] CUL MS Mm.6.50 (Covel transcripts), fos. 339–40, Gregory to Covel, 23 October 1722. In another example, Thomas Madox was observed to be vigorously pursuing subscriptions in 1709 for his *History and Antiquities of the Exchequer* (1711): *The London Diaries of William Nicolson*, 497 (14 April 1709).

[100] *Thoresby Letters*, II, 30 (Bishop Nicolson to Thoresby, 4 September 1703).

[101] Ibid., II, 53, 74 (Strype to Thoresby, 15 May and 4 November 1707). The price was £3 12s

lems beset Strype in 1710, on publication of his life of Archbishop Grindal. Copyright in this was shared between two major publishers, John Hartley and John Wyat, but Hartley had been the more successful in rounding up advance subscriptions, allowing him to set the price, a substantial 8s 7d in sheets; Thoresby's copy would cost him a further three shillings for binding and tiling. The beleaguered Strype complained that he had already been attacked for this book and its cost in a sixpenny pamphlet called *Memorials of Bishop Grindal*, "where I am called an appendix-monger; that the accounts given of his birth and parentage are below the dignity of an historian, and of no use but for the author to fill up the empty spaces of his volume." This had not, to his relief, inhibited early sales, and "This Archbishop's Life is mightily bought up, and I hope the reading of it will do a great deal of good, both by showing the good temper and spirit of the true Church of England, and by making it appear how our men that talk so much for the Church of England do vary from it, as it stood in those best (and I may say primitive) days of it."[102]

These problems appear mild in comparison with the difficulties Strype was already experiencing on another front in putting together a new edition of Stow's *Survey of London*. Building on an abortive 1694 project by the topographer Richard Blome to update and revise the *Survey*, Strype was promised £103 by Awnsham Churchill (previously seen as one of the tight-fisted undertakers of *Camden's Britannia*) and two other publishers to produce a new Stow. Though we are as usual a victim of the far sparser correspondence surviving from that earlier era, things really do seem to have been simpler in Stow's time.[103] Strype ran into difficulties at every turn –

for the two sets (same to same, 7 October 1708, ibid., II, 112); ibid., II, 145 (Plaxton to Thoresby, n.d. [1708]). Hearne wrote to Thoresby in 1710 to try to secure advance orders for the first volume of his edition of the *Itineraries* of John Leland. "I print only just an hundred and twenty copies, (all at my own charge) and, therefore, I desire you would let me know as soon as you can, what friends you have that are desirous to be furnished, that I may reserve copies for them. The book will not exceed ten sheets; but the number being so small, I cannot, I think, afford it under 3s. 6d. or 4s. per book": ibid., II, 260 (Hearne to Thoresby, 8 July 1710). Thoresby also acted as buyer for two friends, putting in their order to Hearne along with his own, ibid., II, 277 (same to same, 3 November 1710).

102 Ibid., II, 255–57 (Strype to Thoresby, 22 June 1710). Booksellers could change prices at short notice. When the publisher of Strype's *Annals* found that the first impression was nearly gone, he raised the price of the remaining copies. "Seven were desired by a clergyman of Dublin, in a letter he wrote to me, but Mr. Wyat [the seller] would not part with them." Strype suggested that Thoresby, who had inadvertently been saddled with two more copies than he needed as a result of having taken defaulted orders on behalf of others, sell them back to Wyat: ibid., II, 297 (Strype to Thoresby, 27 September 1710).

103 Stow himself may have been the first historian or antiquary to profit from advance subscription, after a fashion, since in 1604 he received a letter patent from the king authorizing him or his agents "to collect amongst our loving subjects theyr voluntary contribution and kinde gratuities" to aid in his researches toward a new edition of the *Survey of London*. Parishioners of St. Mary Woolnoth, London, in fact contributed 7s 10d: Pollard and Ehrman, *Distribution of Books by Catalogue*, p. 179.

including civic officials who would not release transcripts of documents till they were certain they contained "nothing . . . prejudicial to this city," a plausible enough legal precaution but one with which Strype can have had little patience. He nevertheless secured over the next few years the assistance of his own bishop, Henry Compton, and that of antiquaries such as John Woodward, George Hickes, and Humfrey Wanley. But in January 1708 Strype experienced every scholarly author's worst nightmare: with the work in press, he discovered that his own publishers were about to issue a rival work by Edward Hutton entitled *The New View of London*. The publishers did not think of the works as directly competitive at first – Hutton's drew on Stow but was much smaller and cheaper. Before long, however, they had realized their error and abandoned the publication. Strype was now out of pocket by £71. It was only a dozen years later, after the deficiencies of Hutton's *New View* had been realized, that Strype undertook a further, minor updating of the 1708 manuscript, and persuaded printers to issue it by subscription. Even then, the six-guinea price (increased, for those who had not guaranteed a price by subscribing, by the late addition of extra sheets) was so expensive that one Cambridge antiquary, Samuel Knight, had to apologize to Strype, a personal friend, for not buying a copy for himself. The price, he admitted, "frightens almost all but wealthy Citizens in the country."[104]

There were other disasters, befalling scholars less famous than Strype. There is the sad tale of Joshua Barnes of Emmanuel College, Cambridge, a cleric and classicist turned historian who published a large *Life of King Edward III*, complete with Thucydidean style speeches, in 1688, notable as being perhaps the first subscription history book printed outside London. The project very nearly ruined him: Barnes backed the wrong political horse in dedicating it to James II. The king only lost his throne, Barnes a great deal of money and his chances at preferment. Fortunately, a successful edition of Euripides six years later and marriage to a wealthy wife brought him a Greek professorship and the need no longer to fret about either patronage or subscription.[105] Other works simply died at the proposal stage, leaving authors with wounded pride but spared the debacle of an unsold print run. Without the weight of a major book publisher behind them, it is no wonder that many privately arranged projects were aborted at this stage, such as the ill-fated scheme to print the posthumous Yorkshire antiquarian collections of the physician Nathaniel Johnston, who had died in 1705. A thousand copies of the proposals and the agreement of their printer, William Bowyer, to help the Revd Henry Johnston of Northamptonshire to collect

---

[104] J. J. Morrison, "Strype's Stow: the 1720 Edition of 'A Survey of London,'" *London Journal*, 3 (1977), 40–54, quotation at p. 49.

[105] Levine, *Battle of the Books*, p. 153; Clapp, "Subscription Publishers Prior to Tonson," p. 168.

subscriptions were insufficient to bring this work to the press.[106]

By the middle of the eighteenth century, subscription had become the subject of literary satire, as Fielding's Mr. Wilson poked fun at impecunious authors seeking support for worthless books that might never appear.[107] Yet the system served would-be historians as much as the booksellers, and it is interesting the number of historical works proposals for which were initiated by authors rather than by potential publishers. Hearne, for example, was a habitual and successful user of the system, employing subscription to self-publish his many editions of medieval and Tudor texts, and to maintain lines of communication with the powerful and intellectually useful.[108] Well before subscription became the norm for historical titles, most Restoration or Augustan historians had long since lost the luxury of royal or aristocratic patronage, at least to the degree necessary to support them in their writing: there were simply now too many of them for the older patronage system to sustain. The career of James Howell, who died in 1666 in the financially meager position of Historiographer Royal, would have profited from advance subscription; so would that of Jean Baptiste de Rocoles (1620–96), a Huguenot refugee and former court historian to the elector of Brandenburg, who was obliged to petition Archbishop Sancroft for some employment as a historian of the English people.[109] And for all the complaints about the subscription system, it is clear that a great number of historical works, especially those with a slightly more everyday use in the library of the educated gentleman or merchant, did enjoy considerable success; Richard Coffin's keenness to subscribe to Chauncy's projected *Hertfordshire*, noted at the end of chapter 3 above, is one example. The enormous and almost immediate success of Clarendon's *History* (1702–4) – which that enthusiastic "modern," William Wotton, deemed superior to Sarpi, Commynes, and most of the ancients – is evident in the number of booksellers who themselves subscribed for copies, which they were confident of selling at a profit.[110]

[106] Keith Maslen and John Lancaster, *The Bowyer Ledgers: the Printing Accounts of William Bowyer, Father and Son Reproduced on Microfiche: with a Checklist of Bowyer Printing 1699–1977* (London and New York, 1991), pp. 69–70, no. 853.

[107] Sarah L. C. Clapp, "The Beginnings of Subscription Publication in the Seventeenth Century," *Modern Philology*, 19 (1931–32), 192–224; P. Rogers, "Book Subscriptions Among the Augustans," *TLS*, 15 December 1972; W. A. Speck, "Politicians, Peers, and Publication by Subscription 1700–50," in *Books and Their Readers in Eighteenth-Century England*, ed. I. Rivers (Leicester, 1982), pp. 47–68, at pp. 48–49, to which essay I owe the reference to Morgan.

[108] E.g. Bodl. MS Rawl. lett. 7, fo. 89, George Holmes to Hearne, *ca.* 27 October, 1716; Holmes, deputy-keeper of the Tower records, was ordering several copies of Hearne's edition of Camden's *Annales*, and Hearne, in the year following the loss of all his university offices for refusing to take the oaths, was to be increasingly reliant on sales of his books to augment his college fellowship at St. Edmund Hall.

[109] Bodl. MS Tanner lett. 39, fo. 112, Rocoles to Sancroft, 4 October, n.a.

[110] *The Notebook of Thomas Bennet and Henry Clements*, Oxford Bibl. Soc., n.s. 6 (1956), appendix 9, pp. 209–11. The *History*, it should be recalled, came out virtually simultaneously in folio (Oxford, 1702–4) and octavo (1703) editions. Thomas Bennet, for instance,

THE SOCIAL DISTRIBUTION OF HISTORY BOOKS BY
SUBSCRIPTION: A PRELIMINARY SURVEY

It is not clear what confidence should be placed in the subscription prices as
advertised in proposals, since the prices of many works would be reduced or
increased subsequently depending on how well subscribed they were. John
Walker's *Sufferings of the Clergy* (plate 6.20) was set at twenty-five shillings
in 1714; when reprinted later in the same year this was reduced by two
shillings. Claver Morris paid £1 4s for his copy, but the more patient Henry
Prescott was able to buy a copy for eighteen shillings less than three years
later.[111] The prices at which the books were advertised are, in any case, not
the most useful information that the subscription system can give us about
historical readership. Much more important are the lists of those who
subscribed, which were frequently printed at the front of the volume when it
finally appeared. The study of these lists is a formidable task, and that has
been underway for some time, involving painstaking prosopographical reconstruction of their contents through the identification of their subscribers
and their locations.[112] For over twenty years the project of analyzing and
cross-referencing titles and their subscribers for all extant subscription lists
has been in progress under the direction of the late Dr. P. J. Wallis of the
University of Newcastle-upon-Tyne and his colleagues in the Project for
Historical Biobibliography (PHIBB). When complete, their database will
allow researchers to evaluate such factors as party affiliation, social status,
and geographic region not only for a single title but for groups of books and
even entire genres, and to analyze and compare the attitudes of particular
famous subscribers (many of whom were themselves authors) to various
topics.[113] Using PHIBB data, for example, Professor William Speck has
demonstrated a strong tendency to party affiliation in certain history titles,
with tories subscribing for particular titles and whigs to others. Strype's
*History of the Life and Acts of the Most Reverend Father in God Edmund
Grindal*, for instance, was commissioned by the whigs in 1710 as a kind of
antidote to the high church feelings generated by the Sacheverell trial, and
the work found little support among tory readers, though thirty-four whig

---

bought volume II, folio, at 15s and subscribed it to buyers at 18s; vol. III (folio) for 16s, and
subscribed for a pound; vol. I (octavo) he purchased for 1s 8d a copy while subscribing it for
2s 9d. For Wotton's comment on Clarendon see J. M. Levine, *The Battle of the Books:
History and Literature in the Augustan Age* (Ithaca, NY, 1991), p. 44; for Clarendon's early
readership in general see Philip Hicks, *Neoclassical History and English Culture from
Clarendon to Hume* (New York, 1996), pp. 45–81.

[111] E. Hobhouse, "The Library of a Physician *circa* 1700," *The Library*, 4th series, 13 (1932–
33), 89–96, at p. 93; *Diary of Henry Prescott*, II, 579 (29 June 1717).

[112] F. J. G. Robinson and P. J. Wallis, *Book Subscription Lists: a Revised Guide* (Newcastle-
upon-Tyne: Book Subscriptions List Project, 1975).

[113] The CD-ROM version of this material, updating Wallis' original work, appeared late in
1995, too late to be taken into account in this study.

Part II.   *The Parochial Clergy.*   251

D U R H A M.

——, ——, . *Gainsford*, V. See the Note at *Abberton* in *Suffex*, under the Letter *A*. One of his *Succeffors*, if he had more than One, was *George Sanderfon*; who was Prefented to it in 1655.

E S S E X.

GOULDMAN, FRANCIS, . *South-Okendon*, R.

He was the well-known *Compiler* of the *Dictionary* which now *commonly bears his Name*. He out-liv'd the *Ufurpation*, and enjoyed his *Living* many Years after it.

In 1654, one Abraham Pinchback was Prefented to this Living.

GRAY, ROBERT, . *Mafhbury*, V. There was one Dr. *Robert Grey*, who was Defended from the Noble Family of *Wark*, great Uncle to the late Earl of *Tankerville*, and a Great Sufferer in thefe Times; being *Plundered, Imprifoned,* and almoft *Ruined.* He was bred at *Chrift-College* in *Cambridge,* under the Famous Mr. *Mede.* He out-lived the *Ufurpation,* became Prebendary of *Durham,* and was living in 1704, but fince, as I hear, is dead. *Quære* whether he was the fame Perfon with this *Robert Gray* of *Mafhbury.* If he was not, he ought to be inferted *diftinctly* at the End of the Counties.

GREEN, ——, D. D. *Littlebury*, R. See Mr. *Tucker* in this County, and a *Note* there. See alfo one Dr. *Green* in *Hampfhire*, and another in *Wiltfhire*, and *quære*.

faid, put funder *Sequeftration* in the late Times of *Rebellion*, during all which, Mr. *Gcodnyn* was the *Rightful Incumbent*, and confequently the *Sufferer*; having been Prefented in 1639, and not Vacating it till by his Death in 1679.

Newe.Rep. Ecclef. Vol.I. p. 806.

GORSUCH, JOHN, D.D. *Walkherne*, . In 1652. He was the Son of *Daniel Gorfuch* of *Lonaon,* Mercer. The Charge againft him was the *Hackney* one of *Drunkennefs*; as alfo *Gaming*; feldom appearing in the Pulpit, and obferving the Orders of the Church. But that which carrieth the greateft Venom in it, is, that he had 'En-'deavoured to hire one *Jones* to ride a Troop-'Horfe for Prince *Rupert*, to ferve under him a-'gainft the Parliament; faying withal, *he had a* '*Snotty-Nofe Jade to fend to the Parliament to* '*Poifon the whole Band*; and had publifhed a 'wicked Libel againft the Parliament, *that* '*fome of the Lords whom he had named, were Fools,* '*Baftards, and Cuckolds*. And if this be not e-'nough to make him *Scandalous* and *Malignant*, I know not what is. He had been Prefented to this Living by his Father; who, if I miftake not, had alfo built a new Parfonage-Houfe from the Ground, before he gave his Son the Living.

Chaun. Ant. p. 149.

Chaun. Ant. p. 149.

——, ——, . *Great Geddefden*, V. I find this Living alfo under Sequeftration.

——, ——, . *Little Geddefden*, R. See the Note at *Abberton* in *Suffex*, under the Letter *A*.

'One Richard Lee was Prefented to this Living in 1655.'

H U N T I N G T O N S H I R E.

GOUGE, THOMAS, . *Covington*, R. In 1657, One *William Donne* was admitted to this Living.

Plate 6.20   Detail of "The Parochial Clergy" from John Walker's *Sufferings of the Clergy* (1714), p. 251.

MPs subscribed. John Oldmixon's *History of England* (1729) was similarly whiggish in support, as were the two volumes of Burnet's *History of his own Time* (1724, 1734). On the other side, the "sturdy Jacobite" Francis Drake found mainly tory subscribers for his *Eboracum: or the History . . . of York* (1736), its few subscribers who were whig MPs being almost all from the region.[114]

My task here is a much more modest one, and focuses exclusively on a cross-section of historical works of different sorts that were subscribed in the late seventeenth and early eighteenth centuries, in order to establish a rough

[114] Speck, "Politicians, Peers, and Publication by Subscription," pp. 51–62. Other titles were more evenly divided between opposition whigs and tories, and Speck argues that this supports the existence of a bipartisan opposition to measures such as the excise bill of 1733.

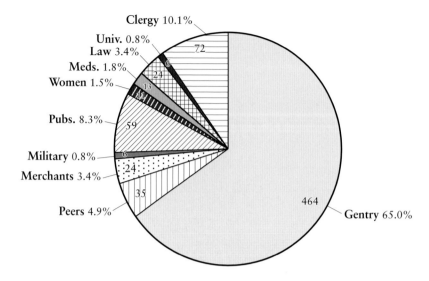

Total of 720 subscribers

Figure 6.11   Subscribers to *The Great Historical, Geographical and Poetical Dictionary*.

sense of the geographical, social, and occupational distribution of the subscribers for these items. A good example of the information that can be gleaned comes from the subscription list printed at the front of *The Great Historical, Geographical and Poetical Dictionary*, a large potpourri principally ascribed to the Frenchman Louis Moréri with revisions by Jean Le Clerc (1694); later English editions were further revised by Jeremy Collier (plate 6.21).[115] The list of subscribers is lengthy, but informative. It includes 720 names, nearly all of them listed by title, and several by occupation and/or location. Of these, there were 470 (about 65 percent) gentry, 35 lay peers, and 113 in the three professions (clergy, including the episcopacy, law, and medicine); 11 women signed up, both the wives of peers and a few untitled. The distribution is given in full in fig. 6.11. Fifty-nine names were men involved in the publishing trade, either as printers or, more commonly, as provincial or London booksellers, and their locations are given in map 6.2.

[115] *TC*, II, 405.

Plate 6.21 (*opposite*)   Title page of the 1701 revision, by Jeremy Collier, of Louis Moréri's *Great Historical . . . Dictionary*. 2 vols., London, 1701. Collier also compiled an "appendix" and a "supplement" to the work.

THE GREAT

HISTORICAL,

Geographical, Genealogical and Poetical

DICTIONARY;

BEING

A Curious Miscellany

OF

SACRED and PROPHANE HISTORY.

Containing, in short,

The LIVES and most REMARKABLE ACTIONS

Of the Patriarchs, Judges, and Kings of the Jews; Of the Apostles, Fathers, and Doctors of the Church; Of Popes, Cardinals, Bishops, &c. Of Heresiarchs and Schismaticks, with an Account of their Principal Doctrines; Of Emperors, Kings, Illustrious Princes, and Great Generals; Of Ancient and Modern Authors; Of Philosophers, Inventors of Arts, and all those who have recommended themselves to the World, by their Valour, Virtue, Learning, or some Notable Circumstances of their Lives. Together with the Establishment and Progress both of Religious and Military Orders, and the Lives of their Founders. As also, The Fabulous History of the Heathen G o d s and H e r o e s.

THE DESCRIPTION

Of Empires, Kingdoms, Common-Wealths, Provinces, Cities, Towns, Islands, Mountains, Rivers, and other considerable Places, both of Ancient and Modern Geography; wherein is observed the Situation, Extent and Quality of the Country; the Religion, Government, Morals and Customs of the Inhabitants; the Sects of Christians, Jews, Heathens and Mahometans. The principal Terms of Arts and Sciences; the Publick and Solemn Actions, as Festivals, Plays, &c. The Statutes and Laws; and withal, the History of General and Particular Councils, under the Names of the Places where they have been Celebrated.

The Whole being full of Remarks and Curious Enquiries, for the Illustration of several Difficulties in Theology, History, Chronology and Geography.

COLLECTED

From the best Historians, Chronologers, and Lexicographers; as *Calvisius, Helvicus, Isaacson, Marsham, Bandrand, Hoffman, Lloyd, Chevreau,* and others: But more especially out of *LEWIS MORERY,* D. D. his Eighth Edition Corrected and Enlarged by Monsieur *LE CLERC;* In Two Volumes in Folio.

To which are added, by way of Supplement, intermix'd throughout the Alphabet, The Lives, most Remarkable Actions, and Writings of several Illustrious Families of our *English, Scotch* and *Irish* Nobility, and Gentry, and most Famous Men of all Professions, Arts and Sciences: As also, an Exact Description of these Kingdoms; with the most Considerable Occurrences that have happened to this present Time.

The FIRST VOLUME.

The Second Edition Revis'd, Corrected and Enlarg'd to the Year 1688; By J e r. C o l l i e r, *A. M.*

L O N D O N,
Printed for *Henry Rhodes,* near *Bride-Lane* in *Fleetstreet;* *Thomas Newborough,* at the *Golden-Ball* in St. *Paul's Church-Yard;* the Assigns of *L. Meredith,* at the *Star* in St. *Paul's Church-Yard;* and *Elizabeth Harris,* at the *Harrow* in *Little-Britain;* MDCCI.

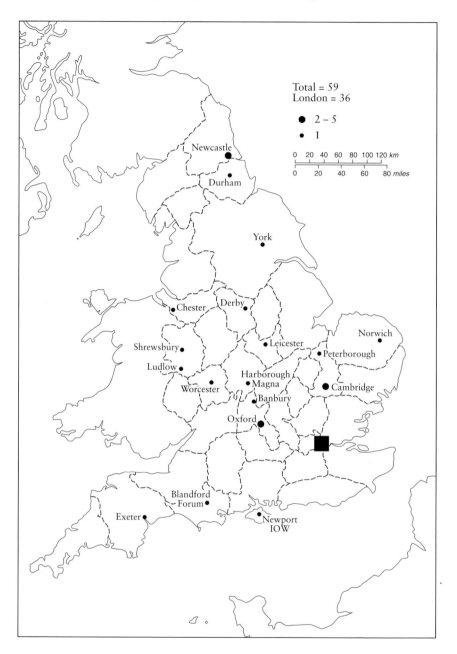

Total = 59
London = 36

● 2 – 5
• 1

Map 6.2   Booksellers subscribing to *The Great Historical, Geographical and Poetical Dictionary.*

The subscription list gives the location of slightly less than half the listed subscribers, though the location of one or two others can be surmised, either from regional surnames, or where they are reasonably prominent and also known to have been active book buyers. Sixteen locations given are unidentifiable, almost always because no shire is given and two or more places with the same name exist: for instance "Hilton." Ninety-three are listed as resident in London, Westminster, or their immediate environs, and in several instances, more than one person in an area signed up: in Ashford, Kent, no less than six copies were subscribed, including one by William Hills, a local blacksmith.

The frequency of subscriptions, excluding all peers and unplaceables (totaling 426) is illustrated in map 6.3. The *relatively* even geographical distribution admits some peculiar gaps – no copies were subscribed in Derbyshire, Staffordshire, and Cornwall, for instance – but is more uniform than that of many other historical works, especially those with a local or specialist interest. The printed subscription list for Tristram Risdon's *Chorographical Description or Survey of Devon*, first printed by Edmund Curll in 1711, shows reasonable advance sales across the south and central part of the kingdom, but, not surprisingly, a preponderance of names from Devon, Dorset, and environs.

Seventeen historical works with printed subscription lists (Moréri's among them), all published in the very late seventeenth century or the first three decades of the eighteenth, have been selected. The major principles of selection were first, that each have a list with sufficient numbers of subscribers and enough information to discuss them; and secondly, that the books together should represent a cross-section of all the different genres within which history was now being presented to the public, from editions of medieval texts like Asser and Geoffrey of Monmouth to political memoirs such as Edmund Sawyer's *Memorials of Affairs of State* and Gilbert Burnet's *History of his own Time*; from an antiquarian–topographical work such as Hearne's first edition of Leland's *Itinerary* to the same writer's reedition of Camden's *Annales* of Queen Elizabeth. The range of books includes both a hugely subscribed work of church history and biography such as John Walker's *Sufferings of the Clergy* (which includes the longest and biographically most detailed list, of over 1,300 names) to a much more narrowly appealing and expensive illustrated luxury book, Robert Castell's *The Villas of the Ancients Illustrated*, which had a mere 117 subscribers. County studies such as Plot's *Staffordshire* and Nathaniel Salmon's *The History of Hertfordshire*, again with a relatively low number of subscribers, are included, together with a classical history, *Lucan's Pharsalia*, edited by the playwright Nicholas Rowe (with the most politically partisan list). Each list was analyzed under a variety of categories. Two of the lists, Moréri's and Walker's, give sufficient

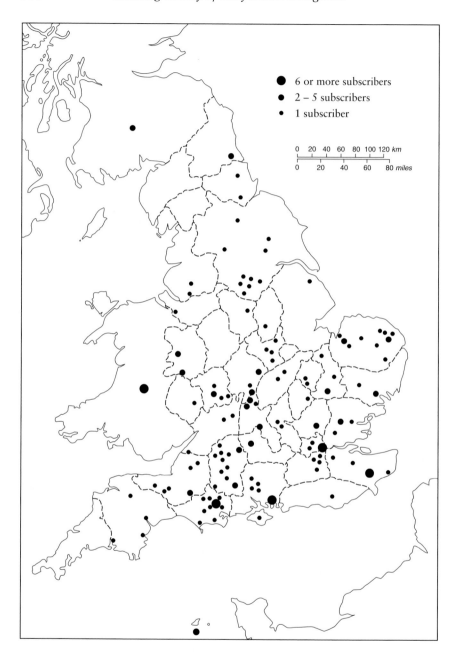

Map 6.3   Location of subscribers to *The Great Historical, Geographical and Poetical Dictionary.*

information as to the addresses of subscribers to permit mapping of the dispersal of copies. In every case, however, the list has been broken down according to the social status or principal occupation of the subscriber. The cumulative results are listed in table 6.17, with absolute numbers on top and percentages below, and exclusions described in the notes.

The following lists were used, principally from copies in the Harry Ransom Humanities Research Center at the University of Texas in Austin: Robert Plot, *The Natural History of Staffordshire* (Oxford, 1686); William Camden, *Annales*, ed. Thomas Hearne (Oxford, 1717/18); John de Fordun, *Scotichronicon*, ed. Hearne (Oxford, 1722); John Leland, *Itinerary*, ed. Hearne (vol. III, Oxford, 1711); Edmund Sawyer (ed.), *Memorials of Affairs of State* (1725); Louis Moréri, *The Great Historical . . . Dictionary* (1694); John Strype, *Annals of the Reformation* (2nd edn, vol. I, 1725); Edward Lhwyd, *Archaeologica Britannica* (Oxford, 1707); John Walker, *Sufferings of the Clergy* (1714); Jeremy Collier, *Ecclesiastical History* (vol. I, 1708); *Lucan's Pharsalia*, trans. Nicholas Rowe (London, 1718 [actually 1719] edition only – this was simultaneously published at Dublin with a different list); Geoffrey of Monmouth, *British History*, trans. A. Thompson (1718); Gilbert Burnet, *History of his own Time* (vol. I only, 1724); Philippe de Commynes, *Memoirs*, trans. T. Uvedale (1712); Nathaniel Salmon, *History of Hertfordshire* (1728); Asser, *Life of Alfred*, ed. F. Wise (Oxford, 1722); and Robert Castell, *The Villas of the Ancients Illustrated* (1728).

Because a number of subscribers in any list could fit under two or even three categories (the only entirely clear and unambiguous category being women), and because it has been deemed preferable not to double-count (and thereby inflate the total numbers), it has been essential to establish rubrics for placing ambiguous cases. In defining the initial categories, I have been guided by the picture of Augustan society and its professions outlined in G. S. Holmes, *Augustan England* (London, 1982). The following assumptions and conventions have been used in analyzing all subscription lists. The result is that the totals reflect the reality of the list, while the categories admit of some elasticity: clerical and gentry counts, for instance, are invariably lower than reality simply because some of their numbers have been placed in the "university" category.

1. Major categories may vary slightly according to the contents of the lists.
2. Clergy includes all persons with "Revd" before their name, clerks, vicars, curates, rectors, prebendaries, etc., of whatever rank or denomination *unless* they have a university position (fellow, head of house, professor, etc.), in which case they and nonclerical university persons

Table 6.17. Breakdown of subscribers to seventeen historical works

Book subscribed	Total subs.	Peers	Gentry	Clergy	Univ.	Law	Medicine	Women	Pubs.	Military officers	Merchants
Leland, Itinerary	97[a]	7	41	11	25	3	8	0	2	0	0
	100	7.2	42.3	11.3	25.8	3.1	8.2	—	2.1	—	—
Camden, Annales	208[b]	7	76	19	39	17	33	1	7	3	4
	100	3.4	36.9	9.2	18.9	8.3	16.0	0.5	3.4	1.5	1.9
Fordun, Scotichronicon	161	13	75	23	16	12	16	1	4	1	0
	100	8.1	46.6	14.3	9.9	7.5	9.9	0.6	2.5	0.6	—
Commynes, Memoirs	520[c]	13	333	20	8	38	25	11	22	28	22
	100	2.5	64.0	3.8	1.5	7.3	4.8	2.1	4.2	5.4	4.2
Collier, Eccles. Hist.	551	11	156	239	35	39	14	11	27	6	13
	100	2.0	28.3	43.4	6.4	7.1	2.5	2.0	4.9	1.1	2.4
Asser, Alfred	346[d]	9	48	15	262	3	5	0	4	0	0
	100	2.6	13.8	4.3	75.7	0.9	1.4	—	1.1	—	—
Burnet, Own time	1195	46	724	136	8	101	14	22	62	28	53
	100	3.8	60.6	11.5	0.7	8.5	1.2	1.8	5.2	2.3	4.4
Castell, Villas	115[e]	18	88	2	0	1	0	3	0	3	0
	100	15.7	76.5	1.7	—	0.9	—	2.6	—	2.6	—
Sawyer, Memorials	315	62	172	24	8	28	3	9	2	7	0
	100	19.7	54.6	7.6	2.5	8.9	1.0	2.9	0.6	2.2	—
Walker, Sufferings	1333[f]	7	383	677	95	16	24	10	60	8	53
	100	0.5	28.7	50.8	7.1	1.2	1.8	0.8	4.5	0.6	4.0
Geoffrey of Monmouth	326	14	131	67	30	3	5	53	7	8	8
	100	4.2	36.9	20.2	9.1	0.9	1.5	17.5	2.1	2.4	2.4
Strype, Ref. Annals	198[g]	5	53	83	2	5	1	1	42	5	1
	100	2.5	26.2	41.1	1.0	2.5	0.5	0.5	20.8	2.5	0.5
Salmon, Hist. Herts.	185[h]	9	110	46	1	4	8	7	0	0	0
	100	4.9	59.5	24.9	0.5	2.2	4.3	3.8	—	—	—

Lucan, *Pharsalia*	387[i]	61	243	8	3	6	4	28	0	33	1
	100	15.8	62.8	2.1	0.8	1.6	1.0	7.2	—	8.5	0.3
Lhwyd, *Arch. Brit.*	203[j]	15	166	12	—	2	8	0	—	0	—
	100	7.4	81.8	5.9	0	1.0	3.9	0	0	0	0
Moréri, *Gt. Hist. Dict.*	720	35	470	72	6	24	13	11	59	6	24
	100	4.8	65.3	10.0	0.8	3.3	1.8	1.5	8.2	0.8	3.3
Plot, *Nat. Hist. of Staffs.*	603	20	266	44	207	13	39	7	0	1	6
	100	3.3	44.1	7.3	34.3	2.2	6.5	1.2	—	0.2	1.0

[a] No booksellers are specified as such, nor counted in the total, but at least two are named with no indication of occupation, Jonah or Jonas Bowyer and Henry Clements. Several private subscribers bought more than one copy. Hearne, whose relations with most booksellers were cool at best, generally relied on the assistance of learned friends such as Woodward or Thorpe. Clements, an Oxford bookseller, disposed of six copies for Hearne, and Henry Prescott of Chester, whose reading habits are discussed above, was among the subscribers. This list comes from vol. III; Hearne printed a new list with each volume as he produced them, but the list differences are inconsequential.

[b] Two institutional subscribers not counted.

[c] One untitled subscriber, Zachary Foxall, is excluded from the count owing to his unclear rank and occupation; few locations are provided.

[d] Three Oxford college libraries excluded from count. All university subscribers were at Oxford, with one exception. Several subscribers at Oxford were students, and three people have been counted as peers rather than under university though they too were then students: Henry Somerset, duke of Beaufort (b. 1707) was only fifteen years of age; Henry Viscount Lewisham; and Sidney Lord Beauclerk of Trinity (fifth son of Charles, duke of St. Albans), who matriculated on 4 December 1721, aged eighteen.

[e] Two institutional subscribers not counted.

[f] Six institutional subscribers not counted.

[g] Four institutions not counted. The sole medical subscriber was an apothecary. Fifty-four subscribers are listed in vol. III (1728), of whom twenty-nine had also subscribed for vol. I, including the sole female subscriber, Mrs. Mary Woolryche.

[h] Peers include the earl of Hertford, to whom the work was dedicated; no publishers, merchants, or officers are listed and few locations are given.

[i] Two institutional subscribers not counted.

[j] Subscriber locations principally Welsh.

are combined under the "university" category. In practice, this means that all clerical counts are lower than the number of persons actually in holy orders. Example: a subscriber to Plot, John Lloyd (briefly bishop of St. David's from 1686 till his death the following year) is counted under "university," not clergy, since he was also principal of Jesus College, Oxford and the university's vice-chancellor (1682–85). But Henry Smith, DD, canon of Christ Church, has been counted under clergy since his attachment was to the cathedral, rather than the college. In all this an element of arbitrariness is inescapable, but it also reflects the complexities of a society in which occupation and social status were no longer synonymous.

3. Officers includes anyone with military title (army or navy) unless they are also a peer.

4. Schoolmasters are counted either under clergy, if they have a clerical title, or under gentry.

5. Merchants includes those specifically called merchants (in the narrowest sense) in the lists, but also anyone in a trade, e.g. vintners, brewers, goldsmiths, haberdashers, etc., *unless* they are printers, booksellers, stationers, or bookbinders, who are all lumped under publishing. It has been assumed that those named as aldermen or mayors in corporate towns fit under this category.

6. Peers is self-explanatory, but also includes older sons with subsidiary titles, Scottish and Irish peers. It includes those aristocrats listed as attached to or resident at a university.

7. Lawyers includes civil and common, judges, solicitors, attorneys etc.: anyone with a legal degree or whose address is an Inn of Court; they did not actually have to be in practice. The exception to this is a combination of legal qualification and clerical title (for instance in the case of the chancellors of some dioceses, who were in orders but also civil lawyers): in such cases the clerical title has taken precedence in the count. Strictly honorific degrees (for instance the LLD and DCL granted to Sir Christopher Wren by Cambridge and Oxford) have not been counted where I have been able to recognize them.

8. "Women" includes women of all ranks, peeresses down and is the one category that admits no ambiguity.

9. "Medical" includes all persons with MD or MB after their name, all surgeons, druggists, and apothecaries. It does not, however, include those who simply have the title of "Dr." but no medical indication unless I have been able to establish from other sources that those persons were in fact physicians (there are a few in this latter category, such as James Yonge of Plymouth, billed simply as doctor but known as a naval surgeon). Persons with a generic "Dr." prefix have been vari-

ously counted under clergy (if also accompanied by a "Revd" prefix, or listed as obviously clerical), lawyers (if attached to a legal address such as Doctors commons); where I have been unable to resolve what sort of doctor they were they have been counted with the gentry. Example: a Plot subscriber, John Lamphire, principal of Hart Hall and Camden professor of history has been counted as medical because he was also a doctor of medicine.

10. University includes anyone with a university affiliation from heads of house down to commoner-students; it includes not only Oxford and Cambridge (the overwhelming majority) but also Irish and Scottish universities, and those attached to institutions such as Gresham College. Those listed simply as "MA" or by degree without a university affiliation are instead counted under gentry, clergy, or whichever is appropriate. Peers and their older sons are excluded; civil lawyers and doctors of medicine are also excluded and counted under their professions. Example: a subscriber to Plot, Sir Thomas Clayton, MD, warden of Merton College, could fit under gentry, university, or medicine, but his medical degree places him in the medical category. A university fellowship, other than a chair or a house headship was, as Holmes reminds us, almost invariably a temporary status *en route* (usually) to a career in the church or one of the other major professions.

11. So far as locations are concerned, these are virtually never complete, even in the most detailed list, included in Walker. Where a list has been mapped, those addresses that are unidentifiable (either no address is given at all, or an ambiguous one such as a commonplace town name but no county) are excluded.

12. Status of individuals is list-specific and does not recognize past status or future mobility: the earl of Macclesfield (formerly Thomas Parker, a lawyer), appearing on a list *as* the earl of Macclesfield, would be treated in this instance as a peer, not a lawyer.

That authors and publishers were consciously targeting particular audiences is dramatically apparent in the substantially different clienteles that subscribed for works of religious history, whether Strype, Walker, or Collier, all of which had overwhelmingly clerical subscription lists (despite the divergent political views of their respective authors) as compared with what we would now call political history. Commynes' *Memoirs*, long respected for its crisp and sagacious account of fifteenth-century diplomacy and politics, appealed to a subscription readership over two-thirds of which were in the peerage or gentry; it also had the second-highest number of military subscribers, just behind a classical work that had similar military appeal, Rowe's *Lucan's Pharsalia*. Sawyer's edition of documents and letters from the early seventeenth century, principally derived from the papers of the Jacobean secretary Sir Ralph Winwood, drew a similar readership though its under-takers were more successful in signing up peers and also attracted a signifi-cant percentage of lawyers (the only professional group that showed no particular preference for political over ecclesiastical history, or even for new rather than old texts, signing up for Collier, Camden, and Fordun's *Scotich-ronicon* in approximately equal numbers). Burnet's *History of his own Time*, despite a critical reception, was written by a cleric and lacked the military appeal (only 2.3 percent officers) but had the benefit of being about recent history; it found its readers, once again, mainly among the gentry and peers, with clergy well behind at 11.5 percent and the other professions represented in very small numbers. University-connected readers, lay and clerical, were evidently unimpressed. Perhaps they shared the views of one don, William Stratford, who read the book while nursing a cold only to discover that it gave him a worse opinion of "Gibby" Burnet's morals and understanding than he already had; he decried it as a "strange rhapsody of chitchat and lies, ill tacked together."[116] It was also rather expensive: the second volume of the large paper version sold to one reader for fifty shillings.[117]

By far the most socially exclusive book, no doubt because of its price as much as its subject, was Castell's *Villas of the Ancients*, printed by Bowyer for the author.[118] Over 90 percent of its small subscribership of 117 were gentry or aristocracy, precisely those owners who had both the financial resources to afford a large, lavishly illustrated folio – the duke of Somerset took six copies – and the magnificent homes, many built on the same classical models laid out in Castell's book, that made the book attractive. The absence of merchants and booksellers (unlikely to venture any capital on such a project) is not surprising, that of university fellows, who might have enter-tained an intellectual interest but would scarcely have the funds, somewhat more so. In contrast, Francis Wise's edition of Asser, which had a respectable number of subscribers at 346, appealed overwhelmingly to the university set, virtually all of whom were at Oxford. Both the editor's connections (he was fellow of Trinity College and, from 1719, underkeeper of the Bodleian) and Alfred's mythical fame as the founder of the university and source of its putative seniority over Cambridge could account for this.

Women are another distinctive group – in this case a sex rather than a rank – within the study, and the sample shows them subscribing in small but relatively steady numbers across the genres. Virtually all were the wives or mothers of peers, or gentlewomen (the occasional female bookseller or an

[116] William Stratford to Edward Lord Harley (15 November 1723), Hist. MSS Comm., *Port-land*, VII, 367–68.
[117] Receipt dated 10 June 1733 at the Temple by T. Burnett for 25s, being half the price of the book. Hist. MSS Comm., *Eighth Report of the Royal Commission on Historical Manu-scripts*, 3 vols. in 5 parts (1881–1910), part I, p. 13.
[118] Maslen and Lancaster, *The Bowyer Ledgers*, p. 107, no. 1357; p. 115, no. 1454.

actress, like Anne Oldfield, who subscribed to Rowe's *Lucan*, being the exceptions). The only books in the sample not to have any female subscribers were Leland's *Itinerary*, Lhwyd's *Archaeologia Britannica* (a learned work that drew an overwhelmingly Welsh subscribership), and Wise's edition of Asser. But another work that was largely marketed in and around Oxford and its environs, Thompson's translation of Geoffrey of Monmouth, complete with a defence of that author's accuracy in the face of over a century of skepticism, attracted an enormous female readership of over 17 percent. The mythical and legendary, the chivalrous and romantic, maintained a greater attraction for women than did the hard-nosed empiricism and linguistic acumen of a scholar like Lhwyd.[119]

Although not as striking a hit as Geoffrey of Monmouth, Nicholas Rowe's *Lucan*, too, sold well among women at over 7 percent.[120] This may be explicable through the translator's dramatic and official connections (he had been a client of both the Prince of Wales and the earl of Macclesfield, and the list includes such figures as Samuel Molyneux, secretary to the prince, the Secretary of State, the comptroller of the royal household and master of ceremonies, Justice Sir Robert Eyre of the King's Bench, Lord Chancellor Parker, and the chancellor of the duchy of Lancaster) and because the work was supported by Rowe's widow, who wrote the dedication to the king.[121] Among the female subscribers, one can find the name of the famous letter

---

[119] The female subscribers to Thompson's Geoffrey included various of the Boyle women: Rt. Hon. Lady Elizabeth, Lady Juliana, Lady Jane, and Lady Harriet; Mrs. Sarah Eyles and Lady Eyles, one each; Viscountess Lanesbrough; Lady Parker; and the countess of Dalkeith (the last two of whom subscribed for several copies). The question of women's interest in various sorts of history is dealt with at much greater length in my article, "A Feminine Past? Gender, Genre and Historical Knowledge in England, 1500–1800," *American Historical Review*, 102 (June 1997), 645–79.

[120] Rowe himself, the poet laureate, was born in Little Berkford, Bedfordshire in 1673 and took to literature after training as a barrister. A great admirer of Shakespeare (whose works he edited in six volumes in 1709), Rowe tried to imitate him in *The Tragedy of Jane Shore* and other plays. A good linguist, he had "read most of the Greek and Roman histories in their original languages, and most that are writ in English, French, Italian, and Spanish." He died on 6 December 1718, aged forty-five. He had married twice, first to a daughter of Anthony Parsons, auditor of the revenue (both a Captain Parsons and a Theophilus Parsons, esq. are on the list); then to Anne Devenish, daughter of Mr. Devenish of Dorset: not surprisingly, there are also two Devenishes in the subscription list, Henry and Joseph.

[121] His widow received a pension of £40 a year from George I for Rowe's *Lucan*. The book commences with a preface about Lucan and Rowe by James Welwood, MD, who was also a subscriber. Like Rowe, Welwood was a thorough whig, and the author of *Memoirs of the most Material Transactions in England, for the last Hundred Years, preceding the Revolution in 1688* (4th edn, 1702), a work written in praise of the revolution, and not very complimentary to the Stuarts. Despite the title page date of 1718, the preface is dated 29 February 1719 [not 1718/19], and a date of 1719 can be independently established from the marital status of a female subscriber, Sophia Howe, who had married Emmanuel Scrope Howe, second Viscount Howe, on 8 April 1719 – just before the book would have appeared (Romney Sedgwick, *The House of Commons 1715–1754* [2 vols., 1970, II, 154–55). Rowe's *Lucan* is more a paraphrase than a translation, and eight editions of it appeared between 1719 and 1807.

writer Lady Mary Wortley-Montagu (and her husband Edward Wortley-Montagu), and Anne Oldfield (1683–1730), the celebrated actress connected with Cibber, Steele, and Rowe himself: she had played the title role in the dramatist's *Lady Jane Grey*, the epilogue of which had been penned by his friend, Alexander Pope, in 1715.[122] Women were the fourth largest group of subscribers (behind gentry, peers, and officers) for Rowe's verse rendition of the *Pharsalia*. As a poem this no doubt held greater interest for them than the hard slogging of a Latin text, which relatively few women could read.

In some instances other factors enter in: women often subscribed in their own right for books that their husbands or fathers had also undertaken to buy. Thus the list for Uvedale's Commynes includes several such combinations.[123] Several peeresses subscribed independently of their husbands to various other works, and the small number of peers subscribed for Walker may also have dragged down the female readership independent of the book's appeal, or lack thereof. The reasons why women, or men, would subscribe a book can vary widely, since the book was not always for personal collection (much less necessarily to be read) but intended as a gift. No women subscribed for Hearne's Leland at first, but eventually the name of Elizabeth Elstob appears in the lists for later volumes. When collecting subscribers for the Fordun *Scotichronicon* in 1722, Hearne made a point of signing up Anne Dodwell, the widow of his own former tutor and fellow nonjuror, Henry Dodwell of Shottesbrook, Berkshire. Mrs. Dodwell was the only female subscriber to that work, and her subscription was probably prompted by devotion to her husband's memory; Henry Dodwell himself appears in the lists for the Leland several years earlier as already deceased, having died while the book was in press. Hearne's Camden similarly drew only one woman, the notorious Jacobite Anna Henrietta Oglethorpe, daughter

---

[122] *DNB*, sub "Rowe, Nicholas" and "Oldfield, Anne." Other female subscribers, twenty-eight in all, included the duchess of Bolton, the countess of Burlington (whose husband the earl bought six), Mrs. Berenger (wife of Moses Berenger, Esq., also on the list), the countess of Carnarvon (and her husband the earl), Mrs. Mary Cartaret, Sir Isaac Newton's stepniece and heiress Catherine Conduitt and her husband, John (see Sedgwick, *The House of Commons 1715–1754*, I, 569–70), Lady Guilford, Hon. Mrs. Sophia Howe; Hon. Mary Lepell (the daughter of Brigadier General Nicholas Lepell and daughter-in-law of John Hervey, first earl of Bristol), the duchess of Marlborough; the countess of Pembroke (together with the earl), the countess of Sunderland (again, with the earl); Lady Rich (probably Elizabeth Rich, *née* Griffith, who married Sir Robert Rich, later Field Marshal Rich [1685–1768, of Roos Hall, Suffolk] in 1710, when he had already succeeded to the baronetcy), Lady Tyrconnel; Lady Jane Wharton (sister of the first duke and daughter of the marquis); and the countess of Warwick (together with the earl).

[123] Dorothea and Norton Powlett subscribed, as did Charles and Mary Long, and Nicholas and Mary Hutchinson. Tyringham Backwell and his wife took a copy each of Geoffrey of Monmouth, as did the earl and countess of Burlington, Earl and Countess Ferrers, Mrs. Ann and Mr. Henry Fenn, the earl and countess of Pembroke, the earl and countess of Hertford, and Sir John and Lady Harpur (she taking more than one copy). William Morice and Mrs. Alice Morice took a copy each (his in royal paper, hers in ordinary).

of Sir Theophilus Oglethorpe and sister of the first baron Oglethorpe.[124]

Other than women, two groups that figure in varying degrees among subscriber lists are the umbrella category of merchants, and members of the publishing trades (printers, stationers, and especially booksellers). Merchants occupy a very small percentage, though not a negligible one. On some lists, names billed as in some sort of craft or trade do not appear at all: Castell's extremely narrowly targeted and expensive *Villas* has already been mentioned, but it was not alone. Among the selected lists, that for Rowe's *Lucan* had only one merchant subscriber while six other works – Hearne's Leland and Fordun, Sawyer's *Memorials*, Salmon's *Hertfordshire*, Wise's *Asser*, and Lhwyd's *Archaeologia* – had none at all. It is probable that some of those listed as "Mr." with no occupational description were in fact members of trading families, especially in light of what Peter Earle has recently written about the emergence of a recognizable middle class in the early eighteenth century, and also of the much looser definition of gentility that by then applied. But since merchants and traders are clearly identified as such where they are listed, this is not likely to represent a very great distortion of reality. Of the titles with no merchant subscribers, it is easiest to understand the lack of interest in Lhwyd's book and the two Latin chronicles, Fordun and Asser, none of which would have qualified as entertaining reading and all of which were without question pitched at small, primarily scholarly audiences; and when presented with an English-language translation, such as Thompson's Geoffrey of Monmouth, or Uvedale's Commynes, merchants did sign up in small numbers. Hearne's Leland, Salmon's *Hertfordshire* and Sawyer's *Memorials* are a bit more difficult to explain: all were written in English and in the case of Leland dealt with antiquities on a national level. But in two of those cases the total number of subscribers is itself rather small, rendering conclusions less reliable, and it is significant that merchants occur in largest numbers absolutely (fifty-three each) and relatively among the most and second-most heavily subscribed books, Walker's *Sufferings* (4.0 percent) and Burnet's *History of his own Time* (4.4 percent). In other words, a paucity of mercantile subscriptions should not necessarily be read as lack of interest, since it may well simply represent the opposite, the failure of authors or undertakers to push their quest for subscribers beyond a carefully selected target audience of their immediate social circles and of prominent persons who could immediately lend names as well as shillings to an enterprise – hence, perhaps, the steady stream of lawyers and, to a lesser

---

[124] See *DNB* sub "Oglethorpe, Theophilus"; *Complete Peerage*, X, 41–42. Anne was born *ca.* 1683 and grew up largely in France as a catholic of Jacobite tendencies. She returned to England early in the eighteenth century and informed on Jacobites, but was created countess Oglethorpe by the Old Pretender in 1722. She died, unmarried, in an unknown year.

extent, doctors, surgeons, and apothecaries whose names fill out lists dominated by clergy, peerage, and gentry.

Printers and booksellers were in a trade themselves but are of course in an entirely different category. A prosperous urban fishmonger or provincial JP who subscribes in advance for a book means to read it, keep it as decoration in his library, or give it away as a gift. A bookseller normally intends to sell it, and at a mark-up, to those who missed the original call to subscribe.[125] It is not surprising, therefore, to find booksellers in greater numbers on most lists. Many of the best-known names in publishing are represented on several lists: Tonson, Lintot, Clements, and the Innyses, for example, were giants who could simply not afford to let a title pass. Thus Wise's *Asser*, which had a very low proportion of publishing subscribers, nonetheless drew orders from the Innyses and Paul Vaillant of London; from Samuel Wilmot of Oxford; and from John or James Waghorn of Durham.[126]

More interesting is the large number of provincial booksellers, like Waghorn, who subscribed, often for multiple copies, of some works. For a general work like Moréri's *Great Historical Dictionary*, the interest of provincial booksellers could run very high, even if inconsistently so across the country. It was strong for Burnet, Collier, and Walker, and keenest of all for Strype's *Annals*, fully a fifth of whose subscribers were in one way or another connected with the book trade. For others, the numbers were much smaller, particularly the more scholarly and antiquarian works that were unlikely to be bought off the shelf and might languish unpurchased, tying up space and capital. The lack of bookselling subscribers for Castell's *Villas* is an extreme case, and the booksellers were probably frightened off by other works such as Sawyer's *Memorials*, or even a little book like Wise's *Asser*. They may similarly have been chary of titles with regional appeal like Salmon's *Hertfordshire* (though this was certainly not true in the case of another county study, Plot's *Staffordshire*). In still other cases an author's personal preferences may have kept bookseller involvement to a minimum. Hearne in fact had at least two booksellers subscribe for his Leland – Jonah Bowyer of London and Henry Clements of Oxford – but neither of them was billed as such in the list, and Clements was included simply as an agent for five other individuals. In most instances, though, booksellers could be found in a comfortable range of 2 to 4 percent, with a book like Strype's

---

[125] Printers may well have bought works as readers, rather than for retail, but it is less risky to include their relatively small numbers together with the booksellers.

[126] Wilmot, listed only as "Mr." is probably Samuel Wilmot, active in Oxford and London from 1715 to 1733, and much mentioned by Hearne, who complained of his prices (*Remarks and Collections*, VII, 257). Waghorn is listed in Plomer *et al.*, *Dictionary of Printers 1726–75* as active in Durham from 1727 to 1730; this title proves him to have been selling there earlier. His wife (probably), the Mrs. Waghorn selling and publishing in Durham in 1733–36, published a work on Durham Cathedral. Cf. C. J. Hunt, *The Book Trade in Northumberland and Durham to 1860* (Newcastle-upon-Tyne, 1975), p. 92.

representing a clear aberration at the other end. In Burnet's case, subscriptions were received from provincial booksellers in Burton, Dublin, Edinburgh, Exeter, Manchester, Newcastle, Norwich, Plymouth, Sherborne, Shrewsbury, Totnes, and York. In larger provincial towns more than one bookseller subscribed to the more attractive titles: among the 696 locations specified in the list for Walker's *Sufferings*, booksellers subscribed from similarly dispersed quarters: Cambridge, Canterbury, Chichester, Colchester, Dorchester, Dublin, Durham, Evesham, Exeter (4),[127] Hereford, Hull, Leeds, Leicester (2), Lichfield, Lincoln, London (23), Manchester, Newcastle-upon-Tyne, Northampton, Nottingham, Oxford (3), Peterborough, Plymouth, St. Edmondsbury in County Dublin, Sherborne in Dorset, Whitchurch in Shropshire, Wolverhampton, Worcester, and York.

Among the reasons that could impel a prospective reader to commit funds for more than one copy of a book, a compulsive desire to have duplicates probably ranks low (biblioholics such as Thomas Rawlinson being relatively rare). On the other hand, many owners divided their libraries between town and country, and writers of marginalia such as Roger Twysden could annotate two identical copies of a work with different material. Within the intellectual community, many readers, either noble patrons or fellow scholars, might so subscribe as a boost to sales, to ensure sufficient numbers for the publisher or author to proceed.[128] Charles Leigh's *Natural History of Lancashire, Cheshire and the Peak in Derbyshire*, another work sold by subscription, actually included only a partial list of subscribers because of "several persons subscribing for different numbers," that is on behalf of other buyers.[129] Several members of Thomas Uvedale's own family subscribed for his new edition of Commynes.[130] Two brothers, Henry and Richard Edmunds of Jesus College, Oxford signed up for copies of Wise's Asser.[131]

The greatest impulse behind multiple subscription may be the above-noted

---

[127] Exeter had a particularly active bookselling trade in the early eighteenth century: William Stukeley visited it in 1723 and was struck by the number of booksellers that made for "a good face of learning," complete with auction sales. SAL MS Stukeley IV/i/336 (Stukeley to the earl of Pembroke, [?]August 1723).

[128] The large, and largely inexplicable, number of medical subscribers (physicians, surgeons, and apothecaries) for Hearne's edition of Camden may simply be a result of having approached one or two working within proximity of several others: aside from a prominent doctor and bibliophile like Sloane, many were associated with St. Bartholomew's Hospital or the hospitals of Bridewell and Bethlehem.

[129] Charles Leigh, *Natural History of Lancashire, Cheshire, and the Peak, in Derbyshire* (1700), p. [1].

[130] *The Memoirs of Philip de Comines*, trans. Uvedale, based on Godefroy's French edition (2 vols., 1712). HRC, copy 2 shelfmark DC 106.9 C723 1712 HRC/QUA is annotated in a contemporary hand.

[131] Both matriculated on 23 June 1715 (age fifteen and sixteen respectively) and were still alive to subscribe in 1722; they were sons of John Edmunds of Llandegay, Carnarvonshire, gent. (Foster, *Alum Ox.*, II, 409).

popularity of books as gifts. A concrete example comes from a copy of one of the books here sampled, Hearne's reedition, in Latin, of Camden's *Annales* of Elizabeth. Among the 208 subscribers for this work, one finds Samuel Mead, Esq. Mead's name shows up on several of the lists, generally with no address, but he was undoubtedly the lawyer of that name associated with Lincoln's Inn. Mead subscribed in 1717 for several copies of the Camden, his name being daggered on that list. We know that the extra copies were to be given away, since the copy at the University of Texas in Austin bears a noble bookplate and is inscribed (on the verso of an engraved portrait of Elizabeth) "E dono Samueli Meade Ar[miger] Ao. 1718."[132] Mead had evidently given this copy, within a year of his receipt of his order, to the recipient, who can be identified from the bookplate and motto, *tuum est*, as William, Earl Cowper (himself a frequent subscriber to such books, though not to this one). Mead also subscribed, as a very young man, to Moréri's *Great Historical Diction-ary* in 1694, to Hearne's Leland and *Scotichronicon*, to Rowe's *Lucan* in 1718/19, to Sawyer's *Memorials* in 1725 (as did Earl Cowper's son and heir), and to a book not in the sample, David Scott's *The History of Scotland* (Westminster, 1727).[133] And Samuel's better-known younger brother, Dr. Richard Mead (1673–1754), who was Alexander Pope's physician and an active whig, also appears on several lists, acquiring during his lifetime a huge collection of books, manuscripts, statuary, and coins that was one of the largest of its day.[134]

Regional disparities such as those discussed briefly above in connection with publishing-sector subscribers are somewhat more difficult to assess owing to the fact that not all lists contain information as to the locations of subscribers and those that do are rarely without ambiguity. There can be little question, however, that regional chorographies, though not devoid of readers further afield, sold best to booksellers and private subscribers in the

---

[132] HRC, shelfmark DA 350 C17 1717 HRC.
[133] J. Venn and J. A. Venn, *Alumni Cantabrigienses: a Biographical List of all Known Students, Graduates and Holders of Office at the University of Cambridge, from the Earliest Times to 1900* (10 vols., Cambridge, 1922–54), part I, vol. III, p. 170 gives him as Samuel Mede or Mead (1670–1733), university counsel to Cambridge 1719–24, second son of Matthew Mead, Stepney, Middlesex, gent. (for whom see *DNB*). Samuel Mead was admitted to the Middle Temple on 12 April 1695; called to the bar on 19 May 1699, and admitted to Lincoln's Inn on 20 January 1712/13. He died on 20 March 1733, aged sixty-three and according to the obituary notice in *Gentleman's Magazine*, 3 (1733), 157, he was the brother of "Dr. Mead." Richard and Samuel's father, also in *DNB*, was Matthew Mead (1630?–99), an Independent divine. Born in Bedfordshire, he was ejected from his Stepney living in 1662 but was still able to live there and teach his thirteen children at home. Samuel, an elder son, was apparently at Utrecht with Edmund Calamy as a fellow student. He became evening lecturer at Salters' Hall but was not ordained and became a chancery practitioner.
[134] Richard Mead's collection sold for £5,518 10s 11d: see *DNB*. He was largely responsible for raising money for and arranging the seven-volume edition of De Thou's *History of his own Time*, buying some papers from Thomas Carte, then a refugee in France.

county so described: this is especially noticeable with a book not in the selection, Tristram Risdon's *Devon*. But there are more subtle regional variations. Moréri, the closest thing in the sample to a general-interest encyclopedia of historical and geographical information, and quite successful given the number of its subsequent editions, appealed in 1694 to a readership confined principally to the south and southwest, with some counties in the north and north-central part of the country unrepresented. The pattern for Walker, the other large list with sufficient information to map subscribers, shows a similar pattern. A total of 490 firmly identifiable locations have been marked on map 6.4 (slightly over a third of all the names), of which fifty-five had multiple subscribers. The most densely subscribed areas were cities and their suburban areas, especially London, Chichester, Colchester, and Exeter – where the author was prebendary – as well as in the two universities, while in the countryside the book sold best in the southwest. In short, the book was most subscribed in East Anglia and the West Country, both areas that had seen considerable ejection of clergy, but also areas, interestingly, with long-standing traditions of antipopery and dissent. Of the identified subscribers, only a handful were based in Wales, and very few could be found north of central Yorkshire, with some conspicuous exceptions such as the growing seaside coal town of Whitehaven, seat of one branch of the influential Lowther family, who are not included in the list. It is probably safer to attribute this disparity less to a geography of taste than to a greater sophistication of bookselling networks in particular counties. An arch-tory of Jacobite sympathies such as Henry Prescott should have been a likely subscriber for Walker's *Sufferings*, which he in fact would buy three years after its publication, but there is no mention in his diary of the proposals, and Cheshire had only a single subscriber. The list for Hearne's *Camden* is too spotty to map, but those persons with addresses specified were overwhelmingly from London, Oxford, Berkshire, and the south (Dorset, Hampshire, Wiltshire, and Sussex), with none further north than Robert Cholmondley of Holford, Cheshire and Christopher Rawlinson of Carke Hall, Lancashire; a Welsh subscriber, Richard Mostyn of Penbedw, also subscribed for the *Scotichronicon*, for Leigh's *Natural History of Lancashire*, and for Thompson's edition of Geoffrey of Monmouth.[135]

---

[135] Hearne had a good many repeat subscribers, in part because several of his works included advertisements of his next project: the first volume of the Camden ends with an announcement, immediately following the subscription list (p. clxxxiv) for Hearne's *Gulielmi Neubrigensis Historia Rerum Anglicarum*, already in press, at a guinea for the large paper version, 15s for the small paper. The advertisement invited buyers to give their money to the "publisher" (Hearne himself) at St. Edmund Hall or to the printer John Rance at the "Theatre" printing house. Only 150 copies (fifty of which would be large paper) would be printed. At this stage Hearne was in particular difficulties with university authorities, who threatened to stop publication of his William of Newburgh: Hist. MSS Comm., *Portland*, VII, 234–35, 245.

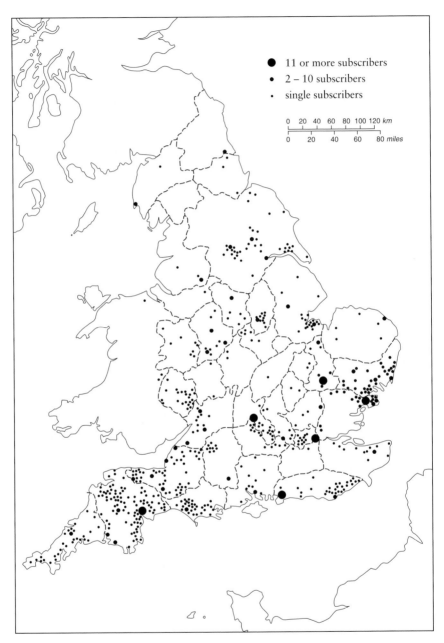

Map 6.4   Identifiable subscribers to John Walker's *Sufferings of the Clergy.*

Thompson's book, even more than Hearne's, relied on a subscription base within a short radius of the translator's base at Queen's College, rarely finding buyers beyond Oxford, Warwickshire, Northamptonshire, and the border counties of Wales. A large number of university-connected persons subscribed, overwhelmingly from Queen's College itself.[136]

In addition to asking what the broad patterns of subscription are, we can also determine the reading tastes of particular individuals across lists. In addition to Mostyn and the Mead brothers, several names appear in a number of the lists. Many were prominent bibliophiles, who could be expected to subscribe to a book that they simply wanted to add to their collections, such as Rawlinson, the Harleys, and Lord Sunderland. Well-known scholars and families of scholars appear throughout: the Gales, for example, Browne Willis, Charles Eyston (whose work on Glastonbury Hearne would subsequently edit), Ralph Thoresby, and Thomas Tanner. Several of these were friends of the authors and in Hearne's case acted as informal agents, typically receiving a bonus copy if they signed up six subscribers.[137] Heralds also appear with regularity, in particular John Anstis, and a variety of Crown and ecclesiastical officials. Henry Prescott subscribed for two copies of volumes one through four of Leland, but the competing demands of his publican had forced him back to a single copy by volume five.[138] The book-hungry ex-sheriff of Devon, Richard Coffin, similarly appears on several early lists, including that for Plot.

Among the gentry of middling but principally local prominence who regularly subscribed to historical books in the first third of the eighteenth century, Thomas Cartwright (1671–1748) of Aynho in Northamptonshire provides a good example. The grandson of a roundhead lawyer whose own father had purchased Aynho in 1615, Cartwright was a tory and a member of the October Club. He sat in every parliament but two from 1695 till his death, consistently voting with the government except on a motion for the removal from office of Sir Robert Walpole in 1748.[139] Among the numerous

---

[136] Merchants/tradesmen include a mathematical instrument maker and a watchmaker, both in London, and several provincial tradesmen. Interestingly, Sir Isaac Newton subscribed for more than one copy, which should be a guard against assuming that every learned reader would have been uninterested in Thompson's attempt to resurrect the Galfridian history of Britain.

[137] Pollard and Ehrman, *Distribution of Books by Catalogue*, p. 189.

[138] Prescott also subscribed to Charles Leigh's *Natural History of Lancashire* (not in sample). He refers to receiving his Leland, via the Oxford carrier as arranged by his son Jack (then a student in Oxford), in *Diary of Henry Prescott*, II, 309, 312. He visited Hearne "close at study in his post in the Bodleian Library" while in Oxford in September 1711: ibid., II, 326. And in November 1715 he paid 4s 6d to the Oxford carrier for delivering his son's box complete with Leland's *Collectanea* in six volumes: ibid., II, 474.

[139] Burke's *Commoners*, vol. II, p. 439 and Sedgwick, ed., *The House of Commons, 1715–1754*, I, 534. Cartwright was sheriff of Northamptonshire in 1693–94 and of Oxfordshire in 1699–1700; Venn and Venn, *Alum. Cant.*, part I, vol. i, p. 303 lists him as adm. fellow-

works to which he subscribed were Thompson's rather low-brow edition of Geoffrey of Monmouth, Sawyer's *Memorials*, Hearne's Fordun (but not the Hearne Leland or Camden), Strype's *Annals of the Reformation*, and Collier's *Ecclesiastical History*.[140] And in addition to works purchased by subscription, Cartwright of course had many other works of history in his collection, including some purchased second-hand. A copy of Robert Cary's *Paleologia chronica* (1677) now at the University of Texas was purchased by Cartwright in 1698 and features his armorial bookplate.[141] In contrast to a mild dissenting whig like Samuel Mead, whose political inclinations apparently played little part in his selection of books (including the unlikely combination of Rowe's *Lucan* and Hearne's various editions), Thomas Cartwright's tory tastes kept his name off the list for books such as Rowe's, though not those for Strype and the second volume of Burnet.[142]

By the 1730s the book trade had matured into the form it would keep for much of the next two centuries, though further developments such as the circulating libraries, themselves bookseller-sponsored, demonstrate that other marketing strategies still lay ahead. The republic of letters that linked the pieces of Europe together at the dawn of the Enlightenment was shadowed in England by a network of booksellers, agents, carriers, and merchants able to distribute books of various sizes with a speed and efficiency that now seems remarkable, particularly in comparison with the situation of a century or so before. Historical works were by not, of course, the only beneficiaries of this network, but the evidence of serialization and subscription, coupled with the remarks of readers themselves, makes it clear that history had a prominent "market share." History was an acceptable and highly valued form of middle-class reading, considerably less suspect than that "frivolous" newcomer, the novel, and read as much for entertainment as

commoner at St. Catherine's, Cambridge, 14 January 1686–87. The son of William Cartwright of Aynho, Thomas was MP for Northamptonshire in 1695–98, 1701–10, and 1748; he died 10 March 1748 aged seventy-seven; see *Gentleman's Magazine* (1748). The biographical sketch in Sedgwick, ed., *The House of Commons, 1715–1754* identifies him as the son of William Cartwright of Bloxham, Oxon., by Ursula, daughter of Ferdinando Fairfax, MP, second lord Fairfax. He married on 30 March 1699 Armine, daughter of Thomas Crew MP, second baron Crew.

[140] With respect to Collier, Cartwright's name is on the list for the second volume of 1714; the "Mr. Cartwright" listed in the first volume of 1708 may or not be the same man, since there is considerable divergence between the two lists.

[141] HRC, shelfmark Wing C.743. This has been annotated in a late seventeenth- or early eighteenth-century hand, perhaps Cartwright's; although Cary's book was among the first sold by subscription, he bought his copy over twenty years after publication and not by subscription.

[142] He is probably the "Thomas Cartwright Esq." who subscribed for the large paper edition of the second volume of Burnet, which was certainly not a tory-favored title. Strype's whig connections have been noted above.

for education. It was the civilized literary subject *par excellence* through the rest of the eighteenth and into the nineteenth century, as demonstrated by the enormous popularity of Hume, Gibbon, Robertson, Catherine Macaulay, and, later, Thomas Babington Macaulay. That popularity owed much, of course, to the indisputable talents of the likes of Gibbon and Hume, but it would have been inconceivable without the marketing tactics of the previous century or so, which pushed history books into the most remote corners of the realm.

Conclusion

This book has been built on a number of fundamental premises. The first is that the history of historiography cannot be told simply through the analysis of the writings of historians, but must also take account of the readers, publishers, printers, and booksellers, among others, who together make up Darnton's "communications circuit," a metaphor I have adopted, with some revision. The second is that historical texts composed by authors are neither immutable and permanent nor identical with the books in which they are contained, but rather are the joint fabrication of several hands in an on-going process of collective creation (physical as well as intellectual) and communication in which, during the early modern period at least, readers were active and important participants. The third is that the forces determining the writing, printing, purchase, lending, reading, and, often, revision and reprinting of individual historical works, and the success or failure of entire genres, were many and complex. They had as much to do with social and economic trends, in particular the changing nature of readership and the evolution of the institutions of knowledge production (including both the publishing industry and libraries) as with the more traditional factors, such as the advent of continental humanism, to which they have generally been ascribed. In chapter 1 we witnessed the decline and virtual extinction of an entire medieval genre, the chronicle, while noting both its successor "parasite genres," and its surviving offshoots outside the realm of print, for instance private chronologies and town chronicles. Chapter 2, which focuses most clearly on reading, explored the fate of history books once they reached readers' hands, by examining the many contexts in which they were read, and the various uses, serious and frivolous, to which they were put. Chapters 3 and 4 turned more directly to the issue of access to historical works, either through ownership or borrowing; the conclusion of these two chapters was, not surprisingly, that history in a wide variety of genres and formats was much more readily available at the end of the period than the beginning. In the final two chapters the focus shifted again, this time to the process whereby a text left an author's hand and became a published book, to the economic constraints and commercial pressures operating in the world of history publishing, and to the various means, formal and informal, whereby history books could be marketed and distributed up and down the land.

In dealing with all these matters we have had to traverse two and a half centuries of profound social, economic, political, religious, and intellectual changes. At the beginning of the period, the Wars of the Roses remained unconcluded and England was a minor kingdom on the outskirts of Europe, in which a tiny minority of the population was literate; at the end, England and Scotland were evolving into Great Britain, an uneasily United Kingdom that, for all its internal tensions, now stood on the brink of European hegemony and overseas empire, with a considerably larger population that was much more complex and stratified. In intellectual and cultural history, no less than political, economic or social history, 250 years is a long time. In the final pages of this history book it may therefore be useful to step back and consider how very different was the situation of the history book as a whole, and of its reader, in the age of Defoe, Swift and Pope, than it was in the era of author/printers like William Caxton and his mid-Tudor successor, Richard Grafton.

In Defoe's posthumously published work, *The Compleat Gentleman*, there is a brief dialogue between the author and one Sir A. B. This knight is a member of the same family of provincial squires as Sir Roger de Coverley and Squire Western, but a little less literate than either. He has a library, in a room all its own, but no books. When asked what books his father had owned (and which he has now sold) Sir A. B. replies with a verbal catalog, many of the items in which will seem familiar to readers of the present work. The books, to which Sir A. B. has not added, included "a great Bible, the register of the house, where all the nativityes and the burials of the family were recorded for about a hundred years pass't." There were also three mass books, since Sir A. B.'s grandfather was a catholic; the family has since converted to protestantism. An "old Book of Martyrs" is on loan to the parish church and beyond any temptation the owner might have to sell it. And, finally, "not to leav out the most valuable things," there was "the old ballad of Chevy Chace set to very good music, with Robin Hood and some more of the antient heroes of that kind." All in all, the list denotes a very small private library of the sort that might have been found in a late sixteenth or early seventeenth-century minor gentry household.

His friend persuades Sir A. B. that it might be prudent to add a few books to his library in case his own sons require education. Seized with a sudden zeal for learning, the squire is advised to consult the booksellers as to "what will suit your library." His enthusiasm is short-lived. On calling at a bookseller famous for "old and scarse books of learning and antiquity and in most languages," he is disappointed to discover that most of the books are "old and dusty and lay in heaps on the counters and on the floore, out of all order." He finds another bookseller whose wares are neatly arranged, "all fair and new," many of them "guilded and letter'd on the back." To this merchant's surprise, the knight offers a flat sum for a whole side of the shop without further inspection, being more interested in the covers than the contents. After some haggling over the price, the books are sold, packed up, and shipped by sea to Southampton, and thence carted overland to Sir A. B.'s house, where the empty room awaits, having been refurbished with new presses and glass doors.[1]

Sir A. B. is a fictional figure of course, and a satirical one at that. But there are elements in him of many of the people we have met: of book collectors like the enthusiastic Richard Coffin; of the fussy arranger of books, Pepys, with his side interest in ballads like Chevy Chase and Robin Hood; or of the earl of Sunderland, Thomas Rawlinson, and the wig-maker Edmund Harrold, spending themselves into near ruin at auctions and booksellers' stalls; and even of the many donors, their names obscure to us, who presented parochial libraries with copies of Foxe's *Acts and Monuments* or other godly histories. Even as a fictional character, however, Sir A. B. seems an anachronism, his meager inherited collection redolent of an Elizabethan or Jacobean minor gentry closet rather than an Augustan manor house.

If the Renaissance was the great age of the Text, and the Reformation that of the Word, then the "long eighteenth century" between the Restoration and the Napoleonic wars was unquestionably that of the Page. Not all printed pages had the shape of books, but books are nevertheless central to the educated culture of the time to a degree unprecedented even in the preceding two centuries. Defoe, an observer outside the religious and social mainstream, once again put his finger on what books in general and historical books in particular represented to their readers. In arguing for an education devoid of pedantry, Defoe thought that it was possible to acquire learning through books, and those written in English, without direct experience where that could not be had. The gentleman who has not made the Grand Tour may "travell by land with the historian, by sea with the navigators." He has all of the past at his hands, too, even though direct experience of it is impossible:

The studious geographer and the well read historian travells with not this or that navigator or traveller, marches with not this or that generall, or making this or that campaign, but he keeps them all company; he marches with Hannibal over the Alps into Italy, and with Caesar into Gaul and into Britain, with Belisarius into Affric, and with the Emperor Honorius into Persia. He fights the battle of Granicus with Alexander, and of Actium with Augustus; he is at the overthro' of the great Bajazette by Tamerlain, and of Tomombejus and his Mamaluks by Selymus; he sees the battle

---

[1] Daniel Defoe, *The Compleat English Gentleman*, ed. K. B. Bülbring (1890), pp. 135–39.

of Lepanto, with the defeat of the Spanish Armada with Drake; with Adrian he views the whole Roman Empire and in a word, the whole world; he discovers America with Columbus, conquers it with the great Cortez, and replunders it with Sir Francis Drake.

Nothing has been famous or valuable in the world, or even the ruines of it, but he has it all in his view; and nothing done in the world but he has it in his knowledge, from the siege of Jerusalem to the siege of Namure, and from Titus Vespasian to the greater King William: he has it all at the tip of his tonge.[2]

Defoe's well-educated gentleman is no scholar in the narrow sense. He lives outside the university, and his reading of history among other subjects is not merely for personal improvement or knowledge, or for civil employment, but for wider social intercourse and even mere enjoyment. Histories are superior in this regard to fiction, for "No romances, playes, or diverting storyes can be equally entertaining to a man of sence." The world of the past is his through history, enlivened by a knowledge of place that he can verify with his maps and globes, to which he can "see the very spot where every great accion was done, however remote in place or in time." By reading both ancient and modern history, "Every scene of glory is there spread before him, from the great overtho' of Senacherib's army at the gates of Samaria . . . to the yet more well fought battles of Leipsick, Blenheim, and Malplaquet."[3] On the face of it, this looks like any Tudor advice book commending the reading of history. There is, to be sure, greater attention to the events themselves, and their imaginative apprehension, than the largely exemplary focus of Renaissance humanism dictated. Nevertheless, there is still a broad similarity in the enthusiastic endorsement of Clio's virtues. We have heard such words from the time of Caxton and Fabyan, through Degory Wheare and Henry Peacham, up to Hearne's *Ductor Historicus* and Nicolson's *English Historical Library*. We catch the scent of Bolingbroke close by; Hume lurks just around the bend. But while the praise of history remained a commonplace in the two and a half centuries after Caxton first printed the *Polychronicon*, the cultural world within which histories were read had changed drastically.

The past that the sixteenth-century history reader could visit was a limited one indeed, both because not very many histories were yet in print, but also because the contexts in which they were read were very narrowly defined. Although there was a medieval tradition of courtly reading of chivalric, military histories in the style of Froissart, reading itself was not an act generally associated with pleasure, much less with leisure, a concept whose day had not yet come. The number of history books found in most sixteenth-century libraries was not insignificant, but neither was it large, and many smaller collections would have had no histories at all. Although many of the

---

[2] Ibid., p. 226.   [3] Ibid., p. 227.

Tudor chroniclers were read for enjoyment as well as consulted for factual information, history was certainly not a "major" subject for either most readers or their booksellers, and in the early decades of print, many histories were read principally as rhetorical and literary models rather than with a view toward understanding the past in its own right. Those Elizabethans who did wish to purchase or read historical works outside the classical canon were pretty much confined to the Tudor chronicles and the small number of medieval annalists who had reached print. This pool increased to some degree at the end of the century with the advent of Tacitean politic history, the history play, and the other "parasite" genres that would ultimately kill the chronicle, but pickings were arguably still slim. This is true even if one factors in the importation or translation of successful continental works by authors such as Sleidan or Sarpi, or allows for the advent of the alternative, antiquarian account of the past which, in the form of *Britannia* and the county chorographies it inspired, added a new element to many pre-civil war libraries.

A century later the picture could not be more different. The reader of the 1730s had a bewildering array of choices to make: choices among subject (history as opposed to religion, science, or fiction); choices among genres of history; choices of particular authors. There were now histories of virtually every known event, and histories of institutions, in expensive folios, and in every other format down to almanacs. The evidence adduced here suggests that history books were, on average, more expensive than other sorts of books, and that there was a vigorous market for expensive, lavishly bound folios among the wealthiest collectors. That should not blind us to the smaller-scale collecting activities, and reading habits of the likes of Edmund Harrold, or of the apprentice Roger Lowe. Moreover, it was considerably easier to find a particular title, even an old or rare one, by the end of the seventeenth century. Auctions, advertisements, serialization, and advance subscription, together with a vastly improved communications network among booksellers and between booksellers and potential clients, at home and abroad, made Sir A. B.s out of a good many gentlemen and aristocrats with money to spend, while catering to the particular interests of more discriminating readers.

History had established itself, both by weight of numbers and social convention, as an essential part of any library, institutional or private. It figured prominently in the leisure reading of most literate persons in the eighteenth century. It did not, of course, have a monopoly on taste, as demonstrated by the success of French romance after 1650 and of the novel three-quarters of a century later. The novel proved a potent rival indeed, and considerable effort was devoted by the most famous historians of the eighteenth century to winning back reading souls lost to the pages of Scudéry and

Haywood, and then to Fielding, Richardson, and Smollett – the last a historian-for-hire as well as a novelist. A very few historians – Clarendon (posthumously) at the beginning of the eighteenth century, Hume in the middle, Robertson and Gibbon in the later decades – achieved an enduring "star" status, a phenomenon that would have confounded a Stow or a Camden, both of whose Tudor works of history had sold, for their day, quite well. Historians now had a visibility and social presence that their shadowy Tudor and early Stuart precursors had neither enjoyed nor sought. We saw in chapter 1 that the medieval chronicler John Hardyng was a phantom who could be depicted in the guise of a German prince by an owner keen to adorn his copy with an authorial image, however false. To most contemporary readers, Camden and Samuel Daniel, even Sir Walter Ralegh and Sir Francis Bacon, were respected names attached to particular books. Clarendon's image graced his *History of the Rebellion and Civil Wars* upon its first publication, three decades after his death (see plate 7.22). But Hume, Gibbon, Catharine Macaulay, Horace Walpole, and a number of lesser lights such as Lord Lyttelton, were public persons who entered into many private homes more than once: first through their books, and then bodily, to dine or drink with their more admiring and affluent readers.

The nineteenth century would witness yet another change, as history and literature, for a time, drew closer together, in the highly rhetorical historical narratives of master storytellers like Macaulay and in what might be described as a new kind of parasite genre, the historical novel established by Scott and continued in Thackeray's *Henry Esmond*, Dickens' *Tale of Two Cities*, and hundreds of lesser works. The vogue for historical fiction proved considerably more durable than the corresponding fashion for history plays two centuries earlier. Even now it saturates the supermarket shelves through popular authors like Taylor Caldwell and Ellis Peters. While it has faded as a genre of "serious" literature, every so often recondite novels such as Umberto Eco's *The Name of the Rose* and highly imaginative histories such as *The Return of Martin Guerre* will strike a chord with readers who would normally know little and care less about the intricacies of scholastic philosophy or the domestic practices of rural French villagers. These are, of course, exceptional, and the market share of straight history, though considerable, pales in comparison with that for mysteries, thrillers, and pop-psychology self-help books.

The change in "academic" or scholarly history from 1475 to 1730 is also remarkable. Although the classics remained the core of the school and university liberal arts curriculum until the mid-twentieth century, the student of the early eighteenth century (one thinks of the future lawyer and frustrated rake Dudley Ryder) was no longer confined to the pages of Sallust, Caesar, and Livy. A great number of modern works lay at hand, ranging from critical editions of those authors by the likes of Gronovius and Graevius, to foreign and domestic surveys of medieval and modern times. Magazines regularly announced the latest publications and eventually offered reviews; new books were discussed in college rooms and in dining halls and parlors; booksellers multiplied the number of readers per single copy of a book through devices such as the circulating library. Eighteenth-century advice books, the heirs to Renaissance works by Richard Brathwait and others, regularly stressed the usefulness of history to male and female sociability.[4] If the problem of the sixteenth-century reader lay in obtaining all of his or her history from a small number of authors, the dilemma of his or her Hanoverian descendant lay in what and how to choose. By the very end of the eighteenth century, the time in which many of Jane Austen's novels are set, one can see a certain fatigue setting in, whether in Catherine Morland's (and Austen's own) dislike of the endless, tiresome accounts of kings and popes "and hardly any women at all," or Fanny Price's efforts at impressing her own historical selections from circulating libraries on her less enthusiastic sister.[5]

The nineteenth century is often called the golden age of historical writing all across Europe, and it may, too, have been similarly golden for historical reading. A good study is needed of the readers of Victorian histories to match the many works by authors such as Stephen Bann, J. W. Burrow, Dwight Culler, and Rosemary Jann concerning the content and language of the great historians.[6] Industrialization, the fulfillment of the consumer revolution initiated a century earlier, together with the modernization of printing techniques, undoubtedly contributed to an even more thorough "historiciz-

[4] D. R. Woolf, "A Feminine Past? gender, genre, and historical knowledge in England, 1500–1800," *American Historical Review*, 102.3 (June 1997), 645–79.

[5] Jane Austen, *Mansfield Park* (London, 1814), ed. Margaret Drabble (New York and London, 1996), pp. 35–36, 363; *Jane Austen's The History of England*, ed. D. Le Faye (Chapel Hill, NC, 1993); *Northanger Abbey* (London, 1818, but completed in 1803), ed. Margaret Drabble (London, 1989), pp. 109–11; Christopher Kent in "Learning History with, and from, Jane Austen," in J. D. Grey (ed.), *Jane Austen's Beginnings* (Ann Arbor and London, 1989), pp. 59–71.

[6] Stephen Bann, *The Clothing of Clio: a Study of the Representation of History in Nineteenth-century Britain and France* (Cambridge, 1984), which is as much concerned with visual as verbal representation; J. W. Burrow, *A Liberal Descent: Victorian Historians and the English Past* (Cambridge, 1981); A. Dwight Culler, *The Victorian Mirror of History* (New Haven, CT, 1985); Rosemary Jann, *The Art and Science of Victorian History* (Columbus, OH, 1985). Cf. Valerie E. Chancellor, *History for Their Masters: Opinion in the English History Textbook, 1800–1914* (Bath, 1970).

Plate 7.22 (*opposite*)   By the early eighteenth century images of authors were much better known to generations now used to collecting portraits, and historians themselves had a much better established public persona, here illustrated in the engraved image of the earl of Clarendon preceding each of three volumes of his *History of the Rebellion* (Oxford, 1702–4): compare this with the image of "John Hardyng," plate 1.1, above.

Edward Earl of CLARENDON, Lord High CHANCELLOR of England.
and Chancellor of the University of Oxford Anᵒ Domⁱ 1667.

ation" of the population than that which I have suggested occurred in the early modern period; the formation of a "British" identity, in part through public celebrations of national victories, recent and remote, naturally magnified the effects of books that in turn reflected different interpretations of Britain's past, and the pasts of the wider world.[7]

It is also arguable, however, that this golden age simply extended trends that began in the seventeenth century. We as readers are not exactly the descendants of Roger Lowe, Henry Prescott, Sarah Cowper, John Ward, and the many other book owners mentioned in this study, any more than, as writers, we are working in precisely the same tradition as Gibbon or Hume, Clarendon or Rushworth, Stow or Holinshed, and before them Edward Hall and Polydore Vergil. The contexts of reading as well as of writing have certainly evolved since the eighteenth century and are demonstrably different now than they were before the post-1945 flood of Penguin paperbacks. Yet when we pick up a history book and read it, we are engaging with our own past in ways that would have seemed strange to a Gabriel Harvey or John Dee, but considerably less so to a Prescott or a Pepys. If indeed there was a historical revolution in the early modern period, it lay less in the texts that historians, biographers, and antiquaries wrote than in the volume and variety of books that appeared under their names, and in the even greater number of English men and women who read them.

[7] Linda Colley, *Britons: Forging the Nation, 1707–1837* (New Haven, CT, 1992); for revisions to this thesis see Colin Kidd, *British Identities Before Nationalism: Ethnicity and Nationhood in the Atlantic World 1600–1800* (Cambridge, 1999).

⟨⟨ A ⟩⟩

A bookseller's inventory in history books, ca. 1730: evidence from Folger MS Add. 923

Folger Shakespeare Library MS Add. 923, which as of late 1999 remains incompletely cataloged, and its authorship unknown, contains what appears to be either the actual "stockbook" of an early eighteenth-century bookseller who both sold books retail and wholesale and bought them on behalf of other booksellers, or, less likely but not impossibly, the author's listing, for some other purpose such as a general guide to prices, of various books and their values. The manuscript bears no indication of authorship,[1] nor any date, but no work mentioned therein is dated after 1730, allowing this to stand as the probable year of composition.

The information the manuscript contains is doubly useful. First, it provides through a large sample of over 2,000 books a good snapshot of the historical (and other) works being traded in right at the end of our period. Secondly, it gives fixed prices in unbound and bound form for nearly all of these, allowing us to establish some sense of the prices of a large number of Augustan historical works at the same time, beyond the evidence of scattered references from different years and multiple sources that are discussed in chapter 5 and elsewhere in this book.

The stockbook itself begins with a list (paginated pp. 1–11) of European printers and their locations ranging back to Gutenberg; this may have been intended as a key to the imprints in the list, and at the very least it offers a clear indication that the author of the manuscript was interested in older books as well as recent titles. The rest of the manuscript is unfoliated, and includes many blank or only partially inscribed leaves interspersed with

---

[1] Two Dutch scholars, Ann Veenhoff and Marja Smolenaars of the Sir Thomas Browne Institute in Leiden, working on the Anglo-Dutch book trade, inform me that the Dutch titles included herein are, in different editions, commonplace, turning up for instance in the somewhat earlier correspondence of the Oxford bookseller Samuel Smith.

more closely written ones. It lists books with generally though not always precise details of edition (place and date), together with what may or may not be – depending on whether the author was, indeed, a bookseller – the price paid for the work by him in sheets (or in some instances, bound), and what appears to be a recommended sale price (the price of the work bound). There is insufficient evidence to identify these prices definitively with what we would now call "wholesale" or "retail" prices, and unbound books could often sell "retail" to private buyers for more than they sold, discounted, to other booksellers. On the other hand, the distinction is here maintained so consistently as to warrant a presumption that this is what is intended, though even the quire books came at some kind of mark-up, since a few were marked as received at "prime cost" (see below).

Tables A.1–A.3 extract from the manuscript nearly all the works on history, biography, antiquarianism, and chronology, together with collected works containing a significant historical component (for example, *Opera* of Tacitus, which would also contain nonhistorical works). Authors and titles are presented *not* as they appear in the manuscript, but in edited form, as identified by the present writer (in some cases, only provisionally, uncertainties being marked with a ?). They have been realphabetized by author, out of sequence with the original (for instance moving Hobbes' translation of Thucydides from *H* to *T*). Square brackets around information denotes a fact that is not given in the MS but which can be either inferred with some certainty or established from bibliographical sources.

Dates of publication are given as rendered in the manuscript, and in several instances do not match dates on title pages of works as given in modern library catalogs. Where dates are not given in the MS, or more than one edition appeared in that year, the editions identified are the most likely, and are based on reference to *STC*, Wing, the *National Union Catalogue: pre-1956 Imprints*, the *British Library Catalogue of Printed Books*, the on-line catalogs of Harvard University, the University of California, and the Library of Congress, and the on-line *English Short-Title Catalogue*; I wish particularly to thank my former doctoral student Mr. Greg Bak for his assistance in the time-consuming task of identifying the works. The purpose is to illustrate the range and prices of histories available at the end of the period of study, not to provide a fully edited version of the manuscript (a task well worth doing but well outside the scope of this book). Latin places of publication have been silently converted to their English-vernacular equivalents: e.g. *Lugduni Batavorum* in MS is here denoted as Leiden, *Trajectum ad Rhenum* as Utrecht, and so on.

Anomalies, including *possible* errors by the author of the MS, are noted item by item as they occur. The word *possible* must be stressed because there is always the chance that he recorded a real book, edition, or reprint that is no longer extant. In the case of multivolume works published over several years, the author invariably records only the year in which the first volume(s) were published; in one or two instances, the absence of a reference to multiple volumes, or reference to fewer volumes than subsequently made up a complete set (as for instance in the case of Michel Maittaire's *Annales typographici* [5 vols., The Hague, 1719–41], only 2 vols. of which are noted herein) suggests a title not yet fully published; this in turn helps to confirm 1730 as the likeliest *terminus ad quem* for the composition of the manuscript.

For foreign works the rates of exchange are taken from John J. McCusker, *Money and Exchange in Europe and America, 1600–1775* (Chapel Hill, NC, 1978), tables 2.5 and 5.1. The rate of exchange for Dutch gulden (guilders) or florijns in 1730 was 1,036.20 gu. = £100 sterling, meaning guilder figures should be divided by a factor of 10.36. There were 20 stuivers to the guilder. The popularity of The Netherlands as a source for books derived both from its comparative freedom of the press and also its very stable currency; the exchange rate appears not to have been a decisive factor for English booksellers such as the unidentified proprietor of this stock, or the earlier Thomas Bennet and Henry Clements in Oxford, in determining whence they obtained foreign books since the French livre had been more or less steadily losing ground against the pound for a century.

Many of the books, or different editions of the same works, turn up in contemporary lists of other sorts: Dr. José de Kruif of the University of Utrecht has been of great assistance in identifying several Dutch books that occur in her database of mid-eighteenth century estate inventories; in the "confraterboeken" (records of transactions with other publishers) and "onkostenboeken" (production cost account book) of the Leiden publisher Luchtens (University of Amsterdam, Zaal van de Vereniging voor de Belangen des Boekhandels); and from the day-ledgers of Pieter van Cleef, bookseller in The Hague at about the same time. It is my pleasure to acknowledge the helpful correspondence in 1997 of Dr. de Kruif, and also of two of her compatriots, Ann Veenhoff and Marja Smolenaars, for independent communication with me concerning the possible identity of the author of the manuscript which, regrettably, remains unknown.

The absence of a price in the quires column, most common among the octavo and smaller format books, suggests an out of print title of which the seller happens to have acquired a copy (quire books were invariably newer books, still in print, and usually purchased unbound). Some titles appear with very little information, suggesting either a failure to record the information or, possibly, an expectation of acquiring an item that never materialized. Books are listed here by format, from folio down, and alphabetically by author within format. For the sake of brevity, I have excluded a number of items in these lists (in particular certain commonplace editions of classical historians) that will still figure in the total count of histories. Conversely, I have for illustrative purposes listed a small number of nonhistorical items (Shakespeare's plays for instance) that are not included in the count. An asterisk (*) indicates title is endorsed "prime cost," that is a book purchased with no mark-up at all,[2] which may mean a work purchased straight from the printer rather than through another bookseller. In the calculation of low, high, and median prices, only those items for which prices are given are, of necessity, counted. Longer titles and obvious words ("Hist." for History and its variants [*Historia, Historiae, Histoire*]) are abbreviated in the interest of space.

One or two further points are worth observing. The list contains very few very old books. Two early Stuart titles, Bacon's *Henry VII* and Dallington's *Aphorismes civill and militarie* are among the earliest works, Valentin Forster's *De historia juris romani libri tres* (1565) earlier still, and the only sixteenth-century edition of a historical work. This would suggest a preference of the manuscript's author, and perhaps also his customers if customers he or she had, for newer editions where available. This is not especially surprising: though the old printed book had value as an antiquity, this was to a small segment of the market, many of whom would have sought such works out through other avenues such as auctions. Another significant point is the relative paucity of historical works in quarto format: the manuscript contains far more octavo and smaller size books than folio or quarto combined, but nearly as many (267) quartos as folios (310); yet there are only twenty-four quarto history titles. Finally, histories are in a far higher percentage among the folios than among the other two formats (amounting to just over a fifth of all folios), once again demonstrating the gravitation of history to the more expensive formats, but also a considerably wider range of prices on history books of all kinds than would have been true a century earlier.

Total no. of books listed in document = 2,155
Total no. of historical works = 304
Percentage of historical works in record = 14%

Format proportion totals
Folio: all works = 310; histories = 65 (20.6%)

[1] Two Dutch scholars, Ann Veenhoff and Marja Smollenaars of the Sir Thomas Browne Institute in Leiden, working on the Anglo-Dutch book trade, inform me that the Dutch titles included herein are, in different editions, commonplace, turning up for instance in the somewhat earlier correspondence of the Oxford bookseller Samuel Smith.

[2] The term *prime cost* was used, for instance, by George Hickes in 1698 when requesting subscribers, who had already paid twenty-two shillings for his *Thesaurus Linguarum Septentrionalium*, to increase their payment to £2 8s because his own "prime cost" had risen owing to expensive engravings: G. Pollard and A. Ehrman, *The Distribution of Books by Catalogue from the Invention of Printing to AD 1800* (Cambridge, 1965), p. 189.

Quarto: all works = 267; histories = 24 (9.7%)
Octavo or smaller: all works = 1,578; histories = 124 (7.7%)

High end values (all books including histories)
Folio: £9 15s 0d Rycaut, *Hist. of Turks* (London, 1721)
Quarto: *Titi Livii Patavini Historiarum libri qui extant* (with supplement by Joannes Dujatius), 6 vols. (Paris, 1679) at £8 0s 0d; Shakespeare's *Works* published by Pope and Sewell, 7 vols. (London, 1726), at £7 7s 0d; Catrou and Rouille, *Histoire romaine*, £6 1s 0d; Paul de Rapin-Thoyras, *Histoire de angleterre*, 10 vols. (The Hague, 1727) is a close fourth at 40 gu. in quires (approx. £4) and £6 bound.
Octavo and smaller: D. Jones *History of Europe from 1660–1714*, 18 vols., 8vo (London, n.d.), £5; *Ciceronis opera omnia*, 9 vol. H. Estienne edn (1557), 8vo, £5; *Cicero opera omnia verburgii*, 16 vols. (Amsterdam, 1724), 20 gu. quires, £3 10s bound; *Acts of the Parliament of Scotland*, 12mo (Edinburgh), 3 vols., £2 6s

Low end values (all books including histories)
Folio: Robert Dallington, *Aphorisms civill and militarie* (1629), 1s 6d
Quarto: Jeremiah Burroughs, *Gospel-revelation*, 1s
Octavo and smaller: Forbes' *Laws of election of members of parl,*, 12mo (1710), 4d; Joseph Alleine's *A most familiar explanation of the Assemblies shorter catechism* (1701), 5d

Median bound prices (histories only), excluding items for which no price is listed, and with values interpolated for even-numbered lists
Folio: £1 5s (3 titles at median of 57 counted prices: Cave, *Lives of the Primitive Fathers*; Hamelow, *Henricus Hamelow Jc. Imperatores Romani*; Tyrrell, *General Hist. of England*)
Quarto: 12s 6d (2 titles at interpolated median of 22 prices: Rowlands, *Mona antiqua restaurata*; Struve, *Historia iuris Romani*)
Octavo and smaller: 6s (16 titles at median of 119 counted prices).

Table A.1. *The price of historical works ca. 1730: the Folger stockbook. Folio volumes*

Author	Title	Format	Place of publication	Date of edition	Price (quires) £ s d	Selling bound £ s d
F. Bacon	*Hist. of Henry VII* (1st edn)	Folio	London	1622	—	0-5-0
R. Baillie	*Operis Historicis et chronologici*	folio*	Amsterdam	1663	0-2-6	0-5-0
J. Basnage de Beauval	"Contin. of Josephus" [*Hist. des Juifs*]a	folio*	London	1708	0-13-0	1-2-0
S. Basnage	*Annales politico-ecclesiastici annorum DCXLV*	fo. 3 vols.	Rotterdam	1706	—	2-10-0
G. Burnet	*Hist. of Reformation*	fo. 3 vols.	London	1715	2-7-0	3-10-0
T.Burnet	*Theory of earth*	folio	London	1697	0-6-0	0-12-0
D. Calderwood	*True History of Church of Scotland*	folio	—	1704	—	0-4-0
W. Camden	*Britannia*	fo. 2 vols	London	1722	2-8-0	3-16-0
W. Camden	*History of [Queen]. Eliz.* (i.e. *Annales*, English, 3rd edn)	folio	London	1675	—	0-10-6
W. Cave	*Lives of the Primitive Fathers*	folio	London	1716	0-16-6	1-5-0
J. Collier	*Eccles. Hist. of Eng.*	fo. 2 vols.	London	1708	2-7-0	3-10-0
R. Dallington	*Aphorismes Civill & Militarie*	folio	London	1629	—	0-1-6
D. Defoe	*The history of the union between England and Scotland*	folio	Edinburgh	1709	—	0-14-0
Diodorus Siculus	*Historical Library*	folio	London	1721	0-12-0	—
L. E. Dupin	*Compendious Hist. of Church*	folio	[London?]	[1713?]	—	—
L. Echard	*General Eccles. History*	folio	—	—	—	—
L. Echard	*Hist. of England*	folio	London	1720	—	2-2-0

Eusebius	Historia (Latin)	fo. 3 vols.	Paris	1678	—	5-5-0
Eusebius	Church History	folio	London	1709	0-13-0	1-3-0
T. Fuller	Holy War	folio	Cambridge	1647	0-1-6	0-3-0
V. Forster	De historia juris romani libri tres	folio	Basel	1565	8 bd[b]	0-14-0
A. Gordon	Itinerarium septentrionale	folio	London	1726[c]	1-0-0	1-10-0
H. Hamelow	Henricus Hamelow Jc. Imperatores Romani[d]	folio	Amsterdam	1710	—	1-5-0
C. Helvicus	Theatrum Historicum	folio	Oxford	1651	—	0-2-6
Herodotus, ed. J. Gronovius	Historia	folio Gk/Lat.	Leiden	1715	—	1-10-0
P. Heylyn	Cosmographie	folio	London	172[e]	—	1-2-0
W. Howell	Institution of General Hist.	fo. 2nd edn	London	1680	—	0-10-0
J. Hughes (ed.) (and W. Kennett)	Complete History of England	fo. 3 vols.	London	[1706 or 1719]	4-0-0	—
Josephus, trans. R. L'Estrange	Works	folio	London	1725	1-2-0	1-10-0
R. Knox	Historical Relation of . . . Ceylon	folio	London	1681	—	0-10-0
R. Lindsey	Hist. of Scotland	folio	Edinburgh	1728	—	0-12-0
Livy	Historia cum notis variorum	folio	Paris	1625	—	1-1-0
Livy	Hist. of Rome (in English)	folio	London	—	0-14-0	1-0-0
[W. Kennett]	Register and chronicle of kings of Engl. from the Restoration	folio	London	1728	—	1-17-0
W. Marryn	Hist. of England	folio	London	1628	—	0-5-0
C. Mather	Magnalia Christi Americana, or, The ecclesiastical history of New-England	folio	London	1702	0-6-0	0-18-0
J. Mencke	Scriptores rerum Germanicarum	fo. 2 vols.[f]	London	1728	—	—
F. de Mézeray	Histoire de France	fo. 3 vols.	Paris	1685	3-3-0	7-7-0
L. Moréri	Grand Dictionare historique[g]	fo. 3 vols.	Amsterdam	1724	42 gu. = 4-1-4	5-0-0

Table A.1. (cont.)

Author	Title	Format	Place of publication	Date of edition	Price (quires) £ s d	Selling bound £ s d
J. Morton	Natural Hist. of Northamptonshire	fo., engr.	London	1728	—	1-10-0
J. Nalson	Impartial Collections	fo. 2 vols.*	London	1682	0-10-0	1-8-0
W. Nicolson	English Hist. Library	folio	London	1714	—	0-12-0
J. Norden	Speculi Britanniae pars, a Topog. and Hist. Descrip. of Cornwall	folio	London	1728	—	1-1-0
J. Ogilby	History of China[h]	fo. 2 vols.	London	16—	—	3-0-0
J. Ogilby	History of Africa[i]	folio	London	16—	2-0-0	
B. Walton (ed.)	Biblia sacra polyglotta	fo. 7 vols.	London	1657	—	8-0-0
J. Oldmixon	Hist. of England under the Stewarts[j]	folio	London	1730	1-1-0	1-10-0
L. de Pontis (trans. C. Cotton)	Memoirs of the Sieur de Pontis	folio*	London	1694	—	0-9-0
W. Ralegh	Hist. of World	fo. bd.	[London?]	n.d.	0-4-3[k]	1-0-0
J. Rushworth	Hist. Collections	fo. 8 vols.	London	1721	6-6-0	9-15-0
P. Rycaut	History of Turks	folio	—	[1700?]	—	—
J. Selden (ed. D. Wilkins)	Opera omnia	folio / 3 vols. in 6	London	1726	—	8-0-0
J. Sleidan	General Hist. of the Reformation	folio*	London	1689	0-11-0	0-15-0
J. Stow (ed. Strype)	Survey of London	fo. 2 vols.	London	1720	4-4-0	6-0-0
J. Spottiswood	Hist. of Church of Scotland	fo. "best edn"	London	1655	—	1-0-0
J. Tyrrell	General Hist. of England	fo. 3 vols.	London	1700	—	1-5-0[l]
Tacitus (ed. Gordon)	—	fo. 1 vol. only	London	1728	0-18-0	1-6-0[m]
J. Taylor	Life of Christ	folio*	London	—	0-6-0	0-12-0
J. Ussher	Annales vet. & nov. testamenti	folio	Geneva	1722	—	—
Abbé René Aubert de Vertot	History of the knights of Malta	fo. 2 vols.	London	1728	2-12-6	3-10-0

| A. Wood | Athenae Oxon. | fo. 2 vols. | London | 1721 | 1-11-6 | 2-10-0 |
| A. de Wicquefort | L'Histoire de l'établissement de la République des Provinces-Unies | folio | The Hague | 1719 | 6 gu. 10 st. = 12s 6d | 1-0-0 |

[a] See further below for an octavo-format edition of this work.

[b] Unconverted: currency of canton of Basel.

[c] Annotated "to subscri[be]."

[d] MS indicates an edition of the *Historia Augusta*; this is the edition of Hamelow's work (MS: "Chamelou") bound together with J. P. Lotichius (ed.), *Historia augusta imperatorum Romanorum*, (Amsterdam, 1710).

[e] *sic* in MS.

[f] Also Leipzig, 3 vols, 1728–30; the absence of reference to the last volume in the manuscript is further reinforcement for the date 1730 as the year in which the MS was compiled.

[g] Rotterdam written, struck out, and replaced by Amsterdam in MS; *NUC* records the edition of Moréri's book published by Peter Brunel in 1724 as being in 4 vols.

[h] No such work: perhaps John Ogilby's translation of Arnoldus Montanus, *Atlas Chinensis* (1671) intended.

[i] Similarly no such work: Ogilby, a geographer and cartographer rather than a historian, published his *An Accurate Description of Africa* in 1669. He also published in 1682 a *History of America*, and the author may intend either of these; the lack of dates makes identification difficult.

[j] MS: "By the critical historian."

[k] This quire price crossed through in MS but not revised.

[l] Price crossed through in MS.

[m] Bound price unclear owing to smudge in MS.

Table A.2. *The price of historical works ca. 1730: the Folger stockbook. Quarto volumes*[3]

Author	Title	Format	Place of publication	Date of edition	Price (quires) £ s d	Selling bound £ s d
J. Arbuthnot	Tables of ancient coins	quarto	London	1727	1-10-0	1-15-0
[Elie Benoist]	Histoire de l'Edit de Nantes	quarto 5 vols.	Delft	1693	—	3-0-0
[Elie Benoist]	Hist. Edict of Nantes (English)	quarto 2 vols.	London	1694	—	—
F. Catrou and P. Rouille	Histoire romaine	quarto	Paris	1725	66 gu. = 6-7-2	6-18-0
J. Cluverius	Historiarum totius mundi epitome	quarto	[Leiden]	[1639]	—	0-3-0
P. Danet	A complete dictionary of the Greek and Roman antiquities	quarto	London	1700	—	0-9-0
G. Daniel	Histoire de France	quarto[a] 6 vols.	Amsterdam	1720	—	—
Einhard	De vita et gestis Caroli Magni cum notis variorum	quarto	Utrecht	1711	—	0-5-0
T. Godwyn	Romanae historiae anthologia recognita et aucta	quarto	London	1661	—	0-4-0
J. H. Heidegger	De historia sacra patriarcharum	quarto 2 vols.	Amsterdam	1688[-89]	—	0-14-0
Daniel Le Clerc	Hist. de la médicine	quarto	Amsterdam	1723	4 gu. 10 st. = 0-9-0	0-15-0
Livy	Titi Livii Patavini Historiarum libri qui extant	quarto [6 vols.]	Paris	1679[-82]	—	8-0-0
M. Maittaire	Annales typographici ab artis inventae origine	quarto 2 vols.	The Hague	1719[b]	—	11-5-0
I. Newton	Chronology of Ancient Kingdoms	quarto	London	1728	—	0-10-6
Plutarch	Les vies des hommes illustres	quarto	Paris	1721	28 gu. = 2-14-0	4-10-0

J. Rosinus (annot. T. Dempsteri)	Antiquitates Romanorum cum notis Dempsteri	quarto	Amsterdam	1685	—	0-10-0
H. Rowlands	Mona antiqua restaurata	quarto	Dublin	1723	0-8-6	0-12-0
R. Simon	Histoire critique de vieux testament	quarto	Amsterdam	1685	—	0-8-0
T. Sprat	History of the Royal Society	quarto	London	1722	0-5-6	0-9-6
G. Story	Impartial Hist. of Wars of Ireland	quarto	London	1693	0-3-0	0-6-0
B. G. Struve	Historia iuris Romani	quarto	Jena	1718	4 gu. = 7s 8d	0-13-0
Tacitus (ed. Jacobus Gronovius)	C. Cornelii Taciti opera quae extant	quarto	Leiden	1721	8 gu.[c] = 0-15-6	1-5-0
Abbé René Aubert de Vertot	Histoire des Chevaliers Hospitaliers de S. Jean de Jérusalem	quarto 4 vols.[d]	—	1727	—	3-16-0
G. Vossius	De historicis graecis & latinis	quarto 2 vols.	Leiden	1651[e]	—	0-7-0

[a] Actually 7 vols., 1720–25.
[b] Complete edn was 5 vols., The Hague: Isaac Vaillant, 1719–41.
[c] The publisher Luchtmans bought three copies from another publisher, van Poolsum, for 10 guilders and 10 stuivers (= 30 st.) each on 3 January 1732. Source: J. de Kruif, personal communication.
[d] Actually Paris, 5 vols.
[e] An apparent conflation of two distinct but related titles by Vossius, both published at Leiden in 1651: *De historicis graecis libri IV* and *De historicis latinis libri III* (2 vols. in 1).

[3] Criteria unchanged from folios: note that there are many fewer history titles, and an increased proportion of works imported or printed abroad.

Table A.3. *The price of historical works ca. 1730: the Folger stockbook. Octavo and smaller volumes*[4]

Author	Title	Format	Place of publication	Date of edition	Price (quires) £ s d	Selling bound £ s d
J. Basnage de Beauval	Histoire des juifs	12mo 5 vols.	The Hague	1716	—	1-10-0
Bede	Eccles. Hist.	8vo	London	1723	—	0-6-0
A.Bedford	Animadversions on Sir Isaac Newton's Chronology	8vo	London	1728	—	0-2-6
H. Bell	Historical Essay on origins of painting	[12mo]	London	1728	—	0-2-0
J. Bellegarde	Histoire général d'Espagne	8vo 9 vols.	Paris	1723	—	1-12-0
B. Bennet	Memorial of the Reformation	8vo	London	1721	—	0-6-0
W. Beveridge	Institutionum chronologicarum libri duo	8vo	London	1721	0-3-6	0-6-0
[R. Beverley]	Hist. of Virginia	8vo	London	1705	0-2-9	0-5-0
[Bilton, Henry]	Hist. of English Martyrs	8vo	London	1720	0-3-0	0-5-0
A. Blackmore	Ecclesiae primitivae notitia or . . . Christian Antiquities	2 vols.	London	1723	—	0-12-0
G. Buchanan	Rerum Scoticarum historia	8vo	Amsterdam[a]	1668	—	0-6-0
G. Burnet (abridged by T. Stackhouse)	An Abridgment of Bishop Burnet's History of his own times	8vo	London	1724	—	0-6-6
G. Burnet	Abridgement of Hist. of Reformation	12mo 3 vols.	London	1719	—	0-9-0
G. Burnet	History of Own Times	8 vo 3 vols.	The Hague	1725	—	0-11-0
G. Burnet	Some Passages in Life of Rochester	8vo	London	17—	—	0-2-0
T. Burnet	Theory of the Earth	8vo	London	1726	0-8-0	0-13-0
Caesar (ed. J. Graevius)	C. Julii Caesaris quae extant omnia cum animadversiones	8vo	Leiden	1713	3¾ gu.[b] = 0-7-1	0-11-0

Author	Title	Format	Place	Date		
F. Catrou (trans. J. Ozell)	The Roman History	8vo	[London]	[1725]	—	—
Clarendon	Hist. of Rebellion	8vo 6 vols.	London	1721	1-0-6	1-13-0
Clarendon	Hist. of Irish Rebellion	8vo	London	1720	—	0-5-0
P. de Commynes (trans. T. Uvedale)	Memoirs	8vo	London	1723	—	0-12-0
Cooper	Chronology	8vo	Edinburgh	1722	—	—
D. Crawford (or Craufurd)	Memoirs of Revolution in Scotland 1567	8vo	London	1706	—	0-5-0
D. Crawford	Notes on Buchanan's History	12mo	Edinburgh	1707[c]	—	0-2-0
J. B. Dameto	Hist. of Balearick Islands	8vo	London	[1719]	—	0-4-6
G. Daniel	Hist. of France (in English)	8vo 5 vols.	London	1726	0-16-0	1-6-0
[D. Defoe]	History of Wars of Sweden, or Charles XII[d]	8vo	London	[1715]	0-3-0	0-5-0
[D. Defoe]	History of Apparitions	8vo	London	1727	—	0-6-0
[D. Defoe]	Impartial Hist. of the Present Czar of Muscovy	8vo	London	1723	0-3-6	0-6-0
[D. Defoe]	The political history of the devil	8vo	London	1726	—	0-6-0
L. E. Dupin	History of the Church[e]	12mo 2 vols.	London	1724	0-6-0	0-11-0
L. E. Dupin	Universal Library of Historians	8vo 2 vols.	London	1709	0-5-6	0-10-0
L. E. Dupin	Histoire profane	12mo 6 vols.	Amsterdam[f]	1717	4 gu. = 0-7-6	0-15-0
M. Duncan	Hist. Kings of Scotland	12mo	Glasgow	1722	—	0-2-6
L. Echard	Roman History	8vo 5 vols.	London	1724	0-15-0	1-5-0
L. Echard	General Eccles. History	8vo 2 vols.	London	1722	0-5-6	0-10-0

[a] Criteria unchanged from folio and quarto: well over half the items listed are in octavo and smaller formats.

Table A.3. (*cont.*)

Author	Title	Format	Place of publication	Date of edition	Price (quires) £ s d	Selling bound £ s d
L. Echard	*Hist. of the Revolution*	8vo	London	1725	0-2-9	0-4-6
C. J. de Ferrière	*Hist. of the Roman or civil law*	8vo	London	1724	0-3-6	0-5-6
C. Fleury	*Histoire ecclesiastique*	8vo, 24 vols.	[Paris]	[1728–52]	24 gu.g = 2-7-0	3-15-0
Abbé de Fourcroy (trans. T. Brown)	*A New and Easy Method to Understand the Roman History*	12mo	London	1726	0-1-6	0-2-6
W. Gordon	*History of the . . . Family of Gordon*	8vo, 2 vols.	Edinburgh	1727	—	0-12-0
H. Grotius	*Historia Gotthorum, Vandalorum, & Langobardorum*	8vo	Amsterdam	1655	—	0-5-0
Bp. H. Guthry	*Memoirs of Henry Guthry*	8vo	London	1702		0-3-6
Eliza Haywood	*Mary Stuart . . . being the Secret Hist.*	8vo	London	1725	0-2-0	0-3-6
T. Hearne	*Ductor historicus*	8vo, 2 vols.	London	1724	—	0-11-0
Herodian	*Historia . . . cum notis*	8vo, Gk & Lat.	[Strasbourg]	1662	—	0-5-0
Herodian	*Herodiani Historiarum libri 8*	8vo, Gk and Lat.	Edinburgh	1724	—	0-4-0
Denzil Holles	*Memoirs*	8vo	London	1699	—	0-3-6
R. Houstoun	*Hist. of Ruptures*	8vo	London	1726		0-4-6
L. Howell	*Compleat Hist. of the Holy Bible*	8vo	London	1725	0-14-0	1-1-0
Anon.	*Historical Compendium of Chronol. & Hist., Creation to 1722*	24mo [16mo]	London	1722	0-1-3	0-2-4

Author	Title	Format	Place	Year		
[S. Jebb][h]	Hist. of Mary Queen of Scotland	8vo	London	1725	0-3-6	0-5-6
[D. Jones]	Compleat History of the Turks	8vo 4 vols.	London	1719	—	1-1-0
[D. Jones]	A Compleat Hist. of Europe from 1660 to 1714	8vo 18 vols.	London	—	—	5-0-0
Josephus (ed. R. L'Estrange)	Works	8vo 3 vols.	London	1716	—	0-18-0
B. Kennett	Romae antiquae notitia	8vo	London	1726	0-3-6	0-6-0
J. G. Keyssler	Antiquitates selectae septentrionales et Celticae	8vo	Hanover	1720	1 gu.16 st =0-3-1	0-6-0
I. Kimber	Life of Oliver Cromwell	8vo	London	1725	0-3-9	0-6-0
W. King	Historical Account of Heathen Gods and Heroes	[12mo]	London	1722	—	0-2-6
I. de Larrey	Histoire de . . . Louis XIV	12mo 9 vols.	Rotterdam	1721	8 gu. = 0-15-6[i]	1-8-0
[J. Lawson][j]	Hist. of North Carolina	8vo	London	1728	—	0-3-6
N. Lenglet du Fresnoy (trans. R. Rawlinson)	New method of studying hist. geog. & chronology	8vo 2 vols.	London	1728	—	0-12-0
T. Lewis	Hist. of the Parthian Empire	8vo	London	1728	—	0-5-0
H. P. de Limiers	Histoire de L'académie appelée l'institut des sciences et des arts	8vo	Amsterdam	1723	1 gu. = 2s	0-3-6
Livy (ed. D. Heinsius)	Titi Livii historiarum libri	12mo	Leiden	1634	—	0-1-0[k]
Livy (ed. J. Gronovius)	Titi Livii Historiarum quod extat	8vo 3 vols.	Amsterdam	1679	—	0-1-8
Livy (ed. T. Hearne)	History of Rome	8vo 6 vols.	Oxford	1708	—	1-12-0
J. Le Long	Bibliothèque historique de la France	8vo	Paris	1719	—	1-10-0

Table A.3. (*cont.*)

Author	Title	Format	Place of publication	Date of edition	Price (quires) £ s d	Selling bound £ s d
Lucan (trans. N. Rowe)	*Pharsalia*	12mo 2 vols.	London	1722	0-3-6	0-6-0
E. Ludlow	*Memoirs*	8vo 3 vols.	London	—	—	0-14-0
M. Maitaire (ed.)[1]	*T. Livii patavini historiarum ab urbe condita libri qui supersunt*	12mo 6 vols.	London	1722	0-10-0	0-18-0
M. Maitaire (ed.)	*Justini historiarum ex Trogo Pompeio libri XLIV*	12mo	London	1713	—	0-2-6
M. Maitaire (ed.)	*C. Sallustii Crispi quae extant*	12mo	London	1713	—	0-2-0
M. Maitaire (ed.)	*M. Annaei Lucani Pharsalia*	12mo	London	1719	—	0-3-6
M. Maitaire (ed.)	*C. Julii Caesaris et A. Hirtii de rebus a C. Julio Caesare gestis commentarii*	12mo	London	1716	—	0-3-0
M. Maitaire (ed.)	*Cornelius Nepotis excellentium imperatorum vitae*	12mo	London	1715	—	0-1-6
M. Maitaire (ed.)	*Quinti Curtii Rufi de rebus gestis Alexandri Magni libri*	12mo	London	1716	0-1-0	0-2-0
G. Marcel	*Tablettes chronologiques*	12mo	Amsterdam	1687	—	0-2-6
J. Milton	*Hist. of Britain*	8vo	London	1695	—	0-3-0
D. Neal	*History of New England*	8vo 2 vols.	London	1720	0-5-6	0-9-0
W. Nicolson	*Irish Historical Library*	8vo	Dublin	1724	—	—
W. Nicolson	*Scottish Historical Library*	8vo[m]	[London]	[1702]	—	0-8-0
W. Nicolson	*English Historical Library*	8vo	—	—	—	—
Ockley, Simon	*History of the Saracens*	8vo 2 vols.	London	1718	0-7-6	0-12-0

Author	Title	Format	Place	Date	Price	Price
[J. Oldmixon]	Critical History of England	8vo 2 vols.	London	1726[-30]	0-7-6	0-12-0[n]
[J. Oldmixon]	Clarendon and Whitlock [sic] compar'd	8vo	London	1727	—	0-6-0
Bishop S. Parker (trans. T. Newlin)	De rebus sui temporis commentariorum libri quatuor	8vo	London	1726	—	0-6-6
D. Petau	D. Petavii . . . Rationarium temporum	8vo 2 vols. "best edn"	Leiden	1710	3-10 gu.[o] = 0-6-0	0-10-0
J. Potter	Archaeologia Graeca	8vo 2 vols.	London	1722	—	0-12-0
H. Prideaux	Life of Mahomet	8vo	London	1723	0-2-2	0-3-6
S. Pufendorf	Introduction a l'histoire générale et politique de l'univers	12mo 6 vols.[p]	Amsterdam	1721	6 gu. = 0-12-0[q]	0-18-0
S. Pufendorf	Introductio ad historiam europeam[r]	12mo	[Utrecht]	1693	—	0-2-6
W. Ralegh	An Abridgment of Sir Walter Raleigh's History of the World	8vo	London	1702	—	0-6-0
Sallust	Histoire de la guerre des Romains contre Jugurta	12mo	Paris	1713	1-8 gu. = 0-4-8	0-5-6
Sallust (trans. John Rowe)	Sallustius, the historian	12mo	London	1726	0-1-6	0-2-6
T. Salmon	Review of history of England	8vo 2 vols.	London	1722	—	0-11-0
T. Salmon	Impartial Examination of Bp. Burnet's Hist. of his own Times	8vo 2 vols.	London	1724	—	0-11-0
T. Salmon	Chronological Historian	8vo 6v	London	1723	0-4-0	0-6-6
T. Salmon	Complete Collect. of State Trials	6 vols.	London	1720	1-6-0	2-0-0
W. Shakespeare	Plays	12mo 10 vols.	London	1728	—	1-16-0
S. Shuckford	Sacred and Profane History of the World	8vo [10 vols.]	London	1728[-37]	0-3-6	0-6-0

Table A.3. (*cont.*)

Author	Title	Format	Place of publication	Date of edition	Price (quires) £ s d	Selling bound £ s d
J. Sleidan	*Key to history*	12mo	London	1661	—	0-2-0
F. Spanheim	*Introductio ad chronologiam, et historiam sacram*[s]	8vo	Edinburgh	1727	—	0-5-0
F. Strada	*De bello Belgico*	12mo 2 vols.	Leiden	1643	—	0-4-0
A. Strauch (trans. R. Sault)	*Breviarium chronologium*	8vo	London	1722	0-3-6	0-6-0
R. Steele	*The Romish ecclesiastical history of late years*	12mo	London	1714	0-2-0	0-3-0
W. Temple	*Intro. to the Hist. of England*	8vo	London	[1695?]	—	0-3-6
Thucydides (ed. T. Hobbes)	*The History of the Grecian War*	8vo 2 vols.	London	1723	—	0-11-6
J. Tutchin	*Western Martyrology*	8vo	London	1705	0-2-0	0-3-6
Abbé de Vertot	*Histoire des révolutions . . . Romaine*	12mo 3 vols.	The Hague	1724	—	0-7-0
Abbé de Vertot	*History of the Revolutions that Happened in the Government of the Roman Republic*	8vo 2 vols.	London [and Dublin]	1724	—	0-11-0
Abbé de Vertot	*Histoire des . . . chevaliers de Malthe*	12mo 5 vols.	[Paris]	1727	3 gu. = 0-6-6	0-12-0
Abbé de Vertot	*A Critical Hist. of the Establishment of the Bretons among the Gauls*	8vo 2 vols.	London	1722	—	0-7-6
Abbé de Vertot	*Histoire des révolutions de Portugal*	12mo	Amsterdam	1722	9 st. = 0-1-0	0-2-0
J. Ussher (ed. R. Parr)	*Life and Letters*	8vo	London	[1686?]	—	0-12-0
D. Wheare (trans. E. Bohun)	*Method and Order of Reading . . . Histories*	8vo	London	1694	0-3-0	0-5-0

W. Whiston	*New Theory of the Earth*	8vo	London	1725	0-3-9	0-6-0
J. Woodward	*Essay towards a Natural History of the Earth*	8vo	London[l]	1723	0-2-6	0-4-6
J. Woodward	*An Attempt Towards a Natural History of the Fossils of England*	8vo	London	1728	—	0-4-6
W. Wotton	*History of Rome*	8vo	London	1701	—	0-3-0
Xenophon	*[Memorabilia][n] Greek and Latin*	8vo	London	1720	0-2-9	0-5-0

[a]Perhaps an error: *NUC* records an edition published at Utrecht in 1668.

[b]According to Ms. José de Kruif, working with the Luchtmans archive, this title was published in an edition of 2,100 copies by Luchtmans in collaboration with two other publishers, with the total costs of production (paper, printing, and labor – Dutch workers making no more than 1 gu. per day) amounting to 3,084 guilders, of which Luchtmans share was 1,028, or 30 stuivers (= 1 gu. and 10 st.) per copy. This would work out to a wholesale price of about 2 gu. 5 st. (the price charged to other booksellers). If the MS author was indeed a bookseller, this then suggests a further mark-up, perhaps to cover transportation, allowing him still to make a profit on this book.

[c]In fact, 1708.

[d]Like most of Defoe's "histories" and "memoirs," this is of course fictitious, but is included here for illustration.

[e]Held in some parochial libraries as an alternative to Gilbert Burnet's *History of the Reformation*; see above, chapter 4.

[f]*NUC*: Anvers is the place of publication of this edition, not Amsterdam.

[g]Value of book in a 1753 Dutch estate inventory, 21 guilders. Source: J. de Kruif.

[h]MS gives names of J. Woodman and D. Lyon, the publishers, rather than the author.

[i]A book with this title, but in quarto format, was sold by Pieter van Cleef of the Hague on two occasions in 1740 and 1742, each time for 11 guilders. Source: J. de Kruif.

[j]MS reads T. Cox, but this would seem to be Lawson's book, first published in 1709, three years before his murder at the hands of Indians.

[k]1s 8d emended to 1s in MS (8d crossed out).

[l]For sake of ease, all this continental philologist's editions included herein are here presented together.

[m]Several possible editons of this work; lack of reference to multiple volumes suggests the 2nd edn of 1714; the first, 1696 edition appeared in 2 vols.

[n]Item recorded twice on separate pages, with identical prices; appears to be an authorial error rather than a distinct item.

[o]A copy of this was purchased by Luchtmans from Pieter van der Aa for 4 guilders and 12 stuivers. Source: J. de Kruif.

[p]Actually 7 vols.

[q]An eleven-volume edition was sold by van Cleef for 21 guilders in 1746; the identical title in "franse band" (special binding) and octavo format sold for 10 guilders in 1751. A Dutch estate inventory of 1753 lists an octavo copy with a notary's valuation of 7 guilders. Source: J. de Kruif.

[r]*Bibliothèque nationale*; not in *National Union Catalogue*.

[s]Identification conjectural: MS says "Spanheimii compendium historiae Ecclesi[astic]o," Edinburgh 1727; *NUC* lists the *Introductio* in an Edinburgh edition of 1728. If this is the title in question, it provides an illustration of wide variation in prices for a single title: the same work appears in app. C.i. above in Simon Browne's 1709 list, valued at 16s.

MS says "ib.," implying Amsterdam, the place of the previous entry, but the ibid. is surely meant to refer to London; *NUC* records no Amsterdam editions of the *Essay*, of which the 1723 edition was billed as the third.

Possibly, however, the *Cyropaedia*, an octavo Greek and Latin edition of which also appeared in 1720.

≪ B ≫

History by auction: an analysis of select auction sale catalogs, 1686–1700

In order to measure aggregate historical book ownership and especially the circulation of second-hand books in general, a systematic analysis has been undertaken of forty extant library auction sale catalogs from the last quarter of the seventeenth century. This will provide us with further evidence of the holdings in some notable individual libraries, beyond those noted in previous chapters; it also illustrates the degree to which history books moved from one library to another, either in lots or singly. It should be emphasized at the outset that the complete editing of any single one of these catalogs would be a project in itself, involving such exercises as attempting to identify earlier provenance, and the whereabouts of some of the contents today. It would also involve physically examining each title before placing it in its proper category, rather than relying on often-deceptive short titles. Nothing like this has been attempted here, and it is to be expected that further research on the same catalogs, using more refined categories than we have employed, may yield somewhat different numerical results. The purpose is not to provide a detailed, item-by-item listing analysis of any single catalog but to construct an aggregate profile of the sample as a whole which may, however tentatively, be extended to other catalogs.

The auction of private libraries was known in the early seventeenth century,[1] but only later became a regular means of disposing of large collec-

---

[1] For background see Gwyn Walters, "Early Sale Catalogues: Problems and Perspectives," in Robin Myers and Michael Harris (eds.), *Sale and Distribution of Books from 1700* (Oxford, 1982), pp. 106–25; G. Pollard and A. Ehrman, *The Distribution of Books by Catalogue from the Invention of Printing to AD 1800* (Cambridge, 1965), pp. 216–48; Frank Herrmann, "The Emergence of the Book Auctioneer as a Professional," in Robin Myers and Michael Harris (eds.), *Property of a Gentleman: the Formation, Organisation and Dispersal of the Private Library, 1620–1920* (Winchester, 1991), pp. 1–14. For the later period see Robin Myers, "Sale By Auction: the Rise of Auctioneering Exemplified: in the Firm of Christopher Cock, the Langfords, and Henry, John and George Robins (*ca.* 1720–1847)," in Myers and Harris (eds.), *Property of a Gentleman*, pp. 126–63. For an excellent study of a series of auctions of a particular library, see B. J. Enright, "The Later Auction Sales of Thomas Rawlinson's Library,

tions, where the owner – often but not always deceased – had not left specific instructions for it to be given to named individuals or to an institution. In general, a bookseller would contract to print and distribute a catalog of the books for sale, sometimes amalgamating two or three smaller collections together into a single auction, and by 1700 several booksellers, most notably William Cooper (who auctioned the first library, of Dr. Lazarus Seaman, in 1676) and Edward Millington (who conducted auctions in various provincial towns as well as in London), became specialists in the auction business.[2] The catalogs were then circulated by other booksellers and by professional agents such as Richard Lapthorne to their provincial clients, who would mark off desiderata. Agents provided a useful service by attending the auctions, which could last days or even weeks, and vigilantly waiting for a requested item to come up, then bidding for it; sometimes the agent, as Lapthorne did, would simply acquire an item on the assumption that he could resell it to one of his clients or to another bidder at a higher price. Competition for certain books could be both brisk and fierce: the Essex antiquary James Allen arrived late at a sale in 1723, thereby missing several books on ecclesiastical history and antiquities that he badly wanted.[3]

After 1690 the printed catalogs occasionally include notes of an item's price (sometimes a starting value rather than an actual sum paid). "Fixed-price" sales became more common from about 1715, by which time they were supplanting open-ended auctions in terms of numbers of books sold, but it was only in the mid-eighteenth century that catalogs generally conveyed a printed price next to items; this is the major reason why sale catalog price information is not factored into the discussion of history book prices in chapter 5.[4] H. B. Wheatley recognized the unreliability of auction prices as

---

1727–34," *The Library*, 5th series 11 (1956), 23–40, 103–13. There is an older account of the sales in H. B. Wheatley, *Prices of Books: an Inquiry into the Changes in the Price of Books which have Occurred in England at Different Periods* (1898), pp. 104–25, and in J. Lawler, *Book Auctions in England in the Seventeenth Century (1676–1700)* (1898), which provides a chronology of sales by date, pp. 215–24.

[2] Because some booksellers are known to have disposed of their own stock by associating it with the name of a famous person, the catalogs cannot be taken as absolutely accurate records of the collecting habits of individual Augustan book owners; for an example of this, see F. Korsten, *A Catalogue of the Library of Thomas Baker* (Cambridge, 1990), p. xxviii. For our purposes, however, the catalogs are more than adequate since it is the overall picture of historical book consumption and redistribution that concerns us rather than a precise list of any single owner's books. For a contemporary list of the auctioneers as a subgroup of the booksellers, see John Dunton, *Life and Errors* (1705), 315–16.

[3] Essex RO, D/Y/1//1/8 (Holman letters), James Allen to Revd William Holman, n.d. [1723]; Allen requested that Holman, who was well-connected with booksellers, attempt to obtain the items for him. Notice of auctions spread both through formal advertisement and word of mouth: for a notice of a series of auctions "such as were never before in England," see the letter of the bishop of Peterborough to the earl of Rutland, 27 December 1687, Hist. MSS Comm., *The manuscripts of His Grace the Duke of Rutland . . . preserved at Belvoir Castle*, 4 vols. (1888–1905), II, 117.

early as 1898, pointing out that they could be wildly distorted by competitive bidding or its opposite, the "knock out" whereby prospective buyers colluded not to bid against one another.[5]

The forty sale catalogs selected for analysis were issued for auctions occurring between 1676 and 1700, most of them falling in the 1680s.[6] The catalogs vary considerably in size, the smallest being the 185 books sold outside the Sheldonian by the Oxford bookseller Moses Pitt in February 1679/80, the largest, the nearly 10,000 volumes auctioned in April and October 1686 by another bookseller, Richard Davis, from his own stock.[7] The catalogs are not – and this point requires emphasis – at all representative of English society in the way that a sample of wills might be, though they do include different varieties of elite book owner: eleven clergy, seven booksellers, and a variety of gentry, nobles, and professionals (especially lawyers, doctors), one painter, and one or two merchants.[8] Among the more prominent owners were Francis Bacon, some of whose books were being sold in 1686, six decades after his death, the Oxford orientalist Edward Pococke, the Savilian professor Edward Bernard, and the antiquary, virtuoso, and herald Elias Ashmole. The clerical owners were all ministers with livings (Richard Wallis, for instance, had been rector of Elsborough) and several had higher preferment, such as the noted biblical scholar Brian Walton, bishop of Chester, Matthew Smallwood, dean of Lichfield, and Anthony Scattergood, prebendary of Lichfield. Only one woman, Elizabeth Oliver, is represented, and she was selling her books during her lifetime, probably to raise money by parting with an inherited library. The word *owner* is thus inappropriately applied to these libraries, since several were offered by booksellers rather than private individuals, and since many of the other catalogs included books that may never have actually been owned by the person named – auctioneers were inclined to slip in miscellaneous items, and sometimes entire smaller

[4] Katherine Swift, "Dutch Penetration of the London Market for Books, c. 1690–1730," in G. Berkvens-Stevelinck *et al.* (eds.), *Le Magasin de l'univers: the Dutch Republic as the Centre of the European Book Trade* (Leiden and New York, 1992), pp. 265–79.

[5] Wheatley, *Prices of Books*, p. 125.

[6] For the sake of space I shall not list the titles here: the Wing numbers of the selected catalogs are as follows: A3111; A3981; B273; B1050; B1569A; B1863; B1985; B2820; C1255; C1275; C1257; C1302; C1413; C1416; C1456; C1457; C5119; C6011; C6626; D426; D429; K422; L606; M1029; M1579; M1580; M1581; P399; P614; R1317; S681; S840; S2077; S2173; S3159; S3785; S4010; W621; W656; W2052.

[7] Davis himself auctioned another of the catalogs, that of Edward Pococke, in 1692. The largest collection in the sample that is attributable to a private scholar rather than a bookseller is also the earliest, that of the Reverend Dr. Lazarus Seaman, issued on 31 November 1676; on Seaman, Cambridge divine, minister of All Hallows, Bread Street and a former member of the Westminster Assembly, see *DNB*, sub "Seaman, Lazarus."

[8] Although forty catalogs are listed, there are not forty distinct owners: some catalogs were assembled by booksellers from a number of collections they had acquired, and at least two booksellers handled the books of Charles Mearne, subdivided into English and French titles with an appendix or supplementary catalog to the former.

libraries, under the umbrella provided by sale of a well-known person's volumes; thus the duke of Lauderdale's library, auctioned in 1686, included works published after his death in 1682.[9]

As apparently basic a piece of information as book size can yield interesting results. In the dataset as a whole, which consists of 78,430 identifiable items, the books break down according to the following formats: 21 percent folio, 25 percent quarto, and 54 percent octavo or smaller (it is not possible to separate octavo from duodecimo or sextedecimo with any degree of precision).[10] The distribution is very different for the historical component alone: folios account for 34.90 percent (a full third rather than a bare fifth of all titles), while quartos drop to 20.66 percent and the smaller formats decline to 44.44 percent. This confirms the more impressionistic evidence of private library holdings, and also the evidence of appendix A, above, the "stockbook" in which history fell disproportionately into the folio format. In other words, historical works were more likely than books in general to be found among the larger and more expensive titles, though an even greater percentage, nearly half, were still published in smaller formats.

Similar, but perhaps less surprising, information comes from the language distribution. For the sample as a whole, 50.5 percent were English books, 37.1 percent Latin, 3.0 percent Greek, 8.5 percent various modern foreign languages, 0.8 percent in Hebrew, and 0.1 percent other or unidentifiable. For historical works, the sample breaks down a bit differently: English works

---

[9] Methodological note: the catalogs were analyzed according to thirty-seven variables ranging from informational (Wing number of catalog but not of individual items; identity of owner and bookseller) to quantitative. Each catalog was analyzed item by item to determine the nature of individual books listed and such other details as format (folio, quarto, or smaller), subject matter, place of publication, date of publication (usually but not always given in the catalog), language of books (English, Latin, etc.). Where complete information on an edition was not provided in the catalog, reference was made to *STC*, Wing, *The National union catalog, pre-1956 imprints*, British Museum *General Catalogue of Printed Books*, and other standard bibliographical sources; if ambiguity about a possible "history title" remained and it could not be identified, it was not counted among historical items. Once the historical component of each catalog was identified, it was separated out and resorted according to other variables: historical subject or type of history (political, ecclesiastical, antiquarian, biography, etc.), geographical region covered, time period covered, and the earliest and latest books listed in the catalogs, the earliest in most cases being incunabula and in a few being manuscripts from as early as 1418. Categories and criteria were developed by the author of the present work, who performed analyses on two initial catalogs in 1991. The major part of the data collection is the work of Paula MacKinnon and Susan Hunter, two then postgraduate students in the School of Library and Information Studies at Dalhousie University, working under my supervision over two consecutive summers in 1992 and 1993. While the interpretation of the results are mine alone, without their labors this exercise could not have been attempted. I am pleased also to acknowledge, again, the financial assistance of the Research Development Fund of Dalhousie University for providing an initial grant toward a 10-catalog pilot project, and the Social Sciences and Humanities Research Council for providing funding to enlarge the scope of the sample fourfold.

[10] All percentages are rounded off to the first decimal place.

drop slightly to 46.8 percent, Latin and Greek even more slightly to 35.7 percent and 2.3 percent respectively, Hebrew substantially to 0.1 percent. But the modern languages rise from 8.5 to 15.0 percent, an increase of two-thirds, indicating a relative willingness to read continental historical works written in languages other than English or the classical tongues.

The subject analyses of the whole sample and the historical subsample cannot be directly compared with the language analyses since different variables and values apply. Religious and moral works, buoyed up somewhat by the number of clergy among the "owners," account for 43.1 percent, close to half the total number of books listed. But history in the broad sense (including biography, autobiography, and antiquarianism) is virtually neck and neck for second spot with science and natural philosophy, both falling at about 14.5 percent, with contemporary politics and manuals on political behavior following at 12.6 percent. The category of fiction, poetry, published letters, music, and fine arts weighs in at just under 10 percent. The relatively small numbers of works that we would describe as practical or educational, and of geography or travel books, may be easily explained. The practical works were often printed in smaller formats probably not worth separate itemizing by the auctioneer (just as smaller-still works such as almanacs often eluded the gaze of probate inventory compilers). In the case of geography, it should be remembered that much travel literature came out in the form of histories of particular countries or cities – Giovanni Botero's ambiguously titled *The travellers breviat, or An historicall description of the most famous kingdomes in the world* (1601), or Peter Heylyn's *Cosmographie* (1652) are two frequent examples; such works have been counted as historical (but kept separate within that subsample).

Within the historical subsample (a total of 11,351 books of all sizes), politics, war, and national (British/Irish and foreign countries, past and contemporary) history dominate at 40 percent. Religion, in the form of ecclesiastical history (a broad form that includes both a medieval history like Bede or Eusebius and recent works by authors like James Ussher, William Cave, and Edward Stillingfleet) is a distant second at 18.4 percent, a value that would no doubt be higher were lives of persons connected with the church (those written by Cave and Jeremy Taylor for example, and the various lives of Dissenting figures that occasionally appear in the lists) not hived off into the category "biography." The latter is a substantial category at 11.9 percent, a number that does not, however, include lives of kings or queens, here counted under political history because they nearly always amount to regnal histories.

The other categories are considerably smaller. Antiquarian and chorographical works, older and more recent, count for barely 7 percent in numbers, though the expensive nature of some of these would make them prize items in many sales. An additional 1.7 percent in critical philological works includes books by the likes of Lorenzo Valla, Edward Pococke, and Edward Leigh. Chronicles counted for a mere 4 percent, a staggering decline from a hundred years earlier when the vast majority of published post-classical historical works were chronicles or annals of some sort – but not unexpected given the fate of that genre in the seventeenth century. It is somewhat more surprising, given the early modern interest in ancestry and heraldry, that genealogical and heraldic works counted for less than one per cent of the historical items, but this may reflect the waning of the "pedigree craze" earlier in the century. Chronology, which here includes recondite biblical chronologies like Archbishop Ussher's *Annales veteris et novi testamenti* that otherwise might have found their way under the general rubric of religion, outstripped chronicles slightly at 4.5 percent. The balance of the distribution is made up of several smaller categories: works that combine history with geography but do not fall under the political history sub-category; "poetical" history (not fictional works but rather works *about* literature with a clear historical thrust), and works in the embryonic genre of "history of science or philosophy" (for instance Sprat's *History of the Royal Society* and many of Francis Bacon's works).

The historical subsample can also be analyzed by the time and place to which its items pertain. A solid third (32.3 percent) deal with more than one historical period (and are here called "surveys"). After that, the biggest selection of books fall into the "modern" category, here defined as works dealing with periods after 1485 *but not contemporary with the book itself*. A book printed in the late seventeenth century, dealing with recent events such as a war, peace treaty, or parliament (Thomas May's *A breviary of the history of the parliament of England*, for instance) falls instead under a distinct "contemporary" category of 11.7 percent. In comparison, books about classical and late antique history (both those by ancient authors and those by modern ones) covering periods up to the end of the sixth century AD comprise 21.76 percent of the sample. This is a relatively small quantity given the dominance of ancient history hitherto in the curricula and in humanist notions of historiography, but understandable given a century of vigorous historical publishing about modern events. Works about the Middle Ages, including the medieval chroniclers themselves, follow the chronicle genre itself in a low position, a mere 4.45 percent of all historical works dealing with the period from AD 600 to 1485.

Geographically, the divisions are even more striking in their eurocentricity. For all England's early expansion overseas, the quantity of historical writing about exotic places (as opposed to travel literature not fundamentally historical, such as maps, sea charts, and atlases) was rather small, only 6 percent being devoted to Asia, Africa, and the Middle East and barely half a percent to the Americas (including the works of English authors like Captain John Smith and the various Spanish, Portuguese, and Italian missionary authors such as Las Casas, Acosta, Ricci, and Mendoza). Aside from 7.8 percent of books that purport to be about world history, including the various editions of Ralegh's *History of the World*, and older chronicles like the *Polychronicon* with similar geographic range, over half are about one or more parts of Europe, the rising popularity of the Grand Tour undoubtedly stimulating both historical writing about foreign parts and the vendibility of such books in second-hand form through the auctions. Books on British and Irish history account for a solid third of the subsample at 32.3 percent, a testimony to the amount of narrative and antiquarian scholarship about various parts of the British Isles that had been published in the preceding century or so. A second geographical variable is also of relevance here, and that is the place of publication of individual works (a somewhat smaller number since a few had unsupplied and unidentifiable, or fictitious, imprints). England was consistently a net importer of books, and this is reflected in the number of titles given with continental imprints, nearly 60 percent of the total historical subsample, a slightly greater percentage than that for works *about* Europe. Nearly all the rest came from presses within the British Isles, and a tiny fraction, less than four one-hundredths of a percent, from colonial or non-European locations.

Finally, it can be reported, again with little surprise, that the distribution of subjects within a particular catalog generally conformed to the associated person's occupation if known: lawyers like Henry Parker, the political theorist, and Roger Belwood, serjeant of the Middle Temple, had a high proportion of legal works and political histories; the clerical catalogs are skewed in the direction of religious works relating to religion and, within the subsample, ecclesiastical history and biography.

INDEX

Cambridge Studies in Early Modern British History

Titles in the series

Gender in Mystical and Occult Thought: Behmenism and its Development in England
B. J. GIBBONS

William III and the Godly Revolution
TONY CLAYDON

Law-Making and Society in Late Elizabethan England: The Parliament of England, 1584–1601
DAVID DEAN

Conversion, Politics and Religion in England, 1580–1625
MICHAEL C. QUESTIER

Politics, Religion and the British Revolutions: The Mind of Samuel Rutherford
JOHN COFFEY

King James VI and I and the Reunion of Christendom*
W. B. PATTERSON

The English Reformation and the Laity: Gloucestershire, 1540–1580
CAROLINE LITZENBERGER

Godly Clergy in Early England: The Caroline Puritan Movement, c. 1620–1643
TOM WEBSTER

Prayer Book and People in Elizabethan and Early Stuart England*
JUDITH MALTBY

Sermons at Court, 1559–1629: Religion and Politics in Elizabethan and Jacobean Preaching
PETER E. MCCULLOUGH

Dismembering the Body Politic: Partisan Politics in England's Towns, 1650–1730
PAUL D. HALLIDAY

Women Waging Law in Elizabethan England
TIMOTHY STRETTON

The Early Elizabethan Polity: William Cecil and the British Succession Crisis, 1558–1569
STEPHEN ALFORD

The Polarisation of Elizabethan Politics: The Political Career of Robert Devereux, 2nd Earl of Essex
PAUL J. HAMMER

The Politics of Social Conflict: The Peak Country, 1520–1770
ANDY WOOD

Crime and Mentalities in Early Modern England
MALCOLM GASKILL

The Church in an Age of Danger: Parsons and Parishioners, 1660–1740
DONALD A. SPAETH

Reading History in Early Modern England
D. R. WOOLF

*Also published as a paperback